ADVERTISING FUNDAMENTALS

Third Edition

GRID SERIES IN ADVERTISING AND JOURNALISM

Consulting Editors
ARNOLD M. BARBAN, University of Illinois
DONALD W. JUGENHEIMER, University of Kansas

**OTHER BOOKS IN THE GRID SERIES
IN ADVERTISING AND JOURNALISM**

ADVERTISING FUNDAMENTALS
Third Edition

Philip Ward Burton
School of Journalism
Indiana University

William Ryan
S. I. Newhouse School of Public Communication
Syracuse University

Grid Publishing, Inc., Columbus, Ohio

1 2 3 4 5 6   ▤▤▤   5 4 3 2 1 0

Library of Congress Cataloging in Publication Data

Burton, Philip Ward, 1910-
    Advertising fundamentals.

    (Grid series in advertising/journalism)
    Includes index.
    1. Advertising.   I. Ryan, William, 1932- joint
author.   II. Title.
HF5823.B8722   1979   659.1   79-12110
ISBN O-88244-189-2

CONTENTS

PREFACE

Who knows what will happen before this third edition reaches the booksellers? Will the problem of television clutter be settled? Will advertising to children be outlawed? How much impact will plain pack, or no-name, products have on brand advertising?

Fast-paced and ever-changing advertising creates problems for an author. Change must be reflected, yet certain basic principles must be repeated. On one side, you have the creative world that, essentially, relies on the basic, relatively unchanging, laws of human behavior and psychology. But, on the other side, there is the media world that shifts, changes, and modifies every year, especially television.

Here in the third edition we felt our primary obligation was to answer: "What's new?" Although the second edition was published as recently as 1976, we found many significant developments to add and discuss. An obvious change to chronicle was the increased presence of government on the advertising scene: more government advertising, and more government regulation. And, allied with government are militant consumers, suspicious of advertising and even more so of the business system that supports advertising.

Consciousness of group sensitivities has been heightened in this period. Aggressiveness is the order of the day among women, blacks, and minority elements in our society. Woe to the advertiser who approaches the market heedless of the winds of change. Consciousness of these groups affects the use of the media, packaging, and the phrasing of the advertising message.

As usual, it is in the media that change is most pronounced and thus reflected in this third edition. Broadcast media, as you will see, provide the most dynamic changes. In radio, for example, we have paid close attention to the bewildering profusion of station formats and minority programming. Then, when we reach television, we *really* find change and special problems—the criticisms, the social impact, CATV, children's advertising, clutter, and escalating costs.

Some aspects of this book have *not* changed. It is still, we think, a *teachable* book. From the teacher's standpoint, this means that material is organized in such a way that it is easy to find questions to ask. Guidance is provided, for instance, by the liberal use of subheads. It means, too, that the book can be used logically for a one-semester or two-semester course that covers the field thoroughly without discouraging students in the process. We have tried to make the material readable and possibly even enjoyable for students but tough enough to provide a challenge.

Although this volume is intended primarily for use in basic, or principles-type college-level advertising courses, there are many professionals in the field who could profit from reading it. Numerous persons—especially on the brand management side—are responsible for the direction of the advertising function as well as the marketing function. Quite frequently such persons are likely to know much more about marketing than about advertising. The reading of this book could fill in some of those gaps because, to take MBA training, for example, advertising instruction is given minor attention on the theory that "You can learn what you need to know about advertising on the job." True enough, but the learning would be easier if preceded by the study of this book, or a book like it.

As we looked over the preface for the second edition, we found that what was said about its six sections applies largely to the third edition too. In order that you may know generally what is covered in these sections, we are repeating the preface material about them with little change in the third edition. Remember, however, that each of the sections will include the important changes that have occurred since the writing of the second edition.

SECTION I begins properly (we think) with full attention, not only to the organization of advertising and what an advertising person does, but also with advertising's effect on our society. The social responsibilities of the advertising worker are given close attention along with the regulation of advertising that makes sure that those in advertising live up to their legal and social obligations.

SECTION II considers those factors that enter into preadvertising including budgeting procedure and philosophy, and various forms of research. What with S.I.C. numbers, segmented marketing, and the application of behavioral sciences to marketing and advertising, there is much to be pondered in this section. Although the average business makes little day-to-day use of behavioral sciences or scientists, the serious student should be aware of the potential usefulness of both. Perhaps, because they are aware of their potential in advertising-marketing, such students will bring a new dimension to the field.

SECTION III, concerned with the structure of advertising, discusses in depth the organization and administration of three vital segments of advertising: company advertising departments, advertising agencies, and local businesses. Advertising agencies, because of their importance and because they are interesting and need explanation, are given especially thorough treatment.

SECTION IV, embracing the forms of advertising and the media that serve the forms, is the longest section in the book. This length is inevitable since so many segments must be discussed. Because most of advertising expenditure is concerned with media it seems not unexpected that a discussion of media should be serious and detailed. Anyone attending almost any advertising meeting finds immediately that consideration of media constantly engrosses the attention of persons at such meetings. The length of Section IV simply recognizes the importance of the subject.

SECTION V, relating to often-neglected areas of promotion, is not very long but considers topics that we felt should be given more attention than they are often granted in advertising and marketing books. In addition to having significance to large numbers of advertising men, these topics of contests, trade shows, premiums, and packaging, are also of absorbing interest.

SECTION VI, the creative section, has been placed last. There are some books that place creative advertising first. With all deference to those authors who have placed it thus, we prefer its caboose position because copy is what results after all the other aspects have been considered—media, research, and marketing findings. It will be noted that while copywriting suggestions are fairly detailed for print media, they are given essentially in outline form for broadcast media. There are two reasons for this:

(1) Many of the principles that pertain to print writing apply also to broadcast writing.

(2) On the contrary, some aspects of television and radio creativity cannot be spelled out in rules and writing suggestions. Thus, an outline of suggestions for broadcast media is followed by specific examples that relate to the outline. The person truly interested in broadcast creativity should derive more from this procedure than from a straight exposition that might be headed "How To Write TV and Radio Commercials."

Additionally, the section on creating advertising goes deeply into the production and graphics areas. While this material has been kept as brief as possible, the importance and complexity of the general subject is such that the page count becomes rather substantial.

ACKNOWLEDGMENTS

Many individuals and organizations were helpful in supplying material and ideas for this third edition. We acknowledge their assistance with deep gratitude. It should be understood, however, that persons or organizations who contributed to the book do not necessarily endorse the entire content of the book. To the following we say, "Thanks."

Lawrence Adams, the B. F. Goodrich Company; N. P. Allerup, Pabst Brewing Company; Dean E. Baer, Campbell Soup Company; W. P. Barton, International Business Machines; Maria Beltrametti, Batten, Barton, Durstine, & Osborn; Willa J. Benge, Gulf Oil Corporation; J. F. Betram, the *Geneva Times*; Joseph R. Blackstock, Foster & Kleiser; D. L. Blair Company; Thomas E. Bohan, Benton & Bowles; Alice Boyer, Douglas Leigh Transit Advertising; Robert W. Brown, Eastman Kodak; R.L. Bucher, Thomas J. Lipton, Inc.; J. J. Burgdoerfer, The Hertz Corporation; Tom Burgum, Armstrong Cork; E. Dean Butler, the Procter & Gamble Company; Toni Callahan, E. F. Hutton Company, Inc.; F. R. Cawl, Jr., Outdoor Advertising Association of America; Richard C. Christian, Marsteller, Inc.; D. E. Clark, the *Wall Street Journal*; James F. Coakley, Compton Advertising, Inc.; Peter B. Cooney, Needham, Harper, & Steers, Inc.; Joseph M. Cooper, Xerox Corporation; R. W. Cray, The Rath Packing Company; Robert Cudworth, T. A. Best, Inc.; Douglas C. Dewey, Parma Advertising; Alan M. Deyre, Tennis Feature, Inc.; Sidney A. Diamond, Kaye, Scholer, Fierman, Hayes, & Handler; Lawrence E. Doherty, *Advertising Age*; Richard G. Ebel, Specialty Advertising Association Internation; William Edgley, the Pillsbury Company; Joseph A. Federico, National Trade Show Exhibitors Association; George Feldman, Liberty List Company; Robert B. Ferguson, the Sperry and Hutchinson Company; Daniel W. Fox, Foote, Cone, & Belding; Laurence Frerk, A. C. Nielsen, Company; Jane Fry, T. A. Best, Inc.; Richard Fry, Carrier Corporation; O. T. Gaston, Fetzer Radio Stations; Richard H. Glantz, the Quaker Oats Company; Constance Golden, General Foods Corporation; G. B. Grabow, Public Service Company of Indiana; Benjamin S. Greenburg, the Advertising Council, Inc.; Alden R. Grimes, American Dairy Association; Steve Gritton, Leo Burnett, U.S.A.; Harold W. Gully, Leo Burnett, U.S.A.; Tom Hanson, Ford Motor Company; A. E. Harris, Procter & Gamble Company; Derek J. Holmes, *Christian Science Monitor*; Gerald E. Holmes, Saginaw Steering Gear Division, General Motors Corporation; Cynthia Huffman, Leo Burnett U.S.A.; Saralee Hymen, Radio Advertising Bureau; Mark Johnson, Lanier Business Products; Elizabeth P. Johnston, Kellogg Company; Ashton R. Lee, Leo Burnett U.S.A.; Anthony P. Lepore, O. M. Scott & Sons; Jerry Luboviski, Union Oil Company of California; John Lucas, J. C. Penney Company; Robert M. Lustgarten, Colorite Plastics Company; Carole Ann Lyons, L. S. Ayres Company; Kenneth Mahler, the Sunfloat Company; John R. Malmo, John Malmo Advertising; Marvin Matises, Johnson & Johnson; Will McCracken, Deere & Company; Pat McNamara, Cobra Communications; Robert L. Mercer, National Potato Board; Louis D. Methfessel, American Olean Tile Company; R. E. Mohlie, General Foods Corporation; Hugh G. Monaghan, *Buffalo Evening News*; Joseph E. Montgomery III, North

American Pan American; Campbell B. Niven, *Brunswick Times Record*; Robert J. Noonan, Blue Cross and Blue Shield of Northeast Ohio; David Norton, Syracuse University; J. O'Meara, Star-Kist Tuna Company; Joseph Palastak, Transit Advertising Association; George C. Perry, Mobil Chemical Company; J. S. G. Pigott, Rolls Royce Motors International; Ronald A. Polomoff, N. W. Ayer ABH International; A. B. Priemer, S. C. Johnson & Son; R. J. Ratcheson, Pabst Brewing Company; Peter Reader, Pepsi-Cola Company; William Robertson, Leo Burnett U.S.A.; Danick Rousseau, Printemps; Milt Rubenstein, Syracuse Radio Page; Kevin J. Ryan, Westwood Pharmaceuticals, Inc.; Leda Sanford, American Home Publishing Company; Milton Scheps, Westwood Pharmaceuticals, Inc.; Elly Schoenfeld, Mercedes-Benz of North America, Inc.; S. Schwartz, Caprock Developments; Brian Seavoy, Kenyon & Eckhardt Advertising, Inc.; Stephen P. Seiden, Johnson & Johnson; Pamela Seigal, Bristol-Myers Company; Andrew Shapiro, Metro Associated Services; Norman Simpson, Richard-of-Course Advertising; Dick Smith, Syracuse Mall; Phil Smith, General Foods Corporation; Richard E. Smith, Syracuse Newspapers; Barney Spaulding, New York Subways Advertising Co., Inc.; Trish Spear, May Company; Peter Spengler, Bristol-Myers Company; Eugene J. Sullivan, Borden, Inc.; Byron Taggart, the *Tampa Tribune & Times*; Vincent L. Tofany, National Safety Council; Douglas R. Toler, National Standard Company; B. Stuart Tolley, Newspaper Advertising Bureau, Inc.; Transportation Displays, Inc.; Stephen F. Tucker, Diamond International Corporation; *Vogue Magazine*; Raymond J. Walter, Exhibit Designers and Producers Association; Julie Watson, Givenchy Perfumes; Walter Whetstone III, *World Tennis Magazine*; A. W. White, International Business Machines; Donald C. Williams, Donald C. Williams Advertising, Inc.; Robert S. Yates, Timken Company.

THE PLACE OF ADVERTISING IN OUR LIVES

THE OBJECTIVES AND ORGANIZATION OF ADVERTISING

YOU AND ADVERTISING

You're an authority on advertising.

You're exposed to an estimated 1,500 advertisements each day and have been for years. You watched your first television advertisements before you teethed. When you began to toddle and explore, you literally tripped into advertisements in newspapers and magazines that were lying about. Radio commercials accompanied you on family automobile trips while you noted outdoor posters flashing by. You studied toy advertisements in catalogs before sitting in Santa's lap. Even lying on your back in an isolated, grassy field, you glanced up at the clouds only to be distracted by an airplane pulling a banner, a skywriter or perhaps a famous blimp.

You've never really known a world without advertising, although sometimes you wish you had.

Early in life you formed opinions about advertisements. You liked some and ignored or abhorred others. You may have learned to distrust advertising but didn't regard it as very important. Sometimes you were entertained or amused. Mostly you have been bored and annoyed by the unceasing hectoring, cajoling and the assault on your senses.

When very young you developed conscious, but mostly unconscious defenses against advertising you didn't want to see or hear, much like your response to a parent forbidding you to do something you wanted to do. Eventually, you could turn off those advertisements that were not important or, as popularly expressed "relevant." Now and then an advertisement may turn you on. It is more likely that you will turn advertisements off. How well can you do this? Try to recall one day's advertisements, advertisements you've seen, perhaps while brushing your teeth with an advertised toothpaste before going to bed. You may recall a half-dozen or so advertisements from those estimated 1,500. Even some of those you won't like.

4

Is Advertising a Waste?

Possibly you regard advertising as a waste of money. While you have been influenced by advertisements, you seldom admit it, even though you see advertised movies, eat advertised snack food, drink advertised juices and soft drinks, and wear advertised denim pants while shouldering your advertised backpack.

There is waste in advertising just as there is waste in any economic activity. In part, this reflects the difficulty of measuring the effect of advertising in a precise way. For instance, a retailer, after advertising jogging shoes to you and your friends, counts the resulting sales. To the retailer, advertising works. Sometimes it works well; sometimes not so well. He's not sure just how or why.

Advertising: the Great American Hangup

A manufacturer may distribute a new tennis racket to stores in your area and then advertise to see whether consumers such as you will buy. You and some of your friends may buy and use the racket and be quite pleased with it. This happens all the time. You and your friends, however, will continue to maintain that advertising doesn't influence you. If pressed, you might admit reluctantly that some of your friends might be influenced—but not you.

Our reluctance to admit the influence of advertising is a great American hangup. We approve of political campaigns designed to persuade us to vote for one candidate or another. This is what politics and democracy are all about. We even talk of religious persuasions. We are reluctant, however, to admit that persuasion influences our buying, perhaps because we're supposed to be rational decision makers. We're supposed to buy only in terms of economic values for the money we spend.

Much advertising does talk to us in terms of price and economic value. It also talks to us in social terms, in terms of our families or friends. Sometimes it talks to us as individuals, in terms of our private hopes and goals. So do college catalogs. They are filled with course offerings in sociology, social psychology, psychology and cultural anthropology, to name just a few, which deal with the many influences to which we respond, the way we view ourselves, and the widely differing bases on which we make decisions.

Imagine Your World Without Advertising

We make decisions based on information, and advertising provides this information in several ways. It supports the press. You can demonstrate this to yourself by cutting all the advertisements from a newspaper and then asking yourself whether you'd be willing to pay three or four times as much money for what remains of the newspaper. Do the same with your favorite magazine or place a quarter on top of the television set for every half hour of network entertainment you watch.

You might also speculate what your life would be like without advertising. You'd be paying more for news, of course, but you'd also be lacking the information advertisements offer you about thousands of new products and services introduced each year. In fact, without advertising most of them wouldn't be available, and the few that were would be more expensive. Your world would be much different. So would you. You'd probably have more time to think—about the same old things in the same old way.

Today some suggest advertising is as influential as the church, school or home. They regard it as a pervasive, insistent influence associated with change in ideas but mostly with change in products. Individually these product changes may be slight or significant, but taken as a whole they change our lives dramatically and mostly for the better. They change the way we think about ourselves and our hopes for the future. Because advertising encourages thousands of manufacturers to develop and offer you new or improved products and services, it makes a reality of your freedom of choice.

THE PEOPLE IN ADVERTISING—SKILLS AND TALENTS

Advertising is planned, created and placed by bright, inquisitive, hardworking people in a fast-paced, time-conscious business. They work within limits set by budgets, marketing objectives, research, media deadlines, competitors' actions and a growing list of governmental regulations.

Advertising is an information-intensive business, requiring mounds of information for defining advertising objectives, deciding on creative executions, determining where to place advertisements and finding out how effective they were. Advertising people scan or study research dealing with the latest brand-share information and population migrations and characteristics, including changes in income and family formation, size, and life style. They also sift through surveys revealing attitude and value shifts by potential consumers.

After work, advertising people go to plays, movies, or concerts; or stay at home and watch television, or read widely in magazines and newspapers. They are always on the lookout for new information and ideas. They are fascinated by ideas that express new relationships; for example, making solar collectors from discarded aluminum beer cans.

Using Information and Ideas

Advertising requires people who can use information and ideas in business situations, especially for solving marketing and advertising problems. It needs people who can analytically plot marketing and advertising strategies and encourage and coordinate the talents of writers, artists, and photographers who create the advertisements. It requires people who can locate prospects for the advertisers' product in the audiences of print and broadcast media.

Most importantly, it requires people who create messages designed to influence consumers to buy products. The copywriter is the key person, for the copywriter must assess the consumer benefits offered by a product and relate these to the consumers' self-interest. It is the copywriter who must distill and express the selling message in an attractive, compelling way. The writer may draw on the talents from stage, screen, radio and television as well as from art and photography studios. But in most cases the writer alone is finally responsible for the advertisement.

ADVERTISING IS MARKETING COMMUNICATION
IN THE MARKETING MIX

To the manufacturer of automobile clocks, advertising is unimportant. His salespeople call on designers at the four major automobile manufacturers. If clocks are not designed into dashboards of cars to be produced three years in the future, no amount of advertising will sell the clocks. To the producer of breath mints, breakfast cereals, soft drinks or washing detergents, advertising is very important. It is the only way to reach millions of potential customers quickly and inexpensively.

The person responsible for marketing a product works in a world of traditional and changing influences. Toy wholesalers, for instance, may have traditional pricing practices that the marketing manager must take into account. Food retailers require certain percentage markups, and their requirements cannot be ignored. Industrial and institutional buyers may purchase solely on price and take delivery in train carload lots or tons. Few, if any, packaging decisions are required. Consumers may shop several stores for a new coat but expect a candy bar to be available almost everywhere. These are but a few of the many influences the marketing manager must consider in getting his product to buyers.

A marketing manager selects and uses tools to get products to the market. These tools are elements in what is known as the *marketing mix*, or that combination of personal selling, advertising, pricing, packaging, and other components used to achieve marketing and sales goals. Judgment is at a premium. If any one element is faulty—a package that fails to protect the product, or advertising addressed to the wrong market—it can make the entire mix ineffective.

Packaging

Morton Salt derived an immediate advantage when it brought out a package with a sprinkling arrangement in addition to the spout. It realized another advantage when it sold small containers of salt for lunchboxes and picnics. Campbell's Soups exploited changing patterns of family eating by selling single-portion cans for the eat-and-run family.

Packaging influences consumer buying by attracting attention through size, color, shape, design, and use of symbols. Consumers expect packaging to protect and keep products fresh. They also want convenient food portions and the extra value built into packages usable for refrigerator storage.

Pricing. Advertisers know when the demand for their products is price sensitive. To economists this is demand elasticity. It means consumers may buy one product instead of another if the price difference is small, in the case of gasoline and milk perhaps a penny per gallon. Products consumers think of as substitutes, such as margarine, often are price sensitive. No matter how clever or persuasive the advertising, many consumers continue to buy on price.

Advertising may successfully differentiate some products so that consumers regard them as worth more than competitive products. This is typical for perfumes and other products we use to enhance ourselves.

It is not unusual for marketers to misjudge consumers. The marketer may believe his product is different and worth more to consumers only to find sales

Smooth it on.
JOHNSON's helps make dry
skin feel soft and silky again.

Rub it in.
It helps make knees, elbows,
and other rough spots,
soft spots.

Take it off.
It's a gentle eye makeup
remover.

Think of all the cosmetics
you can do without, with
JOHNSON's Baby Oil.

Johnson & Johnson
© J&J 1976

Primary demand stimulation.

A product may be on the market for a long time but may still be in the primary stage if the manufacturer thinks up new uses for it. Such is the case in this product which strays far from babies in its usage ideas. The picture-caption technique is useful for ideas such as this that feature several ideas.

slowing to a trickle. The consumer sees no difference, and it is the consumer who is in control.

N·W·AYER & SON INC.

CLIENT: AMERICAN CANCER SOCIETY
TITLE: "LT. ROBERT JOHNSON"
PRODUCT: CORPORATE

LENGTH: 30 SECONDS

1. LT. ROBERT JOHNSON: Getting through West Point's no snap.

2. Especially if you get cancer, as I did.

3. But thanks to early detection and treatment, I'm winning the battle.

4. I graduated on time ...

5. And today I'm a lieutenant in the infantry.

6. You know, millions of people, like myself, owe their lives to cancer research.

7. Research made possible with the help of the American Cancer Society.

8. Think about it.

9. We want to wipe out cancer in your lifetime.

Non-commercial advertising.

Advertising agencies, corporations and the media contribute millions of dollars of time, space, and effort to promote worthy causes. Public service advertising, all free, has become a major activity.

Publicity. Publicity is information provided by a company or other organizations to the news media. The information is used by newspapers and other news media as a news story. New product columns in newspapers and magazines often are filled with information supplied by companies and identified as publicity.

Advertising and publicity differ in several respects. Unlike advertising time and space, publicity is not paid for. Nor is the company or other organization identified as the source of the information.

Publicity must have genuine news value to be used by the press. A recent example is provided by a bubble gum manufacturer whose sales dropped rapidly. On investigation, the manufacturer learned that a rumor had started in the market that the gum contained spider eggs. A combined advertising and publicity campaign was used to counteract the rumor. The manufacturer's situation was so unusual the publicity releases were widely used by print and broadcast media, including the evening television network news.

Promotion. A Midwest sugar company, tiny when compared to the giants in the field, was able to outsell its big competitors consistently in the markets it served. Promotion, allied with advertising, made this possible even though the company's advertising budget was comparatively tiny. Reasoning that "sugar is sugar" to most consumers and that it would be impossible to match advertising dollars all year long with its competitors, the company decided:

(1) not to attempt to make it appear that its product was anything but good sugar, just as good but no better than other sugars on the market;

(2) to do all its consumer advertising in two six-week periods during the year; and

(3) to concentrate all this advertising on a promotional device, a contest.

In addition, the company did a modest amount of advertising before and after each contest. This advertising alerted the trade to the forthcoming contest and then gave the results following the contest. In between contests, the company was able, in its local markets, to ride successfully on the momentum built up during the periods of heavily concentrated advertising that appeared in newspapers, on radio and television, and in outdoor, transit, and store displays.

Contests, one-cent deals, premium offers, combination deals, and money-off coupons are all forcing devices that help bring sales in competitive periods and competitive markets. If advertising alone will bring satisfactory sales results, deals will not be used. Sometimes, however, advertising is not enough. Thus, when it becomes necessary to match a competitor's tactics, promotional devices back up the advertising.

Selling. Procter & Gamble, for years the leader in the soap field, knows that its huge advertising expenditures are not enough to ensure its No. 1 position. A well-drilled sales force that calls constantly on every independent grocery store, supermarket, delicatessen, and wholesaler gives Procter & Gamble 100 percent distribution to back up the advertising. No advertisement can do the work of the salesman in closing the orders, in getting good displays of the product, and in telling of techniques that the salesman has seen working for other retailers. In the final analysis, Procter & Gamble advertises to retailers and consumers like any other manufacturer of products sold to the public. But its sales force is constantly urging retailers to order, stock, provide shelf space, and display Procter & Gamble products for consumers.

Product Development. Businesses today prefer to sell a variety of products in several markets because new competitive products, governmental or court action or resource scarcity can quickly make a product unsalable, obsolete, or even illegal. Lasers may replace needles on record players. Hand-held calculators have taken over the market for slide rules. Insecticides are banned; the selling of artificial sweeteners is restricted. Energy scarcity will change the way Americans move about, with smaller cars, van pooling to work, and an increased use of public transportation. New energy-efficient homes will be smaller and better insulated. Heat pumps replace natural gas or oil burning furnaces. Solar collectors deliver energy to hot water heaters in a growing number of American homes.

Because change is so pervasive in America, companies diversify to manage the risk of product obsolescence or a governmental order prohibiting the sale of one or more of a firm's products. Some large businesses diversify by buying small businesses that have developed new products. More likely, large corporations invest in research to develop new products for existing or new markets.

Today there are no stand-still products. While some products enjoy patent protection, patents do run out. Technology constantly yields new and improved products. Consumer demands change. Young mothers demanded baby food without salt and preservatives, upsetting the relatively standardized baby food products that had been marketed unchanged for many years. New diet soft drink brands proliferate in response to consumer desires for sugar-free products. Coffee consumption drops as coffee prices rise, and consumers shift to other beverages. Light beer sales rise dramatically in response to changing consumer tastes.

In the world of marketing, advertising is most frequently associated with new products with a favorable primary demand trend. Why? Advertising tends to work more efficiently for new products with genuine consumer benefits but becomes quite expensive when used to stall a declining consumer demand. Advertising could not convince American men to continue wearing the traditional businessman's hat. With the introduction of cigarettes, advertising could not halt the decline in the sales of cigars.

If the product is not right in the public's eyes, advertising cannot compensate for product shortcomings. This was the lesson of the Edsel automobile, one of the most-discussed new-product failures in American automotive history. Advertising could not persuade automobile buyers to buy Edsels. Now, however, the few Edsels in existence are bought by antique car collectors at prices far exceeding the original price of a new Edsel.

ADVERTISING AND INDUSTRIAL GOODS

All the examples used so far have shown that advertising, even when used by the biggest and most expert advertisers, can do only part of the work of getting products from the factory to the consumers' food shelves, clothes closets, garages, and drug cabinets.

Furthermore, advertising's role is usually even less important in total marketing when we are concerned with the selling of industrial goods. A company manufacturing steam turbines, for example, is normally going to view advertising as unimportant in its total marketing process. There are relatively few buyers. Often such buyers negotiate for years with sale engineering teams. While some producers of industrial equipment may consider the role of advertising vital in their marketing plans, it is in the area of competitive, mass-produced consumer products that advertising plays the most important role.

ADVERTISING SALES OBJECTIVES

First of all, it should be recognized that the eventual purpose of all advertising is selling something. The word *"selling"* here can be used broadly. You are selling, for instance, when you persuade someone to adopt a course of action or a way of thinking. When you have persuaded someone to enter a store, you have "sold" that person on taking that action. All life is made up of persuasion, and persuasion is selling, whether of goods, services, or beliefs, and advertising is a conspicuous form of selling persuasion. Advertising persuasion takes three principal directions:

(1) *It sells goods.* Usually when one thinks of advertising, this selling of goods is overwhelmingly what he considers to be the chief function of advertising. Most retail advertising is concerned with the selling of goods, as is national advertising. From the time that we first read newspapers or magazines or listen to radio or watch television, we are asked to buy goods. Advertising has been used to sell goods since colonial days, and such advertising will always be the most important for advertising people.

(2) *It sells services.* Banks, hotels, laundries, insurance companies, repair services, investment companies, and even advertising agencies find advertising indispensable. If the quality of services offered by these organizations is superb, and excessive charges are not made for these services, satisfied customers often bring much business to these organizations through their enthusiastic recommendations, just as patients help build a big practice for a doctor or a dentist; however, the service organization does not need to entrust the building of its business to the chance recommendations of customers. It can use advertising. Hotel chains the size of the Hilton group or the Statler organizations and auto rental service companies such as Hertz or Avis have not waited for business to come to them from friends of customers. Through aggressive advertising they have promoted their services. "Word-of-mouth" advertising is often praised as the best kind of advertising, but few of the big businesses of this country have been content to depend wholly upon it.

(3) *It sells ideas.* A big company faces a strike threat in one of its many plant areas around the country; it very frequently resorts to advertising to explain its position in the labor situation. Newspaper adver-

tisements and radio commercials point out the contribution of the company to the community and the nation. Careful explanations are given concerning the strike issues, and the position of the company toward the issues and the workers is made clear. Here we have "idea" advertising at work. A product is not being sold, nor is a service. The company is selling the idea that it is fair, that it has made great efforts to settle the issues in question, and that the closing of the plant by strikers will cause a great economic loss to the community.

While idea advertising will always rank a poor third to goods and services advertising, the volume of the idea advertising has increased steadily over the past few years. Companies have used much advertising of this type in the face of labor troubles or difficulties with government. Increasingly idea advertising is used to counter arguments of environmentalists. Although such advertising may seem to be far removed from "selling," it can be considered to be selling the viewpoint of the company on issues important to the company and the general public.

The automobile industry is blamed for air pollution, the oil industry for fuel shortages and price manipulation, the pharmaceutical industry for high prices, the food industry for additives, and the insurance industry for rising automobile and health insurance rates. Some businesses and industry associates in these and other industries currently advertise to explain the size of profits, the cost of finding new energy, or the complexity of adjusting products to new environmental regulations. Some insurance companies are telling us what we all know: inflated automobile damage estimates raise everybody's automobile insurance premiums.

Intermediate Advertising Objectives

Some advertising is designed to accomplish what are called intermediate advertising objectives that may lead to sales. A company may simply want to make people aware that it exists or is known as a research leader or has nationwide parts depots. This is important information to potential consumers. It is also important information to the financial community and to potential investors.

Other advertising may have the goal of showing new uses for an existing product. Much Scotch Brand tape advertising suggests new uses for the already widely used product. The same is true of baking soda. Sometimes consumers develop negative attitudes about genuinely new products without really knowing much about such products. Microwave ovens are one such product. Information on energy use and required cooking times and recipes for gourmet dishes can stimulate the development of positive attitudes toward microwave cooking.

Sometimes the advertiser's major problem is that consumers don't believe an advertised product claim. Many consumers are unsure that clothes can be washed clean in cold water or that a room can be cleared of odors with a single drop of fluid. Demonstrations, tests consumers can make with product samples, or the use of trusted testimonial givers are some of the ways advertisers use to build consumer belief.

It always happens so fast.

And, this time, you're right. It did happen to "the other guy."

You know: The guy who wouldn't hurt a fly, turn down a friendly drink—or take a cab home instead of driving. A nice guy who'd now and then smoke in bed, maybe swim out a little too far, sometimes hurry a little down the stairs.

We know you knew him. And that you'll miss him.

We just don't want you to join him.

"Oops" is a pitiful epitaph.

National Safety Council

If you don't like thinking about safety, think where you'd be without it.

A reminder from the National Safety Council. A non-profit, non-governmental public service organization. Our only goal is a safer America.

Non-commercial advertising.

Television is used dramatically here to demonstrate the wisdom of regular checkups for cancer. Millions of dollars in advertising are devoted to other than commercial selling of products and services.

14

Immediate Action Versus Long-Range Advertising

Most retail advertising urges immediate buying and often stresses price. Exceptions exist, of course, among those retailers selling goods, and especially services, who use reminder or retentive advertising. An example of such a retailer would be a tire shop that merely says over and over again in print and in broadcast media, "When you think of tires, think of Blank's Tire Shop."

National advertising is mostly long range and uses the campaign approach. That is, each advertisement that is prepared is part of a carefully thought-out series of advertisements. Few national advertisers prepare individual advertisements with no consideration of how these advertisements will fit campaign objectives.

The Advertising Council
Help Fight Pollution Campaign

ONE-MINUTE RADIO SPOT - "Botanic Garden"
ANNOUNCER

Riders on a tour train through the South Coast Botanic Garden in Palos Verdes, California, pass through one of the most varied collections of plant life in America. A crystal stream flows through a ravine...and plumed birds sing and feed around the more than 2000 different plant species. And yet, just ten feet below them, lie rusted cars...cracked sinks... 3-million-tons of trash and garbage! For, South Coast Botanic Garden was once a dump.

One thing made this transformation possible. Community involvement. Citizens of Palos Verdes Peninsula raised the money, and did much of the grading and planting.

A dump to a paradise. Impossible? Not when enough people get involved.

Possible. In your community. With volunteer projects that return the land to its natural beauty. We'd like to send you the name of the community team nearest you so you can find out what they're doing and how you can help. Write: KEEP AMERICA BEAUTIFUL, 99 Park Avenue, New York, New York 10016.

People start pollution. People can stop it.

A public service message of this station and The Advertising Council.   # # #   12175

Non-commercial advertising.

Radio has been a very useful medium for non-commercial messages because it is easy to execute and preparation costs are low compared to print media and television.

The Advertising Council, Inc.

In preparing the campaign, the advertiser establishes a theme and then sees that all advertisements tie in with the theme. The "Marlboro Country" of Marlboro cigarettes was the theme line of that product, just as the "flip-top box" was the theme preceding it. Similarly, LSMFT, or Lucky Strike means fine tobacco," was the well-known and long-used campaign theme of American Tobacco.

The themes were designed to meet defined advertising goals. These goals are expressed frequently in terms of awareness of the company, knowledge of its products and services, or perhaps to change peoples' impressions about the company. They seldom relate directly to sales, although consumers may consider the personality or friendliness of the company from which they buy.

Some companies never change a campaign theme. Others use the campaign until it has run its course or until some better campaign approach is found. Others change on a regular basis.

One of the most difficult creative task in advertising is evolving *campaign ideas*—that is, ideas that lend themselves to almost endless repetition in print and broadcast media. Many copywriters can create ideas that are good for one or two advertisements, but the writer who can consistently produce ideas that can be used as campaign themes can make a fortune in advertising.

Many advertising ideas have been rejected with the statement: "Your idea is great, but it's just a one-shotter; it is no good for a campaign." Campaigns can be devised for products in any of the three stages. A campaign for an item in the primary stage will usually, however, be altered as the product reaches the selective stage, and will be changed again as competitive conditions warrant. It is when products reach the retentive stage that campaign themes are longest lasting and may, in fact, never change.

DIVISIONS OF ADVERTISING

Advertising may be classified

(1) by the stage of the advertising,
(2) by the geographical coverage of the advertising, and
(3) by the type of advertising and the media used.

Stages of Advertising

Like people, advertising goes through stages, depending on the newness and degree of development of the products being promoted. The terminology used to describe these stages may vary a bit, but it is generally agreed that there are three principal stages of advertising—primary, selective, and retentive.

Primary. When the first electric toothbrush arrived on the market, it was heralded as a great advance in tooth care, which, of course it was. Despite its obvious advantages, however, it had to be sold to the American public. What was being sold in this initial period was not so much a particular brand of electric toothbrush as the *idea* of the electric toothbrush. It was necessary to persuade people of several facts:

(1) It was safe to put something powered by electricity in the mouth.
(2) The brushing action of the electric toothbrush was far superior to the manual brushing people have used for so many years.
(3) The superiorities of this new device were enough to justify its far greater cost.

During this first stage, therefore, the chief job of the advertiser is to persuade prospects that they want the general type of product represented by the product advertised. Advertising during this period is primary advertising.

Foreign advertisement in United States publication.

With more and more foreign corporations marketing products and services in the U.S., such advertisements as this are becoming common in consumer and business publications. This advertisement appeared in *Fortune* Magazine.

Many products employ a certain amount of primary advertising no matter how long they have been on the market. Other products use it only during the introduction of the product to the market. Television sets, for example, were made known through strong primary advertising that told of the expanded horizons that were possible through this exciting new medium of entertainment and information. In a very short while, when many manufacturers had entered their brands of television receivers on the market, primary selling of entertainment and information was bypassed in favor of emphasis on the technical superiorities of one brand over another. Clarity of the picture, fidelity of the sound, and easy tuning became more important as television came to be taken for granted as a source of entertainment and information.

Electric carving knives, electric toothbrushes, and electric can openers are products that will always need to use a certain amount of primary advertising along with advertising of brand differences. It will always be necessary to persuade people of the merits of these products themselves as well as of the superiority of one brand over the others. Many Americans feel that they can get along without electric can openers, but it is the rare person or family in this television age that feels it can manage without a television set. Thus the stage of a product is determined not so much by how long a product is on the market as by how quickly the product is viewed as indispensable. The electric can opener may use some primary advertising as long as it is on the market; television sets dropped this kind of advertising quickly for black and white sets and then began it again when color television was introduced.

Primary advertising, therefore, must always be used to a certain extent for products that are not considered absolute necessities.

Primary advertising is also necessary for products whose markets change rapidly. Children may chew bubble gum frequently between the ages of five and ten. Every five years there is an almost 100 percent change among heavy users. Retailers likewise face similar turnovers as people move. In some neighborhoods as many as 25 percent of the homes may be sold to new owners each year. The retailer cannot depend on word of mouth. Stores operating near university and college housing and apartment complexes must reestablish themselves with students each year for a maximum of four years.

Selective. When it becomes more important to consider the differences among brands of a product than to consider whether the product itself should be bought, the selective period of advertising has arrived. Thousands of products use this kind of advertising without ever having used primary advertising. A new, unusual product entering the marketplace almost automatically uses primary advertising. But after the new product is established and considered a necessity, manufacturers of new brands of that product will not bother with selling the general kind of product but will hammer hard on the various superiorities of their brands over rival brands. For this reason, selective advertising is sometimes called competitive advertising.

Many more products are in the selective stage of advertising than in any other stage because, in our competitive system, a new and different product that can be sold profitably will rarely have the field long to itself. Just as soon as other brands appear, they will stress the brand differences that they consider superiorities. The first product on the market will counter with advertising that stresses its superiorities and the selective advertising battle is on.

LEO BURNETT COMPANY, INC.
AS FILMED AND RECORDED (5/76)

"Tennis Anybody Rev." :30

STAR-KIST
HZST6090

1. WALLY: Whatchadoin', Charlie?

2. (Sfx: whoosh of Charlie's practice swing) CHARLIE: Playin' tennis.

3. WALLY: Yea, how do ya do that? CHARLIE: You go around yelling...tennis anybody!

4. (Sfx: whiz of balls)

5. CHARLIE: Only not around a octopus.

6. WALLY: Oh.

7. CHARLIE: Anyway, playing tennis shows good taste. Right, Star-Kist?

8. WALLY: But Charlie, Star-Kist don't want tunas with good taste.

9. Star-Kist wants tunas that taste good.

10. (Sfx: zip as hook is jerked away) CHARLIE: Hey! (Anncr VO) Sorry Charlie...

11. ...only good-tasting tuna get to be Star-Kist.

12. Good-tasting one hundred percent tuna fillet.

13. GIRL: This is good-tasting tuna!

14. CHARLIE: Get good taste, (Sfx: whiz of tennis ball, bonk!)...

15. ...get Star-Kist.

Consumer advertising that uses humor.

No one would mistake this television commercial as advertising directed to businessmen. Humor, used correctly and for the right product, can be effective in pulling sales. It is seldom used in business, industrial, or professional advertising.

Foreign advertising.

Many countries, especially Japan, have greatly increased the volume and quality of their advertising, America no longer wholly dominates the world advertising scene.

Fanta..Fantastic!

Out of all this comes constant improvement, since the product that stands still in our competitive system dies. The hardest task of advertising is to sell a product that is no better than its rivals, or possibly somewhat inferior. If inferior, its days are usually numbered, no matter how much or what kind of advertising is used.

Retentive.   Some products, long on the market and generally accepted as everyday necessities—and usually the type of product about which it is not possible to say much—use retentive advertising for the most part, although any one of them may introduce selective advertising when it seems appropriate.

With the trend to the "natural" in products, baking powder advertising has changed from retentive for traditional uses such as baking, to primary and selective as a clothes soaking and washing product, a refrigerator air freshener, and a body powder. In this day of constant discoveries and product improvement there are few products that are so well entrenched that they may dare to rely wholly on merely reminding people that they are available. Almost all products must be sold and resold.

As we look back over what has been said about the three stages of advertising, we find that although selective advertising is the most common form, it is strikingly evident that most advertisers use a combination of primary and selective advertising or selective and retentive advertising.

Sweepstakes advertisement.

Currently, interest in tennis and golf is very high. This advertisement should attract many new users for the product as well as develop more sales among present users.

Groom & Clean will give you a lesson you'll never forget.

Win a day of lessons with Ken Rosewall or Billy Casper during a week's vacation at Hilton Head Island.

Enter the Groom & Clean® Pro-Shop Sportstakes.
And win a week's vacation for two at the exclusive Hilton Head Inn, South Carolina. Plus a full day on the courts with Ken Rosewall, or the course with Billy Casper.

6 Second Prizes
Magnavox 19" Color TV plus the Odyssey electronic sports game you play right on your TV screen. Both provide hours of fun for the whole family.

25 Third Prizes
Full set of Billy Casper "Shotmaker" Golf Clubs or 2 Seamco Ken Rosewall Rackets plus 2 matching Atlantic Racket-Paks®

1,000 Fourth Prizes
World-famed Bausch & Lomb Ray-Ban® sunglasses.

All brought to you by the Groom & Clean Pro-Shop.
Even if you don't win a prize, you can enjoy great Groom & Clean Pro-Shop savings on golf and tennis equipment—like the 37% saving on this Atlantic Deluxe Country Club Bag. All equipment approved by our two great Groom & Clean® users and Groom & Clean Pros, Ken Rosewall and Billy Casper. Look for details on our package.

"GROOM & CLEAN PRO-SHOP SPORTSTAKES" OFFICIAL RULES

OFFICIAL ENTRY BLANK
Please enter me in the Groom & Clean Pro-Shop Sportstakes. I am enclosing proof-of-purchase or the words Groom & Clean printed in plain block letters on a 3" x 5" piece of paper.
Mail entry to: Groom & Clean Pro-Shop Sportstakes, P.O. Box 337, New York, N.Y. 10046

Name _____
(Please print clearly)
Address _____
City _____ State _____ Zip _____

Greaseless control for just shampooed hair.

Even with such a common and accepted item as a record player, for example, combination advertising is at work. Primary advertising is needed to sell the joy of having music readily available through records. Selective advertising is important to make clear the advantages in tone, power, and appearance over competing brands. Primary advertising will be used for new record players that pick up sound from a record by laser rather than by the traditional needle.

Geographical Coverage of Advertising

By rather universal agreement in the industry, advertising is divided geographically into national, regional, and local advertising.

Yet, despite the agreement, the lines are not clear cut. Furthermore, so-called local advertisers may use national and regional advertising, just as a regional advertiser may use national advertising. Still, notwithstanding these variations, there are many advertisers who may definitely be classed firmly under one of the three geographical headings.

National Advertising. When we talk of a national advertiser we mean an advertiser of a product or service who distributes (or makes available) a product or service on a national basis, and uses truly national media, such as network television or radio, national magazines, or newspapers in all major markets.

Such advertising, furthermore, is largely executed by advertising agencies hired by the advertisers to perform such tasks as writing the advertisements, preparing the artwork, and placing the advertising in the media.

When we talk about the big-spending giants of advertising, such as General Motors, Procter & Gamble, General Foods, and General Electric, we are talking about national advertising in its most spectacular aspects: the big television shows, the double-page color advertisements, and all the other aspects of advertising that make it such a talked-about, and criticized, activity in American life.

In any given year, when all the billions spent on advertising are added up, it will invariably be found that more than half the total was spent on national advertising. Yet the number of national advertisers is considerably smaller than those engaged in local advertising, a fact that might not be readily apparent considering how much more is spent on national advertising. National advertising is, of course, because of its scope, the most costly form of advertising.

Regional Advertising. Regional advertising may be used by national advertisers for special regional campaigns to bolster business in areas where sales have been lagging. Truly regional advertisers, who have distribution of their product or service in a fairly well-defined territory, use regional advertising. A baker, for instance, may distribute bread and other products in a five-state area. Because sales people operate only in that area, advertising is done only in the media covering these five states, although there is sure to be some overlapping of state boundaries. Local advertisers, while they do most of their their business in a very localized market, sometimes engage in regional advertising to draw more people to their trading area. A department store with a large furniture annex such as Younker's in Des Moines, Iowa, may use advertising that extends beyond the city limits, because it knows that people in many areas of Iowa are interested in its offerings.

Regional advertising is carried on, also, by makers of products with a highly seasonal appeal. These advertisers may follow the sun in their advertising of antifreeze, suntan oil, and other seasonal products, or the sun and snow with a line of cosmetics for skiers and surfers. It is also used for ethnic concentrations, with Mexican-American foods selling primarily from Texas through Arizona and New Mexico and Southern California.

Great impetus has been given to regional advertising in the past few years by the emergence of regional editions of magazines that once were only national. New fierce competition by the broadcast media has caused these onetime exclusively national magazines to offer regional editions that may enable an advertiser to use the magazine in a single state, or even in a portion of a state.

TV Guide is an example of a big-circulation magazine that has led in the publication of regional editions.

Where once the prestige of advertising in the leading magazines was limited to those advertisers who had national distribution of their products, it is now available for a much more modest cost to much smaller advertisers with limited distribution.

Because magazines divide their circulation in a number of ways the small advertiser can buy one, two, several, or many urban markets, states, or regions to target a selected geographic market.

Local Advertising.   When the word local is used in reference to advertising, it is normally meant to refer to retail advertising done by retail stores, ranging from a small-town hardware store to a giant department store such as Bullock's, Marshall Field's, or Macy's.

Advertising described as local would also be done by hotels, taxicab companies, television repair shops, and other organizations offering services.

Typically, the organization using local advertising does so in media restricted geographically to the trading area in which the business is located. Only media in the hometown are used. To use media outside the town or city would be a waste of money, since the typical organization referred to cannot expect any business from beyond its trading area.

For local advertising the newspaper is king in dollar volume. Other media are used by the local advertiser but the newspaper remains the bread-and-butter medium.

Geographical Breakdowns Indistinct.   Comparatively few advertisers fall strictly into one geographical class. The size of a business is no determinant. A small electronics company, for instance, may have a tiny advertising budget and a limited customer list, but may be considered a national advertiser because it runs an occasional advertisement in an electronics magazine that has a rate of $150 for the quarter-page used. This manufacturer, nevertheless, may draw most of its business from the immediate geographical area and may use some local advertising to draw this business.

A department store may spend most of its money on local newspaper advertising, but in addition to this local advertising, may run national advertising for its fashion goods in *Vogue*, the *New Yorker*, and other magazines stressing fashion merchandise. Sometimes a department store will use a more general magazine, such as *Time*. The point, however, is that a local advertiser can also, if business can thus be obtained, become a national advertiser, or both.

Almost all national advertisers of mass-sold products will at times also be regional advertisers to facilitate the introduction of new products or to bolster business in weak areas, or perhaps to match seasonal buying trends or population shifts. Sometimes a market has unusual prestige. Many clothing manufacturers advertise heavily in New York City and the surrounding surburban market. If a line of clothing sells successfully in the elite New York market area, department and clothing store buyers throughout the nation are more likely to buy for resale to their consumers.

Point of difference.

In a vigorous manner, this advertisement points out a product attribute not possessed by competitive cooking oils. There is no evident primary selling here. The assumption is that the readers use cooking oils and are interested in brand differences.

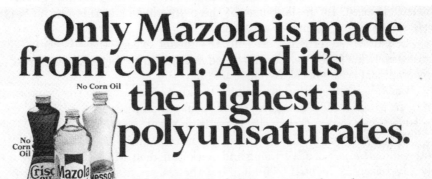

Only Mazola is made from corn. And it's the highest in polyunsaturates.

No Corn Oil

No Corn Oil

100% Corn Oil

Of America's three most-used cooking oils, only Mazola is corn oil.
Neither Crisco nor Wesson have any corn oil at all.

Furthermore, Mazola is highest in polyunsaturates.
And foods fried in Mazola get the delicate, digestible lightness of corn oil.
Only Mazola is corn oil. Wesson and Crisco are not. That's a big difference.*

Mazola. Good for your food because it's Corn Oil.

*Taste the difference in Mazola Margarine, too!

Types of Advertising and the Media Used

There are distinct differences between "consumer" advertising and "business" advertising, and these differences should be understood. There are, furthermore, strongly defined differences within business advertising.

When the word "advertising" is used, consumer advertising is generally meant, whether the user is an advertising man or someone outside the advertising field. The consumer, in this instance, is a person who is interested in the advertised product or products because they answer some personal or household need. In the language of the marketing man, this person is often referred to as an "ultimate" consumer.

Consumer advertising uses all the media except those strictly in the business field. Likewise, consumer advertising may be used in any of the geographical areas—local, regional, and national.

Consumer advertising is, in short, the kind of advertising that is around all of us from our earliest memories throughout our adult lives. Also, it is the kind of advertising that supports the advertising-agency system.

The target of consumer advertising—the consumer—is the object of intense interest on the part of advertising and marketing men. Most of the money spent by advertisers is devoted to finding out the consumer's likes and dislikes, his habits, and his motivations. A slight miscalculation in any market as big as the consumer market can cost millions of dollars, and right judgment can result in fantastic financial success. With the stakes so high, the consumer market is probed, wooed, and analyzed.

Association Advertising to Consumers.   On occasion, the advertisers in an industry find that they must attempt collectively what they cannot accomplish individually. Hence they form an association and pay membership dues; the association then runs advertising on behalf of the entire industry, not the individual firms.

Usually such an association is formed only where there are problems too big for individual companies to handle. When meat sales in the United States declined, for example, the Meat Institute was formed. Foods, including dairy products, citrus fruits, walnuts, and cranberries, are well represented in the association list. Circumstances that would call for association advertising are declining markets, intense competition, and bad public relations.

Association advertising is essentially primary advertising, since it sells the idea of a product or service rather than brands of that product or service. Because it contains no prices, no real urging to buy soon, nor directions about where to buy, association advertising, while effective in promoting an industry, often fails to make a conscious impression on consumers. Its influence is subtle.

Business Advertising.   For years, both by people in business and by outsiders, all business advertising has been lumped under the term *trade advertising*. All business publications, accordingly, were called trade papers. The word "papers" used in this connection has caused further confusion.

The terms *business advertising* and *business publications* are favored these days, although the word "trade" is still applied by many who should know better.

Under the heading of business advertising may be listed four rather well-defined categories:

   (1)   industrial advertising,
   (2)   professional advertising,
   (3)   trade advertising, and
   (4)   vocational and management advertising.

It should be understood that business advertising could be divided into more than these four groupings, since all business advertising cannot be covered by the four groupings without overlappings; most business advertising, however, will fall under these headings fairly well.

Primary advertising.

Many persons must be sold the idea of using a hearing aid. Although the brand name is mentioned here, the big objective of this advertisement is to convince readers to try a hearing aid. This is even more important than the stressing of competitive difference. Many products, as in this case, never get completely out of the primary selling stage because there are always substantial numbers of new prospects who must be sold the "idea" of the product quite apart from the brand name under which it is marketed.

Selective advertising.

Hardly anyone is unaware of the meaning of VW. This brand has become one of the most famous in the world, due largely to advertisements such as these. In both, there is a timely stress, conveyed in a clever yet hardhitting way, on the excellent gas mileage obtained by the Volkswagen.

Industrial Advertising. An industrial advertiser addresses messages primarily to management in an industrial plant or factory. The advertising purpose may be to sell equipment such as machinery to be used in industrial production, or to sell raw materials to be used in production. The company may be selling personal equipment for factory or mill workers, such as safety goggles, or may be selling a service, for example, a washroom towel service or piped music to minimize worker fatigue.

Advertising will be done mostly in industrial magazines that circulate widely among management people who make the buying decisions about industrial equipment. A few of these:

The Iron Age   *Chemical Engineering*   *Industrial Design*
Industry   *Modern Materials Handling*   *Plant Engineering*

An industrial company is playing for big stakes. It may be selling anything from gigantic punch presses to steam turbines or huge traveling cranes. Even if the item it sells is much smaller than these, a single order might include enough units to completely outfit a large mill, or even several mills. It is hardly to be expected, therefore, that industrial advertising will bring in direct sales; the money involved and the arrangements to be made are too big and complex.

Retentive (reminder) advertising.

This advertisement with a humorous copy twist doesn't attempt to tell *how* it carries out its work. Instead, it reminds readers *what* it does hoping that if the situation arises that calls for its services, readers will think automatically of Terminix.

"When you think of pests think of us."

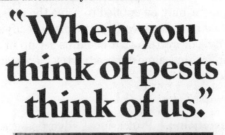

Henry Tobey, President, Terminix International.

"I'm Hank Tobey. I run a company called Terminix. Our business is getting rid of termites, roaches, ants, spiders and other pests that attack American homes. We've been doing this for years. And doing it so well that 94 out of every 100 customers across the country say they'd ask us back again.

"If your home is being invaded by pests, check us out with a neighbor or friend. Then give us a call. We're in the Yellow Pages."

TERMINIX
INTERNATIONAL

The Nationwide
Termite and Pest Control Experts.

Most industrial advertisers are content if their advertising draws some inquiries or requests a visit from a sales representative. In industrial advertising and selling, the roles for advertising and for salespeople are well established.

Sales people simply cannot get to see all the people who can be reached by an advertisement in an industrial magazine. A salesperson might, for example, be allowed to see only the plant purchasing agent and possibly one or two other persons down the management scale. An advertisement in an industrial magazine subscribed to by the company will, in contrast, reach the president, the vice-president, and many management people in the plant and the offices.

Yet, despite the salesperson's inability to contact even a reasonable portion of the people who might have some influence on the purchase of the product or equipment, the salesperson has essential functions.

Advertising can:

- Reach almost everyone who either directly or indirectly influences the buying of the product or equipment. These people are known in the field as *buying influences*, and many more can be reached through advertising than through salesmen.
- Get the buying influences interested in the product or equipment.
- Achieve a recognition of the product or equipment and possibly a preference for it.

Salespersons can:

- Offer a proposal. In this proposal they show the prospect how the product or equipment may be applied to solve the prospect's problem. An example would be an engineering-type plan specifying a new materials-handling conveyor system that could be set up in a factory.
- Close the order, and almost no advertisement can do this in the industrial field.

Professional Advertising. Professional advertising as used here is addressed to those persons who are practicing generally recognized professions that are licensed and operate under professional standards. Medical doctors, dentists, architects, and lawyers form the four most important segments addressed although others are included.

Professional advertising aims directly at professional people. Using doctors and dentists as examples, we find a triple purpose in most such advertising:

(1) To persuade the professionals to use the product (surgical instruments, drills, drugs) in the conduct of their profession.
(2) To persuade them to recommend use of the product (therapeutics, toothpastes) to those who would be swayed by such endorsements.
(3) To persuade them to put the product (which could be anything from cameras to cigarettes) to personal use. If they smoked a certain brand of cigarettes, for instance, it might be considered equivalent to an endorsement.

Typical professional magazines that carry professional advertising are:

Architectural Record	*Journal of the American Dental Association*
The Practical Accountant	*Journal of the American Medical Association*
The Practical Lawyer	*American Bar Association Journal*

Professional advertising, like industrial advertising, seldom makes direct sales but depends upon interesting the professionals enough to cause them to check further into the merits of the product. Professionals have such full working days that it is difficult for salespeople to obtain interview time, but they read the journals in their field, especially those journals, such as the *Journal of the American Medical Association*, that are the official organs of the professional societies. Advertising in publications of this type is carefully screened and so is generally respected by professionals.

Trade Advertising. All retail merchants can find magazines that apply to their business. Trade magazines carry advertisements for equipment and products useful to merchants as well as practical articles that tell how to run their business more profitably. A trade magazine, as distinguished from an industrial magazine, is addressed to retail merchants who are engaged in reselling at a profit the products they buy; the people these merchants sell to are the ultimate consumers.

In addition to the advertising for products to be sold by the retailer, the trade magazine carries much advertising for products used by the retailer in the conduct of business. A mannequin for a clothing store would be an example. A cash register is another.

The advertising in a trade magazine is more likely to result in direct sales or stronger sales leads than the advertising in industrial or professional magazines. The products advertised are less technical than those advertised in the professional magazine, and less costly than those in the industrial publication.

Through an advertisement, a druggist may become interested in a lighting fixture, a butcher in a slicing machine, a candy-store proprietor in a refrigerated display case, a paint store owner in a device for mixing paints, to name a few of the products used in busines that may be advertised in a trade magazine and evoke immediate response from the retailer if there is need for such equipment at the moment.

A retailer may have a similarly immediate interest in a new proprietary medicine, a new packaged meat product, a variety package of candy, or a paint that is guaranteed not to drip from the brush. These products to be sold to customers may cause enough interest to result in an order to the manufacturer or may ask the salesperson to fill an order. Thus trade advertising is not so long range as industrial or professional advertising, and not so reticent about avoiding the appearance of asking for an order directly.

Some typical trade publications are:

Drug Topics	*Boating Industry*
Progressive Grocer	*Liquor Store*
Hardware Retailing	*Chain Store Age*

Vocational and Management Advertising.   Many persons engaged in specialized occupations are covered neither by the term professional nor by the terms trade or industrial. Advertising people are in this group of specialists; so are printing salespeople and aviators.

Many of the publications in the vocational-management group are addressed both to the ordinary worker in the vocation and to the person who has a supervisory job. *Advertising Age* is such a publication.

A few magazines, such as *Fortune, Business Week*, and the *Wall Street Journal*, are thought of as primarily management-oriented but even these have a wide cross section of readers.

Advertising in magazines in the vocational-management group is varied and changes its character from publication to publication because of the specialized needs of both the vocational and the management group. Neither by products nor by advertising style can advertising in these publications be classified or described as exactly as advertising in the other classes of publications already discussed.

A form of advertising that is prominent in itself but still must fall in the vocational-management grouping is institutional advertising. There are many magazines classed as institutional. All of these, however, have vocational-management aspects. Among them are *Resort Management, Hospital Forum, Institutions/Volume Feeding Management*.

Industrial advertisement with a management slant.

Most industrial advertisements, such as this one that appeared in the magazine *Plant Engineering,* are aimed at men who can make decisions. This particular advertisement invites the attention of the very top men in the corporations reached by the publication.

Our free plant survey can show you how to cut your plant operating costs

It's still possible today to cut operating costs when you look in the right places. We can help you find some of those right places.

At no cost to you, our "Scotch" Taping Systems Specialists will work with you on a plant-wide survey of your production needs. They will determine where the proper tape and dispensing systems would help you cut time, labor and material costs.

From this free survey you will get all the benefits of a careful analysis by knowledgeable professionals. And you'll have their confidential recommendations in a detailed written report. With no strings attached.

We've got over 600 ways to cut costs with "Scotch" Industrial Taping Systems ...from packaging, joining, protecting and masking to identifying and graphic arts.

Our free plant survey is helping cut costs in many different types and sizes of plants. It can help you.

Call for the helping hand of your professional 3M representative for your free plant survey. Or write to Industrial Tape Division, 3M Company, 3M Center, St. Paul, MN 55101, Dept. IBD-44.

3M COMPANY

"Scotch" and the Plaid design are reg. T.M's of 3M Company

Reprint scheduled to appear in INDUSTRY WEEK, February 18; PLANT ENGINEERING, April 18 and September 19, 1974 issues.

(2) BPH

LITHO IN U.S.A.

To give some idea of the widely diverse character of the vocational-management publications, here are the names of a few selected at random:

Professional Golfer   *The Police Chief*
Editor & Publisher   *World Ports/American Seaport*
The Bowling Proprietor   *Electro-Optical Systems & Design*
Bank News   *Taxicab Management*

Vertical and Horizontal Publications. When an advertising person speaks of a "vertical" publication or "vertical" advertising he refers to advertising that is confined to one class of industry. *Hardware Retailing* magazine, aimed only at those people interested in hardware marketing and selling at the store level, is a vertical publication. *Fortune* magazine, distributed to management people in many industries, reaches a cross section of American business and is truly a horizontal publication.

Some magazines, while having titles that seem to limit them, are actually more horizontal than vertical. *Plant Engineering*, for instance, goes to a cross section of management engaged in factory operation and thus crosses many industry lines. This magazine does not concentrate on any one type of factory but discusses factory construction and maintenance news common to many factories.

An advertiser must study the market carefully to determine how deeply to penetrate a single market, or how widely to spread the message. The findings will determine whether to use vertical or horizontal advertising.

WHERE IS ADVERTISING PERFORMED?

Although advertising is complex and draws upon many skills, the places where the work is carried on are few:

- Advertising departments of manufacturers and service organizations.
- Retail-store advertising departments.
- Advertising agencies.
- Media advertising departments.

In addition to these, there are supporting areas in the field that are either directly or indirectly related to advertising. Among these are advertising-marketing-research organizations, advertising-production firms that sell and produce printing, engraving, and paper. There are, besides, advertising artists who work independently (free lance) or in studios that service the advertising industry. Then there are direct-mail and mail-order houses that perform advertising chores along with other activities.

ADVERTISING DEPARTMENTS OF MANUFACTURERS AND SERVICE ORGANIZATIONS

The advertising departments of firms such as General Electric, General Foods, and Lever Brothers are big. The advertising departments of most manufacturers are, in contrast, quite small. Much of the work of such an advertising department is administrative and planning, with actual execution of the advertisements left up to advertising agencies that do the creative work and place the advertisements in the media. In smaller plants, especially in the industrial field, the advertising department may consist of one person who devotes only part of the time to the advertising task. The advertising agency handles the bulk of the advertising chores.

The big advertising departments found in giant corporations may hire hundreds to carry on the work and, besides, distribute advertising chores among a number of advertising agencies, especially if the corporations manufacture a number of products.

Industrial advertisement with engineerig slant.

Much of the readership of industrial magazines is composed of hard-boiled engineers who are looking for facts expressed in straightforward and often technical language. This advertisement demonstrates the proper way to approach this demanding audience.

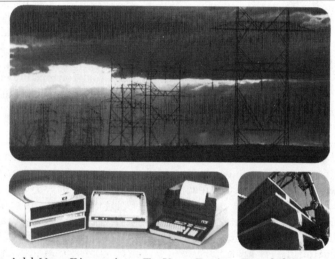

RETAIL-STORE ADVERTISING DEPARTMENTS

There are vast differences among retail-store advertising departments, depending largely on the size of the store. If the store is a small Main Street hardware store, it will have no advertising department, even though it does some advertising. In any given small town, there may not be a single retail establishment with a formal advertising department. Actually, a store must be of a good size to have a full-time advertising manager, let alone an advertising department. In the smaller establishments advertising is a part-time task that is largely carried out by the employee assigned to the work and by the advertising media carrying the advertising. The employee may use materials provided by suppliers of branded merchandise. These are prepared to high standards and the illustrations and identification marks are tied to the national advertising supporting the branded merchandise. Local media salespeople also supply suggestions and materials for the retailer's use.

Big department stores and women's specialty stores, such as Jordan Marsh in Boston or Saks Fifth Avenue in New York City, have busy advertising departments headed by advertising managers. Although they may employ advertising agencies for advertising appearing in specialized media, they prepare most of the advertising themselves, especially the day-to-day advertisements appearing in newspapers.

ADVERTISING AGENCIES

Advertising agencies are among the most publicized of American business enterprises. Despite the publicity, much of it unfavorable, there is a widespread ignorance of what advertising agencies do and how well they do it.

An advertising agency exists only because there is a company or a number of companies which value the services of the agency enough to have that agency plan and execute their advertising. If the agency does the work well, the company will continue to retain it. If, however, the company feels that the agency has not performed its work satisfactorily, the agency will be dismissed. An advertising agency is, therefore, held to a high level of performance and must continually prove its worth to its clients.

Because of the unrelenting demand for results, an advertising agency is a collection of workers who are experts in their field. Most agency personnel specialize in a certain activity, such as copywriting, art, research, media selection.

Almost 100 percent of the national advertising seen in network television, in big-circulation magazine, and in coast-to-coast outdoor advertising campaigns has been created and placed by advertising agencies. Nearly all agencies handling the big national accounts are big themselves, and their dollar volume (called *billings* in the trade) runs into the millions.

Hundreds of advertising agencies, on the other hand, are one- or two-person enterprises, in contrast to the big agencies which may employ hundreds or even thousands of workers. Despite the Hollywood version of an advertising agency as a bustling chrome-trimmed business peopled by handsome, fast-talking men and women, the fact is that most agencies are small businesses that handle

34

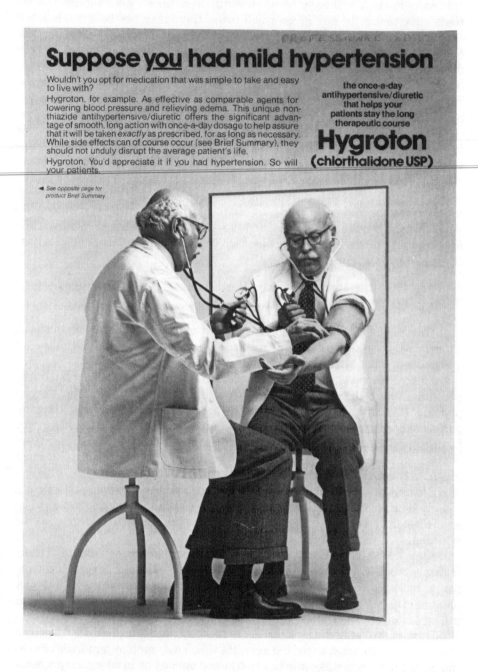

small, unromantic accounts and operate in small, unromantic offices. Advertising agency owners look and work like other business owners except that they work harder and under more pressure than most.

Unlike manufacturer and retail store advertising departments, which are widely scattered in towns and cities throughout the United States, most advertising agencies are concentrated in the big cities, especially New York and Chicago. Most of their business comes from manufacturing and service organizations located in or near these cities. Only a small percentage of the total advertising agency business is obtained from retail stores.

Media Advertising Departments

The advertising department of a newspaper, radio station, television station, or any other medium of communication could more accurately be called a selling department than an advertising department. An examination of almost any media advertising department reveals that selling the medium is the principal activity of the department, and that most of the people employed in the department are primarily salespersons, even though their duties may also require the performance of some creative activities, such as writing copy or preparing layouts.

Even the advertising managers of many media may spend most of their time selling, especially in the business management field.

Creative work by the media is not expected, except by small retailers or by small businesses that have not engaged the services of advertising agencies. Thus, the small Main Street retailer mentioned earlier expects the local newspaper to provide help in preparing newspaper advertisements, just as the retailer calls upon the local radio station (if there is one) to write radio commercials for the store.

As media get larger and deal with bigger clients, they offer services that range from researching the market to providing a wide variety of merchandising services, such as supplying the advertiser's salespeople with route lists, encouraging retailers to display the manufacturer's products, getting retailers to run tie-in advertisements geared to the advertiser's campaign.

To obtain national business, media salespeople call upon advertising agencies and upon advertisers, but particularly upon the agencies. Under a payment system established many years ago, the medium includes the advertising agency's 15 percent commission in the bill sent to the agency, provided that the agency is among the hundreds of agencies that have met certain qualifications. The agency then bills the client the entire amount of the bill and keeps the 15 percent as a commission. Advertising agencies, are, in effect, paid by the media, not by the advertisers. The relationship of the media and the advertising agencies is, accordingly, a very close one, although not always one of mutual friendship and respect.

WHO NEEDS ADVERTISING?

Although the general public has no clear realization of how much it needs and is influenced by advertising, the people who use and pay for advertising have a realistic idea of the power of advertising and its uses.

To answer the question, "Who needs advertising?" it is necessary to examine the usefulness of advertising to (a) the public, (b) the corporation, (c) the retail merchant, and (d) noncommercial organizations.

The Public

Ask most individuals what caused them to buy a certain brand or to use some particular kind of service, and you will very frequently find that they name advertising last as an influence. Yet these same individuals reject non-advertised brands on their shopping trips. A check of their food shelves and bathroom supplies would show an overwhelming preference for advertised goods. Advertising's influence is often subtle. Reaching for the advertised brand is almost a reflex action for the shopper. Many advertising impressions gained from television, magazines, newspapers come into play—often subconsciously—only at that moment when the shopper decides which package or bottle to put into the shopping cart. This "conditioned" buying is one reason why Campbell's soup gets into the shopping basket more often than a lesser known brand.

Besides helping the seller, advertising helps the shopper. It tells the shoppers what goods are available. A perusal of the newspaper, for example, may show that the Ford automobile is now in the dealer's showroom; that Bock beer is making its annual appearance; that Scott's grass seed is ready for purchase. Without this information, the shopper would have to guess what might be found when on a shopping expedition. Especially useful, of course, is the shopping section of the newspaper which gives the supermarket items that enable the homemaker to make up the weekly shopping list. Not knowing what goods were available would make planning much more difficult.

Advertising tells the shopper *where* goods are being sold. One of the greatest problems of shoppers is knowing where to find a number of the products they want to buy. With a product such as Ivory soap or Kellogg's cornflakes, there is no difficulty, since distribution throughout the nation is about 100 percent. Assume however, that the shopper wanted to buy a Macintosh raincoat or a Zenith television set. While both of these products have national distribution, they are not found in many stores; advertising guides the shopper to the outlets that sell them. Telephone classified advertising may provide the information even if the shopper cannot find a media advertisement that will help.

Advertising gives the shopper *facts* helpful in making a final preshopping buying decision. Before making a trip to the downtown department store or the suburban shopping center, the shopper has been made aware, by means of advertising, of such vital information as price, quality of goods, size range, colors, fabrics, design, guarantees. Probably the most helpful aspect of advertising is the opportunity it gives the careful shopper to make a comparison of different products in the unhurried calm of the home, with no salesperson to apply pressure for a quick purchase.

Advertising tells the shopper when *to replace* goods. Before the first snowfall, advertising is run to urge drivers to put on snow tires. Most consumers are well intentioned. They mean to replace dangerously worn-out equipment; they mean to replace old spark plugs that eat gasoline; they mean to replace the ancient refrigerator whose motor runs noisily and constantly. But unless they are reminded, they do not make these replacements when they should; advertising provides the reminders necessary to goad them into action.

The Corporation

Unlike the general public, the businesspeople in corporations usually realize the contribution of advertising. However, there are still those in business who are uneasy about spending money on advertising. Advertising to them is more

Trade magazine advertisement.

"Profit" is the most important word in any advertisement directed at retail dealers. This advertisement not only stresses profits to be made but also another important point—display capabilities. Dealers like products that display attractively and in such a way that they invite easy purchase.

an expense than an investment. These persons when faced with unfavorable business conditions, tend to slash advertising budgets first, since they view advertising as an extra instead of a necessity.

Business people are changing, however, in recognizing that they conduct their business in an environment of public opinion tolerance. If business is slow and sales are down, environmentalists are still vocal, and their challenges must be met. If consumer protectors protest the cost of food packaging, they must be answered and the costs justified.

Even though the sales influence of advertising defies exact measurement, most modern business people use advertising because it enables them to:

Blanket the national or regional markets quickly and inexpensively. Many industrial salespersons are fortunate if they can call on prospects twice a year, and many can manage just one call annually. Furthermore, the cost to the company of a sales call is high. Thus, the industrial sales force covers the market slowly and expensively.

As mentioned earlier in the discussion of industrial advertising, advertisements reach many more prospects than the sales force can hope to, and they do so on a monthly, weekly, or even daily basis. These "calls," furthermore, can be made at a fraction of one cent each.

In the general consumer field, the role of advertising is even more spectacular, since there is no sales force that could match in speed or scope the television commercial beamed into millions of homes, or the copies of a magazine that cover all parts of the United States in one week.

In our distribution system, the company that wants to reach the mass market quickly and at low cost must, with almost no exceptions, use advertising.

Achieve steadier sales and thus eliminate hills and valleys in production. Many businesses sell in cycles, either because demand for their products is seasonal or because the purchase of their products is affected by general business conditions.

Create awareness of a company and its products. In the case of business calls, the prospect may not know anything about the product offered by the salesperson but, if favorably acquainted with the company through advertising, the prospect is more willing to listen to the sales presentation and may be inclined to feel that any product made by the company is likely to be reliable.

In contrast, when the prospect is totally unfamiliar with the company and its products, the salesperson must start from "scratch," as it were. The sales talk must sell not only the product but the belief that the company's sales and manufacturing policies can be trusted.

The Retail Merchant

A grocery store salesperson entered a small corner grocery store. Sitting gloomily behind the counter was the proprietor whose gaze was riveted on the supermarket across the street. When the salesperson attempted to sell him, the store owner shrugged and said: "Those people with their advertising. Look at the people going in there and look at me with no one to talk to but you."

Minutes later the salesperson left the store, but not without learning that

Management advertisement.

Appearing in Fortune Magazine, this advertisement will have a heavy readership among board chairmen, and presidents, of major corporations in the United States, and abroad. The entire tone of the advertisement is correct for management readership of the highest level.

When substantial growth is part of your corporate strategy, consider Morgan Guaranty

In the continuing search for increased profits, your company may have concluded that a program of expansion is essential to continued growth. And your best course may well include multinational moves. Either way, domestic or foreign, you'll face some fundamental questions. For example, what opportunities are there for acquisitions, mergers, joint ventures? What's the best way to finance your expansion or diversification? When is leasing better than borrowing? Which foreign countries offer the soundest economic climate?

Morgan Guaranty's Financial Services group is uniquely experienced in answering questions like these. Based in Morgan offices in major financial centers from New York to Paris to São Paulo to Tokyo, these specialists have broad familiarity with countries, conditions, and companies.

Our Financial Services professionals will help you construct a long-range plan for growth, then assist you with their knowledge of available partners or acquisitions. They'll provide evaluations of an industry, a

market, or a prospective partner— anywhere in the world. They have the experience and innovative talent to counsel you on a variety of financial alternatives, including long-term non-bank financing. In effect, this team acts as your financial adviser before, during, and after negotiations. And they can call on Morgan expertise in such areas as international money management, corporate research, and the Euro-currency market.

For more information, get in touch with a Financial Services officer through any of our offices, worldwide.

Whatever your corporate goal, consider Morgan Guaranty. You'll be in good company. We're already helping 96 of the world's 100 largest corporations, and many smaller ones, too.

MORGAN GUARANTY TRUST COMPANY, 23 Wall Street, New York, New York 10015 • OVERSEAS BANKING OFFICES: London, Paris, Brussels, Antwerp, Frankfurt, Düsseldorf, Munich, Zurich, Milan and Rome (Banca Morgan Vonwiller), Tokyo, Nassau • REPRESENTATIVE OFFICES: Madrid, Beirut, Sydney, Hong Kong, São Paulo, Caracas • INTERNATIONAL BANKING SUBSIDIARIES: San Francisco, Houston

Morgan Guaranty - the corporate bank

the proprietor of this small store (a) had never used advertising, (b) was charging higher prices than the competitor, and (c) had never washed the store windows nor put up selling displays.

Did the supermarket grow to its size because it used advertising? Advertising is undoubtedly part of the reason, an important part. And advertising has contributed greatly to the success of the giant department stores around the country; this is strikingly true of the retail stores of Sears, Roebuck and Company.

Some of the reasons for the use of advertising by retail stores are as follows:

Advertising gives a store character and a "difference." In this day of nationally advertised brands when many stores carry essentially the same lines and offer essentially the same credit terms and other services, it is necessary for retailers to create a "difference" for their establishments. That is, it is necessary if they want customers to come to their stores instead of to those of competitors.

Creating a difference is especially important to department stores and to women's high-fashion shops, yet many such stores never bother to establish such a difference. Thus a shopper can literally decide by the toss of a coin where to shop.

In contrast, consider Neiman-Marcus of Dallas, Texas. Here is a store known throughout the nation. People who have never been to Dallas open charge accounts and do business by mail because, through its advertising, Neiman-Marcus has developed a powerful store personality, a difference that from the start set it apart from the competitors.

A newcomer to any city can look at the advertising for downtown stores and immediately single out the stores that look "interesting" and worth visiting. Copy, art, typography, and the choice of merchandise help establish this preshopping impression.

Creating the difference for downtown stores has taken on special importance with the growth of the giant suburban shopping centers. Luring shoppers downtown is crucial to the downtown merchants. Building store character through advertising can help.

Advertising speeds sales and merchandise turnover. Making fast sales and getting customers out of the store quickly is the recipe for success in many kinds of retail business.

Shoppers acquainted with products through advertising buy more quickly and take less of salesclerks' time. In supermarkets and self-service drugstores, it is vital for sales and turnover to make room for new customers by moving the old ones out in a hurry, an impossible task if each customer has to be "sold" on the merchandise while in the store instead of being at least partially sold before coming in.

In today's competitive market, the profit margin is smaller which makes fast stock turnover even more important. A merchant who turns stock over 20 times on an item giving an 8-cent profit makes more money than the merchant who makes a 10-cent profit with a 15-time turnover. With a greater turnover, the merchant can reduce profit margins and thus prices. With lower prices the merchant can compete better. Any device, such as advertising, that will help speed turnover and lower prices is a tool that must be used.

Advertising is more reliable than word of mouth and more far-reaching than a window display. Many a retailer has been seen to nod wisely and say: "The

Famous advertisement.

In direct, hard-boiled fashion, this advertisement dramatizes the need for advertising to precede the salesman's call.

"I don't know who you are.

I don't know your company.

I don't know your company's product.

I don't know what your company stands for.

I don't know your company's customers.

I don't know your company's record.

I don't know your company's reputation.

Now—what was it you wanted to sell me?"

MORAL: Sales start **before** your salesman calls—with business publication advertising.

McGRAW-HILL MAGAZINES
BUSINESS • PROFESSIONAL • TECHNICAL

best kind of advertising is the word-of-mouth advertising of my customers. That, and my window displays."

Much success has been gained by retailers through this combination, but the ambitious merchant who wants more control over business growth knows that word-of-mouth advertising and window displays do not necessarily build large volume sales.

Just to consider the matter practically, on any given day we might reasonably assume that a downtown store might benefit from the favorable comments of 100 persons to friends. In that same day, the store's advertisement, running in a newspaper with a circulation of 60,000, might be seen by 65 percent of the 30,000 women readers and 20 percent of the men readers for a total of 25,500 persons. A merchant can understandably become much more excited about the possibilities in the bigger number.

As for window displays, no one denies their worth. A good store featuring desirable merchandise in a window on a downtown shopping street obtains much business directly from its displays and a certain amount of business generated by the comments of passersby.

Despite the undeniable drawing power of the department-store display window, we must admit that the number of persons who glance at a window display during any given day is far fewer than the number of men and women who see the store's advertisement in the local newspaper. Furthermore, the newspaper advertisement, unlike the window display, is unaffected by rain, snow, cold, and wind, any one of which will cut the window-display audience drastically.

The Charitable and Noncommercial Organization

Just as the average person needs to be reminded to replace batteries in a flashlight kept at home for emergencies or to replace dangerously worn tires on the family car, that person also needs to be urged by various charitable groups and noncommercial institutions to volunteer, contribute, or participate. This may involve donating blood, volunteering as a hospital aide, or teaching newly arrived immigrants to speak and read a new language.

Although charitable and noncommercial organizations use publicity, they find that professionally planned and executed advertising campaigns present their appeals far more effectively than ordinary publicity releases. Such releases are less likely to be used by a newspaper, for example, or if used may be placed in out-of-the-way positions or edited in a manner that changes the meaning of the information contained in the publicity release.

Many advertising campaigns are contributed free to requesting organizations by the Advertising Council, and media annually provide millions of dollars worth of free time and space. Despite the traditional generosity of the various advertising media in providing free space or time for noncommercial organizations, there is a point at which they must say no to requests from these organizations. Paid advertising by these organizations will, naturally, always find a place in the media, whereas there may be times when publicity will be turned down or given scant notice. The owner of a media business cannot consistently turn down paid advertising in favor of free publicity.

This is one reason why some noncommercial campaigns now depend more heavily on paid advertising than on publicity. The military services, for instance, for many years used media-donated time and space for recruiting campaigns. With legislation requiring the all-volunteer military services and the need to persuade a steady stream of young men and women to join the military, recruiting advertisements could no longer be placed on a hit-or-miss basis. Military recruiting advertisements are now developed and placed by large, full-

National advertisement for retail advertiser.

This advertisement for a famous department store appeared in the *New Yorker* magazine. A number of department stores find national advertising profitable. Through such unusual advertisements as this, a retail advertiser can create a "store personality" that attracts business from customers who have never made a personal shopping trip to the store.

[*N-M scoops Fina by 2 yrs., 1 mo., 12 days, and 7 hrs.!*]

SO IF YOU'RE WALKING DOWN COMMERCE STREET AND YOU SEE A NEIMAN-MARCUS STORE AND IT'S ON YOUR SIDE SO YOU DON'T HAVE TO JAYWALK THROUGH TRAFFIC AND THERE AREN'T 6,000 PEOPLE WAITING AND YOU NEED PINK AIR OR SOMETHING, PLEASE STOP IN.

Neiman-Marcus

YOU recall how Fina has promised to bring you Pink Air, the Additive of the Future, on May 12, 1966 (about 4:30 P.M.; some of their trucks don't get around to the stations until late)?

Well, Neiman-Marcus is tickled pink to announce that we have beat Fina to it by 2 years, 1 month, 12 days, and 7 hours! Yes, as of 9:30 this morning you can buy PINK AIR, the Room Freshener of the Present, from us!

PINK AIR Room Freshener is delightfully scented with the fragrance of pinks (little-bittier carnations of a special species, *Dianthus Petrofinus*). So when you spray it around it will give your house a pink air!

PINK AIR comes in an aerosol container festooned with a sprightly sprig of pinks for $2.00. Ask for it by name on the 1st Floor downtown; or at Preston Center, Fort Worth or Houston, or order by phone; or simply fill in the coupon. If you have a Fina credit card perhaps you'd like a Neiman-Marcus account opened for you also. Under the circumstances it's the least we can do!

PINK AIR ORDERING COUPON

Dear Neiman-Marcus,
Dept. N
Dallas 1, Texas:

Congratulations on breaking the Pink Air Barrier first!

[ ] Please send me_____PINK AIR Room Freshener(s) at $2.00 each *(please add 35¢ for delivery and handling).*

[ ] Please put on your special Neiman-Marcus gift wrap at 65¢ each.

[ ] My check or money order is enclosed.

[ ] Please charge my Neiman-Marcus account.

[ ] I have a Fina credit card (just a minute while I look), No._____. Please open a Neiman-Marcus account for me and charge this to it.

Yours very truly,

Name_____
Address_____
City_____Zone____State____
©1964, NEIMAN-MARCUS

serve advertising agencies. In recent years, recruiting advertising combined with other federal advertising now makes the federal government one of the largest advertisers in the United States. Current federal advertising expenditures account for up to eight percent of the paid advertising volume of some publications.

Advertising's Future

Unless the United States changes suddenly from a free enterprise society to a totally controlled society in which there will be no mass distribution of goods by business entrepreneurs, advertising's future looks bright. The forms of advertising might change. Media may change. Regulations and laws affecting advertising may become more stringent. Possibly there will be less dependence upon advertising agencies than there is today.

Still, despite these possible changes, and others, advertising should be a strong business and marketing force in the years to come. In one respect, however, it will not change. There will not be enough jobs for all those who want to enter the field. Despite this, for the bright, aggressive and imaginative person, the field of advertising should continue to offer an attractive career opportunity in the years to come.

QUESTIONS

1. What would be the consequences if suddenly there was no advertising?

2. Some advertising is not intended to result in immediate sales. What objectives other than sales can you think of?

3. Why are people reluctant to admit that advertising influences them?

4. What are the elements in the marketing mix? Why is it necessary that these elements be coordinated?

5. Why don't consumers buy all products on the basis of price?

6. How does publicity differ from advertising? Explain.

7. Why do companies prefer to sell a variety of products in several markets rather than a single product in just one market?

8. Why are there no "stand-still" products today?

9. Can advertising persuade consumers to buy products they don't like or want? Why?

10. Why is idea advertising increasingly used by corporations and trade associations?

11. Select an advertised product of your choice. Identify the advertising as primary, selective or retentive and give your reasons for so doing.

12. How does national advertising differ from retail advertising?

2

THE ECONOMIC AND SOCIAL INFLUENCE OF ADVERTISING

THE ECONOMIC AND SOCIAL INFLUENCE OF ADVERTISING

In America, such is the faith in the idea of competition, that informal codes or formal rules are adopted and laws are passed to ensure that competition works. Whether on the baseball diamond or in the courtroom, an umpire or judge applies rules designed to ensure a fair contest.

This is the logic behind legislation designed to regulate business. There is little need for laws regulating small retailers in scattered small towns throughout America. If the consumer dislikes a retailer's products, prices, or services, the consumer can patronize another retail store. The small retailer has little or no influence over the consumer. In competition with other small retailers, the small store owner must post prices reasonable to shoppers.

Large manufacturers and sellers can and sometimes do influence the type, quality and variety of products available to consumers. Most importantly, large manufacturers can influence the prices consumers pay for products.

Whether large manufacturers do, in fact, intentionally raise the prices consumers pay is another matter. The potential exists. Sometimes, for example, the very size of manufacturers supplying a market precludes a competitor entering the market, perhaps with a superior product.

Laws are passed to restrict the influence of large manufacturers or sellers in the marketplace. These laws are designed to make price an effective regulator of competition. Some of the laws and regulations deal with the flow of economic information called advertising. They are designed to provide consumers with the information needed to make buying decisions, relating product quality and other characteristics at a price.

THE RAPID GROWTH OF ADVERTISING REGULATION

There are numerous explanations for the upsurge in laws regulating advertising, but two reasons are fundamental. First, it is primarily the large businesses that have the financial resources necessary to originate most of the economic information we call advertising. Second, sophisticated technology is the basis for complex new products consumers can not adequately judge. Few of us are competent to assess the quality of miniaturized electronic components. Even professional engineers and purchasing agents will have difficulty making decisions about laser technology for industrial use. Finally, consumers are unorganized and depend on manufacturers for information about complex products. Therefore, the tendency in regulating advertising today is to require that advertising contain the type of information consumers need to make informed buying decisions.

The Triangle and the Free Enterprise System

Despite antitrust and other laws designed to slow the growth of corporations, large business continue to grow. While Americans are generally uncomfortable with concentrations of business power, or any power for that matter, it is generally recognized today that large-scale or mass production and mass distribution are vital components of America's free enterprise system. Together, they have provided Americans an unparalleled standard of living and a diversity of products unimaginable a scant generation or so ago. To bring a person from a distant, underdeveloped country to the United States today can result in culture shock!

You can think of mass production, mass distribution, and mass consumption as three corners of a triangle. Take away any one of the three and you no longer have a triangle. All three—mass production, mass distribution and mass consumption—are criticized by people concerned about resource scarcity or pollution or by people expressing a particular set of political or social or economic set of values. While mass production is generally, if sometimes begrudgingly, credited with making a vast contribution to our society, mass distribution is often singled out for criticism. Why is this? First, consider the nature of mass production in giving us tangible products we can see, smell, taste and eat, drive, or fly. This includes bulldozers and hairpins.

Mass distribution, on the other hand, tends to provide intangibles. Marketing involves getting products from the factory loading dock into the final consumers' hands. Consumers seem curiously unaware that many thousands of trains, trucks, and airplanes move merchandise toward them. Wholesaling is a hidden, or to many, unfamiliar activity casually dismissed with clichés about "middleman's profit." Consumers even regard retailing costs as mostly profit, ignoring the costs of rent and taxes or utilities and labor. Consumer skepticism about distribution costs is all the more curious because most estimates today indicate that more people work in the distribution of products and services than work in the factories making the products.

Economic Assumptions and Marketing Realities

Consumer suspicion about the need for mass distribution is a blind spot explained in part by widely taught assumptions of perfect competition in the micro-economic theory. This theory makes little if any provision for distribution. It assumes that many small craftsman sell directly the products they made probably from the very shops and stalls in which they made the products. If this were really the case in America today, there would be no distribution costs.

Micro-economic theory also assumes perfect knowledge on the part of all sellers and buyers. Were this assumption true today, every buyer and seller would know everything about all products available and all prices being asked by sellers. There would be no need for advertising.

Why Advertising Attracts Criticism

Advertising is one of the most conspicuous activities of mass distribution. In fact, advertising is one of the aspects most people think of when comparing life in America with life in other countries. The Nepalese with an average per capita advertising expenditure of four or five cents probably don't think of advertising at all.

The very existence of advertising is a constant reminder that business activities are not conducted by many small buyers and sellers dealing at arm's length. Mass distribution does require advertising and other forms of information. The workings of the real market cannot be faulted for not conforming to an abstract theory.

Advertising is also criticized when measured against the assumption in the theory of perfect competition that all selling and buying behavior is completely rational. In economic theory, when we buy rationally, we often focus on a single dimension of product value. We spend dollars *only* for *warm* clothing, for example, or *only* for *nutritious* food.

Much advertising today expresses product appeals which, in the critics' eyes, are not rational. Today, however, rationality is recognized as having cultural, social, and intensely personal or psychological components. Thus, food is not just fuel. Consumers want food to express family or social occasions. Food should be pleasing to the eye and taste. To the young woman being graduated from college and buying clothes to interview for jobs, last year's clothing styles are more likely to be better economic buys in terms of warmth per dollar spent. It is unlikely, however, that last year's clothing styles will help the young woman land a job.

The usefulness of advertising to the person who uses it as a selling tool—the manufacturer or the retailer—is generally conceded by even the most vigorous critics. The economic usefulness of advertising to our consumer society is, in contrast, seriously questioned not only by many ordinary consumers but also by some economic analysts.

These analysts, while granting that advertising helps the consumer in many ways, such as telling where goods may be purchased or giving valuable information about products, often deny that advertising has the right to credit itself with a number of economic contributions it usually claims.

Few of the analysts or critics suggest doing away with advertising. They are more concerned with pointing out its excesses or in exploring such matters as advertising's role in monopoly practices, or in creating a static price structure.

PERILS IN ADVERTISING

Neil H. Borden, in his classic study, *The Economic Effects of Advertising,* listed five dangers in the use of advertising:

(1) A tendency of businessmen to refrain from sufficient use of price as a competitive weapon (in advertising) because they assume too quickly that demand is inelastic.

(2) Insufficient freedom of choice for consumers to buy nonadvertised or privately branded goods on a price basis.

(3) Insufficient freedom of entry of new enterprises into established industries because, in some cases, large advertisers dominate those industries.

(4) Distribution costs may be reaching the point where greater than corresponding declines in the production costs are no longer forthcoming, and where the conveniences and services associated with present-day distribution may be too much for some pocketbooks.

(5) Present-day advertising does not give consumers sufficient information to enable them to buy with full economic effectiveness.

Balancing Arguments for Advertising

To balance these charges, Borden's study declared that: (a) Many firms do compete on a price basis. There are, for example, small manufacturers selling at low prices to private branding distributors, and many large companies putting out goods for sale under distributor brands. Chain stores, too, selling their private brands on a price basis, compete with national advertisers. (b) The consumer movement has helped to offset advertising that stresses emotion and instinct by emphasizing fair prices based upon objective product analysis. (c) Reduction of wastes in advertising and selling through research of markets, budgeting, and advertising techniques, lighten the cost carried by the consumer.

Economic Asset or a Liability?

Advertising's economic service is indicated by Borden's overall conclusion:

> On balance, the general conclusion to be drawn from the evidence is that the functional objectives of advertising in a dynamic economy are socially desirable and that advertising as it is now conducted, though certainly not free from criticism, is an economic asset and not a liability.[2]

For a more modern treatment that confirms many of Borden's conclusions, it is recommended that the student read Jules Backman's, *Advertising and Competition.*[3]

Advertising people may feel justifiably that theirs is a worthwhile contribution to our economic society. They may not view this contribution smugly, however, since too many areas of advertising are still open to the probing of the economist.

Neither should advertising people oversimplify when discussing advertising's effect on price, cost, and the quality of goods. As Borden's study, the most comprehensive ever made, demonstrates, there have been too many erroneous assumptions offered glibly in behalf of advertising.

CONSUMERS PAY FOR ADVERTISING

Although advertisers pay the agency, the printer, and others the advertisers get their money back eventually from the one who really pays for advertising—the consumer. Advertising cost is inevitably reflected in the selling price of a service product to the consumer—just as the costs of the advertiser's rent, delivery, and packaging are also reflected in that selling price.

While it is true that the consumer pays for advertising, it is not usually a large sum when unit costs are considered. For many products the advertising cost is expressed in a fraction of a penny per case. Many consumers, however, conscious of the high total costs of an advertising campaign are likely to assume that advertising expense is greater than it really is. Following are some figures that show some advertising costs:

Company	*Advertising* As a Percentage of Sales
Chrysler Corporation	0.7
Eastman Kodak Company	1.9
Exxon Corporation	0.1
General Motors Corporation	0.6
Kraft, Inc.	2.0
McDonald's Corporation	3.4
Procter & Gamble Company	8.4
Quaker Oats Company	2.8
Sears Roebuck & Company	2.0

As a percent of the gross national product, U.S. advertising usually amounts to about two percent. Venezuela follows the U.S., spending 1.7 percent of its gross national product for advertising. For Hong Kong the figure is 1.5 percent, and for Switzerland the expenditure is 1.3 percent.

Advertising Costs Per Person

More meaningful is the per capita advertising expenditure found in the survey. For the U.S. this amounted to $110.78 per person. For Switzerland the figure is $76.63 per person. In the United Kingdom, the expenditure was $31.09 per person. In underdeveloped countries, the per capita expenditure for advertising often is expressed in pennies per person.

If the per capita advertising expenditure for the United States appears high, this may reflect a number of factors, including the intensity of competition in a mature society, the widespread availability of advertising media or the

50

Trademark advertisement.

This advertisement, published in the magazine, *Editor & Publisher,* not only stresses the value of trademarks to their users but also tells *how* they should be used. Thus the suggestion will be helpful to editors, reporters, and others who may use trademark names in what they are writing. Trademarks, of course, are important not only to the companies that own them but also to consumers in insuring they get what they ask for.

amount of discretionary spending power of consumers. The per capita expenditure also means that you need not spend much time and energy looking for product information. That information is constantly seeking you out.

Typically, consumers envision a *considerable* reduction in the price of an item if advertising were removed. Yet, for most goods the amount represented by advertising in the selling cost is tiny to moderate. One advertising manager who believed that advertising ultimately brings goods to consumers at lower, not higher prices, declared:

No one ever asks me, except in a spirit of honest inquiry, how many salesmen we have, or how many trucks we must maintain, or how many people are in our accounting department. They take these things for granted, as ordinary business expense. No one ever suggests that we could sell our products more cheaply if we had fewer salesmen, or if we didn't have lighted signs identifying our stations.

From experience, advertisers are aware that if they invest too little or nothing in advertising, sales and market shares often decline. They know this because most advertisers test the amount of advertising that must be placed in markets to obtain or maintain sales levels. They want to spend only enough to achieve an objective.

Sometimes an advertiser may run test advertising for traditionally unadvertised brands and discover that increased sales more than pay for the advertising investment. When Nabisco ran such a test for Triscuits, a brand more than 75 years old, sales quadrupled.[5]

BASIC AMERICAN BUSINESS LOGIC: HIGH VOLUME PRODUCTION AND LOW CONSUMER PRICES

Low-cost mass distribution depends upon standardized products produced in long, uninterrupted runs. Both the standardized products and long runs are made possible by wide distribution. If distribution costs (especially advertising) are cut too much, volume may decrease, manufacturing runs shorten, manufacturing costs rise, user prices go up, and profits come down.

Normally, as a producer turns out more and more units, money is saved by buying raw materials in large quantities at lower costs. Through buying and other economies, the producer is able to manufacture at a lower unit cost. In order to take the risk entailed in making more units, the producer must be assured that the larger output will find a market; without the market the producer cannot afford mass production.

Advertising, as one of the most important tools of marketing, helps the producer inform the market of the goods being manufactured. No other means has been found to tell so many people so quickly about those goods—and, in most cases, so cheaply. Thus, by providing a relatively inexpensive means of selling goods, mass advertising enables the producer to reduce unit manufacturing and selling costs.

Were the discussion to end here the advertising exponent could say categorically that the use of advertising automatically lowers prices and, accordingly, justifies its existence in our economic society. The statement would be an oversimplification for these two reasons: (1) Advertising is just one of many distributive forces affecting the raising or lowering of prices. It, along with transporting, financing, warehousing, and selling, constitutes one of the steps between the place and time of production and the place and time of consumption.

The following chart indicates the complex interrelationships in marketing. It makes obvious how many other factors are at work along with advertising in achieving lower prices—or creating higher ones. Poor selling, inefficient wholesaling,[6] or bad timing, singly or in combination, can negate advertising's beneficial effect on prices.

Representative Cost Factors*

Marketing Cost Action Taken	How Manufacturing Costs Are Affected
Product line factors	
(a) Number of items changed	Lengths of manufacturing runs changed
(b) Salability of items increased	Retooling—New methods—retraining operators
(c) Quality of products changed	More or less material or care in manufacture
(d) Packaging of products changed	More or less costly materials
Customer policy factors (direct sale)	
(a) Location of customer solicited changed	Plant location affected in freight costs changed
(b) Size of order accepted changed	Length of manufacturing runs changed
(c) Service and parts policy changed	Lengths of manufacturing runs changed
Channels of distribution factors	
(a) Number of distributors and outlets changed	Size of shipments and lengths of manufacturing runs changed
(b) Location of distributors and outlets changed	Size of shipments and lengths of manufacturing runs changed
(c) Size of shipments changed	Packing and shipping costs affected
Physical handling of products	
(a) Warehousing before shipment	Such marketing policy changes will affect length of manufacturing runs, packing costs, inventory control costs, plant location, intermediate assembly plant possibilities, etc.
(b) Intermediate shipment to distributor and outlet	
(c) Warehousing after intermediate shipment	
(d) Final shipment to customer after purchase	

*As viewed by a marketing man quite apart from any consideration of advertising.

In the case of many products—notably cigarettes—successful advertising tends to hold prices rigid since buying motivation and habitual use has been established on a basis other than price. Frequently, the prices of such advertised goods do not change so much as those of nonadvertised goods. Some advertisers, having created a steady demand for their products, are able to some extent to disregard price competition, even in the face of a general market decline. Such advertisers may, to a degree, disregard price changes on directly or indirectly competing products.

Pricing has many facets, however, some of which we as consumers tend to ignore. For example, the prices posted throughout a supermarket are not necessarily the prices rung up on cash registers for customers with a handful of coupons.

A large number of consumer goods advertisers use coupons to lower prices temporarily and often generously to consumers. Coupons enable the advertiser to give consumers price incentives while maintaining stable relations with wholesalers and retailers and, perhaps most importantly, maintaining what is called the product position in the consumer's mind. *Positioning* a product means influencing the manner in which the consumer perceives, understands and regards the product. Pricing, product characteristics, performance, personality, packaging, where and how the product is sold—all are integrated to influence the consumer's perception of the position. Widely and constantly fluctuating prices can destroy this position, regarded by many advertising professionals as a requirement for repeat sales and brand loyalty.

This is where the advertising professional and the economist come into conflict. The economist tends to dislike price rigidity. Active and flexible price competition, from the economist's viewpoint, is healthful and desirable in the American market.

In both the short- and long-run the economist's desire for flexible prices usually prevails. Price rigidity cannot usually be maintained indefinitely by any advertiser. Sooner or later business rivals using lower prices must be reckoned with, especially in periods of recession. If consumer buying slows during such a period, sales will almost inevitably be lost by the business attempting to maintain high prices.

THE ADVERTISING/PRICE RELATIONSHIP

While it may, as said, be true that for some products and over some period of time, advertising may help to keep prices rigid—even maintaining higher prices for some goods than comparable goods—the forces of competition inevitably work to level the higher prices.

Meanwhile, advertising's overall contribution, *in conjunction with other marketing elements,* has been to help in the lowering of prices. During the period that large-scale production and large-scale advertising have developed, hundreds of products have been lowered sharply in price—for example, 60-watt bulbs selling for 35 cents today that sold for $1.75 in 1905; facial tissue selling for 45 cents today that sold for 65 cents a few years ago. The list is seemingly endless.

Advertising may be given only part of the credit for these price changes. Still, it has been during the period of advertising's greatest growth that they have occurred. It is obvious that advertising did not, in that period, force prices upward.

In attacking distribution costs (and comparing them unfavorably with production costs) the critic sometimes loses sight of the real economic objectives: (1) That the aim is not so much to lower distribution costs as to lower consumer or user prices and still return a fair profit to the producer. (2) That distribution costs (and these include advertising) are closely integrated with other costs, with volume, and with profits. They can hardly be isolated for individual attack.

The consumer is not concerned so much with the ratio between production and distribution costs as in the price paid to obtain the product. If, by adding distribution costs, the long-run prices the consumer pays are reduced, the consumer gains.

While price may be relatively unimportant information to the purchasers of products such as cosmetics, it is the single most important piece of information to young families buying milk for their children, and to elderly consumers who require prescription drugs. Some state courts and legislatures recently have acted to make formerly forbidden price advertising information available to consumers. Some states now require prominent posting of prices for prescription drugs in pharmacies.

Trademark character.

If an advertiser can develop a good trademark character such as the "Doughboy" he achieves instant identification for his product in consumers' minds in print and television. The character, appearing in conjunction with the product or company name, provides strong trademark protection.

LEO BURNETT COMPANY, INC. | PILLSBURY

AS FILMED AND RECORDED | "Roll 'Em" :30 | PBWW5960

1. WOMAN: What do you do with hot dogs...

2. ...besides boiling 'em or broiling 'em?

3. DOUGHBOY: Ever try rolling 'em?

4. WOMAN: What?

5. DOUGHBOY: With Wiener Wrap from Pillsbury.

6. See. It's fresh dough...

7. ...you roll...

8. ...around a hot dog.

9. WOMAN: It's easy.

10. DOUGHBOY: Sure, just pop 'em in the oven...

11. ...while the Wiener Wrap bakes,...

12. ...the hot dogs cook up plump and juicy.

13. HUSBAND: Honey, you're terrific--you even make hot dogs taste great.

14. WOMAN: Well, I had a little help.

15. DOUGHBOY: (Giggles) Wiener Wrap turns plain hot dogs into something special.

Numerous professional associations for years have stressed that professional services should be isolated from direct price competition. Prescription drug and eyeglass prices in states prohibiting price advertising are two, three, or more times as expensive than in neighboring states permitting the advertising of price. Courts recently have turned aside arguments that price competition is ruinous to high-quality professional products and services.

The Supreme Court recently decided that price information is important to people asking legal advice. Lawyers now are allowed to advertise prices for relatively standard services.

The current trend in court decisions acknowledges that price information is important and that advertisements containing price information can help lower prices to consumers.

ADVERTISING AND MONOPOLY

No one denies that heavy advertising, skillfully executed, can create strong brand preference, sometimes so strong that competitors must struggle merely to survive in the sales market. Much of this may be due to the monopoly power control an advertiser has over his trademark. As a seller's advertising investment grows and the trademark becomes identified with a satisfactory product, the value of the trademark increases, along with the value of the monopoly control over it.

Monopoly Is Control of Supply

Monopoly, however, is the exclusive control of a commodity or service in a particular market, or a control that makes possible the manipulation of prices. History teaches that it has been practiced for many centuries and that it invariably invites abuse to the benefit of the monopoly holder.

What's In A Name?

New products often are marketed under new product names that suggest or express product superiority. Glass Plus suggests versatility to the person who uses one cleaner for glass, another for porcelain, another for metal and yet another for woodwork. The name Intensive Care suggests a product superior to competitive hand lotions. It quickly became a sales leader. Or take Slime, a green, viscous fluid designed to delight children and repel adults. The product name and supporting advertising in test markets resulted in such rapid sales the advertising was stopped because supplies ran out.

New products are encouraged in the American economy and are protected to some degree by such monopoly elements as patents and trademarks issued by the federal government. Curiously, then, the government grants limited monopoly protection to encourage competition. Without such protection inventors would be discouraged and investors unwilling to risk their capital backing new inventions.

A Monopoly Based on Persuasion

Can advertising create a monopoly? Until the 1966 Supreme Court decision against Procter & Gamble in the Clorox case gave some substantiation to the monopoly charge, not many people regarded advertising as a monopoly threat. In fact, in that case the court based a divestiture order on the fact that Procter & Gamble qualifies for huge media discounts because it buys such large amounts of media time and space, thereby putting smaller rivals at a considerable disadvantage. Equally as important, the court recognized that Procter & Gamble's skill in marketing and advertising gave that firm a disproportionate advantage against smaller, less skilled companies, even if P & G scrupulously obeyed all laws regulating competitive practices.

A number of obstacles, however, usually preclude achieving monopoly through the mere use of advertising:

(1) No one has a monopoly of ideas for products or for advertising. Microwave ovens are, as Litton advertises, changing the way America cooks. Food processors do more than food blenders. Hand-held calculators are purchased by school systems for use in first and second grade. Wristwatch calculators promise even more convenience. Watches today are more accurate and carefree than ever, using a variety of power devices instead of the conventional mainspring. From ink pens to early ballpoint pens for $12.00 to ballpoint pens for 19 cents to nylon-tipped pens to what next?

Duplicating machines now reproduce by laser beams. A changing natural resource balance makes solar energy more than a toy for basement inventors. Higher electricity rates make heat pumps attractive for heating and cooling while using electricity very efficiently. Hardly a year goes by that new shaver and razor products are not introduced.

(2) No one has a monopoly of the media. It is axiomatic that if a producer has entree to the media and has an idea to sell, it is difficult or impossible to deny him his place in the market. Hundreds of local and regional advertisers compete successfully against large advertisers and many of these small advertisers have themselves become big despite the dominance at first of well-established brands.

(3) No one can dominate all of America—geographically speaking—through advertising. Occasionally we become aware of how much an advertiser pays for a network television program or for a single commercial during a superbowl football game, and conclude that advertising budgets are gargantuan, that major advertisers can literally buy this or that market.

Some corporation advertising budgets are very large. But are they large in comparison to media costs? You can answer this for yourself by looking through *Advertising Age* for the published list of large advertisers and their budgets. Then look through the same publication for network television costs. A few minutes of simple calculation on your part reveals that even the largest advertiser cannot dominate a single medium, much less all media. In reality, network television costs have forced the typical commercial from 60 seconds to 30 seconds, with some advertisers predicting 10 seconds as the basic time unit in the future.

(4)   Advertising that persuades consumers to buy one brand rather than another essentially similar brand is wasteful if not monopolistic. Competitive advertising may be designed to influence brand switching. To say this is wasteful denies consumer free choice or, more bluntly, substitutes the perception and product judgment of the critic for that of the consumer.

To say this is true of all, or most, advertising, is another oversimplification. Usually brand-switching does not occur simply because advertising asks consumers to switch. Advertising men learned long ago that advertising merely urging a change is seldom enough to effect brandswitching. Prospective buyers must be given sensible reasons to buy a product different from the one they had planned to buy, or have been accustomed to buying. The reason may be price, superiority of performance, or any one of countless others.

In short, consumers may make buying decisions for reasons the critic discounts.

(5)   Advertisers are very much aware that a better and/or different product is desirable for successful advertising and quick consumer acceptance. This awareness spurs product improvement efforts. Some improvements are relatively minor; sometimes, however, improvements result in a product that is recognized as genuinely new even by advertising's severest critics. At other times, a manufacturer may market a product essentially similar to a leading branded product but priced much lower. The consumer benefits from these choices.

Product innovation and invention proceed step by step, and these steps are encouraged or accelerated because of advertising. Consumer acceptance of snowmobiles provides year-round sales and employment for formerly one-season boat shops and marinas. Improvements in scuba equipment make diving appealing to larger numbers of people. Information developed elsewhere may make existing products more meaningful. By relating developmental stages to the manipulation of certain toys, child development specialists guide parents in the selection of toys. Whereas building blocks were merely playthings, they now are educational media for learning shapes and relationships and assessing the development of hand and eye coordination in very young children.

IS ADVERTISING WASTEFUL?

Advertising frequently is criticized for being inefficient and wasteful and for encouraging wasteful consumption and obsolescence.

Some advertisers waste money in newspaper advertising when they should be using direct mail. Others waste money because they are advertising to the wrong markets for their products. Some are wasteful in producing great quantities of display material that will not be used. Still others use one copy appeal when they should use another and, to the extent that their advertisements fail to bring sales, they may be considered wasteful, and certainly inefficient.

In these respects and some others, advertising is wasteful. Advertisers fight this problem of waste with many tools—market research, copy testing, budget control, and distribution cost analysis, to name a few—and much improvement has, and is, being effected.

Waste in production is easier to control than waste in marketing and advertising. It is far easier to observe and measure the productivity of ten men versus one machine or to count the number of automobile transmissions rejected by quality control inspectors in a factory than to assess the effective differences between dollars spent for 30 salesmen versus 300 pages of advertising in newspapers.

The past several decades have witnessed remarkable increases in the amount of both marketing and advertising effectiveness . Blind faith, intuition, and hunch have given way to requirements for research information as a decision base. Much research information reveals it can be wasteful *not* to advertise—or not to advertise enough, if this means the loss of potential business. This viewpoint is expressed by an industrialist who said:

> Advertising increases profits faster than it increases costs. Once the breakeven point is passed, profits increase progressively while certain fixed overhead costs remain the same, and the extra advertising dollars that produce more business are producing business on which the percentage of profit is increased.

Does Advertising Encourage Wasteful Consumption?

Does advertising encourage wasteful consumption and obsolescence? Consider the first part of the question—wasteful consumption—and the fact that the modern American family now spends one-third of its food budget in fast food restaurants. This is seldom as economical as buying food at a grocery store for preparation at home. But to the family with two working parents or to the single-parent family the time and convenience are worth the cost.

Advertising may influence the decision to eat out more frequently, but deeper social trends predispose people to do so.

Does advertising cause waste by causing people to buy new goods before the old goods have been utilized fully? Critics of advertising attack manufacturers and advertisers together with an often-used charge that advertising speeds the obsolescence of goods and hence creates waste since consumers get rid of their possessions before they have really outlived their usefulness.

These critics refer to "production for replacement," and say: "It works by planned obsolescence and the degradation of goods." Speaking of advertising's part in this they accuse advertising of fostering various evils and criticize business for making advertising its principal spokesman.

A fact not mentioned is that the consumer—target of the alleged obsolescence—is the final judge of whether or not she will discard last year's vacuum in favor of the new one just advertised in the *Ladies' Home Journal*. No one compels business people to discard dictating machines now being used, for new models. If the new models are better and if the office will operate more efficiently because of their adoption, the change makes sense, but there is no law that says the change must be made.

How evil is speeded-up obsolescence? When car owners buy new automobiles and trade in their perfectly good late year's models merely to take advantage of an inconsequential change of design, they are parties to the "planned obsolescence"—but is even this necessarily bad or wasteful? Such buyers enjoy having the latest car; enjoyment is a form of psychic income that cannot be measured in dollars and cents. Without the cars turned in—and thousands like it—there would be no used-car market to furnish employment to thousands and to be responsible for billions of quick-turnover dollars yearly. Too, without used cars in good condition, many persons not able to afford new cars simply would not drive.

Most so-called obsolete goods are, as in the case of used cars, utilized in some way, usually by buyers who are ever searching the market for used goods.

It may, in fact, be useful to accelerate obsolescence of gas-guzzling automobiles, smelting and refining the useful metal, and converting it into smaller, energy-efficient automobiles.

It may be useful and economical to build new incinerators that both burn trash and provide electricity or heat. It may be more economical to buy new radial tires that can be used in the blistering heat of southwest Texas and perform as well as snow tires in the mountains of Colorado or New Hampshire.

Orthodontists have successfully experimented with a space technology metal, with a "memory," for braces to straighten teeth. This metal, much lighter and less bulky than traditional wires used on braces, exerts a constant pressure to return to a preset form when the memory in the metal is activated by the heat of the mouth. Braces made with this metal require infrequent adjustment and straighten teeth in one-half the time required by conventional braces. Should this new metal be withheld from patients until all existing orthodontal metals are used up? How do we balance economic costs against human comfort and convenience?

Many Americans, it must be noted, who reach out always for the new, the different, and the untried are following a characteristically American pattern. Advertising possibly has accelerated this tendency, but it did not create it and the tendency would exist if all advertising were abandoned. Meanwhile, by accelerating acceptance of new products, advertising has helped to lift our standard of living more quickly than otherwise might have been possible.

ADVERTISING AS INFORMATION

Advertising's Boisterous Language

The language of advertising conforms to this expansive characteristic. It seems that all clothes washing detergents yield the "whitest white." All tires with the same basic construction claim the longest mileage or the greatest holding ability on corners. Competing bubble gums promise unending hours of enjoyment to the youthful chewer. In the land of the biggest burger and the crispiest french fries you can buy a relatively inexpensive watch that ticks unerringly after being ejected from a geyser. How can you refute the demonstrated evidence?

Faced with all these superlatives and the mass of supporting "evidence," the bewildered consumer finds that choosing some products on the basis of advertising claims is difficult indeed.

Many Sources of Information

Out of the consumer's bewilderment have arisen consumer reporting services—Consumers Union, and Consumers' Research. Evaluating of products by the media, such as *Parents'* magazine, and *Good Housekeeping*, is more evidence of consumer need for help in differentiating goods.

Most products live up to advertising claims made for them. Although consumers may be bewildered by rival claims, it would be much worse if no choice were given. Each product can but relate its virtues; the consumer then elects the one he wants. The consumer is king and every advertiser is eager to serve him.

Information Sometimes Inadequate

The assertion is often made that advertisers deal largely in unspecific superlatives, instead of giving solid information that enables a prospect to make a sensible product choice. This is true in the case of some products and types of advertising; it is not true of others. As mentioned elsewhere, for example, mail-order advertisers must supply full information to persuade people to send money for a product they have never seen. Business publication advertising, too, gives information logically and clearly.

Consumer advertising is most frequently guilty of the lack of buying information. Such advertising, however, does not usually even attempt to give complete facts.

There simply is not space in the usual consumer advertisement to supply all buying information; its aims are to arouse product interest, to create recognition for the product and its maker. It is hoped that the consumer will read or hear about the product again in local media (with more specific detail) and will find out where the item may be seen and how much it will cost. The last step is the visit to the store where the item may be compared point by point with competing products.

If consumers read about food mixers in advertisements, they will obtain limited information about the various types. Advertisements may persuade consumers of the need for and profitable use of a mixer but the store demonstration does the final selling. No advertisement can supply the dramatic point-by-point comparison of a salesperson's demonstration—although television comes close.

Required Advertising Information

There is a movement to require prominent displays of price and performance information. In recent years automobile manufacturers were required first to post prices and then mileage figures on window stickers. Air conditioner manufacturers attach energy efficiency ratings to their products, which relate energy use in terms of cooling efficiency.

In response to consumer complaints about the lack of a factual basis for making choices between products, the U.S. Commerce Department is, for the first time, developing methods to measure product performance for home appliances and will require labels disclosing the test results. Such information may be important to some consumers and ignored by others. The energy efficiency rating now on air conditioners does not seem to have unduly influenced consumers. Consumers may consider the ratings in conjunction with quietness of operation, size, style, manufacturer's reputation, and other characteristics or information. An important and unanswered question is whether the test results will be factual information to many consumers who buy for undiscussed reasons or for a product that performs just one function particularly well, such as a washing machine with a thorough rinse cycle for people with sensitive skin.

Consumers do have access to a great deal of product information from government, independent testing laboratories, media, and product producers. One could reasonably argue that there is an information overload. At times, however, the information is presented in very useful ways. Consumers now receive governmental and private industry estimates relating the total cost of driving the family car, including maintenance, fuel, insurance and depreciation for a given year. This suggests what some call the Life Cycle Purchasing concept as a new way to market products. Instead of focusing only on buying the product, or initial cost, this concept would also express operating, service and disposal costs, and in so doing revolutionize the way some products are designed and marketed.

Where advertising must and can supply fuller information, as in the case of business and mail-order advertising, it will do so. Even business-publication advertising, however, factual as it is, rarely attempts to supply all buying information needed. Study after study of advertisement readership reveals the most effective advertisements attempt to make only one point, and a survey of all one-page, four-color advertisements in 47 magazines revealed that only 9 percent of magazine readers read most of an advertisement. The sales person is still required to explain the proposition and to close the order. Advertising is a hard-working partner of this salesperson.

On the point of informativeness of advertising, consumers queried in the American Association of Advertising Agencies study previously cited, had reactions that were encouraging to advertising people:

Why People Should Feel Favorably Toward
Advertising—Major Reasons*

It is informative
It provides specific information on new products
It provides specific information on prices
Advertising is enjoyable, entertaining
Advertising pays for entertainment
No good reason
Other reasons
Don't know or no answer
*Some people gave more than one answer

It is interesting to note, likewise, that when these same consumers were asked why they should feel *unfavorably* toward advertising, there was no complaint about advertising's lack of information. Complaints, instead, were about misleading advertising, too much advertising, and repetitious advertising.

Consumers trust advertised products. Despite some consumer complaints about lack of buying information in advertising, consumers have more confidence in advertised products than in unadvertised, unknown brands. Tests show that consumers given a choice between identical branded and unbranded merchandise lying side by side will consistently pay higher prices for branded merchandise. Why is this?

For one thing, as this table from the American Association of Advertising Agency study shows, consumers think that advertising is at least partially responsible for better goods:

Issue: Advertising Results in Better Products for the Public

Generally agree	52%
Partially agree	22
Can't say	12
Partially disagree	9
Generally disagree	5

Furthermore, consumers have shown consistently that they believe that the manufacturer of an advertised product is more likely to be reliable and thus more willing to stand back of his product than is the manufacturer of an unadvertised product. In this day of repairmen who always seem to be too busy to give quick service, the harried person managing a household leans toward advertised products as more trustworthy.

SOCIOCULTURAL ASSESSMENTS OF ADVERTISING

Because advertising penetrates deeply into American life, it is much more than simply selling products. People quite unconcerned with the economic influence of advertising sometimes look critically at its influence on media content, especially as that content might influence young children. The same people may be uneasy that advertising continuously stimulates desires people can't fulfill in language that is relentlessly emotional.

In the following section, several of these concerns are described and commented upon.

Advertising Influence on Media Content

The critic who finds fault with advertising's failure to effect cultural improvement usually points to radio and television programming. The assertion is that in catering to advertiser demands for ever-larger audiences, program content must be designed for a low level of intelligence, often called the lowest common denominator.

Network programming is filled with daytime serials, game shows, situation comedies or violence-filled adult programs. Whatever the format, many of the programs are predictable, repetitive, unimaginative, and downright dull. To the critic, the educational potential of television has been debased. The cultural product is mundane and pedestrian, with the bad programming driving out the good, because the bad programming develops larger audiences for advertisers.

Much network programming does not engage the mind. If it does not, there are plenty of options. Public television offers quite different programming from commercial programming. Cable TV also offers options. People may listen to a classical music station or read any number of newspapers and magazines written for almost any intellectual level or interest. For the curious and inquiring intellect, boredom can be only a pose in light of the diversity of mass media cheaply available. Advertising, it must be noted, supports the vast majority of these media.

Television commercials themselves frequently are targets of criticism. As selling messages they are designed to make one simple, easily understood claim. Commercials are measured by a variety of research techniques both before and during broadcast to assess their effectiveness, and they are carefully designed to reflect the interests, tastes, and life situations of the people to whom they are addressed. The critic may find the commercial boring because of lack of interest in the product; perhaps the critic even dislikes the product. In either case, the critic (and often each of us is the critic) can express such distaste. If many people dislike the commercial or the product, the advertisement will not be on the air for very long anyway.

Today it may easily be argued that despite the mass of undesirable material used in print and on the air, the overall effect of advertising has been uplifting rather than degrading—that advertising supports media which give large numbers of people the option to develop and satisfy their own interests and tastes. Advertising has brought daytime serials and game shows; it has also brought symphonies, operas, and serious drama to the millions.

Television Advertising and Children

Probably no topic has been more intensively studied and widely discussed in recent years than the effect of television, including commercials, on children. Numerous studies indicate preschool children spend more time with television than they will spend in class through the eighth grade. Social critics, psychologists, and educators believe this influences childrens' approach to school and the world around them. To critics, childrens' television programming and commercials suggest a fantasy world of instant gratification and instant solutions to problems through violence.

Children Learn Through Advertising.   Because you are familiar with a wide range of criticism, you might ask what children learn from television commercials. They gain early experience as consumers in their own right, learning to evaluate products and the value of money. Children develop self-confidence as they learn to know what they want and to exercise independent judgment. Often what adults accept from a commercial children will question. They become knowledgeable very early about a world requiring decisions in the face of attractively and persuasively presented options. This is a preparation for a life filled with decision making, and eventually for voting decisions.

Family Life Is Major Influence on Child.   Critics complain that television commercials force parents to deny their children advertised products. Parents do have a choice. In fact they have several. They can give or deny the requested product. They can turn the television set off. Knowingly or not, parents provide the key interpersonal relations, the primary influence in developing children. In the family structure children internalize the values, goals, and aspirations of the family members.

Television commercials have few lasting effects, if any, on the mental health or emotional development of the average viewing child. Asked what they most enjoyed about childrens' television programming, children often choose commercials as the best part.

Advertising Techniques Widely Adopted.   Curiously, although educators seldom dwell on it, television commercial techniques are increasingly used in the classroom and in childrens' television programming. A variety of these techniques were used from the start in "Sesame Street," a noncommercial, television series for children. This program series, is considered by many to be childrens' programming at its best.

Advertising Creates Unfulfillable Desires

Advertising is often charged with causing individual unrest, unhappiness and frustration by making people constantly aware of what they do not have.

No one denies that one effect of advertising is to make people dissatisfied with what they already have, or to make them want something they do not already have. To some this is frustrating. To others dissatisfaction is a spur to action. People do have a choice.

Such a choice was nonexistent in medieval Europe, for example, where people were born into a class or a station in life with little hope or chance of improving their lives. The controlling ideas and the weight of medieval social structure was to "know thy place". It was a static society, one in which it was unthinkable for a peasant or commoner to aspire to wealth or an aristocratic position. Change was a threat to the existing order of privilege by birth. Advertising in such a society would have few desires or aspirations to influence.

Advertising and Mobility.   Contrast such a society with America today. Americans are encouraged to have desires and aspirations. They move with relative ease both socially and economically, frequently on the basis of work and effort. The only truly recognized and admired aristocracy is that of talent. American society values the striver, the go-getter, the mover, the risk taker. America generously rewards the individual who works because he or she is not content with a place in life or the way things are. This is, in part, the promise of America.

Dissatisfaction is creative in an America that might be characterized as the Land of the Big Carrot. Individual discontent leads to striving on the part of many, frequently resulting in new ideas, products and services. We are all the richer because dissatisfaction, constructively harnessed, results in progress. Business opportunity advertisements in the business and general press invite people to invest their time, energy, and money in new ventures offering the promise of success.

Consumers As Reality Testers.   Frustration may be the reaction to advertising by some consumers. Most buying behavior, however, suggests very rational reality testing by the overwhelming majority of consumers. Many, it must be admitted, are content with a certain type of job, home and car. Many other consumers, it must be recognized, constantly seek out more responsible and better paying jobs. Both the contented consumer and the striving consumer know that, unless they have great wealth, there are some things in life they cannot have. To recognize this is part of the growing-up process.

Consumers often set levels high enough to serve as goals but not so high as to frustrate themselves.

As individuals undertake new business ventures and offer consumers new or improved products and services, each offers a small but incremental improvement in the standard of living. Cumulatively, this means progress. Advertising that provides information about business opportunities and about available consumer products offers information which acts as an incentive to work and to buy. How this information is used is, again, a matter of consumer free choice.

Advertising Charged with Emphasizing Emotional Appeals.

A look at advertising for soaps, cosmetics and many personal enhancement products provides substantial evidence for the presence of emotional appeals. To the critic this means that products are essentially similar or only superficially different, at best, with advertising providing an illusion of real or significant difference.

Advertising people admit that many products are sold through emotional appeals. They know consumers are not interested in the chemical composition of cologne or perfume but in what the product will do for them; that is, how they feel when they put the product on or how others react to the scent. People who buy electric irons do not really care what is inside. They want to know whether the iron will slide easily and lightly and release steam to take out creases. Advertisers attempt to make products desirable in terms consumers understand, in terms of human benefits.

People Are Both Rational and Emotional.   Most people regard themselves as rational, even when buying in response to strong emotional appeals. Advertisers know this and often provide rational selling appeals people can publicly talk about with others when explaining a purchase. Automobile advertisements can present rational reasons for purchasing an automobile, but the manufacturers also know many people buy cars for social reasons, which they are reluctant to discuss publicly, or as a means of expressing mastery, a deep-seated motive the car buyer may be unaware of.

Consumers may buy some products with what might be called intense economic rationality, as if they had computers in their heads. The same consumers may buy other products emotionally, almost as if money was unimportant. People who buy both rationally and emotionally—and most people do—are not split personalities. All their values cannot be contained within a formula dictated by the narrow economic definition of rationality applied by some supposedly objective observer.

Informative-educational advertising.

In consultation with the New York Commissioner of Consumer Affairs, the advertiser published this test advertisement to be helpful to consumers. Advertisers who recognize the validity of the consumerism movement are glad to use such advertising. In addition to running the informative advertisement, the company also offers a free 128-page book that serves as a guide to product information.

4 reasons why you should read the label before you take a pain reliever.

1. Relief
The product provides temporary relief of the specific symptoms listed. And that's all any pain reliever will do—treat the symptoms, not cure the ailment.

2. Dosage
The dosages are precise. Do not exceed them. The label says what it means, but it means nothing unless you do what it says.

3. Caution
This is a non-prescription drug, so if it affects you in some unusual way, you are advised to consult your physician or dentist. It is not for children under six and it is not recommended for prolonged use.

4. Warning
As self-evident as this warning may seem, it is designed to overcome the very human tendency we all have toward carelessness.

The EXCEDRIN formula provides fast, effective relief from pain of: headache, sinusitis, colds or 'flu', muscular aches and menstrual discomfort. Also recommended for temporary relief of toothaches and minor arthritic pains. DOSAGE. Adults, 2 tablets every 4 hours as needed. Do not exceed 8 tablets in 24 hours, unless directed by a physician. For children 6-12, one-half adult dose. CAUTION: Do not give to children under 6 or use for more than 10 days unless directed by physician. If sinus or arthritis pain persists (say for a week) or if skin redness is present, or in arthritic conditions affecting children under 12 consult physician immediately. Consult dentist for toothache promptly. Do not take without consulting physician if under medical care. WARNING: Keep this and all medicines out of children's reach. In case of accidental overdose, contact a physician immediately. Each tablet contains Acetaminophen 1½ grs., Salicylamide, Aspirin, and Caffeine.

Don't take a pain reliever (ours or anyone else's) unless you understand what it can do... and what it can't do. A label may not be great literature, but it's important enough to read.

Bristol-Myers Company
New York, N.Y. 10022

BRISTOL LABORATORIES. Ethical Pharmaceuticals • BRISTOL-MYERS PRODUCTS. Health Care Products and Personal Care Products • DRACKETT. Household Products and Nutritionals • CLAIROL. Hair Care Products and Personal Care Products • MEAD JOHNSON. Ethical Pharmaceuticals and Nutritionals • ZIMMER-U.S.A.. Surgical and Patient Care Products • PELTON & CRANE. Dental Equipment • WESTWOOD. Dermatological Products and Ethical Pharmaceuticals

People Buy for Many Reasons.   People buy products appropriate to their family situation, in terms of peer or aspiration groups. They may buy products because of broad social approval or because of unfelt cultural dictates. They may buy to satisfy a personality need for self-expression or for some deep-seated reason of which even they may be unaware. This does not mean their buying is irrational. It does mean they have reasons for buying that someone may not understand or approve.

Whatever the reason behind the consumer's behavior, the advertiser attempts to learn that reason and starts where the consumer is, or where the consumer wants to get to, or wants to become. If the consumer buys a dentifrice to prevent cavities, Colgate, Crest and Aim are three available brands. If the consumer buys the dentifrice to whiten teeth or to be attractive to someone else, the choices may be Ultra Brite or McLeans. Whatever the reason for buying a dentifrice, the consumer makes the decision. This is one example of how a market segments itself on the basis of advertising appeals.

Emotion is a fundamental component of all behavior, not just buying behavior. Emotion also is most likely found in consumer advertising addressed to large numbers of people. It is consumer advertising which addresses our most personal desire for being physically or socially attractive, for being a graceful dancer or a skilled water skier. Emotional appeals in advertisements tend to be effective because they are quickly understood by the vast majority of people, regardless of education, social class, or how their minds work.

On the other hand, take a close look at retail advertising the next time you leaf through a newspaper. Although local advertisers use some emotion in their copy, close inspection reveals that retail advertising is far more rational than emotional. The primary appeal is price, a rational element. After that are product details. Food advertisements are almost entirely price advertisements. Clothing advertisements are more likely tinged with emotion, but there is specific information as to wearability, washability, and construction details.

Advertising addressed to businessmen, merchants, engineers, and other professionals is almost completely rational. Emotional appeals would repel instead of attract business. Here is a type of advertising that performs a sober, useful service and is almost invariably overlooked by advertising's critics.

Advertising and Debasement of Language

Consumer advertising is written to be meaningful to millions of people, so copywriters work hard to make their writing interesting through the use of short, active words and phrases and to involve the reader through the use of the second person pronoun "you." Copywriters write this way because it is effective.

Copywriters also quickly pick up and use new terms or phrases from the fast-paced world of entertainment. They frequently blend these terms and phrases with the more general language of the popular culture, the words consumers themselves use.

The resulting and evolving language cannot be ignored. It may be lively, engaging, filled with insight, and witty at its best. It may also be common and mundane.

Advertisers are never really sure whether critics disapprove of the consumers who respond to advertisements or just to the language used in advertising. Assuming the latter, it is understandable that a highly cultured individual or someone with a vested interest in written and "correct" language—perhaps a teacher—deplores the slanginess and the violation of grammatical rules.

Spoken Language Is the "Real" Language.   To a descriptive linguist in anthropology, spoken language is the controlling or real language of a culture. Spoken language is incredibly flexible and responsive to the changing needs of people in a changing environment. Television today may have a multiplier effect on the speed and manner in which spoken language is changing. It is spoken language that first gives expression to new ideas, to technological change, with space exploration giving Americans a new vocabulary and a new way of looking at themselves in relation to a universe rather than just a world. Advertising copy uses the informality and naturalness of spoken language.

Language Change Is Accelerating.   Because the world is changing so rapidly today, the grammarian or language purist is always running to catch up with the new reality expressed in language, but is never quite able to do so. Language is too elusive. Today language must rapidly adapt to express an accelerating technology and the proliferation of new products. Advertisers accelerate changes in language meaning and use in the constant search for new ways to express the benefits of new products in ways meaningful to consumers. Consumers themselves are eager to use new terms or phrases as they consciously choose new careers and lifestyles.

The criticism that advertising debases the language is not just an American concern. The prestigious French Academy, dedicated to the purity of the French language, now wrestles with new terms—often anglicized—from the world of technology, fashion, and advertising. The effort to keep the French language pure is valiant but fruitless.

Language Is Tailored to Audience.   Advertising adopts the language most appropriate to its audience. Advertisements in professional journals and even popular scientific publications, such as *Scientific American,* use meticulously precise language expected by the readers of such publications. The disc jockey for a radio program, appealing to teen-agers, may deliver commercials in language that is meaningless to anyone who is not a regular listener to the program.

If advertising invites attention and interest in a product by expressing the self-interest of an audience in simple, direct, engaging language, this is not insulting. Gauged by reading difficulty formulas frequently used in education, there is little difference in the reading difficulty of news between the *New York Times* and less prestigious newspapers.

Copywriters Should Avoid "Ad-dy" writing.   Criticism of advertising copy stems largely from a quality described by George Gallup, research expert, as "ad-iness," or the sum total of the qualities differentiating advertising copy from conventional English. Two of the factors creating ad-iness, for example, are: punctuation (heavy use of hyphens, emdashes, exclamation points, three dots, quotation marks) and multiple adjectives ("Rich full-bodied, hearty flavor").

Overuse of ad-iness language makes one agree that the English language is being perverted. There are two saving factors, however:

(1)   Research seems to indicate that advertisements with a high degree of "ad-iness" are correspondingly low in sales power. If enough advertisers can be shown this, "ad-iness" will decline.
(2)   Copywriters, themselves, are very much against shoddy writing and "copywriterish" language.

The viewpoint of the rebellious copywriter is expressed by an advertising agency head, with a strong background in copywriting, who said: "My whole thesis is that you can write a hard-selling ad without cliche and dullness. The trouble with most copy is that it's written below the average intelligence. I would rather write a little above it. In an upcoming ad for Viyella socks, I have a word 'cognoscenti' in the headline and 'connoisseurship' in the copy. I'd rather flatter the intelligence than insult it."

Another advertising agency head, commenting on the same point, has said: "I honestly believe the people we advertise to are pretty smart. The stuff we find unconvincing because of the cliches they'll find that way, too."

Copywriting has added to the language. Although many advertising men cannot deny the charge of the litterateurs that advertising has caused a certain amount of perversion of the English language, they can say that in the main the copywriter has introduced a new, vigorous form of English prose. He has coined picturesque, descriptive words that have enriched the language. He has encouraged the writing of warm, human, personal language.

Copywriting does not lack its defenders among analysts of writing. When Rudolph Flesch, for instance, wrote his first book, *The Art of Plain Talk*, which described the weaknesses of different types of writing aimed at mass markets, he was far less critical of advertising writing than of other forms. He found that copywriters, as a whole, have instinctively used principles that make for successful communication with mass audiences.

Advertising men are most seriously affected by the consumer's opinion of advertising. Without consumer belief, advertising is pointless. Advertising men, like politicians, are, and must be, sensitive to public opinion. Although a few short-sighted advertisers consider consumers as unintelligent and easily swayed "suckers," most persons in the field know that it is the consumer, not the advertiser, who determines advertising policy. Thus, the following consumer assertions about advertising are viewed very seriously.

Advertising finances the media, hence controls them. Since media—newspaper, radio magazine, television, and others—need advertising in order to continue operating, it is natural that persons with a suspicious bent should incline to the view that advertising is the master, not servant, of the media.

"The newspapers just do what the big advertisers tell them to" is an often-heard charge. Another cynical observation is that television and radio "just give the public the news the sponsors want them to hear; and you never hear anything over the air that is derogatory to big advertisers—such things as

Federal Trade Commission rulings that show that an important sponsor has been found guilty of misleading advertising."

Media men are independent. The greatest safeguard against the alleged advertising influence is the character of the people who head American media. Probably no more independent person exists, for example, than the average newspaper publisher. He has been bred in the tradition that the press is objective and above partisanship, and that the death of the free press occurs when outside influences sway editorial judgment—influences such as government, business, or unions.

Favoring of advertising is usually found not so much in what the media report, as what they do not report. Many times, of course, omissions of this type occur because the editor (also television or radio people) honestly feels that the items lack legitimate news value. Other times, he or she holds back publication because the unfavorable judgment against an advertiser might be reversed at a later date. Meanwhile, if the news had been reported the advertiser's business might have suffered, and the advertiser might later sue the publisher for damages.

There is little direct influencing of media. Advertisers rarely approach the media crassly and say in effect "Do this—or else!" Influence of the advertiser upon the media is more subtle than this. It is an unconscious influence, as it were.

Those heading the media and those heading the companies doing the advertising are likely to have the same outlook. They are employers. They may have the same feeling about keeping government out of business. They have similar problems of taxation, union difficulties, and other matters that, so to speak, put them on the same side of the fence.

Understandable, then, is a natural sympathy of media people with the advertisers. Having the same overall social and business philosophy, it would be surprising if the media did not many times automatically express editorially the viewpoint of the advertisers.

Speaking of advertiser influence over the press, the Commission on Freedom of the Press (financed by Henry Luce's $200,000 and headed by such persons as Robert H. Hutchins, Archibald MacLeish, Charles E. Merriam, Reinhold Niebuhr, Arthur M. Schlesinger) made this statement:

> One of the criticisms repeatedly made is that the press is dominated by its advertisers. The evidence of dictation of policy by advertisers is not impressive. Such dictation seems to occur among the weaker units. As a newspaper becomes financially stable, it becomes more independent and tends to resist pressure from advertisers.

The report emphasizes the well-known truth that the smaller newspaper or radio station has a more difficult time saying "no" to an advertiser than does the big newspaper or radio station. Newspapers such as *The New York Times,* the *Chicago Tribune,* or the *St. Louis Post-Dispatch* are big business. No advertiser is big enough to frighten them. An advertiser attempting to dictate policy to any of those newspapers would be told firmly to take his business elsewhere. The newspaper usually will be able to get along without the advertiser better than the advertiser without the newspaper.

Believable testimonial.

By any yardstick this is a good testimonial. The person giving the testimonial is qualified to discuss the merits of the product and his career as a professional athlete lends interest to what he has to say. The form in which the testimonial is displayed is attention-getting and should insure more readership than if the trestimonial were buried in the body copy.

ANOTHER GOOD STEER FROM A TILT-WHEEL USER

1970 was the first year I tried Tilt-Wheel Steering in my car. My legs have loved it ever since.

Bob Quick
Detroit, Mich.

Bob Quick happens to be 6'7" and a former NBA basketball player. Which explains why he ordered Tilt-Wheel Steering on his last three Toronados.

But no matter how tall you are (or how short), how slim you are (or how chubby), how long your arms (or short your legs), Tilt-Wheel Steering makes driving more comfortable.

It's The Equalizer. It adjusts to you, regardless of your size or shape.

Tilt-Wheel moves up out of the way to help make getting in and out easier.

Then you can adjust the wheel to your most comfortable position, even while you drive.

With Tilt & Telescope Steering, you can adjust the wheel in and out, as well as up and down, for even greater comfort and convenience.

When you're looking at a General Motors car, van or pickup, be sure to look into the advantages of Tilt-Wheel Steering. Ask for a demonstration.

**Saginaw Steering Gear Division
General Motors Corporation**

THE EQUALIZER

A small newspaper in a small town, faced by a boycott of one or two big advertisers, may, in contrast, be in serious financial difficulties if it resists advertiser pressure. Advertiser influence on the medium therefore is often proportionate to the financial independence of the medium. That is one reason why some questionable advertising—patent medicine advertisements, to name one type—is found in small newspapers. Bigger papers can afford to refuse such business. Many smaller papers cannot—especially since they charge and get higher rates for advertising of this type.

High-pressure advertising is tiresome, annoying, and tension-creating. Repetition annoys consumers. The qualities that seem to bother consumers the most in advertising are repetition and exaggeration—especially the former. Repetition, whether of a slogan, a product name, a product benefit, or a singing commercial, is mentioned consistently by consumers as the most maddening aspect of advertising.

The lamentable truth is that there is little prospect of alleviating consumer distress on this point. The whole foundation of modern advertising is to tell prospective buyers something, and then to remind them over and over again—on the assumption that at best the message received only half-attention the first time it was delivered. No advertiser knows exactly how many consumers have heard or seen his message the first time, or even after the second, third, and fourth deliveries. Repetition to make certain of ultimate consumer exposure to the advertising message becomes a competitive necessity.

A possibility exists that the advertiser may repeat so much that the consumer can hardly hear or see his message because it has been used so often. An analogy that might apply here would be that of a mother who says "naughty, naughty" so frequently that her child develops an automatic hearing block when the words are spoken.

Other aspects of advertising offensive to consumers are misrepresentation of goods, or services, bad taste (as in oversexy illustrations, and in too many details of body functions, as in patent medicine advertising), and knocking of competitors' products. Better advertisers are seldom, if ever, guilty of any of these three faults. Apart from ethical reasons, they avoid such advertising because it is bad business.

Bothered by advertising? Yes! Do without it? No! In summation of the point, there is an inevitable annoyance factor in advertising. Repeat something enough and people become bored or annoyed. Work hard to be different, interesting, and original and there is a chance of an occasional misrepresentation or a slip into bad taste. Be aggressive enough and there will almost surely be exaggeration somewhere in your advertising. All these faults advertising will not, and cannot, deny—any more than it can deny that radio, despite its magnificent record in public service and in merchandising, can be a highly irritating instrument, as can television.

Yet, despite their criticisms, consumers want advertising and need advertising. While they complain about advertising's techniques in one breath, in the next breath they say they don't want it eliminated.

It is not unreasonable to conclude, therefore, that despite its faults where consumers are concerned, advertising is heavily on the plus side of the ledger.

QUESTIONS

1. Can there be mass production and mass consumption without mass distribution? Please give the reasons for your answer.

2. What assumptions of pure competition preclude the need for advertising?

3. Why is the per capita expenditure for advertising higher in the U.S. than in other countries?

4. Can manufacturers use advertising alone to hold prices rigid and high to consumers? Why?

5. Several professions are now permitted to advertise price information. What effect will this have on the professions? On prices? On consumers?

6. How effective is a monopoly based on advertising?

7. Discuss the relationship between advertising and product innovation.

8. Can you think of cases where the use of advertising to encourage product obsolescence may be desirable?

9. What do children learn from television advertising?

10. Are people both rational and emotional when they buy products?

11. Is advertising responsible for debasing language?

12. Why, in the American experience, do we depend on competition in the area of ideas and business activity? What outcomes do we expect from the competition of ideas? From business competition?

13. What accounts for the rapid growth in advertising laws and regulations?

REFERENCES

1. Borden, Neil H., The Economic Effects of Advertising (Chicago: Richard D. Irwin, Inc., 1944), p. 36.
2. Ibid.
3. New York: New York University Press, 1967.

REGULATION OF ADVERTISING

REGULATION OF ADVERTISING

Assume that you are asked to write an advertisement for a brand of California-grown olives. What are you going to write? How are you going to describe the size and taste of the olives? Not until you attempt to write an advertisement within the limits of today's numerous laws and regulations do you realize that sentences, phrases, and words can get you in trouble with one governmental agency or another. Years ago, before the invisible grip of law was extended to even our most private activities, this was not so. Today's laws that plague advertisers have ancient roots in English common law.

CURRENT LAW SHIFTS RESPONSIBILITY

One of the most widely recognized common law principles was expressed simply as *caveat emptor*—let the buyer beware. The buyer, under this principle, had very little legal protection in commercial transactions. This caution served buyers and sellers reasonably well when products were simple and easily examined.

Today, with the profusion of laws and regulations applying to marketing and advertising, it is now widely recognized that *caveat venditor,* or let the seller beware, best expresses the shift in responsibility from buyer to seller.

The reasons for the shift in responsibility are numerous. In many cases today, only sellers really know all about the increasingly complex products they sell to consumers. A colonial family purchasing an iron stove really knew what they were getting, compared with today's family purchasing a microwave oven. If the modern oven is complex, the installment contracts signed by consumers buying ovens seem even more so to today's consumer. Many consumers have learned the hard way that the long words in fine print on an installment contract protect only the seller's interests.

Today, the many laws regulating advertising may be divided into those that made modern advertising possible and those that limit or require specific advertising practices.

LAWS THAT MAKE MODERN ADVERTISING POSSIBLE

The first group of laws that make modern advertising possible constitute trademark law, including copyright and branding rules and regulations. Since recorded history, craftsman have put seals or identifying marks upon what they have made. Such marks both identified the craftsman and certified the quality of their products. Now, thousands of years later, identifying marks are still placed on goods. Many of these marks, called trademarks or brands, are widely known through advertisements. They are more important now than ever, for they certify quality between sellers and buyers who never personally meet. It is only because trademarks and brands are protected by a large body of law that modern advertising and marketing exist.

Branding and trademark activity is positively related to both the standard of living and the level of advertising. Without protection for a brand a manufacturer would have no incentive to maintain or offer superior product quality. There would be little reason to advertise. The consumer would find buying products much riskier. Also, without trademark protection, there would be no incentive to develop, much less advertise, new products.

Today even the Soviet Union uses trademarks to enforce quality standards in factories whose production goals were formerly expressed only in numbers of pairs of shoes or watches. Factories often met those goals with shoddy merchandise.

Trademark Protection

Trademarks are registered with the U.S. Patent Office after a thorough search to find out if someone else is already using the mark or one very much like it.

The search can be time consuming and is best done by specialists familiar with the more than 125 principal reference sources published by the United States Trademark Association. There are more than a half-million existing trademarks, and about 20,000 new trademarks are registered each year.

Once registered, the trademark is evidence of the user's claim to the trademark and makes it necessary for a rival claimant to prove that the trademark is invalid or that the user does not own the trademark. Without registration, the trademark loses legal status even though it may have been used and not challenged for many years.

A trademark should be used and identified as a trademark constantly in advertisements. Active and continuous usage of a trademark over a wide geographical area discourages others from the use of a similar mark.

Many outstanding trademarks have been lost because the owners failed to advertise them enough. After two years of nonuse, a trademark is considered abandoned. Others have claimed the rights to trademarks and won when they demonstrated that they had been employing the trademarks while the original user had not.

Some advertisers point out the trademark with stars or asterisks that are explained somewhere in the advertisements.

One advertiser protecting an element within his product uses the following statement at the bottom of his advertisements: "'Gardol' is Colgate-Palmolive Company's Trade Mark for Sodium N-Lauroyl Sarcosinate. R 1964, Colgate-Palmolive Company."

Others, such as Du Pont, have always used a circled R and the "Registered Trademark." Many consumer product advertisers now protect an element within a product by registering a name for the element, for example, "Gardol."

Capitalizing the Trademark. The term "generic" is heard constantly in warnings about the possible loss of a trademark. This term means, when applied to a trademark, that the trademark has become a part of the language because it has been so completely identified with a useful article or a common function.

One of the surest signs that a trademark is, or has become, generic is the spelling of the trademark name with a smaller letter. In 1962, for example, a court ruled that because a Thermos bottle had become so much a part of the American way of life, it was as permissible to spell the word "thermos" with a small "t" as to spell any other common noun in the American language with a small initial letter.

The problem is that, because of constant repetition, whether for advertising purposes or simply because the trademark name is so useful in describing a certain type of product or its function, it becomes almost impossible for the general public to use any other term in asking or talking about the product. Thus the advertiser's success in developing the term is his downfall. Many famous names have become generic and are now spelled with a small initial letter; exclusive rights to the use of these names have thus been lost to their former owners. Some of these are deepfreeze, linoleum, cellophane, kerosene, escalator, aspirin, milk of magnesia, band-aid, kleenex, celluloid, shredded wheat.

Naturally, the advertiser will capitalize his own trademark, but he may find it difficult to get others to do so.

Thus, some advertisers have run advertisements asking, urging, and warning others to capitalize the advertiser's trademark name. Publishers and editors have been particular targets of such advertising. Xerox, Coca-Cola (Coke), Orlon, Dacron, and Scotch Tape have been some of the products so advertised.

By attaching the trademark to the product or its container, the advertiser prevents substitution and provides legal protection. The trademark may be stamped with ink on oranges, or molded into bars of soap.

Intangibles, such as insurance, can use trademarks, too. Examples are the MONY abbreviation of Mutual of New York, or the Rock of Gibraltar symbol of Prudential. Even a sound can be trademarked, like the distinctive sound for each network news program.

Types of Trademarks

When a trademark is being considered, two questions should be pondered: Will this trademark be easily used in advertising or will it be awkward because it is too long, too hard to say, too much like others, or misleading? Does it fit both advertising requirements and legal requirements?

Although there are a number of possible variations, trademarks can be grouped into several classifications.

Dictionary Words. As a rule, dictionary words are considered weak trademarks and their use is discouraged. Premium, Superior, and Gold Label, are so common and undistinctive that they are almost impossible to protect. A good example is Blue Ribbon, which has been registered more than 60 times in the United States Patent Office for many types of goods. It is consequently, virtually unprotectable.

Public issue advertisement.

One of the great problems of our time is what action to take with respect to nuclear power plants. Presented here is one of a series of advertisements aimed at creating a favorable public attitude toward to building of a new nuclear power plant. Advertisements such as this must be executed with exceeding care because the issue is so volatile with its social and economic aspects.

Fourth in a series of reports on Marble Hill nuclear project:

If you don't believe that nuclear plants make good neighbors, just ask the neighbors.

In the U.S., 61 nuclear power reactors are licensed to operate. Some have been in operation for nearly 20 years.

Not a single person has been killed or even seriously injured by the nuclear operation of these plants.

Yet there are those who would have you believe that nuclear power plants are bad news, that they endanger the area in which they're built.

Our Marble Hill nuclear plant will be a good neighbor. If you don't believe us, ask the people who've been living with other nuclear plants. What do they think about their nuclear neighbors?

In Plymouth, Massachusetts, where a nuclear power plant went into operation five years ago, the residents recently voted on whether to have a second nuclear plant in their community. The vote: 4 to 1 in favor of more nuclear power.

Residents of Humboldt County, California, have lived with a nuclear power plant since 1963. And last June all California voters had a chance to vote for or against nuclear power plants. While Californians voted in favor of nuclear power by a 2 to 1 margin, residents of Humboldt County were even more enthusiastic. Seven out of 10 of these nuclear neighbors voted for nuclear power!

"We think the Diablo Canyon Nuclear Plant is a good neighbor," says a former mayor of San Luis Obispo, California, where a majority of residents favor nuclear power. "Many people hear only the scare stories about nuclear," he says, "but those of us who live near nuclear plants are constantly exposed to both sides of nuclear power and the more we hear, the better we are able to decipher the scare stories from the facts."

At LaCrosse, Wisconsin, where a nearby nuclear plant has been in operation since 1969, the mayor considers the facility to be "a good, clean, safe neighbor."

Nuclear power is seen as a vital and safe solution to many of our nation's energy problems by those who know most about it. Here are just a few of the scientific and technical groups that have endorsed nuclear power:

Power Engineering Society (with 18,000 members)
Society of Professional Engineers (69,000 members)
Health Physics Society (3,400 members)
Energy Committee of the Institute of Electrical and Electronics Engineers
(The IEEE has 170,000 members)
American Institute of Chemical Engineers (39,000 members)
American Society of Mechanical Engineers (60,000 members)
American Nuclear Society (10,000 members)

More than 25,000 scientists and engineers last year signed a "Declaration of Energy Independence" urging the use of coal and nuclear power. It was presented to the White House with signatures representing 200,000 man-hours' experience in electric power generation.

And a recent statement signed by 32 eminent scientists—including 11 Nobel laureates—also calls for greater use of coal and uranium to produce electricity. "All energy release involves risks and nuclear power is certainly no exception," says the report. "On any scale, the benefits of a clean, inexpensive and inexhaustible domestic fuel far outweigh the possible risks. We can see no reasonable alternative to an increased use of nuclear power to satisfy our energy needs."

Nuclear power and the Marble Hill plant are essential to the solution of our future energy problems. Responsibly designed, constructed and operated, Marble Hill will be a safe, clean "good neighbor" in Jefferson County. Our future depends on it.

 PUBLIC SERVICE INDIANA

Because distinctiveness is the most desirable attribute of a trademark, it would almost seem as if dictionary words would never be used as identifiers. Yet some of the best-known trademark names are dictionary words. Examples:

Ivory (soap) *Era (detergent)*
Mercury (outboard motors) *Admiral (television)*

A well-chosen dictionary word, such as *Mercury,* can imply a quality of the product without actually describing it, and thus is worth using. Other words, such as *Ivory,* have been used so long and so often that they have a built-in protection against their use by makers of similar products.

Coined Words. Made-up trademark names fall into the strong trademark class since they are distinctive and are easy to protect. Sometimes they are meaningless, as *Yuban* and *Zonite*. Other times they carry some meaning, such as *Kromekote* and *Coke.* Whether they have meaning or not, they are protectable. Sometimes, however, wanting to create a trademark that cannot be stolen or imitated, the creator invents a coined word that is difficult to pronounce or remember. Here are a few coined trademarks:

Anacin (tablets) *Viobin (wheat-germ oil)*
Scripto (lighters) *Alumni-Glow (aluminum cleaner)*
Magnavox (television)

Names. Although one of the most common sources of trademarks, surnames cannot be put in the strong trademark class because persons with the same names are usually (but not always) entitled to use them as trademarks too if they wish.

Sometimes name trademarks can be made stronger if the whole name is used and that whole name is distinctive, as with Fanny Farmer, Elizabeth Arden, or Betty Crocker.

Despite the seeming weakness of a name as a trademark, many of the famous names in industry have been used so long as trademarks that they have developed strength through long, continuous use. In such a category are Parke-Davis, Steinway, and hundreds of others.

Sometimes the trademark is the name of the company founder, sometimes it is an historical name, and sometimes it is a combination of parts of the company name. Examples of each appear in the following:

Goodyear (tires) *John Hancock (insurance)*
Campbell's (soup) *Conoco (Continental Oil Company)*

Foreign Names and Words. From the advertising standpoint, foreign names and words are often highly desirable for many products because they provide an exotic flavor and an air of exclusiveness. From the legal standpoint they often provide distinctiveness that makes for easy protection. On the negative side, though, they can be hard to pronounce and so unfamiliar that they are difficult to remember. Some of the foreign words and names now in use:

Kawasaki (motorcycle)   *Cointreau (liqueur)*
Yashica (Cameras)   *Subaru (Automobiles)*
Arpege (perfume)   *Peugeot (Automobiles)*
Puch (moped)

Symbols and Pictures. Among the very strongest of trademarks are those that combine the trademark name and some sort of picture or symbol. Those are strong not only from the legal standpoint but also from the advertising standpoint. They have memorability. They are immediately associated with the product. They have strong talk value and they are especially useful for visual presentation in print, whether in magazine advertisements, in outdoor advertising, or on packages.

Some of the most famous advertising campaigns of all times have used symbols and pictures, from the famous Fisk tire boy holding the candle near the words "Time to retire" to the Morton Salt girl holding the umbrella. Current combination trademarks:

The name Armco within a triangle
Quick Quaker Oats with a picture of a Quaker
The carriage of Body by Fisher

Geographical Names. A flat "No" may be the answer to a request to register a trademark that includes the name of a well-known geographical location. If, for example, a firm on the West Coast making men's clothing were to ask for a registration of "San Francisco" as the trademark for a brand of clothes, the request would undoubtedly be refused, because this name simply indicates the place of origin. Besides, other firms making products in the San Francisco area would be likely to protest that no one firm should be allowed to preempt an entire geographical area. Protection of the mark would be virtually impossible.

Despite the usual refusals of requests for such trademarks, there are a number of well-known marks which were established long ago and have held on because of a sort of historical right:

Plymouth (automobile)   *Hershey (candy)*
Corning (glass)   *Oneida (tableware)*
Palm Beach (clothes)

Initials and Numbers. Hard to remember and difficult to protect, initials and numbers might be expected to have quite limited usage as trademarks. Instead, they are among the most popular trademarks. A glance at any magazine will reveal that one company after another uses initials as a trademark; in many cases the initials constitute an abbreviation of the company name.

Whether a corporation uses initials or numbers, it is asking consumers for one more memory feat because of the bewildering profusion of initials and numbers that we are asked to remember by the government, our banks, the telephone company, our employers, and almost every other organization that touches our lives. A company should think carefully before imposing this additional burden on the confused consumer. Furthermore, many company abbreviations are so similar that it becomes increasingly difficult to distinguish among them. One issue of a magazine with a moderate amount of advertising carried the following abbreviations: IBM, GE, RCA, TWA, UOP, OP, GM, INA, and NCR. The magazine referred to is in the business classification. Consumer magazines with many more advertisements carry many more initials and compound the rapidly growing confusion.

Trademarks That Cannot Be Registered

Trademarks that cannot be registered include, in particular:

- Immoral material.
- Flags, including those of the United States, states, cities, or foreign nations.
- Fraternal society emblems (without permission).
- Names, signatures and portraits of living persons (without their written permission).
- Material derogatory of persons, beliefs, and institutions.

In general:

- Marks so similar to existing trademarks (for the same or similar goods) that they might confuse or mislead purchasers.
- Marks that are merely descriptive, deceptively misdescriptive, or geographically descriptive (such as the San Francisco clothing company mentioned earlier).
- Marks that are ordinary surnames are usually not registrable because persons with similar names can also use them. If the names are not so ordinary, they may be registered but protection may be difficult.

Guides For Creating Trademarks

Make the trademark imply something about the product, but do not make it descriptive. To call a medicated skin lotion just that—medicated skin lotion—would be descriptive and the words could not be registered or protected. Giving these words registered status would bar makers of similar products from using these words, which actually tell what is being sold. The name Dermassage, however—the trademark name of a medicated lotion now on the market—implies the benefit or use of the product but is not merely descriptive.

Make the trademark easy to remember and to pronounce, but not commonplace. Mercury, Ajax, Hercules, Guardian, Ezy, Magic, Meteor, Reliable, Gold Star, and Pioneer are a few trademark names that are easy to remember, to pronounce, and to make up, but they are commonplace. In originating trademarks minds seem to run in the same channels, as evidenced by all the Blue Ribbons and Gold Medals, and by the more than 50 applications that poured in for atomic, almost before the dust had settled from the first atomic explosion.

Do not make the trademark deceptive or confusing. This point must be emphasized because it is so often forgotten and is the cause of so much trouble. An example of just what kind of trouble is shown by a court case involving the giant corporation Colgate-Palmolive and a small manufacturer in a small California town. The latter, making a liquid detergent called Jeenie, won a court injunction against Colgate-Palmolive prohibiting it from advertising and marketing its liquid detergent, Genie, in 14 western states. This was a serious and costly blow to the big company, which had already spent $1.8 million promoting Genie, including the distribution of 800,000 sample bottles in San Francisco and 2,000,000 in Los Angeles.

When products are similar, the courts are especially sympathetic to the injured party, although even for unlike products there is some protection if it is felt that some loss of business might result from the use of similar names. For instance, the courts ruled in favor of the complainant Sweetheart soap against Sweetheart paper towels; Comet cleanser against Comet floorwax; Seven-Up against Lemon-Up; Midol against Nidol; Seven-Up against Fizz-Up.

Most companies have too much pride to use a trademark or trademark name that capitalizes on the business built up by another company. Still, there are companies that try. It is for protection against these companies that trademark laws exist.

Trademarks and Brand Advertising

In discussing trademarks we have been concerned with the technical aspects of what makes a good trademark and with the importance of the trademark generally in identifying goods and in providing protection for the advertiser.

A more important consideration, however, is the continued existence of brands themselves, and hence of brand advertising.

Despite the amounts spent to establish brand names and despite the importance of those names to thousands of manufacturers and distributors, there are those who would do away with brands. It becomes necessary, accordingly, to discuss the reasons for advertising brands.

Brands are Symbols.   Brands are symbols of quality that give assurance that the branded product the consumer buys in 1980 will have the same quality when it is bought in 1985 and 1990. Brands tell the consumer honestly and openly that the maker feels a responsibility for the product.

Brands supply a ready product identification and thus make shopping easier. Give consumers an array of everyday products bearing unfamiliar names, because they have never been advertised, and you will have provided a shopping puzzle. To solve it, the shoppers must try to read the small print on the packages to decide which products to buy. When, however, products carry advertised brand names, the shopping problem is simplified because consumers already have some assurance of the product quality and performance. For the consumer, shopping has been made easier, quicker, and less risky.

Challenges to Brand Advertising. There are currently two threats to brand advertising of national manufacturers. The first comes from distributor and retailer brands that often sell for less than national brands. If the consumer buys and tries both nationally and locally branded merchandise and finds them comparable in quality, the consumer probably will choose the retailer brand because often it is lower in price. This is to the consumer's advantage.

The second challenge to branding is from the consumer movement, which questions whether nationally branded merchandise is genuinely higher in quality. The consumer movement supports the Federal Trade Commission (FTC) investigation of analgesics, a name for over-the-counter headache, cold-and-sinus-congestion relief drugs, many of which are physically similar, but for which the competing manufacturers claim superiority backed by clinical evidence.

Such investigations become social as well as economic issues. Critics assert that heavy advertising of such chemically similar products is wasteful. Whether through first-hand experience, the recommendation of family or friends, or the influence of advertising, consumers do have preferences and beliefs. They choose one product or, more likely, a brand that works for them, no matter what the critics say.

Distributor Brands. Many manufacturers sell part or all of their products to wholesalers or retailers who then put their own brands (called distributor brands) on the goods. Some very large manufacturers put their own brands on most of what they make and advertise these brands vigorously. Only a minor portion of their output is distributor branded. Other smaller manufacturers do not even attempt to put brands on the market themselves but are content with a permanent arrangement by which they supply goods for others to brand. Under this arrangement they are, in a sense, at the mercy of their buyers who may sometime decide to switch manufacturers.

Present Status of Distributor Brands. Such retailing giants as Macy's, Sears Roebuck, and Montgomery Ward have been especially vigorous in the pushing of their own brands, with Sears Roebuck and Montgomery Ward offering much more (distributor-private) brand merchandise then (manufacturer-advertised) brand goods.

Food chains, too, have worked hard to build distributor-brand business. One chain, for example, has built their own brands up so well that 85 percent of the chain's orange-juice sales are in distributor brands, 33 percent of instant coffee, and 33 percent of light-duty detergents.

Although distributor brands have been increasing in foods, appliances, and other lines, all is not black for advertised (manufacturer) brand names. Some chains, for example, after pushing distributor brands forcefully, have switched their policy and have returned to an emphasis on advertised brands. Just the same, the situation is being watched closely by advertising people.

Some retailers show a marked preference for distributor brands—brands that retailers themselves often own—rather than manufacturers' brands. Other retailers believe they can best run their business by selling both distributor and manufacturer brands. The final choice belongs to the retailers, but there are some compelling reasons, in the retailer's mind, for emphasizing distributor brands.

Distributor brands make more money for the retailer. In many cases the retailer can buy distributor-brand goods somewhat cheaper than comparable nationally advertised brand merchandise. Thus the retailer can price distributor/brand merchandise somewhat lower than the advertised brands, the store giving the customer a bargain and itself a better profit margin. However, the retailer usually has to make an extra effort in the store to give the distributor brands the best positions. Many thinking retailers question whether, under the circumstances, they really do achieve extra profits in the long run through distributor-brand activity, or whether they are merely switching dollars from advertised brands to distributor brands.

Distributor brands give the retailer individuality. Whether we are talking about a food supermarket or a woman's specialty store, the individuality of distributor brands comes into the conversation. The special packaging gives a different look to the offerings of the supermarket, since it sets off the store's brands from the brands the consumer sees in every other store. And if the consumer likes the goods within the distinctive packages, the store offering that particular distributor brand is the only place where the shopper can buy these goods. Thus the distributor brand gives the consumer a reason for shopping in this one store rather than in the many stores that offer essentially the same lines of nationally advertised goods.

A woman's specialty store, such as Saks Fifth Avenue, finds that its own brand means more to customers than nationally advertised brands that can be found in many stores. The private brands have greater exclusiveness, an important quality for a specialty shop.

Distributor brands give the dealer more control. When retailers stress distributor brands, they run their promotions to suit their overall plans. They sell, advertise, and display merchandise as they see fit. On the other hand, retailers who tie in closely with a manufacturer's nationally advertised brands are often compelled to carry certain items in the manufacturer's line and to tie their plans in with the advertiser's promotions. Living up to these conditions may be expedient for one store but not another.

Grade and Descriptive Labeling

One goal of the consumer movement over the years has been to require specific types of information in advertising and packaging. Numerous consumer activists, for example, want more descriptive information about product quality in relation to price so consumers can make more informed purchase decisions. This type of information, consumerists believe, can come only from governmentally developed criteria against which products are measured. The goal is widespread governmental grade labeling of the sort many consumers now associate with meat products.

Grade Labeling. One of the chief aims of the consumer movement is to get government backing for a system of grade labeling. Under this system, numbers or letters on packages or cans would indicate the quality of the contents. Such a system, sponsored by the Bureau of Agricultural Economics, has been established for fruit packed in cans. This labeling system classes contents as follows:

A Grade:	Fancy
B Grade:	Extra-standard
C Grade:	Standard
Off-grade:	Substandard

Arguments For and Against Grade Labeling.   Understandably, there are arguments for and against grade labeling. Some of those for grade labeling are as follows:

- Prices are based on the quality of goods instead of on the name built up through brand advertising.
- Producers can cut marketing expenses, since the cost of using brand advertising to tell consumers of the superiority of their products is eliminated.
- Grade labeling enables buyers to judge quickly the merits of goods, unlike the present brand advertising system, which is more likely to confuse buyers than help them make intelligent selections.

The arguments against grade labeling are as follows:

- A single grade mark cannot describe many products accurately.
- Grades might rob a producer of the incentive to improve his quality or even to maintain it, since a Grade A standard might actually be below normal quality. Thus, the producer would be inclined simply to maintain a Grade A quality even though capable of turning out a product that was actually better than that rating. Thus grades, which themselves tend to be inflexible, would discourage product improvements.
- Grades do not allow for individual preference. A product graded "A" might actually be less preferable to consumers than a product graded "B" or "C".
- The "A" grade reflects the preference of the judgers, not necessarily those of the people buying the product.

Descriptive Labeling.   Another goal of the consumer movement boosts descriptive labeling, which would give much more information on labels than is now given. This kind of labeling, often called "informative" labeling, would attempt to provide information that would help the consumer make a buying decision. It would help also in actually using the product, by naming ways to get longer wear (in the case of clothing products), various uses for the product, warnings, and a detailed listing of ingredients in language that the average person can understand.

One of the largest supermarket chains provides the kind of information on food labels that is demanded by informative-labeling supporters. This chain requires that food labels include:

- Description of processing method
- Instructions for using the product
- Information about the product's maturity, size, variety, color, style of pack, spices, seasoning, and number of servings
- Individual grade
- Brand name
- Accurate picture of the product

Advertiser's View of Grade Labeling.   Although advertisers question that descriptive labeling can always include all the information that is needed, or that the information would be read if it could be included, few advertisers view descriptive labeling as a real threat to the present system of brand advertising.

Grade labeling, however, is not viewed so calmly. Manufacturers who have spent millions of dollars on advertising to build up brand confidence feel that if grades become the buying standard instead of well-known advertised brands, brand differentiation is doomed. Naturally, feeling as they do, they oppose grade labeling vigorously, and with some very sound arguments.

Grade labeling implies a static product, and there are very few of these, even among simple products. Corn on the cob, for example, is a simple product, easily judged by the vast majority of consumers. Grade labels for corn on the cob are unnecessary and could be misleading unless changed as the corn changes. Today's cob of corn is much larger with more uniform rows of kernels than that often pictured on the first Thanksgiving table between Pilgrims and Indians. The kernels are larger and juicier in relation to the cob. Years of experimentation by plant geneticists make today's corn on the cob more unlike than like the corn known to early colonialists.

Put the corn into a can or a package for freezing. Grade labels give reasonable guidance but would have to be altered to keep up with what is put into the can with the corn.

Labeling also attempts to straightjacket diversity. Tomatoes can be huge beefsteak tomatoes, regular, or cherry sized. The pulp-to-liquid content varies according to the strain, as does the taste. Corn and tomatoes are relatively simple products, but they require grading decisions based on criteria that may be irrelevant to consumers. Labels do not express taste as a consideration, although corn of a certain grade may be assumed to have certain taste characteristics. Then again, it may not.

Manufacturers further argue that grade labeling inhibits product innovation and improvement. By ignoring those improvements to consumers which do not fit predefined grades. This, in effect, says the improvement is irrelevant, indeed nonexistent, according to a government definition.

When asked about grade labels currently used for supermarket products, consumers tend to do considerable guessing. Some are quite knowledgeable; many are indifferent, using grade labels only as a casual guide. The same consumer reaction is found with regard to unit pricing, with the important dif-

Advertisement stressing proper use of a trademark name.

Xerox has been vigilant in calling attention to the use of its trademark in order to prevent the name from becoming generic. Other advertisements have emphasized the importance of capitalizing the name and using it as an adjective—not as a noun or verb.

ust was the color of the sky.
Dust was the color of the town.

The young sheriff moved toward the railway platform, pausing only to wipe his moist palms on his holsters.

He watched the Union Pacific engine hurtle around the bend and screech to a clanging, hissing stop. Silently, the Dalton boys swung from the train onto the station platform. Suddenly the sheriff found himself staring down the barrels of three shotguns. The street behind him was empty but for the dust.

There was no turning for help.

As his hands crept slowly toward his gun belt he knew he had to say it now or forever hold his peace. A crooked smile played about the corners of his mouth, as he drawled, "Boys, I want you to hear me and hear me good. Just remember, that Xerox is a registered trademark of Xerox Corporation and, as a brand name, should be used only to identify its products and services."

ference that quite a few consumers find unit prices difficult to understand.

The precise and detailed information now required on packages is ignored by many consumers. Why? Precisely correct information requires long, technical words and graduate degrees in chemistry and nutrition for understanding. Acetyl salicylic acid is aspirin. Which do you ask for when you have a headache?

Those who argue that governmental testing can be objective and impartial now must contend with the accuracy of EPA mileage figures on the windows of new cars. Too many Americans have experienced gas mileage far below what the window sticker officially stated. Had the drivers of new cars taken the sticker figures seriously, they would be angry rather than amused.

Despite the fact that the consumer movement attracts some very active and intelligent people and organizations, actually only a small percentage of the mass of consumers support any change in our present system of brand advertising.

Most people are satisfied with brand-name products and have faith in the advertisers. There has not been, furthermore, any great demand by the public for more information than is now given in advertisements or on labels. Most people realize that advertising is just one of the steps in the selling process and that it cannot do the whole job of providing information any more than the small print on a label can tell everything a consumer needs or would like to know about a product.

The federal government now requires much more information on labels and packages than has been true in the past. Likewise, unit pricing is now found in the supermarkets. These improvements have not come as a result of any huge groundswell of public protest but more as a result of the efforts of various lawmakers who feel that the public must be protected, even if great numbers of the public do not ask for such protection. It has been interesting to note that some shoppers have complained that they don't understand unit pricing and that they are mystified by the long lists of product ingredients, many of them chemicals, found on packages. Still, the trend for more package information must be viewed as a progressive step. Currently, the federal government has been pushing for additional information on labels and packages that will largely satisfy requirements in this respect.

To sum up, the consumer movement, while not likely to change our brand advertising system noticeably, has been useful in making advertisers more conscious than ever of their obligation to supply accurate facts about products, and to provide products that live up to the claims of the advertising. Should advertisers fail noticeably in either of these two respects, then the consumer movement with its grade labeling could truly threaten brand advertising.

Organizations Concerned With Brand Advertising

Brand Names Foundation. A nonprofit membership organization, the Brand Names Foundation, stresses to the public the valuable service provided by brand identification, trademarks, and advertising, not only to consumers but to merchants selling manufactured products.

Overall, it attempts to make clear the values and benefits of the brand system. It is sponsored and supported by brand advertisers, advertising agencies, and advertising media. It was founded in 1943, soon after an attempt by certain government officials to make federal grade labeling mandatory for all products.

Each year, print and broadcast media carry thousands of advertisements that have been prepared to further the objectives of the foundation. In addition to these advertisements, materials are prepared for presentation to schools, clubs, and women's organizations. These materials sell the free competitive enterprise system as well as brand advertising as a part of that system.

Consumers Reports and Consumers Union. Consumers' Union tests goods and services and issue reports of the findings in the publication *Consumer Reports*. Their object is to provide ratings that will help consumers buy more intelligently. Their selling point is their objectivity, which they assert will enable a consumer to buy on the basis of facts, not on the basis of exaggerated claims such as may be made by advertisements.

No one can quarrel with the overall objective of these organizations: to provide unbiased evaluations of products. Such evaluations have proved valuable to many consumers and have caused many manufacturers to squirm whose products actually did not live up to claims.

Manufacturers often assert, however, that the testing methods of these organizations are not always so accurate nor so thorough as they should be. They say also that these organizations are the tool of groups attempting to undermine brand advertising.

Advertisers whose products live up to their advertising, however, usually have little to fear from *Consumers' Reports* or Consumers' Union. By the same token, it is not easy to view either organization as a strong threat to brand advertising—a gadfly, perhaps, but not a threat.

WHY MOST ADVERTISING IS TRUTHFUL

Unless advertising is truthful, it is self-defeating. Only the confidence the consumer can place in the advertiser's word makes possible the success of brand advertising. Advertising's great natural resource is consumer belief, and it is in the interest of all advertisers to protect that natural resource.

Yet some advertising is untruthful, either in whole or in part. Other advertising, while not actually untruthful, stretches the truth or exaggerates to the point where truth is obscured.

Advertising, for the most part, however, is truthful. There are two good reasons for this:

(1) Most people are more honest than dishonest by nature.
(2) Advertisers are businesspeople who know that repeat sales are more important than the first sale. Good sense tells them that, while dishonest or inaccurate statements in their advertising might make the first sale, a buyer who finds that a product does not live up to its advertising will not buy it a second time. Few factories run on one-time purchases. They depend upon repeat sales for their existence. Honest advertising, therefore, is just plain good business and good sense.

Monitoring Advertising

Advertising today is the most closely monitored and scrutinized form of public communication in America. It is regulated informally and formally by advertisers themselves, by their agencies, the media, industry associations, and by governmental agencies. The regulation is done in terms of numerous court decisions that prohibit certain activities and limit or require other activities and types of advertising information. In fact, so detailed are the many, and sometimes conflicting requirements, that some misleading advertising is executed quite innocently by an advertiser who, in meeting the advertising requirements of one governmental agency, violates the advertising requirements of another governmental agency.

A good yardstick has been provided by the United States Supreme Court in a judgment against a magazine in a postal fraud case. The Supreme Court's discussion boiled down to the following points that could serve as general guideposts to all types of advertisers:

(1) Advertising as a whole must not create a misleading impression even though every statement separately considered is literally truthful.

(2) Advertising must be written for the probable effect it produces on ordinary and trusting minds, as well as for those intellectually capable of penetrating analysis.

(3) Advertising must not obscure or conceal material facts.

(4) Advertising must not be artfully contrived to distract and divert reader's attention from the true nature of the terms and conditions of an offer.

(5) Advertising must be free of fraudulent traps and stratagems that induce action that would not result from a forthright disclosure of the true nature of an offer.

REGULATING WHAT ADVERTISING CAN SAY

The FTC and False and Misleading Advertising

The Federal Trade Commission was not established by Congress to regulate advertising. Rather, the commission stumbled into advertising regulation when the Supreme Court upheld the agency in a relatively minor case involving advertising, while rebuffing the commission in cases involving more serious anticompetitive practices.

Because the Supreme Court's decision in this early case represented one of the few victories in an otherwise bleak regulatory start, the FTC allocated increasing manpower and money to curtailing advertising it believed false. Over the years the courts have granted the commission a growing number of decisions. The wording in these decisions provides the precedents which broaden the commission's authority over advertising. Supplementary legislation by the congress further has strengthened the Commission's authority, so that today the FTC is well- —if not over-armed—to move against advertising it believes false or misleading.

Guidelines to the FTC's Approach to Advertisements

Four guidelines express the way the FTC approaches advertising:

(1) Meaning can be determined on the basis of an advertisement's total impression and context, so that while each element of an advertisement—illustration, headline or copy—is literally correct, the interaction between the elements may be misleading;

(2) Literal or technical truth will not save an advertisement that is misleading, if the advertisement can be construed to say one thing but mean another;

(3) Advertising is misleading if it is susceptible of two meanings one of which is false, which in effect makes almost every advertisement potentially misleading if not false; and

(4) Expressions of opinion or personal evaluations of intangible qualities are subjective claims which are mere trade puffing and not deceptive, although the line between subjective and objective is often vague, and the FTC's obvious intention is to limit permissible puffing.

The FTC's Standard of Truth

Advertisements need not be literally false or even misleading but merely have a "tendency to mislead" to be false to the FTC. Couple this mere tendency with the potential, mentioned in the previous paragraph, to read two meanings into an advertisement, and it becomes very easy for the FTC to find an advertisement false and misleading.

Additionally, the FTC can apply a consumer intelligence standard as a measuring rod against advertising content. The standard, according to court-granted precedent, includes the credulous and the gullible, and is at the lowest intelligence level used to measure the meaning of any type of communication content in the United States today. It is little wonder, then, that advertisers run a considerable risk of having simple, direct announcements found false because the advertisements have a "tendency to mislead."

Broad FTC Precedents

Today the FTC's standard of what is false and misleading advertising is so broad that the law, rather than providing certainty for advertisers, creates uncertainty. The cautious advertiser may ask the FTC for an advance opinion about the truthfulness of proposed advertisements before the advertisements are publicly run. The commission will give an advance opinion, but the commission does not consider itself bound by its own opinion. The agency may subsequently charge the advertisements are false.

Relatively recent court decisions have relieved the commission of the traditional legal requirement of developing evidence to show an advertised claim is false. The burden of proof has been shifted to the advertiser. The commission now requires that advertisers develop evidence to back an advertised claim prior to starting an advertising campaign. Then, if the FTC challenges an advertisement, the commission may argue that the evidence submitted by the advertiser is insufficient to back an advertised claim, and the advertisement is thereby false.

The courts also have relieved the FTC of having to develop consumer testimony as to the meanings of advertisements charged with being false by the FTC. Rather, the commission can now determine the meaning of advertisements to consumers on the commission's own "expertise." The only way an advertiser can challenge the commission's expertise is to provide evidence of the meaning of its advertisements to typical consumers. Advertisers, therefore, may survey samples of consumers to learn the meaning of proposed advertisements to consumers. Only when such evidence is developed, are the advertisements run.

In short, advertisers must now have advance evidence of the truthfulness of their advertised claims and of the meaning of such claims to consumers.

Corrective Advertising

In recent years the FTC has ordered a few advertisers to run corrective advertising when the commission finds that claims in an advertising campaign are false or misleading. The commission is testing the legal waters for new powers, requiring the advertiser to devote 25 percent of the space or time in succeeding advertisements to correcting any false information provided to consumers by earlier advertisements.

At present the legality of such orders is questionable. The intent of the FTC act is to prevent unfair acts or practices, and advertisers argue that corrective advertising requirements go beyond prevention to punishment. Additionally, some orders are so broadly phrased they would require corrective advertisements for all product lines for multiple-product manufacturers when the advertising for only a single product is under challenge. Such an order against Coca Cola, for example, would include all soft drinks, canned or frozen juices, wines, and any other products of the company.

Corrective advertising is controversial. Even as you read this book the controversy will continue to unfold. Whether the FTC is allowed to require corrective advertising probably will be decided when the Supreme Court makes a definitive decision concerning First Amendment protection for commercial speech, or advertising. At this writing it appears that the Supreme Court is likely to do so. If advertising is protected speech under the First Amendment, it is unlikely that the FTC will be allowed to order corrective advertising in the future.

*A notable example of such corrective advertising occurred in June, 1978 when the Warner-Lambert Company ended a years-long battle with the Federal Trade Commission and agreed to include the following phrase in the advertisements in a $10-million campaign: "Listerine will not help prevent colds or sore throats or lessen their severity."

The company had advertised Listerine as a cold remedy since 1921 and had fought the Federal Trade Commission off and on since 1941 for the right to continue the claim.

Printers' Ink Statute

The Printers' Ink Model Statute was introduced in 1911 by the advertising magazine *Printers' Ink*. At the urging of advertisers and advertising agencies, it was adopted by the majority of state legislatures. The statutes make it a misdemeanor to use misleading, deceptive or untrue advertising.

Unlike the regulations of the Federal Trade Commission, which are concerned with interstate or national advertising, the Printers' Ink Statute was designed for intrastate use. In recent years the FTC has urged states to move against deceptive advertising on the basis of the state statutes supplemented by the many precedents gained through the courts by the Trade Commission.

SELF-REGULATION

Industry Associations

Some of the most effective regulation of advertising is provided by associations of advertisers who band together to see that, among other things, their individual company members advertise honestly and in good taste. A good example of such an association is the Proprietary Association, composed of manufacturers of proprietary medicines. Its function is to preserve and improve the integrity and stability of the industry, and to improve its advertising.

A number of industry associations have requested the FTC to make specific the meaning of advertising law to association members. When invited, trade commission lawyers meet with industry representatives to reach agreement and publish the meaning of advertising and other commercial laws in terms specific to an industry. Often the rules are designed to give precise meaning to otherwise casually used words and phrases.

In addition to the many manufacturers' associations, there are the associations within the advertising industry itself which help police the advertising activity of their members. Two of these are the American Association of Advertising Agencies and the Association of National Advertisers.

Both call to the attention of the offending member agency any advertising that lacks honesty or good taste; this warning is usually all that is needed to bring about a favorable change.

Advertising Media

Probably the best-known regulation by advertising media is the famous consumer guaranty of *Good Housekeeping* magazine, which says:

> *Good Housekeeping* has satisfied itself that all products and services offered in this issue of the magazine are good products and services. If any product or service is not as advertised herein, it will, upon request and verification of complaint, be replaced or the money paid therefore refunded.

If products do not live up to their advertised claims, the magazine will refuse to accept advertising from the manufacturer. In order to investigate advertising claims, the magazine maintains testing laboratories. Outside testing organizations are used if the *Good Housekeeping* laboratories are unable to do the investigating.

Although most magazines do not have such elaborate safeguards against unacceptable advertising, most of them are vigilant in protecting their readers against untrue claims. In so doing, they simultaneously protect the integrity of the publication.

Other Media Protect Consumers, Too

Most smaller newspapers lack the facilities to do much guarding against dishonest or unethical advertising, but the bigger newspapers, such as the *New York Times,* the *St. Louis Post-Dispatch,* and the *Chicago Tribune,* check advertising carefully for its honesty and, like the magazines, reject advertisements that fail to meet their standards of acceptability. Bigger newspapers often put out booklets that state firmly the regulations governing advertising.

Broadcast media—radio and television—are, if anything, more rigid than the other advertising media about requiring that advertisers employ good taste in their advertising. Both media come into the family circle in a most personal way. Offensive presentations will bar an advertiser from the air, no matter how big his advertising appropriation. Many products are likewise barred from the air because they deal with personal matters, such as bodily functions. Thus broadcast media are likely to stress the need for good taste in commercials just as much as the need for honesty because of the personal characater of both radio and television.

Despite the broadcast medium's once commendable standards in an age of rapidly changing taste and moral standards, advertisers face uncertainty because today networks and individual stations view broadcast commercials by differing standards. A commercial acceptable to one network may be unacceptable to another. Or an individual station may carry a commercial on a network feed but refuse to run the same commercial if the same time slot is bought directly from the station. Current standards of acceptability vary widely and wildly as networks and individual stations attempt to gauge the acceptability of advertisements to their audiences.

Better Business Bureau

A local retail store uses a big type in its advertisement to lure shoppers to a bargain in a certain type of merchandise. Shoppers come in great numbers, only to discover that early on the opening morning of the sale the store was sold out of the bargain merchandise. A shopper suspects that the store never had more than one or two units of the merchandise, and that the advertisement was written in bad faith, with the store never having any intention of living up to the promise of the advertisement.

Our suspicious shopper now reports the incident to the local Better Business Bureau. Investigation follows immediately. If the bureau finds the charges to be true, it will notify the store of its findings and issue a stern warning to avoid such future incidents. It may distribute a bulletin throughout the local community relating the unethical behavior of the store. In especially reprehensible cases, the bureau might give its findings to legal authorities, who can take court action against the store. The Better Business Bureaus do not themselves have any legal authority in such cases. Because of the unfavorable publicity that can ensue from a bureau investigation, however, few local businesses will disregard a Better Business Bureau warning.

Many Better Business Bureaus are scattered in cities throughout the United States and Canada to protect the public against unethical or dishonest advertising, and to help businessmen avoid legal troubles. Retailers, banks, advertising agencies, manufacturers, and media voluntarily contribute to the support of the local bureaus. There is, in addition, a National Better Business Bureau that is concerned with complaints about national advertising. It publishes an important loose-leaf booklet, *Do's and Don't's in Advertising*

Copy, that keeps business people aware of current regulations and laws relating to advertising. Monthly supplements keep the material up to date.

National Self-Regulation of Advertising

The advertising industry has long been an advocate of self-regulation. Currently, such regulation is being done nationally by an investigative body and groups of advertising people who regularly sit in judgment on the work of their fellows. The National Advertising Division of the Council of Better Business and a separate "court of appeals," the National Advertising Review Board, was set up in early 1971 but began to function in mid-1973.

The work of these groups has been labeled "a dismal failure" by consumer groups although it has gone far beyond the more traditional self-regulatory efforts of industry groups.

In the NARB procedure, a panel of five judges rules on the merits of each complaint. The panel is drawn from 50 high-ranking executives on call, 30 of whom are from advertisers, 10 from agencies, and 10 from what might be considered the ranks of consumers in that they are lawyers, college professors, and the like. Each panel is assembled in a 3-1-1 ratio, and members are called in from across the country to make certain the panel does not have an eastern or Madison Avenue bias.

Testimonials

When is a testimonial legitimate? Probably nothing in advertising causes more cynicism among consumers than testimonials and yet, paradoxically, nothing helps sell certain types of products and customers more surely than testimonials. The testimonial has been abused by unscrupulous advertisers. An example of misuse is the testimonial for a patent medicine given by a thirteen-year-old boy who declared that he had been "transformed from an underweight weakling to the center on his football team" as a result of taking a certain tonic. The exploitation of the youngster so enraged people in the state of Illinois that legislators there passed a resolution restraining the use of children's testimonials.

An advertiser is responsible for claims in a testimonial. Defending oneself on the ground that the testimonial is sincere and genuine may not be enough. Statements in a testimonial must be accurate as well as sincere. To aid the advertiser the National Better Business Bureau has set up eight rules for testimonials.

Testimonial Yardstick

- A testimonial should be genuine.
- It should represent the honest and sincere opinion of the author.
- The author should be competent and qualified to express an opinion.
- It should reflect the current opinion of the author.
- Any advertised portion of a testimonial should fairly reflect the spirit and content of the complete testimonial.

- Purchased testimonials should meet the same test of good faith as free-will testimonials.
- When photographs of professional models are used to illustrate testimonials, the advertisement should reveal that fact.

Right-of-Privacy Violations

What does the advertiser need to know about the right of privacy? The "right of privacy" is the right of a person to be left alone, free from unwanted publicity. This right is protected by many states firmly, by some weakly, and by some not at all. Since violation of the law can, in some states like New York result in a prison sentence, advertisers are often nervous on this point. If an advertisement is written about a news event, for example, the law of privacy stops the advertiser from mentioning the name of a living person (even if the person's name was in the news headlines) unless the person gives his consent.

The television camera has created many problems relating to the right of privacy. Is privacy being invaded, for instance, when the camera shows spectators at a football or baseball game? Generally the courts will rule "no" if the spectators are shown as a part of a background scene and are not singled out for special, individual attention. In the case of telecasts of sporting events, such activities may not be telecast without the consent of the owners or promoters. The athletic performers, however, waive their rights to privacy when they knowingly enter an event to be telecast and for which the promoter has signed a contract.

Sometimes the right of privacy and property rights are injured at the same time, as in the case of seven members of the New York Giants who sued two popcorn firms that had put cardboard pictures of the players in popcorn bags without obtaining the consent of the players. The players sued for damages not only because of invasion of the right of privacy but also because the unauthorized use of their names and picture might decrease the revenue the players obtain from endorsing other products.

To protect themselves against suits involving the right of privacy the advertisers must, if there is the slightest question regarding the use of a person in advertising, obtain the written consent of that person for the use of his name or picture. The advertiser must realize, too, that no advertiser is free to use individuals indiscriminantly for any advertising purpose, no matter how innocent the purpose.

Making Good On Advertising Mistakes

What happens when an advertiser makes a mistake? Retail advertisers sometimes find that their advertisements appear with a lower price than was originally planned. This may be due to the merchant's error, or the newspaper may have made the mistake. In either case, who makes good the mistake?

The general rule covering the situation is that an advertisement is simply an invitation to enter into negotiations. It is not a contract merely because the person who read the advertisement decides he wishes to buy at the terms advertised. The advertisement, legally, is only an invitation telling readers or listeners that advertisers are ready to receive offers for the merchandise at prices given in the advertisement. They are not compelled legally to sell at the stated prices. The legal viewpoint is that they can revoke the offer at any time before it is accepted, which they do by refusing to sell.

The merchant thus is not compelled by law to make good to the shoppers for mistakes that were made in advertising. If a shopper sues because the merchant has advertised an item at $8 when the price should have been $18, the merchant will probably win the suit.

What about the other situation—when the newspaper made the mistake? Usually the attitude of the courts is that newspapers have no liability other than a possible refund of the money paid for advertising space. Usually, too, publishers will print a news story telling about the error and will write to the advertiser admitting the mistake. If a newspaper makes an honest attempt to rectify such errors, it will hardly ever lose a suit brought against it by an advertiser.

Agency-Client Responsibility

Who is responsible for misleading advertising—The advertising agency that prepares it? The client under whose name it appears? The media that publish or broadcast it?

Usually the client (advertiser) is held responsible for misleading advertising. When the Federal Trade Commission, to illustrate, takes action in connection with misleading advertising, the action is very often taken solely against the advertiser, and not against the agency that actually created the advertising, nor the media that carried it to the consumer.

Because the advertising company directs and pays for the advertising done in its name, the company usually bears the chief responsibility for the truthfulness of its advertisements. Thus, it is the advertiser who must usually answer to the legal authorities.

Normally, the advertising agency and the media assume that what clients tell them about the product, its uses, and its manufacture are correct. The responsibility for being truthful is the client's. Generally, therefore, the agency and media have been considered innocent if it turns out that the client has not been truthful in its statements about the advertised product or service.

In 1964, however, the hitherto comfortable position of advertising agencies in advertising-dishonesty cases was shattered by an adverse decision in a case centered around the advertising executed by Kaster, Hilton, Chesley, Clifford & Atherton in behalf of Regimen, a reducing pill.

Charging that the agency had written fraudulent advertising copy for the product, the agency along with the manufacturer, was indicted by a federal grand jury and subsequently found guilty. The decision was based on the assumption that the agency had *knowingly* participated in the preparation of deceptive advertising. The word "knowingly" is the key since normally an agency can plead successfully and with justification that they have no recourse but reliance on the honesty of the client's statements about a complex product such as one made chemically. The *Regimen* case has, however, caused advertising agencies of even very sophisticated products to make certain that their work for a client is not, in fact, compounding a fraud.

Despite the implications of the *Regimen* case it is likely in most cases involving fraudulent advertising that the advertising agency will continue to be judged an innocent party since it is inconceivable that many advertising agencies will "knowingly" be parties to actions that can lead to fines, imprisonment and destruction of their business reputations.

In recent years, however, the FTC has tended to hold more advertising agencies accountable along with the advertisers they represent. Media which carry the advertisements have not been held accountable.

AVOIDING LEGAL ENTANGLEMENTS IS DIFFICULT

Today, numerous federal, state, and local laws regulate advertising. In fact there are too many laws to count. For liquor advertising alone there are layers of federal, state, county and city laws and regulations. Since many of these laws deal specifically with beverages, they will have to be changed to handle the new powdered alcoholic beverages.

A growing number of regulatory agencies adopt their own rules and regulations—often with conflicting requirements—applied to products, ingredients, packaging and advertising. The result? It is difficult for even the most scrupulously honest advertiser to avoid entanglement with the law.

Large corporations have legal departments assess proposed advertisements and rely also on their advertising agencies, many of which also have legal departments, to help keep them out of trouble. Small firms rely quite heavily on their advertising agencies to help them avoid legal difficulties.

Certain types of advertising are subject to especially close scrutiny by government agencies. These include food, cosmetics, liquor, soap, animal feeds, medicines and cigarettes. Also, advertisements for any products for children are very closely monitored today. No matter how hard advertisers of these and other products try to live up to regulations, they may be called to account at any time to justify advertising claims. Sometimes this happens, not because product claims are false under existing law, but because a regulatory agency wishes to test a new legal theory which will broaden the agency's authority. A proposed banning of candy advertisements from some childrens' television programming, for example, would be based on a public health argument rather than on advertisement falsity.

Advertising As Regulated Speech

Were you to wonder what would happen were free speech not afforded First Amendment protection, you need only look at advertising. In the 1942 *Valentine vs. Chrestensen* decision[1] the Supreme Court excluded advertising as protected speech in an almost casual and offhand manner, without explanation or reasoning, when it referred to "purely commercial advertising."

This decision provides the basis for an ongoing case history of what can happen when a form of speech is denied First Amendment protection.

Most people think of themselves as authorities on advertising. Thus, many laws and regulations reflect the pressures exerted by individuals and groups with differing philosophies and theories of advertising. Some critics want strict

Public issue advertisement.

A series of such advertisements has been run by the advertiser. With only the slightest mention of the sponsoring advertiser, this advertisement may truly be classed as unselfish. Unfortunately, critics of advertising often fail to mention the extent of such non-commercial advertising.

regulation of advertising, believing the consumer helpless in the face of advertising influence. Others want merely to inhibit advertising so consumers do not act foolishly. Industry groups stress self-regulation, while opponents of advertising want to use legal action to eliminate advertising, believing this form of product information is an economic waste.

Formal and informal consumer activist groups now focus on special problems, often those of the poor, the elderly, or the young, and have been instrumental in placing consumer representatives in federal agencies and in establishing many state and local consumer protection departments.

Ironically, some consumer protectors do not seem inhibited by the rules they want to enforce against commercial advertising. The "case histories" broadcast over WCBS Radio in New York City by the consumer affairs commissioner demonstrated how this government agency vigilantly protected the public against "misleading and sharp business practices." The case histories, it turns out, were fictitious.[2]

It must also be mentioned that the mushrooming growth in advertising regulation has opened a new career area for lawyers with advertisers, law firms, federal and other regulatory agencies, advertising agencies, media, and consumer activist groups.

The low consumer intelligence standard applied to advertising jars common sense. To see this, apply the FTC's standard of false advertising, a mere "tendency to mislead," against political campaign promises. Or, imagine yourself gullible and incredulous—the FTC's consumer intelligence standard—while you read political campaign literature. Then decide for yourself whether political campaign literature and promises would be true or false measured against the two standards. You have to decide in this context: which is more important, buying products or voting?

The FTC chairman, at this writing, regards the amount of deceptive and misleading national advertising to be on the decline. Rather than suggest a curtailment of FTC regulation of advertising, the chairman seeks to expand the already broad authority to regulate advertising, suggesting that certain new categories of advertising may be questionable. Included are those that "take advantage of the 'psychological social vulnerabilities' of consumers."[4] No one is quite sure what the chairman means.

Advertising regulation has taken some curious turns in recent years. The requirement banning sex labels in classified advertising represents the first regulatory intrusion into newspaper content. Proposed laws taxing advertising threaten the lifeline and independence of the press. One result is that several states have passed laws upholding the very right to advertise, and several other states have attempted or considered passage of such laws.

Numerous theories have been suggested as to why advertising is regarded as unworthy of First Amendment protection. It was not specifically mentioned as being protected speech by the founding fathers. But not much was specifically mentioned. Advertising is undertaken for a profit, but so is protected entertainment material, and so are strike speeches, neither of which is usually connected with religious or political expression.

Distinctions between information and persuasion are not logically compelling. Local advertising, estimated at 40 percent of all advertising, is heavily price-oriented. Information to one person may be an attempt at persuasion to another. A status appeal in an advertisement may be information to one consumer and meaningless to another. In fact, were one to argue that advertising is useless, the Supreme Court has stated that, the "Right to receive information and ideas, regardless of their social worth . . . is fundamental."[5]

CONSUMERISM

Cindy Foster threw the can opener into the waste basket in disgust. She had just purchased the opener, and it didn't work. Returning to the kitchen counter, she glanced out of the window at her new car in the driveway. The car didn't please her either; in fact it scared her, but she couldn't throw the car away. It cost too much.

The car sometimes hestitated or bucked when Cindy accelerated from a stop sign. The car didn't hesitate all of the time, just some of the time. The automobile dealer's service manager had personally adjusted the carburetor and timing for Cindy several times before admitting that he didn't know what else to do . It was so minor, anyway. Earlier this morning, while Cindy was on an errand, the car hesitated again at an intersection, almost causing an accident. Cindy was reluctant to drive the car now.

Today, Cindy and others who are displeased with products they have purchased don't sit back helplessly. They call action-line columns in newspapers, or Better Business Bureaus. They write the companies which manufactured the products or call the local consumer protector at city hall or the nearby county building. They want action. Increasingly, consumers are getting action. They are enforcing accountability on business.

Who are the Consumers?

We are *all* consumers. We are all interested in getting satisfaction from the products we buy. Far more often than not we are satisfied. Those times we are not satisfied are frustrating. We remember bad products, and we tell family, friends and neighbors about them. We work hard for our money. We know that others work hard, too. We have a right to expect fair product value for the hard-earned money we spend.

Consumer discontent is not a new phenomenon. What is new is that consumer discontent has, in the past 15 years, become a political, social, and economic issue. There are now consumerist organizations and lobbies. How effective are the new consumer organizations? Initially, business laws were designed to keep competition fair, the belief being that this automatically protected the consumer. The recent activism of consumer groups has spurred Congress to enact laws designed specifically to protect consumers. The rate at which consumer protection laws are being passed is accelerating.

Product Complexity and Company Impersonality

There are two basic reasons for consumer activism. Today's products are more complex and subject to failures that are expensive to repair. Marketing

Idea advertising.

Attacked by consumerism advocates, and often misunderstod by the general public, corporations have more and more used advertising to explain the place of business in our social and economic structure. In this advertisement the company asks for understanding in the face of a threat by the government to break up the oil companies.

This is a monopoly.

Let's say you own this whole pie. And let's just say it's the only pie in the world. You can sell pie at whatever price you want, and people will have to pay it. You have a monopoly. That could be unfair.

But let's say you're a U. S. oil company. No matter which one you are, you only have a small piece of the pie. Not one American oil company accounts for more than 8½ percent of the oil produced in this country, and most produce a much smaller share. Now you don't have

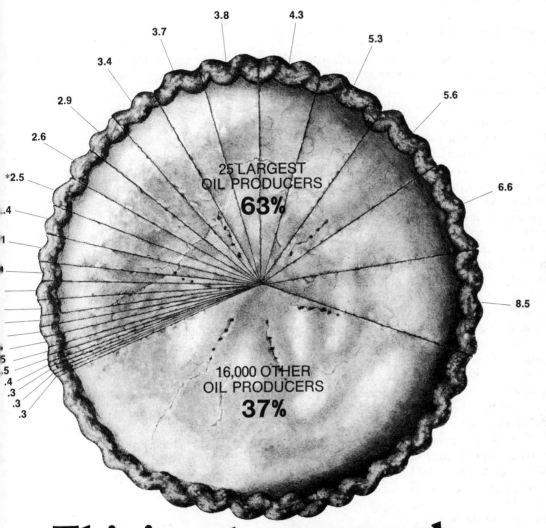

3.7   3.8   4.3   5.3   5.6   3.4   2.9   2.6   *2.5   .4   1   6.6   8.5

25 LARGEST
OIL PRODUCERS
63%

16,000 OTHER
OIL PRODUCERS
37%

.5 .5 .4 .3 .3 .3

This is not a monopoly.

a monopoly—you have competition. In fact, you have very stiff competition. That's fair.

By slicing up a monopoly, the government creates competition.

But by slicing up an already competitive situation, the government only creates . . . a mess.

This is a thought from a company with just a small piece of the pie.

*Our piece of the pie

Union Oil Company of California
Los Angeles, California 90017

likewise is more complex and impersonal, making it more difficult for consumers to get answers or adjustments or service or any sense of satisfaction from distant, large companies that answer consumer complaints with all-too-obvious form letters.

Consumer Activism

Consumer irritation and frustration found natural expression in the activism expressed for many reasons in the 1960s and 1970s. There was activism against an unpopular war, for the rights of minorities and against pollution of the environment. Existing advocacy groups such as the National Association for the Advancement of Colored People and the Southern Christian Leadership Conference became more activist and visible. The National Organization for Women was formed and continuously lobbies for women's rights. The Sierra Club is the best known of the ecology groups, but other groups spring up to protest the building of atomic power generating stations or the building of chemical plants and oil refineries. Environmental protectors make us aware of chemicals in rivers and lakes and the air we breathe. Consumer protectors focus on the chemicals in our homes and foods.

Consumer activism is strongly associated with an individual's name: Ralph Nader. Nader himself has become an institution. He oversees an organization that investigates one consumer problem after another. He testifies before Congress and lobbies for bills designed to protect consumers. Nader, however, is no longer a spokesperson only for consumers. Increasingly, as he investigates the activities of governmental agencies, Nader is regarded as a spokesperson for everyone. Nader, in short, works to make large institutions—governmental and business—responsive to the people they serve.

Nader and other consumer protectors travel widely, speak to many groups, urging the establishment of state and local consumer groups. These groups in turn lobby for the establishment of consumer protection offices in state and local governments.

Not all consumer activism is organized, however. Homemakers spontaneously organize to picket supermarkets against sudden jumps in food prices. Today, whether organized or spontaneous, consumer complaints and pressure are welcomed by a growing number of astute politicians.

Two Critical Gaps

The easiest way to explain consumer discontent is to say that products often do not live up to advertised promises. There is a gap between consumer expectation and product performance. Perhaps the advertising is better than the products. There is another gap revealed by surveys: business leaders and consumers differ in their judgment of consumer satisfaction with products. Consumers are much less satisfied than business leaders think they are.

In a survey of consumers, Harris Research found differing levels of consumer discontent in a sample of 1,510 consumers in response to the following request:

"I am going to read you a list of things which are of concern to some consumers. Please tell me, for each one, how much it has worried you personally—a great deal, somewhat, a little bit, or not at all. I want you to think about your own experiences as a consumer."[9]

TABLE 3-1

(Sample size = 1,510)	A Great Deal %	Some-what %	A Little Bit %	Not At All %	Not Sure %
The high prices of many products	77	17	5	1	*
The high cost of medical and hospital care	69	15	6	8	1
The poor quality of many products	48	33	13	6	*
The failure of many companies to live up to claims made in their advertising	44	32	16	7	1
The poor quality of after-sales service and repairs	38	31	14	15	2
The feeling that many manufacturers don't care about you	36	32	19	12	1
Too many products breaking or going wrong soon after you bring them home	35	29	20	15	1
Misleading packaging or labeling	34	29	20	15	2
Not being able to afford adequate health insurance	32	23	12	31	1
The feeling that it is a waste of time to complain about consumer problems because nothing substantial will be achieved	32	27	20	19	2
Not being able to get adequate insurance coverage against an accident or loss	30	23	14	30	3
Inadequate guarantees or warranties	30	31	17	21	2
Failure of companies to handle complaints properly	29	31	19	19	2
Too many products which are dangerous	26	27	22	22	2
The absence of reliable information about different products and services	26	33	22	18	2
Difficulty in getting insurance claims settled fairly	23	19	15	39	4
Not knowing what to do if something is wrong with a product you have bought	21	28	20	30	1
Difficulty in getting insurance claims paid promptly	20	20	17	39	4
The difficulty of choosing between so many products	11	23	25	41	1

Note: Totals may not add to 100% because of rounding.

"New Harris Consumer Study Causes Few Shocks in Adland, <u>Advertising Age,</u> May 30, 1977, pp. 2, 74.

Business leaders must pay close attention to such surveys because the rise in consumerism parallels another trend in American life. Each year legislative bodies—federal, state and local—pass an estimated 150,000 laws. Each new law, on the average, requires an estimated 10 new regulations. Only some laws and regulations apply to advertising, of course. Many more laws and regulations influence the environment in which marketing and general business decisions are made.

The overall effect of the laws and regulations is to increase the risks of doing business and to slow product innovation. From the consumer protector's standpoint, the laws enforce accountability. They provide a means of exercising social control when traditional mechanisms no longer work.

To many people in and out of advertising the new and lengthy laws are a legislative overkill for relatively minor problems. It is as if the number of words now used in laws is inversely related to the importance of the issue. The Lord's Prayer has 56 words. The Declaration of Independence has 1,322. Over 11,400 words are used for federal regulation of California-grown olives. It is little wonder that today lawyers literally peer over the shoulders of advertising copywriters. Even with expert legal monitoring, however, copywriters are often unsure about what can and cannot be said about a product, because lawyers themselves are unsure.

QUESTIONS

1. Discuss what you believe to be the principal ways that brands and trademarks serve (a) the consumer; (b) the advertiser.

2. What does the term *generic* mean in relation to a trademark? Cite some examples of generic brand names in your explanation.

3. What are some of the important technical and legal considerations involved in creating a product brand name? Choose three modern brand names and analyze them based on the considerations you have mentioned.

4. As a management official at the head of a large chain of retail food stores, you are contemplating stocking only your own distributor brand merchandise. What are the pros and cons of such a decision?

5. "Good advertising is necessarily truthful advertising." Discuss the validity of this statement.

6. Give examples of governmental and of self-regulation of advertising. What are the advantages and disadvantages of each type of regulation?

7. Do you believe advertising should be protected under the First Amendment? Why?

8. Would modern marketing and advertising be possible without current trademark laws?

9. Why is advertising the most carefully monitored and regulated form of speech in the United States?

10. What arguments are expressed for and against governmental grade labeling?

REFERENCES

1. *Valentine vs. Chrestensen*, 316 U.S. 52, 54; 86 L.Ed. 1262; 62 S. Crt 920 (Roberts, J. 1942)
2. *Advertising Age,* Feb. 21, 1977. p. 18.

Section II

PREADVERTISING CONSIDERATIONS

4

DETERMINING THE ADVERTISING BUDGET

DETERMINING THE ADVERTISING BUDGET

To some people in advertising, a budget is merely a set of numbers on paper. To others, it is a sophisticated advertising tool. The budget relates the advertising investment to clearly stated advertising and marketing objectives. Budgets are usually expressed in media costs because the cost of buying television time or newspaper or magazine space often represents the largest part of the advertising budget. Also, because much advertising agency work is paid for by media discounts to advertising agencies, budgeting by media costs automatically includes the cost of making the advertisements.

No One Way To Make Budgets

The way in which an advertising budget is developed primarily reflects company size and the importance of advertising to the company. In some small companies the advertising budget may be what is left over after meeting all other expected costs. Little or no thought is given to advertising. Objectives may be entirely lacking or stated only in very general terms.

Contrast this to large firms where advertising budgets may be based on mounds of information manipulated by computers according to complex mathematical formulas. Major firms with years of experience in marketing consumer products treat advertising investment as an important primary budget input rather than a residual. Advertising and marketing goals are explicitly stated.

Even in large companies, however, past experience and current market information and future goals are assessed and altered, if necessary, through executive judgment.

Experienced advertisers know their judgments are, at best, informed estimates about what we may call the action of variables in the future.

Gauging The Future

Such variables as production levels and manufacturing costs are directly under the firm's control. Other variables, such as price and product placement, may be only partially under the advertiser's control. Wholesalers and retailers influence the price at which many products are finally offered to consumers. Retailers also decide whether to carry a product, and this decision determines whether advertised products are even available to consumers. The way a retailer handles a product also influences sales.

Sales of most supermarket products correlate with what are called shelf facings. A washing detergent with six boxes side-by-side on the shelf tends to outsell a product with only three boxes fully exposed to the consumer. If the supermarket manager stocks breath mints in the candy section rather than displaying the product in dispenser racks near check-out counters, breath mint sales volume is lower.

When developing the advertising budget, the advertiser attempts to gauge the probable action of other variables in the future. These are beyond the advertiser's control or influence. General business conditions influence consumer psychology. If business forecasts are uncertain, consumers may increase saving and defer buying major appliances, for example. If consumers are optimistic and have secure jobs, they may buy a refrigerator, a new car, or higher-priced meats. If consumers are pessimistic, they may buy retread tires for the family car, forego vacations, and buy most groceries on the basis of price.

Each national advertiser learns to anticipate different consumer responses to changing economic conditions. Cadillac sales remain relatively constant whether the economy is good or bad, while sales of other makes of cars are very responsive to the level of economic activity.

General Forecasts

Advertisers can't control general economic conditions, but they reduce budgetary risk and uncertainty through the use of government and industry economic forecasts to plan production levels and sales goals in terms of predicted levels of economic activity. The predictions may vary, however, and sometimes become suspect in the face of unanticipated international tensions and wars or oil embargoes.

For these and other reasons budgets are not cast in bronze and blindly followed. Because budgets express judgments about the action of variables in the future, they are closely monitored as the future unfolds. Whether developed casually or with meticulous care, advertising budgets often are premised on a number of the following stated or unstated considerations.

WHAT YOU NEED TO KNOW BEFORE MAKING A BUDGET

Is the Timing Right?

Knowing how to time the allocation of budget money hangs upon a thorough knowledge of consumer demand for the product—its peaks, its valleys, and its level periods. Some times of the year are far more productive than others. This fluctuation of buying demand is true of hundreds of products.

Some advertisers have studied their products and their markets and have been successful in creating a demand at periods of the year when hitherto the product has not produced sales. Thus, deodorants have increased sales in winter, Florida travel has been promoted successfully for the summer season, watches have been sold in the "off-season," cranberries have been sold in the spring or converted to a beverage for year-round sales.

Despite these and many other successes, the person laying out an advertising budget will usually allot money in accordance with the accustomed buying patterns of consumers. For most products these patterns are fixed. They are the same year after year. Intelligent retailers know these patterns and spend advertising money in conformance with them. National advertisers, in contrast, will ignore the buying patterns to a certain extent. Although the national advertiser anticipates seasonal sales variations for products, advertising is scheduled through low sales periods. The national advertiser wants to maintain continuous contact with the distribution channel and with consumers, in order to maintain awareness of the product brand and brand image.

Is the Product Right?

Some years ago an attempt was made to sell Stillson wrenches to the general public. While the product was of highest quality it was not the right product for the market. The campaign was a failure.

Other products, in contrast, have been right for the market but have not been good products and have been selling failures after starting out with a rush. These failures have been true of products as big as automobiles to products as small as typewriter ribbons.

There is no point in putting money into an advertising budget unless the product is (1) right for the market, (2) a good product that will live up to the claims that will be made for it.

Is the Product Priced Realistically?

Before putting money into the advertising budget the advertiser planner will look at the product's price to see if it is: (1) priced high enough to yield a profit, (2) priced low enough to induce sales, (3) priced in keeping with the economic times and the competition.

When Procter & Gamble was developing the product now widely known as Pampers, the company estimated it would have to sell 400 million Pampers a year at 10 cents each to recover costs. In a test market the company discovered that while consumers liked disposable diapers they thought the 10 cent price per change was too high. The company revised the potential market estimate to one billion pampers a year, calculating that economies of scale in producing the larger number of Pampers would reduce the selling price to six cents per Pamper. Consumer acceptance was immediate, suggesting that the new Procter & Gamble product fitted one of the axioms of advertising: For an advertiser to succeed, the product, timing and price must be right.

"Right" prices, however, are not necessarily the lowest prices. An agency president commenting on price, said: "We all know that price is important. But low prices are not all important. For one thing, a bargain is only a bargain when it represents a saving in money on some known value. A low price constantly advertised becomes an indicator of lesser value."

The advertiser planners must never forget that most people have a price range in which they are willing to buy. They consider whether a product is within, above, or below that price range. Such people may not buy primarily on price considerations. Still they think in terms of certain price ranges; thus price is important as a factor in their ultimate buying decision.

This point is best illustrated by consumer response to the coffee shortage in 1977. As the price of coffee shot up, consumers began substituting other beverages, because coffee prices exceeded what consumers considered reasonable coffee price ranges. Nationwide coffee sales dropped an estimated 20 percent.

Do You Know Your Market?

Every market analysis is quantitative and qualitative. "How many?" is usually the first question advertisers ask about the market. Assured on this point they consider the composition of the market. They will wish to know the market breakdown according to demographic categories (discussed in greater detail in the following chapter):

Men and women	*Living location—city, farm, suburbs*
Age	*Working location—city, farm, suburbs*
Income	*Kind of dwelling—house or apartment*
Occupation	*Marital status*
Education	*Number of children*
Racial origin	*Religious affiliation*

Although it would be sensible for the advertising budget planner to have the foregoing information, and to use it in budget formulation, it would be absurd to think that most people setting up budgets actually do consider *all* these factors. The person, however, who did use them in planning would know better what he or she was doing.

Will Support for Media Advertising Be Given by the Dealer and Sales Organization?

Big spending in the media will often be pointless if the dealer and/or sales organization is: (1) uninformed about the advertising programs, (2) unenthusiastic about the advertising program.

Before media budget spending begins, the people on the "firing line"—dealers and salespeople—should be given full information about the media advertising. They should be "sold" on the backing they are getting so that they, in turn, will back the company's advertising through hard selling, through point-of-sale display, through right pricing of products and the retail level, and through local tie-in advertising.

A budget planner, assured of such dealer and sales department support, can allot budget money with much assurance.

Do Distribution And Media Coverage Match?

A seller of high-quality and expensive marine clocks distributed through exclusive dealers in seaport towns will budget advertising in media that will cover the distribution pattern.

The planner may use *Yachting* magazine because of its selective qualities and will probably pass by general circulation magazines, because they reach millions who are not in the distribution areas. Also omitted will be radio and television network advertising.

The familiar pattern in the case of big advertisers is to set up the distribution first—then the advertising. If a product is being introduced, salespeople load up the dealers in anticipation of demand created by advertising. Even in the case of an established product this pattern may be true if a special promotion such as a contest is being used. Few advertisers have the temerity to advertise first and get distribution second. Distribution coverage and media coverage usually go together.

Have You Set Area Sales Objectives?

Determining sales objectives is really the start of the whole process of budget making. Advertising budgets are not set in a vacuum but in relation to sales goals. Sales forecasts are the first step in budget planning. Exception to this statement may be made, of course, in connection with institutional advertising that creates good will rather than sales. For the usual sales-producing type of advertising, the budget may reflect the advertiser's desire to reach last year's sales goals, or perhaps this year to establish a higher sales objective, and along with it, a higher advertising budget. The important point is that sales objectives be determined in an orderly way and then, in a similarly orderly way, the advertising budget may be fashioned.

How Much of the Selling and Promotional Burden Is to Be Carried by Advertising?

The extent of the budget depends upon the extent of the selling and promotional job it is to do. A patent medicine such as Lydia Pinkham depended upon media advertising to take over almost the entire selling task. An advertising budget of anywhere from 30 per cent to 50 per cent of sales reflected the sales-burden advertising was assuming.

Industrial machinery, in contrast, swings the other way. Relatively few sales of such machinery may be made in any given year. The sellers of the machinery are well known to the buyers, and vice versa. What little advertising is done will often be done principally to keep the company's name before the industry rather than to obtain direct sales. If this approach is satisfactory to the budget planner, advertising's minor role in achieving sales goals will show up in the small allotment for advertising.

A middle point between patent medicine and industrial machinery is represented by many advertisers of consumer products sold in grocery stores or drugstores. The selling burden for these products may be shared on an equal basis between the advertising department and the sales department. The advertising budget will be heavy although its percentage-of-sales figure will not be high.

What Is The Relationship Between the Advertising Budget and Business Condition?

What are budget planners going to do in the face of bad times? Or good times? When bad times come, retrench in advertising spending, or spend more money in order to fight the unfavorable sales situation? If good times are present will the planner say: "Sales are coming easy these days; why waste money advertising for business that's going to come in anyway?" Or: "Now, when people have money is the time to advertise heavily in order to harvest all these easy sales dollars."

There is no clear-cut answer to these questions. Each budget planner answers them according to personal philosophy and experience. The tendency in late years, however, has been to maintain advertising, or even to increase it, in periods of hard-to-get sales. More and more, advertising is being viewed by budget planners as a means of offsetting downward cycles.

In 1975, for instance, the United States experienced a sharp downward business movement. Many businesses cut advertising budgets, a trend that had begun in the preceding year. On the contrary, many advertisers actually increased advertising budgets. Historically, in severe recessions, or full-fledged depressions, marginal advertisers often cut budgets. Big advertisers, however, try to stay close to their normal budgeting patterns.

Will Governmental Actions Affect Your Budget?

Consumer product advertisers face increasing governmental restrictions and prohibitions. Often these regulatory decisions are based on new research information indicating potential environmental or health hazards.

Governmental rulings prohibiting fluorocarbon propellants for deodorants forces advertisers to develop new ways to dispense and advertise deodorants. Regulations governing the sales of artificial sweeteners results in a flurry of activity to develop and advertise new substitutes.

Sometimes, but not always, advertisers can anticipate court decisions and regulatory agency rulings. In either case, advertising budget assumptions can be thrown away. New budgetary decisions are demanded.

The advertiser must now gauge whether regulatory action will declare the advertiser's product, service, or advertising activities illegal. The medical community has reasonably strong arguments against charcoal broiling of steaks. Will this be banned in restaurants? Will the sale of charcoal be banned for home broiling of meats? If so, when? Will regulators ban the advertising of candy and sugared cereals from children's television programming? If so, when? In short, the uncertainties involved in governmental regulation create uncertainties in budgeting.

What Do You Expect From Competitors?

Some advertisers operate in relatively stable markets. Last year's advertising budget may require only a few adjustments to be used for the current year. Independently, competitors in these markets, behave the same way.

Most consumer products, however, are advertised in dynamic and rapidly changing markets where brand shares bob up and down as consumer preferences change, or as new products intentionally disrupt any semblance of a status quo. A baby food manufacturer, for example, may start selling insurance as the market for baby foods drops off, reflecting the declining birth rate. Dog food advertisers develop and promote new and more convenient ways for buyers to use products and offer product variations for young, mature and old dogs.

A large number of new and convenient powdered drink mixes influences the sales of milk and existing canned and bottled beverages. Soft drink bottlers may increase advertising to maintain consumer loyalty, while the American Dairy Association may urge consumers to mix the powdered drink mixes with milk rather than water for summertime refreshment plus nutrition.

When advertising in a dynamic market, advertisers constantly monitor sales and competitors' advertising, often if necessary, reallocating advertising money in an attempt to reach sales goals.

What Is Your Area-by-Area Sales Analysis?

Small neighborhood retailers seldom analyze where their sales are coming from. Large retailers may check charge account or delivery addresses to learn where their shoppers live. Small and large retailers alike find local newspapers and broadcast stations reach the majority of their customers.

Further removed from consumers and serving regional and national markets, large advertisers almost never find an even sales pattern across markets in which their products are distributed. Not too many years ago tanning lotions sold mostly during summer months with some year-round markets in Florida, some in Gulf Coast states, and some in southern California. The rapid growth in winter sports means the products are used in the dead of winter by snowmobilers, campers, hikers and skiers. From experience, advertisers know that markets change and the investment of advertising dollars required to meet sales goals varies from market to market.

A minimum amount of media expenditures may yield heavy sales for a farm machinery manufacturer in Iowa while a maximum advertising effort is needed to obtain comparable results in neighboring Minnesota.

The budget planner, working closely with the sales department, may make a county-by-county, and section-by-section study of the entire sales territory. Perhaps a weak spot will be the Dallas territory, where the company's product was recently introduced. Extra budget will be assigned there to encourage dealers and to encourage sales. Denver, in contrast, may be a long-time market for the product. If sales are good here, the Denver market may be assigned enough budget only to maintain a competitive position.

The regional advertiser or the national advertiser both use the same method to bolster sales in the "soft" sales areas—they emphasize local newspaper, radio, television, or outdoor advertising. Even a national advertiser with heavy big-magazine or big-network coverage will find increased local advertising necessary in order to keep up sales.

The budget planner may assume (if working for an aggressive company) that where sales results are unsatisfactory increased sales effort will be exerted—and where sales efforts are increased, almost automatically extra advertising push will be needed.

Based on Sales Goals Desired, What is the Maximum Amount of Advertising Appropriation That Might Be Approved?

Sound advice to the advertising budget planner is: "Don't estimate how little you can spend but how much." If the advertiser truly believes that advertising helps reduce cost of selling then he or she looks upon advertising as an investment, not an expense.

Most advertisers who have been disappointed in results obtained through advertising have used too little advertising, not too much. By holding down budget expenditure they have not given advertising a fair trial. Thin budgets mean thin advertising—media schedules that are so weak that markets are not even aware of the advertiser's promotion.

"Let's try a little advertising" is the wrong way to approach budgeting. The budget maker must think big, just as big as finances allow. A penny-pinching company treasurer can be a greater threat to successful advertising than any single individual or factor. Responsibility for proving the statement: "This is an investment, not a cost" is, many times, the most important task of the advertiser planner.

What Should You Spend for Advertising?

No question is asked more often by advertisers whether they are retail, regional, or national advertisers. Some, who ask the question, want quick, rough guides that they can apply generally to their situations; others want precise formulas that will enable them to arrive at a systematic budget determination.

Because sooner or later everything that reduces to figures ultimately reduces to percentages, it is a percentage system in one form or another that is more popular with advertising budget makers.

When advertisers ask for percentages they usually ask for industry percentages. That use of such percentages can be dangerous is evidenced in the great variations that can take place within one industry.

Despite the obvious dangers of taking percentages too literally as a guide to budget fashioning, there are some advantages in percentage-analysis. (1) It gives a quick (even though rough) approach to budget analysis. (2) It provides a handy frame of reference. If, for instance, an advertiser spending 12 percent discovered that two rivals were spending only 2 percent, the advertiser might want to find out why such a difference existed. If, in percentages, an advertiser's budget is much lower or higher than that of competitors', the advertiser will usually want to know why.

HOW MOST ADVERTISERS DETERMINE THE ADVERTISING BUDGET

Although there are other systems, five of the most common methods of setting the advertising budget are:[1]

(1) Percentage of sales
(2) Unit of sales
(3) Competitive
(4) Arbitrary judgment
(5) Objective and/or task

Percentage of Sales

In any check made of the budget systems used by advertisers, the percentage method is usually found to be the most often used. Despite its unreliability, it is popular because it is easy to work out.

What is the percentage based on? It is based on (1) past or future sales or (2) gross or net sales. On either basis, there are some obvious weaknesses.

Assume, for instance, that the advertiser had sales last year of $750,000 and that the advertising percentage figure was 4 percent ($30,000). If the advertiser is satisfied with last year's sales results, the easy decision is to allot the same advertising percentage for the forthcoming year. By determining the budget solely on the basis of the past, the advertiser plans for a past rather than a future market.

Assume, however, that the advertiser decides to make an "educated guess" about future sales possibilities. Then the advertiser will decide on a certain advertising percentage for use as an advertising budget for the forthcoming year. While this method is forward looking, the major weakness lies in the fact that no one individual can consistently be right in guessing what the future holds.

From any viewpoint, inflexibility is the greatest deterrent to the use of percentage methods for determining advertising budgets. The percentage figure tends to have an authority of its own. The percentage figure must be adhered to. This is unrealistic when the advertiser's own goals change, when competitors change promotion strategies or introduce new products.

Unit of Sales

Many industries use this method because, like the percentage system, it is easily applied—also, if used over a long enough period it gives the advertiser advertising-to-sales ratios that are reasonably accurate in their predictability.

Advertisers of "big ticket" items such as refrigerators, electric ranges, automobiles, and television sets find the method especially workable. These advertisers assign a certain amount of advertising per unit. The total advertising budget is worked out by multiplying the individual unit figure by the total number of units the manufacturer hopes to sell in the oncoming year. Perhaps the figure will be obtained by multiplying the unit amount by the number of units sold in the past year.

Assume that the unit advertising expenditure is $8 on a television set. A company, using the unit methods, and anticipating sales of 325,000 sets, would have a total advertising appropriation of $2,600,000.

An automobile company, using the unit system, might base its planning on a five-year sales forecast. It will shape the advertising budget to the estimated sales. It may find that long-range goals run 500,000 units (automobiles) annually although the volume at the time of the forecast was 300,000 units annually.

Since the average during the five-year planning period is estimated at 400,000 units, the yearly advertising appropriation is based upon this figure. In dollars the yearly budget would thus total $14 million, or $35 per automobile.

Disadvantages cited for the percentage method are true of the unit methods. The method is arbitrary and inflexible; it does not allow for altered sales conditions.[2] Should there be a fall-off in sales, there may not be enough money in the total advertising appropriation to provide the extra promotional vigor needed. Also, the method is based on the uncertainty of future happenings, or the happenings of a past year that may be vastly different from the year ahead.

Competition

This competitive method—if it can truly be called a "method"—is far less popular than the percentage or unit methods. Under this plan, the advertiser is, in effect, letting a competitor do the thinking, since the advertiser patterns advertising spending after the competitor. After discovering or estimating what the competitor is spending for advertising, the advertiser sets a budget in similar or nearly similar amounts.

If the competitor is facing exactly the same sales conditions and has exactly the same goals, handles advertising in exactly the same manner, and (to complete this set of improbable circumstances) operates the entire company in the same fashion, then the competitive method might be acceptable. Even then, since the competitor might be spending money unwisely, the imitative advertiser could go wrong.

Implied in the foregoing paragraph, of course, is that not only do advertisers not advertise in the same way but also no two companies operate the same way. Several years ago, for instance, one cigarette company was spending (per unit) about one-half the amount spent by some of its competitors, although its sales were billions of cigarettes higher.

The only virtue of the competitive method is that a competitor is usually facing many of the conditions a rival faces. What the competitor allots to advertising, then, is an indicator of his appraisal of what is needed to do an adequate promotional job. If the competitor has a consistent record of advertising and sales success, his example may be a good one to follow. Usually, however, the rule is: Watch what your competitor does. Profit from what he does; but set your own course.

Arbitrary Judgment

A company using this method considers: (1) the sales goal, (2) the competitive situation, and (3) general sales and economic conditions. After weighing these factors, it decides the size of the advertising budget needed to obtain the sales goal. Once the amount has been determined, this becomes the final budget that is followed throughout the year.

Like other methods discussed, this plan suffers because of its inflexibility. Its virtue is that it comes closer to being an actual plan than the others. Still, any method that is so arbitrary can hardly be termed a true plan since implied in "planning" is the allowance for changes necessitated by shifting conditions.

Objective and/or Task

Elements of all the other methods are involved in this method. It will use percentages, it will be based on future sales goals. It will consider the competitive situation. It might use a unit system. It will certainly analyze sales and economic conditions.

Flexibility is the principal virtue of the objective and/or task method. Other pluses, just about equally strong: it requires clearly determined objectives, and a plan for reaching the objectives.

An advertiser using the method decides upon the sales goal for the forthcoming year and then determines how much advertising will be needed to reach that goal.

The advertiser may find, however, as the year progresses that the amount assigned for advertising is insufficient for reaching the sales objective. The budget is then adjusted—upward. Should it seem that the amount assigned to advertising is more than enough to attain the sales goal, the budget may be adjusted—downward.

Although the objective and/or task method is generally praised as the most logical method of setting the budget many advertisers avoid it because it is difficult—difficult to work out in the first place and difficult to adjust upward or downward in the middle of a yearly period.

Another objection to the method is expressed by those to whom continuity of advertising is all-important. Continuity, they say, is upset when the advertising budget is tied so closely to sales. Adjusting the budget upward or downward—especially the latter—is not desirable, according to the continuity proponents. If an advertiser truly believes that the continuity established by a steady advertising program is all important, then advertising should be viewed as long range, not short range, in its goals. Adjusting the advertising volume

Television commercial combining animation with live action.

Somewhere in the budget calculations consideratio must be given to the relative costs and effectiveness of media to be used. A commercial such as this one that combines animation and live action film is very expensive. It may be poor economy, however, not to allow for it in the budget because this type of commercial has great appeal.

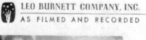 LEO BURNETT COMPANY, INC.
AS FILMED AND RECORDED "Scarecrow" :30 GREEN GIANT GGNB0050

1. (Music: Valley theme up and under) SPROUT: Good morning, Mr. Scarecrow...

2. ...guardin' the Giant's corn, I see.

3. SCARECROW: And an important job it is, Sprout...'cause it's Niblets Brand corn.

4. SPROUT: Niblets...

5. SCARECROW: Uh huh.

6. Only the Giant has Niblets corn.

7. Y'see, it's got a thin skin...

8. ...for extra tenderness.

9. And it's vacuum packed with very little water...

10. ...to stay crisp and fresh-tasting.

11. SPROUT: Well, Mr. Scarecrow, you must have the most important job around.

12. SCARECROW: Thanks, Sprout.

13. SPROUT: Next to the Giant's.

14. SONG: Ho, ho, ho,...

15. ...Green Giant.

because of immediate sales objectives is not compatible, it is thought, with the long-range advertising approach.

BUDGETING FOR A NEW PRODUCT

New-product budgeting, as indicated in the preceding material requires special techniques, and has its special set of difficulties. It is almost axiomatic that new-product advertising, for example, requires a heavy initial investment, heavier, normally, than for an established product being promoted under similar circumstances.[3]

Budgeting for the new product is made especially difficult because the planner has no frame of reference, no previous sets of figures to compare. The planner can, however, use the same budget-determining methods that are used for established products. The big question is usually how much more effort may be required to make the plan effective.

Because of some of the uncertainties connected with promoting a new product, the planner should be flexible. The situation calls for the objective and task methods in order that allowance may be made for unusual first-year circumstances.

Following the heavy initial investment, the new product budget will usually allot money evenly over the remaining months of the year. Exception may be made, of course, for products that peak seasonally, such as auto supplies with peak sales in the spring.

A campaign for a new product will usually budget for heavy support in trade magazines, often in advance of consumer advertising. Such advertising prepares the way for salespeople and creates excitement for the entire promotion.

BUDGETING FOR A SMALL ADVERTISER

Probably the first qualification for laying out a budget for a small advertiser is to be "hard-boiled" about the allotment of money to media. Guidelines to be used include these:

(1)   Select those media that go most directly to the market to be reached. Waste circulation is costly circulation. Advertisers of a product, for example, that is sold almost exclusively in hardware stores will find *The Hardware Retailing* aimed directly at their prospects. They may decide against *Electrical Dealer,* although a fairly sizable number of electrical dealers may also sell the product.

(2)   Given a choice, select those media that have a proved record of sales results. Experimentation is a luxury smaller budget advertisers can seldom afford.

(3)   If one medium offers prestige and the other offers sales, take the latter. This may seem like needless advice but too many small advertisers, because of its boost to their egos, may invest money in a slick, prestige magazine instead of a less attractive, sales-producing publication.

(4)   Look with especial care at how much budget money goes into each advertisement. They might ask (a) If two half-pages will bring more

sales and readership than one full page? (b) Will it be better to eliminate color, thus obtaining a larger black-and-white advertisement, or more frequency? (c) Should "bleed" treatment be used, or should the extra 15 percent charge not applicable to many magazines that no longer charge extra for bleed, be used to buy more space? (d) In a radio spot schedule, will a spot schedule spread over the week be more resultful than a program once a week?

Here again the objective and task method is the more sensible budget approach. Small budget advertisers cannot afford to guess. They should plan their goals, plan the money to be spent, and adjust their spending as the circumstances require. Like larger advertisers, too, they should have a reserve fund for special circumstances.

WHAT CHARGES CAN BE PUT ON THE ADVERTISING BUDGET?

From the time the first advertising budget was fashioned there have been arguments about whether certain charges should be placed on the advertising ledger, or somewhere else. Many sales or promotional expenses are clearly connected with advertising, some are debatable, and some definitely should not be assigned to the advertising budget.

Some years ago (and revised several times since then) *Printers' Ink Magazine* issued "white," "gray," and "black" lists that show the items that do or do not belong in the advertising account. These lists are reproduced here. Almost all advertising media, it will be noticed are on the white list (Table 4-1).

TABLE 4-1
Charges That Belong In The Advertising Budget

(Copyright by Printers' Ink Publishing Co., Inc.)
205 East 42nd Street
New York 17, New York

WHITE LIST
(These charges belong in the advertising account)

SPACE:
Paid advertising in all recognized mediums, including:
Newspapers
Magazines
Business papers
Farm papers
Class journals
Car cards
Theatre programs
Outdoor
Point of purchase
Novelties
Booklets
Directories
Direct advertising
Cartons and labels (for advertising purposes, such as in window displays)

Catalogs
Package inserts (when used as advertising and not just as direction sheets)
House magazines to dealers or consumers
Motion pictures (including talking pictures) when used for advertising
Slides
Dealer helps
Reprints of advertisements used in mail or for display
Radio
Television
All other printed and lithographed material used directly for advertising purposes

ADMINISTRATION:
Salaries of ad dept. executives and employees
Office supplies and fixtures used solely by ad dept.
Commissions and fees to advertising agencies special writers or advisers
Expenses incurred by salesmen when working for ad dept.
Traveling expenses of department em-

(Note: In some companies these go into special "Administration" account)

MECHANICAL:
Art work
Typography
Engraving
Mats & Electros
Photographs
Radio & TV production
Package design (advertising aspects only)

MISCELLANEOUS:
Transportation of advertising material (including postage and other carrying charges)
Fees to window display installation services
Other miscellaneous expenses connected with items on the White List

BLACK LIST	GRAY LIST
(These charges do not belong in the advertising account although too frequently they are put there:)	These are borderline charges, sometimes belonging in the advertising accounts and sometimes in other accounts, depending on circumstances:)

BLACK LIST

(These charges do not belong in the advertising account although too frequently they are put there:)

Free goods
Picnics and bazaar programs
Charitable, religious and fraternal donations
Other expenses for good-will purposes
Cartons
Labels
Instruction sheets
Package manufacture
Press agentry
Stationery used outside advertising department
Price lists
Salesmen's calling cards
Motion pictures for sales use only
House magazines going to factory employees
Bonuses to trade
Special rebates

Membership in trade associations
Entertaining customers or prospects
Annual reports
Showrooms
Demonstration stores
Sales convention expenses
Salesmen's samples (including photographs used in lieu of samples)
Welfare activities among employees
Such recreational activities as baseball teams, etc.
Sales expenses at conventions
Cost of salesmen's automobiles
Special editions which approach advertisers on goodwill basis

GRAY LIST

These are borderline charges, sometimes belonging in the advertising accounts and sometimes in other accounts, depending on circumstances:)

Samples
Demonstrations
Fairs
Canvassing
Rent
Light
Heat
Depreciation of equipment used by advertising department
Telephone and other overhead expenses, apportioned to advertising department
House magazines going to salesmen
Advertising automobiles
Preiums

Membership in associations or other organizations devoted to advertising
Testing bureaus
Advertising portfolios for salesmen
Contributions to special advertising funds of trade associations
Display signs on the factory or office building
Salesmen's catalogs
Research and market investigations
Advertising allowances to trade for co-operative effort

PERSONS INVOLVED IN PREPARING AND APPROVING A BUDGET

Most often, advertising budgets are prepared by the advertising manager (often with help from the advertising agency) and approved by a company's top executive such as the president. Because, however, of the close relationship of advertising and sales, both budget preparation and budget approval may come from some member of the sales department. Even in such a case, the advertising manager or advertising director will be important in budget formulation. Sometimes the preparation of the advertising budget is relatively easy compared to the task of persuading top management to accept the proposal. Frequently, therefore, the company's top advertising and sales personnel join in presenting the budget—after they have agreed among themselves that the budget is exactly what they want.

An important development in recent years has been management's tendency to consider that advertising budgets should be considered within the framework of the total marketing program concept. Numerous corporations have established the title of "vice-president of marketing" within their corporate structure. Where such an executive is established, it is this person to whom the advertising manager will take budget problems. Such an executive will provide a better climate for consideration of an advertising director's budget problems. Most important, if the advertising director has been able to sell a program to the marketing vice-president, a powerful voice is then fighting for the budget in the high echelons of business management.

QUESTIONS

1. Discuss what is meant by "realistic" pricing.

2. As the new advertising manager of a corporation that manufactures camping equipment, you have been asked to devise an advertising budget for a newly developed knapsack. Briefly discuss some important considerations which should enter into your budgetary decisions. Include media and sales considerations in your discussion.

3. Why is distribution of a product usually considered before budgetary decisions are made?

4. Summarize the approaches taken in the five commonly used systems of deriving an advertising budget. What are the weaknesses in each of these methods?

5. Too much advertising is generally preferable to too little advertising. Give reasons for this.

6. What is the rationale behind the current trend of considering advertising budgets within the framework of the total marketing program?

7. Why is it necessary to review an advertising budget frequently during the course of the budget year?

8. When developing an advertising budget, what factors influencing sales are beyond the control of the individual firm?

9. What products can you think of that have recently been changed in some way or prohibited by a court ruling or other governmental action?

REFERENCES

1. Sometimes used also are budgeting plans based on percentage of profits for the past or coming year, or dollars spent per customer or per dollar.
2. In fairness, however, it must be said that some unit-system advertisers underspend in high-volume years by lowering the unit figure by a few dollars. The money thus put aside is then applied in low-volume years to provide an equalizing factor.
3. Many big advertisers introducing a new product knowingly spend so much in the introductory period that they erase any hope for a first-year profit. An example is Procter & Gamble, which spent $15 million for Gleem toothpaste's introductory advertising.

5

MARKETING AND ADVERTISING RESEARCH

MARKETING AND ADVERTISING RESEARCH

Picture yourself suddenly responsible for the national advertising for a product. Sitting in an office in Seattle, Atlanta, Cincinnati, or New York, you become aware that that four office walls isolate you from the world in which your decisions will take effect. You are being paid to make decisions, but you quickly realize that you need some basis for your decisions. You need information to answer the almost unending string of questions that come to mind.

Some answers are close at hand. You have a budget to work with. You can look through the records of previous years to see how advertising was done in the past. You know your advertising decisions have to fit within a framework of general company goals and more specific marketing goals, and this information is readily available.

If the marketing department has a goal of increasing sales or market shares in sunbelt states, this provides some guidance for your decisions. Your advertising decisions will be quite different if the marketing department decides to concentrate only on the 100 largest urban markets. Even with the guides provided by marketing goals, you have different types of questions to answer and decisions to make to coordinate advertising efforts to help achieve marketing goals.

In this chapter, advertising research is considered in the marketing context. Because advertising is marketing communication, advertisers must be familiar with the types of research used by marketing managers. In the following chapter, advertising research is discussed in the communications context, in terms of getting information about advertising messages, media and the effectiveness of advertising.

THE NEED FOR INFORMATION

Because you need information to make decisions, you begin to gather, read and think about information from any available source. Without realizing it, you're doing research, because according to the American Marketing Association, research is the gathering, recording, and analyzing of all facts about problems relating to the transfer and sales of goods and services from producer to consumer.

At first you feel strange because "research" suggests something exotic. In bits and pieces you've picked up the idea that researchers have their own strange language of methods and probabilities. Researchers seem to you more interested in picky points about their methods and computer formulas than they are in getting answers.

If you said research does not yield absolute answers, you would be right. Much marketing and advertising research is done by survey and experiment. Both research methods use sampling and statistical tests that yield chance or probability answers, much like betting. Research answers are never absolutely true, but you can calculate the likelihood of answers being true, say, 95 times out of 100. The main idea to keep in mind is simply this: research is the process of getting answers to questions.

You, as an advertiser, ask a lot of questions. Because you can't get answers in a vacuum, you begin to gather and read information from trade publications, the business press, government reports, and trade association newsletters. You study information from newspaper and other media associations. Probably no other business function has as much information available as marketing and advertising. Your first job, therefore, as an advertiser is to become familiar with the available, free information.

OBTAINING AND USING SECONDARY DATA

Secondary data, in the form of published material, are used much more frequently than primary data. The advertiser can save considerable time and money by knowing where to find and how to use secondary data. Investigations have been made and published on almost every phase of marketing and advertising activity. Many times it is pointless to bother with original research; the answers may be found in research already done and published—material that is waiting for someone to use it.

Where to find secondary data? Some of the major sources of secondary data are:

(1) Libraries. Public and school libraries have much readily available material.
(2) *Federal or state governments*. The various bureaus of the federal government have almost limitless statistical matter on such topics as housing, farming, finance, employment, population, living conditions, education, industry, business conditions, and foreign trade. Among the more fruitful government sources for material on these topics are:

Department of Commerce	Treasury Department
Department of Agriculture	Library of Congress
Labor Department	Federal Security Agency
Department of the Interior	
Permanent Regulatory Agencies such as Federal Trade Commission, Interstate Commerce Commission,	

and the Securities & Exchange Commission

(3) *Trade associations.* An association exists for almost every industry and is usually anxious to give out information relating to its field. In the retail field the Jewelry Council and the National Retail Hardware Association are examples. On the local level, there are hundreds of associations of retail merchants or chambers of commerce.

(4) *Media.* Newspapers, magazines, radio, television, and other media are among the more energetic collectors of market data. Most media will release them willingly to those who have use for them. Many of the media have large research departments whose research for advertising and marketing facts is performed on a continuing basis. Typical of these are the research departments of Time, Inc., Meredith Publishing Company, and the *Milwaukee Journal.*

(5) *Private services.* If the seeker of the data is willing to pay, there are numerous organizations that will provide information. Among these are A. C. Nielsen, Dun & Bradstreet, F. W. Dodge Corporation, and R. L. Polk Company. Large advertising agencies, too, have active market research departments that gather information that is available only to clients, or that is sometimes released without charge to all advertisers who ask for it.

A major problem with secondary sources is that much of this information is already outdated by the time you get it. Products, markets, and consumers change constantly, sometimes rapidly. Much of the information may be too general for your use. You may question the objectivity of the research. For these or other reasons, you may decide that you need additional information. You may buy research or do it yourself. In either case, you are quickly aware that information has a price.

Observation

You're doing informal research when you observe how people use media or buy and use products. You may personally observe these behaviors as a check on information you get from secondary sources. You get an idea of the importance of price by seeing how many buyers compare package prices or look at unit prices in supermarkets. You can note the sex, approximate age and income, and a variety of other characteristics of consumers who choose your product. Sales records and information about goods moving through wholesalers and retailers give additional information.

Observation is a form of research that can be unobtrusive and quite objective. Unobtrusive observation can document behavior; in this case, what people buy, normally and in a natural setting without their being self-conscious. By being unobtrusive, the advertiser bypasses the problems of bias often associated with asking consumers questions. The advertiser can, however, by combining information from secondary sources with observation more precisely define questions for which answers are needed.

LOCATING AND EVALUATING MARKETS

Advertisers compare the relative value of different markets because products seldom sell at the same rate in different sections of the nation. Sales vary markedly between cities and even adjacent suburbs. Examined in detail, each market presents a set of special problems, some of which may require advertising decisions. Advertisements may have to be produced and placed in three or four or more foreign-language newspapers in urban areas with large foreign-language populations. Outdoor advertising may be purchased in Los Angeles to reach commuters and to supplement fragmented television coverage.

National advertisers may define existing and potential markets on the basis of census information, since the U.S. census is the most authoritative and comprehensive source of information about the U.S. population. The census is taken every ten years, however, and many markets change rapidly in the interim.

Census information is adjusted, updated, and published by *Sales and Marketing Management* magazine each July. Using the updated information in *Sales and Marketing Management*, national advertisers can study existing markets and can define potential new markets on a number of bases. Some advertisers may be interested only in the number of people or people of certain ages. Others may be interested in households or families or families with certain incomes. Some advertisers are interested more in the level of retail sales activity, preferring to focus on markets that are more vital and active than the average.

Many advertisers use the Buying Power Index to assess the sales potential of markets. The Buying Power Index (BPI) is a weighted index that relates population, effective buying income (roughly equivalent to the government's personal disposable income, or income after taxes), and retail sales. The BPI expresses a market's ability to buy, or its potential fertility in sales. Many advertisers of mass-produced, widely distributed, and popularly priced products find the BPI adequately predicts potential sales for their products. The further the product is removed from the mass market, the greater the need to modify the BPI by more discriminating factors such as age, sex, income, and other population characteristics. The BPI is also modified to correlate with sales for low, moderate, and premium-priced items.

ANALYZING COMPETITION

The national advertiser is interested in competitors' activities, such as their pricing, distribution policies, advertising activity, and sales. Much of this information is fed back to the marketing department by a firm's sales force. Information of this type may also be purchased from a firm such as A. C. Nielsen. For the advertiser selling through supermarkets or drug stores, for example, Nielsen store audits provide a wealth of information broken down by ten regions of the country by store size and county size. The national advertiser may buy information about the flow of products through small supermarkets in heavily populated counties in New England, or the advertiser may buy such information for the entire American market.

Nielsen reports provide information about in-store displays, retail selling prices, consumer deals, and special prices. The reports also give the number of stores carrying the merchandise by retailer size: small, medium, and large independent and chain stores. During periodic visits to stores in the Nielsen sample, auditors learn how much of a product a retailer has purchased over a given time period, the amount of inventory carried, and the number of stores that are out of stock. Nielsen also reports on national and local advertising support for products.

Using Nielsen information, the advertiser can pinpoint both marketing and advertising problems. Perhaps advertising has been placed in a section of the country where many stores are out of stock. If this is the case, advertising is wasted. Maybe retailers are not using point-of-purchase materials. The advertiser needs to know this, also.

This is just one type of information the advertiser can purchase. With this information, the advertiser learns what is happening at the retail level of the distribution chain. Other services provide information about the flow of products at wholesale. Still other research services provide competitive advertising expenditures by various media. Even so, this information does not tell who is buying the products and in what quantities. To find this out, the advertiser may have to survey consumers.

CHECKING CONSUMER ATTITUDES

Today's typical consumer is no longer typical. Consumers—young and old and in-between—show less and less inclination to think, act, and buy in traditional ways. Consumers have more discretionary income (income after taxes and living expenses) than ever before and tend to buy in less predictable ways with this income. Many consumers today talk about buying to achieve a certain lifestyle, a term formerly used only by advertising and marketing professionals and a small cluster of academic researchers.

Widespread and invisible shifts in values associated with life-styles surface first in buying. This requires advertisers to monitor consumer attitudes towards their products. While a product may be as good as ever, changes in values can alter consumer perception and evaluation of the product. Suddenly a product is viewed as old-fashioned or inconvenient.

Young, apartment-dwelling families backpack children or buy light, collapsible strollers rather than traditional baby carriages. They buy lightweight furniture because they anticipate moving frequently. When young families buy homes, they want no-wax floors and hang washable curtains. At Thanksgiving they cook self-basting turkeys, which they eat with stainless steel knives and forks. If the President of the United States dropped by for a visit, the young couple would serve instant coffee without feeling the need to make an excuse. The young families value convenience above all.

Other value shifts are widely commented upon, with the underlying trends causing these shifts charted by social scientists and advertisers. By necessity or choice, growing numbers of women return to work while their children are very young. They require day care for their children, new clothing, and perhaps a car for work. Many of these women regard themselves quite differently than the traditional in-home wife and mother. Family roles in two-career families tend to become more egalitarian, with husbands taking over work at home formerly done by their wives. More men are doing the family shopping.

The advertiser surveys consumers in the changing U.S. family to learn who buys what products, who uses the products and with what reactions.

Spurred in part by changing work patterns, the changing self-image of the American woman poses problems for advertisers. One woman with a strong career orientation may regard having and rearing children as a temporary interruption of a full-time career. Another woman may regard managing a household and rearing children as a full-time job. Both women may buy the same product for quite different reasons. Additionally, both women may view advertisements with a heightened sensitivity, watching for advertisements they believe insulting.

MEASURING EFFECTIVENESS OF ADVERTISING AND SALES PROMOTION

Advertisers may do their own research or may buy research that measures the effectiveness of advertising and sales promotion. Expensive television commercials may be pretested with theatre audiences prior to being placed on network television. Magazine advertisements may be tested in special copies of magazines given the advertiser a week before the magazine reaches newstands. Advertisers use research to monitor an advertising campaign at certain intervals to learn if consumers are aware of the product, know the product benefits, and think favorably about and are inclined to buy the product. Such studies are often called "consumer tracking" studies. Direct-mail campaigns and couponing of print advertisement are two widely used methods of self-testing advertising.

PRETESTING PRODUCTS

Many firms pretest products in limited markets before spending millions to market them nationally. Research in test markets helps to forecast success or failure in larger markets. Test market results enable advertisers to diagnose and correct unanticipated problems in pricing, packaging, advertising appeals, media selection and intensity to use, and a host of other possible problems. Almost every issue of *Advertising Age* tells of products in one or more test markets.

Sales and Sales Performance Analysis

This is an evaluation of sales results in terms of price lines, package sizes, trading areas, and sales territories, and an analysis of the performance of individual salesmen. This information comes from the firm's own records and may be supplemented by outside information.

STEPS IN MARKETING AND ADVERTISING RESEARCH

To answer some of the questions posed in this chapter, the advertiser may decide that research is necessary. While there is no fixed formula for conducting research, five basic steps are involved in the research process:

(1) Deciding what problem exists and what information is needed to solve it.
(2) Selecting an appropriate research method to develop the required information.
(3) Getting the data.
(4) Analyzing the data to arrive at reasonable findings.
(5) Presenting the findings.

Step I: Deciding What Problem Exists and What Information Is Needed to Solve It.

Defining an advertising problem often appears deceptively simple, but frequently is the hardest and most crucial step. How a problem is defined directs the four succeeding steps. Improper definition can result in useless research, a waste of time and money. For example, a quick, inexpensive pilot study may reveal consumers are aware of the advertiser's product but do not believe the advertised claims. The problem is not advertising awareness but advertising believability.

What Information Is Needed about the Product? Is the product different? Does it offer genuine consumer benefits? If the answer to these questions is yes, the advertiser or salesperson has something to tell the consumer. The consumer is interested in learning about products that wear longer, are more convenient to use, taste better or use less energy.

Even if the advertiser is convinced a new or improved product is superior to existing products on the market, pretests are run with individual consumers, groups of consumers or in one or more selected test markets. Consumer reaction and judgment is the key.

Are new coffee substitutes made from a blend of coffee and grains less bitter than traditional coffee products? Consumers will decide. Will consumers sacrifice some qualities in taste or the convenience of powdered alcoholic drinks sold in foil packs? Consumers will decide.

Advertising Age, a publication serving the advertising industry, regularly reports information about products in test markets. In one issue the magazine reported the following.[1] Campbell Soup Company was testing "no salt added" canned soups. Procter & Gamble was testing Dri-Weve Pampers, said to keep babies drier by wicking moisture away from the skin. Big H was testing a sauce specifically for hamburgers to find if Americans want to add variety to the widely consumed beef patty. Pillsbury was testing Breakfast Lites, a nutritionally complete breakfast bar.

The mid-1970s saw the advertised introduction of a variety of convenient electric kitchen appliances for making french fries, crepes, hamburgers, doughnuts, and pizzas. Coffee-maker sales boomed at the same time, and coffee makers were quickly modified to brew fewer cups as coffee prices soared.

At the same time, and spurred by higher energy costs, mopeds were advertised to the public as convenient and inexpensive machines for running errands. People began seeing advertisements for solar heating devices and other energy-saving products.

No. 100 outdoor poster showing.

To provide a thorough coverage of outdoor advertising viewers in San Diego, the advertiser will use the number of posters represented by the dots on this traffic flow map. With such coverage, the outdoor advertiser knows that the persons in the market are reached wherever they live in the San Diego area. In the legend at the bottom left, PVF refers to "potential viewer family." PV refers to "potential viewer individual."

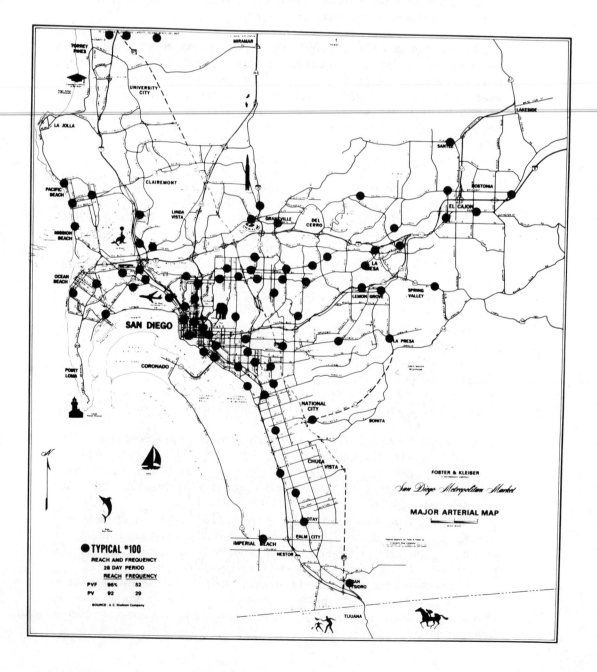

Oftentimes, the advertiser can make a very accurate judgment about the advertised benefits to which consumers will respond. At other times, logic leads the advertiser astray. Many small pickup trucks are used exclusively as recreation vehicles rather than as work vehicles. This was not expected.

What Information Is Needed about the People Who May Buy the Product. If a new product offers genuine consumer benefits, the advertisers seek information about the potential market. The size of the potential market, revealed in *Sales and Marketing Management,* may indicate that from a cost standpoint, it is worthwhile to invest in producing and selling the product.

A number of more specific questions remain to be answered. Who are the people who will buy your product? What are their characteristics? How can these people be described? Information about people in markets is often presented in what are called demographic categories, originally developed by census takers and sociologists for survey work. Potential buyers are frequently described by such demographic categories as age, sex, income, education, occupation, religion, racial or ethnic origin, and family status. Advertisers frequently describe markets using these categories.

The categories may be regarded as simply descriptive. If, however, a company's sales correlate closely with one or another of these categories, the advertiser regards these categories as buying explanatory power; that is, people buy products because they are needed at a certain age, or by one sex, or by people with certain occupations.

Ethnic outdoor poster.

Racial origin is one of the factors to be considered in market research. This 30-sheet poster, placed in Spanish-speaking neighborhoods recognizes that language barriers can hold down sales.

Sex. How many men and women, and how many boys and girls? Nearly all advertisers are interested in this answer. While women buy more goods than men, frequently because they buy family food and household goods, there is considerable crossing of lines. Men often buy perfume for women, especially at Christmas, and women often buy shirts and ties for husbands the year around. Advertisers want to know who buys how much of their product, when, and for what reason.

Age. Radical differences occur in buying as people age. Diapers are needed for the very young, and young men start shaving within a predictable age range. The increasing need for dentures and many other products is associated with age. For diapers and dentures, age explains buying behavior to the advertiser; sometimes social definitions combine with age to explain other behavior. Many people enjoy chewing gum. The 40-year old factory worker may chew while working. The 40-year old factory manager does not chew while working.

The age profile of the American population is changing. The median age of the population will increase from 28.8 to 31.1 years between 1975 and 1985. While this change may not seem large, the importance is more easily seen by understanding that the proportion of the population who are 25 years or older will grow from 56 percent to 61 percent during the same period. Many advertisers are aware of the changing age of the population. Cosmetics manufacturers are now marketing products designed to appeal to mature women. The makers of denim jeans are cutting the traditionally tight-fitting pants more fully and advertising to old consumers.

Income. Markets are composed of people who are willing and able to buy products. Many people may be willing to buy a Porsche, but few are able to afford this automobile. Advertisers know this and define target markets of consumers who are both willing and able to buy their products.

Cadillacs and around-the-world luxury cruises may be aimed at the upper 10 percent of the income levels. Advertisers of soap, soup, and cereal products aim at the entire market, although they know that consumption of their products will be greater at some income levels than others. While it is true that people of different income levels make purchases that frequently are above or below what the advertiser might expect, income levels are fairly consistent determinants of the buying of many products.

Middle-income consumers are the most important to marketers, simply because there are so many consumers in this group. And these consumers have buying power. Typically, within the middle-income market the advertiser selects what are considered better than average prospects for the product. The advertiser must: determine the target income groups in the market areas he wishes to sell, determine how many in these groups may be expected to buy the advertiser's product or service, and finally determine, if possible, how much "premium" business can be anticipated—that is, how many people in lower income levels buy products supposedly priced out of their reach. A surprisingly high purchase rate of so-called high-income products is found among buying groups that do not look promising from the standpoint of income. Some brands of expensive scotch whiskey, for example, are frequently bought by people with very modest incomes.

Along with the previously mentioned changes in family structure, the distribution of family incomes is changing. Families with incomes under $5,000 are expected to decline from 11.7 percent of the population in 1975 to 6.8 percent by 1985. Families with incomes over $20,000 (in 1975 dollars) are expected to rise from 26 percent in 1975 to 45 percent in 1985. This means an improved standard of living for many American families, with more discretionary income available for goods and services that might now be considered luxuries.

Education. Assume you have before you two men of equal age and income. They may even have grown up in the same neighborhood and gone through high school together. One is college educated and in a managerial position with a company. The other may work for the same company, perhaps as an assembly line foreman. If the company in which both men work has an incentive program with prizes, the man in the managerial position will work harder for a Caribbean vacation with his wife than for a motorboat of equal dollar value. The reverse is true for the production line foreman.

Although in many ways similar, these two men will buy products and services in dramatically different ways. Advertising seeks them out in different media and speaks to them using different words keyed to their quite different interests, goals, aspirations, and attitudes toward work and play.

Religion. Although not so important generally as the other considerations already listed, religion nevertheless shapes the market for some products, especially foods. Jewish holidays and Lenten season, for example, are felt strongly in areas dominated by Jewish or Catholic populations. Liquor and cigarette advertisers are aware, too that beverages containing stimulants are not used by practitioners of the Church of Latter Day Saints, nor are tobacco products.

Racial or Ethnic Origin. Advertisers now speak of ethnic markets, and include foreign-born, foreign-language, and black and oriental Americans. In many ways these consumers buy as if their ancestors arrived on the Mayflower; in other ways, advertisers must use special media to reach the markets provided by these people. The advertiser may find sharp differences in product preferences, with some groups demanding fresh fruit and vegetables rather than canned or frozen.

Spanish-speaking Americans in New York City are heavy rice consumers. This is not so for the Spanish-speaking Americans of Mexican origin in California or other southwestern states. In fact, advertisers have learned that a single Spanish-speaking voice for broadcast commercials can be insulting to one or another of the Spanish-language markets. Television and radio commercials for nationally advertised products are now produced with three different voices for the Mexican-American market in the southwest, the Cuban-American market in south Florida, and the Puerto Rican-American market in New York City.

Family Life Cycle. Advertisers for most clothing items and many personal items such as shaving cream, perfume, and ball-point pens, pay little attention to family life cycle. On the other hand, vacuum sweepers, kitchen uten-

Product that answers a consumer need.

Many markets exist for a product such as this. Market research tells the advertiser who will use the product after product analysis reveals the uses and functions of the product. In this case, of course, the target would be mothers whose children present her with an endless array of dirty clothes.

sils, furniture, and many other products are advertised with the wife and/or husband in mind. The percentage of married couples and married couples with children, in any given market is one of the most pertinent figures to many advertisers.

Family formation can be forecast by sellers of engagement rings. Family formation in any given year gives manufacturers a basis for estimating the potential market for baby foods, clothing, diapers, and medicine two and three years in the future. The real estate industry can estimate the demand for single-family dwellings five years later if the young families have more than one child. Many industries closely watch family formation and fertility rates to predict markets one, two, three, five, or ten years in the future.

Family life cycle information often is defined by a combination of age of the household head and the presence of children. The information is presented in the following five stages:

(1) Single or married head under 40 with no children
(2) Married head under 40 with young children
(3) Married head under 40 with older children
(4) Married head over 40 with no children under 20
(5) Married or single head over 40, living alone, with no children

The single or married head (of a household) under 40 with no children may have a modest household income. Obligations are not heavy, and there may be considerable leeway in how money is spent. In the second and third stage family expenses tend to be quite heavy, although income is rising. Usually, when the household head is over 40 and the children are over 20 the household again has considerable leeway in spending money. Income is probably at a peak and expenses, relatively speaking, are modest. In this stage the couple with no children at home may sell their suburban house and one of their cars and move to a city apartment. Replacement furniture may be bought. Deferred vacations are finally taken.

The family life cycle has greater explanatory and predictive power for many advertisers than just the numbers of people of a certain age. Major appliance manufacturers, for example, study the number of marriages more carefully than they watch the number of people between the ages of 18 and 30. Young marrieds are much more likely to buy refrigerators and stoves than are young singles.

The Rapidly Changing American Family.   Many advertisers today are uneasy about the use of family status as a way of describing consumers or as a predictor of future consuming behavior. New ways of describing the family are required to capture the variety of new social arrangements. Today many couples live together and act as if they were married but are not. Young marrieds defer having children and limit themselves to one or two children. As divorce rates rise, single-parent families are becoming common. A frozen vegetable that is a convenience or even a luxury to the in-home homemaker becomes a necessity for the young single parent.

The nature of the change in family structure is best illustrated by the government's own, and often conflicting, figures. The government frequently issues income estimates for the family with a working father, an in-home mother and two youngsters, one teen and one subteen. Many people assume this is the typical American family today. The Bureau of Labor Statistics, however, says this "typical" family represents only six percent of the families in America.

What Do These People Buy?   Some products may be purchased heavily throughout the country by people between the ages of 18 and 49. For other products, sharp regional differences exist. Iced coffee, to illustrate, is more common in the East than on the West Coast. Cakes mixes are more heavily used in the Midwest. Brown eggs are preferred in some localities, white eggs in others. Within the relatively small state of South Carolina, supermarkets near the coast stock plenty of rice, because rice has traditionally been grown and consumed near the coast. Inland, supermarkets stock more potatoes than rice.

Sharp buying differences can exist from region to region and from city to city, even among people having the same demographic characteristics. What customers buy in each of the many markets—whether from tradition, habit, or preference—affects advertising planning.

When do these people buy?   Some products, market research discovers, are inflexibly seasonal in their appeal. Other products, thought to be seasonal, can be promoted and sold, it has been found out, in the so-called "off seasons." Use of ginger ale in the winter, or the consumption of iced coffee in the summer, is a tribute to the market researchers and advertisers who refused to accept tradition.

Although many products have strong potential sales during seasons when customers traditionally do not buy them, advertisers must gear advertising to the time when research indicates consumers normally buy the product. Thousands of retailers, for example, adjust their advertising to big buying seasons. Most of their advertising budgets are spent in those seasons, especially Christmas. Candy shops, for instance, obtaining most of their business at Christmas, Easter, Mother's Day, Valentine's Day, and Thanksgiving, also use almost all of their advertising money at those periods.

Grocery stores and supermarkets plan on a week-to-week basis and, in most towns, assume that the grocery buying days will be Friday and Saturday, thus accounting for the fat newspapers on Thursdays and Fridays. In some towns, however, this is not true, and grocery shopping is heavier on other days. Market researchers have been interested, too, in investigating night openings in the retail business, since night shopping has changed advertising as well as buying patterns.

The U.S. Department of Commerce, trade associations, and the media, to mention a few sources, have many figures to help national and retail advertisers decide when to advertise. Typical of when-to-advertise material is data released each fall by the Newspaper Advertising Bureau, Inc. This material alerts retailers to the potential in the nation's back-to-school market.

Size of the market in dollar figures is given along with suggestions as to what items will find a ready response among the mothers and children buying clothing and supplies for the forthcoming school year.

Where Do These People Buy?   Our population is so fluid, so restless, so mobile that this question is not easy to answer, yet every advertiser wants the answer. Do the consumers in a market do most of their buying at retail stores, or is much of it done by mail order? Are goods bought in the town in which buyers live, or do they travel to nearby towns to buy? Formerly, shopping in the typical retail trading area was done in a central, easily defined downtown shopping district. Much retail activity is now in outlying and especially suburban shopping centers, complete with ample parking, heated and air-conditioned malls, baby sitting, and free puppet shows and concerts. Some centers draw entire families from more than one hundred miles on weekends for what might be called a total family shopping experience.

The advertiser can get a general idea of retail sales activity in a market from the Sales Activity Index in *Sales and Marketing Management*. The index is high for some cities, low for others. People fly to Dallas from surrounding and sparsely populated ranch areas, especially at Christmas. Las Vegas attracts many visitors who shop between visits to gambling casinos. Other markets, perhaps not particularly active, may be known for a certain type of merchandise. People now drive from throughout Michigan and surrounding states to shop for furniture in Grand Rapids, still a center for producing fine furniture.

Many urban markets are now two markets, composed of a central city market and an increasingly affluent suburban market. Advertisers no longer rely on a single central city newspaper to cover a retail market. Suburban newspapers supplement central city newspapers.

Why Do These People Buy?   Determining why people buy what they do is a continuing and often perplexing problem for advertisers, because many consumers honestly don't know why they buy certain products. Sometimes consumers will readily discuss their reasons for buying a product; at other times the same consumers will not discuss their reasons for buying another product. The problem of getting answers to why consumers buy as they do is complicated by the fact that many consumers deny that advertising ever influences them in any way.

Advertisers know, however, that buying behavior is motivated behavior. Advertising and marketing researchers, therefore, sometimes use what are called motivation research methods in an attempt to learn the real reasons behind buying behavior.

It is known that general consumers, in contrast to trade and industrial buyers, are more prone to buy through habit or through impulse. This is not irrational on the consumer's part. Buying through habit is an efficiency technique of the human mind to enable the consumer to focus attention on those buying decisions that present new-product alternatives. Impulse buying is unplanned, but the package or product may have reminded the consumer that a product is needed or desired.

Unsure of the real reasons behind consumer purchasing, many advertisers use saturation advertising for low-cost, convenience goods. The philosophy of such advertising is simple:

(1)   put advertising everywhere the consumer can see or hear it,
(2)   distribute the product everywhere the consumer can buy it.

An advertiser of an acceptable consumer product who follows this two-pronged system will normally build a profitable sales volume. Considerable percentages of drug or grocery store purchases are unplanned. One way for the advertiser to get a share of these unplanned purchases is to make the consumer-buyer so familiar with the name, product, and package that the shopper will, in almost a reflex action, reach for the familiar rather than the unfamiliar.

Are Purchases Made Through Emotion or Through Reason?   Although advertising is frequently accused of being overemotional, most advertisements stress reason more than emotion. This is because we as human beings make decisions which have both rational and emotional components. Very often the cold rational facts of an advertisement arouse an emotional response, a human response. When the U.S. Congress was preparing to cut funds for rat control in major cities, an advertisement urging retention of the program pictured a rat and gave a factual account of the frequency and severity of rat attacks on youngsters. The response in Congress was immediate and emotional. Rat control funds were restored.

Every advertiser of fashion merchandise for men and for women knows that people buy for emotional satisfaction as well as for rational reasons. Fashion merchandise may be bought for pure self-satisfaction. Often enjoyment of the products results from the reactions of others. Frequently, however, fashionable merchandise is presented in very matter-of-fact langauge. The following example is taken from high-fashion advertising:

> Shirtmaker exclusive in go-everywhere wool and cotton tattersal checks. Front buttoning, leather belt. White grounds checked with red and black, blue and black, or brown and green. 12 to 20, 38 and 40.

Step 2. Selecting an Appropriate Research Method to Develop the Required Information.   After studying company records and secondary sources of information coupled with first-hand observation, the advertiser defines one or more problems to be researched. By this time, the advertiser usually has a substantial list of questions, but some are more important than others.

The advertiser's next step is to choose a research method to develop the desired information. Unlike much academic research, advertising and marketing research often is done within very tight time deadlines and as inexpensively as possible. Time and money are major constraints that influence the selection of the research method.

If information is needed quickly, a telephone survey may be completed in one or two days. If there is very little money available for research and the information desired is not needed for several weeks, a mail survey may yield adequate information.

Advertisers use a variety of research methods, fitting the method to the type of information they need. Commonly used methods include survey, experiment, controlled field experiment, and content analysis.

The *survey* method is widely used by advertisers because it fits and supplements the basic methods used to yield broadly based information dealing with nationwide market and consumer behavior. The advertiser choosing to survey must make a number of decisions, the first of which deals with the point

Long copy advertisement with rational approach.

When long copy is skillfully written about an interesting product it will achieve high readership, as the copy for this product does consistently. This advertiser creates high interest advertisements with long, believable copy.

An unbroken line of excellence. Since 1886, Mercedes-Benz has produced one classic automobile after another. Each one is a car engineered like no other car in the world.

The automobiles of Mercedes-Benz.
The legend continues.

Mercedes-Benz invented the automobile in 1886—and in 1895 produced the first 'car ever built on a production line.

Over the generations, Mercedes-Benz has perfected one engineering advance after another.

Add to that an auto racing record of over 4,400 individual victories and you have an automotive heritage unmatched by any other car in the world.

Now Mercedes-Benz offers eight separate and distinct models for sale in the United States. Each one is unique.

Each one continues, in its own way, the Mercedes-Benz legend.

Above, you see almost 50 years in the life of a legend. Look closely. See how nobly time touches these Mercedes-Benz cars. Their appeal is enduring. A characteristic that marks the truly legendary and distinguishes it from the merely passing fancy.

A blend of future and past

Here is disciplined grace, the product of thoughtful evolution in design. When Mercedes-Benz engineers create a new car, their vision is wide. They look backwards to

retain and improve on their worthiest earlier ideas. And forwards as well, to blend in their latest innovative technology.

Thoughtful evolution in design: a mark of Mercedes-Benz.

To the eye, the changes may be subtle. Invariably, though, they are quietly beautiful—which shows how unerringly their "form follows function."

More importantly, the cars of Mercedes-Benz are designed to appeal strongly to your intelligence. They are honest cars. The promises they make relate directly to their primary function: well-engineered, safe transportation.

One of the eight Mercedes-Benz models

currently available in the United States is in the front rank above: the 450SEL Sedan. Our full offering is described in the table, below. Each one is a blending of patient craftsmanship with sophisticated technology.

**Enduring value...
and enduring pleasure**

Many models of the Special Roadster 500K shown here (no. 4, circa 1935) are appraised at over $50,000. The rare 540K Cabriolet B (no. 3, circa 1936) is considered a genuine value at over $75,000. And based on average official used car prices over the past five years, the contemporary Mercedes-Benz automobiles have held their value better than

any other make of luxury car sold in America.

The high retained value of Mercedes-Benz cars is a rational attraction. But they have an emotional raison d'être, too. To experience it, arrange, through your Mercedes-Benz Dealer, to drive one. You'll experience an unrivaled automotive pleasure. One that happens only behind the wheel of this charismatic car.

Truly, the legend continues.

Mercedes-Benz
Engineered like no other car in the world.

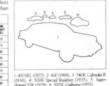

Mercedes-Benz Technical Specifications

MODEL	SEATING	ENGINE	DISPLACEMENT (CU. IN.)	WHEELBASE (IN.)	OVERALL LENGTH (IN.)	CURB WEIGHT (LBS.)
240D (Sedan)	5	Diesel, 4 cyl. ohc (fuel injected)	146.7	110.0	190.9	3210
300D (Sedan)	5	Diesel, 5 cyl. ohc (fuel injected)	183.4	110.0	190.9	3615
280E (Sedan)	5	6 cyl. dohc (fuel injected)	167.6	110.0	190.9	3530
280SE (Sedan)	5	6 cyl. dohc (fuel injected)	167.6	112.8	205.5	3905
450SEL (Sedan)	5	V-8 ohc (fuel injected)	275.8	116.7	209.4	4080
450SL (Sports)	2	V-8 ohc (fuel injected)	275.8	96.9	182.3	3615
450SLC (Sports Coupe)	4	V-8 ohc (fuel injected)	275.8	111.0	196.4	3860
6.9 (Sedan)	5	V-8 ohc (fuel injected)	417.1	116.5	210.0	4390

1: 450SEL (1977); 2. 600 (1969); 3. 540K Cabriolet B (1936); 4. 500K Special Roadster (1935); 5. Supercharged SSK (1929); 6. 300SL Gullwing (1955).

of contact. Each way of contacting consumers has a number of advantages and disadvantages the advertiser must weigh.

Personal Interviewing.   The survey may be done by personal interviewing conducted among any group that can give the information desired. The method may be a house-to-house check or consumers, an in-store check of dealers, an in-the-field check of sales, or others.

Several advantages may be listed for personal interviewing.

(1)   The interviewer generally will get fewer turndowns than the mail questionnaire.
(2)   The interviewer can draw out the respondents more than is possible in a mail questionnaire.
(3)   The interviewer can obtain extra information, not directly related to the questions, that is often more valuable than the answers themselves.
(4)   The interviewer can direct the way the material is put down on the interview form, so that it may be understood and tabulated much easier than is often true of mail questionnaires.
(5)   The interviewer can give advertisements or products to consumers, getting their immediate reactions, and probing for reasons behind their reactions to advertisements or products.

A primary disadvantage of personal interviewing is the cost, particularly if the interviews are at scattered points, or if numerous callbacks must be made, as is often the case in random sampling. Secondly, even skilled interviewers may sometimes unconsciously influence the answers of the respondents, who may often answer what they think the interviewer wishes to hear. Lastly, the presence of the interviewer inhibits some respondents who may be embarrassed to say to a person what they would be quite willing to put down on a mail questionnaire form.

Mail Questionnaires.   Among the advantages that may be listed for mail questionnaires are the following.

(1)   They have entree everywhere, unlike personal interviewers who may not be able to obtain interviews with people who are out frequently, or with people who refuse to grant personal interviews.
(2)   The mail questionnaire reaches the person on a remote Wyoming ranch at the same costs as the Park Avenue resident of New York City. Distance and widely scattered respondents do not affect the mail survey.
(3)   Even the best of interviewers is usually aware of the time pressure in interviews—the fact that the respondents become resentful and less careful in answering if the interview is at all long. A mail questionnaire, in contrast, may be answered at the respondents' convenience.

(4) Questions in a mail questionnaire are set up exactly the same way each "interview," whereas poor interviewers will vary the manner of asking questions from interview to interview in personal contacts. Such switching changes the answers so that in tabulating, different answers are obtained for supposedly similar question.

Most serious among the disadvantages of mail surveys is the fact that the people answering the surveys may not be representative of the entire sample, or of the "population" the researchers are investigating. For one thing, people answering mail surveys unless they are given some incentive to answer are usually a decided minority, since the majority will not usually take time to answer. Also, people who do answer often feel strongly for or against the questionnaire topic. Unless a sampling of the "middle-ground" group is obtained the results will show a decided bias.

Mail surveys, too, often bring a discouragingly low response. Five to 10 percent is about normal expectancy for questionnaires sent to the general public without incentive. The return tends to go higher if the questionnaires are sent to a more specialized list. Returns from mailings to professional and business people, for example, will average about one in four. However, the inclusion of a cash incentive will generally result in a return of nearly 50 percent.

Returns can often be increased by sending a persuasive letter along with the questionnaire. The letter may explain the purpose of the survey and enlist the help of the respondent in a flattering and personal way. An appeal for information is less frequently turned down if it is made on a personal basis.

Use of a postage-free, addressed return envelope helps returns, too. Another help is to inform respondents that their signature is not needed on the reply. Premiums—a pencil or some other useful object—often increase returns, too, as many researchers have already found out.

A mail survey, like other surveys, is no better than the questions asked in the questionnaire. Unless questions are well devised, the survey is useless. Actually, all questions should be pretested by sending out a trial run of questionnaires and analyzing the answers to see if any questions are confusing respondents, or drawing out answers that are not pertinent to the objectives of the survey.

Questions, above all, should not be leading, so that the answer is indicated through the wording of the question. One radio survey, for instance, asked: "Would you like shorter commercials on our program?" The answers, of course, were very heavily "yes." Advised to make a second survey, the sponsor did so. This time the survey asked what was disliked about advertising for the programs. The results revealed that only a small number objected to the length of commercials, but that many disliked other aspects of the commercial treatment, especially the voice of the announcer.

Ambiguity should be avoided, too. Questions should be fashioned to obtain just one answer. As an example, the question: "How often do you go downtown to shop?" may draw replies of "Not very often," "pretty often," "hardly ever," or other vague answers. Either the question should be completely specific, such as "How many times did you shop downtown last week?" (or last month, or last year) or it should be set up in a form that makes it easy for the respondent—such as the following:

Did you shop downtown last week? Yes____ No____
If "yes", how many times? Check below.

One time ____	Four times ____
Two times ____	Five times ____
Three times ____	Six times ____

Questions that ask two things at once create an impossible tabulating job, since it may not be clear which part of the question is being answered. An example is the question "What improvements can you suggest in the merchandise selections of our store, and the way that merchandise is presented?" Answers are certain to be mixed for this question; a mixup that could be avoided by using two carefully phrased questions.

Lastly, questions should be asked in logical order. The respondent should not be compelled to leap from one train of thought to another. Questions that are related should be put together. When one group of questions is finished, then another group should begin.

Telephoning. The use of telephone surveys is growing rapidly. The telephone offers a quick, inexpensive way to reach people, many of whom are otherwise unreachable. By using the telephone, the researcher can find out a person's reaction to something that is happening at the very time of the call. This is called a coincidental telephone survey and is particularly useful to assess broadcast advertising.

Although the telephone is an integral part of millions of American households and homes, there are still some homes without telephones, a fact that may produce bias in the sample. Also, a growing number of homes have unlisted numbers. Researchers can handle this by randomizing generation of phone numbers for specific areas.

Another problem is that many telephone surveys are limited to city zones because of the cost and inconvenience of reaching rural homes by telephone.

This type of geographic bias can be overcome by contracting with the phone company for a limited WATS (Wide Area Telephone Service) contract. WATS service may be contracted for on an area, state, regional, or nationwide basis. The advantage of this service is that calls can be made economically from a single office.

Additionally, unlike personal interviews that take place in a respondent's home, telephone interviews can be monitored unobtrusively by a supervisor, to ensure questions are asked in the proper manner.

Obtaining and Using a Sample. Often the selection of personal interview, mail, or telephone survey determines how the survey sample is selected. Personal interviews may be based on a sample drawn from census areas, tax rolls, lists of charge customers or any number of other bases. Mail surveys may be conducted with samples from the same lists as well as special lists developed by what are called list houses, business firms that specialize in developing and selling lists. Mail surveys also use media subscription lists. Telephone surveys are most frequently conducted with lists of phone numbers randomly selected from phone books.

The researcher decides how the sample list will be developed and the size of the sample needed. A sample is a portion taken out of a total quantity so that the qualities found in the sample may reasonably be expected to be found in the whole—just as several lumps of coal taken from a ton of coal provide a sample that gives an idea of the quality of the whole ton.

In research, a survey conducted on a sample of people who represent a real market for a product or service indicates the response that may be expected. The total group represented by the sample is referred to as a universe or population.

Methods of Selecting People in a Sample.   One of the critical points in sampling is whether or not the people interviewed were selected at random. Where interviewers have an option, they tend to select their friends or people who live in first-floor apartments, or those most like themselves in customs, dress, and language. Since interviewer-control makes such research suspect, a major trend has developed for samples of unquestioned accuracy. This trend has emphasized the value of the random sample.

Informal interviewing is one way to select people. For example, 200 women shopping in a supermarket might be asked whether they cook in an open pan or a double-boiler. Every woman in that supermarket might be questioned. The results would apply only to the women who shopped in that store. No sampling, in the true sense, has been done. The findings, therefore, could not be projected to any other population. Studies of this kind are of little value in serious market research.

Another investigative approach is the quota or stratified method. Using this method the researcher may divide a city into areas, say forty districts. Forty women will be interviewed in each district. An overall distribution is prepared by age, education, and socioeconomic status. An interviewer is sent to a district to interview a certain number of women twenty to thirty years of age, with high school education, and "C" or "D" socioeconomic status. The interviewer is free to interview anyone so long as the quota is filled. Control over the selection of people to be interviewed often introduces a serious source of bias or statistical error.

Despite the fact that much marketing research is done on the basis of quota sampling, probability sampling is gaining favor with market researchers because of its superior objectivity. In this type of sampling the interviewer goes to preselected dwelling units and interviews only those who have been preselected by some random method.

Why Sample? Sampling is something you do when time and money limitations make it impossible to count whatever it is you want to count. The U.S. census, for example, is conducted every ten years and is supposed to be an accurate count of every living human being. No single business could afford to conduct the U.S. census. The information collected requires years to analyze. Additionally, thousands upon thousands of people are missed, even in the official U.S. census.

As with the census, most advertising research deals with people. Unlike the census, advertising research depends on samples, much smaller numbers of people selected according to rules to represent a larger group of people. We live with polls that predict national election outcomes. We recognize that such polls are quite accurate.

For sampling purposes, a group of people is defined in advance and is called a universe. The sample is drawn from the universe. The researchers can define the universe in any way he or she chooses. The universe can be subscribers to *Newsweek*, civil engineers in South Carolina, people 18 years and older in Montgomery County, Maryland, everybody living in New Mexico, or the population of the United States.

No sample perfectly reflects the universe from which it is chosen. Statisticians know, however that repeated random samples taken from the same universe would form a normal curve. Why is this important? Because repeated samplings produce a normal curve, statisticians can calculate the likelihood of error in samples. The calculations depend upon sample design and size. Using these calculations, a statistician can tell you the likelihood of a sample yielding information on which you can rely.

Samples: Reliable and Representative. Much arguing occurs over the relative merits of the sample methods, but the two most important questions about a sample are: Is it reliable? Is it representative? Reliability refers basically to the freedom from large sampling error, and can often be controlled by taking large enough samples.

If in a small sample of twenty golfers, for instance, four men favored Spalding autographed golf clubs, the conclusion might be that only 20 percent of the golfers in the area favored this brand—that is, if the sampling stopped with the twenty respondents.

Extend the sample to 1,000 golfers and now it is found that 450 respondents favor Spalding autographed clubs. Let us say that the actual percentage of people favoring Spalding autographed clubs is 48 percent in the district. We find that the large sample has come much closer to the true percentage figure. The sample is more reliable, a characteristic that tends to occur as the sample size is increased—especially if the sample is representative.

A representative sample is one that gives a true cross section of the characteristics of the population from which it is selected. If our aim in the golf club survey is to find out the characteristics of the entire golfing population, our survey might be thrown off if we interview only those golfers who belong to private clubs. It may well be that golfers who play on public links may not favor autographed clubs because of the higher cost. Our survey then would be guilty of bias if we confined our research to the group known to favor our product. It certainly would not be representative.

Determining Sample Size. Size of the sample depends on the amount of reliability wanted in the results. Once it is determined that the sample design is sound, then, as indicated in the discussion of reliability, the larger the sample, the more accuracy is likely to be attained and the less sampling error found.

A mistake, however, is to assume that bigness of the sample automatically insures reliability. If the hypothetical golf club survey had asked more and more country club members about the autographed golf clubs (and continued to ignore public links golfers), increasing the size of the sample would not have helped at all in achieving the information wanted.

Size of the sample is predicated upon getting the proper proportion of the various components in the population, not directly upon the size of that population. In theory, a survey of five hundred residents of Chicago, Illinois, should tell a researcher about a specific market question as accurately as a survey of five hundred residents of Peoria, Illinois, that is made on the same market question.

In actual practice, however, a much larger sample undoubtedly would be taken in Chicago because of the problems of obtaining a representative sample. The fact that Chicago is about thirty times as large as Peoria does not mean that the sample size must be thirty times as large—if the sample is predicated upon the proper proportion of the various components in the population.

If the probability principle is used in selecting the sample, the researcher will find various formulas and/or tables available for determining sample size. The size of the sample will depend directly upon the amount of error that the researcher considers acceptable. A table might show, for example, that if a sample of one size is used, a limit of 4 percent error is possible, while if the sample size is reduced to another figure the limit will climb to 5 percent. On the contrary, using the principle of geometric progression, the researcher may decide to reduce the error from 4 percent to 2 percent and will accordingly make the sample size approximately four times larger.

Step 3: Obtaining Primary Data By Experiment

Advertisers are increasingly using experimental methods to develop answers to advertising and marketing problems. Experiments may be conducted in offices, stores or cities, and typically involve changing one or more variables while holding all other variables constant. For example, two different headlines may be tested in a single issue of a magazine using a split-run technique. or advertisers may use one appeal in one state or region and another appeal in another state or region, to learn which is the more effective by follow-up survey or perhaps by coupon redemption if both advertisements contained coupons.

Experimentation in advertising poses a number of problems. The experiment may be costly and take a long time to run. Also, the answers yielded may be artificial, or there may be serious questions about generalizing experimental results to an entire market.

An example of the experimental method in action is the testing of the relative sales effectiveness of three different interior store displays. Before the experiment begins, the stores in which the displays are to be placed are picked as typical of the stores in which the displayed products are usually sold. Likewise, the communities in which the stores are located are selected as typical. These are constants. Other constants may be prices used on the displays, and the local advertising in each market.

Variables might be the positions given the displays (on the counters, shelves, or floor) or the in-store promotion used. The variables may be rotated to give each display the same chance under different conditions. The display pulling the greatest percentage increase in sales over the test period is adjudged the most effective.

A variation of the experimental method widely used by advertisers is the controlled field experiment. Rather than testing the effect of one or more variables in a setting under precise control of the experimental researcher, the advertiser tests in a broader arena, such as a test city or region. For example, the advertiser may test the effectiveness of a cents-off-coupon in only one city while continuing to advertise regularly in several comparable cities. Coupon redemptions and sales in the test city reveal the effectiveness of couponing in comparison to sales in the comparable cities.

Consumer and Dealer Panels. A panel is a group of persons who act as continuing sources of information about the buying and/or use of products. The panel members record this information in diaries, which are mailed in regularly to the organizations doing the research. In the case of a dealer panel, the dealers may be tapped for information about the sales movement of goods they stock. This information is gathered by many market research organizations such as A. C. Nielsen, Inc., previously discussed.

Consumers are selected for panels in order to obtain information from them at regular intervals about products or brands bought. To give information that might be considered worthwhile the panel should represent a proper cross section of the population.

The biggest advantage of the panel is its supplying of continuous information that reflects trends and changes in the buying pattern over a period of time. Such trends are more difficult to detect through individual market surveys conducted without continuity and among different groups.

The greatest difficulty is making sure that the panel represents a true crosssection of the population. A corollary difficulty is the replacing of dropouts from the panel with new members who have exactly the same characteristics. Yet another difficulty is the tendency of some panel members to become too conscious of the fact that they are panel members; this may affect their method of buying or even the information they give.

To insure the performance of panel members, most organizations conducting such research offer some material inducement to participants. These inducements may include cash or a variety of premiums. Generally it is found that the absence of some sort of gift causes a lagging in the conscientiousness of panel members.

Step 4: Analyzing the Findings

Interpretation of the results of a market study is usually best done by the person in charge of the study. Despite any convictions he may have had before or during the research, the researcher should approach the interpretation with complete objectivity.

In some cases the researcher is expected merely to give the facts, but not to make recommendations from the information presented. Sometimes the researcher makes recommendations. The latter course is logical, since in the course of the study the researcher learns much about the existing problems and the suggestions have the weight of evidence behind them. The suggestions may be adopted or rejected, but it seems pointless for a sponsor of research not to make use of the opinions of one who has lived very close to the problem.

Likewise, the alert market-research person has an interest in seeing that the findings are used. There is an obligation to follow up the analysis to see that it is correctly interpreted by others. Some cautions for those interpreting the data are:

(1) Favorable and unfavorable evidence should be weighted fairly. Sometimes an interpreter tends to play down unfavorable evidence in deference to the client's feelings. Unfavorable findings are often far more significant than favorable data and should be allocated space in exact proportion to their importance.

(2) Exceptions should not be emphasized disproportionately. Because a few findings are strikingly different, the interpreter may tend to over-dramatize them in the interpretation, thus giving them a significance they do not deserve. Unless they indicate a real trend, or are statistically significant, the exceptions should not be given undue stress.

(3) Opinions should not overweigh fact. People often say one thing and do another, researchers have discovered. An example is given in a milk company's endeavor to find out the milk-drinking habits of its customers. A survey showed that the customers overwhelmingly rejected the idea of having milk bottles on the dining table during a meal. Yet a follow-up survey of the same respondents (made at mealtime) found that a majority of the customers kept milk bottles on their tables during the time they ate.

The maxim "facts speak louder than words" is a good one to remember when interpreting research data.

Step 5: Presenting the Findings

The best market research can be obscured by a jumbled, illogical presentation. Much of the trouble may have been caused by not grouping questions logically in making up the questionnaire form or in not asking questions that obtained a single answer easily tabulated by machine or hand.

A good presentation of the findings should usually include all or one of the following:

- A short presentation of the problem that was to be solved.
- A discussion of the methodology used.
- A description of the persons and/or organization conducting the research.
- The statistical data obtained from the interviews, questionnaires, observation, or experiments. (This should be prefaced by a description of the nature and size of the sample.)
- A discussion and interpretation of the statistical data.
- A summary of the findings, plus conclusions or recommendations.[2]
- An appendix that contains anything from samples of questionnaire forms to explanations that do not fit sensibly in the body of the report.

A covering letter that often accompanies the report and gives the reasons for and objectives of the research may substitute for Step 1 in the foregoing. Likewise, a title page may tell for whom the research was done, the name of the person or organization conducting the research, and the date (very important) and place of the research.

STANDARD INDUSTRIAL CLASSIFICATION CODE (S.I.C.)

No one engaged in industrial marketing research can ever get more than a step away from S.I.C. numbers. Use of the Standard Industrial Classifications numbers is indispensable to anyone who wishes to know precisely the extent and character of the business market. It is especially useful to the advertiser who is deciding whether a certain business publication will reach more prospects than another.

Using a system of coding devised by the Division of Statistical Standards of the U.S. Bureau of the Budget, the S.I.C. assigns appropriate manufacturing industry code numbers to all industries in the entire field of business activity.

So important is the system the federal government adopted it as a standard basis for the collection and presentation of statistics relating to the U.S. economy. Industrial data, gathered and reported by the federal government according to S.I.C. groups, include as a partial list some of these important classifications:

(1) Number of manufacturing plants in operation
(2) Value of products shipped
(3) Value added by manufacture
(4) Employment in the manufacturing industries
(5) Hours worked and wages earned by manufacturing employees
(6) Value of materials consumed
(7) Expenditures for new plant and equipment
(8) Value of fuels and electric energy consumer

Each division of industry—agriculture, manufacturing, transportation, finance, government, and others—is assigned an industry code based on its major activity. This is assigned according to the product or groups of products produced, handled, or serviced.

Under S.I.C., industries are classified by two-digit, three-digit, and four-digit classification. The two-digit classifications are very broad in that they refer to industries as a whole. As the digit numbers grow larger, the industries in question are narrowed down to help the marketer refine specific prospects. Here is how the system works in the case of one type of market:

S.I.C. Number	Industry Definition
33	Primary metal industries
3311	Blast furnaces

Using the foregoing as an example, the advertiser who was content to get figures on the industry as a whole would use the two-digit classification. If however, the advertiser made components for blast furnaces, the two-digit classification would be too broad. Thus the four-digit breakdown would be useful.

Advertisers find that many publishers will break down their circulation figures into three-digit and four-digit subscribers in order that the users of the publications can approach their marketing planning intelligently.

When publications put their listings in Standard Rate & Data Service, they not only break their circulation into S.I.C. industries but also show how many executives and what types of executives are being reached in each S.I.C. category.

An important side result of the standardization represented by the use of S.I.C. numbers in circulation breakdowns is the possiblility it presents for the use of computers in media analysis.

While the uses of S.I.C. figures are almost limitless in marketing and advertising—such as coding consumer lists, laying out sales territories, projecting samples—two of their special values to the advertiser-marketer are

(1) helping determine which industries should be cultivated with special vigor because of the high sales potential, and

(2) helping select business publications for advertising schedules.

In the first case, an industrial marketer is helped greatly if he or she knows, for example, that 85 percent of inquiries resulting from an advertisement came from plants in S.I.C. 3555, printing trades machinery. Then again, if marketing information is needed, a mail questionnaire can be precoded by four-digit S.I.C. numbers before mailing. Returns will then enable the industrial marketer to classify products precisely.

As for the second case (selection of business publications) the circulation broken down by S.I.C. and by the number of executives reached in each classification, gives the advertiser-marketer precise information on which to base media selection.

USING RESEARCH FOR MARKET SEGMENTATION

During the mid-1960's, sophisticated marketers and advertisers became increasingly restive with just numbers of people. Advertisers needed better and more precise information about the consumers who bought everything from typewriters and textbooks to dentifrices, bar soaps, and breath mints. Advertisers know that some consumers buy and use products frequently, some occasionally, and some not at all. Because this information is developed within traditional demographic classifications, the advertiser first thinks of heavy, light or product nonusers in terms of age, sex, income, and other such variables. These are market segments. Segments also may be defined geographically or by social class or in any way other which enables the advertiser to learn more about consumers.

Consumer Segment

The advertiser is following the consumer because it is the consumer who segments the advertiser's market. The logical thing for the advertiser to do is direct marketing and advertising programs to reach those consumers who are frequent product buyers and users. The advertiser adopts a policy of segmenting the market, coordinating product, packaging, distribution, pricing policies, and advertising targeted at certain groups or subgroups of consumers.

Hand-held calculators, for example, may be advertised to many market segments. There is a general business segment, a small and retail business segment. Financial institutions may be yet another segment, as are accountants and engineers. There are college and high school and even grade school market segments. Each segment requires different channels of distribution. Each will require different advertising media with different advertising appeals designed to present situations in which the calculator can be used.

Media Segment

Beyond segmenting by demographics, advertisers may segment markets by interest groups for athletics, hobbies, or home improvement. The proliferation of special appeal or interest magazines show the diversity of segments available. In addition, general appeal magazines, once almost exclusively national in scope, now offer a variety of geographic breakdowns, including regional, city, and suburban. editions. Geographically this is desirable; demographically, however, national magazines still left advertisers dissatisfied.

Time magazine has pioneered demographic segmentation with special editions for doctors, educators, and students. Other magazines began to offer demographic segments within their subscription lists. A number of magazines now offer high-income subscribers, sometimes tied to census data and zip codes, to help advertisers assess marketing areas more accurately. Even farm advertisers can benefit from the zip code selectivity offered in the *Farm Journal* magazine. Business publications may offer selectivity by job title.

Such procedures allow advertisers to segment markets and media. Where once magazine advertisers depended upon editorial character to roughly select their markets, they can now, with the help of magazine circulation figures, control the destination of their advertising with much more precision. By obtaining material from census tracts and feeding it to computers, there is almost no limit to the selectivity now possible to magazines. A marketer can, for example, back up direct mail and sampling operations with media advertising in the same postal zones.

In addition to increased demographic selectivity, geographic selectivity is greatly enhanced, too. In the past, for instance, regional editions of magazines were based upon county breakdowns. While this in itself was a significant advance, the county breakdown was often unsatisfactory since many counties were physically very large and frequently contained diverse populations. Since, however, there are but 3,000 counties and 40,000 zip codes, magazine advertisers can now pinpoint their markets in a way never dreamed possible a few years ago. An almost certain result of this greater marketing precision will be a closer coordination of promotion and sales activities with advertising. Using a magazine's zip code numbers with a mail follow-up, the marketer can run giveaways, sweepstakes, coupons, and samples in the exact area in which a company is advertising.

With increased segmentation, it is possible likewise for the market researcher to investigate markets with much more assurance since samples can be

Product differentiation advertising.

Strong emphasis is placed on the qualities of the advertised product that make it different from (and superior to) competing brands. Although a well-known star presents the commercial there is no chance that the audience will not be aware of the product advertised. The product name is registered in 13 out of the 15 frames and the product points of low cost, strength and size are made strongly.

LEE KING & PARTNERS, INC.

As-filmed Photoboard:	*Client:* Mobil Chemical Company	*Film No.:* MBHB6183
Date: November	*Product:* Hefty Super Weight Trash Bags	*Film Title:* "Battle Stations"
Producer: Haboush		*Film Length:* :30

1. (Sfx: thud!)...

2. ...

3. WINTERS: Say...what are you doing up there?

4. ASST: I'm testing these trash bags...

5. ...for strength! (Sfx: thud!)

6. WINTERS: This is a Hefty Super Weight Trash Bag! It's 33% thicker,...

7. ...so it'll hold 50 pounds of nasty gar-bahj! (Sfx: thud!)

8. The man's a public menace!

9. (Sfx: thud!)

10. Hefty Super Weight Bags are super strong...

11. ...yet they cost less...

12. ...(Sfx: thud!)...than the other heavyweights!

13. (Sfx: thud!)

14. You'll be seeing a lot of this Hefty Super Weight.

15. But this is his last appearance!!

more tightly controlled and the universe more definable. It is a demonstrable fact, for instance, that people of similar interests tend to cluster. Influenced by their environment is their behavior, including their buying habits and attitudes. A market researcher, to supply an example, knowing this cluster tendency finds great help in zip code segmentation that reveals the median family income of a number of Illinois towns in Cook County that were analyzed by studying the families within zip code areas.

TABLE 5-1
Median Family Income of Some Illinois Towns

Zip Code	Post Office	Median Family Income*
60004	Arlington Heights	$15,867
60005	Arlington Heights	15,147
60304	Oak Park	11,185
60035	Oak Park	19,479
60472	Robbins	7,659
60091	Wilmette	20,210

Before the precision of zip code the market researcher doing an analysis of one town in the foregoing example would have had great difficulty in determining the sharp income differences in different sections of the town. When all census data can be assigned to zip code areas, the researcher's work will be made even more precise.

Market segmentation, whether achieved with zip codes or some other means, is the wave of the future in marketing and advertising. Only in isolated cases will marketers promote a "mass" market without regard for its components. As means are found to pinpoint markets precisely—through zip codes, computers, and other devices—the marketer will do research and place media among those market segments most responsive to his or her product or service. This may be an ethnic market, the youth market, the high-income market, the rural market, the low-education market, the blue-collar market, or any one of many markets of peculiar and profitable interest to the advertiser-marketer.

PRODUCT DIFFERENTIATION AND MARKET SEGMENTATION

If, in the preceding example, the advertiser redesigns or modifies the product with hand-held calculators for each of the targeted markets, the advertiser is using product differentiation to fit the product precisely to the requirements of each market segment. Advertisements designed for each market segment can then show how the product is tailored to user requirements.

If entering the dentifrice market for the first time, however, the advertiser faces a somewhat different problem. Demographic characteristics don't reveal much about which brands of paste people buy and use. In this case, the advertiser may survey consumer attitudes towards dentifrices, at the same time learning what products consumers buy and use. Market segments in this case, may be developed by the reasons people give for using dentifrices.

Crest and Colgate are bought to prevent cavities. Close-Up users want white teeth. Pearl Drops is bought as a polish, particularly good for getting tobacco and tea stains off teeth. Consumers buy Sensodyne to clean their teeth while providing protection for sensitive teeth against discomfort from heat and cold, acid, and sweet foods. Other dentifrices are bought for flavor; one is bought by consumers who want a teeth whitener and mouthwash in one.

Assume, for example, the segment who use the product for decay prevention is the largest. The advertiser may attempt to segment this market by a more selective decay prevention appeal. That is what the makers of Aim toothpaste did, developing a product that releases fluoride quickly for children who brush in less than half a minute. Aim is a differentiated product, segmenting an existing market segment by a very specific advertising appeal and benefit that emphasizes product difference.

Sometimes markets quite literally go up for grabs as when, for example, a genuinely new product or process is introduced. The almost instant film prints developed by Polaroid revolutionized photography. The new process of capturing the gas that makes soft drinks fizz in crystals and powders, if sold for home use, will revolutionize the soft drink industry, with serious effects on the bottling and can manufacturers.

Currently, the automobile market is undergoing rapid change. Congress has intervened in America's love (some say love/hate) affair with the automobile. Congress has required manufacturers to make automobiles that get progressively higher gas mileage. Cars are being "downsized" to meet the new and progressively more stringent fuel consumption standards. The traditional product categories of large (Cadillac), standard (Ford LTD), intermediate (Olds Cutlass), compact (Duster), and subcompact (Chevette) will change to describe new automobiles that do not fit the existing categories.

New market segments will emerge and be identified by automobile manufacturers who will then attempt to differentiate their products by designing automobiles to appeal to the emerging new segments.

PRODUCT POSITIONING

Whether based on experience, creative intuition, attitude, or other research, today's advertisers use the military language of strategy and tactics to *position* a product. Positioning is a new and natural outgrowth of market segmentation and product differentiation. Positioning results from assessing the attitudes or reactions of consumers to existing products in a category, for example, popularly priced shampoos for women or sinus-relief products for all adults. Knowledge of consumer reactions to existing products, their associations, and use of these products, can reveal genuine unfilled consumer wants.

The more completely consumer attitudes and reactions are understood, the better the advertiser is able to develop a new or improved product and express the benefit in terms of unfilled wants. The advertising is designed to express the benefits in a basic claim or promise. Dove was first introduced in 1957 as a complexion bar for women with dry skin. Today, many years later, Dove is packaged and advertised as it was when first introduced. The advertisements express the same benefit, and every broadcast commercial uses the cleansing cream demonstration. Another bar soap, Dial, has occupied the same "position" since the product was introduced. The same benefit is advertised year after year. ("She uses Dial. Don't you wish everyone did?")

Positioning, then, means assessing a potential market demand for an unfilled want or desire. The advertiser aligns price, product characteristics, packaging, type of outlet used, and advertising benefit expressed so that the consumer thinks of the product in a certain way. Every advertisement in the campaign for a successfully positioned product carries a distinctive tone and style to support the specific benefit.

Both quantitative and qualitative research is used in positioning products. Quantitative research, such as national surveys, may reveal changing consumer attitudes toward a product or category of products. Women, for example, in growing numbers wanted personal enhancement products such as shampoos with fewer sophisticated chemicals and more natural ingredients.

Shampoos named Earthborn and Sunshine Harvest and several with the name Herbal in the product name won quick consumer acceptance. Shampoo advertising began to stress natural product ingredients rather than miracle ingredients. Qualitative research done with individual or small groups of consumers in informal settings may reveal in the consumers' own words the reasons for changing brands of shampoos or the types of appeals that will get consumer attention in the future. New products supported by new advertising appeals are developed and presented to consumers.

QUESTIONS

1. Distinguish between market segmentation and product differentiation.

2. Why is product positioning a natural outgrowth of market segmentation and product differentiation?

3. What obvious changes are taking place in the U.S. population by age, income, occupation, and other categories that influence the market for products?

4. Why do some advertisers study the rate of family formation (marriage)?

5. Why are advertisers interested in consumer values?

6. How might you go about determining whether the value of a newspaper coupon should be 5¢ or 10¢ for a new bar soap you are introducing to consumers?

7. Advertisers constantly ask themselves why consumers buy the products they do. Choose a product. Now give as many reasons as you can think of why consumers might buy the product.

8. Why do industrial marketers and advertisers find the Standard Industrial Classification Code an invaluable information source?

9. Advertisers are interested in media that serve definable market segments. How do magazines segment markets?

10. Why do marketing and advertising people strive to differentiate their products from competitive products?

11. What information sources can you use to learn about the nature or size of markets for consumer products?

12. What is secondary data? What problems are associated with using secondary data?

13. Assume that you are responsible for advertising a new hand lotion. What information would you want?

14. Can you segment a market by the appeal used in advertising? Give several examples.

15. How would you contact consumers if you needed survey answers quickly?

16. More and more mothers of young children are returning to work. Do these young women differ in what they are likely to look for in products compared with mothers who stay at home with their children? Explain.

17. When advertisers assess the value of survey research, what two characteristics do they look for in a sample? Why?

18. Discuss the advantages and disadvantages of the three ways in which survey respondents are contacted and questioned.

19. Why is information from consumer panels particularly useful to advertisers?

REFERENCES

1. "Last Minute News," Advertising Age, April 20, 1977, p. 105.
2. Conclusions or recommendations should often be put at the beginning of the report in order to save the time of busy executives reading the report. The remainder of the material in the report is then offered as supporting evidence for the conclusions.

6

ADVERTISING RESEARCH: MESSAGES

ADVERTISING RESEARCH: MESSAGES

When F. G. Mortensen, head of a giant industry of some years ago, called in his marketing manager, Tom Fisher, to report on the effect of a new advertising campaign, he was content if Fisher answered: "Sales are up 20 percent over last year, F. G." Similar sentiment was expressed in other industries if sales were up, seemingly a result of advertising, whether that industry was retail, manufacturing, bookselling or service, such as hotels, ski centers, or travel agencies.

ADVERTISING USES THE SOCIAL AND BEHAVIORAL SCIENCES

For years advertisers operated almost on blind faith, knowing that when they advertised, something usually happened. Consumers bought the advertised products. If sales rose, advertisers were relatively content, because sales provided the final measure for advertising effectiveness. Then, as now, the primary question advertisers asked was, "What effect does my advertising have on sales?"

Early descriptions of advertising effectiveness were expressed primarily in economic terms. Money was spent on advertisements to reach consumers. The consumers were regarded as economic entities, digits, or statistics which bought so many units. Consumer purchases could be totaled, given percentage values, and classified neatly by economists and by marketing managers and others engaged in the selling of goods.

Why Consumers Buy

The narrow and relatively simple view of consumer buying used by early economists and marketing people is long past. Such a view was never fully satisfying to those who made advertisements. Too often consumer buying defied prediction. Even if early advertising effectiveness was gauged solely in terms of economic or sales effectiveness, the advertisements themselves reflected an awareness by early advertisers that consumers buy for reasons other than economic reasons. Consumers buy for intensely personal gratification and for emotional as well as physiological reasons; they buy to conform to groups to which they belong, or aspire, or project roles.

Many buying motives or reasons do not fit within the traditional economic assumption of rational buying behavior. Economists formerly dismissed such reasons out of hand, often referring to them as irrational. Often noneconomic reasons or motivations are not irrational. If the economist dismisses such reasons, the advertiser cannot, because the advertiser does not deal with a theoretic model but with actual buying behavior of millions of consumers.

Advertisers have turned increasingly from economics to other academic disciplines that study human behavior in attempts to understand what motivates or influences consumers to buy the way they do. In fact, advertising put social and behavioral science ideas and research to work in more ways and more quickly than any other type of business activity.

In a previous chapter you saw how advertising makes use of demographics, a specialty in sociology, that describes the stability or change in populations according to a variety of classifications. People of differing ages, sex, income, and other characteristics represent markets. Demographic breakdowns are widely used to describe markets, their size, and their character.

Using demographic information, the advertiser locates and estimates the size of potential markets. Media describe their audiences by demographic characteristics.

Advertisers use other ideas and research methods from anthropology, social psychology, and psychology, as well as sociology, and any other academic specialties which study human behavior, individual or in groups, to develop persuasive advertising messages and to locate potential consumers within media audiences.

Buying Behavior and Social and Behavioral Science Ideas

Advertisers borrow from social and behavioral sciences to solve specific problems or develop reasonable explanations of buying behavior. The ideas may be tested with advertising that appeals to a motive underlying buying behavior. Testing often is done in medium-sized markets. The advertiser may test the number of advertisements required in such a market to achieve a certain level of product awareness. In so doing, the advertiser is simultaneously testing perceptual theories from psychology. If the product is advertised for use by families, the advertiser may test for how quickly consumers perceive and learn the desired association. Psychologists call this conditioned learning. If the desired association is not accepted by one market segment, perhaps an ethnic segment, the advertiser may seek an explanation from the ideas examined by cultural anthropologists. Italo-American neighborhoods, for example, traditionally shun frozen fruits and vegetables.

There is another reason advertisers study and use ideas from social and behavioral sciences. Because advertising is a business of ideas, the people in advertising are always eager to examine new ideas from any source. When ideas provide insight into or possible explanations of buyer behavior, the ideas are studied closely. If promising, the ideas may be tested in one or two markets.

Additionally, advertisers never rest with a single explanation of buyer behavior. Markets change, consumers change, and reasons for purchasing a product change. New and refined theories of behavior are constantly offered in the social and behavioral sciences. Advertisers are always curious to see whether these new theories fit the way consumers perceive and buy and use products.

Human Motivation

The rapid growth in the use of social and behavioral theories has given rise to a number of popular misconceptions about consumer motivation. Dr. Steuart Henderson Britt, a psychologist and advertising researcher, has indicated a number of inaccurate assumptions:

(1) Motivation can be divided neatly into rational and emotional categories.
(2) Consumer motivation tends to be on one level only.
(3) Consumer motivation is relatively static.
(4) Most motivation is based on conscious decisions.
(5) By just asking questions and getting answers, adequate information can be obtained from consumers.[1]

Dr. Britt denies the foregoing assumptions, however, by saying that behavioral scientists have demonstrated that:

(1) There is no such thing as a universal set of explanatory motives.
(2) There are many different levels of motivation.
(3) Consumer decisions are relatively changeable.
(4) Consumer decisions are based on both unconscious as well as conscious factors.
(5) Useful information from consumers needs to go far beyond mere question-and-answer procedures.[1]

Perhaps at one point in the American culture it was possible with some certainty to designate people tidily as "typical," and describe buying behavior by using one or two simple theories. Today, however, consumers are regarded as complex and varied. No one who has studied consumer buying talks glibly of a "typical" consumer, for not only is it difficult to classify consumers in ways meaningful to an advertiser, it is even more difficult to assess what motivates consumers to buy.

Fitting Social and Behavioral Science Ideas to Advertising

Aspiration group theories may explain the motivation of high school seniors thinking ahead to attending college. The seniors begin to buy clothes to dress and behave as though already graduated from high school. College seniors study magazine clothing advertisements as they prepare to interview for jobs. Child development specialists know that a nine- or ten-year old child is looked up to by seven-year olds. This is why children used in commercials tend to be slightly older than the children for whom the toys are designed.

The advertising for many products designed to make a person believe they are physically or sexually attractive to others is frequently discussed in Freudian terms. Why? Because the ideas and language of Freud and his followers best explain the response of consumers to advertisements using words and symbols widely understood as Freudian. You see these appeals in advertisements for personal enhancement products such as after-shaves colognes, perfumes, and intimate apparel.

Because consumers are constantly growing and changing and subject to changing influences, several professional advertising research organizations now regularly conduct studies on a nationwide basis. The studies chart the changing values of large groups of Americans. Advertisers can learn the relative importance of work and leisure, and shifts in the importance of saving or education by social class. Such studies provide broad explanations of shifts in consumer buying.

The broad changes influence the ways in which consumers perceive products. If savings are unimportant, consumers buy more products on credit. If leisure is increasingly important, the family spends more for camping or fishing. Rather than living close to work, the family may choose a more restful rural setting with an old farmhouse and several acres.

Value shifts influence the way consumers compartmentalize their lives by work, family, and play, or by time of day, season, or year. Changes in values may come about slowly, at first unconscious or unexpressed. A woman whose children are in school may at first feel uneasy, then realize she wants to finish her own education or wants a job that satisfies her own deferred creative interests in interior decorating. When she returns to work, this woman views herself and her family differently. She dresses differently and cares for the home differently, with an emphasis on convenience foods and low-maintenance household items. An automatic dishwasher may, in her eyes, become a necessity.

Tapping the proper consumer motive is awkward enough in a period of rapid social change. Compounding the advertiser's problem, many products are bought for reasons about which even the consumer is unaware. The projective techniques of the clinical psychologist can give the advertiser a clearer interpretation of meaning of such products to consumers. An automobile may be a way of keeping up with the neighbors or it may be purchased to realize a strong drive for mastery. A person may learn to play tennis supposedly for exercise but really for making social contacts.

ADVERTISING USES ANTHROPOLOGY

Anthropology provides the advertiser with the broadest overview of human behavior, providing an umbrella over the social sciences and the humanities and over the physical and biological sciences.

The synthesizing idea of culture is used to integrate this broadly-based study of behavior. Culture refers to the ways of living developed by a group of human beings and transmitted from one generation to another. The culture of a people includes all forms of social behavior and the values attached to these forms. Culture also includes all products made and used or adopted by a people, a fact of central importance to the advertiser.

We realize the richness of cultural diversity when comparing our own culture with that of others. During the early stages of World War II in the Pacific, numerous isolated tribes, seeing airplanes for the first time, referred to them as birds. An American baseball bat to New Guinea aborigines was a weapon. Today, the differences are more subtle but influential. People in arid Middle East countries refuse to use refrigerators because daily shopping at the market is a time for visiting with friends and neighbors.

Anthropologically, much everyday behavior is prescribed by cultural norms, defined as a standard way of acting and behaving socially. Sometimes norms find expression in law. For the most part, however, norms are not so formal. In fact, the advertiser sometimes has problems defining norms because they are ambiguous or unclear.

Even so, the advertiser knows that products must fit existing norms in a given society. For example, buying life insurance in America is an accepted way of protecting one's family. In Moslem countries, insurance is regarded as a form of gambling contrary to basic religious ideas. Such differences in viewpoint account for the growing use of anthropology by advertisers.

Perhaps casually used by American advertisers for domestic products, the ideas and cultural differences between societies become critical information for the international advertiser.

There are several ways in which the knowledge of the anthropologist is important to advertisers: viewing markets as subcultures, identifying cultural themes, and sensitivity to taboos.

Markets As Subcultures

The knowledge of the anthropologist is used by advertisers who wish to address subcultures, and America today has many subcultures. Traditionally, subcultures are associated with age, race, religion, and national origin. The late 1960's and early 1970's saw the development of a counterculture and conscious attempts to establish subcultures with values and norms quite different from those prevailing with the majority of Americans.

A subculture refers to a manner of behaving that is peculiar to a group that is a part of some larger group. A subculture shares much of the culture with the majority but also has distinctive values and roles of its own. Almost any group may be defined as a subculture, from teenagers to senior citizens, from black middle-class Americans to Southern Baptists.

Media often serve specific subcultures, and the staff of these publications and broadcast stations can advise the advertiser how best to develop advertisements for these markets. Anthropologists who specialize in one or another subculture can also offer advice and insights. The Spanish-language market in New York City, for example, buys food in distinctive ways. This market consumes huge amounts of rice per capita, tends to make heavy use of canned milk and requires special blends of coffee. Traditionally, Puerto-Rican Americans insist on fresh fruits and vegetables and, in general, shop at small neighborhood stores owned by other Spanish-speaking people.

Whether for the growing senior citizen market, a religious market, or an ethnic market, the insights of the anthropologist are particularly important to advertisers. Today more than ever before, markets which may be defined as subcultures are increasingly sensitive to any form of communication addressed to them that might contain a distasteful stereotype or an unintentional insult. The advertiser must understand as fully as possible the attitudes, values, and goals of the subcultures to which advertisements are directed.

If you doubt this, just ask several women what they most dislike in advertisements. You'll most likely hear a catalog of stereotypes women believe demeaning. The problem for advertisers is that many women are intentionally examining their values, attitudes, and goals. Today, women are consciously choosing a subculture. Some are traditional, involving wanting to stay home with young children. Others might be called transitional. These women, through necessity or desire, elect not to have children or return to work quickly if they do. The paychecks are welcome, perhaps even necessary to their family. A third group might be called moderns. These women, if married, regard their careers as being as important to them as careers are to their husbands.

Rather than one fairly broad subculture of women, today advertisers are dealing with at least three subcultures, each of which examines advertisements with a heightened sensitivity to real or imagined slurs or put downs.

Identifying Cultural Themes

Advertising constantly expresses cultural themes that are widely understood. Youthfulness, or the appearance of youthfulness, in thought and action, is a central American cultural theme. Many advertisements stress youthfulness.

The American culture also influences the development of personalities to conform to central cultural themes. For example, in America aggressiveness is an approved male personality trait, a fact often reflected in advertisements. Americans value openness and offer friendship quickly, a characteristic that many foreigners regard as shallow.

In America almost any type of physical activity is regarded positively; in other cultures, quiet reflection by oneself may be equally, if not more highly, regarded.

Sensitivity to Taboos

International advertisers now closely study the cultural, religious and political environment in countries in which they advertise so as not to violate unwritten or written norms and to avoid associating a product with certain symbols.

Colors have cultural definitions. Blue, for example, is the color for mourning in Iran and is not likely to be favorably received on a commercial product. Green is the nationalist color of Egypt and Syria and is frowned on for use in packages.

Showing pairs of anything on the Gold Coast of Africa is disapproved. White is the color of mourning in Japan and, therefore, is not likely to be popular on a product. Brown and gray are disapproved colors in Nicaragua. Purple is generally disapproved in most Latin America markets because of its association with death. Feet are regarded as despicable in Thailand, where any object and package showing feet is likely to be unfavorably received.

The anthropologist can cast light on taboos and on their opposite: favored colors and symbols.

For a valuable and interesting discussion of the pitfalls that can be avoided in international marketing by learning the behavior patterns of each culture, it is almost imperative to read *The Silent Language* by Edward T. Hall. Derived from years of anthropological study, the book points out that with all goodwill and good intentions, the American is often prone in international business to blunder because of lack of knowledge of local customs and to find that the behavioral patterns of citizens of foreign countries continually hamper and complicate efforts to conduct business dealings in those countries.

Without a deep insight gained from anthropological analysis, the American business person simply is not aware of, or cannot understand fully, the behavior patterns of citizens of other countries, patterns they take for granted but which are so often violated almost the very minute business relations begin. In fact, a manner of greeting may get the business deal off to a disastrous start from which it never recovers.

There are a myriad of ways in which the cultural factors come into collision with the "American way" of doing business. The American is likely to be too impatient, too anxious to conduct business dealings quickly, but soon discovers foreign counterparts are unlikely to share the American devotion to schedules and timetables.

In advertising especially, a marketer from the United States must be diligent to avoid causing insult, resentment, ridicule, or some other unwanted reaction. This caution is valid whether we are talking about *how* advertising is presented, or *how much* is used. On the latter point, for instance, a Spanish marketer attending an American graduate school of business, pointed out that in Spain, contrary to the United States, the advertiser who uses a large amount of advertising is likely to be viewed with some suspicion, whereas in this country the large advertiser creates confidence in goods simply because people *do see* so much advertising backing. The Spanish marketer, in contrast, asserted that in Spain the use of heavy advertising was viewed as a cover-up for the inadequacy of the product; that if the product was truly good, it would not be necessary to advertise it so much.

Cross-cultural differences are important to understand when making advertisements. It is not unusual in America to present the head of a major corporation working with his hands at a hobby such as refinishing antiques or gardening. To do so in some Spanish-language cultures would be unacceptable. People of importance or high status do not work with their hands. Or take the placement of models in advertising: illustrations in some Spanish-language cultures will differ from those used in America because the two major cultures have different definitions of social space, with Americans tending to stand further apart when they converse.

Advertisements portraying friendship in America are scrutinized before being translated for international audiences. Friendship in America is casual. In many foreign countries friendship means a lifelong commitment, often with significant mutual obligations.

Television commercial reporting results of product testing.

Product research goes arem in arm with market research. In this instance, the company's product testing result provided a good advertising opportunity.

KENYON & ECKHARDT INC. 200 PARK AVE.. NEW YORK 17, N. Y.

CLIENT _____ MOTORCRAFT _____   JOB NO. ___ FMMA 7357 _____   TIME __ 30 SECONDS

PRODUCT ____ SHOCK ABSORBERS ____   TITLE ____ "SHOCK ABSORBERS" ____   DATE __ 2/3/77

1. (SFX: WIND) LOWELL THOMAS: (VO) Hello, everybody.

2. Alaska. A tough place to test shock absorbers.

3. That's why we took Motorcraft Shocks to Alaska,

4. testing them in fifty GM, Chrysler

5. and Ford cars and trucks.

6. After six months of driving over

7. (SFX: DOGS) the jarring rough roads of Alaskan pipeline country,

8. only three shocks couldn't take the punishment.

9. This is Lowell Thomas reminding you,

10. no matter what you drive, wherever you drive,

11. ask for Motorcraft Shock Absorbers from Ford.

12. Tested tough in Alaska. So long.

Even when cultures appear similar, advertisements may not work well in both. British humor is quite different from American humor, as are many British values. An American manufacturer's attempt to market a biscuit for the traditional British afternoon tea failed, perhaps because the product resembled and tasted more like an American cookie than the dry and relatively tasteless (to Americans) British biscuit.

ADVERTISING USES SOCIOLOGY

Advertising practitioners have long been aware of the contributions of sociology to advertising and marketing. Sociology is the study of human behavior in groups and in social settings. The sociologist studies group-influenced behavior to make generalizations about social interaction and behavior. Since the advertiser wants to reach large groups of people, it is easy to see why the sociologist has much to offer the advertiser.

In addition to demographic studies already mentioned, the sociologist studies social classes, which to the advertiser is a useful way of explaining certain types of buying behavior.

Social Class Theory

Thousands of studies have been made on the implications stemming from the social class structure. While there are innumerable facets to such studies, the marketer wants to know how the class structure affects the buying of goods and services, how the status factor identified with each class will affect an advertising and marketing approach, what attitudes might be expected from each class toward the goods or services offered, and even the way the goods are sold or advertised. A complete knowledge of the motives that cause people to react to a selling stimulus is hardly possible until one can place the consumer in the appropriate social class.

While many sociologists have provided lists of social classes ranging from five to as many as eleven the most enduring of these lists has been that of Lloyd Warner and Paul Lunt who provided a six-class system that has been widely referred to since introduced in 1941.[2] This consists of the following classes:

Upper-upper.	Old families, conscious of their family reputation. Possesing inherited wealth. Would be called "aristocrats" in Europe.
Lower-upper.	A wealthy class that has come into its money recently but is still striving for the acceptance that belongs automatically to the upper-upper class. Includes successful business people and people in the professions.
Upper-middle.	Successful but at a lower level of success than the lower-upper. Composition once again is largely successful business people and professionals. Mostly college educated and "on the make" as they aim at higher status.
Lower-middle.	Although largely white-collar salaried class, also includes owners of small businesses and, in recent years, better-paid blue-collar workers. This group

	has been characterized as the strivers and the respectables. Ambitious for college education for their children.
Upper-lower.	Semiskilled workers. Almost no college education for this class and no worry about being strivers or respectables. Little push for upward mobility. Live for day-to-day enjoyment.
Lower-lower.	Unskilled workers or chronic unemployables, or seasonally employed. Lacking in goals and with little hope for the future.

The marketer, of course, if interested in a mass market, focuses on the lower-middle and upper-lower classes since approximately 70 to 80 percent of the United States population falls in these classes.

Whether the Warner "list" or some other list of social classes is used, it must be recognized that no list is absolute. There are crossings-over and there are always those in a lower level who have higher-level tastes. Then, too, it is found that in the case of certain products the social class will have little influence, even though the money outlay required would seem to assign such products to a higher social class.

Air conditioners in hot parts of the country, medium-priced automobiles, AM radio sets, television sets, most food products, and many other common products are not advertised with an eye on the social-class breakdown. Many others, in contrast, have a social-class orientation. The likelihood of going to college is associated with social class. The way in which people take vacations—where they go and what they do—often fits within one social class or another. Clothing is associated with social class as is the buying of insurance.

Once the advertiser understands the characteristics of a particular social class and makes an estimate of the size of this class, advertising appeals can become sharply targeted to the values associated with each class and media selected that are attractive to that class.

"Trickle Down" Theory

While the subject of some dispute, the "trickle down" theory has been used for years by social scientists and advertising and marketing people. The basic idea is that many types of goods, especially fashion items, are bought first by style or taste leaders and then "trickle" down from one socio-economic level or social class to another. For fashion items, for instance, what finally evolves is less expensive, mass-produced copies. Women's fashion clothing is most often used as an example, in part because it is relatively easy to watch such fashions become widely adopted and because clothing has obvious status and general symbolic values.

Many advertisers believe in the "trickle down" theory, and consciously attempt to position a product to appeal to fashion or style leaders, with the understanding that other consumers will emulate such leaders. Buying emulation may be horizontal within a socio-economic group or social class as well as vertical, moving from one income or social class to the next lower class. A strategy positioning a fine-grade laundry soap, used for washing delicate clothing, built an exclusive image around its product in the belief that eventually a buying impetus would trickle down from the upper class users to those in other classes. The company placed its advertising in status magazines and eventually attained a greater sales volume than the competitor that cultivated the mass market and neglected what might be called the "leader" market.

Products may lose a carefully chosen status position once widely adopted. Venetian blinds originally were associated with upper class or high status home furnishings, but quickly lost that position in the minds of consumers after "trickling" downward.

Automobiles have long been associated with status and the "trickle down" theory. At first automobiles were the possessions of the very wealthy. Eventually, as ownership became commonplace, only the possession of certain automobiles conveyed status. Eventually, high status automobiles such as the Cadillac and Lincoln were bought by consumers who stretched their budgets or attempted to achieve and project status by buying second-hand Cadillacs. Even Cadillac, once the unquestioned leading status automobile, is slipping in the eyes of many who buy Mercedes automobiles instead.

There is some denial of the "trickle down" theory in the very field in which it has always been considered most valid—the fashion clothing world. The speed with which styles are conveyed to the consumer through modern communications and the speed with which the garment industry can reproduce Paris fashions—overnight in some cases—bring the leisurely paced "trickle down" theory into question.

Diffusion of Innovation Theory

As the "trickle down" theory loses some of its usefulness, advertisers are inclined to use a newer and closely related theory called Diffusion of Innovation. Diffusion theory attempts to explain the process by which consumers accept or reject an idea or product. The process of deciding to buy and try a product is called the *adoption process*. The usefulness of the adoption process to advertisers is that the process parallels the mental steps through which an individual passes from first perception of a new product to buying and using the product.

The adoption process posits that a consumer must

(1)   be made aware of the product and benefit and
(2)   be made interested in the benefit,
(3)   be inclined to evaluate (or think about) the product,
(4)   be willing to try the product, and finally
(5)   buy and use the product over time.

Impersonal information sources, including advertising, are important for developing awareness and generating interest. Personal influence becomes important at the evaluative stage, where people often discuss future purchases with friends or people they believe knowledgeable about the type of product.

Advertisers, knowing that they cannot personally contact all prospects for a product, may simulate personal influence in advertisements. In the advertisements a typical consumer discusses the advantages of the advertiser's product with someone regarded as an authority. This was the reason for the now-forbidden use of actors portraying doctors in television and print advertisements.

Diffusion theory is attractive to advertisers because the academic research behind the theory documents the type of findings that fit the advertiser's experience. Diffusion theory suggests that a new product that is obviously superior to existing products will be adopted more rapidly. Most advertisers have experienced this with superior products.

Diffusion theory is useful to advertisers also because the theory focuses on those people in a society who quickly try and adopt new products. These people are called "innovators" by advertisers who make every attempt to identify such people. Some studies identify these people as venturesome. Whatever term is applied, many advertisers believe these people serve as opinion leaders who influence the evaluative activities of more conservative consumers.

Because diffusion theory parallels the series of mental steps through which the consumer passes to arrive at a buying decision, the theory provides the advertiser with an organized way to investigate the progress of advertising for a new product.

Advertisers first survey to learn the number of consumers who are aware of the advertised product and the benefits associated with the product. Advertisers then try to learn whether consumers are interested in the product benefit. Advertisers may then ask for consumer evaluations of the new product, including whether the advertised claim is believed. Then advertisers may survey to learn whether consumers have tried the new product, and if so with what reactions. The final steps, adoption and repeat purchase of the product, can lead to long-term sales and brand loyalty for a product with genuine consumer benefits.

Reference-Group Theory

Because sociology deals with the interaction of people in groups, it is natural that sociologists study the ways in which reference groups influence behavior, including buying behavior. A reference group, simply expressed, is a group referred to by an individual as a sort of frame of reference. An individual's self-definition often expresses membership in a variety of groups. Thinking is done in terms of group norms; groups constantly monitor verbal and other behavior against group norms, especially those groups in which an individual is considered a member.

Reference-Group Concepts.   Closely allied to the social class concepts is reference-group analysis. A reference group, simply expressed, is a group referred to by an individual as a sort of frame of reference. Thinking and actions are related to the group. Most important are the groups in which the person takes part directly. These are sometimes called membership groups.

Under the reference-group concept we assume that a person's behavior is shaped in different ways and to different degrees by other people. In decision-making the individual tends to weigh what some other person of a certain group would do under the same circumstances. Sociological research (and ultimately marketing research) has been concerned with the difficult task of determining which kinds of groups are likely to be referred to by which kinds of individuals,

Advertisement for the ultimate status symbol.

There might be some "trickling down" for other expensive automobiles but very little for the Rolls Royce the cost of which precludes it being bought at lower income levels. It is an upper-upper expenditure.

Rolls-Royce brings back a great name. Silver Wraith II.

The last of the Silver Wraiths was built in 1959. Or so it seemed at the time.

But the richest of Rolls-Royce memories have a way of living on in the newest of Rolls-Royce motor cars. And so it is with the Silver Wraith II of 1977.

The Timeless Pleasure

The long, sleek look of the Silver Wraith II reflects a time gone by.

You can sense it in the graceful lines, the contrasting top, the gleaming bright work, the tasteful craftsmanship and the roomy interior.

And, for the most up-to-date reasons, the Silver Wraith II is a new air of comfort, a new sense of quiet and a new feeling of command.

A new rack-and-pinion steering system makes the Silver Wraith II quick to respond and rewarding to drive, no matter how narrow the road or sudden the curve.

A unique automatic air-conditioning system maintains any temperature you desire at two levels of the interior. And, because the system creates a rarefied atmosphere all your own, its built-in sensors alert you to outside temperatures as well as icy roads.

The Silver Wraith II also offers you the sophistication of an advanced electrical system, the performance of a quiet V-8 engine, the security of a dual braking system and the sensitivity of a self-leveling suspension.

And, to name one of the many other subtle details you'll discover, the electronic odometer will contemplate recording the miles from 000000.0 to 999999.9.

The Priceless Asset

From the distinctive radiator grille to the matching walnut veneers, the Silver Wraith II is built almost entirely by hand.

In tribute to this enduring Rolls-Royce tradition, it is no coincidence that more than half of all the motor cars we have ever built remain very much on the road.

And, in return for the purchase price of $49,000,* it is little wonder that a Silver Wraith II speaks so warmly of the past and so surely of the future.

≪ ≪ ≪

A collection of Rolls-Royce masterpieces is waiting at your nearest Authorized Rolls-Royce Dealership. For further information, call 800-325-6000 and give this ID number: 1000.

*Suggested U.S. Retail Price March 1, 1977. The names "Rolls-Royce" and "Silver Wraith" and the mascot, badge and radiator grille are all Rolls-Royce trademarks.
© Rolls-Royce Motors Inc. 1977.

The heart and soul of a masterpiece

and under which kinds of circumstances. Also to be determined is which decisions will be made under these circumstances. If these various factors can be determined and related, then there is the task of measuring the extent of this reference-group influence.

Likert and Hayes have established several reference groups against which an individual may evaluate personal status and behavior:[3]

(1) They may be membership groups to which a person actually belongs—either face-to-face groups such as families or organizations, whether business, social, or religious.

(2) They may be groups or categories to which a person automatically belongs by virtue of age, sex, education, or marital status. This sort of reference-group relationship involves the concept of *role*. For example, before taking a certain action an individual might consider whether this action would be regarded as appropriate in his role as a man or husband or educated person or older person or some combination of the roles.

(3) They may be anticipatory rather than actual membership groups. Thus, a person who aspires to membership in a group, although not yet a member, may use the group's standards when making a decision. Clothing and housing decisions often reflect such aspirations and are explained in terms of upward mobility.

(4) They may be negative, dissociative reference groups. Thus an individual sometimes avoids a certain action because it is associated with a group from which the person would like to disassociate himself.

In making a marketing application of this reference-group concept, the researcher must determine which products are likely to be bought individualistically and those for which buying is socially conditioned. In the buying of automobiles, for example, the buyer is likely to be influenced by what others do. In beer, too, as between premium or regular, the concept is at work. This was illustrated by a long campaign for a light beer that called itself the "champagne of bottled beer" and which, in contrast to the heavily masculine or strong togetherness themes of the other beers, featured thin, very fashionable women in all its promotion. In short, a popular image was created of one reference group that presumably drank this brand of beer, or this kind of beer. Reference-group slanting was dominant in the marketing approach for Honda motorbikes, the advertising for which showed the young, Honda-riding types another Honda rider was likely to meet if he went out on the road. Reference-group connection was vitally important to make acceptable a vehicle associated in the past with disreputable hoodlums. Marketers of bowling, and later pool-table equipment, likewise were faced with a long-time social disapproval of the people who played these games and the environment in which they were played. Like the motorbike marketers, sellers of bowling and pool-playing equipment found acceptability in a successful application of reference-group theory in their total marketing methods.

Each product must be analyzed to see if purchasing is influenced by reference-group considerations. Sociological methodology is helpful in this analysis. Each subculture in the population, for example, seems to be strongly influenced in the type of clothing it favors whether we consider advertising people, Ivy Leaguers, bankers, or other groups. On the contrary, many products now owned by almost everyone in the population cannot utilize reference-group theory with any significant success. This is true whether we consider types of these products, or brands of these products. Sugar, refrigerators, and television sets serve as illustrations.

The marketer then should use advertising that shows the right people (reference group) using the product but should avoid making the group so narrow that the market is so thin it is unprofitable. That would have been easy to do in the case of Honda, previously mentioned, but fortunately great numbers of young people were emotionally attracted to motorbikes.

Thus, if the product or brand has been correctly assessed insofar as the part played by reference groups in influencing its purchase, how can this help in marketing the product? Here is what one authority has written on the point:[4]

(1) Where neither product nor brand appear to be associated strongly with reference-group influence, advertising should emphasize the product's attributes, intrinsic qualities, price, and advantages over competing products.

(2) Where reference-group influence is operative, the advertiser should stress the kinds of people who buy the product, reinforcing and broadening where possible the existing stereotypes of users. The strategy of the advertiser should involve learning what the stereotypes are and what specific reference groups enter into the picture, in order that appeals can be "tailored" to each main group reached by the different media employed.

The word "stereotypes" used in the foregoing quotation should be explained not only because it is a standard sociological term but also because it is so often put in conjunction with reference groups. Conveniently, but often erroneously, some students of sociology and psychology have divided people neatly into types or "stereotypes" and then just as neatly evolved predictability charts on the basis of the types they are. Stereotypes abound of the "impractical" professor, the "male animal" football player, the "bloodless" accountant, the "prim" librarian, the "glib" advertiser, and the like.

While the concept of stereotypes has been and continues to be useful because people do play their social roles, hardly anyone follows the script faithfully but instead lives up to the role only partly. Thus, people vary within stereotypes as much as they do between stereotypes. As mentioned earlier in this chapter, there is great danger in oversimplifying by referring to people as "typical" and not recognizing the factor of variability within these "typical" people or "stereotypes," whichever terms you are using.

A marketer, guided by the sociologist, will avoid reducing complex individuals into markets of neatly labeled stereotypes when attempting to assess proper approaches for selling and advertising.

Life Style

Life style theory is an outgrowth of both social theory and marketing and advertising theory, and is an attempt to explain the different ways in which consumers spend and save, even when occupying roughly similar life experiences. Several families, for example, may be in the same social class, have roughly comparable incomes, and even live in the same neighborhood but buy in radically different ways. Some may spend a great deal on transportation, while others buy swimming pools or add hobby rooms to their homes. Some save, while others overspend.

Each family or individual has a distinctive outlook on life, and each spends or saves accordingly. A life style is increasingly used by consumers to describe their goals and desires. Life style behavior represents an intentional decision to buy in ways that are not traditional to an income level or social class. Both families and individuals today consciously express and seek new roles in a life style. A growing number of young families elect not to have children in order to maintain a life style.

Roles

Originally, the idea of roles was associated with the idea of playing, suggesting there was something less than serious or fundamental in the fact that we behave in different ways, or adopt different roles, at different times and in different circumstances. In fact, descriptions of role behavior could be dismissed as hypocritical, despite the fact that roles are forced on all of us from a very early age. The scrappy shortstop may be the emotional leader of a little league team, but at a religious service parents expect and demand quiet and reverent behavior from him. Families, friends, and a growing circle of acquaintances all have different expectations of us that require different roles.

Theories that examine the way we develop and mature as individuals with distinctive personalities explain why we assume one role or another. Without thinking, we assume roles. We're one type of person playing tennis and quite another type when interviewing for a job. Advertisers recognize the roles we assume, indeed are required to assume, and present products to help us protect ourselves in desired ways; in short, to play one role or another.

Advertisers cannot avoid using sociological tools and ideas. Markets are described in demographic terms, a working tool of the specialty within sociology called demography. Advertisers depend on surveys—a primary sociological research method—to learn about markets and groups of consumers.

Sociology offers the advertiser a diversity of possible explanations of buying behavior. Advertisements now use the phrase "life style" when urging us to buy an imported sports car or serve a specific liquor. Advertisements offer clothing appropriate for our first visit to Vail or Stowe, so that we may fit the role. Advertisements illustrate furniture appropriate for a social class and inform us that the groups to which we belong will approve of our new bracelets, shoes, belts, or hairstyles.

Advertisers use the steps in the mental process outlined in diffusion theory—awareness, interest, evaluation, trial, and adoption—as a guide to advertising strategy. Each step in the mental process must be accomplished in order. Advertisements must make consumers aware of a product and benefit before the advertisements can make consumers interested. Consumers must be interested enough to evaluate and then try a product. Only then will consumers begin to buy the product regularly.

ADVERTISING USES PSYCHOLOGY

Advertisers look beyond sociology to psychology for additional explanations of behavior leading to buying. While not ignoring group influences, advertisers are interested in studying the behavior of the individual. No attempt will be made to discuss in detail all the divisions of psychology useful to advertisers. Only a few will be considered, with particular stress on perception, attitude, and motivation.

Perception

Defining perception is not easily done in a few words. Briefly, it consists of the very subjective ways in which people perceive their environment. A situation—an advertisement or marketing approach, for example—may look one way to some people and much different to others. Contributing to what an individual perceives are traits, emotions, attitudes, and learning factors. A consumer's behavior in the marketplace is affected significantly by the various ways products and services are perceived.

Perception is shaped strongly by culture. Thus, people of different cultures frequently perceive the same stimuli in different ways. The marketer bringing out a new product, for instance, perceives in it a number of advantages that are seen differently by the consumer, as in the case of a manufacturer of plumber's wrenches (discussed earlier) who gift-wrapped the wrenches hoping to expand the market through advertisements that urged consumers to give them as Christmas gifts. Consumers did not perceive these wrenches as gifts but as utilitarian tools that were too expensive when considered in the light of their infrequent household use.

A number of laboratory techniques and sensitive instruments have been developed primarily to pretest elements in advertisements such as headlines, illustrations, or copy. Sometimes the entire advertisement is, in psychological language, the test stimulus. Some instruments limit exposure to a headline to a second or a fraction of a second to see if the viewer quickly perceives the meaning of the headline from a selected type face or type size. Some eye cameras trace the movement of the eye as it reads the advertisement, to learn what arrests the eye and what the eye skips. Other eye cameras record changes in pupil dilation, an uncontrolled perceiver response which may indicate consumer interest or distaste. When television commercials are pretested, some research organizations will tape electronic sensors to the viewers' wrists to record uncontrolled physiological responses such as skin moisture, or pulse rate. These physiological responses may indicate heightened viewer reaction that the viewer is reluctant to admit or discuss.

Some laboratory devices used by advertisers are adapted from other uses. To check perception of planned outdoor advertisements, the potential consumer may be asked to use a driver-training machine. Planned outdoor advertisements are in the background of the route projected on a screen for the consumer. After a period of simulated driving, the consumer is asked whether any outdoor advertisements were seen and remembered.

When pretesting elements or entire advertisements, the advertiser is testing what a psychologist calls a stimulus or external cue designed to tap and call forth an existing motive within an individual and direct the resulting drive, whether hunger, thirst, or the desire for companionship. Note that the advertisements do not plant a motive within the individual. Motives are already there, a fact some social critics misunderstand.

The advertisements, or elements of advertisements tested are, in the language of psychology, structural factors, or part of the environmental stimuli. They are intended to influence perception. But the selection and presentation of appeals to motives in advertisements deal with only half the equation. Consumer perception is active, not passive. Perception is influenced by the consumer's past experience, present environment, and hopes for the future as well as group factors. These are:

Mental set	A readiness to perceive in a certain way and perhaps to react in a predetermined way to the perception.
Expectation	A tendency to expect that a stimulus situation will exhibit certain characteristics.
Past experience and primacy	A tendency to perceive or interpret new experience on the basis of previous experience; a tendency to organize our perception of later stimulus situations on the basis of initial impressions.
Inner needs	The internal and psychological needs of the individual affect the way the world is perceived.
Role	The role an individual plays in a situation—and his conception of that role—tends to shape perception of the situation.
Status	People of different status may sometimes perceive the same product or company in different ways.
Mood	Our moods affect the way we perceive situations, the elements on which we concentrate, and the elements we ignore, as well as our evaluation of the significance of the situation.
Perceptual constancy	We tend to perceive things in the way we are accustomed to perceiving them, even though the stimulus changes; we thus preserve a relatively stable image of "reality" in a world where things are constantly changing.
Selectivity	We tend to select from a stimulus situation those elements that interest us or are important to us and ignore the rest of the stimuli.
Leveling and sharpening	In remembering things, we tend to simplify them and recall a relatively general and meaningful pattern that is consistent without inner needs by dropping details (leveling) and amplifying or sharpening others.
Cultural and group factors	Attitudes are contagious and they modify our percepts. Group attitudes toward skin color, companies, and products spread through a culture or subculture and influence the way people perceive.

Now, how to *apply* the principles that make up the foregoing list in the everyday world of marketing, advertising, and research. Some of the principles are self-evident to the intelligent, sensitive marketer who recognizes, applies, or is aware of them either consciously or unconsciously. Consider the point of "selectivity" for example. While a ski binding may have a number of admirable qualities that are mentioned in the selling situatioin, the knowledgeable purchaser selects points of interest: A sure release under pressure. Easy to adjust.

A marketer considering "leveling and sharpening" will use this principle in broadcast advertising by insisting that commercials make one idea big or may use the principle to justify an image campaign that eliminates product details in favor of telling prospects that Company A is an admirable organization—therefore, *any* product made by Company A has quality and workmanship.

Attitudes

From the prior list, you will note that attitudes modify what we perceive. Attitudes also influence our evaluation of those stimuli we do perceive. You can reasonably say that we perceive the world around us in terms of our attitudes.

Attitudes are relatively long-lasting organizations of beliefs about an object or situation that predispose us to like or dislike something. To advertisers, attitudes are important because they reveal the reasons behind buying behavior. Attitudes often are sought in survey questionnaires. Advertisers attempt to learn consumer attitudes toward work, play, marriage, child-raising, and a large number of general activities. Advertisers want to learn whether potential new products fit the existing consumer attitudes associated with each activity.

Advertisers closely examine attitudes associated with activities and products because learned attitudes come between a drive and its goal. For example, after a full day's work cleaning out a garage we feel grubby. We have the urge (a drive) to clean up. How we go about cleaning up is influenced by the attitudes we've learned.

Few drives are ever aroused without being accompanied by attitudes that may have a drive value of their own. For example, consumers may quench their thirst with water, hot beverages, or cold soft drinks. We as consumers seldom become thirsty without at the the same time thinking of a learned and preferred way of quenching our thirst. Some people regularly use soft drinks at breakfast; others wouldn't think of doing so.

There is another way in which the study of attitudes is useful to advertisers. Attitudes are visualized as having three components: the cognitive, affective, and conative.

The *cognitive component* refers to the process of perception, including thinking and assessing. The advertiser for a new product develops advertisements in terms of cognition, often emphasizing the package for identification as one of a number of devices to get attention. The copy in such advertisements introduces and explains the product benefits. Advertising research at this stage asks for brand awareness, recognition, and information playback from potential consumers.

The *affective component* includes the emotional reaction to an advertisement. It is this component of attitude that is measured during attitude studies. People express strong likes or dislikes about one product or another. Advertisements designed to change attitudes and feelings may contain competitive appeals, associating a new product with identified consumer likes. Appeals to status frequently are used at this time. Advertisements designed to develop an emotional response may be assessed by research that uses rating scales or measures that associate the product with qualities the consumer believes desirable.

The *conative component* includes the disposition to act or buy. Advertisements designed to impel consumer to buy include price appeals, last chance offers, perhaps testimonials, and the majority of retail advertisements. Research at this point may attempt to measure the consumers' intent to purchase and actual purchase.

Such terms as the three foregoing are not in the working vocabulary of the average advertising man but are useful to the advertising researcher whose long academic training in the social sciences is applied to the analysis of advertising and marketing strategies.

Frames of Reference

A pattern of attitudes toward a product based on past experience is called a *frame of reference*. Understanding consumer frames of reference is critical for the strategic positioning of a product. If the consumers' frame of reference is complete; that is, the consumer has a number of well-established attitudes, the advertiser must make the advertising appeal fit the existing frame of reference. The consumer will reject the appeal otherwise, not because the appeal is false but because the consumer is unwilling to accept the claimed benefit. If consumers don't believe a certain vitamin is an effective ingredient in a deodorant applied to the skin, the advertiser knows the cost of attempting to persuade skeptical consumers would be prohibitive.

Through surveys the advertiser may learn the consumers' frame of reference is incomplete or sketchy. The consumer doesn't know much about a product category. An advertising appeal designed to fit what little the consumer believes and feels may be accepted and acted upon. In fact, this is why the word "new" is such a powerful word in advertising.

When the advertiser attempts to position a product as "new," the advertiser is suggesting that the consumer regard the product through an incomplete frame of reference. The advertiser supplies information to complete the frame. Viewed in this way, advertisers attempt to influence the frame of reference through which consumers view advertisements.

Motivation

Like perception, motivation is not easy to explain. One dictionary definition calls it "an impelling force," and commonly in the business and academic field we apply such words as "drive," and "urges" to explain what is meant by motivation. In the classical tradition, motivation was explained simply as being made up of "needs." Some psychologists have objected to the "needs" concept by saying that if there was nothing more to motivation than the desire for needs-gratification, then this would eliminate behavior not directly aimed at obtaining this result. Still, "needs" is a useful word in the explanation of motivation and will be used here along with other words that help to illuminate this complex subject.

Most simple of the needs are those with physiological foundations, the satisfying of the basic wants for food, warmth. Certainly these basics are considered almost automatically by thousands of marketers whose products are aimed at fulfilling these wants. Where psychological theory can be more useful to the marketer is in isolating and defining the less obvious needs such as: *Social needs*—the need for acceptance by others and for belonging. *Ego needs*—the need for confidence, self-esteem, for status, for recognition, for respect, for admiration, and for self-fulfillment.

While it is possible to make up a list of the drives, forces, and needs that cause a certain behavior in the marketplace, it is extremely difficult to know just which of these factors, single or plural, may be behind the acceptance of a good or service.

Consider, for instance, the popular sport of skiing that has created a huge industry of goods and services. What motivation is behind the almost frightening passion for skiing observed in young and middle-aged people?

It would be difficult for many skiers to articulate the motivation, and others would be unwilling to do so because the *real* reason for taking up skiing is something that would not be admitted. Skiing motivation might be rooted in:

Sense of physical adventure	The thrill of speed and danger.
Ego-building	The dash imparted by attractive ski clothes. The sense that skiing marks one as having flair, as being interesting.
Social acceptance	Skiing is "in." It has talk-value.
Sensory pleasure	In the beauty of the slopes, the sun on the snow, in the ski country itself. In the clean cold, and the rushing of the wind, the sound of the runners over the snow.
Family togetherness	A way to find a common enthusiasm to be shared by mother, father, and the children.
Sex drive	A means of meeting those of the opposite sex who share the same enthusiasms, who are also interesting members of the "in" crowd, and moreover, to meet them under romantic circumstances.
Physical challenge	To courage, to endurance, to muscular development.
Good companionship as in apres ski	Skiing is secondary to the fun after skiing.

Were we to examine the motives behind country club membership, we could find once more a number of reasons that would not be expressed were we to ask direct questions and we would find, as in the case of the skiers, that in most cases *several* motives would impel a person to join a golf club. It should be recognized that when a list of motives is presented to account for the buying of product or service we are, sociologically speaking, really concerned with goals more than the instigating drives or motivations, and that motivations are just one part (albeit an important part) of the determination of behavior.

There is no attempt here to provide a convenient list of motives that drive consumers and that help determine their behavior patterns. Everyone has a different list and many psychologists find themselves unable to agree on a definition of "motivation" or "motive."

Motives frequently are expressed in two lists, one for those having biological or innate origins and one for those motives having sociological or learned origins. Biological motives include hunger, thirst, need for shelter, warmth, and protection. Sociological motives include companionship, welfare of loved ones and curiosity, to mention a few. There is no list that will satisfy all psychologists. For the advertiser, however, it is not so important that there be a correct list or any list at all. It *is* important to try to identify drives and motives, so that advertisements address the real motive impelling someone to action.

MARKET RESEARCH USES PSYCHIATRIC METHODOLOGY

As is evident from the discussion thus far, many of the reasons why consumers act as they do cannot be articulated by the consumers because they themselves are not consciously aware of these reasons, or motives or drives. It has long been apparent that the use of direct questions, while of great value in many situations, is fruitless in digging into the subconscious. Even in the case of many conscious actions, beliefs, or thoughts, the respondent will not answer correctly because of embarrassment, the prestige factor, or some other reason.

Psychology and psychiatry, therefore, have provided methods to obtain information for the marketer that cannot be obtained through direct methods. One of the great difficulties in obtaining usable answers from people is that there is such a gap between what they say, or what they say they think, and their actual behavior. Their avowed reasons for buying products are vastly different in many cases from the real, hidden reasons. A buyer of a high-priced car when asked why a brand was chosen might answer: "Because it's a finely engineered automobile that will give good performance." The real reason might be that this buyer wants to impress neighbors and friends. Unless a respondent is unusually frank, such an answer would never be given an interviewer. How then to get this real reason? The answer is to call upon psychological techniques that ferret out:

(1) real reasons that the respondent is conscious of but would not express to an interviewer;
(2) hidden, subconscious reasons that the respondent is not aware of.

Some of the most-used techniques are depth interviews, word association, pictures and visuals, sentence completion, role playing, and group interviewing.

Depth Interviews

These are long, probing interviews in which the interviewer, skilled in the technique, asks questions, many without any seeming relevance, and lets the respondent talk freely. Such an interview may take two to three hours. It requires patience on the part of the interviewer and respondent alike. It is costly, as any advertiser will testify who has had to pay for 100 to 200 of such interviews. While much skill is required in the interviewing, even more skill is demanded of the psychologist who must interpret the mass of material resulting from the questioning. Many of the answers, of course, have absolutely no value or relevancy and even the significant answers are often hazy and difficult to interpret. Furthermore, since there is often no real system in the depth interview but a sort of "Let's see where this takes us" approach, the task of interpretation is all the more difficult. The statement that there is no "system" does not mean that interviewers have no overall interviewing plan. It does mean, however, that they do not have a neat set of questions from which they do not deviate. It means, too, that if the answer to a question seems to lead to a promising area of exploration, the questions will "take off" in that direction. It becomes obvious that the success of depth interviewing requires skill in

(1) the interviewer in creating rapport with the respondent and in having a feeling for questions that will bring out useful information,

(2) the interpreter in achieving significant meaning out of the mass of replies.

Word Association

This is a seemingly simple test, somewhat like a game youngsters have played for years in which respondents are required to supply the first word that occurs to them for each word in a list of unrelated words. If the word is "ham" the respondent might answer "eggs" or for "automobile" the corresponding word might be "speed."

In addition to analyzing the significance of the replies, the interpreter studies the length of time required for the respondent to respond as well as to determine whether the same response will be given quickly in a second test. The analysis shows how solid the association is between words and measures the respondent's spontaneous emotional reaction in each case. A common use for word association is to check out possible names for a new product, a laborious process. Usually the names under study have been created by the advertising agency and the advertiser. Now, through word-association testing, it is determined what feelings or reactions are aroused. If, for example, the word "cheap" came up a number of times when the advertiser did not want to convey a low-cost impression, the name that elicited such a response will be avoided.

This technique is useful in probing for the respondent's knowledge of current copy claims or advertising campaigns or product knowledge. Likewise, sentence completions can reveal attitudes toward companies, products, and corporate policies. Relatively simple to conduct, the sentence-completion technique like the other psychological techniques described here, requires skill in interpretation. Like the other techniques, sentence-completion testing is used for qualitative research rather than quantitative measurement.

Although the test is very often used directly in connection with specific products and specific situations, the skilled psychologist can adapt the method to more subtle areas. It is especially useful to elicit responses that might be embarrassing to answer through direct questioning. A skillful technician, furthermore, can phrase the test sentences in such a way that neither interviewers nor respondents know the purpose of the study. Thus the method can be as open or as devious as seems desirable.

Role Playing

Used frequently in the testing of advertising copy, role playing in one form consists of showing respondents part or all of an advertisement and asking them to describe the kind of person who would buy the product being advertised. Overfamiliarization with the product creates an unfavorable situation for the test. Likewise, if the illustrations show the kind of people who buy the product, the value of the test diminishes.

One value of the role playing test is to help advertising planners make more certain that advertisements are compatible with the kind of people who are wanted as buyers of a product or service.

Group Interviewing

Such interviewing, often of the "depth" variety and recorded on tape with a hidden microphone, has developed some very interesting information for marketers. In the typical situation, a number of women may be assembled in informal and comfortable circumstances under the guidance of a person who may be called an interviewer, group leader, or moderator. The number of persons in the group may vary but five to eight is a desirable range. More important, the group members should share a common interest in order that they will interact with each other. The moderator typically will introduce some subject for discussion and, if the group members react properly they will "spark" each other in discussing the subject. It is undesirable to have most of the discussion by individual members directed to the moderator.

Subject matter, of course, can be whatever the marketer indicates. It may be reaction to advertising, to a product, to a service. A group discussion of dog food, for instance, indicated that the members felt that their pets were members of the family, that they enjoyed and deserved the kind of food served to family members, that often they were fed milk and eggs in addition to meat. These and many other observations by the group were behind the development of a dog food containing meat, milk and eggs and an advertising campaign with a "people food" stress.

Another group session about retail trading stamps brought out a number of impassioned statements about stamps, including these conclusions: That women felt that all stamps were not alike; that they had different personalities; that stamps made shopping more fun and more adventuresome; that despite the bother of putting stamps in the books the women resented attempts to do away with stamps; that the stamps led to the acquisition of many products that would otherwise not have found their way into the household.

Both group interviews lasted between two and three hours. In each case, there was no interruption in the conversational flow. Women were so eager to talk that the only function of the moderator was to see that everyone had a chance to contribute. Such spontaneity is typical of well-conducted group interviewing on subjects of common interest.

Advantages in group interviewing include:

(1) A frankness and willingness to discuss intimate subjects that is in amazing contrast to the reticence with which the subjects might be discussed in individual interviews.

(2) A volume of ideas and revelations since many of the interviews are somewhat like the celebrated "brainstorming" sessions, in that everyone is encouraged to contribute without any rein put upon the flow of words.

(3) A picture of how solidly some points of view or opinion are held by the group. It is often observed that a certain opinion will seem to be held at the beginning of a group session but after much discussion the opinion of the group will take a swing in an opposite direction, or at least the original opinion will be modified considerably.

On the negative side:

(1) It is often difficult and time-consuming to get a group together that possesses the common interests desired.

(2) There is a tendency for one or two in the group to dominate the conversation; to prevent this from happening takes much skill on the part of the group leader.

(3) At the end of the session, such a mass of material has been obtained that the culling of the material and its interpretation is a formidable task.

(4) Much of the material is worthless, representing a waste of interviewing time and interpretation time.

In summary, each of the various psychological techniques used to obtain information for marketing and advertising research must be administered by people well-trained in sophisticated research methods. It is dangerous for "amateurs" to attempt any of these. All of them fall within that group known as "projective methods" devised by psychologists and used for psychological experiments long before their application to marketing, and advertising. All of them have been used in so-called "motivational research" as a means of finding buying motives not discoverable by conventional testing. In the case of at least a few of the techniques they may be used as a form of exploratory research, preliminary to large-scale surveying. The group interview, for example, can well be used in this way, or can be used at several steps in the process of new-product development as:

(a) to determine the need or desirability of developing the product;

(b) to determine the form and pricing of the product;

(c) to determine appropriate advertising themes, packaging, and even distribution channels.

"Typical" consumers?

Common stock is bought by millions. What psychological or sociological factors would be behind *your* choice of "typical" people to be characters in this commercial? Incidentally, an unusual and effective technique used in this commercial was to have a period of silence to emphasize a point. What with the silence and brief copy, only 39 words of audio were required to put over the sales message.

Client: E. F. HUTTON COMPANY INC.
Product: INVESTMENTS
Length: 30 SECONDS - QHBV3432
Title: "GARDEN PARTY II"

1. (SFX UNDER) WOMAN 1: We checked with our broker

2. and our broker said it seemed like a good idea.

3. What does your broker say?

4. WOMAN 2: Oh well, our broker is E.F. Hutton.

5. And E.F. Hutton says ...

6. (SILENCE)

7. (SILENCE)

8. ANNCR: (VO) When E. F. Hutton talks,

9. people listen.

10. (SILENT)

APPLYING BEHAVIORAL SCIENCES
TO MARKETING AND ADVERTISING

This chapter provides a mere introduction to the subject, so many are the experiments and so many the directions that behavioral scientists are taking in cooperation with marketers and advertising-marketing researchers. There is, for instance, an increasing use of semantic differential testing. A promising start has been made in the wedding of behavioral science concepts and computer simulation to solve problems of marketing and advertising strategy. Social and psychological hazards found in international marketing have only recently been explored.

Analysis of the social classes as an important force in marketing is a relatively recent development for the marketer who had not made much use of the data assembled for years by the social scientists.

With or without behavioral scientists, the marketing and advertising professional will always be faced with vexing, nagging questions because of dealing with people—logical, emotional, rational, irrational, predictable sometimes, and wildly unpredictable at others.

MAKING SOCIAL AND BEHAVIORAL SCIENCES
WORK FOR YOU IN ADVERTISING

Choose a category of products that is available nationwide through supermarkets or drug stores. The category can be anything from hand towels to potato chips. Maybe tomato sauces or snack crackers. Or how about pickles or chewing gums? You choose!

Next, assume you are responsible for the development of a potential new brand for the product category of your choice. What do you do? How do you go about getting ideas and finding out what you have to know? The following process is by no means exhaustive, but is used to illustrate how you can use the theories and research methods from the social sciences to get the answers you need to make decisions.

Develop an Information Base

In the previous chapter you became aware of a number of research sources. Information is available from governmental studies, trade publications, and commercial research companies. You might also use commercial research information based on nationwide samples from Target Group Index (TGI) or Simmons to learn the demographic and perhaps personality (psychographic) characteristics of consumers who are heavy, medium, light, or nonusers of competing brands already on the market in your chosen product category. TGI and Simmons also provide information about media use by consumers, so you get a good idea of what consumers read, listen to or view.

This is your information base, and it is considerable. Already you know the dollar volume of sales for your product category.

If Nielsen Food Index or Drug Index information is available to you from Nielsen audits of food and drug stores, you would know brand shares for competing products. The information is broken down by regions, store sizes, and counties. From Nielsen you might also buy historical information relating the shifting market shares by brand over a given period of time.

You also know a great deal—demographically—about who buys how much of the product and what media might be used to reach consumers with advertisements. You study the advertising for brands already in the market.

Research Consumer Reactions to Products

At this point you will have to do or buy research to learn how well consumers are satisfied with existing brands. You can conduct telephone or in-home surveys with individual consumers in one or more markets. You might also invite identified product users to group interviews. You want to learn consumer attitudes toward existing products and the associations consumers have with the use of each competitive product. You want to know the shortcomings of existing products and whether these shortcomings are important or trivial to consumers.

This information provides an advance indication of the ease of inducing consumers to try and buy a new and improved product. You're using the ideas (for example, attitudes) and research methods (surveys and group interviews) of social scientists to develop answers to advertising and marketing questions.

Identify Product Characteristics for Which Consumers Look

You examine your potential new product through the eyes of consumers to learn the most salient attributes on which brand discriminations (reasons for buying) are made. You want to know how well current leading brands fulfill consumer needs through these product attributes.

One simple way to do this is with the *semantic differential*. You might develop a list of adjectives that are opposites and express the attributes by which people make choices. Words such as heavy or light, cold or hot, creamy or rough, strong or weak may be presented at each end of a 5-, 7-, or 10-point scale. When consumers check a point on the scale they express reactions that evaluate a product attribute. When all consumer reactions are totaled, the result is a configuration of the meaning of existing brands and an insight into product characteristics or meanings to which consumers might respond. Beyond this relatively simple method, there are a variety of sophisticated methods for analyzing product attributes and consumer assessment of attributes.

Perhaps you've isolated one or two product attributes with which consumers are dissatisfied. Ideally, these attributes are strong points for your product. You have, then, a distinctive or unique benefit to be expressed in your advertisements.

You now face another decision: whether to produce a limited supply of your promised new product for in-home use by potential consumers. If you do test your proposed new product in this way, and if, as a result of such a test, you are convinced by consumers' reactions that the product is regarded as superior to existing products, you begin to think of advertising.

Use Social Science Theories and Ideas

From studying the advertising appeals of existing brands, and from consumer reactions during in-home testing with your product, you have some ideas as to which product benefits will be emphasized. Your problem now is to select an appeal to express the benefits.

You are at a critical point in the process of making decisions. You know that simple and physically similar products may be bought for quite different reasons. Take razor blades. One advertiser may stress closeness of shave, another convenience, another safety, another pampering oneself, and another may build in sexual meanings or some other appeal. The appeal and expression of the appeal in the advertising of razor blade manufacturers segment the razor blade market through the advertised appeal. People buy and use shaving products on the basis of the appeal. Consumers think about razor blades in terms of how the product is presented to them.

You must decide whether the appeal you choose to express your product benefit is important and meaningful to consumers. You may make your decision on the basis of research already done with consumers through individual or group interviews. You may also pretest the appeal within the advertisements you develop, so that you're testing substance and form—appeal and advertised expression of the appeal—at the same time.

As a check on existing information you have, you may want research using projective techniques because these techniques provide a range of interpretations and richness of insight into motivation not otherwise available.

Return to the preceding example momentarily. Razor blades, or any other product, have little human meaning in and of themselves. You, the advertiser, give the product meaning. From the social and behavioral sciences you are familiar with the range of potential meanings for a product, from rational to emotional, individual to social, sensory (the way a balanced hammer feels in the hand) to functional. You can present your product to express a role, identify status or perhaps express a life style.

You must present a set of meanings for your product through symbols, such as words and pictures, that quickly express an appeal. For example, the benefit of a close shave may be expressed by an appeal showing approval by a young man's date. The benefit of a self-basting turkey may be expressed by an appeal stressing the ease of preparation or by an appeal showing approval of family members gathered for Thanksgiving dinner as the turkey is brought to the table. The appeal and the set of meanings by which it is expressed become the position for your product in the consumers' mind.

How You Research Advertising

At this point you may proceed to make advertisements on the basis of your professional experience. On the other hand, you've probably already learned from experience that the best way to gauge the effectiveness and meaning of an advertisement is with consumers. Unless advertisements communicate as intended with consumers, the results may be not only wasted advertising but advertising that works against you.

Your approach to testing advertisements can be organized in a number of ways. One of the simplest is to ask yourself what you want to test, when, where and how. You have an incredible variety of options, and the following are simply examples.

What to Test

You can test the elements in an advertisement: headlines, illustrations, copy, typography, color, or models used for print. For broadcasting you can also test spokespersons, testimonial givers, musical themes, and settings. You may test entire print advertisements or broadcast commercials in rough or finished form. Because often you are choosing between two or three possible advertisements, you may place the advertisements in a newspaper or magazine to test the relative effectiveness in whatever way you define, including follow-up mail or phone surveys for awareness or consumer understanding of the meaning of the avertisements. You may coupon the advertisements and count the returns.

Perhaps you have to choose between an unknown actor and a well-known movie personality as a spokesperson. The choice is not casual. The well-known personality may command thousands and even hundreds of thousands of dollars more than a relatively unknown actor. An in-theatre test using both spokespersons can reveal the relative effectiveness of each.

When to Test

You can pretest individual advertisement elements or entire advertisements with individuals or groups. You can also assess advertisement effectiveness and meaning in limited test market situations. During the life of a campaign, you use research to monitor the levels of awareness your advertisements are generating with consumers and to learn why people continue to buy your product, or why they switch to a competing brand.

Today, advertisers also use pretest results as evidence of the meaning of advertisements to consumers, should the truthfulness of the advertisements subsequently be challenged by the FTC, the BBB or perhaps rejected by a television network commercial review board.

Where to Test

If you are using laboratory equipment to pretest your advertisements, you are probably limited to the location of the equipment. Group interviews most likely are conducted in central locations easily reached by consumers. Oftentimes test kitchens are next to conference rooms where interviews are conducted. Recording equipment also is most often in a fixed location because it is complex and requires ample space.

Many broadcast commercials are pretested in rough or finished form in specially equipped theatres located in several major cities.

How to Test

You, the advertiser, may choose to use research that is highly quantitative, relying heavily on sampling and statistical testing techniques, or you may choose other research methods used with carefully selected individuals or small groups of people and involve little or no use of statistics. Some social scientists are ambivalent about the use of small sample studies using projective techniques. Too often, two or more researchers using the same test come up with different answers, raising fundamental questions about the reliability and validity of projective methods. Still, you may choose such tests because of their flexibility and because they yield creative insights into consumer motivation.

Unlike most academic researchers who have an allegiance to one or a few research methods, you are likely to match the research method to the types of questions to be answered. This is your decision, and your problem is that often you are not satisfied with the answers. So you are inclined to use several research methods to get answers. For example, if a nationwide survey leaves you with the feeling that the answers to questions are reasonable but superficial, you may commission a small study using depth interviews to check on the information from the nationwide survey. Or, group interviews with consumers may help you determine the questions to be asked of a nationwide sample of consumers.

You may borrow from the experimental psychologist and work with consumers divided into test and control groups to test an advertising appeal or the believability of a claim. You may use indirect questioning techniques to learn consumer associations with one or another brand of product. You may ask consumers to describe the persons who make heavy use of spices in cooking or who shampoo their hair three times per week. You may want unintentional or uncontrolled consumer responses provided, for example, by sensors attached to the wrists of in-theatre audiences viewing test commercials. Such responses may show involuntary physiological changes indicative of pleasure or disapproval of what the audience is viewing and about which audience members are reluctant to talk.

Why You Should Pretest

Pretesting elements or entire advertisements enables you to isolate and correct problems before spending huge amounts of money. Your advertisements will be more effective. Pretesting also provides evidence of the meaning of advertisements to consumers, telling you the consumer perceives and understands the product as you intended to position the product, while giving you evidence of the meaning of the advertisement should it be subsequently challenged.

While pretesting does lower the risk involved in your decisions, you are aware that much pretesting is necessarily artificial. Consumers using eye cameras in laboratories are not perceiving the advertisement as they would naturally in the environment with many competing advertisements. So you may decide to test market the product in one, but ideally two or more, markets.

TESTING IN THE MARKET

Because every advertiser works in constantly changing markets, last year's decisions may not work for this year's problems. Markets constantly change, presenting every advertiser with new problems, new questions. New decisions are required.

New competing products with dramatic advantages to consumers are frequently launched. Think for a moment of the new products you have heard or read about in the past few weeks. Prices sometimes change rapidly. Look at the advertising prices of hand-held calculators. Then look at the calculator newspaper advertisements from one or two years ago. The prices have changed substantially.

Advertisers are always seeking new retail outlets. Years ago flashlight batteries were sold primarily through hardware stores. Now flashlight batteries and batteries for radios, toys, calculators, watches, and other products are available almost everywhere.

The effectiveness of advertising appeals change. Ten years ago a toy with an educational appeal gathered dust on the retailers' shelves. Today some of the fastest selling toys are backed by advertised learning appeals. Effective hair shampoo advertisements become less effective as hair styles change and men and women require different product characteristics.

Market change and dynamism spur the advertiser to change. Every change, however, is a departure from what the advertiser knows worked in the past. Change, in short, involves risk.

Advertisers manage risk by testing their decisions in carefully selected markets. In such markets the advertiser learns how well a new product will sell and what consumers think of the new product.

Perhaps the advertiser must make decisions about an existing product. The advertiser knows that increasing the advertising for an existing product will increase sales. In a test market, however, the advertiser can learn more precisely the influence of a 10 percent increase in the advertising support for a product.

Posing the Question

The advertiser can construct a long list of points to test. The following are typical:

(1) How well will a new or innovated product sell?
(2) What will happen to sales if the retail price to consumers is increased 5 percent? decreased 5 percent?
(3) What will happen to sales if the product is distributed through additional retail stores?
(4) How much advertising investment is required to increase brand share by 5 percent in the market?
(5) Will a new advertising appeal be more effective than the current appeal?
(6) Which of two (or more) ways of expressing a single appeal—a health appeal, for example—is more effective?
(7) Which single medium or combination of media is more effective in reaching and influencing consumers?

What Can Be Learned?

The advertiser can learn the answers to the prior and many more questions. Testing in the market is simply a more formal and explicit way of getting specific answers to questions the advertiser continuously asks of the sales data crossing the desk.

Testing in the market reveals what happens when something is done in one market that is not done in another comparable market. The key is the comparison in the natural environment of the market. Advertisements are perceived naturally. Consumers selectively perceive some advertisements and ignore others. Consumers clip and use some coupons and are indifferent to other coupons. Consumers buy more of some products when prices are lowered. For other products, sales don't increase when prices are lowered.

Testing Methods

Much advertising testing is done through traditional media. Newspapers, for example, are often used to test advertisements containing coupons. Newspaper coupons are quickly used by consumers. Direct mail advertisements with coupons enclosed may be used by advertisers wanting to reach specific income, age, or other groups in the market.

For an existing product, the advertiser continues planned advertising levels in most markets. In several selected markets, the advertiser may continue the same level of advertising but use different appeals, announce combination offers. Disposable cigarette lighters and razors are often sold as a single unit. New product uses may be announced or coupons offering temporary price reductions may be included in the advertising.

Sales in the selected markets are compared with sales in the markets where advertising continues unchanged. Changes in the advertiser's brand share are compared with changes in competitors' brand shares.

Many advertisers test in three cities, using as many control cities. If severe weather or a natural catastrophe influences sales in one city, the test continues in the remaining cities.

Test Targets

The advertiser decides where to test based on an assessment of several different sets of facts:

(1) Every advertiser knows sales and brand share figures by cities and regions. Some markets buy more of the advertiser's product; others buy less. From experience, professional meetings and business publications the advertiser also knows some markets are more receptive to new products than others. Media advertisements in *Advertising Age* and other advertising publications also provide information about the desirability of various cities as test markets. If the advertiser is testing an existing but innovated product, markets chosen may be those in which sales experience—historically and currently— reflects national product sales.

(2) The advertiser wants markets that are representative and separated from other cities. Advertisers traditionally selected test cities that are separated from other cities for clearer test results. More recently, however, some advertisers intentionally test in suburban markets. If the advertiser has distribution for an existing product, or is targeting a new product for suburban markets, tests may reasonably be run in suburbs. The major problem is that test results may be influenced by activities in adjacent suburbs or the central city around which the suburbs cluster.

(3) The advertiser also looks for household incomes that fit the general income profile in the markets in which the advertiser is interested. Advertisers typically look at the number or percentage of households with incomes from $5,000 to $10,000, from $10,000 to $15,000, and from $15,000 to $20,000. Households in these income categories represent the mass market for most nationally advertised products. The advertiser also is interested in how income is earned. Advertisers tend to avoid one-industry towns. Consumer buying would not be typical if the major industry went on strike. Advertisers also tend to avoid cities where employment is primarily governmental, university or military because employment is too stable, not reflecting general economic conditions. The advertiser looks for household incomes earned from a variety of activities.

(4) Distribution in a potential test market is vital to the advertiser. If, for example, scheduled advertising introduces a product that is not available through retailers, the advertising is wasted. Wholesalers and retailers in desirable test markets become accustomed to handling the initial distribution and display of new products. They know the importance of timing and shelf facings. Retailers can anticipate problems and alert the manufacturer's sales personnel quickly.

(5) The advertiser also examines the media in potential test cities. The advertiser wants a mix of media similar to that in other markets. Media in frequently used test cities also acquire expertise in handling advertising for tests. Media sales personnel coordinate advertising schedules with wholesalers and retailers. The media study their own markets intensively, providing advertisers with information about distribution and sales and how local consumers use the media. Media in test markets also provide advertisers with case histories of prior successful tests in their markets.

How Long to Test

The advertisers must decide how long to test. If the test is restricted to the pulling power of newspaper coupons, one month may be sufficient. If monthly magazines carry coupons, two months may be required. If the advertiser is interested in consumer repurchase rates after a coupon offer expires, three months may be required. If additional information is gathered by surveys, consumers may be interviewed at planned intervals over a four-month period.

Getting Answers

Test marketing is best expressed in a simple example. Assume you are an advertiser of a food product, testing the effectiveness of two different advertising appeals. Your current advertising expresses a taste appeal. Now you want to find out how consumers will react to a social approval appeal in a family setting. You select two cities. In one city, you continue to use advertisements with your present taste appeal. This is your control city. The control city is your measurement base. Increases or decreases in sales in the test city are measured against sales during the same period in the control city.

In the test city you change your advertised food appeal to one of social approval in a family setting.

You can express market test results in both unit or dollar sales. The following example is in dollar sales. You want to find the increase or decrease in sales which can be credited to the changed appeal.

TABLE 6-1
Comparing Control and Test Cities

City	Sales During Preadvertising Period	Sales During Advertising Period in Test City	Increase or Decrease	Increase or Decrease Weighted by Control City Trend
Control City A	TIME 1 200.00	TIME 2 190.00	D or I% 5% decrease	
Test City X	TIME 1X 220.00	TIME 2X 255.00	15.90% increase	22.00%

1. In control city A, current level of unchanged advertising shows a decrease in dollar sales in Time 2. The percentage decrease D is expressed as

$$\frac{Time\ 1 - Time\ 2}{Time\ 1} \times 100 = D\% \text{ decrease}$$

$$\frac{200 - 190}{200} \times 100 = 5\% \text{ decrease}$$

(The same formula can be applied to test city X.

$$\frac{255 - 220}{220} \times 100 = 15.90\% \text{ increase)}$$

2. We say that with current advertising appeals, test city X would have had the same 5% decrease. Therefore, the dollar sales figure for Time 2X in city X would have been

Time 1X   —   (D% of Time 1X)
220   —   (5/100 × 220)
= 220   —   11
= $209

[In this step, if the percentage had been a positive figure, the equation would have been

Time 1X   +   (I% of Time 1X)]

3. However, because of the new advertising appeal, the dollar sales in Time 2× is $255. The difference therefore between the actual dollar sales with the new appeal advertising and the potential dollar sales had the current advertising been continued is expressed as

$$
\begin{aligned}
\text{Time 2×} \quad &- \quad 209 \\
= \quad 255 \quad &- \quad 209 \\
= \$46.00
\end{aligned}
$$

4. The percentage increase therefore due to advertising with the new appeal is

$$\frac{46}{209} \times 100 = 22.00\%$$

The preceding calculation can be expressed more formally in the following equations:

— Percentage increase if the control city shows a decrease in sales between Time 1 and Time 2

$$\frac{\text{Time 2×} - [\text{Time 1×} - (D\% \text{ of Time 1×})]}{[\text{Time 1×} - (D\% \text{ of Time 1×})]} \times 100$$

— Percentage increase if the control city shows an increase in sales between Time 1 and Time 2.

$$\frac{\text{Time 2×} - [\text{Time 1×} + (I\% \text{ of Time 1×})]}{[\text{Time 1×} + (I\% \text{ of Time 1×})]} \times 100$$

QUESTIONS

1. What is rational consumer behavior?

2. Why is the economic definition of rational consumer behavior considered narrow by advertisers?

3. Briefly discuss the ways in which advertisers make use of demographic research.

4. Give an example of a product that expresses a consumer's life style.

5. It is often said we buy and use products to project roles. Choose a product and explain how the product would help a consumer project a role.

6. Diffusion theory helps advertisers define advertising goals. Explain this statement.

7. What is meant by product position?

8. What products might a teenager buy for family approval? What products might the same teenager buy for peer approval?

9. How many different appeals can you think of for a dentifrice? a pair of jogging shoes? a golf ball?

10. Why are projective research methods used by advertisers?

11. For what reasons does an advertiser engage in pretesting appeals and advertising?

12. Why is the word "new" such a powerful word in advertising?

13. Why does advertising borrow from the behavioral and social sciences?

14. What is the role of advertising in the Diffusion of Innovation theory?

15. How does culture affect perception?

16. How is new product development helped by group interviews?

17. Why is human motivation so difficult for advertisers to pin down?

18. The young American woman of today is changing rapidly. In what ways are young women changing? How does this influence advertising?

19. Why might reference groups be important to an advertiser?

20. Why is the sociological idea of roles important to advertisers?

REFERENCES

1. Stewart Henderson Britt, *Consumer Behavior and the Behavioral Sciences* (New York: John Wiley & Sons, Inc., 1966), p. 19.
2. W. Lloyd Warner and Paul Lunt, *The Social Life of a Modern Community* (New Haven: Yale University Press, 1941).
3. Rensis Likert and Samuel P. Hayes, Jr. (eds.), *Some Application of Behavioral Research* (Paris: UNESCO, 1957), pp. 208-12, 217-24.
4. Francis S. Bourne, "Group Influence in Marketing and Public Relations," in Rensis Likert and Samuel P. Hayes, Jr. (eds.) *op. cit.*, pp. 217-24.

7

MEDIA RESEARCH

MEDIA RESEARCH

Joan Cramer's first job after graduation from college was in the media department of an advertising agency. She was assigned as an assistant media buyer for a large consumer goods manufacturer.

To Joan, advertising had always meant the printed advertisement itself, or the television commercial itself. Now, after studying the advertising plan and budget, Joan realized that very shortly she would be making recommendations involving millions of dollars. Joan also realized that she was several persons removed from the individuals who would accept, reject, or modify her recommendations. Her proposed buys would be reviewed by the media chief and the agency account representative responsible for the advertising of the manufacturer. The account representative, in turn, would present Joan's recommendations to the brand managers and advertising director of the consumer goods manufacturer.

How important are the media decisions made by Joan? At each meeting in which the recommendations are reviewed, the proposed media buys are questioned. At each meeting the recommendations have to be justified because, for one reason, it is wasteful if the media selected reach large numbers of nonusers of the advertised product. Also, media costs account for the largest part of the advertising budget, so media investment naturally requires careful study.

MEDIA TIME AND SPACE: AN EXPENSIVE BUY

You can easily illustrate for yourself the reason media buys are carefully assessed. First, assume whatever cost you want for making a 30-second television commercial. Make the cost reasonable. Scan a current issue of *Advertising Age* to find out how much one advertiser or another spent to make a commercial. Use a current figure as your cost.

In *Advertising Age* or other advertising publications find out what the networks are charging for 30-second time slots. The figures vary considerably, depending upon the time slot you want. Assume you want evening prime time or Sunday afternoon football. Also assume that you are going to run the commercial 50 or 100 times during the year—not at all unusual for national advertisers. Now, multiply the commercial time charge by 50 or 100 or however many times you choose to run the commercial. Divide the resulting figure by the cost of making the 30-second commercial and you have a relationship between the cost of commercial production and network time charges. The cost of making the television commercial is small compared to the network time charges.[1]

SELLING TO THE ADVERTISER

The results might surprise you; they don't surprise the advertisers. Admittedly, the network time costs that you used would be adjusted by professional advertising people who know how to take advantage of network volume discounts. Still, the time charges you used, if you worked out the preceding problem using current commercial production and network time costs, express why advertisers avidly study media information and research.[2] The time has no value in itself. The value of broadcast time or print media space is determined primarily by the access each medium provides an advertiser to people who are prospects for the advertised product.

Note that the medium provides access. This means that on the basis of what is known about past audience use of media, a predictable number of people with certain demographic characteristics—age, occupation, and income—will view a specific television channel at a specified time or read a magazine after buying it at a newsstand. Just what does the media buyer know about readers of magazines or newspapers? Or about the listeners to radio? The viewers of television? On what basis are media time and space purchased?

KNOW WHAT YOU BUY

The media buyer recommends that the advertiser buy time or space on the basis of information developed through research. Audience information, however imperfect or questionable, provides the most reasonable basis for media buying decisions. Media research tells what the medium delivers: the number and demographic characteristics of the audience to whom the advertiser is buying access, most often in an environment of news entertainment or information that attracts the audience.

Most media research develops large numbers. Research reports filled with page after page of numbers describing audiences arrive almost daily in the mail of large advertisers and advertising agencies. During sales calls, media representatives offer still more numbers describing the size and characteristics of audiences.

To the person responsible for investing advertising dollars in media time and space a major problem is too much media research information, much of which is contradictory. The media buyer questions the information, wanting to know, among other things, who paid for the research and who carried it out. The buyer studies research findings to determine whether the information presented is the sort reasonably derived from the research method used. The buyer is skeptical of telephone surveys that reveal detailed information of the type consumers regard as confidential. Consumers do not give this type of information over the phone.

The media buyer also checks the definition of terms used in research: circulation is not the same as readership, nor is a broadcast rating the same as a share-of-audience, nor are families and households identical. The buyer must know precisely what the research is reporting in order to compare the findings of one research report with another.

SOURCES OF MEDIA RESEARCH?

Individual Media and Media Associations

Where does the advertiser get information about the size and characteristics of media audiences? First, most media and media associations develop information for advertisers. Sometimes this amounts to little more than audited circulation information for some print media. Large, market-oriented newspapers, radio stations, magazines, and television stations do their own research or commission independent research organizations to do research for them. Media associations such as the Magazine Publishers Association and the Radio Advertising Bureau do general research on behalf of their members. Most media belong to associations that do or sponsor research designed to show how effective the media in each association are.

Media plunge into research in order to establish their competitive advantages. Both against similar types of media—one radio station versus one or more others—and against other types of media—a television station's audience versus the readership of a newspaper. Much of this research is elaborate and expensive. Many of the studies are skillfully planned and executed. Much media-sponsored research, however, is called *advocacy research.* All too often research done by a medium reflects the self-interest of the medium.

Some advertising agencies, in fact, will not permit media-sponsored research to be used by their personnel until the agency's research departments have approved the techniques used. One agency that screens media research in this manner estimated that out of more than 60 studies so evaluated, almost half were useless. To give an example, one classical music radio station printed a questionnaire on the last page of a program guide distributed monthly to listeners. What listeners? Listeners who wrote or called the station requesting the monthly guide, a self-selection bias. Recipients of the monthly program guide were asked to fill in and tear off the pages with the questionnaires, use their own envelopes, and address, stamp, and mail them. Each additional step required of listeners added bias. Not unexpectedly, the people responding tended to drive Cadillacs or expensive imported cars, read *Yachting* and *Gourmet* magazines, belonged to at least one golf club, and enjoyed an income that averaged in the top 10 percent for the county in which the classical music station was located. In one sense, you might expect what advertisers call an "upscale" audience, one with more money than the average. However, many people without wealth enjoy classical music.

Secondly, there are commercial research companies. Some research companies do only media research; others do media, advertising and marketing

Media mix and the use of the computer.

Graphs such as this are used by Simulmatics Corporation, New York, to explain its media-mix approach.

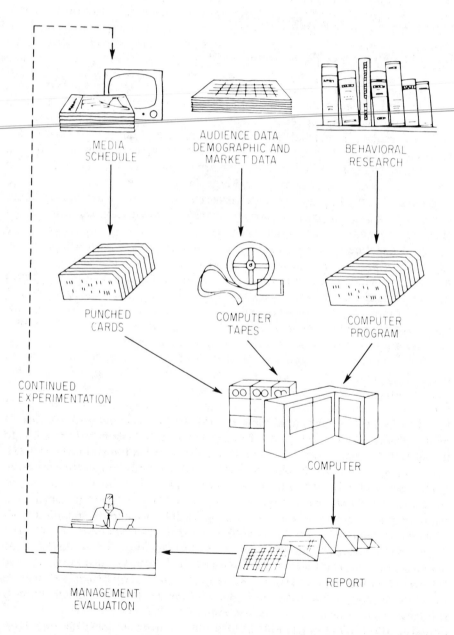

SIMULATION CYCLE FOR MEDIA MIX

research. These companies get part of their income from many advertisers and therefore are impartial in gathering and analyzing data as they must be to continue to service demanding and often skeptical clients. Differences of opinion about their work usually center around the validity of the techniques they employ.

Independent research firms such as Nielsen, Arbitron, and many others provide broadcast audience information for both network and independent stations in major markets. Nielsen audimeters provide quarter-hour audience information year round. Arbitron and Nielsen survey major markets several times a year with a sample of consumers in each market asked to keep track of television viewing in a diary for one week. Other firms use telephone interviews. Some firms use personal interviews. Many firms will do intensive, large sample studies in a market of an advertiser's choice. This might be done for test market purposes.

Auditors from the Audit Bureau of Circulations (ABC) walk in unannounced and pour through newsstand and subscription records to certify that the stated copies of each issue of a publication are, in fact, in circulation. Audited publications themselves pay for the audits. Verified Audit Circulation Corporation (VAC) and Business Publication Audit of Circulation (BPA) audit consumer and business publications.

Using large, nationwide samples, Target Group Index and Simmons collect comprehensive information from consumers that relates media use and product purchase and use. Each service publishes the results of their surveys in many volumes, which are used as information tools by advertisers who want to locate users of their products within media audiences.

Many independent research firms sample among people exposed to print or broadcast to learn whether advertisements are seen or remembered, and if remembered, whether people can actually recall the information in the advertisement.

Advertisers and Agencies

Thirdly, most major advertising agencies and manufacturers conduct their own media research. This varies from elaborate surveys to simple analysis of available data. Such research is usually devoted to the problems encountered by the advertising agency or manufacturer. It is generally not available to outsiders and frequently applies only to a specific problem.

For example, there is not much research information on consumers 65 and over for the manufacturer who may wish to introduce a new branded product to this age segment. The prevailing stereotype is that these people are inactive, have a low income, and are uninterested in new products or couldn't afford to buy the products even if interested. A manufacturer who sponsored research focused on consumers 65 and over would find large numbers travel extensively and own property of substantial value. Because of tax law requirements, the reported incomes for many consumers 65 and over is substantially below their actual incomes. This is valuable information to the manufacturer who sponsored the research. This information is not made available to competitors.

Advertising Research Foundation

A final source of media research is the Advertising Research Foundation, an industry-supported organization that conducts what can be called basic research. The foundation does not do "product-specific" studies of use to one advertiser or another. Rather, the foundation assesses the research methods used in advertising and attempts to develop new methods for advertiser use in a continuing effort to develop valid measures of media and advertising effectiveness.

THE ADVERTISER'S CRITICAL LOOK

An advertisement's effectiveness does not solely depend on the advertisement itself. The medium in which the advertisement is placed influences the number, characteristics, and frame of mind or receptivity of consumers potentially exposed to the advertisement. This is what a medium sells to advertisers: the opportunity to reach the prospects, often in an information or entertainment environment, at a cost.

Only if the situation comedy on network television, or the news content in a newspaper attracts and holds an audience, does the advertisement have a chance to be viewed or read. Only then does the advertisement have a chance of attracting attention to itself and engaging the viewer or reader. For this reason, advertisers study size and characteristics of media audiences and the media environment that draws readers, listeners, or viewers.

Any advertiser can reel off a list of desirable media. The list of media actually used, however, is much shorter because the advertiser's budget restricts what media are bought and how frequently the advertisements are run. The advertiser is forced to choose.

HOW THE ADVERTISER DECIDES

When selecting media and deciding how to use the selected media, the advertiser is manipulating four variables: *reach, frequency, continuity,* and *message.* Each has a cost, and the total cost of all four variables must fit within the budget.

Advertising people use the term *reach* to refer to the number of different households or individuals exposed within a given time period, usually four weeks. If the advertiser decides to emphasize reach, the cost of doing so means that there will be less money for frequency, continuity, and message.

Frequency refers to the average number of messages to which a household or individual is exposed within a given time period, usually four weeks. If the advertiser decides to emphasize frequency, there will be less money for reach, continuity, and message. In this case, for example, the advertiser trades off exposing large numbers of prospects to the advertisement in order to expose a smaller number of prospects more than once.

The evenness with which advertising is run within a given time period is called *continuity.* Often the period is a budgetary period of six months or a year.

If the demand for the advertiser's product is constant throughout the year, the advertiser may decide continuity is important, and make reach, frequency, and message decisions after continuity objectives are established.

Message refers to the costs involved in making one or more advertisements coupled with the space or time cost for a one-time insertion of the advertisement in the medium. If the advertiser decides to use full-page, four-color advertisements both production and space costs will be higher than for a quarter-page black-and-white advertisement for a magazine. Or, if the advertiser makes many different advertisements for different market segments and media, production costs will be high. There will be less money available for reach, frequency and continuity.

Media decisions typically involve a compromise between the conflicting cost requirements of *reach, frequency, continuity,* and *message.* How the advertiser makes the compromises depends upon such factors as the newness of the product, consumer loyalty to existing brands. The advertiser's own distribuiton goals, and a host of other factors. Whatever decisions the advertiser makes, however, are based on information developed through research.

WHAT MEDIA RESEARCH PROVIDES ADVERTISERS

Media research yields several different types of information used by advertisers. Customs, habits, work patterns, and life styles of a society are constantly shifting; media research documents the accompanying shifts in media use. Radio was *the* broadcast medium until the introduction of television in the early 1950s. Evening time on radio developed huge audiences. Radio is now used quite differently by listeners. Despite the fact that more radio sets are sold than television sets, radio today has smaller audiences than television. Today, radio audiences are often segmented by listener musical tastes. Radio prime time is now commuter time. Because radio develops audiences in quite different ways than television, radio commercials are bought on a different basis than in the past.

Quantitative Information

The majority of media research develops information about audience size and characteristics, sometimes with no more than descriptions of audience, sex, and age. Advertisers prefer more detailed demographic information, including occupation, education, buying power, and geographic distribution. (The advertiser's pattern of product distribution is an important planning factor, too.) Some independent research firms provide product-purchase and frequency-of-product-use information related to audience size and demographic characteristics. This gives the advertiser a basis for making an intelligent appraisal of the media needed to reach the buyers of a specific product.

Sometimes a product's nature dictates rather clearly whether a medium is suitable. A grass-seed advertiser, for instance would avoid a medium that was read almost exclusively by apartment dwellers. Even when products seem to have a universal appeal to the mass market, analysis of sales data invariably reveals widely differing market shares by geographic areas and by consumer demographic classifications. Knowing this, media buyers dig into media research to find media that reach the manufacturer's geographic and demographic markets.

Where new products are concerned, some people are more venturesome than others. They will try unknown products more readily. Yet these venturesome people may read and listen to exactly the same media and possess many other characteristics in common with people who are more conservative in their reaction to advertising in the media to which they are exposed. Since selling new products is a vital part of U.S. marketing, it is necessary to determine as closely as possible the degree of venturesomeness that will exist in the audience for specific media. Media identify venturesome consumers by surveying readers, listeners, and viewers to learn how quickly and in what numbers the audiences buy and try a variety of new products.

Following market analysis, the advertiser studies the appropriateness of the product and how the product will be advertised to the characteristics of the various media. Some products depend upon color. Some products benefit from demonstration. Other products require long and detailed copy. The characteristics of the medium and the way the medium is used and regarded by the audience influence where the advertisement is placed.

The advertiser also makes judgments about the effect on advertisements of the surrounding news, general information or entertainment content. This content disposes audiences to see advertisements in certain ways. So advertisers study how audiences use media and what audiences expect of particular media. Advertisers seek information indicating whether audience members regard a medium as authoritative, witty, accurate, informative, tasteful, or entertaining. The way in which advertisement are perceived is influenced by surrounding material. Advertisements are known by the company they keep.

Qualitative Information

Quantitative media research provides the basis for the majority of media buying decisions. Advertisers, however, have insatiable appetites for information. There are times when there *are* no numbers, as when, for example, the advertiser buys time on a new situation-comedy show on network television. In this case, there are no audience figures from the previous year. At best, the advertiser can only speculate what audience numbers to expect.

There are times, also, when numbers are not enough. While numbers enable the advertiser to assess large amounts of data efficiently, the way in which the audience is demographically described, and the numbers applied to the descriptive audience breakdowns may be too abstract to capture the richness and subtlety and sometime intimacy of a reader's reaction to an article in the *Reader's Digest* or a viewer's reaction to a television documentary. The advertiser may want to listen to taped interviews or read verbatim reports to learn audience reactions to media. The advertiser then applies judgment, using both quantitative and qualitative information, to reach media-buying decisions.

A CLOSE LOOK at PRINT

Ingenious advertising researchers have used every technique from hypnotism to lie-detector devices to discover reactions of people exposed to print media. In the welter of different media-research techniques, it becomes difficult to know what may accurately be called *media research* and what may be called *message research.* In other words, what is the effect of the medium by itself and what is the effect of the advertisement by itself?

Some advertisers test the effect of media to their satisfaction by putting couponed advertisements in two or more different magazines. The advertisements are identical in all respects save the address to which the consumer mails the coupon. The difference in coupon return between the magazines is identified by the address to which the coupon is sent and is considered evidence of the influence of each magazine.

Print media research is most easily discussed using magazines as examples. Magazines tend to segment markets demographically, rather than geographically as do most newspapers. Several well-known independent research firms have a long tradition of researching the effectiveness of magazine advertising, and the research is widely understood and used in advertising.

Using Print Media Research

Standard Rate and Data Service publishes magazine circulation figures verified by the Audit Bureau of Circulations. In the absence of additional data, cost comparisons between magazines often are made on a *cost-per-thousand* basis. This is one of the most frequently used terms in advertising. The cost-per-thousand, or CPM for short, is obtained by dividing the cost of an advertisement by the circulation of the magazine in thousands.

$$\frac{\text{Cost}}{\text{Circulation in thousands}} = \text{Cost-per-thousand circulation}$$

This simple calculation enables advertisers to compare media with different space costs and different circulations. Which of the two following magazines, for example, is cheaper on a cost-per-thousand basis: Magazine A with a four-color page cost of $20,000 and a circulation of 2,900,000? or Magazine B with a four-color page cost of $30,000 and a circulation of 4,250,000? You can guess, of course, but calculating the answers gives you precise answers for making media-buying decisions. And it must be admitted that some people have trouble juggling zeros and placing decimals. A working rule of thumb for mass circulation magazines is that the answer will usually be between one and nine dollars and some odd cents.

Advertisers change the bottom portion of the CPM calculation in a number of ways, often on the basis of media research that reveals additional information of interest to advertisers.

For example, purchase of a magazine, either on the newsstand or by subscription is no guarantee that the magazine is going to be read or even looked at. Surveys of a magazine's readers may reveal, however, that the magazine is typically read by two or perhaps three members of the family. In this case, the CPM calculation would be:

$$\frac{\text{Cost}}{\text{Circulation in thousands} \times \text{readers per copy}} = \frac{\text{Cost per thousand}}{\text{readers}}$$

Readers per copy multiplied by the circulation gives the audience for that particular magazine. When this number is divided into the cost of the magazine
space, the result is a cost per thousand readers, a more useful figure for many
advertisers than cost per thousand circulation. This calculation also lowers the
cost-per-thousand figure.[3]

Advertisers adjust the denominator in the cost-per-thousand equation to
reveal the cost of reaching an age, sex, occupation, or some other segment in the
audience of a magazine. Perhaps one manufacturer identifies prospects for a
branded product as adults 18 to 25. People this age may be only 20 percent of
the total circulation of the publication. The circulation adjusted from, say,
100,000 to 20,000 would raise the CPM substantially. To the advertiser, this
may be realistic, for mass circulation magazines seldom deliver an audience in
which all the readers are prospects. For example, the advertiser may find some
magazines which at first glance do not look promising. The cost-per-thousand
computation applied to an age, sex, or other segment of a magazine's audience
may reveal a magazine to be efficient in reaching just those segments within its
total audience.

When the advertiser progressively refines those to be reached in an audience, the CPM increases. From the total circulation or readership of a
magazine, the advertiser may want to reach only women. If women comprise
half the readership, the CPM doubles. Assume further that the advertiser wants
to reach only those women between 18 and 49, and these women represent only
one quarter of the readership. If this is the case, the CPM quadruples.

Cost per thousand readers can be further refined. *Time* magazine, for example, is read by a variety of people from bank presidents to home makers to college students. A campaign aimed at selling electronic accounting machines for
banking purposes would eliminate home makers and college students as serious
prospects. Knowledge of the readers by key characteristics introduces a new
dimension. The cost per thousand readers is now refined to a cost per thousand
prospects by use of the following formula:

$$\frac{\text{Cost}}{\begin{array}{c}\text{Circulation} \times \text{Readers per copy} \\ \times \text{ percent of prospects in thousands}\end{array}} = \text{Cost per thousand prospects}$$

Another important factor that must be considered is *reach*. Reach refers to
the percent of the potential market reached. While it is often expressed by the
media themselves in terms of what percentage of a certain market they will
reach, it must be further refined for the use of a specific advertiser because he or
she will be interested in what specific proportion of prospects can be reached by
the use of a magazine.

Reach is usually evaluated in context with the cost. What percent of the
potential market is reached, and at what cost? In order to compute coverage it is
necessary to know what the potential market is. Then it is a simple matter,
when applied to an individual magazine, to divide the prospects reached by the

potential prospects in the market. This gives the reach and is frequently expressed in geographical terms as follows:

$$\frac{\text{Prospects reached by Magazine } A \text{ in New York}}{\text{Potential prospects in New York}} = \text{Reach of Magazine } A \text{ in New York}$$

Duplication As a Reseach Factor

Since many advertisers use more than one magazine, the problem of reach becomes complicated by overlaps in subscribers or readers called duplication. There are heavy and light magazine readers, some families subscribing to many magazines, some to few and some to none. For professional reasons the purchasing officer of a company may read a half-dozen or more professional publications to keep abreast of the latest developments in a specialized field. The advertiser in consumer, trade, and professional publications wants to know the extent of duplication.

The information is available from Starch and other sources, for example, for consumer magazines. You would expect low duplication between *Catholic Digest* and *The Lutheran* magazine. *Mechanix Illustrated* and *Popular Mechanics* tend to attract an audience with similar interests and offer duplication. Metropolitan magazines such as *Atlanta, Philadelphia Magazine,* and *The Washingtonian Magazine* offer geographic duplication with news magazines such as *Time* and *Newsweek* and *U.S. News & World Report.*

Duplication is not automatically bad or wasted. Duplication can provide frequency, or more than one advertising impression per household, family, or individual for the advertiser who wishes to reach prospective consumers more than once. Suppose an advertisement for a cake mix was inserted in both *Time* and the *Ladies' Home Journal,* and suppose that a specific family subscribed to both magazines. In terms of reach, this family is counted once because reach refers to the number of *different* families exposed to the advertisement. But now the frequency is two instead of one.

Frequency of Exposure

Frequency, or the number of times a reader is exposed to a specific advertisement, depends on two factors:

(1)   the use of successive advertisements in the same publication;
(2)   the use of the same advertisement in several publications.

Few advertisers depend upon a single advertisement to reach consumers, even within a single medium. A rough rule of thumb for a weekly magazine is that the first advertisement will reach 60 percent of the total audience. The second week, 80 percent; the third week 92 percent and the fourth week 98 percent. Running an advertisement in five consecutive issues of a weekly magazine will reach the total audience. For a monthly publication seven consecutive advertisements should reach the total audience. For both weeklies and monthlies, each advertisement after the first means some readers are seeing the advertisement more than once; perhaps a fraction of the audience will see all five insertions in the weekly magazine. Repeated exposures mean frequency of impression.

Most advertisers build frequency into a schedule of media buys; few depend on a single advertisement. Advertisers run the same advertisement over and over again, or use new variations of the advertisement, so consumers who have seen the original advertisement won't get bored.

The advertiser needs media research to know whether each advertisement run is increasing reach—those exposed to the advertisement for the first time—or frequency—those exposed to the advertisement two, three, five or ten or more times. Often when talking of frequency, the advertiser will use the word *weight* interchangeably with frequency. Weight is another way of saying the advertiser is willing to spend money to obtain frequency with an audience the advertiser regards as important.

Only by computing the frequency with which advertisements reach prospects can the advertiser determine the degree of exposure. The advertiser may decide on a frequency level for a defined market segment on the basis of test-market experience. Test marketing often reveals the amount of advertising investment required to introduce a new product. Testing reveals the strength of consumer inertia and habit or resistance to a new brand based on loyalty to existing brands. Happily, testing at times also reveals quick and widespread buying response, as if consumers were hungering for the new brand.

Accumulative Audience Figures

Magazines and broadcast media are more and more reporting their accumulative audience, a set of figures that frequently reveals both reach and frequency over a defined time period. Magazines and broadcast media do not necessarily reach the same people every day or week or month. Some people, it must be noted, wouldn't miss a single issue of a magazine. Many people are uneasy if they miss a single episode of their favorite television daytime serial. Media buyers know that buying popular daytime serials means a great deal of frequency with a loyal audience, but relatively few new viewers are reached with each succeeding daily broadcast. If, however, the media buyer selects a prime-time weekly variety show on television, from past viewer behavior, the buyer anticipates little program loyalty. People tune in and out quickly, expanding reach at the expensive of frequency, and accumulating an audience (increasing reach) week after week. Reach expands, or accumulates, at the expense of frequency, as many new viewers tune to the program for the first time each week.

There are numerous ways in which audiences accumulate. Media research is required to get a handle on accumulation. A magazine such as the *National Geographic* may be kept for years by subscribers. Most members of the family and even visitors may glance at or read the magazine. *TV Guide* is designed to be picked up frequently. Every day of the week a family member may use the magazine, resulting in both frequency of potential exposure to advertisements and audience accumulation as different family members use the publication.

CHECKING OUT MAGAZINE RESEARCH

To the advertiser, the mounds of numbers describing magazine readership and circulation simply represent the potential audience that may be reached. The advertiser wants more specific information that tells how effective an advertisement is in an issue of a magazine. The advertiser may request one or more organizations engaged in studying readership of both editorial and advertising material to study the performance of a particular advertisement. Why more than one organization? Each organization uses different methods and develops different measures of advertisement effectiveness.

The fact that different methods are used has led to controversy about what the various readership organizations are attempting to measure. The Advertising Research Foundation once spent nearly three years and many thousands of dollars examining the most commonly used commercial research services. The study was based on four premises:

(1) For most advertising it is impossible or impracticable to measure sales effect directly.

(2) Just as advertisements that are not read or when seen cannot sell, advertisements that have no impression on the reader will have little sales effect.

(3) Similarly, advertisements that do leave some impression on readers will have more sales effect than those that do not.

(4) Advertisers, therefore, are interested in measurements that indicate the impressions left on people's memories by advertisement reading.

Three methods were studied. The *aided-recall* method measures the number of people who can recall something about an advertisement in the checked publication when the name of the advertiser or product is shown to them. The *recognition* method measures the number of people whose previous readership of an advertisement left at least enough impression for them to recognize the advertisement and possibly to remember having read it when it is shown to them. The *reader-interest* method measures the number of people whose previous readership of an advertisement left enough impression for them to remember—when they see it again—that it was of interest to them. The Advertising Research Foundation study duplicated, as closely as possible, the methods of the leading commercial research organizations employing the three methods described.

The aided-recall method and the recognition method have some points of similarity that differ from the reader interest method and, therefore, will be discussed together.

It is necessary first to determine what a reader is. In the aided-recall method the respondent must be able to describe something in the magazine simply on the basis of seeing the cover. In the recognition method the respondent is allowed to examine the magazine to ascertain whether or not he or she has read it. Determination of a reader, it can be seen, is achieved with more difficulty in the aided-recall methods than in the recognition methods.

When a person participating in a readership survey interview is qualified as a reader, the interviewer then proceeds to determine specific advertisement or

High readership consumer magazine advertisement.

Starch scores were high for this advertisement. Pre-test and post-test scores showed a high level of interest, awareness and recognition for the advertisement. Sometimes, however, an advertisement scoring well in pre-tests does not do so in post-tests.

editorial readership. In the aided-recall method the respondent must describe or tell about some element in the advertisement to an interviewer who shows the respondent product or brand names on a deck of cards. From this a rating called "proved name registration" is obtained and expressed as a percentage of the total issue readers.

In the recognition method respondents are taken through the publication page by page and asked to point out all the advertisements they remember having seen or read in the issue. Results are usually expressed in some variation of the following:

"Noted"—the percentage of readers who recognized the advertisement.

"Advertiser-associated"—the percentage of readers who remembered some part identifying the brand or advertising by name.

"Read-most"—the percentage who remembered reading 50 percent or more of the copy in the advertisement.

Again it is readily apparent that the aided-recall method makes much greater demands on the respondent's memory.

The reader-interest method is somewhat different from the other two in that there is no special effort to prove readership. In most cases the magazine is mailed to the respondent who is asked to mark it as if he or she has read it. The respondent is then asked to indicate which advertisement or article was of interest on reading the publication originally. This method obviously measures something different from the other two methods.

The following figures show the average size of the advertising scores obtained for the various types of studies just discussed:

Type of Study	All Percent	Men Percent	Women Percent
Aided recall	3.0	3.0	3.0
Recognition (noted score)	19.2	17.6	20.7
Reader interest	14.9	14.5	15.3

The figures indicate clearly consistently higher scores obtained from the recognition and reader-interest methods.

While there are many technical conclusions drawn from the Advertising Research Foundation, the important conclusions appear to be that the ratings produced are based on memory tests of different levels or difficulty. Each technique is useful. The recognition method, for instance, has certain advantages, such as:

(1) the way its results can be clearly reproduced;
(2) its lesser sensitivity to hard-to-control variables, such as interviewing skill;
(3) its lesser demanding memory requirement that makes possible a larger and perhaps more representative sample.

For advertisement meanings the aided-recall method can supply useful information from those relatively few respondents who can supply it. The reader-interest method is the simplest and the most direct.

While the Advertising Research Foundation study reached many technical conclusions, primarily of interest to researchers, the most important conclusion to advertisers is that the measured results developed by each method differ by the challenge presented to memory.

Also, as mentioned early in this chapter, sometimes advertising research yields information about both the advertisement and the medium in a single measurement. The relative influence of the advertisement and the medium on the score given the advertisement may vary.

An advertiser, for example, may read Starch recognition scores, regarding them as measures of the advertisement by itself. The same advertiser, on the other hand, may have placed the same advertisement in six different magazines. The advertisements in the six magazines are given different recognition scores by the Starch organization research. Obviously here, the scores reflect the influence of each magazine. The advertiser, in short, can read recognition scores as measures of advertisement (message) effectiveness or as measures of media effectiveness or as a combination of both advertisement and medium effectiveness.

CHOOSING A METHOD

To assess advertising message and medium effectiveness, should the advertiser depend on the aided-recall method by Gallup and Robinson or the recognition method by Starch? The aided-recall method is considered quite demanding of the respondent's memory. Only an unusually compelling advertisement has much chance to be remembered. The recognition method, on the contrary, demands very little of the respondent. In fact, the respondent in a recognition study is exposed to the advertisement longer during the study than during normal reading of magazines.

Which method the advertiser chooses depends on what the advertiser believes important. If the advertiser wants information about awareness or a simple association of a product benefit with a brand name, the recognition method gives this information. If the advertiser desires to learn the impression made on consumers, the aided-recall method is preferable. Aided-recall has the added advantage of revealing whether readers correctly understand the message.

Judge Carefully

Whatever the method of advertisement readership used, an advertisement should not be judged on the basis of a single score. Only by examining the scores given an advertisement in several media and over time can the advertiser arrive at a reasonable judgment.

Also, readership figures provide only one basis for advertising evaluation. A high score does not necessarily mean high sales will result from the advertisement. An advertisement for a do-it-yourself atomic bomb might produce high readership but (hopefully) few prospects. Often sexual appeals are used when not really appropriate. Sexual appeals may generate high scores for advertisements but contribute little toward product sales.

Experienced advertisers tend to look beyond general readership scores for an advertisement in a publication. An experienced advertiser studies scores by predefined age or occupation or other demographic market segment.

Some Things Are Hard to Count

There are many qualitative factors contributing to a magazine's effectiveness. Some, such as editorial leadership and editorial content and appeal, are difficult to quantify for research purposes. The publication might, for example, create a "frame of mind" receptive to certain types of advertisements. Sometimes this is very obvious. *Vogue* and the *New York Times* magazine provide an attractive environment for the advertiser of women's clothing, accessories, and cosmetics. Sometimes, when reading a magazine, the advertiser may have a vague feeling or intuition that a magazine possesses characteristics that are difficult to describe, much less define and count. Seasoned judgment may influence the selection of one magazine over another, when the quantitative research suggests that in many ways the magazines are similar.

Earlier in the chapter it was pointed out that some advertising agencies critically examine the research offered by publications. If you were asked to base a buying decision on media research, here are some of the obvious questions you might ask:

(1) Under what conditions was the study made? Who actually did the study? Who financed the study? When was the study done? What definitions were used for readership and advertisement recall? Is there a complete statement of the research method used?

(2) Was the questionnaire well designed? Is there obvious bias? Were pretests made? Are the choices of answers reasonable?

(3) Has the interviewing been adequate and reliably done? Were trained, mature interviewers used? Were spot checks made to ensure accuracy?

(4) Has the best sampling plan been followed? Was the sample randomly developed? Is it representative? Is it large enough? Has the plan been fully executed?

(5) Are the results reported in a forthright and logical manner? Are small differences emphasized? Is the analysis clear and simple?

EXAMINING BUSINESS PUBLICATIONS

Most of the preceding material dealing with magazine research is applicable to business publications. Business publications are, however, much narrower in appeal than most consumer publications.

Business buyers, to a great extent, purchase on the basis of price, specifications, and test results. Consumers, in contrast, frequently buy for convenience, for example, as much as by price. Determining the number, characteristics, and interest of business publication readers is easier. Readers tend to be more homogeneous than the readers of consumer magazines. Thus, it is easier not only to discover why businessmen buy as they do but also to pinpoint where they are and who they are.

Business publication advertising is often devoted to developing specific leads for salesmen. If this is an advertising objective, the advertiser may evaluate business publications on a cost per inquiry basis. This is done by dividing the cost of an advertisement in a publication by the number of inquiries or coupons received. Most advertising is designed to do more than simply develop leads, so other advertising objectives may likewise be used.

Until recent years, relatively little research was done on business publications; almost all readership research was in consumer magazines. The lack of research activity is explained by the low space rates for many business publications. It was not feasible on a dollars and cents basis for most advertisers or agencies to conduct research. Consumer magazine space rates are expressed in thousands of dollars; business publication space rates are expressed in hundreds of dollars. Thus, cost of research on business publications quite frequently exceeded the cost of space. This is still true.

Today, however, there is a growing demand for business publication research and a number of organizations are now established to satisfy that demand. Business publications are sponsoring research by themselves to fill the research void. There is now a considerable volume of factual material about business publication readers and readership, and more is being supplied each year.

Business publications develop information about buyers and about what is called buyer influence.

Business publications put greater stress on developing what is called *buyer influence* information than do consumer magazines. Children influence the purchase of breakfast cereals, but for many frequently bought household items, if the woman does the shopping, she chooses what she wants. In other cases, the man in the household clearly chooses what he wants. While influence is not always clear cut, determining who is the principal buying influence for a consumer product is, comparatively speaking, delightfully simple when contrasted with making that decision in many industrial buying situations.

An industrial magazine advertisement may be seen by many people in and outside of a factory. Electrical safety equipment, for example, may be of interest to the factory architect, the safety engineer, the purchasing agents, the various executives on the management level, and several operating engineers. Which of these people is the real buying influence? Who originated the order that comes to the advertiser? Who made the final buying decision: an individual or a buying committee? The advertiser seeks answers to these questions in order to reach those who influence buying decisions and those who make them.

A central focus of business publication research, then, is buying influence. Also important is finding out where and how business publication readers read—at home, in the factory or office? Do they consider business publications necessary? If so, how do they view the relative importance of news and advertisements? These and other important questions are being answered by current business publication research.

Although much benefit is derived from the use of business publication research, advertisers should guard against overreliance on readership scores for two reasons:

(1)   The readership studies do not measure how many of those who receive

a copy of a publication actually read it. Each study measures only the relative readership, or reader interest, of the advertisement among those who did read the publication. The starting point for a readership study is a sample of the acknowledged readers of the issue studies. Perhaps 300 subscribers may have to be interviewed in order to find 100 readers. This information is not indicated in the report.

(2) The different readership services use different techniques. Some, by the nature of their questioning, will always yield lower scores than the others. One readership service, for instance, may find that it takes a 30 percent rating to be better than average; another service may consider a 20 percent or even a 15 percent rating to be in the superior group. It would be unwise, therefore, for an advertiser to judge the value of a magazine in terms of the readership scores alone since the lower readership scores in one publication might represent an equal or superior readership than the higher readership scores that appeared in another magazine that used a different readership service.

NEWSPAPER RESEARCH

Much newspaper research is similar to magazine research, providing information about circulation, readership, and audience coverage. Newspaper research differs in several notable ways, however. There is much less newspaper research dealing with the effect of color because newspaper make less use of color than magazines. Because newspapers are read quickly and discarded, there is little research information about the number of reading days. In contrast, information about the number of reading days is important to *TV Guide* or the *Reader's Digest.*

Because newspapers are, with few exceptions, distributed in geographic areas, media buyers regard market coverage or reach as the most important information. Information about individuals, families, or households reached is often presented in combination with market information. Newspapers stress information about retail activity, consumer income, and buying trends. Often newspapers provide research information about the relative sales position (share of market) of advertised and local or retail brands. The combination of newspaper circulation, reach, and market information is useful to advertisers in determining: (1) whether they will find it profitable to advertise in the newspaper's market; and (2) which newspaper, if there is a choice, should be selected.

Few newspapers can afford to provide readership research on a continuing basis. On the other hand, advertisers are reluctant to make newspaper-buying decisions on the basis of one or a few occasional readership studies. What the advertiser may do is refer to Newspaper Advertising Bureau reports, which are based on many studies of the readership of many newspapers.

Numerous studies of newspapers over the years yield much the same basic information relating to the advertising value of position, page traffic, and reader interest by subjects such as editorials, sports, politics, and other types of content. The information is so generally recognized and accepted that individual newspapers can persuasively argue the advertising values of newspapers without the expense of conducting isolated readership studies.

LOOKING AT BROADCAST MEDIA

Broadcast media research necessarily differs from print media research because the media are so different. Basically, the differences are those of time versus space. A broadcast message or commercial is aired for 30 or 60 seconds and gone forever. A researcher who is studying advertising effectiveness with audience members uses different research methods and different types of questions when assessing a broadcast commercial and a printed advertisement. Different questions yield different answers, making it difficult to compare the advertising values of broadcast and print media.

Understanding the various methods of researching broadcast media must be preceded by an understanding of the questions posed by those who buy radio or television time. Some of these questions are:

(1) How can competing measurement services use such different sample sizes in identical markets?

(2) Why is there such a lack of frequency and continuity in local ratings? Some markets are measured monthly, others less often, and some are passed by entirely.

(3) For what reasons are the areas covered in local surveys so lacking in uniformity?

(4) How can a time buyer make intelligent selections on mere audience figures; are not audience composition figures equally important?

(5) How can competing measurement services find such differences in audience sizes?

(6) What can rating services do when local stations attempt to build larger than normal audiences during rating periods? Stations may increase audience size by airing outstanding programs or by using extra newspaper and broadcast advertising, or by running contests with valuable prizes. These practices are called "hypoing." Stations "hypo" to build larger-than-normal audiences. Then the stations can charge advertisers more money for commercial time.

Whether blatant or subtle, "hypoing" is a problem. A rating service can neutralize "hypo" effects by extending the typical one-week rating period beyond that announced. Sometimes secret rating weeks are added by a broadcast research organization.

Although many time buyers in advertising agencies are skeptical about the use of ratings as evidence of audience size, the buyers have no other reasonable way to get this information. Time buyers look for other evidence. Buyers may be influenced by (a) sales success stories, (b) mail-pull figures. Buyers also weigh the value of (a) tie-ins with local broadcast personalties, (b) prestige of the station, or (c) merchandising services offered.

None of these, singly or in combination, gives the buyer the type of yardstick offered by ratings.

Radio/Television: the Data

Generally speaking, the following basic ways of expressing the data on broadcast audiences are widely used:

(1) What is the potential audience—number of sets?

(2) How many are listening or viewing—sets in use?

(3) How many sets are tuned to a particular station—the rating?

(4) Of the sets in use, how many are tuned to a particular station—the share of audience?

(5) How many are listening or viewing—the total audience?

(6) Who is in the audience—the audience composition?

(7) What is the audience size at any specific time during a broadcast—the average audience?

You are already familiar with some of the broadcast-research measures listed.

You read about the ratings of popular television shows. In the past, you were aware of the millions of people (total audience) watching the Apollo 17 launch. Perhaps you're aware that you are one of the millions of people watching the annual football superbowl game. The first televised showing of movies such as *Love Story, Patton,* and *Airport* were viewed by some of the largest television audiences in the brief history of television.

Ratings and total audience figures are but two of several widely used broadcast measures. They are expressed in a context of other types of broadcast-measurement information advertisers need to know.

Fundamental to any television or radio research is a knowledge of the number of sets in working order in households. This information may be determined by special surveys, including that of the U.S. Census Bureau. Set counts are frequently published in advertising magazines, with the information broken down by states and counties. The number of sets must be expressed in terms of sets (AM, FM, UHF, VHF) and may be expressed in numbers of households or as percentages.

Today 97 percent of all households in the U.S. have one or more sets, with 40 percent having more than one set. Approximately 70 percent of U.S. households have a color television set.

The percent of households owning a television receiver expresses the audience that is potentially reachable by the medium. This is the first measure advertising media buyers look for.

Advertisers are interested in the number of households with receivers, but frequently express this and the following measures in percentages. Percentages make comparisons easy and quick. Thus, advertisers often refer to the ownership (sometimes called *penetration*) figure as 100 percent. This makes ownership a convenient measurement base from which other audience measures are calculated.

Sets-in-use is the next widely used figure. This is the number of households in a defined area with their sets on. Sets-in-use may be expressed in numbers of sets. More likely, you will find the figure expressed as a percentage. Assume, for the purpose of a calculation to follow, that 75 percent of the sets in the area are turned on.

Next comes the figure you are familiar with: the *rating.* Ratings express the percentage of all homes in the sample tuned to a particular channel. A rating of 15, for example, is based on all homes in a defined area or in the sample.

Another measure used frequently in the media industry is *share-of-audience*. This measurement expresses the percent of homes tuned to a channel or station based upon the percent of homes with a set turned on (the sets-in-use). Notice that the measurement base has shifted from 100 percent to 75 percent. To obtain the share-of-audience measure, you would divide the sets-in-use, in this case 75 percent, into the rating of 15 percent to arrive at your share of audience. In this case the share is 20 percent.

Why bother with a share-of-audience measure? Why not use just the rating? First, the share-of-audience figure is regarded as more realistic because it represents the reachable audience at any given time. Second, the share-of-audience figure expresses the audience size in a competitive context. The measure reflects the attractiveness or pulling power of one program against others broadcast at the same time. Advertisers find this useful for making current or future buys of broadcast commercial time.

The next measure is *total audience*. The advertiser may know the rating and share-of-audience for a program in which commercials are placed but wants to know whether, for example, anyone was watching the television set at the time. Several broadcast research methods yield this information. If a survey reveals an average of two adults watching a program, the advertiser may then multiply the number of receivers tuned to the program by two. This gives the advertiser the total audience.

Most advertisers, however, are not interested in just numbers of viewers. Advertisers want to know who is in the audience by sex, age, income levels, occupations, and other audience characteristics. Audience information of this type reveals the *audience composition.*.

A final measure you're probably not aware of is the *average audience*. This measure expresses the number of percent of homes tuned to a particular program on a minute-by-minute basis. Average audience information is obtained from recording devices attached to television receivers in a sample of homes. Audience size, on a miute-by-minute basis, enables the advertiser to determine just where to place the commercial within the program being broadcast.

Extracting the Data

There are four common research methods used to obtain radio and television viewing or listening data:

(1) Telephone-coincidental method
(2) Mechanical recorder
(3) Diary
(4) Personal interview

The *telephone-coincidental* method is clearly described by the name. Telephone calls are made to a random sample, and the respondent is asked if (1) the television or radio is on, (2) what program or station is tuned in, and (3) who is viewing or listening. It is assumed that the respondent will give a truthful answer. Since the method is quick, cheap, and easy to execute, it was one of the first methods of broadcast audience research. The telephone-coincidental method has, however, several disadvantages. Telephone surveyors assume, not always correctly, that telephone ownership is synonymous with radio or television ownership. Some people who are called are distrustful; others regard the survey as an invasion of privacy. Also, early morning and late evening calls cannot be made without antagonizing people.

Coincidental ratings can be obtained also by the personal interview method but are much more costly when so obtained. If the cost can be reduced to a feasible level, the personal interview method has much to recommend it since each interview, conducted with a family during the progress of a show, can provide both quantitative and qualitative information about the audience, program, and commercials.

The second method of broadcast-audience research depends upon a device, slightly smaller than a cigar box, which measures sets-in-use and tuning on television sets. These devices, called *audimeters,* record when the set is turned on and to which channel or station the set is tuned. Recording devices can be attached to any or all television sets in a household. Nielsen's Storage Instantaneous Audimeter (SIA) can be connected to as many as four television sets in a household. If a household has more than four sets, Nielsen will use more than one audimeter. The audimeter automatically records and stores information at one-minute intervals.

The information is retrieved via a special telephone line connected to each Nielsen sample household. (If the household has no telephone, Nielsen installs a special line.) A central office computer "interrogates" each audimeter daily. The procedure takes about five seconds.

Audimeter information does not tell whether anyone was watching the television set that was turned on. Repeated telephone surveys by the Nielsen organization suggests the following guidelines: No one is viewing about 4 percent of the television sets turned on during the day. During evening prime time, the figure drops to 2 percent.

The third method of audience research requires respondents to maintain a *diary.* In the diary the respondent lists the times the television or radio was on and the station or channel tuned in. The respondent records, in addition, who was listening or watching at the times recorded. The diary method provides a reasonably economical way of recording audience data, but must depend upon the reliability of the respondent to record fully and accurately the required information.

The fourth method of audience measurement uses *personal interviews* for broadcast-recall information. In this method, an interviewer calls on the respondent to ask what program or station has been heard or seen. Calls are so spaced that morning listening or viewing is asked about in the afternoon. Afternoon listening or viewing information is sought in the evening. Evening listening or viewing is sought the following morning. The respondent may simply be asked what she or he remembers hearing or seeing, or the respondent may be handed a list (often called a "roster") of the actual programs and then asked to report listening or viewing to the listed programs. The personal interview method can also obtain accurate audience composition information. The accuracy of listening or viewing information is more subject to lapses in memory than is the telephone coincidental method.

Reliability of the Data

Broadcast audience measurement uses methods in addition to the primary methods previously mentioned. Different ways of developing samples are used by many researchers. Sample sizes vary. Audience definitions differ, as do the questions asked and the way the data is handled. The result? Often advertisers face mounds of audience measurement information that provide conflicting descriptions of audience size and characteristics. Because the information is developed in so many different ways, the results can not be compared.

In an attempt to develop valid and reliable audience measurements for advertisers, the Advertising Research Foundation set the following standards for broadcast audience research:

Exposure to a broadcast should be measured in terms of set tuning.
The unit of measurement should be the household.
All sets owned by the household should be measured.
The entire reception area should be measured.
The measurement should be representative of all households.
The measurement should report the average instantaneous audience.
The measurement should express the number of households reached.

One of the greatest problems—and one of the greatest sources of controversy in broadcast media audience research—is sampling. There are enormous difficulties inherent in the process of obtaining a representative proportion of a population, gathering the data and then projecting the findings to the entire population. No audience broadcast measurement service is any better than the sampling procedure it employs, no matter what the research method used. Any sample is subject to error, and the degree of error is calculated on the basis of sample size.

Sampling broadcast audiences is done because contacting each of the estimated 68 million television households would be incredibly expensive and time consuming. Furthermore, in handling all this data, the likelihood is that there would be errors larger than calculable sampling errors. Even during the 1970 census, some information was collected from samples of the U.S. population. "Of the 71 questions included in the 1970 census, only 24 were asked of all households. The remaining 47 were asked among a sample of households." The federal government depends on samples to provide us with information on the cost of living, retail sales, wage rates, and unemployment rates.

Broadcast-audience measurements, then, are approximations of true values, because the measurements are developed from samples. How accurate is the measurement? The problem can be stated this way: Many people are skeptical of Nielsen ratings, once they learn the information behind the rating is gathered from only 1,200 households. A rating of 20, for example, means the true rating lies somewhere between 18.7 and 21.3 for two out of three programs. There is error. But you would probably agree, the error is relatively small. How does an advertiser handle this error? Advertisers seldom make decisions about where to place broadcast commercials on just one rating. The advertiser probably will average several ratings of the same program. Because ratings are done constantly throughout the year, the advertiser becomes confident if the resulting audience measurements are reasonably stable.

"Starched" magazine page.

The boxed figures on this page show the reading scores for different sections by men and women. These are based on interviews utilizing the "recognition" type of testing. Best known of the organizations offering such research to advertisers is the Daniel Starch company.

Will we love you in December as we did in May?

STARCH™		Read %
M		15
W		28

STARCH™ AD-AS-A-WHOLE					
Noted %		Associated %		Read Most %	
M	27	M	20	M	1
W	42	W	39	W	5

Choosing a new appliance is ~~~~~ rush into blindly. It's nothing less than a long-term commitment. Whirlpool appreciates that fact. And we think you'll be glad to know Whirlpool makes an important commitment to you. Not just when you buy. But long after. Let us explain.

Quality Controllers who nag, nag, nag.

Our customer assurance staff inspects our products from early design stages all the way to actual in-home use. Demanding, exhaustive tests. Anyone at Whirlpool can tell you, it's not easy working for perfectionists. But it makes darn good sense to buy from them.

A warranty dedicated to you.

Some warranties look like they're written only for lawyers. Not ours. Every Whirlpool letter warranty is easy to read, easy to understand *and* just as easy to use.

Service you can count on.

Whirlpool appliances are designed for years of trouble-free use. But even the best products sometimes need

STARCH™		Seen %
M		25
W		40

repairs. That's why there's Whirlpool ~~~~are®~~~~ service. ~~~~ds are that a ~~~~chised Tech-~~~~erviceman is ~~~~ more than ~~~~inutes away.

Cool-Line for hot tempers.

Toll-free help available to assist you 24 hours a day . . . our Cool-Line® service. If you don't believe us—and our research says you won't—just dial 800-253-1301. In Michigan, 800-632-2243.

A checkup on us.

If you've ever contacted Whirlpool for ~~~~ and Tech-Car~~~~ the Cool-Line, ~~~~ surprised if yo~~~~ back. Right, w~~~~ ourselves with random calls. Just to ma~~~~ satisfied with the job we're doing.

STARCH™		Read Some %
M		6
W		15

"Promises, promises," you say? Well, true. But with promises it's wise to consider the source. Consider Whirlpool.

STARCH™		Signature %
M		19
W		38

Whirlp
Home

STARCH™		Read %
M		4
W		7

We believe quality can be beautiful.

How many American households are tuned in when the rating is 20? Simply multiply the 68 million television households by 20. The number of TV households tuned in is 13.6 million.

The measurement procedures discussed often yield impressive audience figures in the tens of millions. An advertiser wants to go beyond these large audience figures to the portion of the audience that actually saw the advertiser's commercial. Minute-by-minute audience measurement figures provide the basis for an educated guess. Telephone-coincidental studies and personal interviews provide actual commercial recall measures, along with information about the characteristics of people who recalled the commercials.

Cumulative Ratings

Many ratings today are based on the cumulative concept (or "cumes," as they are commonly called). Many radio and television programs can build up large unduplicated audiences over a period of time; that is, many of the same people do not listen to or watch every program. On the other hand, a daytime serial, for example, may have a relatively small but loyal audience. Each viewer attempts to see the program during each weekday broadcast. Each succeeding day's program does not attract many new viewers.

Such a program would have what is called a low audience turnover. The advertiser buying commercial time in such a program would expose the commercial to basically the same people time after time. The result is heavy frequency of commercial exposure to a relatively stable audience. The advertiser might want such an audience.

Television variety shows, on the other hand, tend to have considerable audience turnover, even within a single program. People are pleased with and view one act, but dislike the following act and turn to another channel. Such a program broadcast once a week during the evening would have a relatively high turnover within each program and from week to week. Over the period of a month, such a program will accumulate large numbers of people who have seen perhaps only a part of one program. The advertiser on such a program would be seeking to reach many different people, perhaps once or twice.

A cumulative rating in broadcast gives the total number of households reached over a specified period of time. Only a rating service that measures audiences continually can provide an audience accumulation measurement over a specified time period.

Cumulative ratings are frequently important in the evaluation of low-rated programs. They are especially important today for radio audience measurement where individual program ratings are low. Here, cumulative ratings will show that total audiences become large over a period of time, even for low-rated shows.

A study of radio audience accumulation prepared by the A. C. Nielsen Company indicated the following:

(1) That as a radio compaign is continued there is a strong cumulative growth in the number of unduplicated homes reached. Radio's audience turnover is so great that its total unduplicated coverage increases with great speed.

(2) That as the campaign continues, there is an increase in the average number of commercials heard per home. This was especially noticeable in the three campaign plans suggested for a weekly usage of seven spots, fourteen spots, or twenty-eight spots respectively.

The important finding coming out of cumulative audience studies is that every time a radio announcement is broadcast it reaches a sizable new audience at a greater speed than is the case with television—and that this increase tends to pile up week after week to the inevitable saturation point. Thus radio's reliance in a rating battle with television is not on a strict perbroadcast basis. On this basis, such a comparison will give the average radio station an audience of only about 3 percent of the homes in its area. On a cumulative basis, over a four-week period, a radio campaign may reach, for the average station, a total of 30 percent of the homes in a market.

Cost per thousand households is obtained by dividing the cost of a program or spot broadcast by the rating, times the number of sets in the area being researched. Cost-per-thousand commercial minutes delivered is obtained by dividing the foregoing by the number of commercial minutes.

The out-of-home audience presents special problems, and this is markedly true of radio. Television sets, while common in public places, represent a small proportion of total watching. The rapid rise in car and portable radio sets, on the contrary, has made radio out-of-home listening a sizable proportion of the total listening.

Several organizations are attempting to measure this out-of-home audience. This research has largely been dependent upon some form of diary or personal interview technique; generally the data is not so refined nor as accurate as home listening data.

Evaluating a Media Plan

Most advertisers wish to know what results can be expected from the use of a certain medium, or combination of media. Too frequently advertisers fail to equate a specific piece of advertising to specific sales. This might happen for two reasons. First, the techniques of measurement are not refined enough. Second, there are factors other than advertising at play in the marketplace, and it is not always possible to isolate the effect of these factors. It is not difficult to think of examples. Sales of air conditioners depend upon the weather; a cold summer will produce poor sales in the air-conditioner field, no matter what the amount of advertising. Water hardness in localized sales areas within a larger sales district can create weird sales curves within the same general area. Then, too, product distribution, retail sales effort, and effective point-of-sales material can influence sales results.

All of the known factors must be considered in the evaluation of a media plan. There is no such thing as the "best" medium. Advertisers use test marketing and marketing and media research to help evaluate media for their particular products and their individual sales situations. Bigger advertisers sometimes go to the extent of using sales-test operations in which they set up controlled situations in which one medium can be tested against another, or in

Typical page from a Starch Readership Report.

Figures are supplied in this manner for all the advertisements that were researched in a magazine issue. The Whirlpool advertisement, shown in FIGURE 00, is listed on this page (men readers only). Notice the cost ratio figures on the right that show how much it cost to reach readers in relation to the readership obtained.

READERSHIP REPORT

46 ADS 1/2 PAGE AND OVER
READER'S DIGEST   JULY

MEN READERS

PAGE	SIZE & COLOR	ADVERTISER	COST PENNIES PER READER	RANK IN ISSUE BY NUMBER OF READERS	RANK IN ISSUE BY COST PER READER	PERCENTAGES NOTED	PERCENTAGES ASSOCIATED	PERCENTAGES READ MOST	READERS PER DOLLAR NOTED	READERS PER DOLLAR ASSOCIATED	READERS PER DOLLAR READ MOST	COST RATIOS NOTED	COST RATIOS ASSOCIATED	COST RATIOS READ MOST
		FOOD BEVERAGES												
5	1P4B	BRIM DECAFFEINATED COFFEE	1.0	12	13	53	48	5	106	96	10	125	145	100
156	1P4B	SANKA DECAFFEINATED COFFEE	1.7	28	29	36	30	3-	72	60	6	85	91	60
		CONFECTIONERY/SNACKS												
47	1P4	KRAFT MARSHMALLOWS	1.4	17	19	50	36	5-	100	72	10	118	109	100
		JEWELRY/WATCHES												
180	1P4B	DE BEERS DIAMONDS	1.9	31	36	43	26	3	86	52	6	101	79	60
		CAMERAS/PHOTOGRAPHIC SUPPLIES												
44	1P4B	KODAK TELE-INSTAMATIC CAMERA	.9	5	6	64	57	18	128	114	36	151	173	360
		LUGGAGE/LEATHER GOODS												
148	1P4B	AMERICAN TOURISTER LUGGAGE	1.4	19	21	42	35	3	84	70	6	99	106	60
		MISCELLANEOUS												
185	1P4B	GARDEN GROVE BICENTENNIAL COIN	1.1	13	15	60	46	23	120	92	46	141	139	460
		HOUSEHOLD FABRICS/FINISHES												
166	1P4B	CANNON ROYAL FAMILY PRODS	1.8	29	31	43	28	3	86	56	6	101	85	60
		MAJOR APPLIANCES												
10	1P4	KITCHENAID DISHWASHER	2.4	37	41	31	21	2	62	42	4	73	64	40
27	1P	WHIRLPOOL CORPORATION G P	2.1	38	38	27	20	1	65	48	2	76	73	20
48	1P B	MAYTAG WASHER & DRYER	1.8	32	33	29	23	1	69	55	2	81	83	20
		HOUSEHOLD ACCESSORIES/SUPPLIES												
28	1S	PRESTO PRESSURE COOKERS	2.3	21	40	47	33	3	61	43	4	72	65	40
		CLEANERS/CLEANSERS/POLISHES												
7	1P4B	DRANO INSTANT PLUNGER	1.6	24	26	38	31	6	76	62	12	89	94	120
18	H1/2S4B	TEXIZE GREASE RELIEF	1.4	17	19	42	36	5	84	72	10	99	109	100
		PROTECTIVE COATINGS/FINISHES												
15	1P4B	OLYMPIC STAINS & OVERCOAT	1.5	20	22	42	34	8	84	68	16	99	103	160
		- FEWER THAN 50 WORDS IN AD.												
		MEDIAN READERS/DOLLAR							85	66	10			

READERS PER DOLLAR ARE BASED ON 12,956,000 MEN READERS AND PUBLISHED ONE-TIME SPACE RATES. READER FIGURES
ARE OBTAINED FROM 17,994,151 U.S. A.B.C. CIRC. TIMES MEN PRIMARY READERS PER COPY FROM STARCH ESTIMATES.

which different amounts of advertising can be tried and evaluated. Advertising effect may be evaluated by awareness studies and store audits.

The selection of test towns and the evaluation of the variable constitute a complex problem for the researcher. To provide projectable figures, test towns must be representative. Factors such as distribution must be controlled carefully. Media selection must be applicable to other situations. While the expense of sales testing is heavy, it is considered by some manufacturers to be the best way to arrive at final media evaluation.

Selection of media is sometimes based on factors beyond those that have been discussed. Sometimes a media plan must be sold to the trade and certain types of media are often favored by retailers over others. When retailers' cooperation, is necessary their media choice may be all-important. Certain media, too are much more aggressive than others in contributing merchandising assistance in the form of local promotion, point-of-sale materials, and solicitations of the trade to obtain distribution and support. All these factors must be assessed in media selection.

COMPETITIVE ADVERTISING ANALYSIS

Most manufacturers are interested in their competitors' advertising activity. While keeping abreast of this activity is essentially a mere bookkeeping or recording function, considerable effort is devoted to competitive advertising analysis. Most major media offer some service for recording this information; thus, data are available for specific television or radio commercials and magazine or newspaper advertising. Some services merely report the time or space devoted to a product. In these cases it is necessary to compute the costs; other services report the actual costs. Beginning with this basic data, it is then a simple matter to add up the media expenditures for the promotional efforts of the competitors being investigated.

Measured media generally consist of newspapers, magazines, Sunday supplements, network radio and television, farm magazines, business publications, and outdoor advertising. Media expenditures in these fields are readily obtained. There is much media expenditure, however, that is not accurately measured—point-of-sale material, catalogs, direct mail, premiums, and theater-screen advertising. How much the competition may be spending in these areas can only be guessed. Also, there are other media such as nonnetwork television or radio that are only spot-checked; consequently only partial reports are available.

DEVELOPING AN ALL-MEDIA YARDSTICK

The dream of every avertising researcher is to develop a set of criteria through which all media can be compared accurately and fairly. Many attempts have been made to develop what has come to be known as the all-media yardstick, or the "single" yardstick.

Meanwhile, each media group issues its own yardsticks which, not unexpectedly, result in figures that invariably favor the sponsoring medium.

Such comparisons never fail to elicit shrill cries from the opposition that it is impossible to compare "apples and oranges." The opposing media then proceed to develop their yardsticks which, of course, result in a favorable set of figures for themselves.

Media comparisons and countercomparisons have been occurring for a long time. As one editor has expressed it: "It is inconceivable that this state of affairs can go on forever. A more scientific method of comparing the effectiveness of various advertising media must be developed and more or less generally accepted by the various fields. Then rate and cost adjustments for various media can be made which will permit advertisers to pursue their individual strategies without too much guessing about basic values."

It is dubious that any medium, media association, advertising agency, or company advertising department can ever develop an objective and accurate all-media yardstick. The task, if it is capable of accomplishment, must be done by an impartial organization that has the objectivity, resources, and personnel to accomplish it. The Advertising Research Foundation is such an organization, or possibly the researchers of a large university might be called upon.

Even if the yardstick were developed it would not measure factors that may be important to an advertiser. The yardstick would compare media cost-efficiency and audience figures. Not considered in such a comparison is the unmeasurable prestige of a medium, its suitability for the advertised product, or the peculiar hold it might have on its readers.

One more factor works against the all-media yardstick—the market-by-market individual objectives of each advertiser. The possible media variations resulting from these objectives are infinite. How then can a media yardstick be achieved to cover all these different objectives and the consequent media variations? To this point in time, no one has come close to answering this all-important question.

QUESTIONS

1. For what reasons do advertisers study media research?

2. What does a medium sell to an advertiser or an advertising agency?

3. Why do media associations such as the Magazine Publishers' Association undertake or commission research by independent research firms?

4. Many advertising media provide an environment of news or entertainment for an advertisement. Discuss the environment provided by a magazine you enjoy for a product of your choice.

5. Discuss the relationship of media reach, frequency, continuity, and message cost to the advertising budget.

6. What does media duplication mean? What is the meaning of duplication information to the advertiser?

7. What types of audience information do media offer to advertisers?

8. What does the cost-per-thousand calculation enable the advertiser to do?

9. What is secondary or pass-along readership? Give an example.

10. For what reasons do advertisers adjust the denominator in the cost-per-thousand calculation? Give an example of how you might do this.

11. What is meant by accumulative audience? How is the way in which audiences accumulate important to an advertiser?

12. Why are aided recall scores lower than recognition scores?

13. What checks must a media buyer make in examining research reports?

14. How has radio changed over the years, both in use and in the audience it serves?

15. What are the questions a buyer of broadcast media must ask?

16. Discuss the seven ways of expressing broadcast audiences.

17. What methods would you use to collect data on broadcast audiences?

18. What are some problems that arise with sampling?

19. What is sampling error? How would an advertiser handle it?

REFERENCES

1. For example, a television commercial costing $50,000 to make may be run numerous times, accumulating time charges of $1 million. The ratio, in this case, would be 1:20.
2. The relationship you find between commercial production costs and time costs may appear extreme but is not unusual with the importance of television. Sometimes space costs in limited circulation magazines are lower than the actual cost of making the advertisement. For the majority of media, however, the cost of making the advertisement usually is much smaller than the time or space.
3. Magazine readers can be described as primary and secondary readers. Primary readers are the individuals or households initially purchasing a magazine. Other individuals or households reading the magazines are called secondary or pass-along readers. This pass-along readership may also be described as *projected* readership. Whatever it is called, it adds readers and may be important for the advertiser in determining overall readership. The formula used is the same as the foregoing formula except that readers per copy are expressed in terms of both primary and secondry readership. Some advertisers ignore secondary readers. A number of studies show secondary readers are not so likely to buy products advertised in a magazine as primary readers. For example, dentists may bring magazines from home for their patients to read while in the dental office waiting room. The patients become pass-along readers. Are the patients as likely to buy the products advertised in the magazine as the dentist or members of the dentist's family? In some cases yes; in many cases no.
4. A. C. Nielsen Company, "Everything You've Always Wanted to Know About TV Ratings."

SECTION III

STRUCTURE OF ADVERTISING

8

STRUCTURE OF ADVERTISING

THE ADVERTISING DEPARTMENT

Advertising is people-intensive. The people in advertising come in all shapes and sizes and from all walks of life. This is the first chapter to deal with the people in advertising, what they do, what they are responsible for, and the organizations within which they work.

WHERE ADVERTISING STARTS: THE ADVERTISING MANAGER

The place to start is where advertising starts: with the advertising manager of a company, in this case assume a firm producing a nationally advertised product. To the advertising agency, the manager is the client whose slightest wish is a command. From the advertising manager flows a constant stream of memos, orders, and sudden changes in plans. It is the manager who approves or disapproves budgets, copy and art, media buys, and research proposals. The manager may be a pleasant cooperative partner or a morale-destroying tyrant who complains, rejects, and obstructs the work of the agency.

To top management of the company, the advertising manager may be a highly regarded member of the management team or "that person way down the hall who takes care of advertising." The advertising manager may have complete control of advertising or may make no major decisions. Instead, those decisions may be made by the sales manager, the marketing manager, or the president of the firm. In this case, the manager is simply a buffer between the agency and company management.

Major Responsibilities

Typically, the advertising manager is responsible for starting the advertising process, always within limits set by a budget. The manager makes decisions based on the types of information discussed in Section II dealing with preadvertising considerations.

The manager defines advertising goals or objectives and develops plans to reach the defined objectives. The manager authorizes the creation and place-ment of advertisements, frequently by advertising agencies, and then follows through by monitoring the effectiveness of the advertising.

Advertising Management Problems: Unique and Shared

Each advertising manager faces many unusual problems. This is because each company is unique. Products differ and are distributed in different ways. Pricing, advertising, and the ways in which consumers buy tend to be different for each firm.

On the other hand, some problems are common to most advertising managers. The professional information, and many of the management tech-niques employed, are used by advertising managers for national, regional, or local brands. The same is true of advertising managers of consumer, industrial, financial, service, or retail advertising.

DEPARTMENTS, BIG AND SMALL

In a growing number of companies today, advertising is recognized as im-portant; in some cases, the *key* element in marketing operations, especially for widely distributed, low-cost products that consumers select from open shelves in supermarkets and drug stores.

The advertising department of a manufacturer doing business nationally may employ few or many people, reflecting a management philosophy, com-petitive conditions, and the importance of advertising to the firm.

The department may be small for a business that relies primarily on salespeople and assigns advertising a minor supporting role. This is often the case for industrial advertising. The department may be intentionally lean, even for the large national advertiser for consumer products, with the in-house func-tions restricted to budgeting, planning advertising, and coordinating work con-tracted for with advertising agencies and other outside service organizations or suppliers, such as printers or photography or art studios. A small advertising department responsible for a large advertising budget puts a premium on plan-ning and lead times, coordination and timing.

If the department is large, it may employ many people, perhaps having an in-house capacity for photography or art, copywriting for direct mail, and pro-duct brochures. Direct-mail lists of important customers or prospects may be maintained. Some large corporations have complete in-house production facilities for broadcast commercials and may even place advertisements directly with media. When this is the case, such advertising departments are called "house agencies"—as described in the chapter on advertising agencies. They may qualify for media discounts and may even, occasionally, handle advertising for other companies.

FITTING ADVERTISING TO MARKETING OBJECTIVES

Always within budgetary limits, the advertising manager starts by study-ing the marketing plan and objectives in order to develop an advertising plan. It is important to realize that advertising does not have a life or goals of its own:

Tie-in radio commercial.

Material such as this sometimes may be written by someone in the advertising department of the manufacturer or sometimes by the manufacturer's advertising agency. It is supplied free to dealers in order to encourage them to advertise and to "tie in" with national advertising. In some instances it may be supplied as a part of a cooperative advertising plan in which the dealer and the manufacturer share the media cost of running such advertising.

Radio Script

Time: 60 Sec.
Script No: 10-39-1
Subject: Sound-Gard Body
           Demonstration

Today's John Deere Tractors are full of Sound Ideas. And one of the soundest is Sound-Gard body. The folks at _____ in (dealership)

_____, are anxious to demonstrate why. (location)

So experience the benefits for yourself ... with a test drive of an eighty-horsepower Forty-Thirty, one-hundred-horsepower Forty-Two-Thirty, one-hundred-twenty-five-horsepower Forty-Four-Thirty, or one-hundred-fifty-horsepower Forty-Six-Thirty.*

Sound-Gard cushions out bumps and vibrations. And it has sound-deadening design with generous acoustical padding that keeps interior sound levels at a quiet eighty-three dB(A)** or less. Adjust the atmosphere to your liking ... cool air ... warm air ... pressurization ... dehumidification. Check out the conveniences ... a control console at your right-hand fingertips ... Tilt-Telescope steering column ... stair-step mounting.

Don't overlook the safety aspects ... built-in four-post Roll-Gard protection ... color- and shape-coded controls ... and tinted safety glass.

Stop in at _____ now. And get the feel of Sound-Gard (dealership)

body ... another reason why John Deere Tractors are a sound, long-term investment.

*   DEALER: delete models you do not have
** ANNOUNCER: say "dee-bee-ay"

Advertising is marketing communication. Only when short range and long-range marketing objectives are defined can the advertising manager begin to define and recommend the advertising plan that will best fit and support the marketing effort.

Most organizations are typically confronted with one or more of the four following and basic marketing problems:

(1) introducing a new product or service,
(2) building sales for an established product or service,

(3) stimulating sales for a product with a static or declining sales history, and

(4) changing the consumers' attitudes.

The marketing plan presents a solution to one or more marketing problems. The plan can be brief and in outline form or lengthy and detailed. In either case, the plan is developed on the basis of marketing facts and the types of information or research findings discussed in Section II.

Advertising Objectives: Let's Be Realistic

What is a realistic objective? Actually, there are hundreds of them. They will vary from company to company based upon marketing needs. Some advertising goals are expressed as marketing goals such as sales, brand shares, or a percentage increase in the number of retail outlets or distributors. Ideally, advertising goals are expressed more specifically in advertising or communications terms. Some examples of attainable objectives for advertising include:

(1) *Creating awareness* of the company, brand or product. Awareness levels can be measured very precisely before and after a campaign (long- or short-range) to determine changes.
(2) *Getting customers to specify* a brand name rather than the generic name of the product. In the power tool industry "Skil®" rather than "quarter-inch drill."
(3) *Increase usage by present customers* by showing new uses, providing multiple packs, offering large economy sizes.
(4) *Inciting action.* Getting customers to send in a coupon, ask for a demonstration, visit a retail outlet, accept a free home trial.

Of course, there are many more objectives that advertising can and does accomplish. The important point is that if advertising objectives are to be effective, the following conditions must be met.

(1) They should be stated in terms of what advertising can *realistically* achieve.
(2) They should be put *in writing* in measurable terms (e.g., increase brand awareness by 10 percent or produce a 15 percent increase in demonstrations).
(3) Benchmarks should be established against which results can be measured, whether dollar or unit sales, number of repeat purchasers for a newly introduced product.
(4) Progress toward reaching objectives should be reviewed periodically and changes made if necessary.

Getting It All Together

Advertising objectives can be effective only if they are coordinated with the objectives and schedules of general marketing, as well as manufacturing and engineering. It does little good to prepare a complete advertising campaign only to find out later that engineering has radically modified the product or manufacturing cannot produce it during the allotted time. It is important therefore to set up effective communications lines with other departments of the company to be certain of their day-to-day—and long-range—plans and their effect on advertising.

How important is coordination? Look in the *Standard Directory of Advertisers,* often simply called the "Redbook" in the industry. Find a large, multiproduct corporation selling in a variety of product categories, and the importance of planning and coordination becomes readily apparent.

Just to illustrate, the Borden Company in the mid-1970s worked with 30 different advertising agencies. Glancing at the list of Borden divisional titles indicates the company sells a variety of dairy and beverage products. Food products include bakery, snack foods, and pet foods. The company also sells adhesive tapes and glues, spray paints, and a variety of chemicals and wallpaper. Borden products are sold to consumer, institutional, and industrial markets. Coordination in such a large corporation obviously is at a premium. tion in such a large corporation obviously is at a premium.

In smaller, single-product companies, communications can be most effective since departmental operating heads are generally in the same building and converse daily. In the large, multidivisonal company, however, with hundreds of products, the communications job must be more formalized.

Two of the more practical communication techniques used today are:

(1) *Executive communications meetings.* Called by various names, this meeting is set up for the sole purpose of interdepartmental communication. It has no operating function. Meetings of this type are generally held monthly with representatives of general marketing, advertising, manufacturing, engineering, and administration.

(2) *Task force.* Some companies have established task force groups geared to specific product or market areas. The task force consists of one representative from marketing (usually the product manager), engineering, manufacturing, and advertising. The task force is an operating group assigned with the responsibility for total interdepartmental coordination. They meet frequently (sometimes daily) to discuss current operations as well as both short- and long-range objectives.

(3) Determining how outside services, especially the advertising agency, can best complement and supplement the internal advertising department.

ADVERTISING: WHO'S RESPONSIBLE?

The lines of responsibility for advertising will vary to some degree based upon size of company, the relative importance of advertising to marketing, the size of the advertising budget, the complexity of product lines, and top management's personal interest in the advertising function.

Advertising will usually report to one of these four areas:

(1) *To the Chief Executive.* In these cases, advertising assumes a role equal to the operating heads of other aspects of the business. This type of pattern is generally applied in smaller companies and in companies where advertising is a vital part of the company effort. Also, the advertising manager may report to the head of marketing who, in turn, reports to the chief executive. This is a common approach for companies with several divisions. The organization is structured to provide a centralized advertising department to service the needs of several autonomous divisions of a company. It is a practical organization in cases where product lines are similar but markets vary by division. Such an organization avoids unnecessary duplication of product knowledge and provides a "corporate" flavor to advertising.

(2) *To the Marketing Head.* Many companies today have appointed one person to head up all marketing functions. Whether the title is Vice-president of Marketing, Director of Marketing, or Marketing Manager, this person is totally responsible for all of the company's marketing functions—product line, pricing, packaging, advertising, selling, marketing research, promotions, and a large share of profit responsibility. This has become a popular place to position advertising in recent years, since it places advertising on an equal plane with other marketing functions and coordinates the efforts of all toward a common goal.

(3) *To the Sales Head.* In these cases advertising reports to the head of sales (Vice-president-Sales, Sales Manager) whether or not there is a marketing executive in the company. This positioning is most frequently used when advertising is considered a direct aid to personal selling. It is used when advertising is expected to produce inquiries that can be followed up by personal calls, as in heavy equipment industries (earth movers, bulldozers) or "considered purchase" industries (swimming pools, fencing, remodeling).

(4) *To a Division Head.* This approach is used in multidivisional corporations in which products and markets vary substantially between divisions and where each division is large enough to justify its own advertising department. The division head may be responsible for total marketing or may be a sales head. Here the divisional departments are supplemented by the addition of a corporate staff reporting to the chief executive. The purpose of the corporate department is to coordinate interdivisional efforts, handle corporate advertising, and provide services (research, testing, and media analysis) not practical to obtain at the divisional level.

These various positions for advertising are the most common in use today. The job of the advertising manager is to determine which approach will position advertising where it can most effectively carry out the advertising plan.

FIGURE 8-1
Place of advertising department in overall corporate structure.

Sometimes, especially in smaller companies, the advertising department will report directly to the top executives. In most cases, however, the department will report to the marketing or sales department.

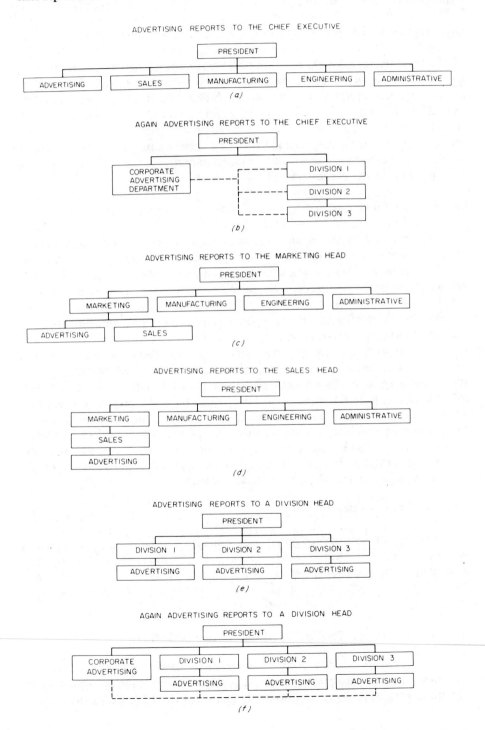

HOW THE ADVERTISING DEPARTMENT IS STRUCTURED

Four basic organization structures are in common use among advertisers today. Organization for any one company may use one of these arrangements or a combination of two or more.

Organization by Function

In this arrangement the division of labor is by the specialized functions required of the department. These functions are advertising, sales promotion, advertising production, and shows and exhibits. This arrangement functions well in smaller companies with relatively simple product lines, since the functions can be shared. For example, in a two-person department the advertising manager may assume responsibility for the advertising and agency contact function. The assistant handles the production and exhibit portions, while the sales promotion aspects are shared.

Organization by Market

This type of organization is useful to companies that manufacture dissimilar products. A large firm making optical products may organize an advertising department for scientific instruments for laboratories, professional people and schools and universities. Another department may advertise products for eyewear and related accessories. Since the products and markets are so diverse, the advertising function is split to provide better advertising effect in each major segment of the business.

When a company manufactures a single product line that is sold in several markets, this approach may be most effective. A large manufacturer of power tools may sell essentially similar tools to four distinct markets. Reaching each market may require different distribution channels. The advertising appeals and media used to reach the markets may vary substantially. To provide advertising focus, the advertising department can be divided to align itself with the marketing divisions. A single agency can be employed, but different account executives are assigned to each division. The sales promotion section also is divided by market to provide specialized assistance.

Organization by Media

This is generally reserved for large advertisers with substantial advertising budgets invested in a wide variety of media. The functions called for are truly advertising functions and specialists are employed for each of the primary media used. Each primary media class has its own section head and specialists in copy, layout, media analysis, budgeting and research.

A WORKING TEAM: THE ADVERTISING DEPARTMENT AND THE AGENCY

Unlike other sections of the company, the advertising department relies heavily on outside services to plan, create and produce a large part of its output.

Advertising department structure by function, product, market and media.

An advertising department is a flexible, multi-sided structure as demonstrated by this chart.

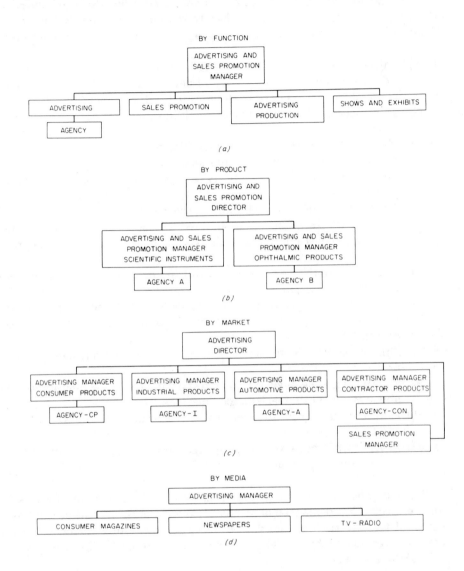

Creative printers are called on to do layouts, specify type, and recommend colors and paper stock on catalogs; commercial photographers contribute to composition of the photographs used; display manufacturers handle the total design aspects of point-of-purchase material, and the advertising agency assumes total responsibility for all aspects of national advertising from the selection of media, through creative planning right down to paying the publication or station for space and time charges.

Well-staffed agencies today give complete advertising and sales promotion service. In addition to media recommendations and preparation of advertisements, many of today's agencies provide backup support in such major areas as market and product research, merchandising, packaging, sales promotion, and public relations.

Both the quality and quantity of work done for a company by an advertising agency depend upon the ability of the advertising manager. In working with the agency, the advertising manager typically is responsible for the following:

(1) Developing and transmitting the advertising plan to the agency. Periodic changes in objectives and newly planned activities to reach those objectives must be communicated to the agency.

(2) Interpreting company policies, attitudes, and preferences to the agency.

(3) Keeping the agency informed about new product developments, sales programs, and competitive conditions.

(4) Arranging periodic meetings between agency personnel and company management.

(5) Providing the agency with most of the raw material for advertising: product specifications, photographs, engineering test data, competitive comparisons, market and product research findings, and pricing information.

(6) Working with the agency in evaluating material available and developing themes, ideas, and campaigns.

(7) Reviewing all layouts, storyboards and copy for approval and, if necessary, obtaining final approval from the proper company executive.

(8) Approving art, proofs and other work requiring official company approval.

(9) Sharing with the agency a joint responsibility for keeping informed about media which reach defined markets.

(10) Auditing all agency invoices to verify charges and to approve payment.

(11) Providing general assistance and direction to the agency in developing advertising campaigns.

There is probably no relationship in modern business that calls for closer teamwork than that demanded of an advertising manager and the account executive of the advertising agency. These two persons represent independent companies bound only by a service contract that can be broken by either party on 60 to 90 days' notice.

LEARNING FROM MEDIA REPRESENTATIVES

The advertising manager supplements information provided by the agency account executive with information from the media.

Most advertising media employ "time" or "space salespeople," often called media representatives (or *reps* for short). These representatives call frequently on both advertising agencies and advertisers. The advertising manager sees as many representatives as time permits, and from them learns about technical changes, for example a magazine may offer metallic inks or tear-out postcards, or content changes—each issue of the magazine may stress a different theme, some of which provide attractive tie ins for the advertiser.

The representative may present the results of new audience studies and other new marketing information of interest to the advertiser. Additionally, most media representatives are veritable storehouses of ideas that have worked successfully in their medium and can be adapted to other products.

Market and Media File

Most advertising managers maintain a Market and Media file, which contains all information on these subjects. The advertising bible, so far as publications are concerned, is Standard Rate & Data Service published monthly in its various sections. However, the buying information in SRDS is necessarily brief and should be broadly supplemented with more detailed reports. A convenient, practical method of setting up the market and media file is first to establish major market headings and then, under each market heading, arrange market data and statistics followed by classified information on media pertaining to that market.

CLIENT EXPECTATIONS COUNT

Some think an agency should stick to making advertisements. Others insist that the agency, as discussed elsewhere, should be involved in the total marketing operation. What *should* the company expect?

First, any agency should provide productive advertising. If it cannot produce advertising that gives more readership, more television-viewer recall, or more inquiries than average, then it does not make much difference what else it can do.

Good advertising, generally speaking, results from an agency's knowledge of a company's marketing situation. Careful study must be given to the company's marketing practices. Only then can customer needs, wants, and desires be translated into the basic appeals used in the advertising copy.

An agency therefore *ought* to be able to write the advertising plan with proper direction and guidance from the client. Whether the agency does write it depends on the client. In some cases, they write entire plans. In others they assist in the development. In still other cases they contribute only information and recommendations.

How far an agency gets into the marketing picture depends on

(1) the abilities of the agency,
(2) the talent available in the company's own organization, and
(3) the marketing situation of the company.

First, as we have said, the advertising manager has a right to expect better-than-average advertising from the agency. After that comes *additional* assistance in the total marketing effort.

Most agencies will provide many services beyond the producing of advertisements. In almost every case agency people will assist in the preparation and presentation of advertising talks for sales meetings before the company sales force and distributors. Unless billing is small, sales meeting assistance is generally provided at no charge.

Many agencies will provide professional assistance in areas such as package design, pricing, research, public relations, campaign development, and sales promotion. In each the agency usually charges a fee.

EVALUATING THE ADVERTISING AGENCY

The advertising manager may be totally responsible for assessing the performance of the advertising agency. Sometimes a marketing department team assembles to review agency performance. Perhaps top management will be involved.

No matter who evaluates the work of the agency, advertising agency people believe the judgments are highly subjective, reflecting a variety of philosophies of creativity, media selection, and general responsibility for sales.

Advertising agency people are aware that the agency is often a scapegoat for poor decisions or problems in the client's own organization.

The Borden Corporation uses an Agency Performance Evaluation Survey. Advertising agency performance is measured by weights in three categories: share of market performance, creativity, and co-operation (see figure 8-2). An advertising agency might argue, for example, that not enough weight is given to creativity and cooperation. Or the agency might argue that too many activities influence sales share and market share to hold the agency so heavily responsible.

Borden believes agency performance must be closely tied to sales growth, market share and the resulting return on investment. If sales, brand shares and returns on investment are not satisfactory, neither Borden nor the advertising agency will prosper. To Borden, this is the final and most important measure. The advertising agency knows this. The agency also knows in advance the criteria the client will use to grade the agency's performance every six months.

Agency Limitations And Bias

Irrespective of how closely the agency works with its clients, there are certain agency limitations that must be recognized in evaluating agency performance. Many agencies today talk of their total marketing orientation and of the wide range of services they offer. This can mislead the new advertising manager into expecting more help than *any* agency can provide. No matter how "marketing oriented" an agency is (or claims to be) it cannot be as knowledgeable about the marketing needs and requirements of its clients as the clients themselves.

In many cases, if an account executive calls on the account three times a week, every week of the year, the company is getting outstanding service. Yet even this account executive cannot be expected to know the intimate workings of a company's marketing department.

A key point to remember is that while the agency and the account executive can provide much help in areas beyond advertising, they should not be considered wizards who can find solutions to all problems.

Another limitation of an agency rests in its creative output. Whether the budget is extremely limited or runs into millions of dollars, creativity will vary. The most creative people in the business have their share of bad advertisements,

Figure 8-2.

Borden Company Agency Performance Survey

EXHIBIT

AGENCY PERFORMANCE EVALUATION SUMMARY

AGENCY

BIANNUAL REVIEW DATED

WEIGHT	ITEM PERFORMANCE EVALUATION	Product Line % Impn't Goal						ITEM POINT SCORE (Item Weight x Evaluation)						TOTAL SCORE
I. 60	**SHARE OF MARKET PERFORMANCE**		%	%	%	%	%							
60	(a) Per cent Improvement Achieved (Memo) Actual Data: Sub Total	%					%						%	XXX
II. 20	**CREATIVITY** (Range: 0 - 100%; 100% = Optimum)		%	%	%	%	%							
6	(a) Marketing Strategy Formulation	%					%						%	
4	(b) Conceptional Ability (Defining & Solving Problems)													
4	(c) Creative Ability in Tv													
4	(d) Creative Ability in Print													
1	(e) Advertising Research Ability (Media & Copy)													
1	(f) New Product Development Sub Total													XXX
III. 20	**COOPERATION** (Range: 0 - 100%; 100% = Optimum)		%	%	%	%	%							
10	(a) Over-all Performance	%					%						%	
5	(b) Service (Deadlines, Cost Control)													
5	(c) Goal Achievement Efforts Sub Total													XXX
IV.	**TOTAL INDIVIDUAL PRODUCT LINE PERFORMANCE** (100 Points = Optimum)	%		%		%		%		%		%		
	A. PLANNED RELATIVE PROFIT IMPORTANCE OF MARKETING STRATEGIES													
	B. TOTAL AGENCY PERFORMANCE SCORE (100 Points=Optimum)													%

(Range: 0 - 100%; 100% = Optimum)

the primary difference being that they produce more truly creative advertisements than poor or ordinary advertisements. For this reason, the new advertising manager should evaluate an agency's creative output over a period of time.

"Hall-of-fame" advertising should not be expected every time the account executive presents a layout. Naturally, if proposed advertisements continue to be below par, the agency should be warned and even dropped if no improvement occurs after warnings.

Another serious limitation with most agencies rests in the area of *media* orientation. Most agencies today continue to derive the bulk of their income from the placing of advertisements in broadcast or print. So long as this practice continues, it is only logical that, as good businessmen, agency people will strive to solve most marketing problems through the use of advertising. This is perhaps the strongest argument for the use of a fee system for agency compensation. Obviously, not all marketing problems find their solution in advertising until the marketing problems have been solved. Yet, an advertising agency will sometimes propose increased advertising appropriations as their solution to a marketing problem, with little consideration for other alternatives. Agency people will take exception to this general statement and yet, it is the rare agency that approaches a client and says, "Please do not do any advertising on this product until this marketing problem has been solved."

Establishment of Togetherness Feeling with the Agency

If the advertising manager expects to get excellent work from an agency, he or she must learn how to build in agency people—particularly the account executive—the same interest and enthusiasm in the company that the manager has. The best way to accomplish a feeling of togetherness with the agency is to convince both company and agency people that the advertising agency is an important supporting arm of the company.

Creative People

Creative people at the agency should be invited to the company on a regular basis to hear firsthand of new product development and campaign strategy. While the account executive assumes primary responsibility for communicating company plans to the creative people, it helps to get writers and artists to the company in order that they can catch some of the enthusiasm and excitement which the company people have for their product.

Advertising managers play an important role in getting top creative work from the agency. Their general attitude and approach to creative work will set a pattern that either encourages or discourages the creative people at the agency. Most people in advertising today are (or think they are) creative. This includes most advertising managers. This simple fact is often the cause for discouraging many creative agency people. The advertising manager who rewrites every piece of agency copy and redos every agency layout is setting the stage for mediocre creative work from the agency. The advertising manager must learn to exercise restraint in reviewing proposed advertisements to avoid stifling top-notch creative effort.

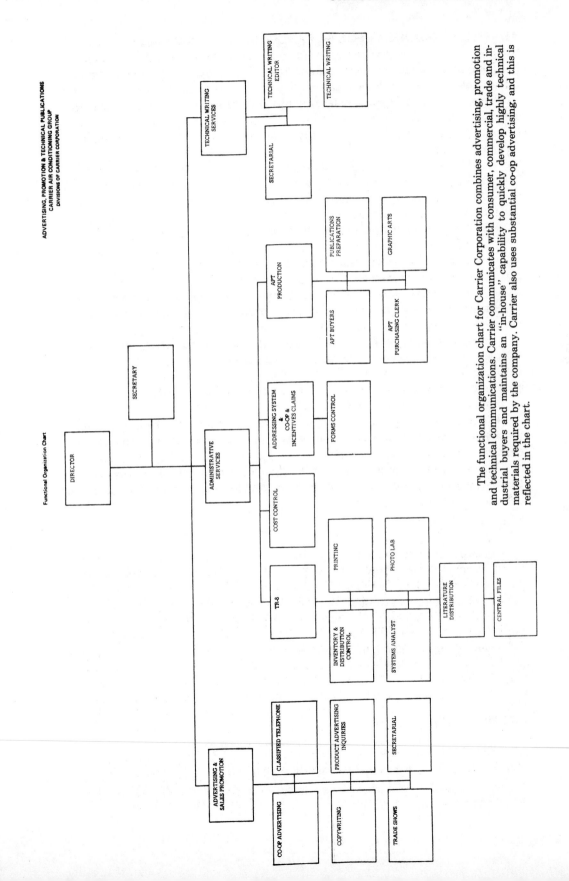

Functional Organization Chart

ADVERTISING, PROMOTION & TECHNICAL PUBLICATIONS
CARRIER AIR CONDITIONING GROUP
DIVISIONS OF CARRIER CORPORATION

DIRECTOR

SECRETARY

ADMINISTRATIVE SERVICES

TECHNICAL WRITING SERVICES

TECHNICAL WRITING EDITOR

TECHNICAL WRITING

SECRETARIAL

APT PRODUCTION

PUBLICATIONS PREPARATION

GRAPHIC ARTS

APT BUYERS

APT PURCHASING CLERK

ADDRESSING SYSTEM & CO-OP & INCENTIVES CLAIMS

FORMS CONTROL

COST CONTROL

TR-8

PRINTING

PHOTO LAB

INVENTORY & DISTRIBUTION CONTROL

SYSTEMS ANALYST

LITERATURE DISTRIBUTION

CENTRAL FILES

ADVERTISING & SALES PROMOTION

CLASSIFIED TELEPHONE

PRODUCT ADVERTISING INQUIRIES

SECRETARIAL

CO-OP ADVERTISING

COPYWRITING

TRADE SHOWS

The functional organization chart for Carrier Corporation combines advertising, promotion and technical communications. Carrier communicates with consumer, commercial, trade and industrial buyers and maintains an "in-house" capability to quickly develop highly technical materials required by the company. Carrier also uses substantial co-op advertising, and this is reflected in the chart.

ADVERTISING BUDGET FORMAT AND PRESENTATION

The advertising manager should develop a budget format that relates budget allocations to specific types of advertising and promotion activities. For example, the advertising and sales promotion functions might be organized as follows in six broad categories:

> *Advertising*
> > National
> > Local
>
> *Sales Promotion*
> > New product introduction
> > New literature
> > "Shelf" literature
> > Advertising department services

Each page of the budget is then broken into three columns to describe the specific *objective*, the *method* to be used in obtaining the objective, and finally the *cost*.

Enough detail should be provided so that it is evident that recommendations are supported by fact, and the final budget can serve as a useful control device throughout the year. To assist in the sales review and management presentation it is helpful to support the proposed budget with an introduction covering general objectives and specific marketing objectives.

For financial review most budgets provide comparison figures showing budget for the new year and current year with dollar variations explained in detail.

Finally, a budget summary is drawn up and a historical comparison table showing expenditures for previous years is provided.

Marketing Review

With budget detail complete, the advertising manager is ready to place specific proposals and figures before the marketing executives. If the budget has been drawn up by the objectives and task method, marketing people will have been involved in establishing objectives and formulating plans and programs for the coming year. As a result, a marketing review of the budget detail becomes a relatively easy step.

Primary objective of a marketing review is to obtain complete agreement on the budget by all parties concerned prior to the formal presentation to top management.

Management Presentation

Depending on the size of the company, these first steps in budget preparation (the plan, the budget, and marketing review) will take anywhere from two weeks to six months. Once the final budget has been detailed and reviewed with marketing, the advertising manager sets out to win management approval.

Budget presentations will range from brief informal discussions between the president and the advertising manager to elaborate presentations using flip charts, film strips, movies, and other visual aids before relatively large management groups. In many cases, the advertising agency is an active participant in the budget presentation. The form a budget presentation takes depends to a large extent upon the personality of top management and the advertising manager as well as the size of appropriation and number of markets served. (See figure 8-3 for sample interpretation of budget presentation.)

FIGURE 8-3
**Comparative budget which includes
explanation of variances.**

DIFFERENCES BETWEEN 19— AND 19— BUDGETS

ITEM	19——	19——	DIFFERENCE	REASONS
Advertising	$———	$———	$———	1) Added TV exposure in (market) to reinforce declining sales.
				2) Increased distribution advertising to announce new division.
				3) Addition of (medium) to cover construction.
New Product Introduction	$———	$———	$———	15 additional products in 19——.
New literature	$———	$———	$———	2 major campaigns required by: ——— division to launch ——— product line.
"Shelf" Literature	$———	$———	$———	Decrease here due to development of master catalog elimination 8 separate specification pages.

Generally, less detail is presented to management in larger companies than in small. Approval of detailed expenses is cleared at divisional level, top management being asked to approve only the broad advertising program in terms of communications, objectives, and total dollars requested.

Whether the presentation is to be informal or elaborate, the advertising manager should prepare the presentation of the budget just as carefully as the budget itself. In presenting the budget the manager should:

(1) Show that the advertising program has grown out of the needs of marketing.
(2) Demonstrate that the advertising program is designed to support the marketing effort.
(3) Prove that the methods used to achieve objectives have been selected to do the job at lowest cost.
(4) Avoid overtechnical language.

(5) Restrict the presentation to essential facts. (Top management, while interested in key points needed to make a decision, can be as easily confused as anyone when presented with too much detail.)

(6) In addition to outlining the proposed advertising plan, point out those products or markets *not* included in the proposed plan.

(7) Provide a copy of the budget or presentation for all persons involved in final approval.

(8) Where the situation warrants, use exhibits to visualize points. Tables or graphs can be prepared to show competitive advertising appropriations, historic comparisons, the split between advertising and sales promotion, measurable results of previous advertising programs, sketches or layouts of new campaigns.

A thoughtfully prepared and professionally presented budget stands a good chance of obtaining management approval if

(1) the company's cash position is good,
(2) prospects for increased sales look promising, and
(3) the past year's business has not been so bad that management is super-cautious.

EVALUATING ADVERTISING: LOOKING FOR RESULTS

Evaluating the effectiveness of advertising is a favorite subject of conversation among businessmen everywhere. More and more, today's advertising manager is being asked to justify advertising expenditures with evidence of results. Almost daily the advertising manager faces questions or challenges like these:

Why advertise? It's profits we're after, not more cost.
We've been in business a long time; our customers are sold on our products.
Instead of advertising, why don't we hire more salespeople?
How do we *know* our advertising is producing results?

The advertiser whose only contact with the customer is through direct mail can give very specific answers to these questions. If many orders are received as a result of a direct-mail advertisement, then the advertisement is a good one. Conversely, if few or no orders are received, the advertisement is dropped. In either case, the advertising manager can say precisely how effective each mailing is, both in units and dollars.

Such precision is not possible with advertisements placed in other media. In fact, few companies today expect sales as a direct result of their advertising. Too many other factors influence sales.

Advertising objectives are stated, however, in measurable terms, so the advertising manager decides in advance what is to be measured and by what research method. The reason for specifying the research method is because advertising effectiveness scores reflect the method used.

Because the first job of advertising is to attract attention, samples of consumers may be asked to name the first brand that comes to mind for facial tissues or mouthwash. Or they may be asked to recall television commercials from the previous evening's viewing.

Interviewers for readership-research firms may go through an issue of a magazine a consumer acknowledges having read to see how many advertisements the consumer recognizes and whether readers associated the brand name with a benefit or whether the reader can give evidence of having read most of the advertisement. This is what researchers call a *recognition procedure* and yields information that enables the advertiser to compare current and past advertising performance for a brand as well as current advertisement performance with that or one other advertisements in the magazine.

Other magazine-research procedures require more mental effort from consumers, making greater demands on memory. As a result, scores are lower, but to many advertisers more meaningful. These are called recall procedures. They are particularly useful in revealing confusion of advertised claims for competing products, a fact acknowledged in Goodrich Tire advertisements expressly mentioning the Goodyear Tire blimp. Because scores of advertising effectiveness vary by the way in which questions are asked of consumers, the expression of an advertising objective—a 10% increase in awareness—should specify the research method to be used.

At predetermined time intervals, the advertising manager may use surveys to trace the mental movement of consumers toward purchase, asking whether consumers are interested in the product, what consumers know or think about the product, whether the benefits claimed are believed and whether consumers intend to try the product.

Beyond asking questions, the advertising manager has a number of particularly useful measures of effectiveness, many of which yield information as a byproduct of some consumer activity.

(1) *Increased sales of a product following a campaign.* Obviously, if sales for a particular product or product line go up substantially following a particular campaign, advertising will have had some effect. When presenting this type of story to management be certain to point out that advertising was *not fully* responsible for the increase. Remember that *decreases* in sales following a campaign can be evidence of ineffective advertising.

(2) *Sales in areas not covered by a salesperson.* While not always traceable to a specific advertisement, such sales may be attributed to advertising, although public relations effort and word-of-mouth advertising may also have had an effect.

(3) *Coupon response.* Coupons are keyed by a department number or post office box address to identify the specific magazine and issue from which a coupon is returned. The same is true of newspaper coupons. The advertiser can measure the pulling power of a medium.

(4) *Inquiries.* This is another behavioral measure. Many industrial publications intentionally stimulate inquiries with a page of inquiry tear-out post cards at the back of the publication.

(5) *Study of guarantee cards.* Many companies ask that the customers return a guarantee or warranty card to register their product. Such cards can be designed to extract information concerning the original cause for the sale. Here again, however, care must be used in such an evaluation since many customers will not report that they decided to purchase as a result of a specific ad or campaign. Still a guarantee card can be used to trace the origin of a *large* order and to learn what part advertising played in obtaining it.

(6) *Field work.* A good place for an advertising manager to determine advertising and sales promotion effectiveness of the company is in the field. Although it may be difficult for the advertising manager to take a day off for the purpose, yet when the manager leaves the office to look a distributor, dealer, wholesaler, or customer in the eye, the manager is facing marketing in its most direct sense. This is the real world. The flow of information developed by surveys and other scientific and not-so-scientific techniques often are undimensional at best, misleading at worst.

Only in the field can the advertising manager learn how advertising is regarded by the sales force, by jobbers, wholesalers, and retailers. Are displays being used? Is coupon redemption handled smoothly, or do retailers have complaints? Is merchandise fresh and frequently rotated? How many shelf facings are there? What is the competition doing?

What about consumers? Are they buying single packages of the advertiser's branded product, or several packages at once? Who is buying? Which member of the household? Do the consumers the manager sees paying for the product in checkout lines fit the demographic descriptions yielded by consumer surveys?

In most cases one solid week in the field will provide the equivalent of six months of committee meetings at the home office. The advertising manager should be in the field a minimum of 10 percent of the time, and an ideal would be 20 percent. Pressures of day-to-day business make this seem impossible, yet it is the best time investment an advertising manager can make. Field work proves to the sales organization and to wholesalers and retailers that the manager wants to make advertising work for them.

(7) *Common-sense measurement.* Another area of measurement is based on the common-sense observations of the advertising manager who will consider the question of effectiveness in all activities and ask such questions as:

Do we have any unsolicited letters from customers on particular ads?
How did the salespeople react to this campaign?
How did our dealers react?
Did dealers complain because the ad program broke too soon and customers were asking for the product?
How did competition react?
Did advertising publications pick up the ad?

Advertisement aimed at establishing company's place in its industry.

A company that it is second in its field (and has a name somewhat similar to its chief rival) has a problem of consumer identification. The advertiser, in this instance, has as one of its principal goals the registration of its name on the consciousness of the tire-buying public.

"JOCELYN" :30

JOCELYN: Whatcha doin' there Stevie?

STEVIE: Checkin' to see the treads wearing evenly on my Goodrich Radials, Jocelyn.

JOCELYN: Why?
STEVIE: My Goodrich dealer said I should.

JOCELYN: Why?
STEVIE: It's safer and I want

the tires to last even longer.
JOCELYN: Why?

STEVIE: They're fabulous tires.

You don't know anything about tires. Jocelyn.

JOCELYN: Hey look.

The Goodrich Blimp.

(SHE LAUGHS)

ANNCR: (VO) Tires you can trust.

B.F. Goodrich. The Other Guys.

Were any awards given by trade associations for a particular campaign?

QUESTIONS

1. What are the responsibilities of the advertising manager?

2. What are some examples of marketing objectives? Advertising objectives?

3. Why should advertising objectives be expressed as precisely as possible?

4. What does the advertising manager learn when meeting with media representatives?

5. What does the advertising manager expect from the advertising agency?

6. How does the advertising manager go about evaluating advertising?

7. What four basic marketing problems face advertising?

8. Why are advertising departments organized in different ways?

9. What advertising agency work requires the advertising manager's approval?

10. If you work for an advertising agency, what arguments would you offer against the evaluation of your agency's performance on the basis of product sales?

11. How can the advertising department coordinate its activities with other departments in the firm?

12. What are some advertising agency limitations?

9

ADVERTISING AGENCIES

ADVERTISING AGENCIES

Joe Fredericks runs a one-person advertising agency in a small town in Iowa. Among his clients are a used-car dealer, a supermarket, a hardware store, and the town's only department store. Fredericks does the advertising planning for his clients, plus all the creative work, media placement, and related assorted odd jobs.

Jason Kilbourn is president of a 500-person New York City advertising agency that has branch offices across the U.S. and in London and Germany. He is deeply involved in the marketing and advertising plans of some of America's largest corporations. In addition, of course, he is responsible for keeping his own organization solvent and the employees reasonably content.

Both men, on different scales, find their work satisfying, challenging, and impossible to handle in the normal eight-hour day. Each feels keenly the need to help his clients prosper in the marketplace. Each is totally involved in the affairs of his clients. Service to the client is the overwhelming motivation that drives both men each day.

Small, middle-sized, and giant agencies all share the "service to the client" guiding principle. If you were to visit advertising agencies in Turkey, India, Japan, Italy, Sweden, or Iran, you would find this same motivation is present. It is the reason why advertising agencies exist.

A young man or woman with a yen for interesting, exciting, and rewarding work will find few activities that match advertising agency work in all three respects.

Hungry for people with ideas, imagination, energy, and common sense, advertising agencies reward such people handsomely, quickly, and while they are still young enough to enjoy such rewards to the fullest.

In the advertising agency we find advertising in its most concentrated and yet most varied form. Here in this one organization we find all the activities that are associated with advertising. No other place where advertising goes on—media, company advertising departments, or research companies—brings together all the advertising skills found in the advertising agency.

Rough storyboard for famous and effective campaign.

Companies "shopping" around for advertising agencies to handle their advertising will be strongly influenced toward agencies that have produced such successes as this campaign. Adults and youngsters alike have learned to look for the "Doughboy" presenter in Pillsbury commercials. His use presents some production challenges, however, because stop motion photography is used to give him movement. Thus, for each second the "Doughboy" appears on the screen, 24 photographs must be taken.

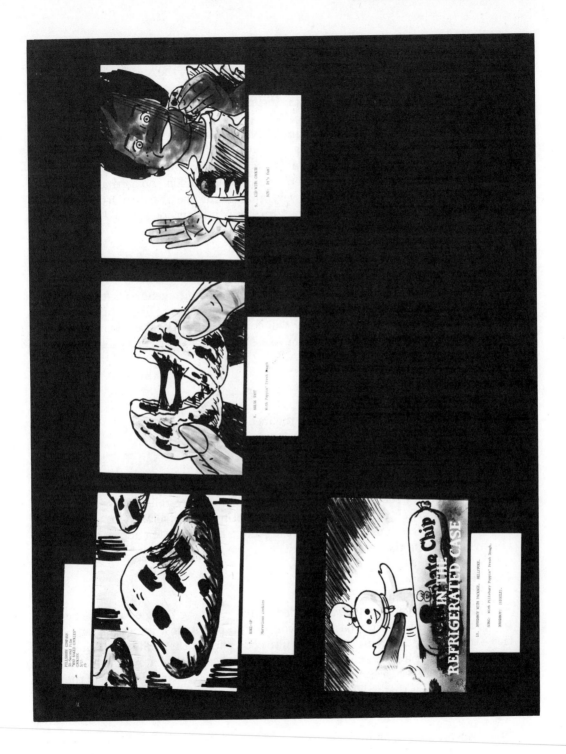

It is this amalgam of talent that makes the advertising agency so interesting to the public and business world at large, and that makes the advertising agency so fascinating to its own workers. A walk down the row of offices in a large advertising agency will take the viewer past artists, writers, musicians, television experts, marketing experts, top merchandisers, show-business experts, and a host of other specialists.

There is hardly any other enterprise that so closely relates hard-driving, hard-headed business skill with the various aspects of show business. An advertising agency account executive who at one minute may be discussing the proper way to enlist the support of food brokers in a multimillion-dollar marketing and advertising campaign, may the very next minute be asked to decide the merits of using a glamorous motion picture star in a television special that can well become the talk of the entertainment world.

WHAT AN AGENCY DOES FOR A CLIENT

There are three basic functions that an advertising agency performs in behalf of a client. These have been the basic functions since the beginning of the modern advertising agency, and they will continue to be despite all the additional functions advertising agencies have assumed over the years. These basic functions are:

(1) To help clients plan their advertising
(2) To prepare their advertising
(3) To place their advertising in the media

Help Clients Plan

Since all advertising that matters begins with a plan, it is natural that the advertising agency should have an important part in the overall planning. Such planning will include every aspect of the marketing and advertising required. Some of the aspects considered will be the selling, the marketing approach, the creative approach, the selection of media, and the research required.

Do Creative Work

Overall creative strategy was decided in the "planning" stage. Now it is up to the agency to perform what many consider to be its most important function—translating the creative strategy into copy and art that will sell goods or services or create a favorable feeling for the advertiser and whatever he has to offer. Part of the preparation detail is selection by the advertising agency of the printing processes that will be most suitable for carrying out the creative objectives.

Place Advertising In Media

After advertising has been planned and prepared it still is without meaning or value until it has been placed in the advertising media—and not in just any media but in the media that will convey the advertiser's message most effectively to the greatest number of buying prospects at the lowest cost. Thus the advertising agency is far from being a neutral figure in media placement. In handling its media obligations the advertising agency has both a mechanical function and a thinking function. It is "mechanical" in the very exacting physical scheduling and placement of the advertising, and in making the billing arrangements. It is "thinking" in deciding which media to use and why.

Other Advertising Agency Services

Although there may be some argument about the major classifications of the additional functions (not to mention that, in some cases, these so-called "additional" functions may be thought of as basic), the important classifications to most agencies are:

(1)   Marketing (including merchandising and sales promotion help)
(2)   Public relations (sometimes merely publicity and sometimes both publicity and public relations)
(3)   Research (advertising and marketing)

WHY MEDIA PAY COMMISSIONS TO AGENCIES

Over the years, good media men have pondered the question of why media pay commissions to agencies. Some have refused to go along with the practice, because they have felt that the business handled by agencies would have come to them anyway.

Others have gone along with the custom grudgingly but have had serious misgivings about the common sense of the system. Still others gladly pay the commission because of certain functions performed by advertising agencies that otherwise, these media reason, they would be forced to assume themselves.

Some of the reasons why media accept the agency commission system:

The creative burden is eliminated. Under the present system, copy and art are furnished by the advertising agencies in behalf of their clients. Were the advertisers to place space and time orders directly thus bypassing the advertising agencies, they would expect much more creative help than is now required of the advertising media. Small advertisers, in particular, would be dependent upon the media for creative assistance. Extension of such help by media would thus become a form of selling expense.

The credit risk is minimized. Advertising agencies are responsible for the media bills run up in behalf of their clients. If this were not so, the media would first of all need to conduct expensive credit investigations of each advertiser. Then they would need to collect from each one and take the loss whenever the advertiser defaulted. Instead, the media collect only from the agency. Defaulting by financially responsible agencies is a rare occurrence.

Sales costs are eased. A big advertising agency may represent 100 or more clients, many of whom will have multiple brands each headed by a different brand manager or advertising manager. Media salesmen, if the advertising agencies did not exist, would need to make constant, well-planned calls on all these different people, no doubt widely scattered geographically.

A typical advertising agency organization chart by function.

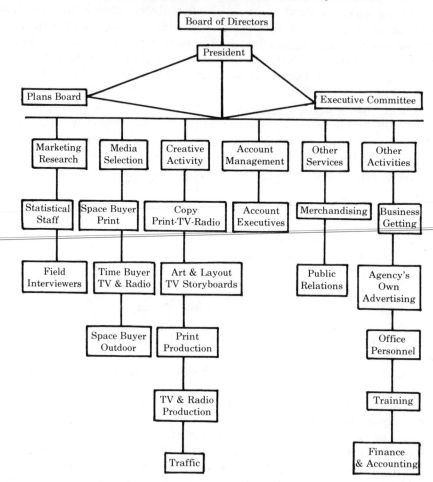

Instead, sales calls can be made at one advertising agency office upon the account executives or media buyers representing all these accounts with their numerous brands. An additional advantage is that, unlike many of the clients, the advertising agencies are located principally in the cities where the important media are operating. In the case of smaller media in nonmetropolitan areas, the sales calls upon advertising agencies are made by national representatives—firms that represent these media in the metropolitan areas.

Scheduling detail is cut. One of the advertising agency's most irksome tasks is making certain that media schedules are met—that the print or broadcast material is delivered on time. The mere keeping of records for the advertising put out by a big agency is a masterpiece of organization. In the main, the job is done well and the great bulk of the advertising is in the media's office in time to meet scheduled dates, and usually with a minimum need for follow-up by the media. Much of this detail would fall on the media were agencies out of the picture.

Mechanical production is handled. A newspaper printed by letterpress receives a heavy package from the XYZ advertising agency. When the wrapper is removed, there is an electrotype of an advertisement produced for the agency's client. Sent to the back shop, the electrotype is ready for putting in the chase (an iron frame in which the electrotpye is locked). Good reproduction is assured and nothing was required of the newspaper in the whole transaction.

By far the bulk of material sent to the media by advertising agencies requires no production effort on the part of the media, whether the material is printing plates for newspapers or magazines, or radio tapes, or film commercials for television.

WHY COMPANIES CONTINUE TO USE AGENCIES

Here and there are companies using national advertising that do not make use of advertising agencies. These are not usually big companies, and there are not many of them. If a company wishes to do its own advertising and to place its advertising directly with the media, there is nothing that bars this procedure. Such a company, furthermore, may produce excellent advertising, since all the creative talent is not necessarily appropriated by advertising agencies. There are, however, some reasons that make most advertisers of any size feel that it is sensible to employ advertising agencies. These reasons are:

A company doing its own advertising requires a greatly expanded advertising department.

Copy, art, media scheduling, production, and research must, if there is no advertising agency, be provided by the company. As it is, most advertising departments, even of some very large corporations, consist of just a few persons. These small departments would not be possible if all the advertising work were done by a company instead of by an advertising agency.

It must be kept in mind, also, that most of the advertising agency's services are provided within the 15 percent commission given by the media. This means that the company without an advertising agency would need to incur the heavy expense of doing its own advertising and still would be required to pay the full media price, since it would not be eligible for the media commission. Thus, the company would find its advertising costing far more than if it engaged the services of an advertising agency.

A company doing its own advertising does not have available the wide background acquired by the usual advertising agency.

Over the years, an advertising agency faces a wide range of advertising and marketing problems. Also, it acquires knowledge of a great variety of products and services. In addition, it piles up experience with media, research, mechanical production, and all the other facets of advertising.

Few company advertising departments, if any, can acquire the rich background of a medium-sized or large advertising agency. So often the knowledge of how to advertise or market one product can be useful in advertising or marketing another product. Agencies use this knowledge constantly in behalf of clients.

A company doing its own advertising lacks the benefit of an objective, outside viewpoint.

Its detached viewpoint is often the strongest advantage offered by an advertising agency. Conceivably a company may approximate other advantages of an agency. It is possible, for instance, for a company to afford an advertising department large enough to provide the equivalent of an advertising agency's service. Also, an advertising department can acquire background sufficient to enable it to match that of an advertising agency.

No company advertising department, however, if it does all of its own advertising, can avoid thinking and reacting the way the company itself does. Sometimes this may be perfectly all right. other times it may result in "company" advertising rather than fresh, daring, and original advertising. If the company president or other top officials are strong-minded persons, it is going to take a courageous advertising manager to insist on what is right rather than to give in to the bosses by approving advertising that is not as good as it should be.

On the other hand, raw courage is not always found consistently even among advertising agencies, despite their repeated claim that they can offer advertising counsel untinged by fearful consideration of what the company's top executives may say. Too much of advertising agency advertising is guided by what the client will "buy" rather than by what the agency knows is right. Thus, except in a relatively few instances, advertising agencies do not have a more outside, objective, fearless viewpoint than might be found in a well-staffed company advertising department.

HOW AGENCIES GET PAID

Although many complicated and ingenious arrangements are worked out between clients and advertising agencies, three payment systems prevail: a straight retainer, a flat fee, and a commission basis.

Straight Retainer

If the advertising agency is relied upon more for counsel than for everyday execution of advertising, it often establishes a yearly retainer arrangement to be paid in monthly installments. Publicity and public relations work by advertising agencies is often paid in this manner. If at the end of the year it is found that the client's demands were very light, or were very heavy, the retainer may be revised accordingly.

The retainer arrangement is quite often used for local accounts, since the advertising agency may not be granted media commissions; or it may be to the client's advantage to obtain a bigger discount by placing advertising direct with local media. He than pays the advertising agency the retainer, since this is the only way the agency will be compensated.

Fee

Fees are especially useful:

(1) where the advertising work to be performed is quite infrequent;
(2) where the work does not involve media commissions. Examples: doing

a motion picture script; turning out a house organ; organizing a closed-circuit arrangement for a company sales meeting

(3) where the 15 percent commission is insufficient compensation.

Here and there, a large advertising agency works out a fee arrangement with a big advertiser instead of the commission form of payment, the commissions being turned over to the client. Those who favor this system say that an advertising agency operating on the fee basis will not be inclined to recommend high-priced media simply to increase its commission payments. Instead, it will recommend only those media that will do the very best job for the client since, regardless of the commission, it will be paid anyway.

This kind of fee arrangement is still on trial. Meanwhile, the big advertising agencies and the big advertisers operate mostly on the media commission arrangement, or on a combination of commissions and fees (and sometimes retainers).

Commission

The importance of media commissions to advertising agencies is apparent in the fact that about 75 percent of agency income is derived from media commissions. The other 25 percent comes from service fees or retainers.

In the relatively short years of its existence the agency commission system (or discount system, as it is often called) has become famous—or infamous, depending on the viewpoint. Generally, as indicated previously, the commission amounts to 15 percent, which is taken off the normal media rate and passed on to the advertising agency.

Although criticism of the media commission system is strong, even stronger criticism is heard frequently about the practice of advertising agencies adding a similar commission on top of actual charges for the various services it renders clients. These services may include anything from furnishing freelance artwork to arranging for the production of a filmed television commercial.

STEPS IN PAYMENT BY COMMISSION

(1) A client of Roswell & Blair advertising agency is Nash, Inc. On behalf of the client, the agency puts through a space order in a women's service magazine. Space charges are $13,800.00.

(2) Roswell & Blair, also on behalf of the client, contracts for some outside production. Charges for this outside work are paid by the agency. These charges are:

Engraving plates and printing. Charges for plates, printing, and the writing of catalogs, booklets, and folders cause continual trouble in agency-client relationships. One reason for this is that arrangements vary so much from agency to agency.

Plates and printing are usually compensated for by the 17.65 percent charge addition. If, however, the printing is very heavy, as for sales manuals, booklets, and catalogs, the addition of the 17.65 percent charge may shock the client into setting up a company printshop or getting bids on the local market.

As for the advertising agency preparing a catalog, it can well get into a bog of time-consuming detail work that makes the job unprofitable unless a heavy fee is agreed upon, or unless the agency can add its commission to the printing costs. Sometimes this commission is set up on a sliding scale, starting at 10 percent and going downward as the printing costs go up.

The writing of booklets, catalogs, or folders is performed free by some agencies, under a fee arrangement by others, and under a commission agreement by still others.

Research. Research is another touchy area. Many advertising agencies are not equipped to handle the various details involved in research, such as determining the sample, devising questionnaires, setting up interviewing arrangements, and tabulating and reporting on the results. Is it right for such agencies to add the 17.65 percent charge for the total cost of the research when their chief contribution was to locate the research organization and get it and the client together? Even if the advertising agency looks over the research as an experienced critic, is this enough to warrant the full advertising agency service fee of 17.65 percent?

Many advertisers feel it is not and, consequently, make their own arrangements with research organizations. The only answer is for the advertising agency to contribute more to the total process. If the agency, for instance helps design the questionnaire and the sample and takes care of the tabulating or possibly the interpretation of the results, this may cause the client to consider that the commission has been earned.

Talent costs. "Outrageous" has been the word used by many advertisers when they find the advertising agency has added its heavy 17.65 percent to talent charges. Once more it is felt that locating the talent is not enough work or trouble to justify the fee.

An advertising agency will counter that knowing how to locate and sign up talent is an art, and that a number of high-priced people in the agency are specialists in this art. Getting the right talent for a big show, moreover, may have such an effect on ratings and increase the exposure to the advertising so much that the commission is a small price to pay.

Many agencies even mark up residual payments. These are payments made to television talent when commercials in which they appear are run beyond a specified period. Thus, each rerun is profitable to the agency as well as the talent.

Copy and art. At one time, advertising agencies did not charge clients for copywriting time or for layout work done in the agency art department.

As agency profits have dwindled and costs have risen, numerous advertising agencies now charge for copy and art on a time basis. Agencies that do not, reason that the basic functions of copy and art are included in the 15 percent media commission.

In many agencies that have adopted cost accounting, every artist, copywriter, research person, and account executive keeps a record of the time spent in daily activities, and this time is then charged against the client in proportion to the hourly compensation of the employee. Only the top executives and the clerical help do not maintain such records.

FEE PAYMENTS AND ALTERNATIVE SYSTEMS

Although there has been much switching to fees, many clients and their agencies are reluctant to get into the complex bookkeeping that often results from the change. A problem is that there are so many variations of fee arrangements. The list of some of them that follows will demonstrate and provide some idea of the possible complexity of administering some of these arrangements:

$ 375.00 Artwork supplied by a free lance artist.
185.00 Typography from a printing firm.
450.00 Engraving plates for color work.

$1,010.00 Total

(3) The agency is billed directly by the magazine. The bill looks like this: $13,800 minus 15 percent, or $11,730. A cash discount is taken off the net amount of $11,730. Thus, the total media bill is $11,730 minus the discount of $234.60, or $11,495.40.

(4) Nash, Inc. is billed by the agency for the gross cost of the space $13,800 minus the cash discount of $234.60 for a total space cost of $13,565.40.

(5) Nash, Inc. is also billed for the gross cost of outside expenses $1,010, plus 17.65 percent for a total cost of $1,188.26.

(6) Total charges submitted by the agency to Nash, Inc. are:

$13,565.40 for space charges
1,188.26 for outside costs. This includes the 17.65 percent.

$14,753.66 Total

(7) The agency's profit in the transaction was:

$2,070.00, which is 15 percent of the space cost of $13,800
178.26, which is 17.65 percent of the outside costs of $1,010.00.

There are several aspects of this billing system that can puzzle the outsider. The 2 percent discount for cash payment is taken from the net media bill, not the gross. Furthermore, it is merely a bookkeeping transaction, since it is passed on to the client. It is not calculated as agency profit unless, for some reason, it is not passed on. Then, too, it does not appear in the billing for outside expenses.

In the example, outside expenses are billed to the client at actual cost plus 17.65 percent, though some advertising agencies bill cost plus 15 percent. In either event the commission on top of outside expenses is often resented bitterly by clients who feel that the agency has not done enough work in such instances to earn the commission. Many critics suggest abolishing the commission charge on all production work. It is recommended that if an agency is losing money on such work, a fee should be charged.

Some confusion exists about the thinking behind the use of the 17.65 percent. It stems from the reasoning that profits and commissions should be based on the total sale price, not on the cost price.

If, for example, the figure involves $100, it makes sense to first add 17.65 percent for a total of $117.65, and then to take the 15 percent, which comes to $17.65. A markup of 17.65 percent is the same amount of money as a discount of 15 percent.

Usually when an advertising agency is arranging for outside work to be done, it will request the supplier—whether a printing concern, an artist, or a television production firm—to bill on a "commissionable" basis, which means that the 17.65 percent is figured into the total bill. In this way the advertising agency is assured of its full commission on the sales price.

FLAWS IN THE COMMISSION SYSTEM

One of the glaring troubles with the commission system is that an advertising agency will be vastly overpaid in some instances and badly underpaid in others.

Anyone, for instance, who has turned out industrial advertisements knows that they require much technical background and great care in the writing. A good industrial advertisement may be much more difficult to write than a consumer advertisement for cereal, soup, or soap. The artwork, also, may be more demanding, since it may well require the execution of complicated graphs and charts, or the use of difficult-to-obtain location photographs of machinery or machines in action.

A consumer advertisement, in four colors, running in *Woman's Day* currently costs around $42,000, just for the space. The advertising agency's commission on that part of the advertisement is $6,300.

The hard-to-do industrial advertisement running in *Metal Progress* costs $1,690 for a black-and-white full page. Four-color process is $645 extra (both charges in effect at the time this book is being published). Commission: $350.25.

From the foregoing examples, it is easy to see that the commission system very often pays the agency for the space used (or actually for the type of space used) rather than for the work that has to be done.

Another weakness in the system is that it encourages some agencies to recommend to clients media that will yield a substantial commission to the agency rather than those media which might be better for the client's promotional objectives.

Newspaper cooperative advertising, for example, is looked upon by some advertising agencies with a notable lack of enthusiasm. Such agencies would rather see the advertising money go into national consumer magazines or into network television, even though, under certain circumstances, the low-paying cooperative advertising would be best for the advertiser.

Commission Payments: Overpayment and Underpayment

Many advertisers tend to accept the 15 percent media commission without objection. They reason that this commission would not be given to them if they ordered space or time directly. Even though the advertising agency is rewarded excessively for some advertisements, they can see that the compensation is insufficient for certain other advertising, notably that which is prepared for the business publication field.

Advertisers are, however, anything but philosophical about some of the charges other than those for space and time.

Point-of-purchase material. Creative work on such material may run much higher than for glossy consumer magazine advertisements. Copy and layout time will not be covered even if the 17.65 percent is added. Clients, shocked by advertising agency charges for turning out such material, often shop for better prices. This may be shortsighted economy, since the advertising agency is more likely to be able to fit this material into the overall campaign objectives than some outside organization. In fact, this material, such as retail-store floor stands, window displays, and counter displays, may be vitally important to the success of the campaign. Sometimes, if the client is willing to let the advertising agency add the commission to printing costs, the agency can make its profit in this manner.

Fixed fees	Minimum-maximum fees
Fees based on hourly rates	Incremental fees
Minimum guarantee fees	Project fees
Fixed fees plus direct costs	Stock or royalty fees
Fee plus media commission	Fees based on reduced commissions
Cost plus profit	Fees based on volume rebates

Despite inherent complexities, advocates of the fee system laud it for increasing cost consciousness of the client as well as the agency. They point out, for example, that when fees are charged for specific services, there is less likelihood of clients themselves being capricious in their demands. As it is now, the demands may often be unreasonable because they are made under the commission umbrella and viewed in a sense as "free."

Alternatives

One big company uses the 15 percent as a yardstick and even though it is on the fee arrangement pays up or down from the 15 percent according to the type of work. Under this system, they may pay 21 percent for services on industrial accounts and 14 percent on consumer accounts.

Another uses a sliding-scale payment based on

(1) the number of advertisements and campaigns prepared for each product;
(2) the services provided for the client and the depth of the service provided.

Incentive plans are favored by some advertisers. In one of these the client pays a profit bonus for an outstanding contribution to its business success. Another has a cost plus profit system with profits related to increased sales at a lower advertising-to-sales ratio.

Behind these various methods is the philosophy that the agency is entitled to a fair profit, but that the system should be in the best interest of the client, as well as fair to the agency. Implicit in this feeling is the thought that agencies should not be rewarded merely for how hard they work but for what they accomplish. If the accomplishment is there, the incentive will be there.

Will the Commission System Continue?

Critics of the commission system have been predicting its demise for years, but advertising agencies continue to use it, with modifications, because to this time no truly better system has been evolved. Publishers and broadcast media likewise have failed to offer a better system. Mixed into the situation is a sense of tradition. It is the tradition to allow a 15 percent commission, and breaking tradition is not easy. Furthermore, payment by commission is simpler than that for alternatives.

Should the commission system be abandoned, inevitable chaos would follow. Advertising agencies, advertisers, and media find it easier for the present to go along with the existing system, which, despite its obvious faults, has worked rather well. Should the system be abandoned, the present client-agency relationship will be drastically changed.

PEOPLE: AN AGENCY'S CHIEF COMMODITY

A bright young man or woman turned down by an advertising agency may be hurt or baffled. Neither would be if it were understood that advertising agencies, whether soliciting new business or holding on to present accounts, are always selling people. If a shift is made in the agency personnel working on an account, the client will usually ask quickly: "Who's the new person on our account? Good background?"

Faced by such questions, it is the brave advertising executive who will reply: "We're putting a newcomer on your account. No experience, but bright."

If the client is normal, either there will be apprehension about the ability of the inexperienced newcomer to do satisfactory work, or the client will be resentful that the agency thinks so little of the account that it will let a low-priced beginner learn at the account's expense, as it were.

Skill, personality, ideas, energy, and experience are the material sold by advertising agencies. In equipment, offices, and location, one advertising agency is just about like another agency. Only the people and their abilities are different.

Ordinarily, advertising agency people work in one of four general areas, though some will work in two or more areas at the same time. The four areas are:

(1) Client contact
(2) Creative
(3) Administrative
(4) Miscellaneous services

Client Contact

Account executives, management executives, and new business people are involved in client contact.

Closest to the client is the account executive whose job consists of helping the client plan the advertising, including budgeting, media selection, creative approach, and overall marketing strategy. In addition, is the very important job of keeping the client "happy" with the "A.E." (account executive) and the rest of the advertising agency.

Back at the agency, the account executive, as the chief spokesman for the account, gets the agency people to do their very best in copy, art, production, research, and marketing planning. It is part of the job, furthermore, to see that deadlines are met.

Some account executives are what are known as "copy-contact" types, which means that they write copy for their account as well as performing the contact work. Most advertising agencies, however, do not add the copywriting chore to the account executive's duties.

Lastly, account executives are often used to solicit new business, especially if their account load is light.

Account executives are among the busiest and best paid of the agency personnel, and usually they obtain their jobs only after acquiring considerable experience either as assistant account executives or in a good background of company advertising work.

Especially for important accounts, the management executives of advertising agencies will not involve day-to-day details but will be concerned with overall objectives. Very often the contact will be between the very top level executives of the client and the agency; that is, president to president, or chairperson to chairperson.

Many an account has been lost, and many accounts have been saved, because of such contacts. "Mending fences" is a very useful function of the agency president, more of it could be done.

Since most advertising agencies lose a certain amount of business each year because the accounts switch to other agencies, or because some accounts do less advertising in one year than in other years, it is vital that an advertising agency add new business.

Although, unofficially, establishing new business contacts is the duty of everyone in an advertising agency, the work is most often handled by account executives, management executives, or persons especially hired for the purpose.

Good new-business types have a wide background in business in general and special knowledge of the business of the prospective clients. They must be strong sales types; forceful, pleasant, and persuasive. If account executives pick up new business, they often will handle the accounts they bring in.

Naturally, a person skilled in getting new business must have a thorough grounding in advertising, media, and marketing. These skills will be put to work in the preparation of a new-business "presentation" that will be given to the prospective client. There will be more on presentations later.

Creative

Copywriters, artists, production managers, and radio-TV directors are included in the creative area.

Although copywriters ply their art in many places other than advertising agencies, agency copywriters are the "elite" in the advertising creative world. They are better paid, and their work is seen in more glamorous media than that of the copywriters, for example, who write for mail-order houses or for newspaper advertising departments.

Copywriters, both male and female, are usually in two categories. There are those who are fast, skillful writers who know their trade but are not especially creative in getting original ideas. They work best when supplied with a copy theme or "slant." The second group, relatively few in number, is composed of "idea" people who can also write well.

Although there is much talk of specialization in advertising agencies, the copywriter most assured of making a living is the one who can write for various media and about a number of different types of products.

Copywriters usually work up the ladder from the "cub" copywriter stage up to the position of creative director, who has overall supervision in many agencies in art, production, and radio and television, as well as copy. In between there are such titles as senior copywriter, copy group head, and copy chief.

Agency copywriters must not only be good writers; they must also be *fast* writers, because much advertising agency writing is against deadlines.

Most advertising agency art departments furnish layouts, not finished artwork. Artwork is usually farmed out to free-lance artists. There is nothing derogatory in following this practice, however, because advertising layout artists are skilled workers who are imaginative and yet practical enough to make art fit the needs of campaigns and sales objectives. Layouts may range from "rough roughs" to the comprehensive ("comp") that approximates the finished artwork.

In many advertising agencies the copywriter works first on the advertisement and indicates the possible direction to be taken by the art department. Good layout artists, however, usually regard such suggestions as starting points only. They are able through experience and artistic ingenuity to improve upon the copywriter's ideas.

Typography, engraving, and photography are three subjects in which the advertising agency layout artist is thoroughly versed. A good piece of layout design can be spoiled by poor typography or photography.

There are not many titles in the advertising agency art department. There is the art director, sometimes a vice-president as well, and assistant art directors.

Some specialization exists, however, with some artists more oriented to consumer art than industrial art.

Although not creative in the sense of copywriters or artists, production managers work in the creative sphere. They are in constant touch with artists about the appropriate typefaces, photography, and reproduction processes to use. In smaller advertising agencies the lone artist may assume the production manager's role as well."

Production managers must not only have a creative flair; they must also be business-minded in their search for good prices on all bids of printing shops, engraving companies and other production concerns. They live in an atmosphere of crisis, because most production work is put through "rush."

Their experience eventually gives them deep knowledge of printing, paper, inks, engraving, lithography, and photography plus a shrewd judgment of just how much the advertising agency must pay to obtain satisfactory mechanical production.

The position of radio-TV director has many variations. In some advertising agencies the position is concerned principally with the writing of radio or television commercials. In others, all or almost all of such writing will be done by copywriters.

In smaller or medium-sized advertising agencies, the demands of the broadcast media work will not be enough to keep the radio-TV director busy all the time. This person will be expected at times to write print copy and may even serve as an account executive on small accounts doing heavy broadcast advertising.

In the bigger advertising agencies the radio-TV directors will be more concerned with overall planning of the use of broadcast media. They will be expected to have full knowledge of production techniques and to know all the tricks of film, videotape, and animation.

When the advertising agency is preparing television storyboards, such directors will supervise them and provide overall direction. Once these look satisfactory, they will draw upon their background to select the best producer and then will work with the producer to see that the client gets the best possible production for the lowest possible price.

They will be equally versed in radio production and will perform the same general functions in that medium.

For background, the radio-TV director should know the theatrical arts, photography, motion picture film production, and radio and television studio procedures. He or she has usually worked in radio or television or both. Within the radio-TV area of the advertising agency the titles may range from radio-TV director to radio-TV producer, to business manager of the radio-TV department.

In advertising agencies having multimillion-dollar expenditures in television, radio-TV directors (often just television directors) have as one of their chief responsibilities the selection of shows that will be winners in the ratings race. Although others will be involved in this selection, they are experts whose judgment will carry much weight. When the show is in the production stage, they will represent the agency in seeing that the producer does the best possible job.

Administrative

Under the heading of administrative fall a number of titles, including president, chairman of the board, chairman of the executive committee, executive vice-president, secretary, treasurer, and account supervisor.

These people have the usual responsibilities of the company executive. Account supervisors, however, will take more active part in day-to-day activities than might be true, for example, of a corporation executive.

Also included in the administrative area are accountants, billing clerks, and all the miscellaneous clerical jobs to be found in any business.

Miscellaneous Services

Media directors, media buyers, research directors, marketing directors, traffic managers, public relations personnel, and lawyers all provide a miscellaneous service to the advertising agency.

In big advertising agencies *media directors* are usually vice-presidents as well. They supervise the work of the media buyers and usually are important members of the agency planning groups. Almost invariably they have long experience in media work, either as advertising agency media buyers or as executives in print or broadcast media.

It's not creative unless it sells.

If anything came out of the so-called creative revolution of the 60's and the recessions of the early 70's, it was a clearer understanding of what advertising is and what it isn't.

By the time those years were over, many advertisers and their agencies had been painfully reminded that advertising was not an art form but a serious business tool. And that "creative advertising" really was advertising that created sales and not just attention.

You might say creativity grew up in those years. And one would think that the mistakes made then would never again be repeated.

Yet here we are, a short time later, and like war and politics, advertising seems to be repeating itself. You need only look at television or pick up a magazine to see the frivolities and ambiguities that are passing as creative selling.

It seems such a pity that many advertisers are still learning—the hard way—what some of us have always known:

Not an entertainment medium.

During those crazy 60's, the ambience of television rubbed off on the advertising message and more and more advertising tried to become as entertaining as the programming in which it appeared—very often at the expense of the selling idea. One can still see a rash of imitative commercials following the advent of popular new television programs and feature films. Extravagant productions featuring everything but a concept are still prevalent. Movie stars and athletes continue to serve as substitutes for selling ideas.

Awards for what.

Awards for creativity conferred by juries of advertising people often have nothing to do with advertising that sells. Certainly, in recent years, the importance of advertising awards has diminished. Their value seems to have decreased in direct proportion to the proliferation of festivals. At the same time, many began to question the worth of honors bestowed out of context of sales results.

But as long as advertising will continue to be written by people, people will continue to give each other awards. And that isn't all bad. George Burns once said of Al Jolson, "It was easy enough to make him happy. You just had to cheer him for breakfast, applaud wildly for lunch, and give him a standing ovation for dinner."

You don't have to be loved.

Criticism of an advertising campaign has little bearing on selling effectiveness. There are many examples of advertising which are disliked by the very people who are reacting to the message.

By the same token, much advertising that is

beloved by the critics and consumers alike fizzles badly.

This is not to suggest that advertising need be grating or irritating or hated to be effective. Wouldn't it be great if we could always write advertising that would win awards, that people would love and talk about, and that would sell the product, too?

But, alas, this magic combination is very elusive. And remember, the main objective is not to win awards, not to get people to love your advertising, but to get them to act upon it. In the process of meeting that objective, you may not endear yourself to some consumers but you may become very popular with your stockholders.

Watch out for distraction.

A selling idea runs a very real risk of being swamped by its execution. It's a cliché of the advertising business, but how many times does someone describe a commercial to you almost verbatim and then fail to remember the product? Humor is most often involved. A good joke, a funny piece of action, a great punch line—all can undermine the strongest selling idea. And yet humor, judiciously used, can uplift a piece of advertising, increasing its chances of being remembered while actually enhancing the selling idea. A good test: Is the humor relevant to the message?

Explore the alternatives.

There is no sure way to sell anything. There are many ways to approach the sale of a product—strategically and executionally. Some ways are better than others and you really don't know for sure which is best until you copy test and market test.

The time is long past when an ad agency can deliver a single advertising campaign to a client without examining and presenting alternatives. Every client has the right to take part in the selection process that an agency goes through in leading up to a creative recommendation.

And the most creative campaign is the one that ultimately proves itself in the market.

Don't overshoot the audience.

A lot of words have been written and spoken about advertising catering to the lowest intelligence level of its prospects. That of course is as untrue as it would be unwise.

But equally ridiculous is advertising that wafts over the head of the prospect. We still see and hear commercials and ads that are so cleverly obtuse that they reflect no more than the private narrow world of their creators. For every potential customer who reacts to such "sophisticated" advertising, there are countless others who just don't get it.

There is no "soft sell."

The one factor that did more to end the creative revolution and topple the "creative crazies" from power was the recession of 1970. It was a very sobering experience for many high-flying businesses and advertising agencies.

Creative philosophies seemed to change overnight. "These are hard times that call for hard sell" became the watchword.

But the truth of the matter is: All times are hard times and all times call for hard sell. Hard sell meaning the presentation of a cogent, persuasive idea, stripped of any distracting or irrelevant elements, that will convince people to buy a product. Is there any other kind?

There can be no doubt that advertising today must be more intrusive, more imaginative, more innovative than it has ever been. In a business riddled with sameness and clutter, there is a great virtue in being "creative."

Yet, if ever a word was subject to misinterpretation and confusion, it is the word "creative."

To some it means advertising that wins awards. To others it is advertising that makes people laugh. And there are those who think to be creative, advertising must be talked about at cocktail parties and joked about by comedians.

But "creative" can also mean dramatically showing how a product fulfills a consumer need or desire. Or it can be something as simple as casting the appropriate person for a brand. A unique demonstration of product superiority can be creative. So, of course, can a memorable jingle.

There are probably as many opinions of what is creative as there are people who conceive and judge advertising.

But no matter what your interpretation of the word, one thing is irrefutable:

It's not creative unless it sells.

That, in six words, is the philosophy that guides Benton & Bowles.

If you're a major advertiser in need of truly creative advertising, please call or write to Jack Bowen, President, Benton & Bowles, Inc., 909 Third Avenue, New York, New York 10022, (212) 758-6200.

Benton & Bowles

New York, Chicago, Los Angeles, and other major cities worldwide.

Media directors necessarily become acquainted with every account in the agency They are concerned with the broad advertising objectives of these accounts and with what combination of media can best achieve those objectives.

For the man or woman who does not mind detail, has an analytical mind, and has no dislike of figures, the buying of time and space offers an exciting career. Usually, *media buyers* in large advertising agencies are assigned to certain accounts. It is up to them to keep abreast of the constantly changing media picture. Both the media buyers and the media directors are besieged by media people. Separating the real facts from the enthusiastic sales talk is one of the more trying aspects of the work. Young persons who enter media buying in larger agencies are often earmarked for future account executive work.

In smaller advertising agencies, there may be no one who is classed as a media director or a media buyer. In one-person agencies these duties will be handled along with other agency activities. In somewhat larger advertising agencies the account executives will interview salespeople from the media and will make the buying decisions after consultation with the clients.

An agency must be of fairly good size to be able to support a full-time *research director.* Only the larger advertising agencies carry on enough research to justify putting a research director on the staff.

The research director's function is to initiate research in behalf of clients, to supervise it, and to analyze results. Sometimes research will be done for various agency departments, especially the creative department. This work may be done in advertising, marketing, or media research.

Because of the constantly changing research techniques, the research worker must keep current with current methodology. Usually research directors are scholarly, analytical persons with strong backgrounds in statistics and the social sciences. Frequently, they have Ph.D.'s in these areas.

Once again, only the larger agencies will have *marketing directors.* These persons usually come to the agency with a strong background in marketing and selling. They may well have been marketing or sales managers, or both, for corporations before beginning their advertising agency careers. Their chief function at the agency is to give marketing counsel to agency personnel, especially the account executives, and to work closely with clients in marketing planning, setting up sales quotas, distribution channels, pricing, and all other aspects of marketing a product.

Marketing managers can be especially useful in new-business presentations because their background enables them to provide a useful approach to the marketing, advertising, and selling problems of prospective clients. They can, of course, work out the marketing section of a presentation.

In many advertising agencies, especially those too small to afford both a research director and a marketing director, the functions are combined under the title of marketing and research director. These two activities go together quite naturally.

The function of the *traffic department* is to follow the jobs going through the advertising agency and to see that all the departments concerned are kept aware of deadlines. In a large advertising agency, it requires a masterpiece of organization to keep the work flowing so that no insertion dates are missed.

Many agency beginners start in the traffic department because nowhere else can one see the entire agency operation so clearly. In the effort to move the jobs in progress, traffic department people must work closely with the copy department, the art department, the production department, and the account executives.

In most agencies that have a *public relations department* (many advertising agencies do not have such a department), the work is more concerned with publicity releases than with broad-gauge public relations.

Almost always the men or women in public relations have had newspaper work and sometimes work in the broadcast media too. Although the public relations department very often works closely with other agency departments, it is customary to give the department a certain amount of autonomy.

Frequently, for instance, the department will do its own new-business solicitations and will get new clients who sign up only for the public relations service of the agency, not for its advertising service. In other cases, when the new-business team wins a new client for the advertising services, the new account signs up for public relations services at the same time. At one time public relations work was done mostly by special public relations firms, and cooperation with the advertising program was difficult to achieve. When, however, both functions are performed by the client's advertising agency, there is a better chance for close coordination.

Organization of the public relations department is somewhat like that of the advertising side, with its use of account executives, account supervisors, and similar positions. One difference, however, is that usually the account executives will do the writing as well as the contact and planning work.

Work performed may include product publicity and dealer—jobber promotion; stockholder reports and meetings; employee publications and relations; community relations; sales promotion; supplier relations; public service activities; annual reports; speech writing; trade show management, and many other activities.

Because of the increased complexity of laws governing business, and advertising along with it, a number of the larger advertising agencies have full-time *lawyers* on their staffs to keep the agencies and their clients out of trouble. Their work is concerned largely with keeping advertising copy from running afoul of Federal Trade Commission regulations or the provisions of the Food and Drug Act. Agencies that devise numerous contests for clients also find their own staff lawyers a valuable asset.

Personnel Training and Hiring

In view of the great stress on the importance of its personnel, the lack of interest of the average advertising agency in training personnel seems odd and, indeed, short-sighted. Because of its insistence on hiring experienced people only, the agency loses bright young people who go to other fields of work or, ironically, to manufacturer advertising departments where they become clients of the agencies that had no use for them.

Only about 20 percent of advertising agencies have training programs. Of these, many are so superficial that they are meaningless.

Two advertising agency heads interviewed for this book talked about hiring college graduates without experience or training: No. 1 said: "Too disruptive. We're not running a school here. Let someone else train them. We can't afford to give them schooling and without experience we can't put them to work on our accounts." No. 2 said: "Hiring a limited number of people right out of college is good for the agency. They're eager and we can train them in our way of doing advertising. We find hiring such young people is especially good in media and account training. It's harder to train copy people."

In still another opinion, William A. Marsteller, chairman of Marsteller, Inc., a large international advertising agency said in a *Wall Street Journal* advertisement (in *Advertising Age*, July 18, 1977) "We've grown our own talent. More than 50 percent of our senior people have never worked at another agency. We believe we can recruit bright, intelligent college graduates who are serious about an advertising career and train them very quickly to take over major responsibilities."

One noticeable change in recent times has been the hiring of more women for management work in agencies. Formerly, women college graduates were told: "Start as secretaries and wait for the break in copy." Copy departments have always used many women. If not in traffic, women worked mostly in lesser jobs in media or research. Today, however, sees many young women being hired for account management and moving rapidly into top management levels.

Location of Advertising Agencies

Most advertising agencies are located where the greatest number of business prospects are to be obtained. New York City dominates as the most important advertising agency location. Chicago is a strong second. After these two cities come Detroit, Los Angeles, St. Louis, Minneapolis, Cleveland, Philadelphia, San Francisco, Boston, Kansas City, Dallas, and Atlanta.

Although the presence of large-scale industry, such as the milling industry in Minneapolis and the automobile industry in Detroit, is decidedly the most important factor in determining advertising agency location, concentration in certain big cities is also influenced by still another factor—supply of talent.

Chicago, New York, and Los Angeles, for instance, are centers for artists, musicians, film producers, television, and radio and motion picture stars and technicians. Advertising agencies draw upon such talent and find it useful to have them nearby. Los Angeles and Hollywood, for example, long before the Los Angeles area boomed with commercial industry, were the locations of many agency offices. These offices were first established to serve as liaison between the motion picture talent and later the television talent.

Importance of Branch Offices

When an advertising agency opens for the first time, it is usually one office located in a place where it can reasonably expect to develop business.

As business prospers for the new advertising agency, the agency adds more personnel and office space in the one office. If, however, it manages to land some big-spending clients in another city—or even just one very big client—it may decide to open an office in that city. This is often called a "service" office, as well as branch office.

Eventually, as the agency expands, it may open offices in a good number of principal cities. It is common, for instance, for big agencies to have offices in

New York City, Chicago, San Francisco, and Los Angeles, even if their main offices are in some other city.

Branch offices have two clear purposes. One purpose is to "service" national accounts that may have been originated in the home office or one of the other branch offices. Services offered by the branches can take many forms—local market studies, local research, media analysis, checks on the movement of clients' goods in retail outlets, and publicity work for client personnel, offices, and factories in the branch office area. The other purpose of branch offices is to initiate new business in the branch office area. This is the paramount goal of the branch office manager, since new business makes the office more important.

When a branch office lands an account it will usually provide creative services for that account out of its office. Likewise, it will handle media scheduling and other agency routine. Some advertising agencies, however, require that all creative work be performed in the home office. If it is necessary for the creative people to have meetings with clients and branch office personnel, they will travel to the branch office city.

Branch offices sometimes obtain greater billings (the term for the dollar volume done by an advertising agency) than the home office.

Advertising agencies generally, despite speeded-up jet travel, prefer to solicit accounts that are close to the home office, or the branch office. To waste the expensive time of an account executive in travel is uneconomical, unless the billing of the account is big enough to justify travel time. An example of the latter is Procter & Gamble, located in Cincinnati, which is not noted as an advertising agency center. The various advertising agencies serving Procter & Gamble are located in New York and Chicago. Because of the amount of business involved, advertising agencies are usually quite willing to make frequent trips to Procter & Gamble's Ohio headquarters. Likewise, the soap company's advertising people make numerous trips to the advertising agencies' offices.

Many clients, too, favor the nearby or local advertising agency, reasoning that such proximity will be advantageous for meetings, and for sudden changes that must be made. They are aware, also, that unless they offer considerable billing, their account may be serviced by a less expensive and less experienced account executive, since the advertising agency is not inclined to send its top talent on low-profit trips.

With the demand for increased marketing services, many accounts have been shifted because various advertising agencies have not had enough branch offices. As a result, in the last few years the number of multioffice advertising agencies has increased sharply. Sometimes the offices have been added one by one as evidence of natural growth. In other cases, the number of offices has grown with dramatic suddenness because of a merger between two advertising agencies.

A Quick Way To Grow—Merge!

One of the more striking developments of recent years has been the rash of mergers in the advertising agency field. Sometimes these mergers are between two agencies of equal stature. More often the merger joins a smaller organization to a much larger one. In this case the smaller one is often swallowed by the big organization and loses its identity. Sometimes the smaller one becomes an affiliate instead and retains its name.

Generally the reasons for the mergers are fairly clear. The most common ones are:

(1) *To fight the rising costs of advertising agency operation.*

If the Jones Company, with 35 employees, merges with the Smith Company, with 45 employees, one of the first acts of management will be to cut off a number of employees who have been doing similar work in the separate agencies. Most likely to go will be certain artists, copywriters, account people and others who will not have enough to keep them busy in the merged organization. Within two years, unless much new business has been acquired, the total of 80 employees may very likely be pared to about 50 or 60 without any real loss of agency efficiency or service.

(2) *To answer demands of clients for total marketing service in the client's total marketing area.*

With increasing stress on the need for an advertising agency to offer strong marketing services has come client demand that this service be offered in all-important marketing areas. A number of advertising agencies have met this demand through mergers that have given them widely scattered offices that can service their clients' marketing and sales department personnel working in these areas.

(3) *To pick up new accounts.*

New-business solicitations are costly and uncertain. At best, the acquisition of new accounts is a slow, agonizing process. Through a merger, 20, 30, or more accounts may be gathered at one swoop.

(4) *To achieve a balance in the kind of accounts.*

An advertising agency may suffer for years in its new-business aims because it is tagged as a certain kind of advertising agency. Very often, for example, an agency is thought of as an "industrial" agency; that is known to specialize in industrial accounts. Consumer product manufacturers may, therefore, reject the agency's overtures because they feel that it would not be knowledgeable about consumer marketing and advertising.

Such an advertising agency will find it a very attractive idea to merge with an advertising agency that has long been noted for outstanding work with consumer products.

Both agencies may profit from this alliance of the industrial and consumer products accounts, and the merged company may be able to obtain business that the separate advertising agencies might never have acquired.

(5) *To achieve the bigness that is alluring to some clients.*

Many corporations have a distrust of the small or middle-sized advertising agency. Even though a smaller agency might do good work for the company, it will be passed over for the bigger agency.

In some cases corporations are fascinated by what might be called "giantism," or the urge to be the largest or almost the largest of a kind. There is a tendency to go with the leader, or leaders, in any field. This is certainly true in choosing advertising agencies, despite many arguments that can be offered against this tendency.

THE BIG AGENCY VERSUS THE SMALL ONE

A continual and often grim battle goes on between large and small advertising agencies for accounts. Of the approximately 4,000 advertising agencies, most are small if considered in terms of their personnel or their billings. Most advertising agencies, in fact, bill less than $1,000,000 each year.

These smaller agencies must fight hard for survival in the face of the merger trend, which is making the relatively few large agencies even larger. Not only does the smaller agency do badly in competition for accounts, but it also has difficulty holding accounts against the bigger agencies. It is a bitter fact of advertising agency life that many a smaller advertising agency has been chiefly responsible for the growth of an account from a small business enterprise to a large one. Then, as the billings of the account have grown along with his business, the smaller agency is dropped in order that the account may utilize an agency that is "big enough to handle the increased responsibilities of our account."

Advantages of the Big Agency

There are many advantages that an advertising agency can offer because of large size. Four of these advantages are:

(1) It can usually afford to pay better salaries and fringe benefits, thus attracting abler, more experienced men and women.

(2) It can offer greater depth of services in research, marketing, public relations, and the other extras.

(3) Because it has offices throughout the United States, and in foreign lands, it can spread its service geographically. There are not too many advertising agencies, however, that have a large number of United States and foreign offices. This advantage is therefore enjoyed by only the very largest advertising agencies.

(4) Larger agencies have had greater depth of experience with many different kinds of products, from which they have gained greater knowledge of media and advertising generally.

Advantages of the Smaller Agency

Among the advantages offered by a small agency are these:

(1) Each client's business is more important in terms of total income and is thus valued more. A client's business will be given more attention, an advantage especially gratifying to smaller accounts that would be lost in the big agency's account list.

(2) Because there are few or no committees, the smaller agency can sometimes move faster.

(3) The location of the smaller agency is sometimes better, since the client, when not in a big city, may prefer a smaller advertising agency in his hometown to a bigger one some distance away in a large metropolitan area.

The Agency Network: an Answer to a Problem

A number of the nation's smaller advertising agencies, stung by some of the claims made for the bigger agencies, especially by the assertion that smaller agencies cannot match their bigger rivals in range and depth of service, have achieved something of an answer in the agency network.

By banding together and pooling creative, research, and marketing services and ideas, the smaller agencies in such networks have made themselves much more attractive to prospective clients who may be big-agency oriented.

There are now several nationwide advertising agency networks. Member agencies meet regularly to exchange viewpoints and to work out individual and group problems. Any individual advertising agency in the group can call on other members for assistance. A small or medium-sized agency in the Midwest may, for example, need to obtain market data pertaining to a New England city. A call to a member agency in the New England area will produce the information quickly at a minimum expense or possibly at no expense. Thus the prestige and facilities of the Midwestern unit gain in the eyes of its clients.

An almost unlimited range of services is available to network agency clients. These services include personal calls on customers; information about good distributors, manufacturers' agents, and dealers or jobbers; lining up local television and radio talent; obtaining information from prospects; local interviews and testimonials; obtaining photographs and data on product installations; assistance to salespeople or factory personnel visiting the area; advice on the productivity of local media; and confidential information from local financial and business contacts.

For many smaller agencies, doomed by location and the limited business potential in their area, the network offers the only possibility of matching the competitive sales talk of the big agencies. Up to the present time, however, relatively few of the nation's smaller advertising agencies belong to networks. Consequently the question of the small versus the large advertising agency has been only partially answered.

HOUSE AGENCIES, CREATIVE BOUTIQUES, AND BUYING SERVICES

Most advertising agencies, known as "full service" agencies, because they offer all normal services, are independent of any direct advertiser control. Over the years, however, a number of companies have been dissatisfied with the full service agency system. Two factors usually account for this:

(1) The method of compensation.
(2) The lack of direct control over agency work, especially in the creative area.

Out of the dissatisfaction have emerged house agencies, creative boutiques, and buying services.

A *house agency* is a creature of the advertiser in that it is set up within the company, usually on the premises. It may do all the usual tasks of an advertising agency, or only some of them. Very often it comes into being when a company has been doing all, or most of, its creative work and has used the agency for other functions.

Many companies opening house agencies have been disappointed and have gone back to conventional client-agency relationships. Sometimes they have found that they were not able to save money working through a house agency. Other times they have discovered that working within the company denied them the rich variety of talent and experience offered by a full service agency. Lastly, the house agency employee is, after all, a company employee. As such, he or she may not be able to offer an outside viewpoint. There may be a loss of independence, too, because a company employee is not likely to say "No" very often to superiors in the company.

With so much worship of creativity, the work of many small agencies with extraordinary ability to stun the beholder with their copy and art ideas *(the creative boutique)*, has been the subject of much admiration. Many such agencies concentrate on turning out outstanding advertising. They leave marketing, media analysis, research and other tasks to big, full-service agencies.

Sometimes such organizations are hired by companies with house agencies. In such instances, the company may perform all the functions but the creative, leaving that to the creative boutique. On occasion, too, a company using a full-service agency may farm out some of its creative work to a boutique.

An interesting development sometimes occurs when a creative boutique is so good that its services are in great demand. Eventually, and often with genuine reluctance, the boutique grows to the point where it finally offers all the conventional services. It acquires the bigness it once deplored, even though it may still do outstanding creative work. Unwillingly, it has become a full-service agency.

Although referred to as *buying services*, the term should be *media buying services*, organizations that presumably can buy media (especially spot television) at lower rates than media departments of full-service advertising agencies. These organizations, used by about 10 percent of clients, are discussed fully in the television advertising chapter. Their growth and existence are mentioned here only because of their frequent association with house agencies and creative boutiques.

A house agency sometimes may perform all agency functions but media buying. A media buying service will be hired for that, or the house agency may farm out both creative work and media buying. In another instance, a company may utilize a full-service agency for all services except media buying. In other cases, it may look outside merely for creative work, either wholly or in part.

AGENCY HIRING AND FIRING: AN OUTSIDER'S VIEWPOINT

When Clarke Landon was graduated from a small liberal arts college, he went on to acquire a master's degree in business administration at a leading university. Because many big advertising agencies require the MBA almost as a ticket for interviews, Landon was interviewed by several top agencies. After listening to the agency men sell their organizations and, subsequently, doing much personal pondering about the matter, Landon decided against agency work. When asked for reasons, he replied:

"Too frantic and unsettled. I don't like the constant switching of accounts and the way new accounts are acquired—all the politics and uncertainties. It's all pretty crude, hit-or-miss, and undignified with everybody scrambling to snatch accounts from each other. I'd rather be on the client side so I can have a hand in hiring the agency, not on the other side where I'm running scared all the time."

Selection of an Advertising Agency

Selecting an advertising agency in most cases means "replacing" an advertising agency, since most corporations of any consequence have been using advertising for a long time and have employed advertising agencies to direct that advertising.

When the time comes to replace its present agency, how can a company be certain that the new advertising agency will perform the advertising function any better than its predecessor? The answer is that it cannot be certain. There are, however, a few dependable guidelines that help in the selection.

One of the hardest and most unpleasant tasks of any company advertising manager is the replacement of its present advertising agency with a new one that has a reasonable chance of being more satisfactory.

Sometimes the advertiser invites solicitations by advertising agencies that are known to him or her or to others in the company. The list of agencies invited may consist of only two or three names, or it may contain as many as 40 names. If many agencies are invited the process of selection may extend over an exhausting period of months.

Typical Questions Asked of Agencies

Some typical questions actually asked by companies of agencies soliciting accounts include these:

(1) What is the background experience of the person who will handle the account?

(2) What amount of time will this person spend servicing the account, not including layout, copy, and production? Where will headquarters of that person be?

(3) Give a detailed statement of the basis of charges for other than space, including: (a) copy and layout; (b) roughs and visuals; (c) mechanicals and paste-ups; (d) comprehensives and art, including photographs; (e) creative work purchased outside; (f) production revisions and reprints; (g) other services.

(4) What is your practice in submitting ideas and programs to the client? Give three examples of ideas or programs originated by the agency or developed by it to promote the sale of high-unit merchandise through specialty distributors and dealers.

(5) Please state briefly what is the conception of your agency of the social and economic responsibilities of advertising as a tool of management, and what general recommendations have you made to your clients along these lines?

(6) What were your total billings last year? What are your anticipated billings this year for your office located in this city? What are the individual billings of your top five accounts?

(7) Please list your current accounts, their billings last year, and how long you have serviced each.

(8) Give a brief summary of your agency, including when founded, the names and ages of your corporate officers, how long each officer has been associated with the agency, whether your agency has multiple offices and, if so, where they are located, the total number of employees by type now employed locally, and financial references.

(9) How do your billings divide up between the various media?

(10) What merchandising, media, copy, and art and research personnel would be assigned to our account? Please indicate what share of each person's time would be available to our account, as well as a brief statement regarding each persons's experience.

(11) Tell us why you feel you are the best agency to handle our account.

(12) Would you be willing to make a formal presentation in which you recommend an advertising program for our company, assuming you were one of a few agencies being considered for the account?

(13) What accounts do you have that are closely allied in market, outlets, or sales appeal to our business and products?

(14) How many people are in your organization?

(15) How do you rank in size among all agencies, or agencies in this city?

(16) Are you a member of the American Association of Advertising Agencies? Or any other agency organization or network?

(17) How long has your agency been in business?

(18) Do your account executives do the creative planning and writing on accounts they serve, or do they handle only contact between client and agency?

(19) How many members of your staff have been sales, advertising, or sales promotion managers?

(20) Do you feel that a substantial proportion of our advertising budget should be earmarked for dealer advertising and collateral material?

(21) To what extent is your agency departmentalized? Please list departments and outline how their work is coordinated in serving clients.

(22) To what extent are principals (partners, executive officers, or main stockholders) active in serving clients?

(23) How many of your accounts have been with you over 5 years? Over 10 years? Over 15 years? Over 20 years?

(24) On what basis of compensation do you operate? Fee? Percentage of billing? Other?

(25) What would be your procedure in handling our account if we appointed you?

Fundamental Questions Necessary to Ask

Now and then the advertiser composes a long, involved checklist or questionnaire that competing agencies are asked to fill out. Some of the agencies are eliminated by reason of their answers, and those remaining are than asked to make personal presentations.

No matter how complicated or how simple the advertiser makes the solicitation process, here are the fundamental questions that the advertiser must ask:

(1) *What is the quality of the agency's creative work?*

In many cases the question of creativity is the one most easily answered, since each competing advertising agency will have numerous samples to show. Furthermore, it may have been an agency's outstanding creative work for other accounts that in the first place caused the advertiser to issue an invitation to an agency. Dissatisfaction with the present agency's creative work may, in fact, be the chief cause for replacing it. Thus evidence of high quality in creative work is often the most important attribute sought in the new agency.

(2) *What kind of people, in general, head and staff the agency?*

It has been said before that people and ideas are the important commodities that an advertising agency has to sell. Does the agency have an aggressive, efficient leadership? Do its people, in general, seem of high character and ability? These are difficult questions to answer after two or three meetings, but usually the advertiser will form some important overall opinions about them.

(3) *Who are the people who will work on our account?*

Many advertisers want a detailed background of all key people who will be assigned to their account—account executives, copywriters, artists, and account supervisors. In a sense the advertiser will have to "live" with these people for a long time. Assurance is needed about their ability and personality. Are they the kind of people who will wear well day after day, year after year? Are they capable of sustained and high-level work? Contact people especially are given a close scrutiny, since no sensible advertising manager will hire an advertising agency whose contact people are repugnant.

(4) *What kind of experience has the agency had with our kind of product or service?*

Marketing experience with the client's product may be considered even more essential than advertising experience. Does the agency know the prospective client's channels of distribution, the selling problems, the pricing problems, and the general peculiarities of marketing this particular product?

(5) *How important will our account be in the agency's account list?*

A client who has an advertising budget of only $50,000 to $100,000 a year will have a natural skepticism about an agency's willingness to go all out if most of the agency accounts are in the $250,000 to $1,000,000 range. If, on the other hand, the client's advertising expenditure is such that it puts it well up on the billings list, there is more assurance that the agency will work extra hard on the account.

(6) *What is the range of agency services and how does the agency charge for them?*

Some clients insist that their advertising agencies be able to handle every type of assignment, including such "extras" as marketing planning, publicity, point-of-purchase material, and research. Completeness of marketing, advertising, and public relations services provides a sort of "one-stop" agency arrangement that appeals to the advertising manager who hopes to be able to dump the whole communications load on the advertising agency.

(7)   *Is the agency's account list made up of leaders, or also-rans?*

An advertising agency's account list is revealing to the prospective advertiser. If it is loaded with top concerns, the advertiser cannot help thinking that these respected firms must have had good reasons for selecting the agency to represent them. If, on the contrary, the account list is composed of unknown "cats and dogs," there is little to inspire confidence.

(8)   *Does the agency have case histories that demonstrate its skill?*

Nothing succeeds like success—or a success story. A consistent record of success, portrayed in a number of case histories, can help sell the most skeptical prospective advertiser.

Miscellaneous factors. The miscellaneous factors that an advertiser considers include the age, size, location, credit standing, reputation, and supplementary services of an agency.

Age. The fact that an advertising agency has been in business for a long time may be an advantage if it has retained a youthful outlook. If age has brought stodginess, it can be a handicap. The youthful agency marked as a "comer" finds its lack of years in the business no handicap.

Size. To be the biggest advertising agency in any given city is a help. Most prospects are attracted by size, all other things being equal.

Location. As already discussed, nearness of the advertising agency to the client's office is usually a marked advantage.

Credit standing. If an advertising agency has a shaky credit standing, it reflects badly on the business skill of those who run the enterprise. A client will hesitate to become involved with an organization whose financial standing is dubious.

Reputation. An advertising agency's reputation can soon be ascertained by the prospective client through conversations with media men, with other advertisers, and with printers. Every agency tends to develop a fairly clear-cut reputation for something—be it integrity, ideas, reliability, marketing skill, outstanding copy, or a thoroughly professional approach.

Supplementary services. Model kitchens, TV studios, and model grocery stores are a few of the supplementary services offered by the larger advertising agencies. Usually these will not have a major effect on prospects, but they do help to create a favorable total impression.

Important Criteria

These are the criteria listed by an executive in a large packaged goods company that was asked by the authors of this book what criteria are important in selecting an advertising agency.

(1)   *Creative Ability.* This is obviously important, and I believe we are moving towards placing greater emphasis on this factor and somewhat less emphasis on overall marketing planning and services. However, other factors outlined below also play a vital part in the selection of an agency and probably eliminate from consideration the smaller agencies who have a reputation for being "highly creative."

(2) *Market Research.* Our agencies do virtually all of the copy research and must be adequately staffed and competent in this area.

    (a) *Market Research.* Our agencies do virtually all of the copy research and must be adequately staffed and competent in this area.

    (b) *Media.* Obviously a key since we use a substantial amount of spot TV, and the agencies do the buying.

    (c) *Market Planning.* This includes such things as a fairly well-staffed merchandising, planning, or whatever else you want to call it, group, in addition to a well-staffed account group. As noted above, this is getting somewhat less attention in our current thinking, but it's still quite important.

    (d) *Programming.* This is a less important factor but still worth noting, since we rely rather heavily on our agency for programming recommendations and control.

(3) *Competitive Conflicts.* This is an increasingly difficult problem due to the proliferation of products marketed by the major package goods companies. We have to be concerned about other accounts directly conflicting with our products within each division, and to some extent accounts that concern brands in other company divisions. Several of our agencies do handle some accounts that conflict with some of our products so this has to be flexible, but we do try to keep such conflicts to a minimum.

WHY ACCOUNTS MOVE FROM ONE AGENCY TO ANOTHER

So much publicity has been given account shifting in the advertising agency field that many persons considering advertising agency employment have been frightened away. While it is true that there is constant changing of clients among advertising agencies as a whole, most advertising agencies have managed to hold their clients for a respectable number of years and are serving the same clients today that they began with years ago. Few agencies, furthermore, are affected so seriously by client loss that they actually go out of business.

Still, fear of losing clients is an ever-present condition of advertising agency life. It colors the entire relation of the advertising agency with its client, and it gives certain agency personnel, especially the account executives, many anxious moments.

Every issue of advertising trade magazines relates client shifts. Many reasons are given (although frequently both agency and client decline to comment), but the *chief* reasons follow.

Personality Conflict

Although many times other reasons will be assigned for the dropping of an advertising agency, personality clashes will be behind the move. Most frequently it will be difficulties between the advertising manager and the account executive that have sparked the trouble. These two must work together so closely that if they irritate each other, or if the advertising manager has lost respect for, or faith in, the account executive, the situation may become unbearable for both.

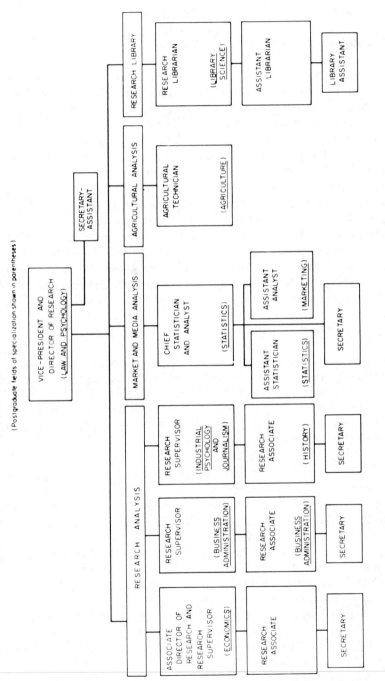

RESEARCH DEPARTMENT ORGANIZATION

(Postgraduate fields of specialization shown in parentheses)

Organization chart.

This chart shows the organization of an unusually impressive research department of an advertising agency. The department is composed of highly trained professional people.

Interviewers and tabulators are hired on the outside, thus holding down the size of the department.

Usually, however, an account executive, to keep the account will go to great lengths to reconcile differences. The advertising manager on the other hand, too often sees no need to make the best of a bad situation; the problem is solved by hiring another agency.

Unsatisfactory Creative Work

Dissatisfaction with its creative work is the most frequently named cause for dropping an advertising agency. "We want a fresh look for our advertising." "Our advertising's been in a rut." "We'd like to try something new."

These are the comments made by clients. Sometimes an advertising agency bursts into the field brimming with ideas, fresh sparkling copy, and electric creativity. If a client's copy has been getting "ho-hum" instead of "O boy!" the client can hardly be blamed for switching to another agency in the hope that the advertising will be revitalized.

Still, it is often the clients' fault that copy is not good. Frequently, they have not given proper guidance or have forced the agency to do advertising that suits management's ideas rather than advertising the agency knows is right.

Proof of the foregoing statement is found in the fact that the new agency so often fails to do any better creatively than the agency that was fired. Since the fault lies with the clients the copy never will improve, no matter which agency produces it, unless the clients change their own creative approach.

Loss of First-Place Sales Position by Client

Advertising agency people say cynically: "When sales are good, everything and everybody gets credit except the advertising. When sales go down, the word is out: "It's that lousy advertising. Fire the advertising agency."

It does seem true that few persons in most corporations are inclined to give advertising much credit for a fine sales position. It is true also that they tend to find fault with the advertising when sales fall.

In highly competitive fields—automotives, beverages, drug products, soaps, and others—there is much firing of advertising agencies if sales decline. A striking example of this took place some years ago in the automobile industry when a major manufacturer fired its agency of many years. There was nothing wrong with the advertising as events revealed. Instead, the sales decline could have been attributed to two definite factors:

(1) a poor design that was heartily disliked by the automobile-buying public;

(2) a dealer organization without morale, skill, or proper guidance from a factory sales department that needed revamping.

Still, no matter how many reasons an advertising agency may be able to give for the sales decline of a client's product, the agency knows that loss of a first-place, or near-first-place, sales position is a time for it to begin worrying.

Conflict with Other Accounts

One of the rules of the advertising agency business is that the same advertising agency cannot serve competing accounts, such as two dog-food accounts or two razor-blade accounts.

It is reasoned that, advertising agency avowals to the contrary, it will be impossible for an advertising agency to prevent confidential material about one account from leaking in some way to its rival. Furthermore, one of the two accounts may ask how it is supposed to feel when the agency devises an outstanding campaign for its rival, a campaign the company regards as far superior to the one it has been given.

Competing accounts, in the past, were handled only if each one had its own region of the country and did not go into other regions. If an advertising agency, for example, had three regional beer accounts and one of them went national, it would be compelled to choose between servicing the national account and servicing the remaining regional accounts.

Because of the recent trend toward advertising agency mergers, however, advertisers and their clients are reviewing the traditional stand about competing accounts. Some very large advertising agencies have established the agencies with which they have merged as affiliates that in many ways operate independently of the mother agency. This independence of operation is reassuring to clients who would otherwise object to having a competing account represented by their agency.

Not only advertising agencies, but corporations also, have been vigorously merging or affiliating in the last few years. This trend has made the problem of competing accounts more acute, as the following illustration will show. Suppose, for instance, that the North Star advertising agency services the East Side Manufacturing Company, manufacturers of the Shutterbug camera. Suppose, in addition, that this same agency serves the Agro Products Company, manufacturer of farm feed. The products of these two companies are as dissimilar as they can be; seemingly no product conflict can ever arise. Suddenly, however, Agro Products begins expanding and diversifying, in keeping with modern trends. One of the companies it acquires manufactures a little-known camera, a rival nonetheless of the Shutterbug camera.

What to do about the product conflict? Should the agency resign East Side Manufacturing? Resign Agro Products? Will the agency be fired by one or the other of the companies? These questions are being asked with increasing frequency either because agencies merge and acquire competing accounts, or because accounts themselves diversify their products. Up to this time, most clients have been distinctly unhappy about product conflicts and usually they have resolved the problem by replacing the agency.

Stature of Client Greater Than Agency's

One of the sharp ironies of the advertising agency business is that an advertising agency is often too successful in building up a client's business. Many a small company has been helped immensely in its growth by its advertising agency, but, after achieving stature in its field has replaced its agency of long standing with a larger organization.

Unless the smaller advertising agency can manage to match the growth of such an account, the agency will almost inevitably lose the account because it simply does not offer facilities varied enough to service the account fully. Despite a successful sales record by the company, that company eventually will select an advertising agency of a size appropriate to the greater size of the advertiser.

Agency Losing Money on Account

Loss of money on an account causes the advertising agency to resign the account. Possibly the client has cut the budget to the point of no profit for the agency. Possibly so many extra services have been demanded that the agency cannot perform them and still make a profit. Perhaps the fault lies with the agency in promising, at the time it solicited the account, more than it could deliver without making extra charges.

Now and then an advertising agency will resign a smaller account in order to pick up a bigger one, sometimes on the basis that it is losing money on the smaller account. Advertising agency men, in general, frown on the discarding of a smaller account in order to solicit the bigger one. There is no rule against the practice, however; it is only a question of business ethics.

Marketing Services Too Limited

Limited marketing services has been given as a reason with increasing frequency in the last few years. This is because many advertisers have begun to demand that some advertising agencies become full partners in the marketing as well as the advertising of their goods. Such advertisers look for marketing guidance and strong merchandising help from an agency. They expect the agency to provide people who will work in the field with their own people. They incline toward agencies that will provide these services out of their various offices around the country.

Misunderstanding about Charges

Suspicion and dissatisfaction with agency charges provide a constant source of irritation to many clients. Trouble is especially frequent in the matter of production costs, or in the cost of services not embraced by media commissions. Even media commissions enter the picture. Advertising agencies are often accused of advising the use of media on which they can make the most money rather than the media that will be best for the client's promotion.

Client Perversity

One large advertiser was noted for a demanding, impulsive top executive who directed the firing of eight advertising agencies in a period of ten years. In some cases the replacement agencies lasted only a few months, despite the fact that these were big, successful agencies. Another advertiser consistently changed agencies every other year. There are many such cases.

It is a fact of advertising agency life that some accounts are impossible to satisfy. Perhaps the advertising manager is at fault, or perhaps it is the president of the company who holds autocratic sway over the advertising.

Sometimes agencies, faced with unreasonable and costly demands by clients, resign the accounts. Usually, however, no matter how unpleasant and demanding a client is, so long as there is a profit in handling the account the advertising agency will hold on to it. This makes for a trying relationship, but getting along with account people, no matter how impossible they may behave, is one of the crosses the advertising agency must bear.

CONTRACTS BETWEEN CLIENTS AND AGENCIES NECESSARY

Much trouble has been caused by informal agreements between clients and agencies, even though highly successful relationships have existed without formal contracts. Although letters of agreement will suffice for many clients and their agencies, a formal contract drawn up by a lawyer will give both parties even more assurance.

Points to be covered in a complete, well-thought-out contract include:

(1) Duties or responsibilities that the agency is to assume.
(2) Length of the relationship.
(3) Compensation of the agency, whether by fees, monthly or yearly retainer, commissions, or a combination of these systems.
(4) Basis of compensation, when the work is of such character that the agency must go outside its own organization for assistance.
(5) The men or women in the agency to be responsible for certain work.
(6) Executive or department head in the advertiser's organization who shall be responsible, on behalf of the advertiser, for original authorization and final approval.
(7) How surveys, work among merchants and salespeople, rough drawings, finished artwork, and so on, should be authorized and approved. Most advertisers prefer not to be responsible for published advertising, or even for preliminary artwork, unless every important item has had the approval of some designated executive.
(8) Working basis on which direct-mail, original printing and succeeding editions, and so on, shall be handled.
(9) What traveling and hotel expenses shall be borne by the agency and what will be paid by the advertiser. Most agencies expect to bear their own expenses for trips to the advertiser's place of business but not traveling and hotel expenses for other trips.
(10) If the agency is to assume responsibility for any kind of sales effort, for editorial work on house organs, or for work in connection with packages, patents, copyrights, publicity articles, radio programs, sales manuals, and so on, how it will be compensated.
(11) Length of notice required in case of severance of relationship. This is sometimes 30 days, sometimes as much as 90 days.
(12) Manner in which accounts are to be paid.
(13) Items with respect to ownership of approved drawings and authorized plates and those that were not approved for completion.
(14) Agency's responsibility for drawings or plates held in its own office for advertiser's convenience but possibly not fully insured.

HOW AGENCIES GET NEW BUSINESS

Speculative Presentations

One of the great evils in new-business solicitations is the costly speculative presentation. This is a presentation that is complete with finished art and copy for print advertising, with ready-to-broadcast radio tapes or transcriptions, and a complete advertising, marketing, and merchandising plan worked out to the last period. Such presentations may cost many thousands of dollars. Furthermore, a number of advertising agencies may be matching dollars with each other as the prospective client invites a series of presentations by agencies over a period of weeks or months.

Although, understandably, advertising agencies are eager for new business, why are they willing to spend so much money and time on what so often is a futile try for new accounts? The answer is that usually they are not willing to do this, but prospective clients make it known that this is the way they want the presentation made. Also, if one agency leads the way by offering this kind of presentation, others feel compelled to compete on the same basis.

Strong opposition to expensive speculative presentations has been voiced many times by the American Association of Advertising Agencies. Leaders in the agency field have echoed this opposition, but still some agencies persist in the practice.

Some advertising agencies refuse to submit plans in competition with others and will not submit plans unless they are paid for this prelimimary work.

It is not unknown for advertisers to invite a number of advertising agency presentations, in order to "pick the brains" of the agencies, and then eventually to utilize the better marketing and advertising ideas in future promotions.

Despite the fact that some of the very best and biggest of agencies refuse to make speculative presentations, prospective clients continue to feel that the speculative presentation enables them to see what the agency will do with *their* problem and to judge how much better the approach is than the one that had been used by the agency being fired.

On the positive side, if the client accepts the work offered in the presentation, then the agency has a good head start for the critical early months of working for the new account.

Solicit Accounts of Other Advertising Agencies

A number of advertising agencies make constant calls upon advertisers who already have advertising agencies. In some cases the solicitation will be made because the "grapevine" has indicated that the advertiser is dissatisfied with his current agency.

In other instances the agency call is made "cold," since there has been no indication that the advertiser has any fault to find with the agency handling the account. Some agencies will make such cold calls for years, hoping that some day dissatisfaction will set in and the advertiser will be receptive.

Calling upon advertisers who are already being served by an advertising agency is frowned on by many agencies, especially those who have enough billing that they can afford to insist that the initial overtures be made by the advertiser. There are, in fact, a number of advertising agencies who have never solicited new business; the advertisers must always make the first move. Usually, these agencies will be big, successful leading organizations, or they will be agencies noted for their creativity and for being selective about the kind of accounts they handle.

Presentations to Present Clients

Some clients stay with campaigns that use an unchanging theme year after year. Even the media used do not change much. Such procedures often make sense if sales continue to rise and the general image of the advertiser is good.

Other clients expect their agencies to pop constantly with new campaign ideas and like to change the theme and general approach every six months or, at the longest, each year. Unfortunately, it is too often true that the only ones tired of the campaign are the client people. Because they see the advertisements constantly and were in on their creative birth, they view them as "old hat" and are prone to criticize the agency for not coming up with something "fresh."

If the client people are this type, and the agency is unable to talk them out of their mistaken viewpoint that campaign themes need constant changing, then change the campaign it must. In working up the new campaign the agency will follow procedures not unlike those described for new-business solicitation.

GETTING GOOD WORK FROM THE ADVERTISING AGENCY: WHAT THE CLIENT SHOULD DO

Most agency-client difficulties may be traced to bad handling on the client's part. A few changes in attitude and procedure can bring satisfactory work from almost any advertising agency, since most agencies are staffed by competent people, or can hire competent people who will be acceptable to the client.

Here are a few suggestions which, if followed, can develop a pleasant working relationship between client and agency and good advertising:

Treat agency people as equals, not subordinates

Too many clients use the "crack the whip" approach. A perfectly normal person who becomes an advertising manager too often then becomes a bully who plays constantly on the agency's fear of losing the account to "keep them in line."

Do not change for the sake of change.

Advertising managers often seem to feel that they must change, if only slightly, everything submitted by the advertising agency, whether creative work or plans. Usually there are many ways to present something in advertising. If the advertising manager's way is no better than the agency's way, then the advertising manager should not discourage the advertising agency by changing the agency's work for no real purpose.

If the agency is not doing satisfactory work, let it know precisely what is wrong.

Many times an advertising agency is aware that the client is not satisfied with the agency, but the client never indicates specifically what is wrong. If it is the creative work, the service, the charges, or whatever, it is the obligation of the advertising manager to tell concretely what changes can and should be made.

Unfortunately, an advertising manager will frequently begin looking about for another advertising agency instead of working with the present agency to correct the situation.

There have been many cases where the advertising manager never once indicated dissatisfaction. The agency's first intimation that anything was wrong was its firing without ever having been given a chance to correct its errors or procedures.

Speak up to company management.

Once the advertising manager and the advertising agency have both decided on something, it is the advertising manager's obligation to back the advertising agency in talks with company management. Whether the matter agreed upon is the creative approach, media selection, or the budget, the advertising manager should be strong enough to make management hesitate before lightly changing an advertising agency recommendation. Otherwise the agency feels a sense of futility as it works out plan after plan only to have each succeeding plan changed because the advertising manager is weak and thus overridden.

Give the advertising agency the full facts.

Agencies are, in a sense, full partners with their clients. If confidential information that will make for better agency understanding of the client's marketing and advertising is held back, the agency's work suffers.

Sometimes information is held back not because the client does not trust the agency but because everyone is "too busy" to give the necessary product information. Some account executives return from client meetings with so little useful information that the creative department has a desperate time writing a specific, interesting advertising.

Praise as well as criticize.

"How are you going to keep 'em on their toes if you tell 'em their work is good?" Many clients are silent about good work and loud about work that does not please them. Especially in dealing in the creative areas of the work, the client can obtain an extra measure of enthusiasm for the account by occasionally writing a note about the copy or art that says: "This is great, keep it up" or "A fine idea."

Give prompt, firm decisions, and give time to plan.

Waiting until the last minute means that the agency must work under pressure and over weekends to get jobs done. Sometimes poor work is the consequence. Likewise, indecision, often behind lack of promptness, causes trouble at the agency, since having to do work over because the account changed its mind is one of the sure ways to crack morale, especially the morale of creative people. Because an advertising manager does not plan work well, the agency may always have its back to the deadline wall. Putting the agency people in this position will result in nervous wrecks and poor work.

Remember that the account executive and the advertising agency have other work to do.

In most advertising agencies account executives have more than one account, just as do the agencies. In their excessive demands for service, with no consideration for the profitability of the account to the agency, some clients demand 24-hour-a-day service and all kinds of extras. Intelligence and consideration must be used to decide how much service can justifiably be expected.

MAKING CLIENTS SATISFIED: WHAT THE AGENCY SHOULD DO

Clients expect agency men to be pleasant, hardworking, and willing to pick up luncheon and entertainment bills. These attributes are not enough, however, to enable an advertising agency to hold off competition. Both small agencies and large agencies can be more certain of holding their accounts if they keep the following always in mind:

Be in constant touch.

This rule is most abused in the case of small accounts. There is much "fussing" over a big account, but the smaller account frequently complains: "I never see anybody from the agency." This is one of the most common causes of the loss of small accounts. Since it is not profitable to make frequent personal visits, phone calls, memos, and letters make certain the account does not feel neglected.

Get more than one person involved with the client.

Too frequently the only agency person seen by the account is the account executive. Occasionally, the account executive should take other agency personnel along when visiting the client's office. It might be the research and marketing director; it could be someone from the creative department. If the account uses television, the agency's television director might go along.

Above all, the agency president should make it a point to visit the client at least once a year. A talk with the president of the company in which the agency president asks the former how satisfied the company is with the advertising can bring out invaluable reactions. This gives the agency president a chance to convince the client that the agency is sincerely interested in the account.

Another useful technique is to get as many client people as possible to come to meetings at the agency and to take the "tour," during which the company personnel get acquainted with agency people and facilities.

Hold down costs and let the client know about what has been saved.

Some clients suspect advertising agencies of wringing every ounce of profit out of an account. They are especially suspicious of production charges. All service charges should be held as low as possible. All expenses should be discussed and approved in advance with the client, and all charges should be itemized in writing.

Clients sometimes complain that the advertising agency seems interested only in putting through advertising in mass media, where commissions are high. They charge that the agency lacks enthusiasm for creating dealer materials for cooperative advertising, and for other less glamorous and less profitable activities.

Become an expert in the client's product and marketing approach.

Some account executives and copywriters work so closely with their accounts that they are almost looked upon as staff members by the clients. The quicker an account executive can get to the stage where it is not necessary for the client to "background" any more, the better. This knowledge of products is especially important in the industrial field, where products are technical and where the account executive sometimes, by working with product managers, ends up knowing more about the client's products than the advertising manager—especially if the account executive has had a technical background and the advertising manager has not.

Be willing to make field trips.

This advice is directed especially at account executives, who will never learn all there is to learn about a client's business by running back and forth between the client's office and the agency office. If, for instance, the account markets a grocery store product, the account executive who is worth his money will make store checks to see how the product is moving, how it is displayed, how it is priced, what the competition is doing, and what the retailers think about the product, the company, and the advertising. A check will be made with the wholesalers, as well as occasional trips with company salespeople to learn their problems and to see how the selling and advertising are coordinating.

Sell creative work enthusiastically.

A client's attitude toward the agency's creative work is going to be shaped strongly by the way the account executive, or others, present that work. It is important for the agency personnel to sell the advertising manager on the merits of the creative work because the latter will usually need to sell company superiors. "Selling" here does not refer to the ability to palm off poor work but to present enthusiastically and convincingly the good creative work of the agency in order that the advertising manager will feel assured that the company is being given a consistently high level of creativity.

Write full call reports.

Each time a call is made upon the client, the account executive writes a call report that gives in detail what took place and what action was agreed upon, and that confirms various understandings. In some cases a copy of the call report goes to the client; in some cases it does not. Other copies go to various agency personnel, including the account supervisor.

Sending call reports to the client is a highly desirable procedure. If the account executive misunderstood any statement made by the client, or if the understanding was inaccurate in any way, the client can quickly rectify the error.

The careful writing of full call reports, and careful reading by the client, has kept relations between many accounts and advertising agencies on a basis of mutual understanding.

MULTIPLE-AGENCY CLIENTS

A number of the larger corporations, those offering a number of products, break up the advertising task among several agencies. Some companies will use as many as eight to ten agencies at one time.

One of the notable examples of such a corporation is Procter & Gamble, which has a profusion of items in the form of detergents, foods, drugstore, and paper products. By splitting the promotion of these products among different agencies, the company feels that it avoids sameness in the appearance of its advertising. Also, a sort of unspoken competition among the different agencies spurs all of them to do a spirited job for the giant soap company.

There is no feeling among Procter & Gamble agencies that there is anything demeaning about having to share the company's business. In fact, much of the growth of certain Procter & Gamble agencies has been direct growth of the products themselves. When the company, for instance, brings out a new product, it usually assigns the product to one of its present agencies. If the new product succeeds—and most Procter & Gamble products do succeed—billings may shoot up quickly into the millions of dollars.

Before this happens, however, the advertising agency has been steeped in test marketing planning and execution, since the company believes strongly in trying the product out in local and regional markets before going national. The company's agency is involved in every arduous step of this test period.

Despite the multiple-agency arrangement, usually there will not be too much cooperation between advertising agencies hired by the same advertiser. It is considered desirable for each agency to maintain its independence. In the company's advertising department this same independence is found. Each brand manager is trained to compete just as hard against company brands sold in the same markets as against those manufactured by rival companies. This kind of rivalry extends to the company's agencies. Unless ordered otherwise by the company, each advertising agency of the company is just as close-mouthed and secretive about its activities with other company agencies as it is with agencies in general.

SPECIALIZED AGENCIES: PRO AND CON

Most advertising agencies do not wish to specialize in certain types of accounts. Yet many agencies, without planning to do so, develop a high degree of specialization.

One agency, to give an example, specializes in advertising for commercial banks. Known widely as a "financial" advertising agency, this organization represents scores of these banks. In doing so, it has established a syndicated service. Print and broadcast media advertising is the same for all banks on its client list. Each bank, however, is the only one in its area served by the advertising agency. This eliminates the possible embarrassment that two banks in the same district will have the same advertisements.

To its client list the agency's specialization is useful for two reasons:

(1) The agency is a real expert in financial advertising and in the field of banking generally.
(2) The advertising service, because the advertising is syndicated, is often less costly than if a local advertising agency were preparing the advertisements.

On the negative side, the advertising agency's syndicated service is certain to lack the local touch, since it is created for many banks in a widespread geographical area. Furthermore, such advertising is often charged with having a "canned" look. This charge is usually made by other advertising agency men who might be suspected of prejudice. Usually the general public is unaware that syndicated advertising is different from any other.

Another area for advertising agency specialization is in products advertised in the medical journals. Advertising for these products requires a specialized knowledge. Advertising agencies engaged in such professional advertising may have a client list made up completely of pharmaceutical houses and surgical supply firms.

Still other advertising agencies, especially in the Midwest, may have a strong concentration in farm products, including various animal feeds, and farm machinery.

Then, as mentioned earlier, some agencies are known as "consumer" or "packaged goods" specialists, while others are known as "industrial" agencies. Either type of agency may find it difficult to break out of its "rut," since its reputation for specialization may cause companies not in its area of specialization to avoid it. Usually it is the industrial advertising agency that is more likely to break away from its specialized mold, because there is more money to be made in consumer goods promotion. To accomplish the breakaway the industrial agency must have people with successful consumer-goods advertising and marketing experience, and then it must, on the strength of these people, pick up some consumer-goods accounts which, in turn, it must serve successfully. Even with all this, the industrial advertising agency will find that it will be a long time before it shatters the conviction that it is not especially gifted in consumer marketing and advertising.

LOCAL ADVERTISING AND THE AGENCY ROLE

Although many advertising agencies, especially smaller ones, have retail-store accounts, the sum total of all these accounts does not amount to a significant sum in dollar volume.

Most of the big spenders—the giant department stores—use advertising agencies only for the preparation of advertising for national magazines, radio, and television. For the big-money, bread-and-butter newspaper advertising, they utilize the services of their own advertising departments. This procedure is followed because the sliding rates given by newspapers to retail advertisers make it possible for the department stores to buy space at a very low rate—at a much lower rate, in fact, than the rate at which the advertising agency can buy the same space with its 15 percent discount. Thus, it is more profitable for department stores to do their own advertising and to buy their space directly.

Because retail accounts demand minute-by-minute service for their daily advertising, many advertising agencies are not interested in their business anyway. One form of local advertising, however, that is sought eagerly by advertising agencies is that of banks. Agencies get around the low local advertising rates here by charging banks a service fee that makes it profitable to devote time to their accounts.

Smaller agencies tend to be much more interested in retail or local advertising than bigger agencies. These small organizations will usually work entirely on a fee or retainer basis and will have as clients only the small or medium-sized local businesses. Such agencies can make a good living from local accounts, but the work is hard, demanding, and constant, and it is filled with just as much pressure, if not so much profit, as that devoted to bigger accounts.

WHAT AN AGENCY FACES ON THE INTERNATIONAL SCENE

One of the striking developments of recent years has been the growth of international advertising. This growth, while striking, is not surprising, since it mirrors the growth of U.S. manufacturing and distribution in Europe, Asia, and other parts of the world. U.S. manufacturers, lured by these enormous new markets, have entered vigorously into the international field, especially in the area embraced by the Common Market.

Entrance into these various international markets is always attended by a sharp realization of the need to gain acceptance for the products of manufacturing, since for many of these nations the experience of having a surplus of goods is a new one. Advertising, of course, is one of the instruments to be used in helping to solve the distribution problem, and here the advertising agency plays an important part.

Foreign advertising agencies have experienced a rapid growth. In Germany, England, and Japan, to cite a few, are some of the world's great advertising agencies. In Tokyo alone are two of the world's largest advertising agencies, Dentsu and the Hakuhodu agency. These agencies, of course, create much of the advertising that is done in their countries.

Added to the efforts of the foreign agencies are those of the branches of United States advertising agencies. Some U.S. agencies have only recently become interested in foreign branches. Others, such as J. Walter Thompson and McCann-Erickson have had many years experience in international advertising.

An advertising agency in the United States that wishes to set up a foreign branch will often affiliate with an existing agency in the other country. This kind of affiliate-merger has been especially popular in London, where advertising agencies have been strong and well established and the language and the general way of doing business are similar to our own.

In English affiliates, management may be left entirely to the English staff or else a few management persons may be sent over from the States to help in running the office.

Branches in other countries will normally be staffed completely by nationals of the country in which the offices are located. Help from the agency's main office will come in the form of advice and finances, though occasionally an executive may be sent from the home office to assist in running the foreign office. This executive will usually be a high-caliber person who knows the language of the country and who is at home with its marketing and advertising requirements.

Although the main office in the United States has much to offer the branch office, it is usually best to leave most of the running of the branch office to the nationals who make up the staff. Following are some of the problems faced by the U.S. advertising agency person assigned to a foreign office.

(1) *The foreign office has to deal with a different culture and with different patterns of habits and of likes and dislikes.*

In some countries, for instance, heavy advertising by a manufacturer is construed by the public as evidence that the advertiser is trying to "cover up something." They believe that if the product is all right, people will find out about it without so much advertising. Advertising is viewed as a sort of smoke screen.

(2) *All media are not available.*

Not only is there the difficulty of knowing which media to select, but there is also the fact that certain media available in the United States are not available for advertising in foreign countries, notably radio and television. Likewise, the profusion of media choice is lacking, since the United States leads the world in the number of magazines, newspapers, and broadcast outlets.

(3) *It is hard to conduct research in the normal way.*

Different research techniques are required, since the people of foreign lands are not accustomed to the kind of prying into their thoughts, habits, and personal life that Americans accept so easily. Research interviewers, in fact, are often viewed with suspicion.

(4) *Pressure in selling or advertising is frowned upon.*

The push and drive of American methods are resented in foreign lands. Soft sell amounting to just about "no sell" characterizes much foreign advertising. A hard-sell American advertising man will find that bulldozing methods will not only not work but will actually cause resentment.

For the average advertising man or woman who thinks romantically that the work in a foreign advertising agency branch would answer dreams of experience in foreign lands, while permitting a continuation of work in the exciting field of the advertising agency, there is just one piece of advice: "Forget it!" Average people are not sent from the United States to foreign agency branches. Only persons with unusual experience or qualifications are sent, and not many of these.

MODEST AGENCY PROFITS

Because of advertising agencies' highly publicized salary scales and the often exaggerated stories of lush expense-account living among agency personnel, a generally unrealistic idea is held about the size of advertising agency profits. In reality, advertising agencies as a group make less profit, often considerably less, than the clients they serve. This truth often comes as a surprise to clients who, like others, have had grossly inaccurate ideas about agency profits. It is sensible procedure, in fact, for an advertising agency to remind clients on occasion that it is not making unwholesome profits. By so doing the agency may be able to protect itself against unreasonable and costly demands for extra services, many of which are sought on the basis of "These fellows are making money hand over fist from our account; they can afford to give a few extras."

Too many advertising agencies refrain from talking about their small profits as if there were something indelicate in the subject. It has been said before that the chief sales commodity of the advertising agency is people, their skills, imagination, and energy. To get the kind of people that clients want, and often insist upon, takes money. This is the reason why payrolls run around 70 percent of the total expenses in the average advertising agency.

Profits before United States income tax have averaged around 6 percent.

Net profits have averaged from 3 to 4 percent, but net profits as a percentage of billings have averaged less than 1 percent.

Despite the low profits for advertising agencies, the mortality rate among agencies is not excessive. Few disappear altogether. Should an agency find itself in difficulties, mergers, affiliations, or new men with additional capital often keep the organization going, though not always under the same name.

"GOING PUBLIC"

A significant development in the 1960's was the issuance of advertising agency stock to the public. Two well-known advertising agencies—Foote, Cone & Belding and Papert, Koenig, Lois—were among the pioneers in "going public," as it has been called in the trade.

This limited movement is still being watched with interest by other advertising agencies. Some have declared they will never follow the example; others indicate they might.

Although the issuance of stock to the public is a tempting way to raise operating capital, this development has caused questions to be asked that can be answered only as time passes:

(1) Can a business so volatile, and subject to so many ups and downs, provide a proper climate for investors?

(2) What happens to stock value when important accounts switch advertising agencies?

(3) What will be the attitude of investors toward the agency if, as sometimes happens, the agency resigns a large account because of disagreement with the philosophy of the client?

(4) Is the obligation to stockholders going to interfere with obligation to clients?

On the other hand, it is entirely possible that an advertising agency may have a low-profit year but still do well on the stock market, thus providing a balancing factor not possible before going public.

ACCOUNT STEALING: HOW TO PREVENT IT

Some years ago what was known as the "Duane Jones case" shook the advertising agency world. Duane Jones, head of an avertising agency bearing his name, lost 50 percent of his billings and 90 percent of his skilled personnel when several of his executives departed from the agency taking a number of accounts with them.

After a long-drawn-out legal proceedings the court found in favor of Duane Jones, who had sued the new agency formed from the billings taken from him. His charge of a conspiracy to ruin his busines was upheld and the former top executives were compelled to pay a huge sum to make up for Duane Jones' losses.

In many cases, such departing employees have not only persuaded accounts to switch business to their newly formed agencies but have also set up shop with many of the key personnel of their former employers. While still working for those employers they have persuaded both the accounts and the employees to leave.

Although such practices had been occurring for a long time, the Duane Jones case represented the first attempt to stop them in the law courts. The judgment in Duane Jones' favor caused a change in the practice but did not stop it. Part of the change was in the timing. Instead of openly soliciting the accounts while still working for their present agency, those about to leave waited until they had formally resigned from their agencies before attempting to take business away from them, or at least there was nothing to indicate that a solicitation had been made while they were still employed by agency No. 1.

So long as there is an advertising agency business, there will be a substantial amount of switching of accounts because accounts that are satisfied with their account executive will transfer their business if the account executive leaves to go to another agency. (Rarely, however, will such a switch ruin an agency, as in the Duane Jones case.) If the account executive has been almost the sole contact between the agency and the client, it is natural for the account to go where this person goes. To the client, the account executive *is* the agency.

One way to thwart this tendency is to make certain that the client is exposed to many more agency people than the account executive. A method to accomplish this is to use the group system of handling accounts. Under this arrangement, an account executive, creative people, and others will be assigned to the account. The advertising manager or product manager will be made aware of this group activity on the account and will become acquainted with all the members of the group. For the manager the agency will then consist of more people than the account executive.

Another way to involve more personnel than account executives in the affairs of the different accounts is to utilize the skills of a plans board in behalf of the accounts.

A plans board is composed of the better brains of the advertising agency—persons with successful experience in advertising and marketing. On the board will be people from the contact side, the creative side, and the management side. On some boards may be found the president of the agency, the chairperson, or the executive vice-president.

ACCOUNT SWITCHING: ITS DARK SIDE

People in and out of advertising have always looked aghast at the turmoil caused by account switching (which is allied with account grabbing). With unhappy agency workers thrown out of work and agencies sometimes forced out of business, the practice has given the agency field, and advertising as a whole, a reputation for instability, excessive opportunism, and general lack of character. At no time have these feelings been more apparent than in 1977 when occurred one of the largest account switches of all times. In this, the Parker Advertising Agency lost the $45 million Datsun account at a time when Datsun's business was booming.

Hiring a consultant to screen agencies vying for the account, the company put these agencies through the tortuous and expensive ritual of staging speculative presentations. Two of these were reported to have cost $100,000. At the end of a long, drawn-out screening a good agency was declared the winner. The question asked by the advertising community, however, was whether the new agency could actually do better work for Datsun and whether it was necessary to put Parker out of business, the calamitous result of its being fired.

Instead of hiring a consultant to screen new agencies, why could not the consultant be hired to work out arrangements or changes that would make it possible for Parker to continue as Datsun's agency? Unfortunately, clients too

Advertising Agency call report.

Each time a contact is made between the agency and the client, the agency (usually the account executive) prepares a report of the meeting that, in addition to naming the time, place, and participants, gives the details of what occurred. The report goes immediately to the client. It is the latter's responsibility to tell the agency immediately if there are any inaccuracies, especially in

SERVICE REPORT NO. 98 CLIENT XYZ COMPANY

DATE August 30   **PRODUCT** PRODUCT X

A record of contacts with client, a report of status of work in production, and a memorandum of ideas discussed and work to be performed **Leo Burnett Company**, Inc.

This reports a meeting held in the offices of the Leo Burnett Company on Monday, August 30

Present:

XYZ COMPANY	LEO BURNETT COMPANY
Mr. A. B. Barnam	Mr. J. T. Able
Mr. T. V. Strong	Mr. R. S. Baker
Mr. C. B. Fox	Mr. C. D. Easy

1. <u>BUSINESS PROJECTIONS</u>

   Agency presented Product X Sales Projection Report for next ten-year period, utilizing varied assumptions. Conclusions suggested a series of aggressive marketing actions -- tests and implementation of actions related to the quality of distribution, ad spending, price actions, product difference sort-out and actions, broker evaluations and upgrade possibilities.

   <u>Next Step</u>: Client consideration of individual recommendations and Agency implementation procedure development. Anticipated Client/Agency agreement 9/15.

2. <u>PERMANENT END-AISLE DISPLAY PROGRAM</u>

   Aspects discussed in detail. A number of varied ideas, approaches and pitfalls were discussed. It was agreed that salesforce involvement and input would be helpful in terms of establishing program viability and incentive-to-authorize costs.

   Ideas developed and to be considered included test cell activity to develop specific evidence of increased level of sales, chain-breaker techniques.

   Following an afternoon meeting with broker representatives, it was agreed that the basic program would be pilot presented to representative factors by salesforce and broker personnel and that following these exploratory meetings program strategies and ingredients would be finalized.

   <u>Next Step</u>: Broker representatives (John Howard and Frank Sullivan) to discuss program with market factors and report findings and reactions to Corporate Management on or before 9/15

3. <u>TELEVISION COMMERCIAL ROTATION</u>

   It was agreed that the Agency will rotate "Half Slice" and "Nuance" commercials for the East Coast feed beginning immediately and until prevent. No changes for West Coast feed at this time.

   Probable start date for national introduction of new "Ventriloquist" campaign is 12/15 matters where some action was agreed upon or where there was a supposed agreement on budget. A call report should be accurate and thorough to protect both parties, especially the agency in case later the client, for example, denied the authorization of a certain expenditure, or media schedule.

XYZ COMPANY - PRODUCT X
Service Report #98
August 30
Page 2

4. "ADAMANT" RADIO REVISED SCRIPTS presented and taken under consideration by Client. Agency repeated its position -- preference not to produce. Cost for production quoted at $1100.

   Next Step: Client decision anticipated on 9/8.

5. "VENTRILOQUIST" RADIO CAMPAIGN discussed. Agreement reached to produce Archer execution for communications (CRW) test.

   Next Steps: Agency to arrange for Alice Smith to come to Chicago, and production of this single spot will take place locally. Five follow-up commercials tabled pending production and CRW results for Archer.

6. BUDGETARY - MEDIA.

   Agency and Client data was reviewed to achieve dollar agreement.

   Next Step: Agency will develop monthly dollar flow projections and submit week of 9/7. Client will review proposition to release additional funds for 1st, 2nd, 3rd Quarters upon receipt of dollar flow information.

7. RESEARCH

   Agency will develop proposal for research procedure to update knowledge of consumer attitudes relative to Product X and major competitors. Submission week of 9/7.

8. MAGAZINE MERCHANDISING (Holiday Period Campaign)

   Agency to contact publication for 5M and 10M quantity prices for 8½ x 11" color reprints (display cut included) and report costs to Client.

   Client to determine if scotchprints can be made available for display illustration.

9. MEDIA

   Agency reported options not currently possible for network purchases during 2nd and 3rd Quarters. Agency will proceed with negotiations and placement of authorized funds. Purchases will be concluded on or before 9/8.

10. MISCELLANEOUS

   -- Agency provided photoscripts of two recent competitive commercials.

   -- Client reported broker incentive recommendations are being favorably considered. Time span continues as a question. Final decision week of 9/7.

                              C. D. Easy

often have a firing complex, a sense of power they use unwisely. Probably 90 percent of agency firings are unnecessary but still the cruel and wasteful practice continues — to the detriment of the advertising industry as a whole.

LIABILITY OF THE ADVERTISING AGENCY
FOR FALSE CLAIMS

From the very beginning of the advertising agency system it has been assumed by the advertising agencies that the facts supplied by clients for the writing of advertising copy are accurate and truthful. Agencies have had to make this assumption, since in thousands of instances it is literally impossible for the advertising agencies to conduct the research or investigation that would be necessary to verify the truthfulness of material furnished by clients.

Yet in 1964 two cases caused advertising agency men considerable worry, because in each case not only was the client held liable for statements in advertising, but the advertising agency along with the client was also held responsible. One of these cases involving fraudulent advertising was brought forth by the state of New York; the other originated with the Federal Trade Commission.

In the first case, the advertising agency was indicted along with its client because a section of the New York State Penal Code made the placement of an advertisement a crime regardless of whether or not the agency had any knowledge that the advertisement was untrue, false, or misleading.

Such a ruling put an advertising agency at the mercy of a dishonest client. This agency vulnerability is especially true if the client makes a product so complex in its formulation that the agency is forced to rely upon the client for the complete accuracy and truthfulness of product facts that are supplied.

Should other legal bodies have taken the New York State view of the responsibility of advertising agencies for the accuracy or honesty of their advertising for clients, it is difficult to see how advertising agencies as a whole could permanently stay out of legal trouble.

To look at the matter practically, one wonders what the advertising agency can do in the case of:

(1) A producer of hybrid seed corn who for five years has tested the seed under varied climatic and soil conditions on hundreds of test plots.
(2) A manufacturer of animal feeds that contain antibiotics. Testing has been done in School of Agriculture laboratories, as well as in the client's laboratories and on hundreds of farms. Figures from all these tests are reflected in the material given to the advertising agency.
(3) A manufacturer of toothpaste that contains a special chemical formula that inhibits tooth decay. Tests have been conducted for years by the manufacturer and by reputable dentists. Finally, results of these tests are given to the advertising agency, which is instructed to center copy around strong claims for prevention of tooth decay.
(4) A manufacturer of cough medicine that, like the toothpaste, has been tested in laboratories and by many professional men. The advertising agency is told to write strong copy claims for the ability of the new product to knock out persistent coughs.

Any reasonable person can see that in these situations, and in thousands of situations like them, the advertising agency must believe in the accuracy and honesty of its clients. Here and there it is possible that an advertising agency may be a party with the client in using copy claims they know are not true. The law should be invoked in such cases. Where it is not possible for the advertising agency to do anything but accept client information as true, it is difficult to see the advertising agency as anything but an innocent party.

On the other hand, despite the former[1] New York state law, the Federal Trade Commission and the federal courts will not hold advertising agencies responsible if it is established clearly that they have no knowledge of, or reason to know, of a client's deceptive or untrue claims. Notice the phrase "reason to know." This implies an earnest attempt on the part of the advertising agency to ascertain the truth, not to close its eyes to the possibility that the copy claims could be disproved were the agency to conduct a normal investigation of their validity.

Still, there are two situations wherein an advertising agency might legitimately be judged guilty of legal misdoing: one is the rigged demonstration as in the famous shaving cream-sandpaper case. In this instance, the agency, to demonstrate its client's shaving cream, showed in a commercial how the product could soften sandpaper sufficiently to shave it. Actually, plexiglass sprinkled with sand, was substituted for sandpaper. The second is the situation wherein the agency takes an active role in working up copy claims and thus should be responsible for verifying their accuracy and truthfulness.

AGENCY-CLIENT RESPONSIBILITY FOR MEDIA PAYMENTS

In the preceding chapter, the advertising agency's responsibility for paying client media bills was listed as one of the reasons why the media continue to favor the agency commission system wherein the media allow a 15 percent discount from media bills paid by advertising agencies.

For many years, this responsibility to pay media bills was accepted as a foundation of the advertising agency system. Recent court cases have càst a shadow on the concept. Here are typical situations that are causing nervousness among clients and agencies alike:

(1) A television network sued a company to recover money the network was owed by the now-bankrupt advertising agency of the company. The company had paid the agency an amount to cover the network charges but the agency had never used this money to pay the network. The company refused to pay the network on the grounds that if they did so, they would be paying the same bill twice.

(2) A city retailer went bankrupt. There was a substantial newspaper advertising bill that had not been paid. The newspaper thereupon sued the retailer's advertising agency on the assumption that the agency had sole liability for paying the newspaper advertising bill.

In the foregoing cases, we saw a bankruptcy occur in an agency, and then in a company. Each situation brought up the question of responsibility. Unfortunately, agency-client relationships too often are informal with no clearly-expressed written contracts. Frequently, verbal agreements rule.

Most advertising agencies, especially the bigger ones, favor sole liability by the agency as the guiding principle. Normally, then, it has been assumed that unless there is a written statement to the contrary that the advertising agency is liable for payments of media bills.

To avoid trouble it is obvious that a written client-agency contract should state clearly whether the agency has sole liability for payment of media bills. If not, then it should be stated that the agency *is* merely an agent for the client. The latter will then be responsible for payment of media bills even though the agency is billed by a medium. If the agency has gone out of business, the medium then collects from the client.

QUESTIONS

1. What reasons other than personality conflicts are behind the shifting of accounts?

2. What is the attitude of most big advertising agencies toward the sole liability of agencies in the payment of media bills.

3. Put down as many as you can of the "fundamental" questions an advertiser should ask an agency soliciting the company's account.

4. Discuss personality conflicts as a reason for agency shifts.

5. What other reasons are behind the shifting of accounts?

6. Name some points you think should be in an agency-client contract. Now check your suggestions against those in the book to see what you have missed.

7. Name positives and negatives for speculative presentations.

8. List a few suggestions that will help a client get along with the advertising agency.

9. Suggest some procedures to be followed by an advertising agency if it wants to keep the client satisfied.

10. Why and how do agencies specialize? Is such specialization desirable or undesirable? Explain.

11. What basic reason is responsible for the fact that big department stores almost always set up their own advertising departments instead of hiring an advertising agency to do their work?

12. For what reasons might a U.S. advertising executive find it difficult to work in the foreign office of an advertising agency? In short, what are some of the differences he might expect to face?

13. How good are the opportunities for jobs if a U.S. man or woman wants to work in a foreign advertising agency?

14. What questions arise when an advertising agency "goes public?"

15. What safeguard should be taken if an advertising agency executive plans to leave an agency and take some accounts to the new agency?

16. Under what circumstances will an advertising agency be held liable by the FTC and federal courts, along with the client, in a situation in which misleading advertising is charged?

REFERENCES

1. The section of the New York Penal Code referred to was revised in 1965 and concluded with the statement that: ". . . in any prosecution under this section, it is an affirmative defense that the allegedly false or misleading statement was not knowingly or recklessly made or caused to be made."

10

ADVERTISING FOR LOCAL BUSINESS

ADVERTISING FOR LOCAL BUSINESS

Grace Lonergan, flicked a worried glance at her watch as she hurried along Center street to the Lonergan Beauty Salon. One of her best and most demanding customers would be in at 9 a.m. for a hair set.

On her way, Grace passed Jim Laslo as he swept the sidewalk in front of his suburban hardware store. This chore was part of the daily ritual of getting ready for the day ahead.

Twelve miles away in the city, John C. Maddox, president of the area's largest commercial bank, sat in his luxurious office pondering some disappointing figures sent up by the accounting department. A slight frown accompanied his decision to increase the advertising budget in order to acquire more savings and checking accounts.

Also, in the central business district, Hugh L. Danforth, managing director of the city's biggest hotel, was wrestling with a long-time problem—how to increase occupancy in the face of stiffening competition from the motor inns on the city's borders—Howard Johnson's, Holiday Inn, Travelodge, and others. All of these were snaring travelers before they reached the downtown area.

Despite the vast differences in the levels of their responsibilities, the four persons described have one factor in common. They are "local" advertisers. Only one of them fits the commonly-used term "retail" advertiser. That is Jim Laslo, the hardware store proprietor.

Usually the advertising for local business establishments is lumped under the one classification of "retail advertising." This term immediately brings to mind the advertising for retail stores that sells goods over the counter.

"Retail," however, cannot be applied accurately to such important local advertisers as banks. Neither can it be applied to beauty shops, automotive service shops, hotels, and many other local business enterprises.

"Local" advertising, accordingly, is more applicable to the kind of advertising being discussed by this text. Likewise, it provides a clearer contrast with "national" advertising. Local advertising, as the term is used here, refers to advertising done by businesses that expect to obtain most of their business from the retail trading area of a village, town, or city. National advertising obtains business wherever it can be found throughout the nation. Another classification, "regional" advertising, is applied to advertising that covers a sizable section of a state, a whole state, or possibly a number of states.

In this chapter, chief stress will be on retailers who sell goods. Such retailers fall into three classes:

(1) *Promotional.* Establishments in this group stress price, many sales, and clearances. They make up for their low mark-up through volume and quick turnover.

(2) *Semi-promotional.* Although the semi-promotional store, represented by the conventional department store, runs sales, it does so on a predetermined schedule. In between, it offers goods at regular prices. A sale in such a store has real meaning to its customers.

(3) *Nonpromotional.* Very ultra expensive stores fall in this group. It is made up of exclusive high fashion shops, jewelry stores with many years of tradition, and some fine furniture stores. Relatively few retail establishments have reached the prestige level that enables them to be nonpromotional.

HOW IS LOCAL ADVERTISING DIFFERENT FROM NATIONAL?

The most important difference, and the one that is at the root of almost all the differences between local and national advertising, is the size of the territory covered. This difference affects media selection, amount spent by individual advertisers, advertising approach, use of price, and speed of buying response.

Media Used Differently

Because overall the most powerful local advertising medium is the newspaper, newspaper advertising is most used by local advertisers. Not for the local advertiser are the network television and radio shows, nor the lavish spreads in national magazines. Each medium used by local advertisers must deliver the maximum coverage of the surrounding trading area from which the establishments may expect to draw customers. Coverage outside that area is meaningless and wasteful—unless advertisers aim at obtaining mail order business. But even so they still select the medium that gives them the best coverage in their immediate trading area.

Budgets Are Smaller

Although total dollars spent in local and national advertising are comparable, the amounts spent by individual local advertisers tend to be smaller. Budgets, as will be demonstrated in the section on local advertising appropriations, can be very modest. With a smaller territory to cover there is no need, except for the big department stores and women's specialty stores, to spend huge amounts in advertising to obtain sales.

Local television commercial.

Despite the dominance of newspapers for local advertising, many local businesses find television useful, especially for institutional approaches such as the one used here.

LANDO

LANDO INC
600 GRANT STREET 39ᵀᴴ FLOOR
PITTSBURGH, PA. 15219
412 456 2500

TV Copy

CLIENT THRIFT DRUG		JOB NO. TD-9444-CA	
DATE TYPED	**TITLE**	**SCRIPT NO.**	**LENGTH**
11/17 R-5	Professional/personal service (VERSION #2)		:30
RECORDING DATE	**SCHEDULE**		

VIDEO	AUDIO
1. SLOW PAN ACROSS BOTTLES OF DIFFERENT PRESCRIPTION ANTIBIOTICS	1. ANNCR: (VO) Thirty-five prescription antibiotics. Why buy yours at Thrift Drug instead of someplace else?
2. WOMAN AT R$_x$ COUNTER PHARMACIST BEHIND HER OUT OF FOCUS	2. WOMAN: (SYNC - CANDID IN FEELING) Well, I like the fact that I'm never treated like a number. My Thrift pharmacist
3. CLOSE UP OF PHARMACIST FILLING R$_x$	3. really makes a point of knowing me and giving me personal attention...
4. DISS TO WOMAN, FUMBLING IN PURSE, PULLING OUT HER PENNEY'S CARD	4. I like Thrift Drug's prices, too. And charging with my J.C. Penney card.
5. DISS TO SIGNATURE SHOT-- TYPEWRITER TYPE APPEARS IN SYNC WITH AUDIO ON OVERSIZE THRIFT LABEL. Just what the doctor ordered. At just what the price should be.	5. (TYPEWRITER FX BEHIND) ANNCR: (VO) For just what the doctor ordered, at just what the price should be -- trust Thrift Drug.
6. (POP ON IN SYNC) The R$_x$perts	6. The R$_x$perts. (SFX)

Copy Is More Intimate And Informal

Because of the proximity of the local advertisers to the people who do business with them, the local advertiser is much more a personality to customers than the national advertisers who, no matter how they try, never achieve the local flavor of the advertiser who is part of the customer's hometown.

Copy in the local advertiser's advertisements, therefore, is likely to be much more informal than that of the national advertiser. This breezy excerpt from the advertisement of a local advertiser illustrates the point:

> Get 'em while last. We warned you last time they wouldn't be around long, but a flock of you didn't show until the last item had been carried out the door. This time better get here bright and early 'cause all we can do is take care of people as they show up. Sorry.

Likewise, the advertising of the local advertiser works much harder to build the image or personality of the establishment, whether it is a bank, a hardware store, or a tire shop. As an institution that is just as local as the newspaper or the community fire department, the business that is able through its advertising to create a "difference" for itself has a better chance to succeed.

Price Is Stressed

Price is the most powerful sales tool in advertising. National advertisers, because prices may vary from dealer to dealer, or from territory to territory, rarely use prices in their advertising. In contrast, local advertisers very often go almost too far in building advertisements around price. Still, the fact that the local advertiser can use prices in advertising gives local promotion more interest, vitality, and buying information than is found in national advertising.

Response Is Quick

Some national advertisers never have the thrill of seeing anything happen quickly as a result of their advertising. All their advertising is of the long range type that builds up an impression over the years.

A local advertiser almost always expects immediate response to advertising. As a rule of thumb, the average retail advertisement is "dead" after 48 hours, since few sales will come in after that time.

Everything about retail advertising is geared for the quick sales reaction: "Buy now," "Hurry while they last," "First come, first served," "4-hour sale," "These low prices only this week."

A retailer advertiser depends upon quick response. A national advertiser rarely does.

FEW LOCAL ADVERTISERS USE ADVERTISING AGENCIES

Whereas national advertising is dominated by advertising agencies, local advertisers make relatively little use of them. The principal reason for the minor role of advertising agencies is the newspaper rate structure. Newspapers give local advertisers quantity or frequency discounts which greatly reduce the cost of advertising for those local enterprises that use enough advertising to benefit from these discounts.

Agencies, on the other hand, obtain only a 15 percent discount from the media. This contrasts with the 50 to 75 percent discount that can be earned by the local advertisers who advertise regularly. Because of these generous allowances, these local advertisers can afford to set up their own advertising departments, which do the work normally performed by advertising agencies.

Most local advertisers do not spend enough money on advertising to justify having an advertising department or hiring an advertising agency. For those advertisers with heavy advertising expenditures, the advertising agency is useful, not for the day-to-day newspaper advertising, but for the specialized advertising if the local business uses such promotion. Such advertising includes radio, television, outdoor advertising, or advertisements in national magazines.

Many advertising agencies, on their part, shun local advertising because of low budgets, and because so many local advertisers are viewed as "nuisance" accounts with their daily crises and their constant demands for service.

WHY LOCAL BUSINESSES USE ADVERTISING

Whenever the faint-hearted, faced with advertising bills, begin to view advertising as an extra expense rather than an investment, or as a luxury rather than a necessary cost of doing business, in the same category as other overhead items such as electricity, heat, and salaries, they should consider the following reasons for using local advertising.

To Build Character

Establishing store character through advertising is a long process and is made up of many elements. The kinds of goods selected for advertising, the kind of copy written, the illustrations chosen, the typography used—all these and other elements contribute to the character that a store builds up through its advertisements. Finally, the advertising of a local business makes it a familiar friend to old customers and helps introduce it to new customers who, unless the advertisements are completely neutral and undistinguished, can establish some idea in their minds as to whether they would like to do business with the advertiser.

A service organization, such as a savings bank, a savings and loan association, or a commercial bank, also creates character for itself through advertising. Even more than retail stores, savings institutions have nothing different to sell customers. No bank is distinguishable through its services, but all can be different through advertising. The same is true of dry-cleaning establishments, dairies, auto repair service shops, beauty parlors, and other businesses selling services.

To Attract New Customers

Although almost any local business values highly the steady customer—the type who comes back time after time—the business will die eventually if it does not attract new trade. Old customers are lost in time because of moving, death, or a myriad of other reasons. Any progressive local business must try constantly to obtain "first-time" customers. Must a store or a service organization advertise in media to get these customers? Not necessarily. Word-of-mouth advertising may bring in business. A display in a store or bank window may cause new customers to walk in. A superb location will insure some new business; this is especially true of banks, since many of the public, thinking that "banks are all alike," patronize the bank that is easiest to reach.

Notice, however, that each of these three business builders—word of mouth, display, and location—leaves much to chance. Old customers may produce the word-of-mouth advertising that brings in new customers, but building a day-to-day volume by this means is highly uncertain. Likewise, the display and location of a business, although important, can hardly insure steady and diversified new business. On a rainy or snowy day, for example, few persons may notice, or even go by, a retailer's attractive window display. But thousands will see the newspaper advertisement regardless of the weather.

Steady advertising removes much uncertainty. It tells new residents where a business is located and what it has to offer. It keeps old-time residents (but noncustomers) aware of the business. Any time, therefore, that they cease to stop in at their accustomed places, they will think of the store because they know what it has to offer and how to find it.

To Hold Present Customers

Even an old customer can be wooed away if she sees tempting offers in other advertising and no counter offer by her present store. Banks have found this true when they see depositors lured away by rival banks that offer merchandise to anyone who opens a new account. A constant barrage of advertising by other advertisers, while the one business is silent, can make old customers forget, or cause them to wonder if the nonadvertiser is as progressive as the others.

An old customer, too, needs to be given information about a store. Although she may know its general policies and merchandise, she needs to be informed about new merchandise just received or new services being offered. She will be grateful for information about special money-saving prices.

One of the surer ways to lose old customers is to do nothing to remind them of you. The saying "out of sight, out of mind" is quite applicable to the store or service organization that fails to keep itself in the consciousness of old customers, who may become "lost" customers because no attempt has been made to keep up with competitors' advertising.

To Cut Sales Costs

Advertising reduces sales expense (1) by increasing the speed of stock turnover, (2) by making the sales job in the store easier.

Successful retail advertisers know that the combination of good merchandise and good advertising will clear shelves quickly. These people know, too, that they could probably "get by" without spending money for advertising. If, however, advertising makes their stock turn over three times to the one turn-over they would have without advertising, then advertising may be considered to have reduced sales expense and to have increased the chance for profits.

Suppose, for example, that the monthly picture for a two-month period looks like this on a certain item:

First month:	No advertising.
	Profit from one turnover, $50.
Second month:	Advertising costs, $50.
	Profit from three turnovers, $150.

It would be hard to deny that sales expense for the second month was great-ly reduced. Remember, advertising expense can hardly be viewed as intolerable if it reduces sales costs through increasing stock turnover.

Too, advertising is a form of preselling that lightens the sales job in the store. Many customers sold by an advertisement come into the store ready to put down their money. This makes for quicker sales and gives the manager, the owner, or the salespeople more time for other activities, or for working on those hard-to-sell customers who have not been softened in any way.

To Combat Periodic Slumps

Anyone in local business has encountered buying lulls. They may come at different times for different types of buinesses. Some will feel the pinch right after Christmas, and before and after income-tax time. The after-Easter period hits some. Others, unless selling hot-weather items, may suffer the summer doldrums.

Yet there is a buying potential all the time among any given set of customers. Encouragement and reminding through advertising can sometimes turn the potential into buying action.

What can the local business person do? Let nature take its course? Be idle at some periods and overly rushed at others? Or fight the lulls with promotional advertising that goes out aggressively after the customer's buying dollar.

No one, of course, can completely eliminate seasonal buying peaks. People's buying habits follow a definite pattern year after year. Through advertising, however, the seasonal peaks perhaps may be made to look less extreme.

To buy intelligently, to run a store more profitably, those up-and-down buy-ing periods must be leveled off. One way to achieve the leveling off is to select good merchandise and to use good advertising to make people want the goods. Battling a seasonal trend is one of advertising's hardest tasks, as any local businessman knows. Although advertising is not the only available weapon in the battle, it is one that should not be overlooked.

To Help Sell Items That Are Not Advertised

Certain grocery store items, such as soap, have traditionally been the lures that bring shoppers into a store. Once in the store, the shopper picks up the other items on the shopping list.

FIGURE 10-1
Chart that shows when sales are made.

Year after year demand for products is consistently about the same in the different months. Observant retailers key advertising to these monthly buying patterns. In this instance, product sales climb steadily from the early months and peak in December.

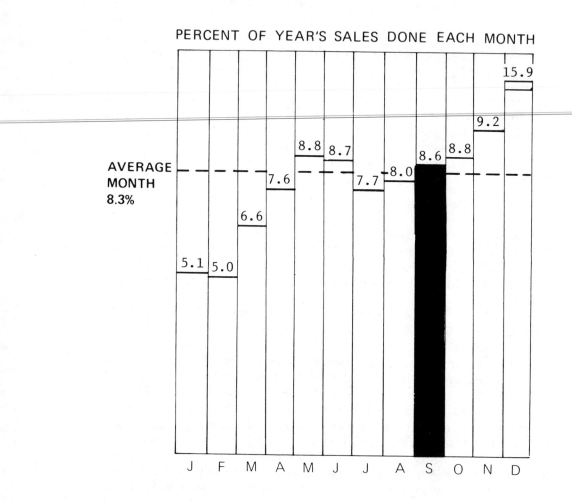

PERCENT OF YEAR'S SALES DONE EACH MONTH

AVERAGE
MONTH
8.3%

This practice of making one item attractive through price or some other inducement in order to attract shoppers to a store and thus cause them to buy other items is a long-standing device of merchandising and advertising. Yet this important advertising fact is often overlooked by retailers who, because a certain advertised item has not sold well, are inclined to write off the advertising as a total loss. They forget, or ignore, the effect the advertising has had on the sale of other items.

Sometimes an advertisement for a certain item may not interest a person in that item but may arouse buying fever for the type of article, thus getting the shopper into the store after all. A man may not care for the rake his hardware dealer is advertising, but he may be reminded that he needs a shovel. His wife may not want the clothing store's special on babies' flannel shirts but may be reminded of a need for diapers. Once in the store, either of these persons may buy other completely unrelated items.

Advertising builds traffic and traffic sells good in all lines, not just the ones advertised. It is important to give people a reason to be in a store. Advertising provides that reason.

To Identify With Nationally — Advertised Goods

National advertising creates a tremendous momentum. Pounded from the air by the broadcasting media and attracted by print advertising in magazines, newspapers, outdoor posters, and transit cards, the customer has been conditioned to ask for nationally advertised products; and to be wary of nonadvertised goods.

Yet all the advertising weight means nothing if the customer does not know where to buy the goods locally in her own hometown or neighborhood. Every time a local advertisement features nationally advertised merchandise, it is performing a two-way function: (1) Providing real shopping help to customers by telling them just where to buy favorite brands. (2) Helping the dealer take advantage of the preselling done by the national advertisers.

Despite recent growth of private brands, enormous numbers of consumers want and trust nationally advertised brands. Stores that offer these brands utilize an already aroused interest.

To Build Trust in the Company

Seeing the name of a business constantly in the newspapers, or hearing it over the air, breeds confidence. Most people are inclined to distrust the unknown. A store's advertising makes its name familiar, acquaints shoppers with the way it conducts business, and informs them about the kind of goods sold. Once the store has become familiar to shoppers they will be more likely to trust it and to buy from it.

MAJOR CRITICISMS of LOCAL ADVERTISING

Uncertainty over advertising is probably the most outstanding characteristic of local advertisers. They are fatalistic, too. Some advertisements pull and some do not, they say. Having said this, they shrug and continue advertising, or stop it altogether.

Here are some of the major troubles with local advertising. Find answers to these and local advertising may become less of a puzzle; its results may become more certain.

1. *Not given equal prominence with the buying and selling functions.*

Too often advertising is treated as a stepchild, as a minor activity that does not deserve the attention given buying, selling, merchandising arrangements, and other store functions. This downgrading of advertising, of course, is truer in smaller stores than in the larger ones.

Some of the local advertisers who unquestioningly spend heavily in advertising and pay out hundreds or thousands of dollars for such advertising each year will haggle sharply over relatively minor purchases of equipment or merchandise. Before either is purchased, information about the exact performance of each will be demanded. A guarantee may even be requested.

No such demands are made of advertising. The lack of knowledge behind the spending of money for advertising by otherwise astute local businessmen is disturbing.

Largely responsible for the local advertiser's attitude is the nature of advertising itself. When merchants, for example, buy merchandise, they have something solid to demonstrate the wisdom of the purchase. When they sell the merchandise, they once again have something to show: cash receipts.

When they advertise, on the contrary, there is much outgo and not necessarily any income. An advertisement, furthermore, can be put together with little effort and time. The minimum time needed for the buying and selling functions is likely to be much greater and such functions, consequently assume more importance. Should an equal amount of time be devoted to advertising? In the case of smaller stores with smaller advertising expenditures, the answer is obviously "No."

Many of these smaller merchants should, however, take a different attitude toward advertising: to think of it as more equal in importance to buying and selling activities; to want to know why they advertise; to want to be able to measure the results obtained from advertising; to be willing to give their advertising planning the serious thought, if not the time, equal to that customarily given to buying and selling.

2. *Often handled by unqualified persons.*

It is often said that the field of retailing is filled by many people who know nothing of retailing. Whether that statement is correct will not be discussed here. But it is certainly true that thousands of retailers are not qualified to conduct retail advertising assignments.

Smaller or medium-sized stores usually have no advertising manager or anyone else qualified by experience or knowledge to direct the advertising efficiently. Instead, the assignment is taken over by the store owners or store managers, who view advertising as one more annoying chore. These persons harried by the many jobs that make up the task of running a local business, can only consider advertising as one more job to be disposed of during a busy day.

If persons must get out the advertising in addition to many other tasks, it would seem imperative that they had better be advertising experts in order to do the advertising well. Most store owners or store managers, however, are not experts. Most will admit, as did one owner: "I know I don't know nearly enough about advertising. But, I don't have time to spend on it, either."

3. *Advertising efforts are uncoordinated.*

Advertising will seldom succeed if (a) merchandise advertised is not wanted by customers; (b) timing is wrong; (c) it is not backed up by the whole store; or (d) it is not used continuously.

Advertising must be thought of, not as a separate effort, but as an important step in the sales process and a part of the total merchandising activity. It is not an individual effort but a cumulative action. It is part of the general overhead, not an extra expense.

A strong reason for the lack of coordinated effort in advertising is the ignorance of advertising found among the unqualified advertising personnel. Too many retailers do not know how to achieve the needed coordination. For instance, it is found consistently that big numbers of local advertisers do not work out in advance the amount of money to be used for advertising. The budget is stretched, according to one retailer, "as the spirit moves me." Another, in explaining why newspapers were used gave a somewhat typical answer: "I suppose I use the newspapers because everybody else does."

Some methods of coordinating are obvious. One procedure that could be expected from local advertisers, for instance, is that they be able to make an intelligent appraisal of what results might be expected from advertising in order that they might know how much or how little use of advertising can contribute to the sales objectives of the business.

Another coordinating factor that should be considered is the close cooperation of advertising with the whole store. A well-coordinated advertising plan includes making certain that the clerks, the interior and window display, and the prices all reflect the current local advertising. Coordination also means that someone sees that enough goods are on hand to satisfy the needs of those customers who are brought into the store by the advertising.

Another element in total coordination is the tying-in of local advertising with the store's promotion of merchandise currently being promoted vigorously in national advertising. The alert merchandiser will plan ahead in merchandise ordering, and in preparation of the advertising, in order to make newspaper advertisements tie in closely with current magazine advertising. Such tie-ins supply a one-two punch. Coordination like this will tie in advertising with all departments—a whole-store viewpoint that local advertising so often lacks. Surprisingly enough, even some very large local advertisers fail to achieve this sort of viewpoint. Thus one department may go one way, while other departments head in another direction.

HOW OFTEN TO ADVERTISE

It can be assumed that it is nearly always better for sales results to advertise frequently instead of infrequently. The word "nearly" is used because under certain circumstances it might be better to use bigger space more infrequently than it would be to use small space more frequently.

Usually, however, local advertisers should advertise daily if the budget will support such advertising. If not daily, then six times. If not six times, then five times.

If local advertisers have goods or services worth advertising, they cannot afford *not* to advertise frequently. Newspapers and radio stations have thousands of case histories that demonstrate that local advertising success is firmly associated with consistent advertising. These histories show that sales volume, if other factors are normal, goes up in almost direct proportion to advertising frequency rate.

Like so many local advertisers, the owner of a prosperous women's specialty shop in a town of 50,000 had this to say: "We advertise daily. I've never been able to figure out a way to tell just what results we get from our advertising, but I do know this: If we cut advertising out for even one day, we can notice a fall-off in sales. And if we're out of the paper for two days, sales go way down. So we stick with our daily schedule whether or not we can measure exactly what our results are."

Another local advertiser, a large hardware store owner from the Midwest, explained: "We've got a large stock here. There's something for everybody. If we advertise daily with our fourteen-inch ads we're sure to present items that someone's going to want to buy. I'd rather hammer away on a daily basis than shoot my whole advertising budget in end-of-the-week page ads. I keep salesclerks around all week. I might as well keep them busy Monday through Friday, as well as Saturday."

In local advertising, some sort of minimum advertising frequency must be the rule. Life of a newspaper advertisement is short and that of a radio or television commercial even shorter. Other advertisements and other issues of a newspaper wipe away previous advertising impressions.

Frequent advertisements keep readers or listeners from forgetting. A selling message must be kept strong and fresh in shoppers' minds. Perhaps once a week should be the local advertiser's advertising minimum; advertising can hardly be less frequent than that and be business-producing. If the advertiser wishes to build cumulative effect, it would be desirable to think of advertising as a 52-time minimum venture.

A 52-time formula will save the retailer from the lure of saving advertising efforts for one time of the year. On the one-season-of-the-year basis, almost no advertising is run between special seasons, such as Christmas and Easter. Another temptation for the let's-put-all-our-eggs-into-one-basket type of advertiser is to eliminate small advertisements in order to run big "splash" advertisements at widely spaced intervals.

If necessary, it is advisable to cut down the size of daily or weekly advertisements in order to have advertising money for the seasonal push. As said previously, no one will argue that it is not desirable to devote a sizable portion of the advertising budget to special seasons. Attention, however, must also be given to the rest of the year. Special season promotions are going to bring greater results if they have been backed up by consistent day-to-day or week-by-week advertising messages.

WHAT TO ADVERTISE

Deciding what to advertise is one of the retailer's most important advertising functions. He must remember, in making decisions, that advertising rarely does a good job of selling goods that people basically do not want. Interest in the merchandise advertised is one of the big requirements if the advertisements are to be successful. Advertising's role is to inform people that the goods they want are on hand, and to fan their already-existing interest into buying action.

Advertising's job is not that of "educating" people to want certain things but of telling them about those things they want in the first place. Neither is advertising a vehicle to enable local advertisers to foist on people their ideas of what they should buy. Local advertisers must be like politicians, their ears must be attuned to the murmur of the crowd. What the crowd wants, and when it wants it the local advertiser (or politician) gives them.

Although selecting the right merchandise to advertise is a personal, individual job, there are general rules for such selection that apply to the local advertisers. These are:

(1) Advertise best sellers.
(2) Push traffic items.
(3) Feature nationally advertised brands.

Use Advertising for Fast Movers

One of the hardest lessons for many retailers to learn is to restrain their natural desire to use advertising to sell merchandise that is slow-moving. Their reason: "The fast-moving items are going to sell anyway, so why not give the slow-moving items an extra push through advertising?"

The trouble with this thinking, of course, is that customers who have already shown through their nonbuying that they do not want the merchandise are going to have no interest in advertising promoting the merchandise. Enough such advertisements, devoid of personal appeal, will cause them to quit altogether looking at the merchant's advertising.

In selecting merchandise for advertising, then, the first rule is to narrow the selection to a relatively few items that are sure sellers. Estimates indicate that about 70 percent of retail sales are made on 30 percent of the stock. Wise retailers do not try to promote all the stock but concentrate on those items they know are certain to have appeal at the time they are advertised. Once more this demonstrates the principle of advertising goods people want at the right time.

What makes items "sure sellers" in their advertising appeal? Two major considerations are that the merchandise is current and that it is priced right.

First, *if merchandise is "current,"* it is tied in with events, the seasons, the weather, and the particular needs of the local market. An example of tying in the advertising of merchandise with events is afforded by the good fortune of the Oklahoma City retailer who sold out a big supply of boys' sweatshirts the day after the escape of a leopard from the local zoo, a news story that made headlines all over the country. Why did these sweatshirts sell so fast? Because they had on the chest the imprint of a ferocious leopard. The merchandise was "hot" because the event was hot, and the merchant profited because he was alert enough to hammer away with advertising at just the right time.

Part of being current in advertising is to concentrate advertising on items that are natural for a particular month. Going back to the hardware store discussed previously, its owner will find May a good month to promote such items as lawn and garden supplies, fishing equipment, and builder's hardware.

A wide-awake local advertiser always has an eye on the weather in making decisions about what to advertise. Preparing emergency advertisements that can be substituted at any time of the year for regular advertisements is part of good planning. In the fall, standby advertisements can be ready for seasonal items such as snow shovels, overshoes, snow tires, and any number of other items that will have current interest following the first heavy snow. In the spring, when spring rains might burst any time, standby advertisements can replace regular advertising for such rainy weather specials as raincoats, rubbers, umbrellas, and all-weather hats.

Being current by being completely keyed to the needs of the local market is essential. If retailers know a community and all its activities, they will advertise those goods that can be used in those activities. To illustrate, suppose the city is opening its summer on the weekend. What does this mean to merchants?

To the sports store—swimming suits, bathing caps, tennis rackets, baseballs, and so on.

To the drugstore—sunglasses, thermos jugs, suntan oil, and so on.

To the food store—picnic hams, cold cuts, potato salad, frankfurters, paper plates, and so on.

To the camera shop—film, cameras, photographic accessories.

Second, *if the prices in advertisements* are not in line, those fine illustrations and that fine copy will not pull enough business to pay for the space. Promotable prices are just as much a part of successful advertisements as the advertiser's signature, headlines, and other elements. A price policy should be set that will make the advertising interesting to all portions of a local advertiser's potential market.

Use of certain selling prices that have built-in sales appeal has been called "psychological pricing." A local advertiser who is a "planner" does not choose a price simply because it offers the desired markup or because it seems "right." Prices are chosen, instead, that seem to be able to create a bargain impression in the customer's mind.

Pricing goods right is very often the advertising planner's most important task when selling goods at retail. From every source, figures should be obtained and studied before a price is put into an advertisement.

Stress Items That Build Traffic

"Traffic" items frequently are not big profit items but are constantly in demand. Their virtue is that they build store traffic that results in heavy selling of items other than the ones advertised. These latter items may often return a greater profit than the traffic items. In some cases, traffic items fall in the "loss-leader" class; that is, the local advertiser is willing to sell them at a slight loss or the break-even point in order to get people into the store to buy other, higher-profit goods. Examples of traffic items for grocery stores are soaps and shortenings; for drugstores, toothpaste and shaving equipment; for camera stores, film and film-developing needs.

A good rule is to have at least one such traffic-building item in every multiitem advertisement. A variation of this is to have at least one traffic item every week. Most people reading local advertisements (unlike people reading national advertisements) are "price shopping." Their eyes have acquired the habit of comparing the prices of certain key items. Most frequently the reader looks first for the traffic item—like soup in a supermarket advertisement—and then compares the price with that offered by competing stores. If this one price is high, the conclusion, often wrong of course, is that the store is going to be high in other lines also.

Good planning, then is (1) to include traffic items in advertisements and (2) to see that these traffic items are competitively priced.

Emphasize Items That Are Nationally Advertised

Markups for nationally advertised brands may be smaller, and sometimes one is put in the uncomfortable position of being dependent upon a supplier's goodwill. Likewise, since the manufacturer will normally sell to other local advertisers (all competitors) also, the one local advertiser often has nothing to talk about that a competitor cannot talk about in advertising, too.

Despite these drawbacks, and there are others, there are advantages in featuring nationally advertised merchandise in the advertising. Some of them are:

(1) *Obtains quick attention for advertisements of the local advertiser.* Just as the presence of a well-known name catches the eye quickly, almost automatically in a news story, so does the nationally advertised trade name in an advertisement have the same attention-capturing power. These names have been pounded into the public's consciousness from childhood. They are attention-getters in the same way that one's own name or signature can be picked out quickly from a page of type matter.

(2) *Takes less explaining.* A number of nationally advertised brands have become synonymous with high quality, a specific type of performance, the inclusion of a certain ingredients, or other characteristics.

A local advertiser stressing an unknown brand might need to eat up valuable space or time explaining the attributes of the brand. This kind of explanation is unneeded for a well-advertised brand already known to the trade of the local advertiser.

(3) *Helps build a reputation for the local advertiser.* Most retailers are not big enough to create a reputation for their own brands. If they attempt to push distributor brands (not nationally advertised) in their advertising, they obtain little attention. Unless they are careful about how they push them in the store itself, many shoppers may resent what they consider to be high-pressure selling. There is a danger that shoppers will question the quality of the unknown brand and the reputation of the business that attempts to sell it.

A big store, on the other hand, can have such a reputation that the distributor-brands it promotes, with or without the store's own name on labels or packages, will automatically achieve the reputation and reliability of the store itself.

A small store without any particular reputation of its own will do better to feature goods already known. Thus it will be capitalizing on the millions of dollars that have already been spent promoting the items. Many times a smaller store has been recommended in these terms: "That's not a very big store but they carry all the well-known brands."

ELEMENTS IN ADVERTISING PLANNING

In planning how to advertise, advertisers must first decide what kind of impression they want to make. Then they plan advertisements to suit. A promotional store will use different advertising from the institutional type of store. Indecision in this matter will be reflected in the advertising and local advertisers will thus have failed to make clear their kind of operation in the minds of potential customers.

A good-sized millinery store in a town of 40,000 affords an example of the indecision mentioned. This store had been following a merchandising policy that stressed price, but its advertising was wholly institutional. Faced with stock that was not moving, the owner finally made his advertising fit his merchandising policies. In an advertising turnabout, he promoted his brands and his prices vigorously in newspaper and radio copy, and in his window displays. On radio alone, a three-month stress on price sold 5,000 hats. In the words of the store owner: "Sales have jumped tremendously ever since we switched to a price policy."

Using a price story does not mean, however, that the "sale" technique should be overused. To make sales mean anything, they must be spaced out and heavily promoted each time. Sales may be used consistently but should not be run one after the other at close intervals.

Major elements in the planning of advertising are:

(1) Gearing the store to the market
(2) Examining the competitive situation
(3) Working out a suitable creative approach
(4) Making the advertising take the "whole-store" viewpoint
(5) Making departments work together through related-item selling
(6) Sticking to the plan

The Market

If the advertiser is operating a neighborhood store, drawing customers only from the immediate section, then advertising should reflect exactly the buying needs, the mental level, and the financial status of the neighborhood. If the trading section is dominated by one nationality group—for example, Jewish, Polish, Italian—advertising must reflect its needs and customs.

If a retailer has a downtown location and the trading area is more widespread, advertising cannot be centered so specifically on one group as in the case of the merchant serving the immediate neighborhood. Even so, the townspeople may have shopping habits that are different from those of other communities.

Knowing preferences of customers is a must. Many local advertisers for example, are certain that price is the only consideration with their customers. In most cases they are right. There may be, however, many customers to whom price is only one consideration in the advertisement. They may be interested in prestige and performance factors that subordinate the price story. Certainly this should be true of most Cadillac buyers, to name one group.

Here are some questions about the market. The answers to these questions will help determine the proper advertising approach:

- What are the principal occupational breakdowns—farmers, factory workers, office workers, professional men?
- What are the principal financial breakdowns—poor, average, well-to-do?
- What are the principal nationality and religious breakdowns?
- What is the educational level of the market?

This information will guide the local advertisers in the kind of copy they write, the kind of goods promoted, and the kind of prices used. Without these facts, the advertisers approach their market blindly.

Competitive Situation

A local advertiser cannot ignore competitors in the same line. When store owners read the newspaper or listen to the radio, they see or hear what the competitors are saying. Even walking to work they may be compelled to look at competitors' window displays.

There are some who say: "Pay no attention to the competition. Do your own job well and the competition will take care of itself." This is bad advice. Competition being what it is, a local advertiser cannot exist in a vacuum. A store must keep pace with competition, but cannot do so unless it knows its rivals' use of price, advertising copy, and the selection of goods.

An entirely different approach from rivals may be desirable in order that advertising may stand out. An example of this is seen in the advertising of a retailer whose jewelry store was located in a North Carolina town. Four jewelry stores, including his own, were lined up in one block, two on each side of the street. The other jewelry stores were directly competitive with him. Each, like his own, was strongly promotional in its advertising. Sales, strong price appeals, and pressure characterized each. He began to think, "How can the shoppers in this area tell one of us from the other by our advertising? All of us say the same thing."

With a certain sense of daring he decided to change his whole approach. He switched to institutional advertising. Stress was put on his reliability, craftsmanship in repair work, and quality merchandise. While he hammered away with this kind of advertising, the others continued their slam-bang promotional approach. The result? He went far ahead in sales.

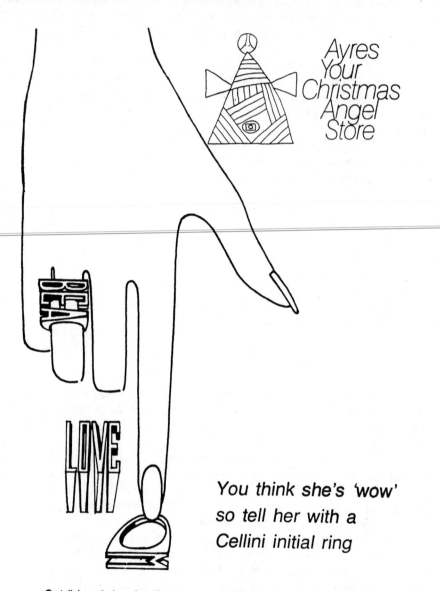

Ayres
Your
Christmas
Angel
Store

You think she's 'wow'
so tell her with a
Cellini initial ring

*Or tell her she's a fox. Send a message like Ooh! Aah! Hey! Spell out something, using initials, that only the two of you know about. Or maybe you think she's one of the BP's (beautiful people, that is), then tell her. We can spell most anything, including her initials, of course, except words with Q-U-X-Y-Z. In sterling silver, sizes 5-6-7, **5.00 each.** Fashion Jewelry, Street Floor, Downtown, all Indianapolis Branches and Lafayette, Indiana.*

Advertising in behalf of local business.

All advertising of this advertiser aims at getting customers into retail establishments to buy the product. A local advertiser needs such support because often he lacks the money to do an extensive advertising promotion of the individual products he sells.

N.W. AYER & SON, INC.
1345 AVENUE OF THE AMERICAS, NEW YORK, N.Y. 10019

CLIENT	De Beers Consolidated Mines, Ltd.	PROGRAM	
PRODUCT	Diamond Jewelry	FACILITIES	
TITLE	"Snowflake"	DATE	
NUMBER	QZBZ0134	LENGTH	30-second
	For Production		

VIDEO	AUDIO
1. FADE IN ON CU OF ROTATING DIAMOND WITH GLINTS OF LIGHT SPARKLING FROM ITS FACETS.	1. (MUSIC THROUGHOUT) ANNCR. (VO): A diamond...
2. DIAMOND RECEDES INTO DISTANCE TO BECOME VERY SMALL.	2. even the smallest one sparkles in its own special way.
3. MAN'S FINGERS ENTER AND WE SEE WE HAVE BEEN ADMIRING A TINY DIAMOND. FINGERS PUSH DIAMOND OVER TO GROUPING OF SIX OTHER SMALL DIAMONDS.	3. Each one as individual as a snowflake. Except diamonds
4. DISS TO: CU DIAMONDS "SNOWFLAKE" PIN. THE SEVEN DIAMONDS IN THE PIN MATCH THE SEVEN IN THE GROUPING. MAN'S HAND LIFTS PIN TO DISPLAY IT AND TAKES IT OUT OF FRAME.	4. are forever and a day. This diamond snowflake was designed to sell for just two hundred forty dollars.
5. CUT TO: MED. SHOT OF HAND PINNING "SNOWFLAKE" PIN ON WHITE FUR HAT OF BEAUTIFUL WOMAN. ZOOM IN TO CU FRAMING WOMAN'S EYES AT BOTTOM OF FRAME, PIN ABOVE AND SUPER TITLE AT TOP OF FRAME. TITLE: "CATCH YOUR WOMAN A DIAMOND SNOWFLAKE. DE BEERS."	5. Your jeweler has a special Christmas Diamond Collection now. Catch your woman a diamond snowflake.

To analyze a competitor's method systematically, the local advertiser can list on one side of a sheet of paper everything a competitor has to offer. Listening to customers can often provide this information.

On the other side of the paper, opposite each attribute a rival offers, can be listed the comparative service offered by the retailer. A review of the two lists should then show one of these three possibilities:

    (1)   That the retailer's services are so superior that they provide a wealth of advertising material.

    (2)   That the services are so similar that certain improvements must be made in order to have something to advertise.

    (3)   That the competitor's services are so superior that the retailer must change policies and/or price structure completely.

Creative Approach

Creativity, as applied to copywriting and advertising layouts, is a subject that requires a book for itself. When a local advertiser considers the creative approach as part of the planning, care must be taken to assure that advertising:

    (1)   *Is distinctive.*

          Distinctiveness can be attained through the physical appearance of the advertisement, the kind of copy written, the kind of goods offered. Advertisements can be so distinctive physically that readers will not even need to look at the signature to know who is doing the advertising. Such advertising will not be confused with that of competitors. A caution: the local advertiser must not let efforts to be distinctive alter the long-range store character that has been built.

    (2)   *Uses the right appeals.*

          Because one knows merchandise well does not necessarily mean that one knows what advertising features are strongest in that merchandise. Is the store featuring price in women's shoes when it should be stressing style? Is the store featuring reliable timekeeping in watches, when the appearance of the watches should be emphasized? An analytical examination of each selling line is necessary in order to dig out the right advertising appeal.

    (3)   *Appeals to the right people.*

          Should the advertising be slanted to men or women? The entire direction of an advertisement is affected by the answer to this point. Consider cooking stoves, for example. Should advertising for this product be slanted toward women? Toward men? Surveys indicate that both men and women buy stoves. Whether the local advertiser is running a drugstore, an electrical shop, a gift shop, a music store, or a photography shop, the question of "who" buys the merchandise must be considered carefully in planning.

          Even in the case of services the point is important. Bank advertisers, for example, have had much difficulty in making up their minds about whether men or women should be appealed to. On one side, there are many impressive figures about the importance of women in the financial affairs of the nation—their holding of stocks, their keeping of family financial records, and the number who do the family banking. Yet, the banker who is advertising is aware that while the woman does the banking, it is the husband who very often decides what bank should be used. The woman is, in effect, merely carrying out orders from her husband when she deposits the weekly paycheck. How, then, to decide to whom to advertise?

Women are said to do about 80 percent of the purchasing in this country and to hold about 50 percent of the financial assets. These figures may vary somewhat, according to who is releasing them, but no one denies the dominant role women have in buying. Still, it is dangerous to oversimplify. Women, for example, may buy many hardware-store items, but it is their husbands who may specify the items. Also, as any supermarket operator knows, a surprising number of men do the family grocery shopping, a trend that has been increasing in this period when so many married women are working.

Many retailers have observed that it is the man who often determines that a commodity or product will be bought and that it is the woman who selects the brand.

(4)   *Gives complete information.*

To make buying easy for the customer, enough information should be given to make a buying decision possible before the trip to the store. Sometimes the person handling the advertising function will find it useful to refer to a checklist of points to be included in advertisements. These points, of course, will vary widely according to the merchandise. Appliances will require one type of checklist, clothing another. For soft goods, for example, some of the points would be:

Colors • Fabrics • Sizes • Length • Width • Design

No matter how long a person has been preparing advertising copy, it is possible occasionally to forget to include essential information. Checklists will help overcome this tendency.

The Whole-Store Viewpoint

Local advertising requires teamwork. Coordinating advertising and other promotional activities with all the departments of a big store is a difficult, complicated task. Even in a smaller store, it is no easy assignment. It entails a number of steps.

Newspaper, radio, or television advertising has made contact with the potential buyers in the market. An important outside step has occurred in the sales process. The next steps occur inside the store. Answering the following questions will help assure that the advertising promotion does not end with that outside step.

(1)   *Is there an ample stock of the advertised goods?*

Hardly anything will gain a reputation for trickery faster than to feature an item in advertising, only to tell customers who come in that day. "Sorry, we're out of that item, but here's something that's just as good."

Occasionally there will be a sensational seller that runs out of stock with unexpected speed. Normally, however, there is no excuse for being out of an advertised item while the advertising is running—not if the stock is carefully checked before the advertising breaks and a count is kept while the advertising runs.

A good practice is to keep an ample number of the advertised items on view during the advertising day. Some stores get themselves put on the "suspected" list because they keep most of their advertised stock hidden. So few of the advertised items are displayed that shoppers think the stock is low even early in the morning of the advertising day. Complaints have been made in such cases to local chambers of commerce. Although the merchants are usually innocent, the word goes around that, "They were running out of that advertised item just an hour after the store was opened." Shoppers, in these instances, feel that the advertising was just a "come-on" to lure them into the store—that the local advertiser never did have enough of the advertised item to take care of customers who came to the store to buy it.

(2) *Are displays of the item set up?*

In one rather large store, the advertising manager and the display manager were not on speaking terms for a number of years. Throughout this time, the window displays went their way and the advertising took another path.

Coordination, obviously, is lacking in such a situation. A local advertiser with the necessary time and help should never fail to display in the windows and in the store the items featured in the advertising. If advertising a great many items at one time, the store may not have enough windows to display all the items, but just as much as possible it should display the items stressed in the current advertising. Increased sales are the reward of such coordination. Advertising, the first contact, informs. Display, the second contact, sells.

(3) *Have the advertisements been displayed?*

People believe what they read in the newspapers. A retailer should remember this faith when running a newspaper advertisement by displaying the advertising currently being run. Such displays are a powerful spur to buying. To the person who has seen the local advertiser's advertisement in the newspaper, the display of that advertisement is a potent reminder. To the person who has not seen the advertisement in the newspaper, the display gives the item stature simply because of the fact that it has been promoted in print.

Displaying of local advertising is one of the finest and most inexpensive forms of promotion. All that is needed is a set of placards headed by the words "As advertised in (name of local paper)." Such placards can be designed so that new advertisements can be inserted and old ones removed. Used liberally in windows and the store interior, the displays can give the promoted item an air of "something special."

(4) *Have the shelf prices been changed?*

Although this is a relatively small point, it is a good one to have in any checklist of things to do. To the customer, the store looks uncoordinated and inefficient if the advertising has one set of prices and the shelves still another.

(5) *Do store employees know about the advertising?*

If the establishment has only one or two employees, unawareness of advertising is not likely to be a factor. If, however, there are a number of employees, there may be a discouraging lack of knowledge of the advertising throughout the store.

A striking fact of retail store operation is the number of times that clerks fail to read the advertisements of the store for which they work. Reading of the current advertising should be mandatory for everyone in the retail establishment, from the personnel in the department featuring the advertised goods to the cashier. All personnel should know the items being advertised; the prices at which they are offered; the specials; the styles, sizes, and colors; just where in the store the item can be found; and how much stock is on hand.

A customer who comes enthusiastically into a store for an advertised item can be cooled off quickly by an indifferent clerk not interested enough in the job to read that day's advertising.

A store manager or advertising manager, should not, however, depend upon the initiative of the personnel to read the advertising. Copies of the advertisements should be distributed to each department. In addition, the "As advertised" placards, previously mentioned, should be distributed throughout the store.

In bigger stores, department buyers (who also supervise the selling in their departments) review the day's advertising with their salesclerks if that advertising contains items for their departments. Other stores may call attention by loudspeaker to the day's specials that are featured in advertising.

Related—Item Selling

A shoe manufacturer speaking about the need for selling-advertising coordination, observed wryly: "Stores want to sell that extra pair of shoes to a woman, a shoe wardrobe to men, and to participate in Foot Health Week for children. But they often defeat themselves by failing to follow through and to coordinate the item with related apparel in the store. The buyers for the store prefer to have their own separate straight shoe ads instead of tying in with apparel advertising. Because of this, the customer is deprived of a fashion-right presentation of related items, and the store loses sales."

If a store is departmentalized, it can coordinate the departments through advertising. In food lines especially, there are countless case histories of increased sales through the use of related-item selling or related-item display. The same sort of success is found in other lines, too, such as hardware; automotive supplies, garden supplies, or apparel.

Nowhere is the whole-store viewpoint better illustrated than in the store, large or small, that emphasizes related-item selling in its advertising. It is the happy way to get departments working together and to make the advertisements create the impression of a unified organization. Such advertising requires planning not only in the advertising but also in the buying and selling.

In related-item selling a store often uses bigger-space advertisements called *omnibus* (or multi-item) advertisements. Unlike radio or television commercials, the newspaper advertisement can offer a big spread of items in space that may take less than a page but often will take a full page or a two-page spread. These advertisements that are suitable for related-item selling may take several forms.

One can offer a huge assortment of similar items such as cutlery. Another may have fewer items that are not related but represent a number of different departments. Still another may feature related items. These, for example, could be safety items associated with National Fire Prevention Week, or the advertisement could stress cold-weather items or garden items for the spring. If the advertiser runs a related-item omnibus advertisement, the following format can make it especially productive:

- A headline that serves as an umbrella by indicating the commonality of purpose served by the items.
- A short unifying copy paragraph that elaborates on the headline and sells the items in general.
- Separate illustrations and copy blocks for the items with each copy block introduced by a strong-selling subhead.

Adherence to the Plan

Once the character of the advertising has been decided upon, all advertising should reflect this character. Deviation from the selected promotional pattern should be rare.

Suppose, for instance, the quality or institutional advertising has been used consistently. A sudden switch to "borax" advertising (loud, crude advertising with heavy black headlines and price figures), because the advertiser had some special prices to offer, would be unwise.

While stressing prices it is well to keep the same overall character in the advertisements. If a store is big enough to have a basement or budget floor, hard-hitting price advertisements can be confined to the floor while the quality-institutional approach is retained for the other departments.

The important principle is: *Stay* with the store character as established by advertising.

One caution: If a local advertiser finds that the overall policy simply is not working, it may be wise to change it. If changed, however, all advertising henceforth reflects the new policy, whether institutional or price.

BUDGETING for ADVERTISING

No matter how small a store's advertising expenditure, it should be planned to give the maximum return. Because some advertisers spend as little as 0.2 percent for advertising, they are likely to dismiss the sum as not worth bothering about. Any money spent on advertising is important because it is one of the retailer's expenditures that can yield a return.

To a big advertiser, setting up an advertising budget is a complicated procedure involving merchandising and accounting. To many small advertisers, the procedure is no more involved than taking money out of the cash register and saying: "Let's run an ad." An executive of one of the largest companies in the country servicing retail accounts remarked: "The small retailer is, in many lines, a rather slovenly individual in the matter of budget planning. Operating his advertising on a hit-or-miss basis, or as he feels the need to simulate sales, he fails to find a pattern of expenditures that results in wise spending of the advertising budget."

Despite the gloomy picture of the small retailer—which can be applied to many medium-sized retailers, too—there are thousands of retailers who try hard to evolve sensible budget planning. When retailers get together, one of their most often-asked questions is: "How much should I spend on advertising?"

An advertising budget is an intensely personal matter involving knowledge of one's own business and community. Use of averages may be dangerous, since there is no pat formula that will enable a local advertiser to set up an advertising budget without reference to individual circumstances.

A 3 percent average for one store, for example, may be too high for another store and too low for still another. Yet these percentage averages give an approximate idea of the budgeting of other local advertisers. If advertisers find themselves far to one side or the other of the average, they may wish to check reasons for the variance.

Average Advertising Expenditures of Different Types of Local Business

Each business wants to know industry averages in order to position itself. True, the average can be misleading. Substantial diffferences may exist between the biggest spender in a category and the smallest category. Yet, averages provide general guidelines.

Here are averages for a few types of local enterprises as gathered from a number of sources and reported in a brochure of the Newspaper Advertising Bureau entitled: "The 'I Wonder-How-To-Set-Up-An-Advertising-Program-And-How-Much-To Budget' Book." The budgets are expressed in the average percentage of ́sales invested in advertising.

Such figures as have been presented in the foregoing section represent whole-store budgetary allotments. A whole-store budget figure has been preceded, let us hope, by planning that considers sharp differences in the requirements of different departments. Each department's budget should reflect its own sales trend. Once departmental budgets have been worked out, a meaningful whole-store budget can be fashioned—and *only* then.

BASIC FACTORS in BUDGET PLANNING

Two factors are so basic that they might be taken for granted: (1) the sales goal, and (2) business conditions.

A store's sales goal will influence greatly how much it is willing to spend for advertising, and the amount will vary according to how close or how far the store is from achieving this goal.

Unfavorable business conditions lower a community's spending power and, hence, the sales expectancy of the merchants. Advertising expenditure will be lowered in such periods, but not in direct proportion to sales decreases, since

TABLE 10-1
Average Advertising Expenditure for Selected Local Businesses

Category	Average % of sales invested in advertising
Banks (commercial)	1.3
Banks (savings)	1.5
Book stores	1.7
Department stores	2.8
Drug stores (chains)	1.7
Furniture stores	5.0
Hardware stores	1.6
Jewelry stores	4.4
Mens' wear stores	2.8
Motion picture theaters	5.5
Music stores	1.8
Office supply dealers	0.8
Real estate	0.6
Savings and loan associations	1.5
Sporting goods stores	3.5
Tire dealers	2.2
Travel agents	5.0

competition will be fiercer than ever. Good business conditions, on the contrary, stimulate advertising spending.

Two other factors are basic to some retailers and not to others. These are: *cooperative advertising and the need to promote branch stores.* If heavy use of cooperative advertising is planned, it can cut down media expenditures significantly because the retailer is thus cutting newspaper and other media costs in half, and sometimes more. Although local advertisers have something to lose and something to gain in the use of cooperative advertising, there is no disputing that one of the gains is financial.

In the past, a typical department store usually had one building. It was downtown, and one newspaper advertisement could cover its offerings. Now, with big-city stores (and other establishments such as banks, too) having branches in shopping centers, coverage of the market can be a problem and certainly may add to the advertising expense. For instance, it may be necessary to run advertisements in suburban weeklies and shopping newspapers to cover all the outlets. The same is true of supermarkets. Adding to the advertising expense even more are additional media such as radio and television.

OTHER IMPORTANT CONSIDERATIONS

Once having weighed these basic points, other aspects are considered in arriving at the advertising budget. Some of these are given here.

The Real McCabe.

Ed McCabe. Outspoken. Caustic. Brilliant. The youngest individual ever elected to the Copywriters' Hall of Fame. A founding father of Scali, McCabe. Sloves, Inc., one of the most talked-about and successful agencies of our time. Here, in his own words, are some of Mr. McCabe's views on subjects of interest to the advertising community.

On standards:
"Our only standard is excellence. In everything we do. And every time we do it. A matchbook cover deserves as much effort, as much work, as a 30-second network television commercial."

On headlines:
"Monosyllables work best. Say it simply. Don't beat around the bush."

On people:
"People who want to work hard, to be excellent in everything they do, who are willing to make that kind of commitment to this business of advertising—those people are happy at Scali, McCabe, Sloves. For those who don't, it's a miserable place to work."

On working:
"We don't have an agency way of doing things. If an art director and a copywriter can do great work together, that's fine. But if an art director can turn out great advertising locked up in a room by himself, that's fine, too. The only thing that counts is what you put into the space you buy."

On great advertising:
"It's surprising that virtually all of the great advertising is most remembered as it appeared in print. It's tough to play back great television commercials in just a sentence—and, if you can, the same advertising is probably far more powerful in print."

On rules:
"I have no use for rules. They only rule out the possibility of brilliant exceptions."

On agency growth:
"We're making a product. If that product is good—consistently good—more and more people will let us make that product for them. That's what our growth is all about."

On The Wall Street Journal.
"It's a great publication, a highly productive medium. Somehow, our kind of advertising works particularly well in The Journal. I read The Journal myself. I believe Journal readers are people who have the money to buy, and the intelligence to buy on the basis of logical facts. And they read The Journal—just as I do—with a real sense of anticipation. That's why it works!"

The Wall Street Journal. Over five million American decision-makers—including Ed McCabe—read The Journal every business day. And as many of the brightest, most successful, most respected advertising professionals—including Ed McCabe—have discovered, The Journal is a potent advertising medium. For, as their experience has shown, a single truth sums up America's only national daily:

**The Wall Street Journal.
It works.**

Type of Product or Service Sold

Certain products and services demand more advertising than other. They might be sharply competitive products, such as furniture, groceries, men's clothing, or electrical appliances. In the services there are the 24-hour cleaners, banks, auto rental companies, and laundries.

A local advertiser in a competitive business will be forced into heavy advertising simply to keep up with competitors. Advertisers in less competitive areas will need less advertising to do equally effective promotion. Such establishments as antique shops, drain and sewer pipe cleaners, furniture rebuilders, and bookshops can employ less frequent and smaller space reminder advertising to obtain business. Such advertising cuts down budget requirements.

Location of Store

A store located outside the central business district will need to spend more money than its better-located competitors in order to induce shoppers to travel the extra distance.

Even this greater expenditure, however, will bring no results unless the outlying business has something quite special to offer in goods or services. Better services, better parking facilities, variety of merchandise, or special prices might make it worthwhile for the advertiser to spend more money to reach them.

Unless the outlying store does have something special to offer, it should avoid expensive mass media such as city newspapers, radio, and television in favor of highly localized media such as handbills, neighborhood shopping papers, and direct mail. This is usually true even if the store is located in an active shopping center.

The local advertiser with a good location has a reason for advertising steadily and maintaining a respectable advertising budget. If the trading area is limited, the store will spend less money, however, than if the advertising must cover a big area that forces the use of many outlying media to cover the market.

A big-city merchant has an enviable location insofar as potential customers are concerned, but the very excellence of the location requires additional advertising expenditure. Big cities have a profusion of media. A merchant to make an impression on the big population is forced into the use of more than one medium and, accordingly, into a bigger advertising budget.

Branch stores, as discussed earlier, have created a new set of problems because of the monstrous growth of shopping centers. Thus, the central location is no longer the big boon it was when big stores conducted their entire operation in the downtown area. Even smaller towns now have shopping centers. Thus, the branch store advertising coverage is a problem for smaller stores as well as the retailing giants.

Many shopping centers carry on cooperative campaigns for the center as a whole thus doing for member stores what they cannot afford to do individually.

Department store television.

Although broadcast media are often used by department stores solely for institutional messages, they are frequently used for item selling in busy selling periods such as Christmas holidays or store-wide sales. Such is the case with this simple, low-cost television commercial that uses the same opening and closing for a series of Christmas commercials and then employs slides in between.

Byer&Bowman
Advertising Agency, Inc.
Member of American Association of Advertising Agencies

**RADIO
TELEVISION**

Date:		**Script Number:** AT-2409
	Client: AYRES	
	Promotion: CHRISTMAS-- LEVI'S	
	Air Week:	
	Air Date:	
	Stations:	

VIDEO	AUDIO
CHRISTMAS ANIMATION OPEN	CHRISTMAS JINGLE UNDER ANNOUNCER
	ANNCR.: The joy of Christmas is the joy of giving, from your Christmas Angel Store!
WIPE TO SERIES OF MOVES ON SLIDES	Looking for what he really wants? Look no further than Ayres selection of Levi's Panatela the year 'round favorites of every man in your life.
SHOW LEVI'S PANATELA LOGO	Take it from the top, with the Panatela cotton flannel shirt, classic plaids, super comfort, and only $15.
	Levi's cotton corduroy Panatela slacks go great with 'em everywhere... for just $18.
	This season...any season...give Levi's. And get Levi's...at Ayres!
DISSOLVE TO CHRISTMAS CLOSE ANIMATION	MUSIC UP FULL FOR TAG The difference is Ayres...
	ANNCR.: ...Your Christmas Angel Store.

Sales fluctuation graph.

Many goods are subject to violent fluctuations of demand, as this chart shows. "What" to advertise is often dictated by the season of the year.

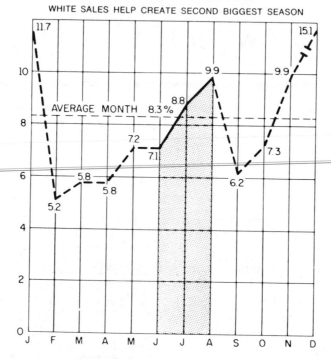

LINENS AND TOWELS
WHITE SALES HELP CREATE SECOND BIGGEST SEASON

Figures indicate % of year's business done each month.
Source: Federal Reserve Board.

Length of Time Store Has Been in a Business Location

Fred Jones opens a new shoe store. Will he sell high-fashion lines only, or will he sell from low price to high price? Will he concentrate on women's shoes, or will he stock a complete line of men's shoes also? Is he open any night during the week? Does he stock special items such as slippers, boots, tennis shoes, and overshoes? What brands does he carry? Does he have a wide range of sizes?

Customers of a well-established store know these facts from past advertising, from shopping in the store, or from word-of-mouth advertising. The new store, in contrast, must make all this clear quickly. Heavier advertising is required in the introductory period. Here is one more reason why a new store, at least, cannot take "average" budget figures too literally.

New products in the national field often require twice as much advertising exposure during the introductory campaign as later, when they are established. A new local business likewise must spend more at the beginning than a well-entrenched competitor. Advertising budgets for the first one or two years may run about twice as high as in the following years. What is disheartening about this double expenditure is that it may obtain results that are no more, and possibly less, than those of established rivals.

An older store cannot, of course, rest on its established reputation. It can, however, assume the role of a familiar neighbor, no longer needing to devote the bulk of its advertisisng to selling its whole operation. Instead, it can concentrate on item selling.

Character and Size of Store

Store policy, it has been said earlier, shapes the planning of advertising and merchandising. If the policy calls for fast turnover by selling to many customers at low prices, the store is almost certain to require a fat advertising budget.

If the store does not push price and has a steady list of customers who have a habit of shopping there, or if it is a high-price store with a limited clientele, a more modest advertising budget may be employed. With clientele and sales volume relatively assured (as compared to the low-price, big-turnover store,) advertising pressure is not so intense.

Fashion stores, featuring short-lived fashion items, must get quick turnover. To achieve this, they spend more money in their advertising than stores with more ordinary merchandise.

What about large stores? To bring crowds of shoppers into the aisles, they will spend more money for advertising. Such stores must reach out into the far corners of their trading areas, in order to build traffic. This reaching out takes strong advertising budgets, as will be recalled from the discussion relating to the effect of a store location on advertising budgets.

Usually it is axiomatic that the more a store has to talk about (low prices, parking and other facilities, quick service, variety of goods, pleasant surroundings), the more money that store can justifiably spend on advertising. Many retailers really have nothing to shout about in advertising. For those establishments offering many shopping advantages, advertising will let people know about their offerings and will bring in business.

The truly big retailers, while spending a bigger total sum in advertising, will usually spend less percentagewise than the smaller specialty stores. The reason for this is simple. If a big store were to spend 4 percent of its huge sales in advertising, it would oversaturate the market. A specialty store, on the other hand, has a much smaller sales volume. Four percent of that volume will provide an adequate advertising coverage but certainly will not oversaturate the market.

Availability and Quality of Media

A one-newspaper town without television and radio stations does not offer enough opportunity for advertising expenditure to cause advertising budgets to soar. If the town has a profusion of media and consequently is jostling with media all working to persuade the local advertiser to spend money in advertising, the budgets are certain to be larger because (1) the retailer yields to the sales pressure of the media, (2) the retailer must advertise in more than one medium to

Call report.

Such a report—also called a "Service report" or "Contact report," is written by the account executive following a meeting with the client. It sums up what occurred at the meeting. No good account executive fails to write his report quickly and fully after each meeting. Such diligence prevents future misunderstandings about decisions and agreements that were made.

N.W. AYER & SON, INC.

☐ **CLIENT MEMORANDUM**

☒ **CLIENT REPORT OF CALL**

Dept

Date 5/16

Date of call 5/16

Date dictated

cc to

Client: AT&T Long Lines

Product or Division:

Client People: Hutchins, Forney

Ayer People: Clark, Robinson, Davis

Keith	
Reed	
Riley	
Marsh	
Stone	
Ossola	
Siano	

Subject: Submission of Four Long Lines Television Commercials

"Direct Dial Story" was well received, though the client did a little scratching on the script. Paragraph 2 was slightly altered by the client to read as follows: "Well! I gave the operator her number. The operator, the dear, told me I could save money if I dialed the call direct." Paragraph 5 was altered very slightly to read: "Now that we both know we can save by dialing direct, you bet we're gonna keep in touch from now on."

Mr. Hutchins feels that casting is extra important in this commercial, since the woman kind of splits the difference between a spokeswoman and a character. She must be immensely believable. She is not too old (perhaps 60 to 65) and not too sophisticated or upper class. She is a believable, sympathetic, ordinary person.

"Cupid" was well liked and is approved.

"Race" was also well liked and is also approved. Client took both of these latter two scripts with him and could possibly call back with small suggestions, but the commercials are approved for production.

"Report Card", being of the same brother/sister theme as "Cupid", won't be produced at this time, though the client seemed to like it. "Race" is approved for production.

We then looked into the commercials available for network use in September. "Dandelions" and "Friends" are the emotional commercials which will carry over into the new season. We will produce "Maid of Honor"; "Work of Art"; "Race"; and "Cupid" to round out the package and the relationships. "Blessed Event", previously approved, will not be produced at this time.

With these four new emotion commercials and "Direct Dial Story", we have five commercials to produce this summer. We are all agreed that we start soon on the first package, probably of two commercials. For the moment, that's it. Thanks to all involved.

Howard Davis

pf

F 525 Rev. 5/73

A GOOD REPORT: 1. Quotes client's words exactly.   2. Interprets client's meaning   3. States action to be taken.   **10 PARTS**

ACCOUNT MANAGEMENT: Use this form for all house correspondence which concerns client advertising.

be competitive, and (3) most important, the retailer finds that the additional advertising brings increased sales.

Another point connected with media: rates vary sharply sometimes from town to town. The rates available to the retailer may be so high that the budget is higher than that for a similar business in another town, even a business that may be doing more total advertising.

Pulling Power of Advertisements

Too often local advertisers blame the media for the lack of pulling power of their advertising. The best newspapers, magazines, or broadcast stations cannot make people buy if the advertising given them by the advertiser is poor. Before the store blames the media it must examine its advertising. Is it messy typographically? Is the copy forceful? Do the illustrations command attention? Quality of advertising has much to do with the advertising budget, since if the advertising is poor, more will be spent for promotion than the sales results seem to justify. A good small advertisement, for instance, can bring more results than a large, bad, and expensive advertisement.

INSTITUTIONAL ADVERTISING—SHOULD IT BE USED?

Some big department stores allot a certain portion of the advertising budget to institutional advertising. Others use no institutional advertising. Because big stores are in a constant fight for identity, a certain amount of institutional advertising can help to remind the public of that identity. High-level department stores, of the semipromotional type, are likely to think that institutional advertising—or a certain amount of it—is useful. Thus, they may on occasion devote an entire advertisement to the institutional approach, or they assign a portion of the copy in big-space advertisements to an institutional message.

A promotional store, in contrast, with its constant bargain atmosphere, may assume that readers of its advertising will soon recognize what type of establishment it is.

As for the small store, unless it has an unusual line of goods, or something about it that makes it truly different, it is somewhat pretentious for it to write institutional advertisements. Furthermore, quick turnover and money return are too important to the small store to allow it the luxury of using institutional advertising aimed at long-range image instead of short-range immediate sales.

WHERE DOES SALES PROMOTION FIT IN?

Emphasis in this chapter is on advertising but some retail establishments put sales promotion on an equal plane with advertising. The obligation of the sales promotion department is to conceive events, large and small, that will not only build character for the store but also, more important, attract crowds. On a simple, individual basis it may consist of having celebrities on hand to meet the store customers. These celebrities may be from the worlds of sports, music, literature, fashion, or entertainment. Their presence is, of course, well covered in the store's advertising.

Promotion, however, may be on a much bigger scale than celebrity appearances. On a truly staggering scale the promotion might entail the cooperative effort of all the downtown merchants such as the huge extravaganza that took place in Chicago in the summer of 1977. In this instance, a period was set aside and named "People's Week." This was a cooperative effort of the State Street Council that was planned to bring in customers from the entire Chicago-land area. In addition to countless forms of entertainment—puppet shows, bridge lessons, cooking demonstrations, fashion shows, circus acts, and so on—each store on State Street, contributed special attractions of its own that were devised by its promotion department.

Occurring almost at the same time in St. Louis was a giant promotion initiated by a single store (Famous-Barr) that attracted 700,000 to the city's business area. Tied in with the 50th anniversary of Lindbergh's flight, the three-day "Sky Spectacular" included air shows, fireworks, concerts, and other stirring events.

An integral part of such promotions is massive advertising that calls attention to what is going to happen. Thus, the two—advertising and promotion—are inseparable in many establishments. An imaginative, energetic sales promotion director can keep his organization in a constant state of excitement and activity and provide the advertising department with subject matter for much of its advertising.

Questions

1. Distinguish between a "promotional" and "semipromotional" store?

2. How does the size of the territory covered make local advertising different from national advertising?

3. Why are advertising agencies not a significant factor to most local advertisers?

4. Give as many reasons you can think of why local businesses use advertising.

5. Criticize the way much local advertising is conducted.

6. Discuss the question: How often to advertise?

7. What is the reasoning behind the advice to advertise best sellers?

8. What advantage to the retailer is there in promoting nationally-advertised goods?

9. Six major elements were given for the planning of advertising. Discuss as many as you can.

10. What are some of the factors that make for a successful creative approach?

11. What is meant by the "whole-store viewpoint"? How do you achieve it?

12. Why must cooperative advertising be considered in planning the budget?

13. Name some other considerations in budget planning.

14. Under what conditions should institutional advertising be used? Under what conditions should it not be used?

15. What effect can sales promotion have on advertising?

References

1. How to work out a budget is discussed in the chapter on budgeting. Two plans, with many variations of each, are used: (1) percentage of sales, and (2) objective and task.
2. Many shopping centers carry on cooperative campaigns for the center as a whole, thus doing for member stores what they cannot afford to do individually.

Section IV
FORMS AND MEDIA
OF ADVERTISING

11

NEWSPAPERS: WHY AND HOW YOU BUY SPACE

WHERE ALL THE MONEY GOES

e advertising dollars have been invested in oup of media. Surprised? As a consumer you is the leading advertising medium. Perhaps advertisers spend more money in newspapers combined.

e importance of newspapers as an advertising how much a single commercial minute costs n movie or for a spot during baseball's World essive, and so we assume television gets more edium. Perhaps we just take newspapers for ly newspapers we read. What is a part of our aracter of what we think of as national media.

ht call glamor, year after year advertisers con- vertising dollars in newspapers because adver- per advertising is effective. Newspapers have itution. While we tend to think of institutions as unchanging, in reality today newspapers are undergoing rapid change.

The Changing Newspaper

Many of these changes have been occurring in newspapers and newspaper advertising. Some are beneficial, such as the increase in the availability and quality of color. On the other hand, there are some disturbing trends that worry newspaper people and outsiders alike.

(1) The number of daily newspapers has been decreasing. What with mergers, papers buying out other newspapers, or newspapers giving up because their revenue did not match rising costs, the number of

newspapers has declined drastically since the turn of the century. This decline has occurred despite the enormous increase in population and is offset in part by the growing number of suburban newspapers, "shoppers," and other publications with some of the characteristics of daily newspapers.

(2) As a direct result of the decline in the number of daily newspapers, great numbers of American cities are now served by only one newspaper instead of two, or three or more newspapers as in the past. In addition, newspaper owners often own radio and television stations; some own magazines as well. This has resulted in a public issue discussed as "cross-media" ownership. Many people are uncomfortable with a single owner controlling many of the media we depend on for information.

Despite newspaper industry problems, Americans by the millions continue to pay for daily and Sunday newspapers. Each copy of the newspaper is read by at least two adults. The daily newspaper is read in over 80 percent of households with incomes of $15,000 and over. About 88 percent of adults who have completed college read the daily newspaper. Thus, newspapers reach a broad and a demographically "upscale" (higher income and better educated) audience. Even if the number of daily newspapers has been declining, the overall circulation of daily newspapers is high and relatively stable at more than 60 million copies on any weekday.

ADVERTISING IN NEWSPAPERS: WHY IS IT SUCH A GOOD DEAL?

Newspaper advertising offers different advertising values to different advertisers—local, regional and, national. All advertisers appreciate newspapers as an advertising medium for the following reasons.

(1) Newspapers are a "shopping" medium.

Newspaper advertising is, more than any other form of advertising, actually sought and used as a shopping aid. Only a few specialized magazines are so used. Broadcast commercials are almost never sought out as a shopping aid.

Readers have a "voluntary interest" in newspaper advertising, in contrast to the forced interest in broadcast commercials. This voluntary interest is shown in (a) willingness of readers to pay money for the daily newspaper, and (b) their seeking out of advertisements that will help them make buying decisions. When asked, more than 60 percent of women readers indicate they would be less satisfied with newspapers without advertising.

(2) Reading the newspaper is a daily habit.

The morning newspaper goes naturally with the morning cup of coffee for many Americans; the evening paper has equally strong habit associations. On any given weekday 77 percent of American adults 18 and over read a newspaper, with each copy of the newspaper read by at least two adults. Newspaper reach grows from 77 percent for one day to 89 percent of all adults in just five days. Because newspapers are read thoroughly daily, an advertisement run during each of five days will be seen by the typical reader over four times. To the advertiser this is a high level of advertising frequency in such a short time period.

(3)   Advertisements are news.

The very term NEWSpaper means the medium is concerned with events of the moment. The "right now" immediacy of the news embraces not only the news content of a newspaper but the advertising as well. Advertisers are well aware of the daily excitement of news. The news environment is a desirable environment in which to announce new products, new services, and new money-saving ideas.

(4)   Newspapers reach the market.

The newspaper is read by the great majority of people in any given market and over 90 percent in many markets. Contrast this with the fact that no single high-circulation magazine is likely to cover more than 15 to 20 percent of the name market. Even such big circulation, widely read publications as *TV Guide* or *Reader's Digest* fall far, far short of blanket coverage of any market area. Among print media, only newspapers reach the majority of adults—day after day after day.

It must be admitted that the very large markets of New York City, Chicago, and Los Angeles will not be dominated by any one newspaper. In these areas a combination of newspapers may be bought to reach the majority of adults. In smaller metropolitan markets, one can usually provide the reach needed by advertisers with mass distribution.

Newspapers and Local Advertisers: Natural Partners

Newspaper advertising is very important to the local advertiser for many reasons:

(1)   Showing the Product

For many local advertisers, advertising lacks full effectiveness unless the products can be shown in some detail. A women's wear shop, a department store, or a credit jewelry store depend upon illustrations of their products. Radio cannot provide this opportunity and television may be too expensive for their budgets. Other print media may not be used practically on a daily basis to provide visualization opportunities. Thus, newspaper advertising must be used.

(2)   Making Quick Sales

For the local advertiser, no other medium rings the cash register so consistently and so quickly. Quick sales are imperative for the local merchandiser, who depends upon fast turnover to move goods and to produce cash to buy more goods and to meet overhead expenses. Newspaper advertising is "bread-and-butter" advertising to most local advertisers, who in most cases are inclined to use other media to supplement newspaper advertising.

(3)   Offering Variety of Products

Outside of distributing "flyers" (printed sheets delivered by crews to homes and apartments or handed out on street corners), there is no medium available to the local advertiser, with the exception of very expensive catalogs, that enables the advertiser to list the many items available to consumers. Actually, the newspaper is the only medium the advertiser can use on a day-to-day basis to offer many products to consumers in a single advertisement.

For the local advertiser with many items to sell, it is very important to use multi-item advertising, even on ordinary days when possibly the advertiser has only a few items to sell. During sales, or clearances, when the advertiser may have hundreds of items to call to the attention of consumers, the newspaper advertisement is indispensable. Then, of course, there are the big supermarket advertisements from which homemakers make up their shopping lists.

In this era of television and radio there is a tendency to overlook the unique advantage offered by the newspaper to the advertiser who wants to advertise, or must advertise, many items at the same time. This advantage is certainly not offered by the broadcast media, which have a hard enough time getting the viewer or listener to concentrate on the one item being advertised.

In addition, of course, the newspaper advertisement, that presents all these items can be retained just as long as the reader needs the information for shopping purposes. This gives it another huge advantage over the broadcast media (and over shopping circulars that are thrown away so quickly and in such numbers), which present their messages about single items in fleeting seconds that are not repeated.

Newspapers' Dual Personality: National and Regional Advertising

Newspaper advertising is important to the national and/or regional advertiser for several reasons:

(1)   Newspapers localize national advertising.

Nothing is more local than the daily newspaper that chronicles the names and events close to us. This fact is recognized by newspaper editors, who headline a local accident and bury deep in the paper a story about 3,000 persons having been wiped out by a flood in central China.

National advertisers recognize that localizing their advertising makes it more effective. National advertising in magazines or on network television makes consumers aware of merchandise, perhaps even interested in the products. Newspaper advertising urges consumers to buy the readily available merchandise.

National advertising in local newspapers uses prices and identifies local stores carrying the nationally advertised brands. If the national advertiser arranges for the local retailer to place the advertisement, the product is associated with a local institution consumers know and trust. The association benefits both the national advertiser and the local merchant.

(2)   Newspapers provide advertised price information—a strong incentive.

Because dealer arrangements differ widely, and because shipping costs to some geographical areas cause goods to cost more in some places than others, most national advertising in magazines and on the network broadcast media does not mention prices. Since price is the greatest single influence in selling, this lack of price mention is one of national advertising's greatest handicaps.

National advertising in newspapers provides the price information needed to persuade consumers to buy.

(3)   Newspapers offer audited circulation.

Most daily newspapers have their circulation audited by the Audit Bureau of Circulations. There is, consequently, no guesswork as to the newspaper's circulation. The advertiser knows the circulation by newsstand sales and by home delivery. If desired, circulation figures are available by neighborhoods. The advertiser knows who is being reached.

(4) Newspapers provide targeting and testing opportunities.

Many national advertisers distribute their product region by region (sometimes called a "roll out") before distributing products nationally. Newspapers can be used to cover population concentrations by regions.

National advertisers may also use newspapers to put extra advertising effort into a city or regional market where sales might be lagging.

Newspapers can be used for city or regional test markets. If the product, given the sales and advertising support, does well in a city or region, the decision will then be made whether to advertise and sell the product nationally.

From all the foregoing uses for regional advertising it can be seen that such advertising is important to the national advertiser. Newspapers have always been a strong medium for regional advertising. Because newspapers provide blanket coverage in the key metropolitan areas so important to nationally advertised goods, they enable national advertisers to cover each of these markets as they wish. In addition, newspapers are found in all the important secondary markets.

There are, of course, a number of regional advertisers who will always remain regional advertisers. Beer brewers, baking industries, and dairies are examples of regional operators who, in most cases, will never go national. They may, however, cover a number of metropolitan key markets, and they may distribute and advertise in a number of states. Newspapers figure strongly in their regional approach, for the same reasons that they do for national advertisers.

Drawbacks in Newspaper Advertising

Like every other advertising medium, the newspaper offers the advertiser advantages and disadvantages. The disadvantages may not concern some advertisers; other advertisers, however, will find the disadvantages serious enough to lead them to use almost all other local media *but* newspapers.

(1) It is a complicated medium.

Assume that you are responsible for buying space in 1,000 newspapers to introduce a new product. Here and there you may find a state press association that will help you deal with all the newspapers in a state; the Iowa Daily Press Association helps national advertisers. Or, you may deal with several newspaper chains that own anywhere from a few to many newspapers.

In the main, however, you must deal with most newspapers individually. You will find that each newspaper seems to have a different space rate structure, different mechanical specifications, and different billing practices. You are faced with a mountain of detail. It is much easier to make a single telephone call to a television network and send some commercials by a single messenger.

Such complications do not discourage some national advertisers who value newspapers advertising. Many advertisers, however, are discouraged by the complexity and difficulty involved in dealing with many newspapers.

(2)   Newspaper advertising can be heavy on a small advertiser's budget.

If the advertiser is a local bank with a definite limit on the advertising budget, the bank will sometimes hesitate to use newspaper to the extent it would like because of the cost. It should be said quickly that, in terms of value received, newspaper advertising may be well worth the cost. Still, the bank will find it must advertise less frequently and in smaller space than it would like.

In addition to the space costs, which might include between $25,000 and $30,000 of the bank's $100,000 total advertising budget, the bank must also be prepared to pay additional heavy charges for rough layouts, copy, finished art, typography, and engraving, and for any proofs that it may use for further promotion.

Even so, the bank will not be using large-space advertisements on a daily basis. Its newspaper advertising will probably consist of an occasional big-space advertisement and a number of smaller ones used two or three times a week.

Because it cannot afford big-space newspaper advertising on a daily schedule, the bank may find radio attractive because of its low preparation costs. There is also the fact that, for the same amount spent in newspaper advertising, the bank can buy all, or most, of the radio stations in the city and can use them on a daily basis to achieve the continuity it wants.

Department stores, on the contrary, can handle much of the expensive advertising preparation in their own advertising departments. Also, they can see tangible results coming from their advertising in the form of sales that directly defray the cost of the advertising. Banks, on the contrary, seldom see direct results from advertising.

For the very small local advertiser, newspaper advertising is not only too expensive for the budget, but it is also wasteful, since it covers thousands of readers who will never trade with the advertiser.

(3)   Advertisers must fight for attention.

News matter will usually run to about 35 percent of a newspaper's content; advertising matter will take up the other 65 percent. In some newspapers the ratio is even higher in favor of advertising. To show how this actually works here is how the percentages broke down in a newspaper of 244,000 circulation:

Reading matter (news, comics, features, etc.)	35.16
Local advertising	40.86
National advertising	7.26
Classified advertising	16.72

As these figures show very plainly, each advertiser fights for attention in competing with all other advertisers. Big advertisers who can afford large-sized advertisements, perhaps even several pages of advertisements, can stand up against the competing advertising. Such advertisers, furthermore, usually occupy the same position day after day; newspaper readers know where to find their advertising.

Smaller advertisers, on the other hand, find the going very rough for their small advertisements, which must do battle with big-space advertising. Their small advertisements, may appear anywhere in the newspaper. Thus, they lack the advantage of the fixed positions of the big advertisers. Also, in this day of newspapers that run 50 to 90 pages even on weekdays, the small advertiser finds it even harder to make certain his advertisement will be seen. Even the biggest advertisers find the thick newspapers (thick because of advertising) have a tendency to smother their advertisements, especially in the Sunday and the grocery advertisement editions.

(4)   Newspapers are read quickly.

Despite the evergrowing thickness of newspapers, there is nothing to indicate that, in this television age, readers are spending any more time in reading their newspapers. This means that the average newspaper reader, always a "skimming" type of reader, who spends possibly 15 to 18 minutes a day reading the newspaper, is skimming even more rapidly over today's thicker newspapers.

Quick reading of newspapers imposes a great demand upon those persons who create advertisements for newspapers. It is imperative that advertisements give an impelling message quickly. Many advertisements fail to do so. Thus, much newspaper advertising is wasted simply because readers do not pause over advertisements long enough to read the message or even to grasp or respond to the headlines.

(5)   Newspapers are not very successful in reaching the teen-age market.

Local advertisers, hungry for a bigger share of the growing teen market, feel that advertising fails to reach this market, simply because many teenagers do not read newspapers. As one retail store advertising manager said: "We have run checks on this and found it to be true. But we try to reach teenagers through ads and features on the amusement pages, which we feel they do read."

Other retailers, skeptical of advertising in newspapers directly to teenagers, aim their advertising more at parents than "nonreading" teenagers.

Still others favor radio for teenage advertising, while some merchants stress in-store events, such as charm and modeling courses, fashion shows, and design contests.

ORGANIZATION OF THE NEWSPAPER ADVERTISING DEPARTMENT

Although there is an enormous difference between the advertising departments of large- and small-circulation newspapers, almost all newspapers will have separate departments to handle local display (such as department-store), national, and classified advertising.

Local Display Advertising Department

The local display advertising department is the mainstay of any newspaper. It is the source of most revenue. By "local display" is meant the advertisements of local advertisers in display form, which usually (but not always) includes headlines in large type, illustrations, and white space. These advertisements ordinarily will appear anywhere in the newspaper except on the front page, editorial page or the classified advertising section.

Charges for such advertisements are based upon the cost per agate line (to be explained later) or the column inch. The latter is the more common basis for most newspapers.

Most of the business done by the local display advertising departments will be with the following types of stores:

Department stores. Department stores offer in one advertisement, a wide range of merchandise. They generally provide the heaviest, the most constant, and some of the best-looking advertising in the newspaper. This advertising is generally prepared by the stores' own advertising departments.

Specialty stores. Although this term "specialty stores" is generally thought of as referring to "women's" specialty clothing stores, catering to the high-fashion needs of women shoppers, it refers also to "specialized" stores in other lines, such as luggage and hardware. In the case of the women's specialty clothing store, most of the stores that do a volume business will prepare their own advertising. Usually the finest illustration work in a newspaper will be provided for such advertising.

Chain or multiple-unit stores. Supermarkets, chains, or independent supermarkets allied under a cooperative arrangement, such as the IGA or the Red-and-White group, make up this classification. Sometimes these organizations do all the preparing of their advertising; in other cases they supply material about items and prices and let the newspapers use their judgment in setting up the advertisements in the back shop.

Independent supermarkets, grocery stores, and drugstores. While advertising for these stores, and for other types of independent stores, may be important in smaller towns, it is usually less important in big-circulation, big-city newspapers simply because owners of these enterprises find it wasteful to advertise in city-wide newspapers that reach so many thousands outside their marketing area.

Servicing the larger accounts. A newspaper space salesperson working in the local or retail display advertising department performs largely what is a service function insofar as the larger advertisers are concerned. These advertisers, through their own advertising departments or through their advertising agencies, will do their own planning and execution of the creative work. Some newspaper space salespeople, therefore, become nothing more than high-priced messengers for such accounts. Their work consists largely in picking up the advertising from the accounts and taking it back to the newspaper to be run.

Even where local newspaper advertisers do their own planning and advertising, however, an enterprising newspaper space salesperson can be more useful and sell more space performing the following services:

(1) Keeps accounts informed of special editions and shows them how it will profit them to tie in with these editions (which usually offer tempting rate reductions).

(2) Sees that accounts buy economically at the lowest possible rates. The alert salesperson will show accounts how they may save considerable money over the year if they buy a few more lines of advertising and thus put themselves in a lower rate bracket for the year. The salesperson will thus sell more space, save the customer a considerable amount, and earn the customer's goodwill.

(3) Makes suggestions as to what items are selling well around the country. Newspapers are given much material about what is selling and supply it to the salespeople.

(4) Tells accounts of special promotions that are working well elsewhere. Once again, during the course of year, a newspaper advertising department will receive hundreds of such ideas from other newspapers and

from various advertising services to which the newspaper subscribes. If the salesperson shows initiative, he or she will suggest some of the better ideas to the accounts.

(5) Gives the accounts information on creative work, budgeting, pricing, and timing, all of which is supplied by the retail division of the Newspaper Advertising Bureau, Inc. of the American Newspaper Publishers Association. Not all the newspapers belong to this organization, but if they do, a salesperson using their material can make invaluable suggestions to accounts, no matter how large or how small they may be.

(6) Helps accounts get good positions for their advertisements. For the very largest accounts such help will usually not be necessary, since, by tradition, these accounts will be given certain fixed positions that they will occupy day after day. For medium-sized or smaller accounts, however, the enterprising salesperson can see that advertisements are placed in positions that the accounts like (even though the usual attitude of newspaper people is that any position is a good position so long as the advertisement advertises goods people want at the right price and the right time).

(7) Corrects any mistakes that might have cropped up. Sometimes the advertiser may have made a mistake in pricing or in the date, or in some other important information, quite apart from the typographical and spelling errors that will be caught by the newspaper's proofreader. The space salesperson will be the last person familiar with the account who will go over the advertisement before it appears in print. Corrections of major errors are important.

(8) Gives a realistic and honest picture of how newspaper advertising compares with other local media, especially in regard to the impact of television versus newspapers. Without "slamming" the rival media, it is part of a good newspaper salesperson's obligations to the advertisers to give them information that will enable them to weigh intelligently the relative merits of the various media. The salesperson will make a mistake to pretend that the other media do not exist—an ostrich-like approach used by a great many media salespeople.

(9) Helps the advertiser to obtain good reproduction from newspaper's back shop. If the salesperson fights for the client by demanding and getting the best kind of reproduction for advertisements, the salesperson will have performed a most useful service. To get such reproduction may be the result of a constant back-of-the-scenes battle between the salesperson and the printers in the newspaper's back shop. Some salespeople have made themselves very unpopular in that area of the newspaper by being persistent in behalf of their advertisers, but they have won the gratitude of their advertisers by so doing.

Giving the Smaller Advertiser a Hand—A few salespeople may service nothing but the larger accounts. These are usually the sales veterans who have earned a special status. Some salespeople will be given a mixture of small and large accounts. Beginners may have nothing but small accounts, which they are to service and develop. Still other salespeople will specialize; some, for example, may service the bank advertisers.

The space salesperson who handles a small advertiser will find that he or she is, in a sense, the advertising manager for the account. The salesperson will give all the help to the retailer, knowing that, in most instances, the retailer has no knowledge of advertising and may not do enough advertising unless the salesperson offers encouragement and down-to-earth help. This "down-to-earth" help will take at least two forms:

● Doing the planning and budgeting for the advertising. The planning may consist not only of deciding how much and when to advertise, but also what to advertise. To give such advice, the salesperson must become intimately acquainted with the merchant's stock and general business problems.

● Preparing the advertising by actually writing the copy and by doing rough layouts that will be turned over to the back shop of the newspaper for setting in type.

In order to do the rough layouts, the salesperson first obtains illustrations from the mat or proof service subscribed to by the newspaper.

Another possibility is that the newspaper space salesperson will pick up all the facts from the retailer about the products to be advertised and will relay this information to the newspaper's copy service department. The latter will then prepare the copy and layouts for the advertisements to be run. These are taken

Figure 11-1.

Proof from newspaper advertising service book. Once these were referred to as "Mat service books" when all newspapers were printed with hot type and plates were made from mats. Now, with newspapers rapidly converting to offset, or cold type printing, the mat is vanishing. Proofs such as this are used by the newspaper in behalf of advertisers and cover practically every type of retailing establishment. The name of the local business is placed on the advertisement, along with price figures, if the latter are needed.

(Courtesy of SCW, Inc.)

by the salesman to the advertiser for approval. Only a relatively few newspapers, however, have a formal copy service department.

Some newspapers load their salespeople with many small accounts and keep them so busy, consequently, that it becomes quite difficult for the salespeople to do a good job of both selling and servicing them.

Mat Services. Mats, previously referred to, are supplied to newspapers by many companies in the form of a complete "mat service." This consists in supplying sheets of mats and a mat proofbook. Code numbers on the mats and on the proofs enable users to pick out quickly the mats they want.

Under the "service" arrangement, mats and proofs are usually supplied on a monthly basis. These cover various major lines of merchandise advertising, including such lines as hardware, furniture, men's and women's clothing, groceries, and various dry goods. Also, there may be illustrations and advertisements for service businesses.

"Major" services, bought by bigger newspapers, offer fewer pages than the "Junior" mat services designed for smaller newspapers. Either service is usually sold on an exclusive franchise basis as a monthly arrangement or on the every-other-month schedule often preferred by smaller newspapers. Cost of a service ordinarily depends on the size of the city and on the newspaper's circulation.

Every newspaper makes constant use in its retail display department of mat services, not only for the use of the material that is sent but for the ideas in copy, art, and merchandising that may be found from careful examination of the monthly proof book. Because of the highly skilled creative and marketing people employed by the mat service companies, the proof books reflect the latest thinking in the retail field. A newspaper space salesperson who knows little about advertising can obtain a good education by studying the work of the mat service companies.

National Advertising Department

In the picturesque language of the newspaper, national advertising is sometimes called "foreign" advertising. It is also called "transient" or "general" advertising. Whatever it is called, it has the following two characteristics.

(1) National advertising is in behalf of advertisers who operate nationally or regionally. Included among these advertisers will be manufacturers, distributors, and wholesalers. Other national advertisers will be large service organizations such as insurance companies.

(2) Advertising for all these organizations will almost without exception be executed by advertising agencies and furnished by them to the newspaper in the form of glossy proofs, regular mats, plastic plates, or metal printing plates, called electrotypes. Newspapers, again almost without exception, will deduct 15 percent from the gross bills sent to the reputable advertising agencies for the space they have contracted for. This will reimburse the advertising agencies for services con-

sidered useful by the newspaper, such as preparing the advertising, scheduling it, and carrying the credit burden. In addition, most newspapers will usually give advertising agencies a 2 percent discount off the net space bill (after the 15 percent has been deducted) for paying within a certain time period. Advertising agencies are quite zealous about paying promptly enough to earn this additional 2 percent.

Special Representatives.   Since only the very largest newspapers can afford their own sales representatives to obtain national advertising in the big cities throughout the country, most newspapers obtain such business through "special representatives." These special representative companies, with offices and salesmen in the key business centers, solicit advertisers and their advertising agencies in behalf of their "list" of newspapers.

When they succeed in persuading the advertiser or the agency to advertise with one of the newspapers they represent, the newspaper usually pays them 10 to 15 percent of the net billing. Occasionally, the special representative company will operate on a fee basis. There are some newspapers that do not use special representatives because of the cost.

A small newspaper that wants to build national advertising linage is almost forced to use a special representative firm, since the cost of soliciting national advertising across the country is prohibitive even for newspapers with substantial circulation.

Special representatives keep a vigilant eye on the advertising and marketing activities of national advertisers. When these activities look promising they make calls upon the advertising agencies representing the advertisers, to show them how advertising in their newspapers can fulfill the advertiser's marketing objectives.

Special Duties to Be Performed.   Usually a national advertising department is headed by the national advertising manager. In many smaller newspapers, however, the work is handled by an overall advertising manager who directs local display and classified advertising as well. In some other cases, the publisher might handle the activity. More often than not, the national advertising department will consist of just one person, the manager. The national advertising department is expected to:

(1) *Provide research*

    This would usually be market research about the area served by the newspaper. It would include information about the various industries, population groups, retail sales, number of retail outlets, and other facts important to advertisers.

(2) *Provide facts about the newspaper itself*

    These facts would include circulation figures, the percentage of people and households reached in the city and the surrounding counties, and the kind of people who read the newspaper by age, income, family status, and occupation.

(3) *Provide merchandising service*

    Merchandising embraces many activities. A few of the merchandising services that a newspaper might be expected to offer national advertisers are given here. Many others could be named.

(a) *Calls on trade.* Calls are made on the trade by someone in the national advertising department to inform retailers and wholesalers of campaigns by national advertisers that are soon to break in the newspaper. In giving this information, the newspaper usually attempts to persuade the retailers to run tie-in advertising in connection with the campaign and to stock merchandise in anticipation of the sales that it is hoped the campaign will spark.

(b) *Trade surveys.* Trade surveys may be conducted at the request of the advertiser, or they may be originated by the newspaper. Such a survey may attempt to find out how widely stocked a certain product is, or how it or the advertiser are regarded. Since it is on the local market level, the newspaper can furnish much valuable information to the national advertiser, if it has enough manpower to conduct such surveys.

(c) *Letters to the trade.* Letters to the trade may serve in lieu of personal calls where the newspaper's staff is too limited.

(d) *Displays.* As an expensive form of cooperation, the newspaper may supply floor displays or window displays to the retailers. These displays will tie in with the advertiser's national campaign running in the newspaper. Displays may also be run in the windows of the newspaper itself.

(e) *Route lists.* One of the more valued merchandising services is the furnishing of route lists to manufacturers and distributors. These list dealers in various retail fields, such as grocery stores and drugstores. Arranged geographically, the lists enable a salesperson to spend the minimum amount of time in covering prospects. Some lists contain the dealers' sales volume and give the area's basic market data.

(f) *Talks to meetings of trade.* Sometimes a representative of the national advertising department will join representatives of the advertiser and the advertising agency in giving a "pep" talk about a forthcoming promotion. The meeting might be attended by food brokers, by wholesaler representatives, or by others connected with local business.

Merchandising efforts are expensive, but sometimes a smaller or medium-sized newspaper may find aggressive merchandising to be the final factor that will cause a national advertiser to buy space. Some advertisers, however, are unimpressed by media merchandising, no matter whether offered by newspapers, radio, television, or magazines. They say flatly they prefer to do their own merchandising. They suggest none too gently that the media will do better to cut down the expense of "useless" merchandising and use the money saved to reduce space or time rates.

Turning to Classifieds

To many of the public, the classified—or "want-ad"—section is the most interesting part of the newspaper. Within this section there may be anything from a message from Mabel saying, "Come home at once, all is forgiven" to an invitation to buy a used tractor.

Classified advertising is a form of business activity that the newspaper has largely to itself, since the broadcast media cannot duplicate this kind of advertising, and since magazines offer only token opposition.

Newspaper classified advertising now runs over $2.25 billion a year, accounting for almost 27 percent of total newspaper advertising revenue. There are estimates that classified advertising revenue will soon grow to about 36 percent of newspaper advertising revenue.

It is the mark of aggressive leading newspapers to have a big classified advertising section.

There are two types of newspaper classified advertising—regular and classified display. The former is the type that the average person uses when attempting to sell a used washing machine or some other personal item. This kind of advertisement will be sold by the word, the line, or the inch. The price will be on a sliding scale, depending on the size of the advertisement and on how many times it is run.

A classified display advertisement will look much like a local display advertisement, except that it will not appear in the news section of the newspaper but in the classified or want-ad section. It will have big type, illustrations, and white space. Like the regular classified advertisements, however, it will fall under some classification, such as real estate, used cars, or some other heading. Business using classified display will usually settle upon a format they like and then run the same advertisement without change for a long time, generally on a contract basis.

Some successful classified users, however, believe in changing copy frequently in their daily classified advertisements. Also, they find best results with advertisements that shun trickiness in favor of straightforward copy that answers questions about the what, the why, and the how much of the product, as well as where it can be bought.

Making and Getting Classified Advertising Sales. Classified advertising is either voluntary or solicited. Organization of the classified advertising department reflects this two-way street to classified volume. Voluntary sales are promoted through advertisements that usually appear in the newspaper, often as success stories of classified users who found classified advertising resultful. These voluntary sales may come in

(1) over the counter, in the newspaper office itself or at classified "stations" set up in locations outside the newspaper office or

(2) over the telephone.

Solicited classified sales may be obtained from telephone salespeople who make an enormous number of telephone calls in the pursuit of busines, or by

Fashion advertisement featuring a new trend.

Close coordination of copy and art is needed in this advertisement in order to make clear just what is entailed in this mode of dressing. "New" is the magic word in fashion. Newspaper advertising by very nature is suited to conveying the excitement of product news.

pareo

A new mode of dressing for summer ...in scarves! South Seas style. Start with a bright splash of cotton by Anne Klein for Robinson and Golluber. Tie it on as a slip of exotic sunfashion, a fluttering skirt, a halter. As a cover-up over your swimsuit... over your shoulders, your hair. Over and over. So many, many ways! Come see them **demonstrated at Glendale Saturday**, 11:30-2:30, in the department. Pick from the pareo collection of Batiks and Polynesian prints and coordinating solid tones in 43x55-inch oblongs **10.50**, and 36-inch squares **8.50**, at Ayres right now in Fashion Scarves, Street Floor, Downtown, all Indianapolis Branches and Lafayette, Indiana

Ayres we've got it for you!

Shop Ayres Today Downtown 9:30 to 5:30; Glendale, Greenwood, Lafayette Square, Washington Square and Lafayette, Indiana, 10.00 to 9:00

street salespeople. The latter usually work in assigned districts or in certain classifications, or both. A salesperson might, for example, concentrate on automotive sales; another might be assigned real estate. Solicited sales are usually on a contract basis, which provides big reductions from one-time rates.

Running Legal Advertising

Legal advertising could more correctly be called "legal notices." These notices of such matter as city ordinances, summons and complaints, notices to creditors, minutes of governmental meetings, calls for bids, and many other items to inform the public of governmental activities.

In some states certain newspapers are "county official newspapers" and automatically get all legal notices of county governments. In some places newspapers that can run legal avertising are appointed by government officials; in other cases, bids are issued to competing newspapers.

Very large newspapers usually do not get, nor want, legal advertising. Most daily newspapers do not obtain this kind of advertising, but many weeklies do. Income from legal advertising is a relatively small source of advertising revenue, though some small newspapers are glad to get it. On bigger papers the legal advertising activities are handled by the classified advertising department; on the weeklies the publisher may handle the details.

Copy Service Department

In the discussion of the work of the local display advertising department, it was said that sometimes the creative work for smaller accounts is turned over to the copy service department.

Many newspapers, even rather large newspapers, do not have copy service departments and do not believe in such departments. Other newspapers that have established these departments are strong boosters. Why should there be this difference over what appears to be a useful service to retailers and to the newspaper itself?

Opposing copy service departments are those newspaper advertising people who say "the best person to write copy and to otherwise prepare advertising for the account is the salesperson who is constantly calling on that account and who knows more about the account than anyone else."

Those who have a copy service department assert that freeing the salesperson from creative duties makes possible more time in sales work and in sales planning, both of which are more important to the newspaper than making layouts and writing copy.

Furthermore, say the copy service department advocates, most salespeople are not very good copywriters or layout experts, whereas the copy service personnel are hired for their creative abilities.

More Departments

Where a newspaper has a big circulation, it is likely to have a merchandising department which will carry out the functions described previously in the discussion of national advertising.

The newspaper may also have a research department that will execute various types of studies, including readership studies (to show how and what the men and women read in the publication) and market studies, concerned with anything from the demographic characteristics of the newspaper's marketing area to a pantry check that will reveal not only what items may be found on the food shelves of area residents but also how they sell (bathroom items may also be included). Some newspapers with especially active research departments, such as that of the *Milwaukee Journal,* conduct pantry checks year after year as an invaluable service to advertisers.

A large newspaper may also have a promotion and publicity department, the main function of which is to sell the newspaper to subscribers and advertisers. One activity in this area is to run advertisements about the newspaper and its services in other media and in the newspaper itself. Much of this kind of advertising consists of testimonials by users who have been satisfied with the newspaper in some respect. Advertising trade magazines are used to reach prospective advertisers.

It should always be understood that there are great many small-circulation daily newspapers that combine all "departments" in one person. This individual may be the business manager, the publisher, the advertising manager, or the editor. For this person the advertising task is one more chore in a busy day. On the way to work in the morning, he or she may pick up the advertising material from the local merchants on Main Street. Upon reaching the newspaper, this material is handed to the head of the print shop, who gets it in shape to be printed. Classified advertising may be assigned to a secretary, who will take voluntary calls over the telephone. If the secretary is not around for over-the-counter classifieds, almost anyone in the editorial or business side may help out.

National advertisers will be entrusted to the special representatives, with only billing arrangements and an occasional bit of letter-writing to constitute the activity on this side of the newspaper's advertising.

CHARGING FOR SPACE: RATES TO REMEMBER

Before getting into the mechanics of how newspapers charge for space, it is necessary to have some understanding of the physical aspects of the newspaper. A newspaper reader may read newspapers for an entire life time and be unaware of the number of columns found on a page. The reader may also have only the haziest idea of how many inches wide or how many inches deep the newspaper is.

For a long time almost every newspaper had 8-column pages, and column widths were 2 inches. Currently, however, many newspapers are switching to a 6-column format. Furthermore, column widths for 8-column newspapers are almost all less than 2 inches. While the depth of newspaper pages varies it is usually around 300 agate lines (approximately 21 inches). Thus, for easy estimating, you can assume an 8-column newspaper has around 2,400 agate lines and a 6-column newspaper around 1,800 lines. Tabloid newspapers, such as the *New York Daily News,* however, have 6-columns of 200 lines depth. Thus, a page has 1,200 agate lines. Because of their widely varying mechanical measurements, newspapers present a constant challenge to advertising agency production people responsible for the preparation of advertising that will be placed in hundreds of newspapers.

An agate line is somewhat less easy to understand. The origin of the agate line as a space-and-rate unit goes back to the early newspapers, which crowded a great amount of typography on a page. Much of the reading matter of the early days of newspapering was set in agate type, which fit 14 lines to the column inch.

Although a modern newspaper reader will hardly ever see type set in such dense measure as agate type, the term "agate line" has descended from the early days. An agate line does not refer to a line of type. It is merely a space measurement used in establishing rates, mostly for national advertising. It is 1/14 in. deep and 1 column wide.

If the national advertiser, for example, were to take the 10-in. advertisement previously mentioned, that advertisement would measure 140 agate lines. If the "line rate," as it is called, were 10 cents an agate line, the advertisement would cost him $14.00.

To arrive at the 140 agate lines, think of an agate line as 1/14 in. deep and a column wide (no matter how wide the column might be). Each column inch, therefore, contains 14 agate lines. To arrive at the total agate lines for any advertisement, multiply the number of column inches, and fractions thereof, by 14. Then multiply that total of agate lines by the agate line rate to obtain the cost of the advertisement.

Most newspaper columns run between 285 lines deep to 300 lines, although some run as high as 315 lines. Figured at 300-agate lines, this would give an 8-column newspaper 2,400 agate lines, and a 6-column newspaper 1,800 agate lines.

Local Display

One fact of newspaper advertising is that local advertisers are rewarded by the newspaper for advertising heavily and steadily. This fact will be evident in the various rates shown hereafter. All rate arrangements, called sliding-scale rate schedules, are given in detail in local rate cards supplied by the newspaper to local advertisers (Fig. 11-2). These rates, as will be shown later, are different from the rates given national advertisers. The latter obtain their rate information from the newspaper section of Standard Rate & Data Service that gives rates and other information about all the daily newspapers in the country.

Reduced to the simplest terms, most sliding scale rates are either bulk—based on buying stated amounts of space in a contract period, or frequency—based on buying at a certain frequency in a contract period.

For the purpose of planning, a newspaper may value its frequency contracts even more than bulk contracts. Frequency contracts ensure a regular pattern of advertising. Based on this pattern a newspaper can plan the number of pages to print each day.

Classifieds

The business that uses classified on a regular basis or in quantity will buy more cheaply. Classified rates are computed on a cost-per-word system or a cost-per-line system used for the want ads placed for personal purposes. In the first, a fixed price is charged for each word no matter how many lines there are in the advertisement. In the second, the newspaper estimates how many lines the advertisements will take by counting the number of words or characters in the advertising and allowing a certain number of words per line. Rates for display classified are always on a per-line basis.

Local Display Advertising Contracts

There is nothing very legal or binding about the usual space contract signed by a local advertiser and the newspaper. Its most important functions are to protect the advertiser against rate increases during the contract year, and to give the newspaper some assurance of regular advertising on the part of the advertiser.

Many advertisers advertise without contracts and still earn the sliding-scale discounts, but newspapers prefer to have signed contracts.

National Advertising Rates

Most newspapers charge national advertisers "flat" rates , which means that no matter how much space is used by the advertiser the rate remains the same. Under the flat-rate arrangement there is no sliding-scale inducement that lures the local advertiser to earn lower rates.

As might be expected, many national advertisers profess annoyance or anger that they are thus "discriminated" against. They have argued for a lessening of the rate differential between national and local advertising or, as has been heard with increasing frequency, a single rate for national and local advertising.

In terms of advertising dollars the stakes are high, since the differential between the lowest local rate and the national rate can exceed 100 percent in some cases. Among 400 newspapers recently checked, the differential was approximately 60 percent.

In arguing for a "fairer" rate, national advertisers declare that national advertising in newspapers supplies 25 percent of the revenue, but only 10 percent of the linage. National advertisers also point out that the reason for the small percentage of the newspapers' linage represented by national advertising revenue is the inflated rate charged national advertisers. Many national advertisers also insist that they do not buy newspaper advertising because of this "punitive" rate differential.

Another complaint sometimes heard is that the national advertiser paying a higher rate is at a position disadvantage, since 50 to 60 percent of each newspaper's space for any given date is already committed to local advertising.

Local rate card for small newspaper.

Retailers, unlike national advertisers, are usually accustomed to buying by the column inch instead of the agate line. Thus, in this rate card, the display buying is shown in column inches.

OTHER ADVERTISING TERMS

● It is of vital importance to The TIMES and its advertisers that the public have confidence in this newspaper's advertising. For this reason, the publisher reserves the right to reject or revise, at his option, the copy or illustrations in any advertising submitted for publication.

● No alcoholic beverage or tobacco advertising accepted.

● No ads will be run in any freak or out of the ordinary manner not in good newspaper practice.

● A column inch is space one column wide and one inch deep. A page is 6 columns wide and 21 inches in depth.

● Advertisements must be at least as many inches in depth as columns in width.

● Double trucks of full page depth with a minimum of 8 columns in width will be accepted. A full column will be charged in addition to the actual space occupied due to extra mechanical and make-ready work required.

● Advertisements over 19 inches in length will be extended to 21 inches and charged as such.

● Excessively intricate or tabular composition will be charged 25% extra.

● The advertiser will be billed for production costs on any ad set but canceled before insertion.

● All advertising similar to editorial copy or news photos will be plainly marked "Adv.".

LET US HELP YOU

1—The country's leading advertising illustration services are purchased by The TIMES and available free of charge.
2—The TIMES advertising staff will gladly furnish advice on layout and copywriting.

The Geneva Times

Geneva, New York   **Phone 789-3333**

DISPLAY ADVERTISING RATES

Basic Rate . . . . $3.32 per col. inch

Cash Discount		**Net Cost**
Up to 500 col. inches per month 8%		$3.05
From 500 col. inches per month 12%		$2.92

Miscellaneous Rates

● Up to 15 column inches - daily or three times per week. Weekly copy change. Discount 12%.(13 wk. agreement)

● Ads at least a half-page in size may be repeated three times within one month of the first insertion. Repeat ads will be billed at half the inches of the original ad.

● Geneva Shopper: Distributed free each Wednesday to over 21,000 area families who are not regular Times subscribers. Rates upon request.

● Saturday T.V. Guide. Rates upon request.

● Public Notices. As provided by law.

● Spot Color. (Press capacity permitting) $100.00 per page, one color and black. Additional information upon request.

● Pre-Printed Supplements. Rates upon request.

● Hi Fi Pre-Prints. Charges at advertiser's earned monthly rate.

All discounts are based on cash payment by the fifteenth of the following month providing there are no balances due. Cash must accompany order in those cases where an advertiser has not established credit with The TIMES.

UNIT PRICES (NET)

¼ page	(32 col. inches)	$97.74
½ page	(63 col. inches)	192.43
Full page	(126 col. inches)	384.85

Additional advertising in the same calendar month can earn a higher discount and result in a lower unit price.

PHOTOGRAPHY

The TIMES display advertising representative should be consulted early in the planning stage when photographs are to be used in advertisements. Releases from persons in ad photos must be supplied by the advertiser with the copy.

DEADLINES

The normal deadline for advertising copy is noon, two working days before publication.

Half page size ads and larger, involving layout and significant composition, have a noon deadline, three working days before publication.

Ads involved in city-wide promotions such as Good Neighbor Days, Dollar Days, etc. have a noon deadline, four working days prior to publication.

COPY CHANGES

Additions or changes in original copy will be made if time permits, but will be charged to the advertiser at the current composing room hourly rate with a minimum charge of $5.00.

POSITION

Position is not guaranteed because of the varying number of pages in each issue and because of conflicting requests by several advertisers for the same position. When position is demanded as a condition of publication, a premium of 25% will be charged.

ERRORS

The newspaper's liability for error in any advertisement shall not exceed the cost of the space actually occupied by the item in which the error is made.

TABLOID SECTIONS

- Width of column 13.4 picas (2 3/16")
- Depth of column 13¾ inches
- Four columns to a page
- Full page, 55 column inches
- Double truck, 123 column inches
- An extra charge of $75 will be made on all tabloid sections to cover added mechanical and handling costs.

Why a Difference Between National and Local Rates?

Although a few newspapers are offering single rates or sliding scales to national advertisers, most are holding firmly to flat rates. These are some of the important reasons for their stand:

(1) Selling costs are greater in getting national advertising. Besides paying the 15 percent agency commission in connection with national advertising, newspapers also pay special representatives 10 to 15 percent. These charges alone add 25 to 30 percent to the cost of handling national advertising.

(2) Additional services are given national advertisers. The cost of merchandising, for example, is wholly assigned to the national advertising department. Also in the special service class are the special editors hired for classifications such as food, travel, and automotive. These editors are put on the newspaper payroll almost exclusively for the benefit of the national advertisers and the industries they represent.

(3) Whereas the local advertising appears on a regular, dependable basis, there is little predictability about national advertising. Local advertising is dependable revenue that makes possible intelligent planning by the newspaper. National advertising schedules, by contrast, are far more hit or miss. There may be a large advertising expenditure one month and almost no money spent the following month. Such uncertainty of volume makes future planning equally uncertain.

(4) There is no evidence that giving sliding scales or lower rates to national advertisers would result in any appreciable increase in national advertising linage.

Despite the bitterness expressed about the higher national rates, it is unlikely that most newspapers will, for the reasons given, either adopt a single rate for local and national advertisers, or make any significant rate concessions to national advertising. Newspaper people reason that if newspapers are an efficient advertising medium for national advertisers, newspaper advertising will be used regardless of the local-national rate differential. They asume furthermore, that most national advertisers will consider the reasons for the differential logical even though they wince at the extent of the difference.

Milline Rates

The thinking of national advertisers using newspaper advertising is greatly influenced by the following milline formula:

$$\frac{1,000,000 \times \text{rate}}{\text{Total circulation}}$$

In theory the formula represents the cost of putting one agate line of advertising before a million persons. Going beyond the theory and speaking in the terms that the usual national advertiser would use, the milline rate makes it possible to compare the real cost of reaching this mass market.

If the national advertiser did not have the milline rate with which to compare newspapers, there would be no choice but to buy newspapers with low agate line rates. If the advertiser did, however, there would be nothing but low-circulation newspapers on the list, since they are the ones with low agate line rates. It becomes obvious, then, that low line rates are not necessarily economical for an advertiser who wants to reach many people. In fact, a newspaper with a low line rate is almost always going to be a newspaper with a high milline rate—thus very often not a good buy for the national advertiser.

The following examples will demonstrate the principle.

Paper A has a circulation of 320,000. Its rate is 90¢ per line.

Paper B has a circulation of 25,000. Its rate is 22¢ per line.

There is no question. Paper B will cost the national advertisr far less if judged by its line rate. When the milline formula is applied, however, a different conclusion must be reached:

$$\text{Paper A:} \quad \frac{1,000,000 \times 90\text{¢}}{320,000}$$

This gives a milline rate of $2.81.

$$\text{Paper B:} \quad \frac{1,000,000 \times 22\text{¢}}{25,000}$$

This gives a milline rate of $8.80. (Thus, by the Milline Yardstick, Paper A is the better buy.

Many a small-circulation newspaper has been cut off the national advertiser's list by this kind of merciless arithmetic. Although the newspaper with the smaller circulation may have many admirable attributes, it has no chance of being used by the kind of advertiser who buys by the slide rule.

Another approach is to use the cost-per-thousand circulation, which for years has been the guide in assessing the cost of magazine advertising. At this time, however, the milline rate is more popular with national advertisers who are comparing the cost efficiency of newspapers.

Short Rate

Anyone buying space from a newspaper should pay close attention to the wording in the space contract. If, for instance, an advertiser is buying space on a quantity basis, the advertiser will contract to use a certain amount of space within a stated period. If the advertiser does not use the amount contracted for, the advertiser will pay the difference between the rate contracted for and the higher rate charged for the smaller quantity actually used. An example of the short-rate process follows:

(1) The rate schedule is:

Number of lines	Rate per line in cents
0 - 1,000	14
1,000 - 2,500	12
2,500 - 5,000	10
5,000 - 10,000	8

(2) Advertiser contracts for 2,600 lines at 10¢ per line.

(3) The advertiser uses only 1,900 lines and is charged $190 (1,900 lines × 10¢).

(4) Since the advertiser should have paid for 1,900 lines at 12¢ per line, the newspaper (because the advertiser did not meet the contract) charges the advertiser the difference between the rates.

(5) The newspaper, therefore, charges the advertiser 1,900 × 2 *, or $38 (the difference between the higher and the lower rate), in addition to the $190 in step 3.

(6) The "short rate" is the difference, or $38 in this instance.

Short Rate in Reverse. Sometimes the short rate system can work in reverse. It may be possible that, by taking just a few more lines of space, the advertiser can save a substantial amount. Suppose, to illustrate, that the advertiser used 910 lines of advertising at 10¢ per line. This would have cost $91.

If the advertiser had taken but 90 lines more, the advertiser would have earned the 1,000-line rate of 8¢. At this rate the total cost would have been $80. Thus, the advertiser could have used more space at a lower total cost.

Usually the newspaper space salesperson will protect the advertiser in such cases by calling attention to the fact that, by taking a few more lines, the advertiser can earn a lower rate. An advertiser should remember, however, that the salesperson has many accounts to think about and, accordingly, should not depend wholly upon the newspaper to protect the account.

Rateholders

Often heard in connection with contract advertisers is the term "rateholder." A rateholder is a small advertisement run by an advertiser to enable the advertiser to live up to the terms of the contract. If the advertiser, for example, has agreed to advertise with a certain frequency, the advertiser may run a small advertisement on occasion—perhaps an advertisement of only a couple of inches—in order to protect a rate arrangement. The advertiser may do this because he or she is planning to run big-space advertisements later. The small advertisement is run simply to enable the advertiser to fulfill a contract if it has a frequency clause.

Combination Rates

Until two court decisions ruled against it, newspapers under the same ownership in the same city were able to force national advertisers into a *forced combination*; that is, if a national advertiser wanted to use newspaper advertising in a certain city he was forced to use both newspapers even though he would have much preferred to advertise in only one.

Combination rates are still offered, but they are now wholly optional. Under the combination rate, the advertiser uses both the morning and evening newspapers at a lower combined rate than if he were to buy space in each paper individually. In addition to saving on space costs, the advertiser likewise saves on mechanical costs, since the same plates or mats are used for both papers.

That it often pays advertisers handsomely to take advantage of the combination rate is shown in the following example of two newspapers that offer such a rate:

Evening newspaper bought singly . . . . 53 cents
Morning newspaper bought singly . . . . 45 cents
Both newspapers bought in combination . . . . 70 cents

Open Rate

A casual retail advertiser who advertises only once or twice a year may be charged the "open" rate. This is a rate on which no discount is given. Many times it is the same rate that is charged national advertisers, though sometimes it is a lower rate.

Sometimes the open rate is charged if the retailer buys less advertising space than a certain specified amount. It may be listed, for example: Open rate, 0 to 1,000 lines. This means that the discounts do not begin until the buyer has used a thousand lines. The cost is just as much per line for 980 lines as it is for one line. It is clear then, that the open rate is the highest rate, and that space bought on the open-rate basis is bought on the most expensive basis.

On the other hand, both for national and local advertisers, the very term "open rate" signifies that the newspaper is "open" to bargaining, and that if the advertisers will buy enough space, there will be discounts offered. This, of course, is exactly the opposite of the situation when "flat" rates are offered. In the latter case, no discounts or sliding scales are available.

More Rates

In its long existence the newspaper has piled up many traditions, many odd terms, and a bewildering variety of rates, special charges, and mechanical specifications. Some of the more common rates are discussed here:

Classification Rates. Classification rates include special rates—some higher and some lower than regular rates—to churches; amusement places; fraternal, political, racing, and travel organizations; schools and camps; and utilities.

Church and school rates will usually be lower. Political and amusement will be higher. Political advertisers must often pay in advance because it has been the experience of newspapers that political candidates, especially the losing candidates, have not always been careful about paying bills run up during their campaigns.

Position Rates. Some newspapers refuse to sell certain positions. An advertiser, unless an old-time advertiser with a fixed position that is occupied through tradition, must be willing to accept whatever position the newspaper gives.

Other newspapers charge extra whenever an advertiser specifically requests a certain position. Newspapers will not charge if the advertiser's order requests a certain place in the newspaper "if possible."

Position charges are fairly substantial, since almost all newspapers view special-position requests as a nuisance, especially because so many advertisers want the same positions.

An example of the special-position rates charged by a newspaper with a circulation of about 17,000 follows:

Next to reading matter	15 percent extra
Full position (minimum 42 lines) ...	25 percent extra
Specified page	25 percent extra

"Full position" is the top of the page next to reading matter.

Preprints and Multipage Inserts.   Throughout the newspaper section of Standard Rate & Data Service there is a phrase used by many newspapers that reads: "Inserts and preprints. See tabulation at beginning of book."

Preprints and inserts (and the latter, too, are actually preprints) are pages printed in advance, usually in color, and included in a regular run of the newspaper. Rates for these special pages are given in the tabulation referred to in the preceding paragraph.

Split Runs.   An increasing number of newspapers are offering split runs to advertisers who want to try out the effect of different copy approaches or different offers in different sections of a newspaper's run.

One such newspaper offers split-run advertising on the following basis:

95 cents per 9-pt line. 8 lines to inch, minimum charge 2 lines. Marked "adv" following copy. Imitation reading notices, first word boldface run in special column in main news City News in Brief.

Color Rates.   As more newspapers offer color to advertisers, the question of color rates grows in importance, since usually there is a significant difference between color and black-and-white rates. Color advertisements, furthermore, are required by newspapers to be in larger space units. Small advertisers, therefore, almost never use color advertising in newspapers.

THE NEWSPAPER LAYOUT

For very small newspapers the makeup, insofar as the placement of news and advertising material is concerned, is left to the compositor in the back shop who, through long experience, lays out the pages quickly, if not always to the best advantage of the newspaper or the advertisers.

For large newspapers, a "dummy" is made for each page, usually by someone in the advertising department (Fig. 12-3). That "someone" might be anyone from the advertising manager to a person who has as one of his or her chief responsibilities the most pleasing and effective laying out of the newspaper.

On pages where advertising is to appear, the spaces to be occupied by specific advertisements are marked off on a "dummy" for each page of the newspaper. The "dummy" is a sort of rough blueprint. Each space to be occupied by an advertisement is "X'd" off, and usually the name of the advertiser or advertised product is written in the space. The space not occupied by advertisements is left for news stories, columns, or various features.

The person who dummies a page has three objectives:

(1) To give every advertisement a good position. "Good position" means to get the advertisement adjacent to reading matter and to avoid "tombstoning' it (having it completely surrounded or "buried" by other advertisements, which sometimes happens to small advertisements placed in the lower corner of a newspaper page).

(2) To achieve an overall pleasant design for the page.

(3) To observe any requests that have been made for special positions, or to avoid putting certain advertisers next to competitive advertisers, or certain kinds of advertisements next to unsuitable news material, such as liquor advertisements next to church news, or airline advertisements next to stories of crashes.

Anyone dummying a page will, if no one else has noticed, make certain that advertisers observe the newspaper's rule about the proportions of advertisements which are almost as deep as they are wide. Generally, the most pleasing proportion for advertisements will be about 3 to 5. Expressed in columns, this would mean that the advertisement was 3 columns by 10 in.*

A newspaper will refuse advertisements of irregular shapes, or advertisements that, for example, are 2 in. deep and 14 in. wide. Were newspapers to accept advertisements of freak shapes or proportions, the job of making up a pleasing newspaper page would be impossible.

Dummying a Page

Most readers have never noticed that almost all newspaper pages are set up in a "pyramid" design. With this arrangement, advertisements build up from left to right on a page, with the largest advertisements appearing on the bottom right. Not only is the pyramid design pleasing to the eye, but also it provides a way to get advertisements next to reading matter—considered very desirable, since the first interest of newspapers is to read news material. If advertisements are next to reading matter, it is logical to assume that they will have a better chance to be read than if they are next to nothing but other advertisements.

Sometimes right-hand pages may be pyramided to the right and left-hand pages to the left.

Sometimes when a paper is jammed with advertising, or is "tight," as newspapermen say, a double pyramid may be used. This will see a half-pyramid on the right of the page and a small half-pyramid on the left. In this way the newspaper gets the maximum amount of advertising on the page but still places

Dummy for newspaper page.

Advertisements are placed on this page in a pyramid going from left to right although the pattern is a bit different here because of the two columns of advertisements on the extreme left-hand side. See FIGURE 00 to see the printed page that resulted from this dummy.

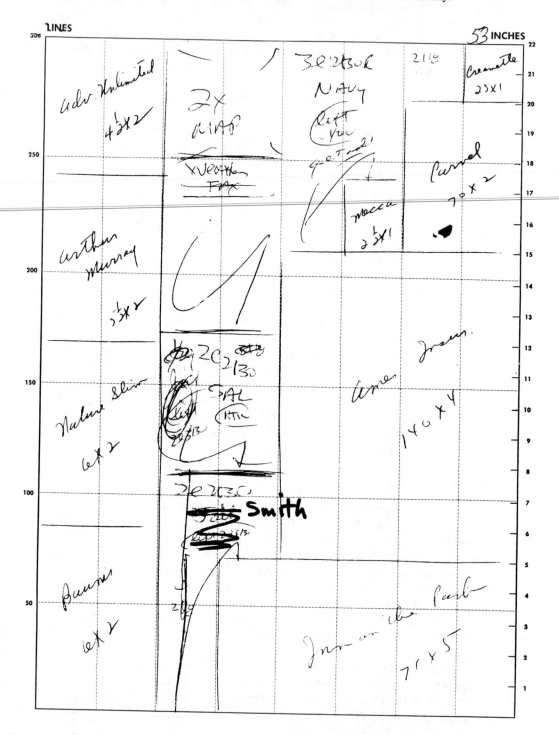

Newspaper page showing pyramid placement of advertising.
Here is the advertisement that resulted from the dummy shown in FIGURE 00.

NATIONAL WEATHER SERVICE FORECAST to 7

UPI WEATHER FOTOCAST ©

NATIONAL WEATHER — Tuesday night will find thundershowers in the western area of Washington and por-

tions of t valley, w will domi nation.

☺ U. S. Weather

For Buffalo and vicinity: Considerable sunshine today with high about 70. Clear tonight. Low about 50 but in the mid 40s in most suburban sections. Sunshine and low humidity with high 75 to 80 Wednesday. Northwest winds 10 to 20 m.p.h. subsiding under 10 m.p.h. tonight. The chance of rain is 10 per cent today and near zero tonight and Wednesday.

Extended Outlook For Western New York Thursday Through Saturday: Mostly sunny Thursday. Chance of a few showers Friday and Saturday. Lows about 50 Thursday and near 60 Friday and Saturday with daily highs within a few degrees of 80.

Buffalo Temperatures

1 pm	68	9 pm	63	5 am	56
2 pm	65	10 pm	66	6 am	55
3 pm	70	11 pm	61	7 am	56
4 pm	66	Midnt	60	8 am	59
5 pm	67	1 am	58	9 am	63
6 pm	69	2 am	56		
7 pm	66	3 am	56		
8 pm	63	4 am	56		

LOCAL DATA

Temperatures		Data at 9 AM	
Normal	67	Humidity	80%
Low 1897	44	Wind veloc.	WNW-8
High in 1953	93		
Excess, 1977	+162	Precipitation	
Mean, June 20	65	24 hours ended	
Departure from		at 7 AM	.20
norm June	-35	Since June 1	.96
Degree days		Norm this mo.	
June 20	0	to date	-1.47
Degree days		Since Jan. 1	13.34
since June 1	87	Def. 1977	-2.55
Lake temp.	62		

This Date 1976 | News Almanac
Maximum temp. 68 | Sunrise today 5:36
Minimum temp. 55 | Sunset today 8:57
Character of day: | Sunrise tomor. 8:36
Showers

TEMPER
Temperatu
daytime high

City
Albany
Albuquerque
Anchorage
Atlanta
Baltimore
Birmingham
Boston
Buffalo
Charlest'n, SC
Chicago
Cincinnati
Cleveland
Dal.-Ft. Worth
Denver
Des Moines
Detroit
Honolulu
Houston
Jacksonville
Juneau
Kansas City
Las Vegas
Los Angeles
Louisville
Memphis
Miami Beach
Milwaukee
Mpls-St. Paul
New Orleans
New York
Omaha
Orlando
Philadelphia
Phoenix
Pittsburgh
Portland Or.
St. Louis
St Prbg Temp
S. L. Cty
S. Fran.
Seattle
Syracuse
Washington

TEMPERATI
Athens 2
Berlin 1
Dublin 1
London 1
Manila 8
Moscow 3

First
June 24
12:44 PM
For loc
Mercury invis
rises before su
rise; Saturn set

Buffalo, Lackawa Sued Over Arres

A Buffalo man who was mistakenly arrested for murder and robbery and later released,

copy of a
Smith fro
files and a

Lose it...
naturally

almost all advertisements adjacent to reading material.

Sometimes makeup on smaller newspapers, or in special sections of large daily newspapers, will put advertisements in a line along the sides. News material is thus in a "well" in the middle, accounting for the name, "well makeup," by which this system is described.

Still other newspapers, but not too many, use a helter-skelter system that places all advertisements next to reading material. Advertisements may be placed in the corners and smaller advertisements put above, below, and alongside the big advertisements. Advertising so clearly dominates such a page that the news editors find it difficult to attract attention to their stories. Furthermore, unlike the pyramid design, this arrangement is not pleasing to the eye.

*For an 8-column newspaper the resulting advertisement would have just about the classic proportion. It would be less so if the newspaper had 6 columns, because the columns are wider.

NEWSPAPER TECHNOLOGY IS CHANGING RAPIDLY

Anyone associated with newspapers in recent years has had to adjust to the overwhelming rush of technical advances in the production processes used in putting out a newspaper. These changes are affecting news-side workers as well as advertising department personnel. Those in the advertising business who become involved with newspaper advertising should make frequent trips to newspaper plants to find out what changes are occurring. Reading such industry publications as *Editor & Publisher* is useful, too, because this magazine carries much material about the advances in newspaper production.

DECIDING TO BUY SPACE AND TIME

Space buyers know that newspapers differ in a number of significant ways. Some newspapers have broad popular appeal, often expressing the viewpoint of blue-collar workers. Others, such as the *New York Times* and *The Christian Science Monitor*, reach audiences with higher levels of income and education, reaching many professional and managerial people.

Space buyers may analyze the press runs of major metropolitan newspapers to determine other circulation characteristics. If, for example, much of the circulation of an evening newspaper is distributed before noon, it is likely that many of these newspapers are not taken home for family reading. Early editions are often bought for late news or for sports results. Such circulation, while of some value, is not so thoroughly read as later editions. Often the person buying the newspaper is the only reader. Thus, in early editions, which are published primarily for newsstand sales, the advertiser will not reach so many people.

Newspapers also develop reputations with advertisers. In some cities, one newspaper may carry the majority of retail and national advertising. In other cities, one newspaper may lead in automobile advertising while another may carry the bulk of the department store advertising.

KNOW YOUR NEWSPAPERS

Assume you are suddenly handed an assignment to make space buying recommendations for newspapers to a manufacturer planning to distribute a new product nationally for the first time. How would you go about deciding which newspapers to recommend? You would examine the newspapers yourself and then look at information sources that detail information about newspapers.

If a nearby library receives newspapers from many major cities, you can go to the library and start studying the newspapers. What do you look for?

A large number of retail advertisements in the newspapers you examine tells you that the newspaper is a desirable advertising medium. Retailers depend heavily on newspapers and place their advertisements where they bring results. Same-day or day-after sales by retailers who have just advertised provide quick and continual measures of newspaper effectiveness.

You study the advertisements themselves. Is the newspaper filled with "last chance" offers and advertisements for relatively inexpensive merchandise? Are there department store and fashion advertisements which downplay price? The chances are the newspaper carries a blend of both types of advertisements. Your key question concerns the balance between the two types of advertisements.

You may check the actual space bought by different kinds of retailers in each newspaper you examine. If, for example, the majority of mens' wear advertising in a market has been placed by a few quality stores, and if these stores have put the bulk of their advertising in one newspaper, this tells you that the retailers believe the newspaper reaches consumers who buy higher-priced mens' wear. Newspapers will supply figures on retailer advertising on request.

Additional figures can be obtained from Media Records, an organization that monitors and reports advertising linage. The information is presented in various classifications for both national and retail advertising space.

You might question the circulation claimed by the newspaper. Hundreds of newspapers have their circulation audited by the Audit Bureau of Circulations This organization certifies the accuracy of a newspaper's claimed circulation, checking whether the circulation figures were pumped up through some quick but temporary circulation-building scheme similar to "hypo-ing" in the broadcast industry.

Insist on Quality

Advertising agencies placing space for clients carefully examine advance proofs of advertisements submitted by newspapers to agencies. Poor quality reproduction of advertisements may mean dropping a newspaper from a schedule of newspaper buys.

Question the Rates

Are the rates out of line? Inconsistency in rate structures is one of the oddities of newspaper advertising. Newspapers in nearby locations, with approximately the same circulation and with no discernible audience or other differences, will often have radically different rates. This has long been a cause of concern to advertisers.

Watch That Duplication Figure

Is newspaper coverage duplicated? An analysis of newspaper circulation sometimes reveals that the use of one morning and one evening newspaper will actually give more than 100 percent family coverage of the market, with many families receiving both newspapers. This means that there is considerable duplication in the market.

A family receiving both a morning and an evening paper usually selects newspapers of the same character. When selecting newspapers, an advertiser must decide whether to emphasize duplication (and frequency) or reach. If the advertiser wants to reach certain types of families frequently, morning and evening newspapers of the same character may be the choice. If the advertiser wants to reach as many different families as possible, the advertiser avoids newspapers with overlapping circulation.

If the advertiser is marketing a frequently purchased, low-cost product that requires little consumer thought—soap, cereal, salt, bread—the advertiser probably wants to reach as many people as possible with a single message. Newspapers with minimum circulation are chosen. Products consumers regard as important may be advertised in newspapers with high duplication; the advertiser wants to present the reasons for buying the product more than once.

MORNING OR EVENING NEWSPAPERS: DAILY DILEMMA

Some advertising people argue that morning newspapers in general are a more desirable advertising medium than evening newspapers. Some argue the reverse. The arguments are futile because newspapers vary so much from city to city.

One of the striking facts of the newspaper business is that the proportion of evening to morning newspapers becomes greater as the years go on. There are currently about 10 times as many evening newspapers. This might lead one to believe that evening newspapers are, therefore, overwhelmingly dominant in the various newspaper markets. The argument is strengthened by the fact that in many one-newspaper cities, the one newspaper is almost certain to be an evening newspaper.

Yet on the national scene, and especially in the big cities, many of the richest, biggest circulation newspapers are morning newspapers. Among these are the *New York Times*, the *New York Daily News*, the *Chicago Tribune*, and the *Los Angeles Times*.

When considering the differences between morning and evening newspapers, therefore, it is wise to think of specific newspapers and specific markets and to think in terms of "characteristics" rather than advantages or disadvantages.

What the Morning Newspaper Is Like

The morning paper is *more likely to be delivered to the home*, especially in the bigger cities. Although evening newsstand sales are likely to be greater in percentage terms in big towns than in small towns, there is still enough differential in home deliveries in favor of the morning newspaper to make the point worth considering, even for the small town.

Home-delivered newspapers can be counted more certainly as genuine circulation, for the home market is definitely reached by the home-delivered newspaper. A newspaper bought at the newsstand, on the contrary, may never reach the home. It may have been bought only because of a momentary interest in a news item. Circulation figures for home-delivered newspapers seem more trustworthy to advertisers to whom one newspaper in the home may be worth more in sales than two in the local cigar shop, or ten left on subway seats.

Morning newspapers are generally conceded to be more *suited to the sale of impulse goods*. Low-cost items—cosmetics, women's hose, ties, belts—are just some of the many quickly purchased items advertised successfully in morning newspapers.

It would be foolish, of course, to think that morning newspapers cannot sell anything but impulse items, but they do have an especial suitability for goods that can be bought soon after advertising appears.

What the Evening Newspaper Is Like

The evening newspaper is more likely to be read by more members of the family. In the average American home with school-age children, the morning period from 6:30 to 8:30 tends to be two hours of scrambling. Shaving, showering, dressing, and eating breakfast leave little time for newspaper reading and, to make things more difficult, there is much listening to radio news, or watching early-morning television.

Because there is more possibility that the evening newspaper can be read by all members of the family, it is generally *considered more of a family newspaper* than the morning newspaper, even though the morning paper is more likely to be home-delivered.

Evening newspapers, furthermore, are generally *more departmentalized* than morning newspapers. Each member of the family, young and old, is likely to find some section of particular interest in his evening newspaper.

In the evening newspaper, *decision-type products can be advertised* to advantage. Although the rule is certainly not inflexible, the evening newspaper is favored by those who advertise goods that require considerable prebuying thought.

Furniture, refrigerators, musical instruments, and other merchandise requiring individual and family thinking and consultation are advertised heavily in evening newspapers.

Even with the distraction offered by television, the evening newspaper is likely to be *read more intensively*. Also, the family can be assembled for joint consideration of the purchase of a product. Although it is true that the purchase must be delayed until the following day, the evening newspaper allows more time for reading the advertising and for consideration of the purchase of the merchandise being advertised.

The circulation of evening newspapers is more likely to be *concentrated in the immediate shopping area*. This point is of less interest to the national advertiser than to the local advertiser, who sees little profit in customers who will

Tie-in newspaper advertisement.

In this case, the manufacturer of farm equipment supplies its dealers with advertising material that can be placed in local newspapers. The dealer puts his name at the point where the words DEALER IMPRINT appear. Thus, the dealers, without effort on their part, will be represented by professional-looking advertising and can, if they wish, tie such advertisements in with national advertisements that may running at the same time.

Are big 4-wheel-drive tractors practical around here? A John Deere is!

The increased power and traction of a new 4-wheel-drive tractor are really attractive. But how can you justify the cost of a new 4-wheeler, if all it can be used for is primary tillage? Well, many times you can't. That's why John Deere 8430 and 8630 Tractors are designed to do much more than pull a plow. These tractors take big power (275 engine hp/225 PTO hp in the 8630; 215 engine hp/175 PTO hp in the 8430) and put it to work on a season-long basis. They're loaded with the kind of features that make them productive throughout the year. Take the 1000-rpm independent PTO, Load-and-Depth Control draft-sensing hitch, rack-and-pinion wheel tread adjustment, and variable-ratio power steering system. These are just a few examples of row-crop features that let you get full use of 4-wheel-drive power. Stop in for a lot more reasons why a John Deere is a good investment.

DEALER IMPRINT

seldom, if ever, shop in the city in which the newspaper is published. Morning paper circulation tends to fan out wider than that of evening newspapers.

THE SUNDAY SCENE

Sunday newspapers have all the advantages of evening newspapers and some others in addition. More than even the evening newspapers, the Sunday newspaper *is a family newspaper*. Since more time is spent by the whole family in reading the Sunday newspaper, it is even superior to the evening newspaper for advertising goods that require family consultation, or long individual deliberation.

Another advantage that makes Sunday newspapers appealing is that almost always they offer *greatly increased circulation over weekday editions*. Because of this fact, many retailers save much of their advertising for this day. Since so many retail stores are open on Monday nights, it is profitable for retailers to reach a bigger audience on Sundays.

Although Sunday newspapers are so thick these days that no one can read completely through many of the Sunday editions (the Sunday *New York Times* is an example), this seeming difficulty is more than overcome by the *sharp departmentalization* of Sunday newspapers. Each family member tends to focus on different sections.

Tied in with the departmentalization is the *longer sales power* of Sunday newspapers. A special travel section, garden section, home building and accessories section, or automotive section will be retained for reference by Sunday newspaper readers. Sales resulting from these sections might come long after the reading of the section. In this respect the Sunday newspaper has one of the magazine's characteristics—long life.

Another attribute of the magazine possessed by Sunday newspapers is the *offering of first-rate color* in the magazine or supplement sections. These sections, almost always printed by rotogravure, are produced outside the newspaper plant and offer both local and national advertisers the kind of color reproduction that is not available except through the preprints described previously.

Most advertisers have found the Sunday newspaper an especially *good medium for mail-order selling*, especially in the case of big-city department stores that like the additional out-of-the-city circulation that reaches potential mail-order buyers who cannot shop personally but who like to buy from well-known stores even if it must be by mail.

Traditionally retailers expected to sell merchandise advertised on Sunday during the following week. Many retailers now open on Sunday, especially during holiday buying seasons. Many consumers now spend a Sunday afternoon in a shopping mall, combining family shopping and pleasure.

THE POPULAR TABLOID

Discussion in this text has centered on standard newspapers—those with eight columns. Since out of hundreds of daily newspapers only around 50 are tabloids, most of the advertisers' attention is centered on standard newspapers, too.

Yet tabloid newspapers, which are usually very lively and hard-hitting newspapers, are a force to be reckoned with because of their vitality and, in many cases, because of their big circulation. The country's largest-circulation newspaper, for example, is a tabloid, the *New York Daily News.*

Standard size of the tabloid is 5 columns by 200 lines, in contrast to the standard newspaper of 6 to 8 columns and 300 lines depth.

SYNDICATED SUNDAY SUPPLEMENTS AND SUNDAY MAGAZINES

At one time the Sunday supplements represented yellow journalism at its worst. Their content was made up of pseudoscientific articles and of intimate glimpses into the seamy lives of famous or notorious individuals. Much of the advertising in the supplements was of the same low character as the feature material.

Over the years, however, the supplements have become more like general consumer magazines. Today supplements are an attractive advertising medium for the advertising of many highly regarded products.

People connected with supplements much prefer that they be called magazines, a terminology that completely divorces such publications from the stigma once attached to Sunday supplements. Despite the fact that most advertising men still use the word "supplements," these publications are officially called "newspaper-distributed magazines" and are so listed in both the newspaper section of Standard Rate & Data Service and the magazine section of this same reference source.

For the marketer who wants advertising to be exposed to dense population groups in urban areas, the syndicated supplement offers one of the very best means of achieving such coverage. Among the printed media, these publications provide circulation that ranks them close to the top. *Parade*, to take an example, has consistently been among the top ten of the printed media in terms of people reached. This circulation, furthermore, is right where many companies want it, in the cities and the suburbs where advertisers have their best distribution.

In addition to the conventional supplements there are Sunday magazines that are locally owned and edited. Unlike the national supplements, these magazines contain local news and local advertising, along with the national advertising. Many of the newspapers offering such magazines have participated in a national network which is called "Sunday magazines." Total circulation of this group is greater than that of any supplement such as *Parade*. While the individual newspaper magazines have a strong local appeal, they lack the prestige of the big supplement. On the other hand, they are liked by the bigger local advertisers, such as department stores or the big furniture stores, and they are heavily supported by these organizations. Because their rates are high for most local advertisers, smaller retailers do not use them extensively.

NEWSPAPER NETWORKS

Ever since the first radio network and, subsequently, the first television network, it has been the dream of newspapers to organize a strong network of newspapers that would compete with the broadcast media. One of the important purposes of such a network would be to make newspapers an easier medium to use than at present, when each newspaper represents an individual purchase by the advertiser.

Most ambitious of all newspaper network attempts was the forming in the mid-1940's of the American Newspaper Advertising Network (ANAN), which was composed of about 50 metropolitan newspapers and an additional 100 newspapers located in smaller towns.

This network caused great excitement in the newspaper field and among some advertisers. It seemed as if the network offered many pluses to national and regional advertisers because it would simplify billing, would cut down overhead, and would offer a package deal that would compete strongly with the broadcast media.

Unfortunately, amidst much bickering and ill-feeling, the ANAN died in 1949. Chief criticism of the network was that it destroyed newspaper advertising's flexibility. This charge was made both by newspapers and by advertisers. Advertisers, in particular, said that the network concept interfered with the market-by-market selection of newspapers that enables newspaper schedules to match exactly their distribution plans.

Another sore point was one that has been mentioned before in this text—the crazy pattern of different rates charged by newspapers. Because newspapers operate in a highly individualistic manner, there was nothing uniform about the rates charged by the various newspapers belonging to the network.

Newspaper 1

Another effort was made to offer advertisers the advantages of a group buy of newspaper advertising through Newspaper 1 (now defunct), made up in 1963 of 30 large-circulation newspapers with a total circulation of approximately 30 million.

One of the principal objectives of the group members was to supply research and marketing information to advertisers and their advertising agencies. Also, the group showed advertisers not only how newspapers could compete with television and magazines but also how they could be used in combination with other media in order to obtain the best "media mix."

NEWSPAPERS ADD COLOR

Run-of-Paper Color

Each year more newspapers throughout the country offer ROP color. Today slightly more than 90 percent of all daily newspapers offer black and white and one color; 85 percent offer black and white and three colors. "ROP" is a newspaper abbreviation for "run-of-paper," meaning that the advertising material, color or otherwise, can be put anywhere in the newspaper.

Yet, despite the growth of newspaper color advertising, great masses of readers have either seen no color advertising or do not see it on a regular basis in their newspapers. Numbers of small newspapers do not offer color advertising, and even very large newspapers sometimes are without ROP color. Some New

York City newspapers, for example, have only recently "broken the color lines"—that is, have begun to offer color to advertisers. Other New York newspapers still do not offer ROP color.

Lack of color opportunity in newspaper advertising has been a serious drawback to many advertisers who depend upon color to sell their goods, such as national manufacturers who need color for package identification, or retail advertisers who need it for selling women's clothing, drapes, rugs, and countless other items.

There is no doubt that newspaper color not only attracts attention to advertisements but also sells merchandise, especially when the product is one that can actually be shown better in color than in black and white. Thus to advertisers color can be a great boon, and for newspapers it can be a great moneymaker.

Yet, despite the appeal of color advertising to the advertisers and the newspapers themselves, there have been serious limitations that have hampered the growth of newspaper color advertising.

From the newspapers' standpoint, color has two drawbacks:

(1) It requires the acquisition of expensive color equipment—presses and other equipment which, in the case of big newspapers, can run into millions of dollars.

(2) It is relatively messy in production, and furthermore, it requires considerably more care and makeready time than black-and-white advertising.

Advertisers, for their part, have had these criticisms of newspaper color:

(1) It costs more. This has already been discussed insofar as newspaper rates are concerned. In addition, there is extra cost in the color plates that must be prepared for printing. Even the artwork will usually be more expensive.

(2) Bigger space units are required. Newspapers will not run small advertisements in color. This fact does not bother the bigger advertisers, but it stops small advertisers almost completely from using newspapera color advertising.

(3) Some newspapers do not offer color every day nor in every section of the newspaper. There are a number of newspapers that have "color" days when color advertising may be run. Still others offer color just in certain sections of the newspaper. Others do not offer full color.

(4) Reproduction is poor. For many advertisers this is the most serious complaint about newspaper color. Although there are some newspapers that offer good color reproduction—although none of it is truly comparable with that offered by high-grade magazines—there are too many that run color advertising that is disappointing to hopeful advertisers. Greens may be a bilious yellow, or reds may be pink, or rich blues may become pale blue. Colors are too often "out of register," which means that the color areas do not match the illustrations. The color for lips, in such instances, may appear just below or just above where it is supposed to be.

Comic page advertisement.

Cheerful, active and aimed directly at young readers, this advertisement on the Sunday comics page is typical of such advertisements.

COLOR SUGGESTIONS

Preprints

Almost all newspapermen and newspaper advertisers have yearned for color advertising in newspapers that would rival that appearing in magazines. As pointed out, however, ROP newspaper color, despite never-ceasing efforts by the newspaper industry, has always lacked the quality of magazine color and probably always will.

An answer sems to have been found in preprints—at least where the quality of reproduction is concerned—even though the costs are disturbing.

A preprint is a full-page, four-color advertisement of magazine quality that is an actual part of a daily newspaper. This is unlike an "insert," which requires that presses be stopped in order to allow it to be inserted in the regular newspaper.

Preprints are printed in outside printing plants and come to a newspaper on rolls with one side blank. Fed into the presses to print the page of the reverse side, the preprint, usually produced by rotogravure printing, comes as a regular part of the paper. In contrast, of course, ROP color is printed on regular newsprint paper, to the detriment of the color reproduction.

Spectacolor Printing

One of the interesting developments in newspaper color advertising is Spectacolor, a superior form of rotogravure preprinting that enables newspapers to offer color and printing quality formerly available only in quality magazines. Spectacolor advertisements are designed much like other advertisements and are printed on a long roll of paper. An electronic sensor on printing presses cuts the paper to include the full advertisement centered on the page.

Another color process used by newspapers is called Hi-Fi color. Over 90 percent of daily newspapers offer Hi-Fi. Hi-Fi advertisements are designed like wallpaper. No matter where the paper is cut, consumers will see the complete advertised message.

Spot Advertising

ROP color, preprints, and other new newspaper techniques are evidence of the newspapers' efforts to maintain their competitive position. Another such development is found in newspaper spot programs for national advertisers. The term "spots" refers to the practice of running a number of small advertisements in a single issue of a newspaper. These programs are especially desirable for advertisers who wish to saturate a market with advertising messages. Under the plans now being offered, the advertiser can use spots in newspaper advertising the way spots are used in radio or television.

Advertisers most likely to use spot newspaper advertising are those with limited advertising budgets who want to stretch them by getting more advertising frequency, and by those who use large-space advertising and employ small advertisements to supplement the bigger advertisements.

Readership studies indicate that spot advertising offers advertisers a chance to reach the majority of readers again and again.

WEEKLIES

In terms of sheer numbers, the weekly (and sometimes semiweekly) newspapers overwhelm the daily newspapers, with around 10,000 such newspapers. Circulation is another story, however, since the 10,000 weeklies have a total circulation of less than half that of the dailies.

In the last 50 years there have been great changes in the weekly newspaper picture. Once the weekly was primarily a country newspaper that reflected rural life, with its news material consisting of the everyday doings of farm folk or of the small towns in which they were located. As the farm population has dwindled, along with the small towns, so have the country weeklies.

Today's weeklies fall mostly into three groups: suburban weeklies, country weeklies, and neighborhood weeklies (in sections of big cities).

There can be great differences in weeklies. One may have slick, coated paper stock that provides fine reproduction for the smart metropolitan stores it services. Such a suburban weekly is a far cry from a struggling rural weekly that does the best it can with cheap paper stock, limited resources, a broken-down press, and shrinking circulation.

Suburban Weeklies

As city populations migrated to the suburbs, a whole new pattern of living evolved that has had profound effects on the weekly newspapers. As suburbs grew in population, existing stores expanded and new stores sprang up. Many branches of big-city stores have opened in the suburbs to serve old and new customers. Frequently these branches have settled down in the big shopping centers that dot the surrounding areas of big cities.

Suburban stores now serve a large, still growing and often affluent segment of the population. Estimates indicate almost 60 percent of America's effective buying income is now suburban income. There is no more optimistic argument for the continued growth and influence of the suburban press.

To serve this greatly expanded population, the old weeklies have increased their advertising and their circulation; in addition, many new weeklies have been started. If the central city newspaper is strong and aggressive, it will continue to be the chief shopping aid for ex-city dwellers who have moved out of the city, but who still shop there. Sometimes it is also an important shopping medium for those who shop in the suburbs. It accomplishes this by having special suburban editions.

In many areas, however, the weeklies have become the chief shopping medium for those persons who do most of their shopping in suburban shopping centers.

Most weeklies obtain the big bulk of their advertising from local businesses. While weeklies would like to obtain much more national advertising, the national advertisers have not been a big factor in weekly advertising revenue. Usually about 75 to 80 percent of a weekly newspaper's advertising will be local display. The ordinary weekly does well, on the other hand, to obtain 10 percent of advertising linage from national advertisers. As for classified advertising, this may run around 10 percent also for numerous weeklies, but more aggressive weeklies may increase that percentage greatly. As in the case of daily newspapers, the better published, more prosperous weeklies can very often be identified by large classified advertising sections, sometimes amounting to pages.

Neighborhood Weeklies

In a number of big cities there are weeklies to serve the interests of their thickly populated neighborhood sections. These papers carry a small amount of very localized news and a large amount of advertising from neighborhood merchants who cannot afford to advertise in city-wide newspapers, and who probably would not advertise in them if they could afford to do so, because most of the big newspaper's circulation would be wasted.

Sometimes one publisher will put out a number of neighborhood weeklies (often called "community weeklies") out of one plant. The news reporters will cover "beats" in each of the neighborhoods and advertising salespeople will follow the same procedure. In appearance, all the newspapers will look alike, and all will have similar designations, such as *Maplewood News, Ravenswood News,* and so forth. Each day will see the publishing of one of these newspapers, until at the end of the week each section will have its newspaper to use for shopping.

DAILY OR WEEKLY?

The whole pace of the usual weekly newspaper is more leisurely. There is less pressure in getting the news and advertising, and in making up the paper. There is less pressure in reading. The newspaper is likely to be read more slowly, and usually there is less to read, a factor that makes for more intensive readership of news and advertising matter. A weekly newspaper is retained longer around the house than are most daily newspapers, which succeed themselves so quickly.

Advertising Subject Matter May Be Different

In rural weeklies, farm subjects may predominate. Much advertising will concern farm feeds, farm machinery, and other agricultural products. In either the suburban or city weeklies, while there is no farm advertising, there may be absolutely no national advertising or very little. Likewise, especially in the city community newspapers, there may be many "puff" stories, or publicity stories that appear in the news columns as regular news stories but which, in reality, are simply advertisements in news form. These stories are often the price the editor must pay for getting the advertisers to run paid display advertising.

Reproduction Quality Is Uncertain

As indicated at the beginning of this section on weekly newspapers, here and there a weekly newspaper will be found that has superb reproduction because of the expensive paper it uses and the fine press equipment in its back shop. Unfortunately, there are hundreds of weekly newspapers that do a very bad job of reproducing advertising, especially any advertising that uses photographic illustrations. Ancient flat-bed presses are found in many of these newspapers. Since paper costs are one of the greatest expenses in the operating of a newspaper, the weekly newspaper is likely to be printed on cheap, coarse paper. To the readers, part of the charm of the weekly, especially the country weekly, is its crude, homespun character. This charm is lost on advertisers who see their advertisements reproduced badly.

The advertiser who must use the weekly newspaper anticipates production problems. The advertiser will avoid halftone illustrations, using line drawings instead. The advertiser may also have an outside typesetter make the advertisements in advance in either mat or plate form. These premade advertisements are then given to the weekly newspaper.

Few Weeklies Are ABC-Audited

Many advertising agencies are reluctant to recommend weekly newspapers to advertisers because so few of the newspapers are audited. Some weeklies have been found to use grossly inaccurate circulation figures. Also, weekly newspaper publishers are often uninformed about the size and composition of their market.

"SHOPPERS"

Throughout the United States, in both, cities and suburbs, there are many publications that are mailed free to every person in the area. These publications, often called "throwaways" by their contemptuous competitors, the regular newspapers, contain nothing but advertising, though in some cases they make a gesture of supplying news, usually in very small amounts.

Some of these publications are supported almost entirely (in the big city) by the large downtown department stores. In other cases the advertising will represent a cross section of the local advertisers.

"Shoppers" are often read with real interest. Readership differs from that of the regular newspaper, where reading the news comes first and reading the advertisements comes second. The shopper is designed solely to tell what goods are being offered and nothing else.

PENNYSAVERS

A special form of shopper has had strong success around the United States. This is the "Pennysaver," a weekly publication composed entirely of advertising and very often turned out on newsprint stock by the mimeograph process. If not mimeographed, Pennysavers are usually produced by offset printing.

Pennysavers are mailed to all the homes in their districts. They have flourished especially well in small towns or suburban towns that do not have weekly newspapers, or that have weak weekly newspapers. Strong readership and complete coverage of the market are the two attributes Pennysavers have to offer, and these attributes have been well received by local advertisers, who, in many areas, have turned from the weekly newspapers and have given the bulk of their advertising to the Pennysavers. Competition has become so deadly for many weekly newspapers that they have frequently begun publishing Pennysavers to supplement their newspapers.

Advertising content is made up largely of classified advertisements, which to persons reading Pennysavers are so interesting that they take the place of the news stories of the conventional newspapers. Classified advertisements cause readers to go all the way through the Pennysavers. Along the way, the display advertisements will also be read. Most display advertisers sign half-year or yearly contracts for their space units.

"SPECIAL" EDITIONS

Anyone who has bought local advertising space must decide what to do about special edition advertising. To retailers it seems that every other day the newspaper space salespeople are making enthusiastic sales talks for the latest "special."

For the advertiser with a closely worked-out budget, putting advertisements in special editions may divert money planned for use to achieve other advertising goals. For the newspaper advertising department, special editions create excitement, sell extra linage, and give the salespeople something new to present to advertisers. Typical events that call for special editions are:

Retail rate card for good-sized newspaper.

On the cover page of this local rate card, we have the rate expressed in agate lines and in column inches. Also, note the bulk rates given to advertisers who use a big volume of advertising in a 12-month period.

Advertising Regulations

COPY

All advertising copy is subject to the approval of the Advertising Manager. The Buffalo Evening News reserves the right to alter or reject any copy. All orders are subject in all respects to The News rules on content of advertising matter, make-up and availability of advertising space.

PRINTED PAGE AND COLUMN SIZES

Width of column 11 picas. Depth of column 308 agate lines or 22 inches. Eight columns to the page. Full page contains 2464 agate lines.

For display advertisements on Classified page contact Retail Advertising Department.

Ads must be at least as many inches deep as columns wide.

Copy over 280 lines deep will be set 308 lines. Minimum for step-down layout is 132 column inches.

The advertiser shall designate the width in columns and exact depth in lines or inches. The advertisement will be published and billed in space ordered, measuring from cut-off rule to cut-off rule.

Double trucks consist of two full depth pages using gutter.

Advertisements requested from the center fold on facing pages must be full depth of page and at least seven columns on the right hand page.

PRINTING MATERIAL

Velox prints or similar material suitable for cold type reproduction should be used. Do not use extreme black type, black or reverse cuts; use Benday instead. Halftone screen required, 65-line.

CORRECTIONS AND CANCELLATIONS

Deadline for cancellations and size changes is 12 noon of day preceding publication, except for special or advance sections. (Wednesday noon for TV Topics).

Proofs will be furnished if copy is received in accordance with The News established proof service schedule.

Alteration in copy after first corrected proof has been furnished, and advertisements set and canceled before insertion are subject to a charge for composition.

There are no guarantees covering composition, correction, service, proof delivery, position or reproduction of advertisements.

NO CHANGES ON DAY OF PUBLICATION

374-1176A

HENRY Z. URBAN
President and Publisher

WILLIAM M. FALLIS
Vice President

CHARLES L. SANDS
Manager, Retail Advertising

BUFFALO EVENING NEWS

Western New York's Great Newspaper

RETAIL RATE CARD

Card 33-Rates effective February 14, 1977

Includes R. O. P. Color, Hi-Fi and SpectaColor; Week-End Edition Color Comics and TV Topics

Retail Display Advertising Rates

RETAIL STORES

These rates apply to establishments within the Buffalo 'RETAIL RATE AREA' advertising a variety of merchandise or services available to the general public through their own retail outlet or outlets. Map available upon request. Rates are net.

	Agate Line	Column Inch
Single or occasional insertions	$1.55	$21.70
Regular schedule totaling less than 10,000 lines within one year	1.01	14.14
10,000 lines within one year	97c	13.58
25,000 lines within one year	93c	13.02
50,000 lines within one year	90c	12.60
Retail stores outside Buffalo area	$1.55	21.70

BULK RATES — Available to a retail store using required number of lines within a pre-determined 12-month period.

First 100,000 lines	90c	12.60
Next 400,000 lines	89½c	12.53
All over 500,000 lines	89c	12.46

NOTE: Retail rates also apply to Buffalo area churches announcing regular services; recognized charities; schools offering resident instructions in Buffalo area; real estate offerings of residential property; restaurants not offering entertainment or dancing.

(1) Special shows. If the town has a big convention hall, there may be many events throughout the year which the newspaper will urge advertisers to affiliate with in their advertisements. These can be auto shows, home-building shows, and many others.

(2) Special merchandising events. These would include Dollar Days, Downtown Days, and Sidewalk Sale days.

(3) Community events. Regattas, big football games, and soapbox derbies fall in this category.

(4) Anniversaries. An outstanding example of this is any centennial celebration.

In some cases, newspapers block off space for advertisers on a number of pages devoted solely to advertising. The spaces will be in different-sized units. Usually the cost will be lower than normal for these units, but at the same time, the retailer's identity will be submerged in a complete page of advertisements. There is no adjacent news material.

Another technique is to devote an entire section, such as a special garden section, to news material and advertising that concerns the one topic. Although these sections will be read by the real enthusiasts, they are likely to be ignored entirely by the ordinary newspaper reader. Also, with so many advertisements, the advertiser often tends to become "lost" unless using large space advertisements.

Advertisers, despite pressures from newspaper salespeople, who understandably want to sell more advertising space, should use special-edition advertising sparingly. The low cost of space is not a bargain if the retailer's advertisement is lumped in with similar advertisements or if the retailer is distracted from investing in advertising to reach primary objectives.

REACHING READERS THROUGH ADVERTISING

How many readers see the retailer's advertisements? The retailer cannot answer this question. Rather, the retailer depends on sales to indicate advertisement readership. Still, the reader prefers some locations and positions in the newspaper to others.

The "Best" Location

First of all, here is what *advertisers* rather generally think about the location of advertisements:

(1) Advertisements on right-hand pages are better read than those on left-hand pages (or sometimes vice versa).

(2) Advertisements below the fold are not so well read as those above the fold.

(3) Advertisements at the back of the newspaper have relatively poor readership. (In the case of larger newspapers, advertisers clamor to be "forward of page 7" because of the tradition that readership falls off after this page. Many of these same advertisers demand page 3 positions for their advertisements).

Specialized products, such as beer and sports equipment, need to be placed in a special section to attain full effectiveness.

Now to take up each of the issues just raised.

Right-hand versus left-hand. Psychologists tell us that the natural eye movement in looking at two advertisements is first toward the left. This follows the ordinary reading habit of glancing first at the upper left area of printed material. Perhaps the foregoing will seem to favor the left-hand page. Yet many newspaper advertisers prefer right-hand pages—insist on them, in fact.

In reality, when an advertisement is on the right side, the chances for dollar volume are just as good as if it were on the left side; others give that edge to the right side. Consensus of investigators is that, for obtaining results from newspaper advertising, there is no significant difference between left-hand and right-hand pages.

Above or below the fold. Advertisers worry too much about this point. For one thing, the pyramid style of page makeup makes it certain that big advertisements will be at the bottom of the page. Size alone will keep them from being unnoticed even if they are at the bottom. Then, too, news or feature material usually touches every advertisement, no matter where the latter is located. Such reading material helps draw readers to advertisements below the fold.

Forward or back of page 7. Newspapers can take just so many advertisements in one section. As one newspaper man has said ruefully, "We'd have nothing but page 3's to make room for all the advertisers who want page 3 position, or who must be forward of page 7."

Every advertiser cannot be in the front of the newspaper. Since almost everyone wants to be, the newspapers for years have been battling this point with angry advertisers. Yet readership studies have shown consistent reading throughout newspapers, and this whether newspapers have a few pages or many pages.

Pulling power of advertising and the attraction of news material create this rather even distribution of reading throughout a newspaper. A position in the front of the newspaper is no ticket to high readership, nor is a position toward the back doomed to light readership. If newspapers could not deliver readership beyond page 7, there would be no newspapers beyond that size.

Placing specialized products. Many advertisers pay special-position space rates to get their advertisements on the sports page, or in the women's section. Often the advertiser is wasting money. First of all, if newspaper readership is rather even throughout the newspaper, what difference does it make whether an advertisement is in one part or another?

An objection to placing the advertisement ROP might be: "But I'm running a sports shop (or a dress shop). It seems to me to make sense to advertise my goods to an interested audience on the sports page (or in the women's section)."

Perhaps it will in either of these cases. Yet this specialized advertising should be tried in the regular news section, too. If there is no real difference in results, a premium should not be paid to have advertisements placed in a special position.

Misplaced Emphasis. Retailers will continue to believe that their advertisements reach more readers when on the left- or right-hand page, or above or

Volume fashion advertisement in newspaper.

The news quality of newspaper advertising is especially important in fashion advertising. Fashion-conscious readers eagerly seek news about the latest styles. Most fashion magazines publish once a month; the daily display of fashion merchandise in newspapers moves great quantities of fashion goods.

Once upon a time there was a dress with a full sweeping skirt and soft billowy sleeves

A dress that made every girl who wore it feel exactly how she had always wanted to feel. It was made of ruffles and bows and bright peasant prints that liked to dance in the sun. Well, that same very happily-ever-after dress can be yours for the asking. Red and gold print of polyester and cotton in jr. sizes 5-13 by Jody of California **$44**

jr. dresses 94 — all may co stores

below the fold. Retailers will insist that their advertisements be in the first few pages of the newspaper, and some research suggests advertisements in the first pages will reach about 5 percent more readers than the same advertisement placed elsewhere. The slight falloff in advertisement readership at the end of the newspaper may be due to the specialized content, often financial or classified advertisements.

What Is Important? Advertisers are well aware that advertisement effectiveness varies by product interest and editorial environment. Men tend to read tire advertisements more than women. Place tire advertisements in the sports section of the newspaper, and this is probably the optimum position for such advertisements. For high readership, women's cosmetics advertisements will do well in the Women's or Life Style section.

Advertisers are also aware that readership increases as the size of the newspaper advertisement increases. The increase, however, is not proportional to the increase in size. A full-page newspaper advertisement may have higher readership than a half-page advertisement, but not twice the readership.

Despite production problems, ROP color advertisements are growing in number. Increasingly, research findings indicate color is so effective in attracting attention that it is worth the additional cost.

The single most important factor influencing newspaper advertising effectiveness is the content. Creative advertisements have doubled readership scores of typical newspaper advertisements.

Fixed Positions

The fixed position (which the advertiser has permanently) saves readers the bother of hunting for the advertiser's advertisements. It gives a feeling of permanency to advertising. The fixed-position advertising becomes a looked-for feature, like other items that run regularly in the same locations in the newspaper—the columnists, the comic strips, the picture pages, and the weather report.

Although the foregoing paints an attractive picture for the fixed positions, the chances are strong that a fixed position will not be available to the average local advertiser and will never be available to a national advertiser. A newspaper simply cannot give fixed positions liberally, if at all. Some newspapers say "No" to all requests for fixed positions. Some charge extra for such positions. Others will give them without extra charge but only to consistent, day-by-day, year-after-year advertisers— and they must be large-space advertisers at that. Even then, the position is given without charge only after the advertiser has been with the newspaper for years in the same position.

In such cases as the latter, the maximum number of fixed-position advertisers in any given newspaper would probably be not more than three to six. Normally, however, the retailer will do just as well anywhere in the newspaper, whether the product or service is, or is not, specialized or the advertisements are large or small.

THE "COOPERATIVE" ADVANTAGE

When a national advertiser shares space costs with a retailer, both may benefit. The practice, called cooperative advertising, means that the retailer buys newspaper space at the lower local or retail advertising rate and runs an advertisement for the national manufacturer's product tied to the local retail establishment. The retailer and the manufacturer both receive bills from the newspaper after the advertisement is run. The manufacturer then pays a portion of the space cost.

There are problems with cooperative advertising. The national manufacturer and the retailer for example, share some, but not all, advertising objectives. Cooperative advertising is used, however, because it offers advantages to both parties. For example, assume the retail space rate is 50 percent of the national rate (actually, it is somewhat more). Next assume the retailer and the national manufacturer each pay half the cost of the retail space the retailer buys to advertise the national manufacturer's product. Under such an arrangement and with the manufacturer's contribution, the retailer can buy twice the advertising space for the same amount of money.

Note also that the national manufacturer pays half the cost of the retail advertisement, which in turn costs half as much as what the national manufacturer would pay for the same space at the national rate.

The mutual advantages—simply from a cost standpoint—provide a strong bond for retailers and national manufacturers.

Newspaper people tend to approve of cooperative advertising. Almost all newspapers obtain extra revenue from cooperative advertising. Cooperative advertising linage may run all the way from 5 to 20 percent, though the upper figure is quite unusual.

Some of the reasons why cooperative advertising is looked upon favorably by newspapers are as follows:

(1) Offers quality advertising, often better than that supplied by the retailer's own advertising department. Much cooperative advertising is supplied in mat or proof form by the manufacturer. Such advertisements are usually clean and well laid out.

(2) Makes more consistent advertisers out of retailers. To earn certain cooperative discounts, the manufacturer's dealer must run a specified amount of linage within a time period. Infrequent advertisers may become steadier advertisers because of this inducement.

(3) Represents "extra" revenue in the case of some retailers. Many retailers continue with their regular advertising program. Their cooperative advertising is on top of the usual advertising.

Newspaper complaints about cooperative advertising are usually confined to the paperwork involved. Newspapers must provide manufacturers with checking copies (the actual page on which the advertisement is run) or affidavits that the advertising was actually run. The newspaper must also bill the manufacturer as well as the retailer.

Some newspaper people are concerned that extensive cooperative advertising means manufacturers cut back on their national advertisements in newspapers. Since the national rate is far higher than the retail rate paid for cooperative advertising, a newspaper may lose some revenue in this way. The prevailing opinion, however, is that a newspaper obtains increased revenue from cooperative advertising that will more than offset any possible loss from national advertising revenue.

DEALER TIE-INS

Dealers often "tie-in" with national advertising by running their own advertisements for the advertised product. These will appear next to the national advertisement, or on another page of the issue in which the national advertisement appears.

Sometimes retailers may not be able to afford to run their own tie-in advertisements. Frequently, in such cses, they will have their names included in a listing next to the national advertisement. This listing will, of course, enable readers to determine whether their favorite stores carry the advertiser's product.

Usually a national advertiser with dealer listings will be large and will attract substantial reader attention and interest. Even more attention is generated if other tie-in advertisements of local advertisers are scattered throughout the newspaper.

A major difference between tie-in advertising and cooperative advertising is that tie-in advertising is placed and paid for at the retail rates by dealers and retailers. The manufacturer does not share the cost of tie-in advertisements.

Preparation and placement of manufacturer tie-in campaigns are worked out between the manufacturer and its advertising agency. Dealers and distributors are notified about the advertisement content and size, the media to be used, and the dates the advertisements are to be run. Dealers are invited to tie in their advertising with that of the national advertiser. The media selected often are urged to encourage retailer and local dealer participation.

KEEPING UP WITH THE "FUNNIES"

Readership studies for years have shown consistently that the comics are among the best-read parts of any newspaper. Consistently, too, these figures have shown that men read comics somewhat more than women.

Advertisers have taken advantage of this high readership by tying in daily and Sunday advertising with comic pages. On Sunday these advertisements are most often set up in comic panel style, using the same humorous or adventure approach of the comics themselves.

A good many of these are written with extreme simplicity, showing first a problem exists and then how the use of the advertised product solves the problem. (The young man has no dates, learns he has bad breath—or might have—buys a mouthwash, and soon he has many dates with attractive young women). It is easy to make fun of such advertisements but many frequently produce outstanding results.

Many daily newspapers sell advertising space on the comic pages. In this case they are not comic strips or panels but conventional advertisements, usually for low-price items of high appeal. A number of advertisers have reported outstanding results from these advertisements. Usually advertising space is limited in these sections, and those advertisers who are found in the sections very often have fixed positions which they almost never relinquish.

One great advantage of a comic page location for an advertiser is that readership is both high and loyal. Readers follow the antics of their favorite comic strips. High and steady readership is reflected in the consistently good response to advertisements in comic sections.

We've caught it for you

TWA

Visit our TWA Travel Booth and register for a TWA Getaway Vacation for two to sunny California. *A winner each store! Winner also receives a Samsonite tote.* **Today Downtown (Thursday Glendale) demonstrations** *in Housewares! 12:00-12:30 Cantonese Wok Cooking, 12:30-1:00 coffee beans and serving pieces, 1:00-1:30 Nordic Ware and Mexican foods.* **Tomorrow** *Downtown at Date at 12,* **meet Helen Rose,** *fashion designer to the*

stars who will autograph her book, "Just Make Them Beautiful". Also tomorrow at "Date", Third Floor, the California **designer, Janor,** *showing her new separates' looks. For the children tomorrow, the lovable* **Magic Mountain Trolls,** *meet them at Lafayette Square 11:00-12:00, Glendale 3:00-4:00, and Washington Square 6:00-7:00. And at Greenwood tomorrow (Downtown Thursday, Friday Lafayette Square, Glendale and Washington Square Saturday) 11:00-2:00 in Housewares; Oster Juice Maker, Farbers new Food Processor and Shish-ka-bobs On the Rotisserie, Mirro Silver Stone Cookware, Mexican omelette, Imperial knives, and Cuisanart®.*

MAKING THE CAMPAIGN WORK

In any extensive advertising campaign certain decisions and actions will precede the actual scheduling and running of the newspaper advertisements. Some of these are:

(1) Determining the extent of market coverage and studying each market to determine in general the weight of advertising to be assigned to these individual markets.

(2) Arranging for distribution through distributors and dealers by supplying them with adequate stocks of the goods to be advertised.

(3) Deciding how much to invest in advertising. This will involve assigning the needed budget and establishing in general the size of advertisements and the frequency with which advertising will be run.

(4) Setting the copy theme, preparing the advertisements, and sending them to the newspapers in the form of mats, or plastic or metal plates.

After these, and other considerations, the advertiser will get down to the specifics of scheduling the advertisements.

Scheduling the Advertisements

When analyzing the costs of newspaper advertising space size and frequency, the advertiser frequently realizes that there are not enough dollars available for the advertising job. What the advertiser often does then is develop several different schedules for a campaign, classifying them as A, B, and C. These schedules represent priorities, usually allocated according to the size of the city and the circulation of the newspaper to be used. This procedure is followed because of the larger sales potential in bigger markets. Also, smaller circulation newspapers in smaller cities frequently have higher milline rates. The smaller the market and the higher the cost of reaching the market, the lower the priority given to the market by the advertiser.

Example of Scheduling

An advertiser decides that the best newspaper in each city of more than 100,000 is to get an *A* schedule; remaining newspapers in those markets are to get a *B* schedule.

Each leading newspaper in each city of 25,000 to 100,000 will be assigned a *B* schedule; other newspapers in those markets will get a *C* schedule.

Lastly, all newspapers in towns of under 25,000 will get a *C* schedule.

If the schedules are prepared on the basis of space units of the same size for all newspapers, with only reduced frequency for some newspapers, the schedules will run like this:

A schedule:	280 lines	26 times
B schedule:	280 lines	20 times
C schedule:	180 lines	13 times

If the schedules are based on reduced space units but with the same frequency, the schedule will run like this:

A schedule:	280 lines	26 times
B schedule:	210 lines	26 times
C schedule:	140 lines	26 times

Both frequency and size of advertisements can be reduced if needed. Each advertising campaign requires individual decisions on these points.

PROVIDING NEWSPAPER ADVERTISING DATA

Many organizations have been established to provide advertisers with data relating to newspapers. Some of these are:

Audit Bureau of Circulations. This organization, which verifies circulation of member publications, serves not only newspapers but other publications as well. Operated by advertisers, advertising agencies, and publishers, the ABC audits circulation report of nearly all daily newspapers, plus many weeklies. Two reports are given: (a) The Publisher's Statement, covering average circulation for each 6-month period. (b) The Audit Report, covering average circulation for a year.

The information in these reports helps advertisers by telling them the amount of circulation to be found in each city and town covered by the newspapers on their advertising schedules. Also, as mentioned earlier in this text, the ABC indicates whether this circulation is obtained without artificial forcing devices.

Newspaper Advertising Bureau, Inc. Benefiting from membership in the bureau are daily newspapers in the United States and Canada. Its function if twofold:

(1) To develop effective use of newspaper advertising by supplying market analyses and research services to advertising agencies and national advertisers, and

(2) To give retail advertising planning helps to member newspaper staffs.

Through its Retail Services Department the bureau is especially helpful to retail display advertising departments and, indirectly, to the retailers they serve. This department provides case histories, help in budget planning, much material about proper timing and pricing of goods, monthly planning schedules, and much other material. This material, if used constantly and intelligently by newspaper staffs, should help them to increase retail advertising linage, and it should help retailers themselves to do a better job of advertising and merchandising.

Media Records. This is a newspaper advertising linage report published by an independent organization and released on a subscription basis to advertisers, advertising agencies, and publishers. Issued every three months, the reports give linage totals for several hundred newspapers in more than 100 cities, and, furthermore, it breaks these totals down into more than 151 classifications. Chief classifications are retail, general (national), automotive, financial, classified, and legal.

Advertisement stressing importance of food advertising to newspapers.

Supermarkets and other food advertisers are vital to daily newspapers. In smaller towns, a local newspaper can be dealt a grievous blow by the linage loss resulting from the departure of one or two supermarkets. Strength in food advertising is a mark of the vigorous newspaper. Thus, it is emphasized in this advertisement directed at media buyers who read *Advertising Age* magazine.

agency people

TLK boosts Birn to ceo; Brookbanks to Van Leeuwen

CHICAGO—Jerome F. Birn has been elected chief executive officer at Tatham-Laird & Kudner, succeeding Charles R. Standen, who will continue as chairman of the management committee. Mr. Birn, formerly chief operating officer, becomes the agency's fourth ceo in its 31-year history and the first

with a creative background. Mr. Birn joined the agency in 1955 and was promoted to creative director in Chicago during 1963, exec vp in 1968 and chief executive officer of the New York office in 1969. He was elected president in 1971 and returned to Chicago in 1975 as chief operating of-

ficer, a title he retains.

■ Ian Brookbanks has been named to the newly created post of senior vp-management supervisor for all accounts at Van Leeuwen Advertising, New York. Mr. Brookbanks joins Van Leeuwen from Young & Rubicam, where he served as a vp-account supervisor, handling several brands in the health care division of Johnson & Johnson. A native of England, Mr. Brookbanks began his career in Y&R's London office in 1964.

Other people moving:

William R. Hodus to new post of vp-communications, dealing with foreign governments and corporations for Doremus & Co., Washington. He had been assistant chief of protocol, U.S. State Department.

J. Fred Hedding Jr. to senior writer, Industrial Group, Meldrum & Fewsmith, Cleveland, from creative supervisor, McCann-Erickson.

J. Fred Hedding   R. C. Doerner

Russell C. Doerner to creative director from vp-associate creative director, D'Arcy-MacManus & Masius, St. Louis. At the New York office: **Bart Blum** to vp-creative services director, a new post, from vp-creative director. Also, **David Krutchik** to vp-associate creative director from vp-creative director. **Charles Blustain**, the agency's remaining vp-creative director, retains that title. **Betty Lev** to vp-research director from associate research director and **James Riley** to account supervisor from account exec.

Bob Reedy to creative supervisor from art supervisor and **Marilyn Lewis** to copy supervisor from copywriter, Needham, Harper & Steers, Chicago.

Alfred A. Duz to vp-group media, Ross Roy Inc., Detroit, from associate media director, D'Arcy-MacManus & Masius, Bloomfield Hills, Mich. Mr. Duz is succeeded by **Edward Coosaia**, formerly associate media supervisor, J. Walter Thompson Co., Dearborn, Mich.

Alex Jesudowich to senior art director, Webb & Athey, Richmond, Va., from art director, Humphrey, Browning, Boston.

Theodore S. Zwier to director of operations, a new post, William Eisner & Associates, Hales Corners, Wis., from vp-administration, Hurvis, Binzer, Churchill/-Van Brunt, Chicago.

Wally Griffin to assistant to the president, Givaudan Advertising, New York, a new post. Mr. Griffin, a former stage and tv performer, was producer of the Candlewood Theatre in Connecticut.

Marc Shenfield to copy chief, Smith/Greenland Inc., New York, a new post, from copywriter.

Harold Bennett to media director, William R. Biggs Associates, Kalamazoo, Mich., from associate media director, N W Ayer ABH, Chicago. Mr. Bennett replaces **Ralph Bachman**, senior media director, who is going into semi-retirement.

Robert D. Brandon to direc-

tor-merchandising, J. Walter Thompson Co., Atlanta, from vp, Einson Freeman Inc., a sales promotion and p.o.p. organization based in New York. Also at Thompson's Chicago office: **Jeffrey Palmer** to account supervisor from account exec, Needham, Harper & Steers.

Thomas E. Brauer to creative director, judy anderson & associates, Battle Creek, Mich., from free lance copywriter.

Walter M. Bagot to exec vp from senior vp-operations, Garrison, Jasper, Rose & Co., Indianapolis.

Reo Kanogawa to senior art director-department head, Ayer Baker, Seattle, from senior art director, Leo Burnett U.S.A., Chicago.

Harry Reingold to vp-account supervisor, Al Paul Lefton Co., New York, from vp, McGlone Nightingale Reingold & Spellman.

Kenneth J. Flint to copy supervisor, Lesly Associates, New York, from a similar post at E. T. Howard Advertising.

Donald W. Bolster, M. Jeffrey Holmes, Bruce N. Leonard and **George L. Stockman**, all to vp-management supervisors from vp-account supervisors, Horton, Church & Goff, Providence, R.I.

Robert Schancupp to copy supervisor, Keenan & McLaughlin, New York, from a similar post at McCaffrey & McCall.

Raymond F. Dundas to media supervisor, Weightman Inc., Phil-

adelphia, from a similar post at W. B. Doner & Co., Baltimore.

Robert Reed to vp-associate creative director, Sawdon & Bess, New York, from executive art director, succeeding **James Marks**, who has left the agency.

Pete Lustig to president and board member from senior vp, McColloch, Bryan, Cipriano, Miami, succeeding **Sam McColloch**, now chairman of the board.

Stephen C. Kahler to chief financial officer, a new post at BBDO International, New York, assuming duties relinquished by treasurer **John H. McQuade**, who will retire at the end of the year. Mr. Kahler had been manager of the corporate planning coordination division of the corporate planning department at Exxon Corp., New York.

ELECTED DIRECTORS

Terrence G. Parmelee, vp-account group supervisor, Meldrum & Fewsmith, Cleveland, and **Richard H. Herrmann**, vp-creative director, Detroit. #

These reports give a full picture of the kind of advertising appearing in each newspaper in each city covered. Especially useful to an advertiser is the chance to study the extent of newspaper advertising activity of competitors. The reports also give the opportunity to determine the relative standing (as an advertising medium) of each newspaper in a market.

Ayer Directory of Newspapers and Periodicals. Containing detailed information about almost every newspaper and periodical poublished in the United States, the *Ayer Directory* is sold to and used by advertisers, advertising agencies, and other interested organizations.

In addition to much data about newspapers and periodicals, the *Directory* furnishes maps and figures that give population, geographical location, industries, and other information indicating the size and importance of each town and city in the United States in which at least one newspaper or periodical is published. The *Directory* is especially useful for supplying information about weekly newspapers, since there is no other single source that gives so much information about these publications.

Standard Rate & Data Service (newspaper section). Issued in thick monthly volumes, this service supplies detailed information about the daily newspapers in the country and the same kind of information about a limited number of weekly newspapers. Published by a private company on a yearly subscription basis, the paperbound volumes are sold to advertisers and advertising agencies, which make constant use of them in arriving at media decisions and in scheduling media.

QUESTIONS

1. Why might space buyers analyze the press runs of major metropolitan newspapers?

2. What can you tell about a newspaper as an advertising medium when you study the newspaper?

3. What information about newspaper advertising is supplied by Media Records? What uses can you make of this information?

4. Why might an advertiser buy space in a morning and an evening newspaper in the same city when the advertiser knows many families receive both newspapers?

5. Why is the evening newspaper more likely to be considered a family newspaper than the morning newspaper?

6. Why has the Sunday newspaper become an even more desirable advertising medium in recent years?

7. What is a Sunday supplement?

8. What problems might be faced by the advertiser who uses ROP color in newspapers?

9. What is meant by "spot" advertising in newspapers?

10. What is meant by ABC-audited? What types of newspapers are unlikely to be audited?

11. What is meant by "fixed position"?

12. Why is cooperative advertising advantageous to the retailer? to the national manufacturer?

13. How does tie-in advertising differ from cooperative advertising?

14. Why might an advertiser develop different schedules for a campaign?

15. What types of information does each of the following organizations provide for newspaper advertisers?
    (1) Audit Bureau of Circulations
    (2) Newspaper Advertising Bureau
    (3) *Ayer Directory of Newspapers and Periodicals*
    (4) *Standard Rate & Data Service* (newspaper section)

(See Color Photo Section (pages 403-406) following page 410).

Public service advertising.

Advertising sells causes through the efforts of advertisers, their agencies and the media. This television commercial is typical of the thousands of public service advertisements contributed free by the advertising industry.

POLICEMAN: For more than two years now, people have been trying to get you to slow down to 55 miles an hour.

Down to the speed limit.

They've told you that slowing down will save millions of gallons of gasoline.

They've told you that slowing down saves thousands of lives and they've got the figures to prove it.

I think those are pretty good reasons.

Some of you obviously do, too. Because some of you have slowed down.

But an awful lot of people, for one reason or another haven't.

They seem to think the fifty-five mile an hour speed limit is something they can take or leave.

But it isn't. It's the law.

With tickets and fines and all the rest, just like any other law.

From where I sit, there's no way around it.

The fifty-five mile an hour speed limit can do a lot of positive things. And it's my job to make sure it gets a chance to work.

Not just because it's a good idea.
(SPEEDING CAR PASSES)

But because it's the law.
(CHASES SPEEDER)

It's not just a good idea. It's the law.

(Your message here)

:5 open end for local signature with live voice over.

Humorous television commercial with a serious message.

Humor can sometimes succeed in putting over a serious idea. This 60-second commercial aroused much interest and, at the same time, entertained viewers. Much of the action, of course, is not conveyed by the six frames of the photoboard.

MUSIC CARRIED THROUGHOUT COMMERCIAL.

ANNCR: People make monkeys of themselves every day.

Eating too much, smoking too much, drinking too much, not getting enough exercise.

Please don't monkey around with your health because keeping healthy is one way to control health care costs.

A job that together, we can do.

Your Blue Cross and Blue Shield Plans in Northeast Ohio.

Produced by Carr Liggett Advertising, Inc., for Blue Cross and Blue Shield in Northeast Ohio.

Straight-selling, long-copy advertisement.

If copy is written well and the product is interesting to large numbers of people, the writer will find that long copy may get far better readership than short copy. Such is the case here. Each spring millions of homeowners feel the urge to get back to nature and to have a good lawn. This advertisement, therefore will obtain fine readership. The long copy will be read eagerly.

The dandelion is one of nature's prettiest villains. It's not only good to eat, there was a time when people took it as medicine.

But here in Marysville, Ohio where we have our main grass research farms, it's just another weed.

In fact, it's a bully. It pushes the good grass out of the way and takes the food in the soil for itself. This is one weed that doesn't die every year. It's a tough perennial with roots that go down as far as two feet.

And that pretty yellow blossom turns into a white puffball full of seeds that the wind carries all over your lawn.

You can't stop dandelions from coming in, the way you can with crabgrass.

You have to get this pest to get rid of it. But it's easy to lick.

Leave one bit of its root and the dandelion will be back.

We'll get these dandelions out of your lawn and that's a promise.

And don't make it hard on yourself by trying to dig it out. Leave one bit of that root and back she'll come.

But just spend 30 minutes with your spreader and our Turf Builder® Plus 2.® Your dandelion population (and a lot of other actively growing weeds) will be on the way out in a matter of days. That's our promise.

And the Turf Builder in this is our own slow-release fertilizer. It will also feed your lawn for up to two months.

In fact, if you spend 30 minutes with our straight Turf Builder every couple of months — your grass will be so thick there just won't be much room for weeds. Good thick turf helps crowd weeds out. That's just survival of the fittest.

We sell Turf Builder Plus 2 with the plainest guarantee we can think of. "If for any reason you are not satisfied with results after using this product, you are entitled to get your money back. Simply send us evidence of purchase and we will mail you a refund check promptly."

You might also like to get our quarterly, Lawn Care® It's free and it's filled with good things to know about grass.

Just write us here in Marysville, Ohio 43040. You don't need a street address. We've been here for over 100 years.

Headline related to illustration and opening copy.

All elements should work together as they do in this advertisement. Too often, however, one or more of the elements will not be tied in with the others.

(Gaines Top Choice is a registered trademark of General Foods Corporation and this advertisement is reproduced with permission of General Foods Corporation)

Careful investigation proves Top Choice chopped burger looks amazingly like hamburger.

It's elementary! Gaines® Top Choice® Chopped Burger For Dogs looks almost identical to hamburger.

And there's no mystery why. Top Choice is made with beef by-products and real beef, so it's moist and meaty. It even holds together just like hamburger.

But it's better for your dog than hamburger, because it also contains vegetables, vitamins and minerals for a fully balanced diet.

Which brings us to Country Style Top Choice. The only chopped burger for dogs with real cheese flavor and protein-rich egg, the equivalent of a quarter of an egg in every serving.

Original Top Choice and Country Style Top Choice. You don't need an investigation to prove they're both great for your dog. **Original Top Choice® and Country Style® Top Choice®. For dogs who love hamburger, they're better for them.**

12

MAGAZINES AND ADVERTISING

MAGAZINES AND ADVERTISING

Magazines reflect us in ways a mirror cannot. Magazines reflect the real us behind the external appearances. Every time we open a magazine, we are seekers. We reveal the unseen personal dimensions of interest, attitude, and aspiration. Magazine content appeals to our need for information, for instruction, and for solving problems. Magazine editorials are congenial to our attitudes, interests and outlooks. Articles inform us how to realize our desires and aspirations, tell us how to maintain our cars, make furniture or fix electrical appliances. More than any other major medium, magazines provide the information we need to help us understand our rapidly changing world.

To learn what interests Americans have, just scan the magazines racks at a newsstand. Magazine cover photography and art are carefully chosen to attract our eye and engage our curiosity. The quotes and article titles, called coverlines, are designed to motivate us to buy the magazine. At the newsstand the cover must succeed in a few short seconds. Millions of magazine covers persuade us to buy week after week. More and more Americans are buying magazines. Millions more buy subscriptions.

MAGAZINES: ARISTOCRATS OF THE MEDIA

Among advertising media, magazines are the aristocrats, whether we are talking about mass circulation magazines, about haughty fashion magazines such as *Vogue* and *Gentlemen's Quarterly*, or the very selective publications such as *Town and Country* and *Yachting*. Whether the appeal is to mass or class, magazines tend to reach what advertisers call "upscale" audiences. Magazines appeal to young, educated, and affluent audiences. Readers tend to be upwardly mobile and their outlook to be optimistic. Readers tend to be doers and thinkers with occupations that are professional or managerial.

In contrast to magazines, newspapers are daily workhorses; direct mail is hardworking but not glamorous; television is tiresome and repetitious but an effective mass medium because of its extraordinary reach into U.S. homes.

Magazines are influential out of proportion to their circulation, reaching opinion leaders and other influentials. Magazines provide audiences for the conversative and liberal intellectual. Magazines provide the fullest discussion of new ideas, new technology, and new social arrangements. In so doing, magazines shape thought.

CONSUMER MAGAZINES

More than any other major advertising medium, magazines develop audiences on the basis of interests. *Newsweek, Time* and *U.S. News and World Report*, for example, are general news magazines. While some of the news may be directly relevant to our work, for the most part these magazines enable us to monitor broad political, economic, social, and technological developments.

Most magazines serve more sharply defined reader interests and thus sharply segment audiences according to interests. We all have a range of interests, some of which are specific to the way we earn a living; some are specific to our world away from work.

To an engineer the first magazine to come to mind may be *Plant Engineering*, a publication aimed at industrial engineers. To a farmer "magazine" may mean *Wallaces Farmer*, if the farmer is in the midwest. But if the farmer is in the citrus business in Florida, "magazine" may mean *The Citrus Industry*.

It is apparent that magazines appeal to many specific interests and to many people. Because there is so much to say about business and farm magazines, they are discussed separately. In this chapter the discussion will be about consumer magazines. Since, currently, billions of dollars are spent annually for advertising in consumer magazines, the subject is important to anyone in advertising.

THE MAGAZINE ENVIRONMENT

Magazines are written to appeal to us in many ways. Some people read the witty and sophisticated *New Yorker*. Others prefer the concrete and folksy down-home appeal of *Grit*. For the serious intellectual there is *Scientific American, Atlantic,* and *Harper's magazine*. Men who tinker enjoy *Popular Science*; women who are creative with their hands get ideas from *Pack-O-Fun*.

Each magazine appeals to its audience with a unique combination of subject matter and treatment. Each develops a rapport or special relationship with an audience, sometimes long-lasting. Many families keep the *National Geographic* for years. Deciding to throw out back copies of the *National Geographic* is seldom easy.

In many ways magazines are the most desirable and credible mass medium we use. Magazine readers are inclined to think and speak positively of their favorite publications. Study after study of mass-media credibility reveals that readers believe in what they read in magazines. This is one reason people actively seek information in magazines.

Advertisements benefit from the belief people have in the surrounding news and entertainment material and from the reputation of the magazine itself. Readers actively involved in seeking information and ideas find magazine advertisements informative and add to reader interest in the adjacent articles.

In the magazine environment, advertisements are regarded as part of the magazine's information. Given their choice of receiving magazines with or without advertisements, the majority of magazine readers vote to keep the advertisements in the magazines. Additionally, magazine readers describe themselves as more attentive to magazine than television advertisements.

If asked to rate their attentiveness to advertisements in various media, women, for instance, describe themselves as more attentive to magazine than television advertisements. This tendency is more marked as the education and income levels of women rise.

Magazine readers frequently discuss magazine content with others, clip coupons, and sometimes remove entire advertisements to show others. All of this suggests an involvement with and response to the medium that is both thoughtful and personal. Among all media, magazines score high on the importance and accuracy of information. Consumers regard magazines as highly believable and authoritative, an environment most attractive to advertisers.

Advertisers are very much aware of the special relationship between magazines and their audiences. Advertisements are designed with appeals and executed with a tone and style appropriate to the magazine. If the advertisement does not "fit" the magazine, the advertisement may be refused. Many magazines make every effort to maintain the integrity of their relationship with their audiences. Advertisements deemed potentially misleading or lacking in taste are not run lest they undermine the special relationship between the magazine and its readers.

A more positive environment for advertising is hard to conceive. Readers want the information in advertisements and regard advertisements as believable. Magazines may be the only appropriate medium for hard-to-believe advertisement claims.

MAGAZINES: ADVANTAGES TO ADVERTISERS

Like all other media, magazines have their shortcomings. Some advertisers do not find magazines a good investment. Other advertisers would be ruined if magazine advertising were not available. Many advertisers would describe the chief advantages of magazine advertisers as described in the following.

Selectivity

Almost any advertiser will say that the number one attribute of magazines is "selectivity"—the ability of the magazine through its editorial policy to select the kind of people the advertiser wishes to reach.

No other advertising medium, except direct mail, offers the kind of selectivity found in magazines; no other true mass medium approaches magazines in this respect. Selectivity includes a number of dimensions worthy of mention.

Audience Selectivity.   The advertiser desiring to reach prospective brides would be at a loss without magazines. National census, state, and city figures might provide estimates of young women of marriageable age. This information is general and vague.

The majority of readers who purchase *Modern Bride* identify themselves for advertisers as persons preparing for marriage. The magazine will reach those with "upscale" demographics, the type likely to have large and formal weddings with follow-up receptions. By advertising in *Modern Bride,* the travel agent, the manufacturer of silverware, as well as manufacturers of hundreds of other products for young brides, may reach an otherwise unidentifiable and unreachable market.

Many other examples can be cited. Interest in CB radio grew rapidly a few years ago. Several magazines started quickly to serve the growing interest. The manufacturer of CB radios can monitor sales figures to learn what is happening in the market. The manufacturer also watches circulation growth trends of CB publications to forecast continued and growing interest. The pattern of circulation is also revealing. A sudden circulation upsurge in the Pacific Northwest alerts the CB manufacturer to build a regional inventory of CB transmitters and receivers in that area.

Time, for example, offers a number of city and state audience options to advertisers. The magazine will sell space in the 6,000 circulation going to Ashland, Kentucky; 3,700 circulation to Flagstaff, Arizona; 7,500 circulation to North Platte, Nebraska. *Time* also offers what are called *demographic* editions to advertisers wanting to reach only certain parts of *Time's* audience. The advertiser may buy *Time* circulation going only to college students, only to physicians, only to top management, and only to businessmen. The *Time* Z edition goes only to upper income households identified by zip code.

The *Reader's Digest* also offers advertisers many options to buy advertising space only in those copies of the magazine circulated where the advertiser's product is distributed. The advertiser may reach one or more up to ten of the largest urban markets. These markets contain about one-fourth of American households and account for more than one-third of all retail sales. The advertiser can buy one or more of the ten regional editions serving clusters of states in the Northeast, Mid-Atlantic, North Central South East, and so on.

The advertiser may also buy circulation in one or more of 50 test markets to test a new product or new advertising appeal. The advertiser may test the pulling power of two different couponed advertisements in the national, regional or major urban markets. As do many large-circulation magazines, the *Reader's Digest* also offers selective circulation to high-income households.

Even large circulation magazines, then, continue to offer the advertiser selectivity within the medium, providing geographically and demographically defined audiences within their total audience.

Offering selective audiences with a large magazine audience helps keep circulation giants robust. Advertisers sometimes are a little suspicious of magazines which are circulation giants. Several, such as *Life* and *Look*, lost their appeal with audiences. Others, such as *TV Guide*, prosper with about 20 million copies of each issue. The *Reader's Digest*, not far behind with more than 18 million circulation, is regarded as a stable U.S. institution.

As a rule, when a magazine reaches multimillion circulation, it becomes less selective. *Better Homes and Gardens*, however, with a circulation of more than 8 million, does a remarkable job of selecting an audience whose chief concern is the care and beautifying of the home. The advertiser's concern remains, however. The reasoning is that the larger the circulation of a magazine the more

likely the circulation includes readers only casually interested in the magazine's content and the products advertised in the magazine.

Geographical Selectivity. Most media develop audiences within a geographical area. The majority of newspapers cover a geographical market comprised of a central city and surrounding suburbs, although a few major newspapers are considered national newspapers. Copies of the *New York Times* and *Christian Science Monitor* circulate nationwide. Television and radio sta-

Consumer magazine advertisement that is helpful to consumer.

Clearly, and with no attempt to be clever, this advertisement gives useful information to the reader. The combination of helpful copy and attractive illustration is found in all advertisements of this company. If more advertisers provided so much help to consumers there would be less criticism of advertising.

tions also reach out for a geographical audience, their coverage being determined by station transmitter power, height, surrounding terrain and other factors. Organizing local television stations into networks makes the audience part of a national or regional audience. Much programming and therefore, audiences, remain local, however.

Some magazines also reach geographical markets. *Los Angeles Magazine* and *Boston Magazine* are two of numerous city magazines with articles of interest to city and suburban residents. Some states now publish magazines to promote in-state tourism by state residents. *Sunset* appeals to a West Coast audience and shuns circulation east of the Rocky Mountains. Magazines for surfers will circulate most heavily where the "surf's up."

Interest Selectivity. While the names of general appeal and general news magazines come rapidly readily to mind, the overwhelming majority of consumer magazines are distinctive in their appeal to more sharply defined consumer interests. The following examples provide only an overview of some of the clusters of interests served by magazines.

People interested in making their homes more comfortable, energy efficient, attractive or versatile may select *American Home, Apartment Life, Better*

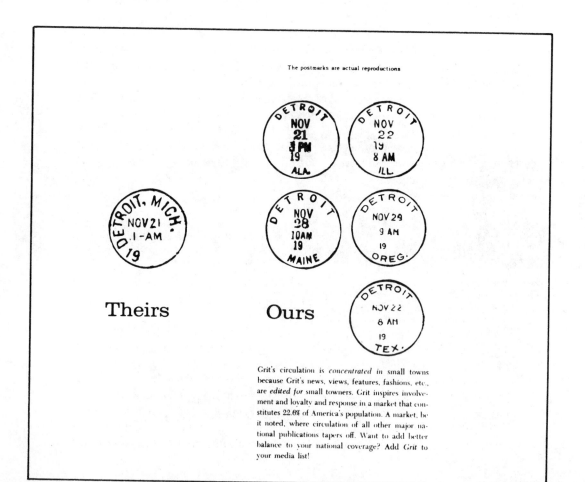

The postmarks are actual reproductions

Theirs   Ours

Grit's circulation is *concentrated in* small towns because Grit's news, views, features, fashions, etc., are *edited for* small towners. Grit inspires involvement and loyalty and response in a market that constitutes 22.6% of America's population. A market, be it noted, where circulation of all other major national publications tapers off. Want to add better balance to your national coverage? Add *Grit* to your media list!

Homes and Gardens, The Family Handyman, House Beautiful, Southern Living, Sunset, or *Architectural Digest* and still not exhaust the list. Many other women's magazines also carry frequent articles about the home.

In advertising, these are called "shelter publications." Such publications appeal to audiences who enjoy adding a room, finishing a basement, or changing their homes in other ways. Not incidentally, audience members have the money to invest in their homes.

Some magazine material is even more specific to sections of the home. *Better Homes and Gardens*, for example, publishes *Bedroom and Bath Decorating Ideas* and *Window and Wall Decorating Ideas*, to name two of the numerous special publications.

For those interested in sports of active leisure, there are *Basketball Digest, Black Belt, Golf Magazine, Horseman, Ski, Skin Diver Magazine, Tennis, Sports Illustrated*, and *Sail and Motorboat*. There are more magazines of the same genre, of course.

Magazines may serve our interest by age and stage in the life cycle. Senior citizens may read *Retirement Life*. Men may read *Field and and Stream* or *Esquire*. Women may select *Harper's Bazaar* or *New Woman*. Teenage boys may subscribe to *Boy's Life*; girls may choose *Seventeen. Jack and Jill* attracts young children. Young women anticipating a child may receive a publication appropriately titled *Expecting*. When the baby arrives, the young mothers may read *Baby Care* or *Baby Talk*.

Environmentalists may subscribe to *Audubon, Pacific Search*, and *Sierra*. If the environmentalist enjoys being out-of-doors rather than just reading about it, *Backpacker* and *Wild Country* are two of more than twenty camping and outdoor recreations magazines.

Most major religious groups publish magazines with articles addressing the spiritual needs of readers. Numerous travel and automotive publications reveal the U.S. love affair with the automobile and the restless desire to move about and curiosity about what lies beyond the distant line of mountains. Craft and hobby publications tell us how to build model railroads, collect coins or find unusual rock specimens.

Long Life

Television and radio advertising are transitory. If you missed the broadcast commercial, you missed it forever. With newspapers you'll sometimes find the rare person who saves old newspapers for rereading. Along among major advertising media, magazines may be retained for weeks, months, and even years. Magazines are the only medium to measure the number of different times or days a reader picks up a publication.

Some magazines are designed to be used frequently. *TV Guide* can be a daily reference source for the viewer. If you want an anecdote to put a visitor at ease, scan the *Reader's Digest* before your visitor arrives. If you're planning your first garden, the publications you buy will be read time and time again. If you are following the instructions and drawings in *Popular Science* while building something in the basement, the magazine becomes a reference tool.

Monthly magazines often contain too much material to absorb in one reading. Sometimes difficult material requires rereading in order to understand

it. Sometimes lengthy articles are serialized over a period of several months. It is almost mandatory for the reader to keep the first installments of a mystery series. Clues overlooked in the first reading may be found later.

Many advertisers have evidence of the long life of magazines. Inquiries, orders and coupons are returned years after the appearance of the advertisements.

Magazines As Authority Channels

Magazines are valued by Americans for numerous reasons. More than any other media, magazines explain our rapidly changing world to us. They tell us the "why" behind the "what." Magazines explain why Americans are migrating south and west, why so many women are joining the work force, why children have trouble with the new math, why flexible work hours are popular in some industries and not in others.

Magazines give us instruction. Editorials and articles in *Better Homes and Gardens* are measured by whether the reader can do something after reading the material. Instructions given in *Popular Science* often include detailed blueprints for the home hobbyist.

We read magazines for reasons and explanations. More so than any other mass medium, magazines invite us to think. Articles and editorials often are acknowledged authorities, giving magazine articles authority and high credibility. Advertisers respect the editorial environment of magazines. People read magazines to seek information, and magazine advertisements frequently offer substantial and detailed information for this thinking audience. The advertisements become part of the magazine's information package.

Outstanding Mechanical Reproduction

Part of authority of magazine advertising, just discussed, is due to the near-flawless reproduction of advertising in quality magazines. This kind of reproduction, especially of color advertising, is the envy and despair of newspaper advertising men. While newspapers have progressed rapidly in the last few years in the quantity and quality of color advertising offered, their only real challenge to the quality of magazine color is the costly insert pages printed outside newspaper plants.

Skilled pressmen, quality coated paper stock, and presses that do not have to run at the shrieking velocity of high-speed newspaper presses, account for the consistent fidelity of magazine advertising reproduction.

Such reproduction is vital to certain products that are sold solely through exact reproduction of colors, including shades of lipstick and asphalt roofing shingles. The first consideration in the sale of asphalt roofing shingles, for instance, is the attractiveness of the colors offered; after this point is settled, buyers get down to price and how long the shingles will last.

Other products or services, while not sold solely through color, are made so attractive through the use of color that it is almost unthinkable for some of the advertisers not to use color in their advertising. Travel advertisements offer an example. Another is cigarette advertising that uses color in order to invest smoking with a feeling of fun and pleasure; the same is true of soft drink advertising and the advertising of hard liquors such as whiskey or gin.

Comparatively Reliable Research Data

Compared to the research performed for some other media, magazine research is more stable and precise. This is because magazine subscribers can be traced through subscriptions to determine the nature of the readership and of the readers themselves more accurately than is possible in the case of the broadcast audience. Other media, for example, outdoor, transit, and broadcast are handicapped because they cannot pinpoint their shifting audiences precisely.

Even small publications, which are bought largely through subscriptions, can offer advertisers accurate data about readers—age, income, occupation, religion, location, buying habits, and other personal data. These magazines can, in addition, usually tell just how the readers read the publications. They can tell, for instance, what readers find interesting or uninteresting.

While magazines have no monopoly on good research and meaningful data about themselves, there is not much doubt that they supply more of each to advertisers than any other medium. In addition, numerous characteristics of magazine audiences are described by independent research organizations using large national samples. Axiom Market Research Bureau, Inc. and W. R. Simmons publish multivolume reports widely used by advertisers interested in reaching consumer magazine audiences.

Several years ago the W.R. Simmons research firm reorganized the way it presented information about media audiences to reveal more sharply media preferences of consumers. The national audience was broken into four segments on the following basis:

> Magazine Imperatives—those who do the most magazine reading and view television the least
>
> Television Imperatives—those who view television frequently and seldom read magazines
>
> Duals—those who frequently read magazines and watch television
>
> Neithers—those who infrequently read magazines and watch television

This way of organizing audience information is important because television and magazines sell most competitively against each other. Advertising decisions often come down to using either network television prime time or several magazines, or sometimes a combination of television prime time in conjunction with a few magazines.

Almost 47 million adults have been identified as Magazine Imperatives. These adults can be reached efficiently through magazine advertising. A somewhat larger number of adults, slightly over 54 million, have been identified as Television Imperatives. While Television Imperatives outnumber Magazine Imperatives, magazine advocates say, "Look behind the numbers. Look at audience quality."

Although there are exceptions, the demographic information generally reveals Magazine Imperatives to be significantly different from Television Imperatives. They are younger, more highly educated, have higher incomes, and tend to live in suburbs. The working woman tends to be a Magazine Imperative.

She has less time for casual viewing and wants the maximum information provided by magazines for her career and home interests.

Merchandising Support

Many of the leading magazines do an outstanding job of supplying merchandising support for their advertisers—usually, of course, for their more important advertisers. This support is valuable not only because it brings the advertising to the local level, but also because it capitalizes on the previously discussed prestige of the magazine. An "As Advertised in *Vogue*" sign in a retail store indictes to the fashion-conscious shopper that here is an item that is in the "in" group of fashion merchandise, such is the prestige of the magazine.

Among the merchandising helps offered national advertisers by the magazines with vigorous merchandising departments are:

(1) *Dealer display cards.* These cards will show the advertisements as they appeared in the magazine, and they can be placed on counters or in windows. Possibly they will not show the advertisement, but instead will be conveniently small and will merely indicate that the item has been advertised in such and such a publication.

(2) *Package and envelope stickers.* These also call attention to the fact that the item was advertised in some national publication.

(3) *Direct mail.* Direct mail can include the furnishing of letters, cards, and folders sent to a store's customers. These will feature "As seen in ____" advertisements. Some of this material may be free while some may be billed at cost to the merchant. the imprinting, addressing, sorting, and mailing of such material will often be done at cost for the merchant, who has nothing more to do with the mailing than to say "yes" when the representative from the magazine explains the merchandising proposal to him.

Going along with the saying "All busines is local," magazines not only provide every encouragement to retailers to tie in with national advertising but also are assiduous in reminding national advertisers of this service.

(4) *Newspaper mats.* Mats or proofs, which are usually furnished free to the merchants, feature the national manufacturer's merchandise and call attention to the fact that the merchandise was advertised in magazine advertisements.

Slower-paced Reading

Magazines are savored. They are picked up, put down, and picked up again. Unlike the frantic atmosphere surrounding broadcast advertising, or the eye-on-the-clock reading of newspapers, the slower-paced reading of magazines provides a fine chance for the use of long, well-written, and often sophisticated copy. Thus many products can be advertised in magazines that will not find a home in other mass media. Also, they can be advertised in a way not possible in other media.

Media advertising in consumer magazines.

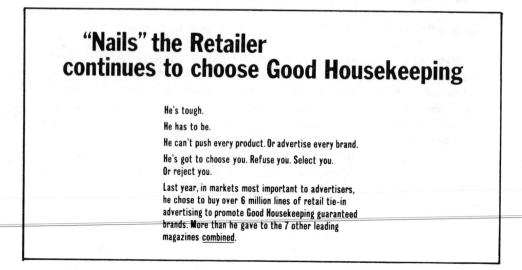

"Nails" the Retailer continues to choose Good Housekeeping

He's tough.

He has to be.

He can't push every product. Or advertise every brand.

He's got to choose you. Refuse you. Select you.
Or reject you.

Last year, in markets most important to advertisers,
he chose to buy over 6 million lines of retail tie-in
advertising to promote Good Housekeeping guaranteed
brands. More than he gave to the 7 other leading
magazines combined.

MAGAZINE LIMITATIONS

While magazine advertising offers many measurable and intangible benefits to advertisers, there are some drawbacks that advertisers usually discuss under two headings:

(1) inflexibility, and
(2) total costs.

Inflexibility

Although many major consumer magazines publish regional or metropolitan editions, enabling advertisers to buy part instead of all of a magazine's circulation, there are still many magazines that offer only a single edition. Consequently, many advertisers avoid using magazines because so much of the circulation goes to areas where the advertisers may not have product distribution or to individuals who are not reasonable prospects.

In addition to geographic inflexibility, there is a time inflexibility. Magazines typically require that advertising material be submitted to them long before the publication date. For big-circulation magazines, the material must be submitted as follows

(1) For weekly magazines: About five weeks ahead of publication date for color material. About four weeks ahead for black-and-white material.
(2) For monthly magazines: For color material, about eight weeks in advance of publication date. About seven weeks ahead for black-and-white material.

Compared with other media, these are long lead times, especially in rapidly changing markets where prices and products change rapidly. By comparison, almost any other medium offers shorter lead times, especially radio and newspapers, which often permit last-minute or last-day changes.

Total Costs

Most magazines, especially the big-circulation magazines, can demonstrate to advertisers that the cost per person reading the magazine is low. Still, many advertisers do not use consumer-magazine advertising, or use it in a limited way because of the high total cost, not only for magazine space but also for the high cost of preparing the high-quality material, such as four-color plates.

Thousands of small-budget advertisers whose products or services are suited for magazine advertising bypass this medium because they cannot justify the total costs. Many others, desiring magazine advertising, will:

(1) Use small-space advertisements when their products would be better shown in big-space advertisements.
(2) Use infrequent insertions.
(3) Use black-and-white advertisements, although their product might be shown to far better advantage in color. For the small advertiser, there are two reasons for not using color, even when advantageous:
   (a) Color advertising costs more than the same amount of black-and-white advertising.
   (b) Usually magazines require that color advertisements be a half page or larger, thus making the costs prohibitive for small-budget advertisers.

MAGAZINE CLASSIFICATIONS

Magazines may be classified by content, by physical size, and by issuance frequency.

Content

To the advertiser, content is the most important gauge of the suitability of a magazine for advertising his product or service. The content of a magazine determines what kind of readers a magazine will attract. Once these people are studied, the advertisers can determine if they are the ones who buy their products or will buy them.

Much has been made about selectivity as the outstanding attribute of magazines as an advertising medium. It is a magazine's content that creates this selectivity or, as it is sometimes called, the magazines "editorial policy" or "editorial atmosphere."

Standard Rate and Data Service (SRDS) publishes the authoritative information source used by media buyers seeking to reach audiences through magazines. In the volume containing consumer magazine information, a brief look at the magazine titles reveals the breadth of topics and audience interests.

Magazines are organized into descriptive groupings, starting with Airline In-flight which includes about fifteen publications. Next comes Almanacs with about ten publications and so on through to Women's Fashions, Beauty, and Grooming with eleven publications and, finally, Youth with sixteen publications. Some magazines are listed in several groupings because they carry material appropriate for different groups. Within each grouping, magazines are identified as to whether the circulation is audited or nonaudited.

Some of the most important groupings, and some of the magazines in each grouping, are:

Grouping	*Magazines representative of the group*
General editorial	*Reader's Digest*
Home service	*Better Homes and Gardens; House Beautiful; Sunset*
News	*Newsweek; Sports Illustrated; Time; U.S. News & World Report*
Women's	*Family Circle; Good Housekeeping; Ladies' Home Journal*
Women's Fashions	*Harper's Bazar; Mademoiselle; Vogue*

Issuance Frquency

The advertiser is interested in the frequency with which a magazine is issued. The advertiser selects magazines, in part, on the match between publication frequency and advertising requirements. For example, a low-cost, mass-distributed product that is frequently purchased requires frequent advertising exposure. A quarterly or annual magazine is of no interest to the advertiser.

Depending upon campaign objectives, the amount of money to be invested in advertising and the kind of product being advertised, an advertiser may schedule advertisements so that a constant barrage of messages is aimed at prospects. If magazines are used, they must be weeklies. For more expensive and infrequently purchased consumer products, monthly magazines may be appropriate. With monthlies the advertiser has the greatest choice of publications. There are about twelve times as many monthly magazines as weeklies.

MAGAZINE RATES AND/OR MECHANICAL OPTIONS

Magazine Rates Closely Competitive with Each Other

Magazines that are similar in appeal (shelter publications, for example) and circulation and reach similar audiences tend to have similar rates for advertising space sold to advertisers. Space rate differences between such magazines are usually determined by circulation differences. This is demonstrated by the following rates and circulations for two big-circulation magazines:

	Circulation	Rate per Black-and-white Page
Magazine *A*	1,600,000	$ 8,900
Magazine *B*	2,904,000	$15,365

Are the rates different? Yes and no. There is a substantial difference in dollar cost. If you relate the space rate to the circulation in the cost-per-thousand calculation discussed in earlier chapters, you'll find the costs are quite similar: Magazine A has a CPM of $5.56 while Magazine B's CPM is $5.29.

There are exceptions to the general rule that similar magazines tend to charge similar space rates. Two magazines in the women's fashion field provide an example of such an exception. The circulation and rates of these magazines are as follows:

	Circulation	Rate per black-and-white Page
Magazine A	596,332	$3,450.00
Magazine B	498,272	$4,350.00

A glance at these figures shows that Magazine A, with almost 100,000 more circulation, has a page rate that is $900 less. When this is the case, study of audience demographic characteristics usually yields the reason behind the exception. Magazine A in this example, while celebrated in the women's fashion field, is read primarily by college and young career women. Magazine B, although it reaches some of these same younger women, also reaches a large and slightly more mature and fashion conscious audience of women with higher incomes. Advertisers wishing to reach those who can afford more expensive clothing and accessory fashion merchandise will pay the higher space rates for Magazine B to reach the women with higher incomes.

Sliding Scales

Where once magazines, like newspapers, seldom offered sliding scales, numerous magazines now offer volume and frequency sliding scales. An example of a frequency sliding scale for a magazine of about 1.5 million circulation is shown in table 12-1.

Table 12-1
Frequency Sliding Scale

Space Unit	1 Time	3 Times	6 Times	12 Times
1 page	$3,960	$3,840	$3,720	$3,555
½ page	2,010	1,950	1,880	1,790
¼ page	1,015	980	945	900
⅛ page	510	495	455	
1 inch	260	255	250	235

In the case of another mass-circulation magazine of multimillion circulation, discounts are based upon the dollar volume of advertising used within a contract period of 52 consecutive weeks.

Even in cases where the magazine offers no sliding scale for frequency or quantity buying, it will most always charge less proportionally for larger space units. This is demonstrated by the rates shown here for a smaller circulation magazine. It will be noted that, proportionately, the rates go higher as the page units become smaller.

Space Unit	Rate
1 page	1490
½ page	260
¼ page . . . . : . .	135
⅛ page	70

Unlike newspapers, magazines offer "guaranteed" circulation. A statement will often be found in the SRDS listing which says that, effective with a forthcoming issue, there will be a guaranteed total net paid circulation of a certain figure. Should the magazine's circulation fail to reach the guaranteed figure, the publication will make a pro rata rebate to advertisers. Happily for advertisers, on the other hand, there is no extra charge for circulation increases during the contract period. Usually, however, if the circulation average is consistently higher during the yearly period, a rate rise is likely to occur.

Magazines Rates More Consistent Than Newspaper Rates. Hard-to-explain newspaper rate differentials are not so likely to occur in the magazine field. Magazines of the same type, circulation, and audience will rather consistently have the same rate structure. Circulation is usually the chief determinant of rates. An examination of rates for magazines will reveal that they are in close proportion as the magazines are smaller or larger in circulation. This is demonstrated by the following rates and circulations for two big-circulation magazines:

	Circulation	Rate per Black-and-white Page
Magazine A	1,600,000	$ 8,900
Magazine B	2,904,000	$15,365

Cost-per-thousand (CPM) Reveals Cost of Reaching Audiences

Advertisers buying magazine space use the same cost-per-thousand calculation they apply against other advertising media. The resulting information is the same. Multiplying the space rate by 1,000 and dividing the result by a magazine's circulation yields the CPM. By doing a number of these calculations for magazines with widely differing circulations and space rates, the advertiser can tell which magazines are most cost efficient. The following reveals the relative cost efficiencies at a glance:

	Circulation	Rate per Black-and-white Page	Per-thousand Cost
Magazine A	290,000	$ 1,400	$4.83
Magazine B	8,200,798	31,000	3.78
Magazine C	1,135,934	3,620	3.19
Magazine D	3,359,988	14,640	4.36

As with other media, the advertiser may manipulate the above figures, computing, for example, on the basis of half-page rates or full-page, four-color page rates. Or, the advertiser may adjust the magazine circulation to reflect only a portion of the total audience. For example, if women 18 to 49 years old are the advertiser's primary target, and such women make up 40 percent of a magazine's circulation of 500,000, for the advertiser's purpose the circulation is 200,000. The cost-per-thousand is computed using 200,000. The result, of course, is that the CPM increases substantially but may more realistically express the cost of reaching the primary target audiences.

CPM Should Not Be Sole Criterion

While CPM rates provide a quick, easy way of expressing the cost of reaching an audience, unthinking use of the calculation has led to what, in the advertising business, is often called a per-thousand fixation. Advertisers become so used to thinking in per-thousand terms that they tend to overlook other magazine advertising values such as:

Intensive readership given some publications
Authority of the magazine with its audience
Reader loyalty
Reader demographics
Ability to generate coupon response

Were Magazine A in the previous example to be judged only by the results of the per-thousand calculation, it would never be used by an economy-minded advertiser. If, however, the advertiser considered the magazine in terms of the foregoing factors, Magazine A might prove to be an outstanding buy. The astute advertiser always examines as much information as possible about magazines, or any other medium.

Other Rates

Regional Rates. The advertiser who distributes a product only in New England may reach a New England audience by advertising only in the New England regional edition of a national magazine. In this case, buying regional circulation rather than national circulation enables the advertiser to match the product distribution and magazine circulation.

The cost differential between regional and national space buys can be illustrated as follows. The advertiser may buy a page of space in the New England edition of a national magazine for $2,098. Regional circulation of 315,000 goes only to Maine, New Hampshire, Vermont, Massachusetts, Rhode Island and Connecticut.

If the magazine did not publish a regional edition and the advertiser bought space in the magazine, the advertiser would pay $27,110 for a national circulation of 6,200,000. Dollar and circulation differences between the regional and national buy is waste.

Regional editions do cost slightly more on a cost-per-thousand basis. While the publisher's cost of handling mechanical plates, general paperwork and billing might be similar for advertisements placed for national or regional circulation, magazine makeup and production coordination costs are higher.

Color Rate. Not all magazines offer color. Those which do offer color advertising, do so only in the larger page units, usually full pages and half pages. Some magazines, however, offer color in units as small as quarter-pages or third-pages.

Rates vary according to the number of colors used, but the extra cost for color usually runs from one-third to one-half more than the basic black-and-white rate. Though occasionally there is a flat sum charged for each additional color used, more frequently the rates will be scaled as in the following:

Two Colors ROP
(Basic black-and-white page rate for this publication is $2,575.)

1 page (black and one color)	$3,0785
2/3 page (black and one color)	2,500
1/2 page (black and one color)	2,100
1/3 page (black and one color)	1,580
4-process colors, ROP — 1 page	3,885

In addition to asking more money for color advertising, magazines also ask more "make-ready" time, usually about a week more.

Split-Run Rates. A number of magazines offer advertisers the opportunity to reach half the magazine audience with one advertisement and half with another advertisement. This is called a split run. The term is a shorthand way of saying that every other copy of the magazine coming off the printing presses (during a press run) contains one or the other of two advertisements.

Why split the press run this way? Why not just stop the presses in mid-run and change the advertisment plates? Typically, the first copies of every issue of a magazine are quickly distributed (and sometimes flown) to those areas furthest from the one or more plants where the magazine is printed. If all such copies contained just one of the two advertisements to be tested, the result would be a geographical bias.

Because of added production costs, magazines charge more for split run advertisements. For a national magazine with a circulation of 3 million, the advertiser may pay a premium of $15,030.

The cost of a split run may be nominal to the advertiser who wants to test two different advertising appeals in the same magazine at the same time. Frequently, the test is to see which of two couponed advertisements generate the larger coupon return. If the advertiser finds that one advertisement generates three times the coupon response of the other advertisement, the advertiser then knows which of the two advertisements to use in other magazines.

For example, assume the first advertisement generates a coupon response of 25,000 and the second advertisement generates a coupon response of 10,000. Assume also the advertiser tested the two advertisements prior to buying space in a substantial number of magazines, perhaps a dozen with a combined circulation of 20 million. The added cost fo the single split-run test becomes a very modest investment to learn which is the more effective advertisement.

Cover Rates. "Cover" is magazine terminology for not only the front and back cover pages of a magazine but also for the inside of the front cover and the inside of the back cover. Since the front cover pages of magazines are rarely sold, advertisers are concerned with the other "covers," called second cover, third cover, and fourth cover, respectively.

If a magazine offers color, the covers are almost invariably sold only in four colors and usually bleed. With almost no exceptions, the most expensive single page of any magazine is the fourth cover. But despite their high cost the back covers of important magazines are signed for in long-term contracts because this position is considered by many advertisers to be the most desirable in a magazine. Since the demand for covers is so great, covers are usually sold on a noncancellable basis.

Even big advertisers, however, sometimes find that weekly use of the fourth cover swallows up too much of the advertising budget. They may, accordingly, as in television, use the position on an alternate week basis.

Short Rates.   Most of us are familiar with the idea of volume discounts. If we buy 10 units of something we pay less per unit than if we bought just one unit. If we bought 20 units, we pay still less per unit, and so on. The same idea is used by magazines when selling space. The more frequently the advertiser buys space, for example, in a weekly magazine during the course of the year, the less the advertiser pays for each unit of space.

Planning advertising for the year in advance, the advertiser may sign a contract to use a certain number of pages in order to earn a discounted rate for each page as it is used. The advertiser pays less for each page. The magazine publisher grants the discounts to encourage frequent advertising. The contracts also enable the publisher to plan the number of pages in each issue of the magazine long in advance.

However, if an advertiser uses fewer than the number of pages contracted for, the advertiser pays what is called a "short rate." To illustrate how the short-rate payment works, here is an example. At the beginning of the year the advertiser consults the rate chart for Magazine A. For the basic black-and-white page, the sliding scale looks like this:

Space Unit	1 Time	6 Times	12 Times	18 Times
1 page	$235	$221	$199	$188

The advertiser decides to advertise 18 times at $188 per page and signs a contract for this schedule.

During the year he cuts back his advertising schedule to 12 insertions. He pays for these insertions each time he runs his advertisement at the $188 rate.

At the end of the year the magazine, in making its final billing, finds that the advertiser has not lived up to his contract agreement. Since he has not earned the 18-time rate, the magazine sends a "short-rate" bill to the advertiser.

To arrive at the short-rate bill, the magazine credits the advertiser for 12 × $188, which is the amount already paid, or $2,256. Since, however, the advertiser should have been paying at the higher 12-time rate, he is charged the difference, or 12 × $11. The 12-insert rate, therefore, is $132 more than the 18-insert rate or $2,388.

From the foregoing it becomes obvious that the short-rate principle in magazine billing is exactly the same as that in the newspaper field. The short rate is actually the difference between the discount contracted for and the discount actually earned.

Bleeds

To make an advertisement appear more open and spacious within the confines of a printed page, advertisers may pay an additional 10 to 15 percent to make the advertisements occupy the entire page, including margins. Advertisers call these bleed advertisements.

Bleed advertisements have become so popular and common that a number of magazines regard them as typical and no longer charge extra for bleed.

Bleed is attractive for cosmetic advertisers and other advertisers who desire to create a mood. Many readers unconsciously associate the technique with certain products. Even nonsmokers enjoy the "big sky" scenery in Marlboro magazine bleed advertisements. Confining Marlboro advertisements within white margins would alter our perception of the seemingly boundless space. The nonverbal meaning of the advertising message would be different.

The advertiser's decision to pay for bleed advertisements, if the magazine charges extra, often is based on aesthetic judgments rather than a traditional efficiency measure, such as attracting measurably more readers.

Inserts

The advertiser may use magazine advertising in ways that result in substantial differences in readership, if not sales. The cost of inserts in magazines may be high, but readership surveys consistently demonstrate the high readership of inserts, often the highest readership achieved by any commercial material in the magazine. High readership can result from high inherent interest in the insert-advertised product, the superior reproduction of the insert, or the fact that when casually opened, the magazine opens naturally to first reveal the insert.

Mail-order Inserts

Possibly the fastest-growing of the mechanical variations is the mail-order insert, used heavily by such coupon advertisers as record clubs, book clubs, and vitamin distributors.

The most popular among mail-order inserts consists of the following combination:

(1)   A $4\frac{1}{2} \times 6$-in. insert piece that carries a detachable business reply card.
(2)   A selling message carried on an accompanying one-page or two-page advertisement. (The offer is repeated on the stub of the insert card.)

Many mail-order advertisers have found that insert cards of the kind just described have increased returns three to six times over what would be pulled by a page advertisement using the conventional coupon. As the use of these cards has increased, the rate of return has gone down somewhat, but not so much that the cards may not still be considered very effective.

Unlike the coupon, the mail-order insert card is a self-mailer complete with stamp, and address of the advertiser. The insert can be detached instantly; it does not need to be cut out with scissors. And, as said before, the magazine holds open at the point of the insert, making it visible and easy to cut out.

Because of various production problems, the use of the insert is expensive, but so spectacular have been the returns that inserts used by mail-order advertisers have still managed to make substantial cuts in the cost of such advertising when considered in terms of the cost per reply.

A late development in the use of such cards has been their employment in the contests and sweepstakes that are so often advertised in the big-circulation magazines. Here, too, they have been responsible for greatly increasing returns from this kind of promotion.

Other Variations

Advertisers may use a number of mechanical options. Gatefolds that open to create a three-page spread, often as used with the second cover to introduce new model-year automobiles. Advertisers may use cutouts that enable you to peer through at the contents of another page. Each of these is costly. Each sufficiently novel to command reader attention.

"Free form" advertisements are probably the most costly of all. These advertisements are often preprinted and precut in other than conventional square or rectangular shapes and then integrated into the magazine. Free forms may often use geometric or large typographic letter designs.

DECISIONS ON HOW TO USE THE MAGAZINES

Magazines are published in a variety of sizes.

Although postal regulations in recent years have forced the majority of magazines to use one of three sizes, magazines still vary by their internal makeup, by size of border, number of columns, and column width and height. Preparing advertisements for production can be costly and time consuming, if the advertiser uses a large number of magazines, most of which use different advertisement size requirements.

Vertical-horizontal Units

The offering of horizontal space units is another difference from newspaper advertising. Most newspapers refuse advertisements that are decidedly wider than they are deep. Such advertisements would ruin the pyramid design used on most newspaper pages.

Horizontal units in magazines are accepted, although both advertisers and the publishers prefer vertical advertisements that are deeper than they are wide. Some publications show their preference for this kind of shape by charging somewhat more for the same size advertisement when it is horizontal.

In any event, advertisers, when they ask for less-than-page units should always indicate whether they want vertical or horizontal space. Whenever reference is made to such units, the width should always be given first.

MAGAZINE POSITIONS

The position of advertisements in magazines is one more factor to be considered in evaluating the success of magazine advertisements. Although there seems to be insufficient evidence that the position of advertisements in newspapers has a substantial effect on readership of those advertisements, the effect of position on magazine advertising readership is much more clear-cut. Still, even here it is a difficult research problem to determine with any sort of precision whether high or low readership of an advertisement is caused by the advertisement's position, or instead by interest in the product or by the creativity of the advertisement.

Covers

There is little argument about the value of cover positions. Despite their premium rates of 25 to 33 percent, back covers are considered a bargain by most advertisers. Extra expense is offset by the higher noting of readers, which may be anywhere from 40 to 70 percent greater.

An even better bargain according to researchers can be the second cover, which also draws very high noting by readers, but which, except for a few publications, does not cost advertisers any more than any other color advertisement.

Left-hand Versus Right-hand Pages

Daniel Starch and a number of other respected researchers say that the placement of advertisements on right-hand or left-hand pages makes no difference in readership scores nor in inquiry returns. This finding for magazines confirms similar findings for newspapers.

Yet there are a number of advertisers, especially in the mail-order business, who declare that the difference between success and failure of an advertisement may depend upon position, and especially on whether or not the advertisement is on the right-hand page. These advertisers often strongly prefer the right-hand page facing the second cover page. After that they like right-hand pages far forward in a magazine. An exception to the distrust of left-hand pages is a liking for the left-hand page facing the third cover.

Advertisers using coupons avoid the second cover, not because it is a left-hand page but because returns are affected by the reluctance of magazine readers to clip or tear out the coupon and thus mar the front cover. General advertisers on the contrary, when they do not use coupons, show a strong preference for the second cover. Left-hand, right-hand—it makes no difference to them.

Forward or Back in the Magazine

At one time magazines rather generally used a format that put a solid block of advertisements in the front of the publication, to be followed by solid editorial material consisting of articles and stories. The remainder of the publication consisted of advertisements and carry-overs of the editorial material. Readership of the advertisements in this last section was largely dependent upon how many readers bothered to finish the carry-over articles or stories.

When most magazines followed the foregoing format, all ideas about the value of a front or back position were based upon this way of setting up the magazine's content. The latest development in magazine makeup, however, is to open (that is, to begin) major articles and stories throughout the magazine. This has tended to spread reader traffic more evenly throughout a publication. It has, at the same time, smashed to some extent the old idea that good readership for advertising is fairly well confined to the first dozen pages in the front and the last dozen in the back.

Recent testing by readership experts indicates that placing an advertisement in the first dozen or last dozen pages will give it only a slight advantage, if any. It is granted, of course, that cover positions, and pages facing cover positions, will normally obtain greater attention than pages deeper in the publication. Also, returns from the first 10 percent of the magazine's pages have been slightly higher in many of the tests. In the main, however, outstanding work in copy and layout is much more important for obtaining attention for an advertisement than where it is placed.

Placement of Advertising Next to Editorial Material

Oddly enough, advertisers have worried:

(1)   if they were placed next to high-interest editorial or
(2)   if they were placed next to low-interest editorial material.

In the first case they feared that readers would be so much interested in the story or article that they would not see or read the adjacent advertising. In the second case they felt that low-interest articles would fail to generate reader traffic; thus, advertisement reading would suffer.

Given a choice, the advertiser should choose to be next to high-interest material. So long as advertisements have something important to say to readers and say it well, there is nothing in research findings which seems to support the idea that lively editorial material will take readership away from nearby advertising material. Furthermore, proximity to well-read editorial material ensures heavy traffic, always to be preferred to having only a few readers to whom to expose the advertising message.

One type of magazine editorial material advertisers should certainly try to place their advertising near is that material which has some relation to the product being advertised. Researchers have observed that putting a food advertisement in the food section, or advertising for an automotive item near an article about cars, will often increase readership for the advertising. Some magazines in fact, stress the breaking up of editorial material into subject sections or departments. *Better Homes & Gardens* is an example of such a publication. Before the advertiser of any product advertises in a magazine that has strong sections relating to certain subjects, he should make known his desire to have his advertisement placed in or near such a section.

Better Homes & Gardens, along with a number of other magazines, has a strong mail-order section at the back of the magazine. This section carries many small advertisements that contain coupon and other offers for a variety of products. Since mail-order sections of this type have their own built-in interest for readers, who seek them out eagerly, it makes no difference whether nearby editorial matter has any product connection, or whether that editorial matter consists of high-interest or low-interest material.

MAGAZINE DIMENSIONS

Thick Versus Thin Magazines

As magazines become more successful in attracting readers, they also become more successful in attracting advertisers. Suddenly the successful magazine is thick with advertisements and editorial material. When advertisers look at these bulky magazines they begin to wonder if readership is not going to suffer because the magazine has become too successful. Are advertisements being buried, they ask themselves, by the sheer bulk of the publication?

There are two indicators that will show whether the thickness of a publication is having an adverse effect:

(1) studies which show the extent of the advertising readership, and
(2) returns from mail-order advertisements that may or may not contain coupons.

With respect to readership, the many studies that have been made have found only a moderate drop-off in advertising readership. Researchers point out, however, that it is difficult to determine this drop-off with any precision because when a magazine becomes very thick—say about 150 to 200 pages—it is almost impossible to conduct a page-by-page reading interview with respondents without causing resentment and boredom on the part of the person being interviewed. This reluctance of respondents to go patiently through an examination of 200 pages to see what they remember is often reflected in answers that are given quickly in order to terminate the interview. Thus researchers are not sure whether respondents actually did not read many of the advertisements or whether they deny reading it in order to get rid of the interviewer.

As for coupon returns, Dr. Daniel Starch, in his *Analysis of 12 Million Inquiries*, found that such returns were affected only slightly by the number of pages in a consumer magazine. Specifically, he discovered that when magazines were between 100 and 125 pages the advertiser could expect about 104 returns. In bigger magazines of about 175 to 200 pages, the inquiry rate dropped to about 98 returns. The drop-off rate accelerated somewhat as the magazines exceeded 200 pages.

Very often a magazine has a large number of advertisements, and consequently more editorial material, because the advertisers have found that they obtain good results regardless of the magazine's bulk. There is nothing about a magazine that is thin, because of the absence of advertisements, to inspire confidence. Many consumer magazines, moreover, are read just as much for their advertising as they are for their editorial material. The college issue of *Mademoiselle* in September, and the Christmastime issue of *Esquire*, loaded with gift suggestions, provide two examples of such magazines.

There is a feeling of success about the thick publication and a feeling of failure about the thin one. Few advertisers are satisfied to work with the failures.

Proportion of Advertising to Editorial Matter

Just as do newspaper readers, magazine readers sometimes complain: "That magazine's all ads. You have to search to find any reading material."

It is quite likely that the successful magazine during good economic times will have a much greater proportion of advertising material to editorial material. The figures given here, which were supplied by the advertising director of one of the nation's largest circulation weekly magazines, show the variations in advertising-editorial material in good and bad economic times, in the summer, and in the post-Christmas period.

Good Economic Period		Bad Economic Period		Summertime		Post-Christmas Week	
Advertising	Editorial	Advertising	Editorial	Advertising	Editorial	Advertising	Editorial
60.8%	39.2%	36.1%	63.9%	34.2%	65.8%	13.1%	86.9%

Normally, the thicker the magazine the greater will be the proportion of advertising material to editorial material.

The proportion of advertising material to editorial will be influenced, of course, by the type of magazine. Fashion magazines, as already noted, attract readers who have a high interest in the advertised goods. Were the advertisements to be cut down, the readers would feel cheated.

Effect of Size of Advertisements

One of the most vexing decisions facing the low-budget magazine advertiser is what size to make advertisements. The advertiser knows that space must be bought in fractions of pages rather than full pages or spreads.

Time after time, readership surveys reveal half-page black-and-white advertisements are more efficient proportionately in reaching readers than full-page, four-color advertisements. Readership does not increase in direct ratio to increase in advertisement size in print (or time in broadcast).

Knowing this, the low-budget advertiser can focus on the real problem involved in small-space advertising: the creative problem. Small space advertisements demand succinct headlines and copy. Illustrations and logotype must also be skillfully executed to compete effectively for attention in an environment of full-page advertisements.

Large corporations prefer full-page advertisements for impact, greater readership, and to give more room for long, persuasive or explanatory copy. We, as readers, expect large-space advertisements from major corporations. In fact, a half-page advertisement from U.S. Steel, General Electric, or some other industrial giant would strike us as odd.

A small corporation, on the other hand, can gain prestige by using a half-page advertisement in a general news magazine such as *Time* or a general business publication such as *Fortune*.

There is no definitive answer to the question: "Is it better to use big space and advertise less often, or smaller space and more often?" The answer must be in terms of the advertiser's objectives. If the advertiser wants impact and space to develop a unique creative story, big space may be mandatory. If the advertiser wants reminders wherever readers look, the smaller, more frequently run space units may be appropriate.

MULTIPAGE ADVERTISEMENT

In any consumer magazine, readers will find spreads of two pages or more. Occasionally they will find a spread of many pages. How does the multipage advertisement work? Is it resultful? Why is it used?

First of all, whether the spread is two pages, or more, it will usually command extra attention and readership if it is well executed in copy and layout—and most spreads are. Their cost is so high that much thought is given to the nature of the offer and how it is presented.

IT HAS IMPACT

A two-page spread is almost certain to be noticed, especially since it is usually given four-color bleed treatment. When more than two pages are used, and the reader goes through many pages of the dramatic and persuasive selling of a product, the effect is similar to that generated by the television spectaculars—those superextravaganzas that advertisers put on once a year and that may cost as much as a million dollars, or more.

It Does A Total Selling Job

Almost any copywriter will say, when finished creating a certain advertisement: "If only I had had the room to put in all the selling arguments!" The multipage advertisement provides that chance. All the illustrations, all the copy points, and all the strong selling headlines and subheads can be included to do the complete sales presentation, or to sell everything in the advertiser's line.

It Provides a Mailing Piece

Mailing costs absorbed by magazines make multipage advertisements seem less costly than at first glance. Furthermore, the mailing list provided by the magazine would cost many thousands of dollars were the advertiser to attempt to buy a similar one.

It Is a Natural for Merchandising

The "talk" value of big multipage advertisements is great, especially with the trade. Tie-ins on the local level create additional sales impact. Here again the multipage advertisement resembles the television spectacular in that it is something so unusual that it jars dealers out of their customary apathetic attitude toward national promotions.

It Can Serve As a Catalog

The use of multipage advertisements as catalogs has had an increasing appeal to big-budget advertisers. Such use is found especially during the gift-buying seasons, when the advertisers, in effect, let magazines handle the production and distribution problems of getting out gift catalogs by putting them in the form of multipage advertisements.

It Can Dominate the Medium

Few advertisers ever find the chance to use a medium in so spectacular a way that they truly dominate it, even momentarily. A big multipage advertisement provides this opportunity.

EQUAL IMPACT FOR "DIGEST"-SIZE ADVERTISEMENTS?

This subject of page size became of pressing interest to advertising men soon after the *Reader's Digest* began to take advertisements in 1955. It was difficult for advertisers to believe that advertisements appearing in big-page magazines could be matched in effectiveness by advertisements in digest-size magazines.

A well-known advertising research firm, Gallup & Robinson, was assigned to settle this question by making a study in which they were given absolute freedom in doing the research and in releasing the results, no matter how they came out. Some of the conclusions of this study are given here:

(1) In general, the absolute size of an advertisement has little to do with the number of readers who perceive and recall it.

(2) A single-page advertisement in a magazine of smaller page size is perceived and recalled by the same proportion of readers as a single-page advertisement appearing in a larger magazine. (This assumes, however, that both magazines are about the same in advertising and editorial content.)

(3) In addition to matching the bigger page advertisements in perception and recall, the smaller page advertisements also match the bigger ones in the number of sales points played back to researchers; that is, in the registration of sales messages.

(4) Readers view an advertisement in the perspective of the magazine in which it appears. It is not the number of square inches that counts.

ADVERTISING PRODUCTION TERMINOLOGY

Although reference to the agate line is made in magazine terminology, where the meaning of the term is the same as in newspaper advertising, this unit of space measurement is used much less in magazine advertising.

Customarily, an advertisement that is a smaller size than the smallest page unit offered (for example, 1/16 of a page) will be figured in terms of the number of agate lines. Most magazines provide an agate line rate along with their other rates. Sometimes a magazine will indicate that for "nonstandard" sizes the advertiser should use the nearest lower standard unit plus the agate line rate for the additional space.

Magazine space, it is apparent, is usually sold in page units, not in agate lines and column inches, as in the case of newspapers.

To further confuse the advertising beginner, there are three page sizes to consider, mechanically speaking.

(1) *Plate size*. The plate size is the part of a full page filled by the advertisement. It does not include bleed pages. When plate size is indicated, it refers to the size that page plates should be made.

(2) *Trim size*. The trim size is the actual size of a magazine page after surplus margins have been trimmed.

(3) *Bleed size*. When the advertisement extends to the edge of the page, instead of being surrounded by a white border, it is called a bleed advertisement. Bleed-page size refers to the size that bleed plates must be made.

MAGAZINE DECISIONS AND INFORMATION

When you casually pick up and scan a newsstand magazine, you are not interested in how the magazine reached the newsstand, how it was produced, or whether there is any plan behind the selection of articles. If asked, you would disclaim any interest in the advertisements.

If an advertiser strolled up next to you, picked up a copy of the same magazine and also began to scan it, would the advertiser look at the magazine the same way you do? Hardly! The advertiser might scan the article titles and photographs looking for information of personal interest. By training and experience, however, the advertiser knows articles are selected according to an editorial policy, that only a portion of the copies are sold at newsstands, and that magazines use different types of paper and printing processes.

The advertiser also knows that each advertisement is in the magazine because someone decided the magazine appeals to the type of person who might buy the advertised products.

FACTORS TO CONSIDER

Just how does the advertiser go about deciding to buy space in a magazine? What information does the advertiser want? Where can the information be found? What does the advertiser do with the information?

Much of the information required by the advertiser was presented previously. As you read this, asume you're the advertiser. You must decide whether to advertise in magazines. Which magazines will you use? How will you use the magazine to reach the audience you want?

First, you will get copies of the magazines you might want to consider. You will glance at the table of contents, select a title of interest to you, and begin to read.

Editorial Policy

When you think of buying space in a magazine, you ask yourself: "Is the content and writing in this magazine designed to appeal to the kind of people who will buy my product?" You attempt to read the magazine through the eyes of people you already know buy your product.

Article titles and subject matter, the way the articles are written—these, and numerous other characteristics of the magazine, reflect what is called the editorial policy. If the writing is sophisticated, readers will likely be also. If your product is a high-fashion cosmetic, you may want your advertisement associated with a sophisticated magazine environment. You make your advertisement "fit" a magazine environment through your selection of artwork, type faces, writing style, and other elements used in your advertisement.

If the magazine is written for owners of high-performance automobiles, the writing style is taut and punchy. Headline typefaces selected for advertisements in such publications are bold, often slanted to suggest action and speed. Art, photography and writing must fit the editorial environment.

Assume that for one or another reason, you personally do not like the magazine you are reading, even though you know the magazine would reach the audience you want. your personal tastes are left aside. You will be investing dollars to communicate product and service benefits to people who make up their own minds. Therefore, it is your professional assessment that influences your decision.

Reader Feedback

Magazines often survey readers to get audience feedback. Magazine editors and publishers want to know what readers think of the publication. Are articles interesting? Is the information authoritative, believable, accurate, and fair? These and other characteristics reveal reader satisfaction. The more positive the reader feedback the higher the magazine's franchise with the readers, and the more attractive the editorial environment is for advertisers.

Magazine Prestige and Advertising

Your advertisements often can be presented to readers in magazines with outstanding reputations for honesty in dealing with readers and advertisers. The appearance of your advertisement in such a magazine gains an implicit endorsement by association with the magazine.

Several magazines make the endorsement explicit. *Good Housekeeping* and

Idea advertisement for women.

Several elements make this a strong advertisement. (1) It offers recipes. (2) It contains an offer. (3) It sells several units of the product. (4) The approach and subject matter are appropriate for the audience and editorial approach of a magazine read primarily by women.

Give me main-dish soups
I don't have to start from scratch.

Start with Campbell's for all the flavor you want. Without all the work.

BEEF NOODLE MAIN-DISH SOUP
1 medium onion, sliced
2 tablespoons dried parsley flakes
½ teaspoon salt
Dash garlic powder
Dash pepper
2 tablespoons butter or margarine
2 cups cubed cooked beef
1 can Campbell's Beef Broth
1 can Campbell's Old Fashioned
  Vegetable Soup
2 soup cans water
1 can (16 ounces) tomatoes, cut up
1 cup uncooked wide noodles
1 small green pepper, diced

In large saucepan, cook onion with seasonings in butter until tender. Add remaining ingredients. Bring to boil; reduce heat. Cook 10 minutes or until noodles are done. Stir occasionally. Makes about 9 cups.

CALICO MAIN-DISH SOUP
1½ pounds ground beef
½ cup diced green pepper
⅓ cup chopped onion
2 tablespoons chili powder
1 teaspoon ground cumin seed
1 teaspoon salt
2 cans Campbell's Golden Mushroom
  Soup
1 soup can water
1 can (16 ounces) tomatoes, cut up
1 can (about 12 ounces) corn, undrained
1 package (10 ounces) frozen cut green
  beans
1 cup quick-cooking rice, uncooked

In large heavy pan, brown beef and cook green pepper and onion with seasonings until tender. Stir to separate meat. Add remaining ingredients. Bring to boil; reduce heat. Cover; simmer 20 minutes or until rice is done. Stir occasionally. Makes about 11½ cups.

Cookbook Offer: Get more than 600 exciting recipes in Campbell's "Cooking with Soup" Cookbook. Send $1.50 and any two Campbell's Soup labels with your name, address and zip code to: COOKBOOK, BOX 494, Maple Plain, Minn. 55348. Offer good only in U.S.A. May be withdrawn at any time. Void where prohibited or restricted. Allow six weeks for delivery.

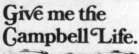

Give me the Campbell Life.

Parents' magazine offer widely recognized seals of commendation or approval for products and services advertised with regularity in the magazines. *Good Housekeeping* maintains a laboratory or has other laboratories test advertised products before awarding the seal. Products tested must live up to advertised claims. *Good Housekeeping* has turned down millions of dollars of advertising because products under test failed to perform as claimed. Both the cost of testing and the refusal of advertisements represent a substantial investment in creating consumer confidence.

Each issue of *Good Housekeeping* carries the following Consumers' Guaranty, which is given in its entirety here because it makes understandable the overall purpose of the seal.

> We satisfy ourselves that products and services advertised in *Good Housekeeping* are good ones and that the advertising claims made for them in our magazine are truthful. If any guaranteed product or service advertised in *Good Housekeeping* proves to be defective, it will upon request and verification be replaced, or the money the consumer paid for it will be refunded. Insurance, realty, automobile, public tansportation, travel facilities, and institutional advertisements are not guaranteed.
>
> The following points should be noted as practical applications of the Guaranty in certain areas: Advertising claims of taste, odor, beauty, etc., are subjective, and accurate measurements are often impractical. Unless such claims are patently in error, we permit them to be made in our pages, even though we may not share the advertiser's opinion. Some products must be installed, used and serviced as the manufacturer directs to give satisfactory performance. We cannot be responsible for faulty installation or service by dealers or independent contractors.

Retailers have found that merchandise carrying the seals will sell noticeably faster than comparable merchandise without the seals. National advertisers, well aware of the seals' selling power, eagerly seek out the magazines' endorsement in order to utilize this additional selling tool.

Circulation

After studying the magazine, you next look at the magazine's circulation. You study numbers and the facts behind the numbers.

The advertiser selling a low-cost, mass-produced, and widely distributed product bought frequently by millions of consumers of all ages, incomes, and occupations might use what appears to be a shotgun approach to advertising. The primary interest, whether in broadcast or print, is simply numbers—large numbers and the larger the better.

The problem with this approach is that each product typically has a core of heavy users. Sometimes the core can be defined geographically. Rice is preferred to potatoes, for example, in several regions of the American south. Sometimes the core can be defined demographically. Age, for example, is the best predictor for bubble gum chewers. Even for regular chewing gum, a shotgun approach using a single advertised appeal may be ineffective. Gum can be chewed for fun, out of habit, for tension relief, for taste or as a substitute for smoking. Magazines may reach audiences who chew gum for different reasons. Advertised appeals should be tailored accordingly.

Even the advertiser interested in a highly selective magazine, using what might be called a rifle approach, is still concerned with the total circulation of the magazine. The advertiser must decide whether the circulation includes enough prospects to warrant advertising in the magazine.

Matching Circulation and Markets. As an advertiser, you also study whether magazine circulation reaches readers where the product is distributed. Some products have quite uniform national distribution and sales. A large circulation magazine may reach substantial numbers of consumers. Often products have a regional or urban or suburban appeal. In such cases you examine circulation specific to such markets. Some magazines even offer you zip-code breakouts of circulation keyed to household income. Such information gives you insight into the characteristics of magazine readers in sharply defined geographic areas.

How Magazines Are Sold. *TV Guide* and the various motion picture magazines enjoy heavy newsstand sales. *Reader's Digest,* by contrast, sells 34 subscription copies for each 3 copies sold singly at newsstands. *Family Circle* sells over 8 million copies of each issue through supermarkets. Advertisers want to know how magazines are sold, knowing this reveals different things about the magazines and their audiences.

Newsstand Sales

Newsstand sales provide sensitive measures of the editorial vitality and appeal of magazines. Figures for weekly publications quickly reveal whether circulation is rising, stable or declining. The figures also quickly reveal regional, suburban, or other shifts in the demand for magazines.

Newsstand sales figures are current and compelling evidence to advertisers. For each sale, someone somewhere was motivated enough to reach into pocket or purse and pay cash for the magazine. For the same reason, magazine editors avidly study newsstand sales. Each copy sold is a vote of confidence in the editorial vitality of the magazine.

From the publisher's standpoint, newsstand circulation is more profitable circulation than subscription circulation because subscriptions often are obtained at reduced rates.

Stress on the value of newsstand sales is evident in the advertising copy given here for *Seventeen* magazine. The copy also stresses the importance of the magazine's editorial policy and the involvement of the magazine's readers in that policy.

"Because our readers are in a rapidly changing period of development, the editorial content of *Seventeen* is tailored to anticipate their needs . . . to prepare them in advance to meet new situations. *Seventeen* helps to enrich each reader's world . . . to broaden her scope . . . to inspire her to excel.

Response at the newsstand . . . where editor and reader meet . . . traditionally indicates true performance of reader service rendered. *Seventeen's* single-copy sales . . . accounts for 68.4 percent of total circulation."

Subscription Sales

As an advertiser, you look up subscription circulation as evidence of a strong commitment on the reader's part. One-, two- or three-year subscriptions are reasonably expensive to most people. Subscription circulation also tends to be stable, important to you for advertising planning six months to a year in advance. On the other hand, circulation stability may not quickly reveal weaknesses in editorial vitality

In addition, consumer magazine subscriptions invariably are mailed to the home, where more than one family member may read the publication. The magazine may subsequently be given to a neighbor, friend, relative or taken to the office for what advertisers call pass-along or secondary readership.

Audience research is conducted primarily with subscription readers, making such readers the best-known portion of the magazine audience. Also, reaching readers frequently through repeated use of the same magazine is accomplished with subscription readers.

Subscription readers are generally a better market for advertised goods. In general, the subscription readers are more likely:

(1) To have a higher income and be made up of a higher percentage of executives and professional people
(2) To own their own homes
(3) To be married
(4) To have bigger families
(5) To have more education
(6) To be somewhat older

Circulation Stability and Growth

You have to make judgments about the circulation figures you study.

Subscription renewal ratios indicate the continued appeal of a magazine to an audience already familiar with the magazine. Audience research previously conducted is usable for longer time periods.

You also ask for the percentage of new or renewed subscriptions gotten at reduced rates or through combination offers in concert with other magazines. Magazines that maintain their subscriptions through one or another form of price reduction may have:

(1) lost part of their editorial appeal, or
(2) expanded circulation beyond the natural core of interested readers and maintain large circulations through very low subscription rates.

Special Editions

The term "special edition" is used in a number of ways in magazine publishing and advertising.

Sometimes the term is used to describe one or more editions of a magazine that both magazine readers and advertisers regard as unusually important. The

December issues of *Esquire* and *Gentlemen's Quarterly* and the *New Yorker* are valued for both fashion and gift ideas. A summer issue of *Marketing Management* includes revised census information of value to marketing and advertising people. That one issue is used as a year-long reference source.

"Bonus" editions are sometimes interchangeably called special editions. Sometimes a monthly magazine may have so much advertising that it publishes a thirteenth issue, called a "bonus" issue.

Special edition also is used in a general way to describe demographic editions or other editions of a single issue, characterized by different advertisements delivered to different target audiences.

Audience Size and Selectivity

Circulation refers to the number of copies of an issue of a magazine, not the readership. Because of their general appeal, consumer magazines often are read by more than one person. A readership survey may reveal an average of 2.4 readers per copy of a magazine. Or it may define the existence, size, location, and other characteristics of the interest market. The readers-per-copy survey research may also reveal unexpected facts about an audience. More women read *Playboy* than might be expected. Women's publications are picked up and scanned by men at home. Knowledge of these unexpected audience characteristics may provide new advertising opportunities.

Demographic Selectivity. As you might expect, *Money* magazine is bought by people with incomes substantially above average. The *Ladies' Home Journal* is read primarily by women. Retirement publications reach mature audiences. Scouting publications will reach youthful audiences. *Catholic Digest* appeals to Roman Catholics. All these are obvious.

Traditional demographic categories of age, income, and occupation often are modified for marketing purposes to include activities or ownership, often with regional appeals. *Welcome to Miami* and *The Beach* are edited for business people and conventioneers visiting Miami, Florida. Dog owners and veterinarians can be reached by *Dogs* magazine. Hunters, campers, and others interested in outdoor activities in nine eastern states would find *Eastern Outdoors* of interest. *Southern Boating* appeals to boatowners from Texas to Florida, the Bahamas, and the Caribbean.

Psychographic Selectivity. When magazine readers are surveyed, the readers sometimes are asked to describe if they agree with sentences such as "I enjoy buying and trying new products," or "I like to buy products I'm familiar with." The reader who agrees with the first statement can be described as venturesome or innovative. You, the advertiser introducing a new product want to reach venturesome readers, believing they are more likely to try new products. The reader agreeing with the second statement can be described as brand loyal, and an obvious target for the advertiser of an established product.

Psychographics is a casually used term in advertising and in marketing. Psychographic information is derived from statements such as those in the preceding paragraph. Responses to such questions reveal something about the

Leg-shaving, face-washing, and other outrageous ways to help save your softness with JOHNSON's Baby Lotion.

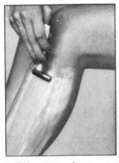

1. Shave your legs. You've probably never thought of shaving with a lotion. JOHNSON'S, however, is the thickest lotion, so it stays right where you put it. And it penetrates the hair to set it up.

JOHNSON'S penetrates the hair to set it up.➤

You'll get a close shave. And afterwards you won't even need to apply lotion to have really beautiful, really soft legs.

2. Wash your face with gentle JOHNSON'S. Specially if your skin tends to be a little dry. Just generously smooth JOHNSON'S all over your face. Massage it into your skin. Rinse lavishly with water.

JOHNSON'S special ingredients will go deep ...help lift out the daily grit and grime...and then leave your face feeling clean and soft.

3. Protect your cheeks against chapping with JOHNSON'S. Smooth it on underneath makeup on cold, wintry days. After all, it's the lotion made to protect the most delicate skin there is.

4. After bath or shower, use JOHNSON'S all over your body. Massaging JOHNSON'S into your skin will help relax and soothe tired muscles; while the lotion will help soften dry skin.

5. Soften your hands with JOHNSON'S lots of ways. Use JOHNSON'S to soften rough, scraggly cuticles. Or, try it on your hands under plastic gloves or even sandwich bags. See if you don't think JOHNSON'S is a good way to pamper your hands anytime.

6. Moisturize after sun with JOHNSON'S. Its rich creamy emollients help soothe the sun-drenched skin. And since it's non-greasy, you can put it on anytime to help keep your beautifully tanned skin, beautifully soft.

JOHNSON's Baby Lotion helps save your softness lots of ways.

Johnson + Johnson

respondent's personality and about the respondent's values, beliefs, and general orientation to life.

Advertisers try to classify orientations to reveal or make specific just how and how many consumers view products. Currently, considerable media research is being conducted on the changing orientations of women. The meaning of their roles as wives and mothers and the meaning and importance of marriage and work are quite different for women who might be described as traditional, transitional, and future-oriented.

Ms. obviously appeals to women with strong career orientations who place higher vlaue on their work and career goals than on the role of mother and housewife. Other women's magazines appeal to women fulfilling traditional roles and holding traditional values. Some women's magazines even now are changing their editorial content, appealing in part to the woman who might hold traditional values while holding down a full-time job as well. Why? Because the majority of married women now work.

Primary and Secondary Readers. Primary magazine readers are those who purchase or subscribe to a magazine, and for many years the only magazine audience research consisted of the circulation figures. When the advertiser wanted more than just circulation numbers, magazine publishers surveyed subscribers. Occasional studies attempted to reach newsstand magazine buyers. Sometimes, large-sample market research studies revealed the characteristics of both subscription and single-copy newsstand magazine buyers.

With the rapid growth of television audiences, magazine publishers realized their formerly large circulation figures were miniscule compared with the tens of millions of television viewers. Advertisers began to develop audience information relating readership-per-copy, giving rise to several principal questions: How many readers of a single copy of a magazine are there? As readers, do secondary readers read with the same degree of intensity as primary readers? Are these additional readers good prospects for advertised products?

Faced by the challenge of television's huge audiences, magazines went beyond circulation figures to projected audiences figures. The figures were projected because they were based on samples of readers, and the results projected to represent the entire audience.

While this move by magazines has been criticized by some advertising people, principally because of uncertainty as to the accuracy of the projected figures, there is no disputing the fact that there is a large secondry or projected readership for many magazines. In fact, it makes no sense to deny secondary readership exists and is important.

Some magazines, of course, have almost no pass-along readership. Usually the more selective and specialized a publication may be, particularly if that specialty is some kind of hobby or avocation, the less likely it is that the magazine will have a high pass-along rate. It may have 100 percent or almost 100 percent primary readership.

Although advertisers want extra readers and magazines like to be able to claim such extra readers, it is rather generally agreed among advertising men that secondary readers do not read the magazines and their advertising with an interest equal to that of the primary readers. Studies made of the two types of readers have indicated that the pass-along audience tends to recall less advertising than the primary audience, that they are less responsive to advertising, and that they pick up and read the magazines fewer times.

An important consideration is that the magazine with a low pass-along audience may have a reader interest among its primary readers that makes those readers worth much more than a magazine made up largely of far less devoted secondary readers.

According to a study made by the Alfred Politz research organization, there is little difference between the readership of the primary readers and the secondary readers who do their reading in the home. *Where* the reading occurs, apparently, is more important than whether the reading is done in a primary or secondary household. This statement is borne out by the Politz findings that showed a drastic drop when the secondary readers did their reading out of the home.

It has been suggested, as a result of these figures, that instead of judging readership simply in primary and secondary terms, it be judged three ways:

(1) In-home primary readership
(2) In-home secondary readership
(3) Out-of-home secondary readership

Repetition in Magazine Advertising. In the discussion of the characteristics of the subscription buyer of magazines it was noted that advertisers are more likely to find repeat impact in this group than in newsstand buyers, who are more sporadic in their purchasing and reading of magazines.

Any discussion of advertising, no matter what medium is being considered, will inevitably come to the point where the question is asked: "But what about the opportunity for repeat messages?" The answer of magazines must be: "Very good."

This repeat exposure of magazines is first of all found in the regular appearance of the magazine on a weekly or monthly basis. Most successful advertisers are frequent and steady advertisers.

Second, and possibly more important when considering magazines versus broadcast media, there is the fact that magazines have a strong "pick-up" factor in their favor. By that is meant the tendency of a magazine reader to read the magazine over a period, to put the magazine down and pick it up again during the course of that period.

This tendency of magazine readers to stay with their publication over an extended period is an advantage that magazines have over television, where advertisements come and go quickly and are seen no more, unless the advertiser can afford to advertise on additional time periods.

Duplication in Circulation. As an advertiser you study the number of readers who receive two or more of the magazines you consider buying. This circulation overlap is called duplication.

In itself, duplication is neither good nor bad. You simply make an assessment of whether it is worthwhile to you for certain readers to see your advertisement two, three or more times in different publications, not to count the number of additional times that may result if the reader uses the magazine on several occasions.

Duplication is higher for magazines than for any other medium. If you are selling a low-cost, simple item, your campaign planning may center on reaching as many different people in the total population as possible. In this case, you may try to avoid duplication as much as possible.

Some advertisers, on the other hand, make no effort to avoid duplication. Costly or technical products may benefit from repeated exposure to the same group of readers. A high-priced automobile, for example, is sold through a wearing-away process—through continued exposure of its many selling points.

Because magazines are "up-scale" demographically; that is, they reach a higher income, better educated audience, there is a tendency for duplication to be heavier in high-income families. Such families read more and can afford more advertised products.

Sometimes duplication is not a problem. Readers of *Catholic Digest* are unlikely subscribers to *The Lutheran. Retirement Living* has no editorial interest for the readers of a youth publication such as *Campus Life*. In many cases, however, you as an advertiser may have to decide what to do about duplication. Do you want it? If not, what can you do?

You may minimize duplication by using the same advertisements in alternate months of publications with substantial circulation overlaps. You may use different advertisements in the magazines, although this can be expensive. Or you can relax and view home duplication calmly, since of the two magazines that go into a single home, one may be read by the man and the other by the woman.

Magazine Reproduction of Advertisements

There is so little difference in the reproduction skill of the major magazines that this product point is of little significance to advertisers in these publications. Among the lesser magazines, however, the factor becomes more important. Also, if we are to consider Sunday newspaper supplements as magazines the factor becomes quite important. Despite the superiority of color reproduction in supplements over ROP daily newspaper color, the supplements have far to go before they match the quality magazines in color advertising.

Campaign planners for a product that cannot be sold with full efficiency unless color reproduction is absolutely faithful—lipstick, floor covering, roofing, paint, and so forth—may wish not to risk the inferior quality of supplement reproduction. Thus, for them the reproduction of advertising is a major consideration, and it may be high among the factors that cause them to invest in one publication rather than another.

If you are planning a campaign for a product that requires absolute fidelity in color reproduction—lipstick, floor covering, paint and so forth—you will not risk the lesser quality of supplement reproduction. In fact, if quality reproduction of advertising is of major importance to you, regular consumer magazines may be your only realistic medium.

Other Magazine Inducements for Advertisers.   What if you wanted to run something other than a standard advertisement? For perfume you might want a "scratch-and-sniff." You might want metallic inks or a piece of foil glued to the page. One advertiser included a bandage sample; another affixed material to show fabric texture and color. The insert and the insert reply card are forms of "extras" which have gained favor with advertisers, and which more and more magazines are willing to offer. Magazines will also cooperate with you if you want to make multipage advertisements that can serve as catalogs for consumers.

Just ask, and you'll find many magazines eager to cooperate with you in developing ingenious and attractive new ways to appeal to readers.

Advertisement Position

As a mail-order advertiser you may experiment for years with various posi-tions within a magazine until certain what positions will yield the greatest results. Rarely will you accept positions other than those specified in the space contract with a magazine.

Other advertisers may be less demanding but may still consider this point if they have certain positions they favor. Once they obtain such positions with cer-tain major magazines, the continued obtaining of these preferential positions has an important influence on their long-time use of a specific magazine. This is especially true of cover positions on which the advertisers stake out a claim, as it were. Back covers, in particular, are sought and held on to by major advertisers in major magazines.

Sometimes, within the trade, you buy the same position so frequently that the position is referred to by your name. Such was the case with the "Campbell's Soup" position in the *Saturday Evening Post* of some years ago. The position was the right-hand page following editorial material. Over the years, the adver-tisement position became familiar to readers who knew, when they saw the Campbell's advertisement, that they were at the end of the section of the magazine containing articles and at the opening of the fiction stories.

Advertiser Use of Magazines

One tip-off as to the desirability of a magazine is its use by well-known advertisers, and especially by successful firms who sell products or services of the same type as the advertiser.

Few advertisers like to be experimenters; they prefer to advertise in magazines that others have already found successful. One way to determine this point is to learn through observation how many advertisers are long-time "repeaters" in the magazine. Another is to read the numerous case histories that will be supplied by the magazines themselves, that can be found in the various trade magazines, or that may be supplied by the Magazine Advertising Bureau that publishes, in behalf of the magazine industry, a long list of successes attained by advertisers who have used magazines.

No advertiser contemplating the use of a magazine for a campaign should fail to study closely:

(1) the editorial character of the publication (a suggestion made earlier), and

(2) the kind of advertisers using the publication and how they use it. At the same time, naturally, the campaign planner will be taking a sharp look at competitors' use of the publication in question.

Some magazines may devote an entire issue editorially to a specific topic—perhaps travel, international problems, a world's fair, fashion, or some other topic appealing to certain advertisers. Such an issue will be an irresistible attraction to an advertiser whose campaign objectives are tied in with the topic. Although the special issue is rarely a major factor in advertising campaign planning, it must be mentioned here for its occasional use.

Reader Response

As an advertiser, you have several ways of gauging reader response to a magazine and the advertisements in it. Readership surveys reveal how completely a magazine is read. Readers may also indicate how accurate, current, and authoritative they believe the magazine to be. Additional information is available from Gallup & Robinson, Starch, and other media research firms that measure the effectiveness of magazine advertisements.

You can test a magazine for yourself with direct-response or couponed advertisements. Response rates vary by magazine, time of year, and nature of offer. The mailing address in couponed advertisements is the advertisers' key to identifying the magazine from which the coupon was clipped. If you don't have time to test, the magazine sales staff usually has abundant evidence of the results obtained by prior advertisers using direct-response or couponed advertisements.

DOLLARS AND READERS: MAKING THE DECISION

You will find the cost-per-thousand formula useful if you

(1) are a large-budget advertiser who uses the formula chiefly for cost comparisons with other media, including magazines, or if you

(2) first must determine whether the page rate falls within your planned budget.

In actuality, only a relatively small number of advertisers can be nonchalant about the cost of full-page advertisements in big-circulation magazines. Thus, although in the long run advertisers may compare magazines by the cost-per-thousand, initially they must consider the actual page cost.

For some advertisers, perhaps you in this case, the cost may mean you must dispense with magazines altogether. Or, you may resort to alternate-month or alternate-week use, enabling you to maintain continuity of contact with readers. You may also combine less frequent use with half- or third-page size advertisements.

Using small advertisements and employing alternate insertions, you can still reach the audience you desire.

Prestige advertisement in consumer magazine.

Products with inherent prestige find magazines the best medium for providing the proper background and audience. This product with true prestige often is advertised in this manner—a small amount of copy, elegant atmosphere, and a dignified, non-busy layout format.

In some cases, advertisers engage in "pulsing," which means that they run heavy advertising in bursts and then cut out advertising for a period. Pulsing is also found in other forms of advertising such as television, outdoor, radio, and newspapers.

FINDING OUT ABOUT MAGAZINES

Industry Information Sources

Any complex, fast-paced industry usually is served by a number of organizations that compile information and do research. The magazine industry is no exception. Research results and other information provide insight into the industry and reference information for those who do business with magazines, in this case advertisers.

There is information available about magazine circulation, advertising volume, and editorial content. Some research firms describe audience size, provide demographic and other audience characteristics, and relate both size and characteristics to media use and product purchase. Other research firms measure magazine advertising effectiveness in various ways.

The following constitutes just a small selection of the numerous organizations to which you might look for information, along with information about the types of information developed by each.

Publishers Information Bureau.   The chief work of this bureau, composed of publishers of magazines and magazine sections of newspapers, is to issue monthly reports of the volume and character of advertising carried by consumer and farm magazines and by newspaper sections and supplements. These reports are in detail and presented account by account.

Typical information includes:

(1)   Total advertising pages and revenue for the current month and for the corresponding month of the preceding year.
(2)   Cumulative advertising pages and revenue, since the first of the year, for the current year and the preceding year.
(3)   Breakdown of magazine advertising totals by 29 types of major advertisers (for example, apparel, food, automotive advertisers).

The value of these reports lies in helping advertisers stay aware of competitive activity; in tracing the popularity of certain publications with various classes of advertisers; and in discovering sharp changes, upward or downward, in the total advertising volume of a magazine.

The Advertising Checking Bureau, Inc.   Concerned entirely with magazine advertising, the Advertising Checking Bureau supplies information in two principal forms. One of these two forms is that of tear sheets, which are advertisements torn out of publications as they appeared. The other form is a report that is custom-designed to supply whatever facts might be needed about a specific campaign, or about the advertising in a certain classification, such as soft drinks, detergents, or shoes. The bureau concentrates on the advertising in the consumer magazine field.

Magazine Publishers Association (MPA). This organization, founded in 1919, has about 100 publisher members who put out many types of publications, including around 300 consumer publications, business publications, agricultural publications, and a number of specialized magazines.

For years the Magazine Publishers Association worked principally in matters concerned with circulation, transportation and distribution, business management, and editorial liaison. The functions of the organization were broadened in 1958, when the MPA was merged with the Magazine Advertising Bureau (MAB). This latter organization, composed of magazine publishers concerned mostly with consumer advertising—and almost all members of MPA—engaged in promotion and research for the consumer magazine industry. Now, under the new arrangement, the MAB will act as a division of the MPA.

Audit Bureau of Circulations (ABC). Since 1914, as was indicated in the text on newspaper advertising, the ABC has been verifying the circulations of newspapers and magazines in its capacity as a cooperative association of several thousands of advertisers, advertising agencies, and publishers.

In the magazine field the ABC members are consumer magazines, business magazines, and farm magazines, with far fewer farm magazines than the other two categories.

There are two types of ABC reports—the *Publisher's Statement* and the *Audit Report.* Circulation claims are found in the *Publisher's Statement.* Issued by ABC for six-month periods ending June 30 and December 31, they are printed for easy identification on colored paper.

An *Audit Report* covers a 12-month period embracing the two latest *Publisher's Statements.* In it are the findings of the field auditor and a section showing how the publisher's claimed circulation compares with the findings of the auditor.

More specifically, the *Publisher's Statement* contains:

(1) The circulation of a specific issue during the year by subscription and single-copy (newsstand) sales. This circulation is analyzed by population-size groups and by states.
(2) Circulation by issues and average circulation for the period—in total, and expressed as subscription; single-copy sales, or bulk.
(3) Subscriptions sold during the six months' period. These are broken down by prices; channels; duration; sponsorship of sale; and use or nonuse of premiums. In addition, the ABC reports the extent of arrears and extensions.

Standard Rate & Data Service, Inc. (SRDS). Standard Rate & Data Service performs the same service for the magazine field that it does for the newspaper field. That is, it supplies information on magazine rates, agency commissions, contract and copy regulations, mechanical requirements, issuance and closing dates, circulation, representatives, and the publication's executives.

Oddly enough, the consumer section of the *Standard Rate & Data Service* lists not only the approximately 800 consumer publications but also the complete lineup of farm magazines. It would seem more natural for the farm magazines to be listed in the business publication section of SRDS.

Now Simmons just gave us match-point.

-WORLD TENNIS-
LEADER IN ITS FIELD
IN TOTAL AUDIENCE
AND CPM

SIMMONS 1977

We've won the big one!

For the first time ever, Simmons has concentrated only on the true tennis enthusiasts in their 1977 U.S. Tennis Market Study. The result: World Tennis has the largest total audience in its field . . . 1,722,000 readers! And the lowest CPM . . . just $2.17*

Simmons also discovered that our readers are more than tennis enthusiasts . . . they're fanatics! Even when they're buying products. They spend way over the average in all consumer categories.

And they love the good life. They have a median household income of $22,090 per year. So every reader's a prime target, not only for tennis products, but all products that add to their active, affluent life-style.

Like to see the new 1977 Simmons Tennis Study? Call Walter Whetstone III, Advertising Sales Director, World Tennis, 383 Madison Avenue, New York, New York 10017, (212) 975-7214. When it comes to tennis magazines, we want you to know the score.

*Based upon current b/w page rate

Reach more of the tennis world in

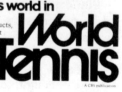

World Tennis

A CBS publication

N. W. Ayer and Sons Directory of Newspapers and Periodicals.   More than 20,000 magazines and newspapers are listed in this thick directory, which has a hard binding, unlike the sections of the *Standard Rate & Data Service.*

Consumer magazines, business publications, and farm publications are all listed, along with all the daily, weekly, and Sunday newspapers.

Each publication is listed according to the city in which it is published. Among the data supplied are facts about these cities, including population figures, principal industries, transportation facilities, and much other information. In addition, of course, there are data about the publication, including mechanical requirements, circulation, frequency of issue, and other needed information. The Ayer Directory, as it is familiarly known, can be found in almost every advertising agency, in media offices, and in most libraries.

Lloyd H. Hall Company.   The Lloyd H. Hall Company publishes monthly reports classifying the editorial content of a number of magazines by subject matter. These reports are called *Magazine Editorial Reports.*

All this information is broken down into the number of lines, pages, and percentage of total editorial content for each magazine for each month and for the current year. Other totals of great interest to advertisers are the ratios of total editorial content to total magazine content. This information helps advertisers determine the balance of the magazine.

Information supplied by the Lloyd H. Hall Company enables advertisers to judge the editorial offerings of magazines. This helps them to determine whether a publication is likely to provide the right editorial climate for the goods or services to be advertised. It will be recalled that the editorial policy of magazines was asserted to be the most important factor to be considered by the advertiser. While the Hall reports do not attempt to judge the quality of editorial content, they indicate the subjects that typical readers of each magazine seem to find interesting.

Consumer Magazine Research

Many organizations develop research about consumer magazines, including the magazines themselves. The research is of two types:

(1)   information about audiences, and
(2)   information about advertisement effectiveness.

Audience Research

Some of the most widely used audience research is provided by Axiom, publishers of *Target Group Index,* and by W. R. Simmons and Associates Research, Inc.

Target Group Index analyzes 120 magazines carrying advertisements for packaged goods and more expensive products, called durables. Magazine audiences are described by traditional demographic characteristics in terms of product usage—heavy, medium, light, and nonusers. Consumers who are brand loyal and brand switchers are likewise identified. More than 30,000 individuals complete the questionnaire booklet from which *TGI* information is extracted.

Simmons *Selective Markets and the Media Reaching Them* describes audiences for 69 magazines and 5 newspaper supplements among other media, including all network TV programs. The report details ownership or usage of more than 500 products and services by demographic characteristics.

Advertising Effectiveness Research

Daniel Starch & Staff, Inc. conduct advertising readership studies on over 100 consumer, general business, and farm magazines. The firm also studies daily newspapers and Sunday supplements from time to time.

Between 100 and 200 respondents of one sex reveal whether they "noted," "associated," or "read most" of the advertisements. Results are expressed in three ways—percentages, readers per dollar, and cost ratios. Each advertisement is given a ranking of its ability to attract readers.

Starch also publishes a *Magazine Adnorms Report*, which reports typical advertisement effectiveness for advertisements of different sizes, color, and position for more than 100 different product categories. Advertisers can measure the performance of current advertising against the adnorms.

Starch uses a "recognition" procedure, whereby readers who can provide evidence of having read a magazine go through the publication page by page with an interviewer. Scores are higher than those achieved by the Gallup & Robinson method of asking readers questions about advertisements with the magazine closed. Although lower, Gallup & Robinson scores reveal more about readership. An advertisement is important to the person who can recall it. What the advertisement actually communicated, including sales point recall, is revealed, as is possible reader misunderstanding of the meaning of the advertisement. The Gallup & Robinson research method places greater demands on the reader's memory. Advertisement persuasiveness is measured by the reader's buying attitude.

Opinion Research Corporation magazine advertisement studies reveal information similar to that developed by Gallup & Robinson. Opinion Research uses follow-up questions to identify target consumers.

Before a new issue of a magazine is circulated, Audience Studies, Inc., gets and distributes advance copies to samples of households after first glueing in (called "tipping-in") copies of new advertisements to be pretested in the natural magazine environment. Subsequent questioning of readers reveals advertisement recall, product interest, and brand preference. An adjective check list is used to gather detailed information.

QUESTIONS

1. (a) What does the "per thousand rate" refer to in magazine advertising?
   (b) Of what significance is this to the advertiser?
   (c) Why is it not wise for an advertiser to select a publication solely on the basis of its cost per thousand?

2. The cost of a full page black-and-white advertisement in a magazine with an estimated circulation of 12,500,000 is $26,300. What is the cost per thousand (to the nearest cent) of the ad?

3. Discuss ways in which each of the following factors has been shown to influence the readership of magazine ads:
   (a) position of ad
   (b) thickness of magazine
   (c) proportion of advertising to editorial matter
   (d) size of ad.

   Answer to question 2:

   $$\frac{\$26,300 \times 1,000}{12,500,000} = 2.02 \text{ (answer)}$$

4. Why are magazines considered the aristocrats of the media?

5. Discuss how magazines develop audiences.

6. Besides cost, what other values would you look for in determining magazine allocation?

7. (a) What is a split run?
   (b) How does a split run work?

8. How might an advertiser gauge advertisement effectiveness in magazines?

9. What is a demographic edition of a magazine?

10. You are considering buying space in a magazine. Why should you examine the advertisements already in the magazine?

11. Discuss the statement: "Duplication is neither good nor bad."

13

BUSINESS ADVERTISING

BUSINESS ADVERTISING

You can hardly wait to get out of school and start working. You look forward to your own career, paycheck, apartment, and independence. For the first and last time in your life you look forward to car payments.

On the job, however, you quickly learn you are still a student. You have joined the largest informal post-graduate educational system in the world. Your campus is both at work and at home. You study during regular working hours, evenings, and weekends. Your texts are what are called business publications.

BUSINESS PUBLICATIONS: LARGELY UNKNOWN BUT INFLUENTIAL

Although many people ignore or are unaware of business publications, these magazines provide the latest, most accurate information for workers of all types, including members of recognized professions. The influence of some small circulation publications is far out of proportion to their circulation. Business publications are scanned, read, studied, and saved for future reference.

Working Information

If you are motivated to excel and advance in your chosen career, you have no choice: you must read business publications.

The term *business publication* is a misnomer describing the magazines that serve the need for working information in their readers' lives. That is the common denominator of the business publication: working information. Whether the writing is in the slangy, breezy style of *Variety* or the meticulously precise language of *Surgical Neurology,* the appropriate business publication is studied with equal care by the entertainer and the surgeon.

Some business magazines are easy to read. *Business Week* reads much the same as *Time* or *Newsweek.* Many publications, however, contain highly technical articles and advertisements not understandable to the reader without a degree in chemical engineering or microbiology.

Rapid Spread of Technology

Business magazines are in a large part responsible for the rapid spread of new technology, new ideas and new manufacturing processes. Thousands of general and specific industry functions are revealed in such titles as *Mining Engineering, Savings Bank Journal, Shoe Service Wholesaler, Vending Times, The Welding Distributor, Modern Brewery Age, Management Leisure Time, Modern Tire Dealer, Leather Buyers' Guide, The Journal of Micrographics, Current Podiatry, Design News, Dental Products Report,* and *Agribusiness Fieldman.* These are just some of the more than 3,100 titles in the SRDS Business Publication volume.

Anything new reported in business magazines is avidly read. The most important research from university, government, or private companies is studied. The import of new tax, regulatory agency, and judicial decisions is examined in detail. Each magazine selects and writes material tailored to reader needs, whether in manufacturing, distribution, finance, service industries, or the professions.

Knowledgeable Readers

For the most part, business magazines are written for small, very knowledgeable audiences. The language is precise, and often technical for people with specialized training or experience in a profession or job specialty.

Scan some business publications at random and you will find them intensely rational and fact-filled. Each serves an audience of experts, some of whom have contributed articles to the magazines in the past. Some magazines serve exclusively professional audiences of doctors, lawyers, accountants, and engineers. Hard, current facts and no-nonsense writing are demanded by such audiences.

Typical Small Circulations

Compared with consumer magazines, business magazine circulations are typically modest. *Business Week's* 750,000 circulation makes that publication a circulation giant. The circulation of many business publications, however, is simply a few thousands. *Compost Science,* a magazine for industrial and municipal officials responsible for the disposal of organic waste, has a circulation slightly over 7,000. *Colorado Municipalities* circulates slightly over 4,000. *Supermarketing* circulates just over 80,000. *Shopping Center World* circulates about 20,000. *American Industrial Properties Report,* edited for those responsible for selecting factory sites, circulates about 30,500. *Alaska Industry* circulates about 8,000.

Intense Reader Interest in Articles

While business publication circulation is small, reader interest is intense. Each sharply focused magazine is written for readers who have common problems to solve.

The majority of readers are well educated and have acquired high levels of competence in their occupations. Readers are both interested and questioning. They measure the usefulness and accuracy of editorial content against what they already know.

Business publications often provide several types of information. Articles provide general economic and industry long-term trend analysis and commentary. Recognized industry leaders may write about the latest environmental or factory safety regulations. Authoritative stories describe new techniques in well drilling for geologists searching for natural gas and oil. Supermarket and institutional feeding publications study the growing fast-food trend. The problems and prospects of each industry or function are examined in detail. In fact, a business publication may assume a position of industry leadership, speaking out, for example, on behalf of the natural gas and oil industries. On occasion, a business magazine may argue that some industry members are engaged in activities that are not in the industry's self-interest. *Advertising Age* sometimes chastises advertisers and advertising agencies for questionable advertising.

Readers are Interested in Advertising

Advertisements in business publications fit the many differenct environments provided by such publications. Often advertisements are fact-filled and highly technical, citing objective research much as students do in term papers. Diagrams, blueprints, engineering specifications, and even mathematical formulae are common. Often advertisements include the first published information about new production processes and machinery, new packaging materials, new lubricant additives, new medical techniques for diagnosing and treating disease, and new techniques for making use of solar energy. These and thousands of additional technical innovations are published every month in thousands upon thousands of business publications.

When critics of advertising level charges at advertising, they often do so completely unaware of the existence of business publication advertising. From readership studies, however, advertisers know that advertisements in business publications are frequently studied with as much care as editorial material in such magazines. The information is often the newest available. Readers have learned to study advertisements for ideas of products that can be used to solve problems at work.

WHY ADVERTISE IN BUSINESS PUBLICATIONS?

Advertisers buy space in magazines for many reasons, some of which are similar to the reasons for buying consumer magazine space. Advertisers want to build market share, sell new market segments, introduce new products and brands, or build a reputation or company identity and awareness with readers.

Many advertising goals are unique to business magazines. The manufacturer of cosmetics may use business publications to solicit new wholesalers and retailers. The advertisements differ from those placed in consumer magazines. Cosmetic manufacturer advertisements tell of the profitability of handling the product line, rapid turnover, ease of selling and use, of high consumer interest and cooperative advertising arrangements, dealer displays, and supporting promotional materials.

Business magazines are used to introduce new corporate names and symbols. Rapidly changing identities, acquisitions and new product lines demand this. Research ability may be advertised to firms requiring new product line versatility, firms needing advice on packaging, or to firms that must meet rigorous clean air standards. Advertised after-sale service may also build a reputation.

To find information about thousands of different product needs, business magazine readers pay as much attention to advertisements as to articles. Advertisements frequently present the newest product development information, whether for information-processing or solar energy. Business publication editorials often are inspired by newly advertised products and processes.

Changing Content

New ideas, techniques, or processes first reported in business publications are often quickly adopted by readers to solve manufacturing or distribution problems. Readers then look for other new ideas to solve other problems. The very success of the business press, in short, requires that editorial content changes constantly to serve the ever-changing needs of readers—changing needs business publications themselves often helped bring about.

Curiously, on the surface it appears that the business press is relatively static. Yet, the number of business publications has grown 10 percent to just over 3,100. The industry has not, however, experienced the tremendous growth enjoyed by television.

In reality, the content of business publictions is undergoing constant and rapid change. Today, for example, entire sections of business magazines report new tax laws or regulatory agency actions important to an industry or job function.

Admittedly, some business publications appear outdated in title and format. *Variety* was a vaudeville publication when founded shortly after the turn of the century. The publication still looks like and retains the flavor of vaudeville.

Variety did not go into eclipse with vaudeville because the magazine changed to serve a broader audience of entertainment professionals. Today *Variety* is avidly read by people who make their living in movies, television, radio, recording, and the personal appearance circuits.

Some business publications change names as the editorial content changes to reach and serve new audiences. *Drug Trade News* changed to *Product Management* and is today known as *Product Marketing. Sales Management* became *Sales and Marketing Management* to reflect the broader range of responsibilities assumed by the traditional sales manager.

Changing Audiences

Many business publication readers traditionally move to top management from manufacturing and engineering backgrounds. During their careers, these readers develop a professional loyalty to the business publications that serve their information needs.

While many business decisions, including buying decisions, are still made at lower and middle management levels, top management ranks are increasingly filled with people who have marketing, financial, or legal backgrounds. Such managers have no tradition of reading the many manufacturing and engineering magazines.

The new breed of top managers operate in a world of increasingly rapid change. Companies change names as they drop one or another product line. They begin manufacturing products quite unlike and unrelated to their traditional products. Mergers and acquisitions accelerate this trend. Companies may shift focus to serve expanding insulation markets and the new market plan for solar energy.

Top management today tends to read business publications and news weeklies appealing to broader audience interests. Corporate advertisements, and the growing number of advocacy advertisements, are placed in general business magazines that deliver a management/executive audience with reasonable cost efficiency. The result: a shift in advertising from sharply defined to more broadly defined management target audiences, delivered by magazines such as *Business Week, Fortune, U.S. News and World Report, Newsweek,* and *Time.*

BUSINESS PUBLICATION AND CONSUMER MEDIA ADVERTISING

Business and consumer advertising differs in several ways, primarily because products and services advertised are bought and sold in different ways. Target audiences in business publications are more precisely identified and buying motives often reflect intensely rational economic and efficiency judgments.

While consumer advertising often carries the entire selling burden, business advertisements are more likely to support personal selling of specialized and often expensive products to sharply defined markets.

The glamour media, such as network television or consumer magazines with colorful center spreads, are bypassed for publications bearing such down-to-earth names as *Locksmith Ledger* and *Feedstuffs.*

Although the majority of business advertising is placed in business publications, for a variety of reasons advertisers sometimes use general appeal or consumer media.

Other Types of Media Used By Business

Radio. Some industrial companies use radio commercials during morning and evening 'drive time' to reach the relatively small number of industrial, institutional, or other buyers in the radio audience. The advertiser may reason that the buyers are receptive to ideas as they prepare for the day's work or that the commercial may suggest a solution to a working problem encountered during the day. The advertiser may want to reach buyers with advertised information that is timely or even urgent.

Where radio is used for business product advertising, it will ordinarily be limited to metropolitan stations in highly industrialized areas.

Imagine what you could do with <u>wire</u> that is...

an electrical conductor with the strength of steel

or hard enough to cut granite

or as fine as human hair

or stronger than any other form of metal

or stiff enough for grinding

or cut into short lengths for reinforcing

or straight enough for push-pull controls

or shaped like a teardrop

or steel-cored with a nickel coating

Use your imagination. Maybe wire can improve your product or solve your problem. Write or call 616/683-8100 for information that helps transform your imagination into reality.

NATIONAL-STANDARD COMPANY
N-S Wire Division
Niles, Michigan 49120

Newspapers.   Business advertisers using newspapers prefer metropolitan dailies in important business centers. Daily newspapers with strong business and financial sections usually attract business people and provide a good working environment for business advertisements.

As with radio and other general-appeal media, the advertiser using newspapers regards the majority of the audience as waste circulation. The advertiser accepts this, reasoning that those prospective buyers who are reached are very important potential customers.

Tennessee Eastman Company used general newspapers for business advertising promoting its plastic, Tenite. Because so many industries use plastic, the company wanted to reach a wide spectrum of management people. Tenite advertisements in *The New York Times,* for example, reached management people in numerous industries.

Consumer Magazines. When business advertisers use consumer magazines, they usually have two choices. One is the big-circulation magazine that has no business section, and which does not make any apparent effort to attract business product advertising. The other choice is the consumer magazine that has a business section or a business slant. Examples include *U.S. News & World Report* and *Time.* A growing number of business advertisements are appearing in news magazines because business publication readers are changing.

Outdoor.   Across the street, not more than 70 yards from the purchasing offices of a major automobile manufacturer, a huge, painted outdoor advertisement displays the name and phone number of a major automotive steel supplier. Every time purchasing personnel look out their windows, they see the advertisement. Many others who pass by see the advertisement also. The advertiser is uninterested in casual passersby. The advertiser wants only to constantly remind steel buyers of the company name and phone number.

Some business advertisers buy outdoor advertisements on major traffic routes to inform salespeople how to reach administrative or factory offices. Companies which give factory tours to the general public also use outdoor advertisements to announce tour times and give directions to reach the factory.

Target Audiences Sharply Defined

Most business advertising is aimed at sharply defined target audiences. The target audience may be composed of electronics engineers, purchasing agents, accountants, or hardware retailers. Media selected reach each of these audiences.

For more general audiences the advertiser may select media that serve varied industries in the same field such as *Iron Age* or a general business publication such as *Business Week.* Sometime the advertiser will select several media knowing that the advertised product is so important and/or expensive that the buying decision is made by a buying committee composed of company financial officers, engineers, production specialists, quality control people, and maintenance people. In this case, the advertiser may create advertisements that address the particular interests of each committee member, placing each advertisement in a business publication appealing to each of the different work interests.

Advertisements Packed with Facts

Consumer advertising, critics claim, does no more than create a "mood" or "feeling" for the product. Were these same critics to read advertisements in business publications, they would find the advertisements packed with hard facts and far more detail than they might want. Some of the advertisements require very specialized graduate study in a physical science for the reader to absorb the meaning of the advertisement.

The Modest Budgets of Business Advertising

Advertising budgets for business advertising are puny when compared to the consumer advertising budgets of Coca Cola, Procter & Gamble or the automobile companies. A million-dollar advertiser in the business field is a giant.

Budgets are modest for several reasons. Business advertising is often assigned a support role for the professional salesperson. The number of possible buyers for machine tools, industrial dyes, and conveyor belts is much smaller than the number of toothpaste and chewing gum buyers. Media space costs are often modest compared to consumer magazine space costs.

Indirect Sales

Business advertising is seldom expected to obtain direct sales. There are many stories of business publication advertisers, especially in the industrial field, who have advertised for 10 to 20 years, or more, who have never been able to trace a direct sale to the advertising.

Questions about the profitability of business advertising become especially sharp among advertisers of components—for example, small parts that make up only one section of a big machine.

Then there are those in the contracting business who get all their business through bidding. An example might be a construction firm specializing in footings for bridges. This firm is one of relatively few firms engaged in such work. Every job of any significance is announced in bid-proposal sheets. Thus, whether the firm advertises or not, it has a chance to obtain such business through successful bidding.

Why continue advertising in cases such as the preceding? There are a number of possible reasons, including maintaining visibility in an industry, reminding buyers of product lines, informing readers of new applications for well-known products, inviting inquiries and sales calls, and identifying potential new customers. Most business advertising supports sales personnel. Direct sales from advertisements are the exception rather than the rule.

Importance of Business Advertising

Business advertising is often viewed as less important than consumer advertising by both company management and advertising agencies. Budgets and media costs are small relative to consumer advertising budgets. Results, as already said, are seldom measured in direct sales.

Because media costs are low relative to consumer media, advertising agencies realize less revenue. After all, fifteen percent of a $3,000,000 consumer advertising campaign is much more attractive than fifteen percent of a $100,000 business advertising campaign. In fact, fifteen percent of a $1,000 page in a business magazine gives the advertising agency so little return that the work often is done under another financial arrangement, such as fee plus costs.

Business advertising is critically important to the company that does no business with consumer markets. Agencies that specialize in business publication advertising regard business advertising equally, if not more, challenging than consumer advertising. Part of the challenge is to accomplish advertising objectives with very modest advertising investments.

KINDS OF BUSINESS ADVERTISING

By business advertising is meant advertising that appears in business publications. Thus this section of the chapter is actually describing the kinds of business publications. As was said earlier, business advertising can use catalogs, radio, newspapers, and other media, but when business advertising is mentioned to the average advertising workers they think automatically of business publications. Other media are usually not even considered in initial discussions.

Because of the peculiar terminology that characterizes the advertising industry, there has been much confusion about what to call business advertising. Many people in the industry solve the problem simply by calling all forms of such advertising by the one term "trade advertising." As will be seen from the following discussion, use of this sweeping term can lead to difficulties. The same people who use the term "trade advertising" to cover business advertising in its many forms will usually refer to business publications as "trade papers." This causes even more confusion since (1) most business publications are not "papers" in any sense of the word, and (2) there are many business publications that do not even approach the meaning of the word "trade," such as the magazines serving the medical profession.

A breakdown of the kinds of business advertising is given here. It must be understood, however, that some magazines in the business field will not fall conveniently into any one of the classifications. Still others may serve two or more of the classifications. Despite these variations, it is useful to have some kind of classification to make discussion of the subject easier.

General Business Publications

Usually such publications will take a strong management slant and will cut across industry lines. They should be classed as horizontal publications, therefore. Among the most prosperous are:

Fortune	*Barron's-National Business*
	& Financial Weekly
Business Week	*Wall Street Journal*
Forbes	*Nation's Business*
	Dun's Review

Specialized Business Publications

Numerous publications fall in this category, which actually embraces many publications listed under other headings. A number of these, like the general business magazines, have a decided management slant. Among these publications are:

Advertising Age	*Journal of Accountancy*
Modern Office Procedures	*Personnel Journal*
	Purchasing Magazine

Industrial Publications

Another large classification, industrial magazines, very often adds another group of interested readers, the engineers. Many of these publications assume that the readers, in addition to having a management interest, will also have a deep knowledge of technical subjects such as engineering, physical science, physics, and electronics. Included here may be:

Industry Week	*Plant Engineering*
The Iron Age	*Consulting Engineer*
Electronic News	*Assembly Engineering*
Power	

Trade Magazines

Those in retail, merchandising, and mercantile activities are served by trade magazines aimed largely at retailers but also of interest to those who supply or service the retail trade. Found among the many publications in this class are:

Progressive Grocer	*Supermarket News*
Hardware Retailing	*Office Products*
Drug Topics	*The College Store Journal*
	Supermarketing

Professional Publications

Aimed at doctors, dentists, architects, lawyers, or teachers, among others, these publications seem far removed in their editorial content from the world of business, but their advertisements seek business just as unmistakably as the more obviously commercially oriented publications.

ADVERTISING OBJECTIVES

Business publication advertising objectives range from general to specific. Target audiences may be broadly defined to include general consumers or narrowly limited to civil engineers in South Carolina or to trucking industry managers in Arizona reached through the *Arizona Roadrunner.*

General

Lumbering and paper products advertisers serving primarily an industrial and business market may wish to reach general consumers to relate how reforestation works in harmony with nature.

Some product manufacturers with wide and diversified lines may find it impossible to advertise each product they make. The company may define advertising objectives designed to enhance the corporate image by conveying information about research and product development and quality control. When advertising of many individual products is impossible, the corporation may attempt to influence buyers to regard the company, and therefore all its products, as reliable and trustworthy.

Specific

Many companies, especially small ones, have a single objective in business publication advertising: to obtain *inquiries.* To achieve this objective the advertisers may coupon every advertisement. Offers of sample materials or literature may be included. The objective, of course, is to develop sales leads. This type of advertising tends to be the most measurable. Advertisers keep track of inquiries generated by different advertisements in a variety of business publications. The number of inquiries subsequently converted into sales provides another measure of advertising and publication effectiveness in reaching and motivating the right prospects.

Sometimes business publication advertisements do the entire sales job, generating orders for simple products often sold in bulk. In such cases the buyer often has done prior business with the advertiser.

Support Objectives

For the most part, business advertising is assigned support objectives, or objectives designed to make salespeople more effective. Salespeople traditionally have been and remain the key for selling products to business buyers.

Often salespeople are formally educated in engineering or chemistry or biology. Often the company provides additional specialized training. Only then are salespeople allowed to call on customers as highly trained and paid representatives who offer expert advice and counsel to buyers.

To support the efforts of salespeople, advertising objectives such as the following may be used:

(1) Make buyers aware of the company and its products so it is easier for salespeople to meet prospects.

(2) Introduce new products and special services to prospects.

(3) Identify key prospects through couponed advertisement returns requesting product brochures or sales calls.

(4) Suggest new uses for existing products to increase the number of new buyer accounts.

(5) Announce a company's entry into a new market.

The Need of Salespeople for Business Publication Advertising. Diaries kept by salespeople reveal that only about 40 percent of their time is spent in face-to-face selling. The remainder is absorbed in travel, waiting for interviews, filing reports, attending meetings, and making service calls. Salespeople also know the toughest sales call is a "cold call;" that is, a sales call made on a buyer who does not know the salesperson, the company, or product. What the buyer often says is summed up in a McGraw-Hill advertisement directed to business advertisers. The copy reads:

You don't know who I am.
You don't know my title.
You don't know where I work.
You don't know what I do.
You don't call on me.
You don't mail things to me.
You don't even know that I exist.
But—I can make or break your sale.
MORAL: You make more friends than you know—with business magazine advertising.

The copy quickly expresses what is going through the buyer's mind. Each statement is an argument against buying.

Reaching The "Unreachables"

McGraw-Hill's research department has found that the "typical" company salesperson calls on:

    Only 6 percent of the management people

    Only 6 to 8 percent of the production and plant services group

    Only 15 percent of the purchasing agents

Business advertising, therefore, fills in for salespeople, reaching many otherwise unreachable buyers or people who influence buying decisions.

Buying Influences

Children influence what breakfast cereals their mothers buy. Wives influence family car-buying decisions. Teenage peer group membership influences what teenagers buy and wear. These and other influences are well known and taken into account by advertisers of consumer products.

Business advertisers face much more complex buying influence problems. Expensive machinery, for example, often is purchased on the recommendation of a buying committee after lengthy discussion. It is difficult, sometimes impossible, to learn just who is on the committee and who has the most influence in arriving at a buying decision. In time, committee membership changes. Companies may have several buying committees working on the same or different purchase decisions.

Reaching all these people is impossible for the machinery salesperson. In one plant, for example, the advertiser discovered that business publication advertisement reached 150 people who were possible buying influences. The advertiser's salesperson, in contrast, had access to only 3 of those 150 persons reached through advertising.

DEVELOPING BUSINESS PAPER CAMPAIGNS

A number of fairly clear-cut steps must be taken in setting up a campaign. These steps include:

(1) Determining objectives—goodwill, image building, inquiries and developing sales.

(2) Deciding who will be targets in the campaign and determining how to buy—analyzing markets served; considering other channels of distribution; learning whether buying decision are made individually or by committee; finding out if there is a long lag between sales contact or advertising exposure or both, and buying action; and locating the prospects in order to determine whether they are scattered or clustered.

(3) Deciding how much advertising impact and saturation is needed—alternative markets, inserts, duplication.

(4) Deciding in general the business publications best suited to reach advertising objectives and markets, whether vertical or horizontal.

(5) Setting up the schedule—how often to make insertions, how big a space to use.

But before anything is done, some preliminary work should include: (a) a thorough analysis of the product to determine its quality and suitability for the intended markets and (b) an assessment of the overall job to be done that will enable planners to determine roughly what kind of budget will be required to accomplish objectives. If such a preliminary assessment is not made, the objectives may be too ambitious or not ambitious enough.

In planning the development of sales the business advertiser establishes marketing goals. This has complexities enough, if there is just one product, or one product line. In the case of many industrial producers, however, there may be a large number of product lines that include thousands of products. Despite the added complexity in such cases, goals should be established for each product line. The best procedure is to assign the major part of the advertising budget to those products that offer the most promising opportunities for increased volume or profit, or both.

Determining Target Audiences And Reasons For Buying

No advertising or marketing objective will ever be attained if there is a faulty knowledge of buyers for the product. Even this knowledge, however, is not enough. It is necessary to know, in addition, the Who, What, Where, When, and How of the buying process. Some steps to take in achieving this knowledge are described in the next paragraphs.

Details should be obtained that will indicate, vertically and horizontally, the markets served. Vertically, taking the textile industry as an example, there would be the fabric mills, converters, dyers and finishers, end-product manufacturers, jobbers, and wholesalers, and retailers. Horizontally, using the office equipment market as an example, the ultimate buyers would be at many different levels in many industries or fields.

Although there are numerous way to locate markets, two are especially usable by business marketers: (1) Standard Industrial Classification, discussed earlier in this book, and (2) circulation statements of business magazines that are appropriate for the industries or fields concerned.

Standard Industrial Classifications, most frequently called S.I.C., were established some years ago by the federal government to provide a way of categorizing industries so that everyone concerned with business would be able to refer to industries in the same way. Thus, under the S.I.C. system, each industrial category has been given a numerical designation. Small-digit classifications refer to the basic industry. As digits get larger, the classification breaks down the industry into smaller, more specialized units.

An example of the S.I.C. system at work is afforded by the primary metals industry, which is given a two-digit classification of 33. While this designation might satisfy some marketers, there are others who want a further breakdown. This is provided by a four-digit breakdown in the primary metals industry. One of the four-digit classifications is, to illustrate, 3362, which covers copper and brass foundries in the primary metals industry.

More than 400 industries have been classified by the government. The classification lists the number of plants and the county location of the plants.

Sales Management magazine also supplies useful information by listing shipments and employment in each S.I.C. industry by county and plants.

Circulation statements of business magazines will, in many cases, provide breakdown by S.I.C. classifications, as well as by geographic location. Even where the S.I.C. classifications are not furnished, the circulation breakdown is an invaluable guide not only for determining the suitability of the publication but also for determining the extent and breakdown of the market. This kind of breakdown is not possible in consumer publications, which have far less well-defined readership than business magazines.

Tables 13-1 through 13-3 show the circulation breakdown for *Chemical & Engineering News*. The circulation is broken down by three-digit S.I.C. numbers in table 13-1. Subscriptions also are presented by the type of job the subscriber does (called function) and (in table 13-3) by major chemical processing industry (CPI) companies.

After the "who" has been satisfactorily determined, it is necessary to ascertain what distributive channels are suited for reaching different elements in the market. These might include anyone from a wholesaler or a jobber to a distributor or manufacturer's representative. When these channels are known, it is then important to know the number, geographic location, and dollar volume of goods and services distributed in each of the categories.

TABLE 13-1
Industrial Subscribers, by S.I.C

S.I.C.	Process Industires	Plants Covered	C &E News Subscribers
281, 289	Chemicals	4,639	18,510
130,290	Oil, Gas, Petroleum	1,017	4,807
282	Plastics	1,285	7,474
300	Rubber	682	2,840
283	Pharmaceuticals	1,035	7,419
200	Food & Beverages	1,355	3,055
220, 230	Textiles	425	1,591
240, 260	Paper & Pulp	635	1,672
284	Soap & Cleaners	758	1,975
285,286	Paints & Allied Products	604	1,520
287	Fertilizers & Pesticides	356	1,421
320	Stone, Clay, Glass	472	1,231
330	Primary Metals	651	1,585
340	Fabricated Metals	330	1.098
350	Machinery (non-electric)	561	1,019
360	Electrical Machinery	890	1,073
370	Transport Equipment	330	757
380	Instruments	568	1,255
009	Nuclear Plants	33	655
	Other Manufacturing	379	1,125
900	Government	....	9,009
490	Public Utilities	....	585
	TOTAL INDUSTRIAL (only)	17,005	71,676

Note: A complete *four*-digit breakdown is available.

table   13-2   and   table   13-3

TABLE 13-2
INDUSTRIAL READERS, BY FUNCTION:

Function	Primary Industrial Subscribers	Total Industrial Pass-along	Industrial Readers
Management	17,489	22,076	39,565
Process Development	13,834	20,471	34,305
Design & Construction	2,222	4,014	6,236
Production, Plant Operations	4,874	8,830	13,704
Product Research & Development	25,086	23,280	48,366
Marketing, Technical Service	6,953	7,225	14,178
Other Job Functions	1,218	14,450	15,668
INDUSTRIAL (only) READERS	71,676	100,346	172,022

TABLE 13-3
Subscribers, by CPI Companies

CPI Company	C & E News Subscribers
E. I. Du Pont	3,538
Goodyear	418
Union Carbide	1,743
Procter & Gamble	274
Dow	1,237
General Electric	978
Shell	845
Monsanto	1,013
CPC International	287
Eastman Kodak	934
Merck	436
American Cyanamid	1,197
Celanese	532
Exxon Corp.	967
Hercules	533
PPG Industries	305
Rohm & Haas	559
Pullman Kellogg	75
3M Company	408
Olin Corp.	490

Learn whether buying decisions are made individually or by committee. If a buying decision is made by a committee, the advertising and selling job is more complicated. Instead of reaching one person, a number of persons must be influenced by the advertising. Possibly more than one publication must be included on the media list, even though all members of the committee are working for the same organization, since their job titles and functions may differ sharply.

Find out if there is a long lag between sales contact or advertising exposure, or both, and buying action. Some products are bought quickly; with others there may be a time lag of several years between original contact and the issuing of a purchase order. Such a time lag is likely to occur in the buying of expensive machinery, but it can happen with simpler and less expensive items. In order to understand what may be expected from advertising, it is necessary to have a reasonable idea of the purchasing time lag.

Locate the prospects and determine whether they are clustered or scattered. If sales are along the Atlantic seaboard in close accordance with sales coverage patterns, the use of national business publications might be questioned. Perhaps direct mail or some other more selective medium should be used. The answer to this question will depend somewhat on how high space costs are. If they are not very high, the advertiser may reason that it is worth spending money to reach prospects through business publication advertising despite the wasted circulation going to parts of the country where there is no distribution.

Advertising Dollars and Use

There are no clear-cut rules that say how much money should be invested in advertising. Each company is unique and has unique marketing and sales problems. Each company solves problems in different ways. The only truism advertising managers agree on is that there is never enough money for advertising. The challenge is to make each advertising dollar work as hard as possible.

The advertiser examines the options: "Should I use small advertisements in several publications? Big advertisements in a few publications? Do I cut advertisement size or the number of publications to advertise frequently? Do I advertise during alternate months only? Should I try an insert for a change because insert readership is high? Because inserts are costly, if I use inserts, where would I cut back?"

The advertiser also studies the duplication, or audience overlap, of business publications. For a simple, inexpensive product—a cleansing agent for factory floors, for example—high duplication may be wasteful. Buyers give little thought to purchase decisions. For expensive, automated machinery for factory assembly lines, duplication may be desirable. Buyers think long and hard before buying. Repeated advertising to such buyers may influence their decisions.

Selecting Publications

A manufacturer of aircraft compasses may buy space in a small number of what are called *vertical* publications. The compass manufacturer relies on a small number of publications because the number of manufacturers is relatively small. Vertical publications are those written for all people, from top management to production line workers, in a single industry. Advertisements may be written for all readers or for aeronautical engineers or instrument panel designers and/or assemblers.

A manufacturer of plastic products for many industries, on the other hand, may use a large number of business publications, often choosing what are called *horizontal* publications. Horizontal publications appeal to people who perform the same basic function in many different industries. *Purchasing World,* for example, is read by purchasing executives in companies making a wide range of products, including adhesives, bearings, chemicals, electronic components, lubricants, and power tools.

Examining Business Publications

While space in business publications generally costs much less than comparable space in conusmer magazines, the business advertiser examines business magazines as carefully as any consumer advertiser. The business advertiser, in fact, has a considerable advantage over the consumer advertiser. Business publications usually have a great deal of precise audience information.

Editorial Environment.   The advertiser first studies the business publication with following question in mind: "Does this publication make itself indispensable to readers by providing current and usable information for people at work?" The advertiser knows that an editorially strong publication almost always attracts the number and kind of readers who are responsive and profitable for the publication's advertisers.

Market Coverage.   Usually in any field one business publication is the recognized leader. The advertiser must decide whether that single publication reaches most or all of the target audience.

The advertiser's problem may be relatively simple. It has been shown, for example, that in most industries 50 percent of the firms do 90 percent of the business and will buy about 90 percent of the equipment, raw materials, semifinished products or components and supplies. Business concentration is even more obvious in several industries, where 10 percent of the companies may do 50 percent of the business and so represent 50 percent of the advertiser's market.

If the marketing objectives guiding the advertiser's decisions stress maintaining contact with a relatively small number of current major buyers and if one business publication reaches those buyers, the advertiser may use a single business publication.

Typically, however, marketing objectives express other goals such as reaching new (and perhaps smaller) buyers or entering a completely new market. If this is the case, the advertiser may buy space in several business publications for different reasons.

Business Publication Use by Other Advertisers.   Business publication advertisers sometimes appear to play follow-the-leader. Manufacturers of industrial instruments and controls, for example, may concentrate their advertising in one, tow, or three publications. If this is the case, it is because these publications have proved effective in reaching and influencing buyers.

Where competitors are advertising is an important clue for the first-time advertiser of a new industrial instrument. The advertiser entering a new market knows there must be good reasons for the use of some publications and not others. Business publications salespeople are questioned sharply about audience size and characteristics. Case histories of successful advertisements and advertising campaigns and numerous other types of evidence are studied before the advertiser reaches a media buying decision.

Circulation and Audience Information.   Circulation and audience characteristics are what business publications sell to advertisers. These may be judged in a number of ways, such as by:

(1)   The number of copies mailed out for each issue
(2)   Where the copies go geographically and by company address
(3)   To whom the copies go by title and job function
(4)   Whether the magazine is subscribed to or distributed free to recipients
(5)   How subscriptions are sold and for what length of time
(6)   How many subscribers renew their subscriptions

Current, accurate information about size and other circulation characteristics of business publications can be obtained from independent auditing organizations such as the ABC (Audit Bureau of Circulations) or the VAC (Verified Audit Circulation) Corporation. Additional information about these organizations appears in later pages.

The Cost of Reaching Audiences.   Both the business advertiser and the consumer advertiser relate space costs to audience size through the cost-per-thousand computation. The business advertiser, however, operates under the smaller space costs and audience figures characteristic of business publications. Also, because the advertiser knows much more about business publication audiences, the CPM computation can precisely reveal the cost of reaching readers in each of ten corporations in Delaware or twenty large institutional food services in Michigan.

Mechanical Versatility.   Business publications offer advertisers more mechanical flexibility than other print media. Both consumer magazines and many business publications offer advertisers split runs, previously discussed in the chapter dealing with consumer magazines. Both offer quality color reproduction.

Business publications are more likely than consumer magazines to devote a page to the listing of advertisers, including company addresses. Business publications are more likely to offer inserts, foldouts, cutouts, and other customer-designed techniques to obtain extra attention for advertisements.

The most distinctive characteristic of business publications is the use of reader service cards, called "bingo" cards, in numerous magazines. The cards make it easy for readers to send for additional information about products or services advertised in a specific issue of a publication.

Paid or Controlled Circulation?

Among readers of business publications these days has evolved an almost universal agreement that valuation of a business publication should be based upon its editorial worth rather than upon whether it has a *paid* or a *controlled* circulation. Many businessmen readers, in fact, are unable to tell, if asked, whether a business publication's circulation is mostly paid or controlled. If the publication is useful to them in their work, they, as the expression goes, could not care less whether the publication has a paid or a controlled circulation. They are however, still interested in whether the circulation is audited.

For years, however, the paid vs. controlled argument has taken up the attention of business publication advertisers. It is always a heated topic in the business press, and the publications themselves keep the topic alive. Suffice it to say that there are many good paid publications and many good controlled publications. The final judge of the worth of one or the other is the advertiser who says: "Let's use this one. It gives us better results."

How To Determine Circulation — Auditing

Because business publication advertising space rates are based upon circulation, advertisers require accurate circulation figures. Several independent organizations exist solely to audit circulation, thereby assuring the advertiser that the circulation charged for is indeed delivered. Some of these are:

Audit Bureau of Circulations. The ABC audits hundreds of business publications on behalf of a membership composed of publishers, advertisers and advertising agencies. For a business publication to qualify for ABC membership, at least 50 percent of its circulation must be from paid subscriptions.

Business Publications Audit of Circulations. This organization, known as the BPA, verifies circulation claims, whether a publication's circulation is paid or "controlled."

Controlled circulation is circulation that goes free to a selected list of people in a certain industry or trade, even if the recipients do not ask to receive the publication. Many advertisers question conrolled circulation, believing readers pay more attention to publications the readers are willing to pay for.

Standards have been established for measuring controlled circulation. Circulation information must show geographic distribution, sources of names, functions and titles of recipients, and other useful information.

The BPA verifies the circulation of even more publications in the business field than does the ABC.

Verified Audit Circulation Corporation. This organization, called the VAC, is smaller than either the ABC or the BPA. The VAC audits both paid and controlled circulation publications, including some publications that combine these two types of circulation. The VAC makes its circulation audits available to all publications without regard to the field served, the amount of paid or controlled circulation, or the manner of distribution.

All audit organizations, in brief, provide advertisers with proof that the circulations of audited publications actually are what publishers claim.

Publications That Are Not Audited. Some publications are not audited because they are not members of the ABC or the BPA. Some publishers just refuse to join, while others do not meet membership requirements in the two organizations. Such publications often are headed by stubborn or very independent publishers who issue their own sworn circulation statements. These statements, the publishers believe, should be just as reassuring to the advertiser as statements verified by an independent auditing organization. Many advertisers do not agree.

ADVERTISING IN BUSINESS AND FARM FIELDS

At first glance you might think buying space in business publications is all the same.

After all, many business publications and consumer magazines look alike. You can use many of the same terms when talking about both groups of magazines. You even make the same type of decisions about advertisement size, locating the advertisement in the publication, the use of color, and/or inserts and advertising frequency.

BUSINESS PUBLICATION ADVERTISING AND CONSUMER MAGAZINE ADVERTISING DIFFER

For a number of reasons, however, your business publication advertising will differ from your advertising in consumer magazines. From the previous chapter, you are aware that the illustrations or art, the appeals and the language used to express the appeals in headlines and copy will be different. The information on which you base decisions often differs from that available for consumer magazines. Your advertising objectives differ. Your markets are much more sharply defined, and sometimes a single buyer may account for 20 or 30 percent or more of your sales.

Also, business publications are read with different expectations, often with a seriousness seldom encountered in consumer magazine readers. Then there is the complex problem of identifying and reaching buying influences. For these and numerous other obvious and subtle reasons you advertise differently in business publications than in consumer magazines.

Maintaining Contact

Business publication advertisers usually stress repetition more than consumer magazine advertisers. The business advertiser knows the existing market in great detail. Subscription circulation breakdowns reveal magazine reach in industries and individual companies. If requested, business publications can provide advertisers with circulation breakdowns by function or job title within a single company.

Assume for the moment that you sell to the chemical products industry. Information in the previous chapter revealed the number of subscriptions *Chemical and Engineering News* sends to such buying giants as Du Pont, Shell, Dow, and Goodyear. You already know your sales volume with each of these companies. You also know what additional sales you want to make to each company. These companies, in fact, represent the most logical buyers of your products. You must maintain contact with these important customer companies.

Or, think of it another way. The loss of business with even one of your top twenty major buyers would represent a substantial business setback. You must maintain contact with such companies as often and in as many ways as possible. You might well advertise in every issue of *Chemical and Engineering News.*

Reader Selection and Repetition

You use repetition also because readership studies indicate that even the most successful business publication advertisements are seen only by perhaps 25 to 30 percent of readers. Only about 9 percent read most or all of the typical advertisement. Knowing this in advance, you repeat advertisements, unwilling to chance that major buyers of your products may miss your single advertisement in a single issue of a business publication.

Many advertisement readership studies reveal that readership actually increases when a good advertisement is repeated. With each additional insertion, a growing number of readers will see the advertisement for the first time, while another group of readers will recall having seen the advertisement before.

Each advertiser decides how many insertions of an advertisement are enough. One way to do this is watch the coupon returns of requests for information generated by advertisements. The advertiser stops using an advertisement when coupon returns or information requests taper off.

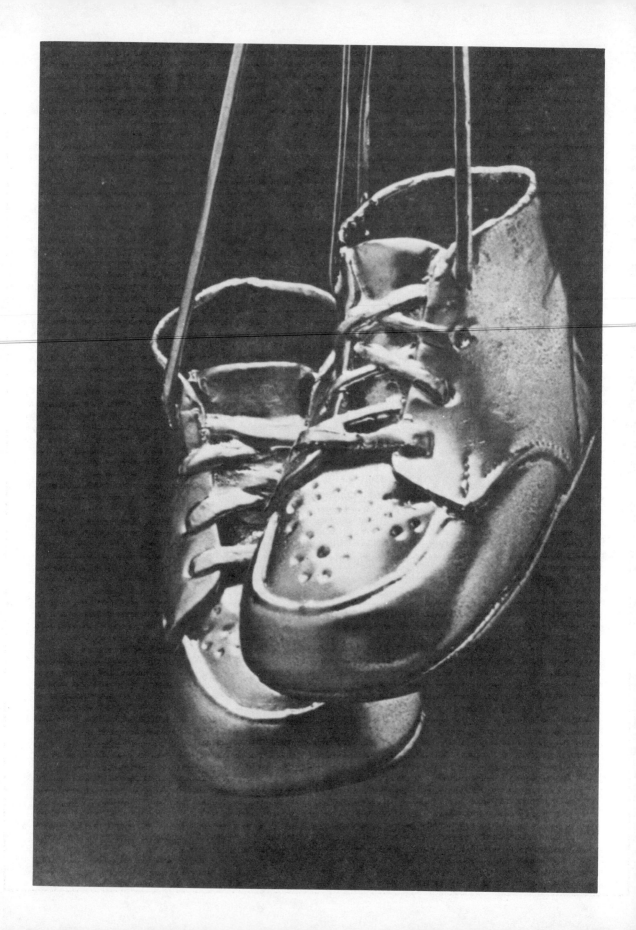

ALL THE TIME WE WERE GROWING UP, WE WANTED TO GROW UP SMALL.

When The Timken Company got into the steel business back in 1916, it was strictly a family affair. We made our steel to go into our bearings.

We gave our steel plenty of tender loving care. Just to make sure we made it just right.

Pretty soon, other companies started asking for Timken® steel. We started to grow. And we kept on growing, until today we make steel for hundreds of companies besides our own.

But we never lost sight of our small beginnings, and we still make steel the way we made steel then — with tender loving care.

We still treat every heat of Timken steel as if it were in the family — from scrap to finished product. We test every order every step of the way — up to 30 times in all — to make sure that it fits your specifications exactly. That its quality stays uniform, order after order.

To us, that's the only way to make steel. After all, we wouldn't have gotten as big as we are if we hadn't grown up small.

The Timken Company, Steel Division, Canton, Ohio 44706.

Steel. As you like it.

TIMKEN®

REGISTERED TRADEMARK

You might argue against using the same advertisement more than once, believing that readers must see something new each time they come across your advertisements. The counterarguments are as follows:

(1) Even a good advertisement reaches on the first time run only about one-third of the readers.
(2) Several exposures to the advertisement may be required before the message is learned, especially for advertisements using long copy to explain complex products.
(3) The advertisement must appear about the time a prospective buyer is getting ready to buy because memories are short, and an advertisement noted three months prior is long forgotten.
(4) Magazine readership is not stable and varies from month to month as people vacation or as subscriptions lapse and new readers buy subscriptions.

Making Advertising Decisions for Business Publications

Advertisers in business publications and the consumer magazine advertiser ask themselves many of the same questions. The decisions they arrive at may be quite different. After all, research information differs. The importance of target audiences may be quite different. The way in which each group of publications is read is quite different. Even so, many of the types of decisions advertisers make are similar.

Which Page? Left or Right?   The question of left-hand versus right-hand pages has been battled in newspapers, consumer magazines, and business publications. In business publications the evidence seems to point to a slight advantage for right-hand pages, as indicated by studies by Starch, McGraw-Hill, and Readex. Only the Industrial Advertising Research Institute has found a *significant* advantage for the right-hand pages, but these findings came from a preliminary study, the results of which change after further investigation. Still, it seems quite probable that here, too, some advantage will continue to show up for the right-hand page.

Why Buy a Cover?   Although readership findings for consumer magazines tend to vary from those for business publications, there is one point of agreement—cover positions in business publications command more readership than inside pages.

One study of Starch scores, for instance, found that the "noted" scores (the scores indicating how many readers had seen the advertisement) gave scores of about 15 points higher for the second cover, 12 points higher for the third cover, and 20 points higher for the fourth cover, which is the outside back cover. In addition, it was found that advertisements facing the third cover gained about 10 points from being in that position.

Despite the increased readership so often found for covers, they do not always give enough increase to make up the extra cost, with covers costing somewhat over one-third more than a two-color page. A McGraw-Hill study, for instance, showed that the readership advantage for covers ranged from 14 to

100 percent. Thus, it becomes evident that, while some of the advertisements yielded a bonus readership, it was not enough to justify the extra cost of this position.

Do You Buy Space in Thick or Thin Publications? As publications, whether business or consumer, become thicker and thicker with advertisements and text matter, you, as an advertiser, become concerned. You check to learn whether advertisement readership declines in thick magazines, smothered by the sheer weight of other material competing for the reader's attention.

Publishers of successful business publications (almost always thick publications) have a strong interest in this subject, since they must answer advertisers who worry about decreased visibility of their advertisements in the multipage magazines.

To answer this question, *Purchasing* magazine analyzed Starch scores for each page of an issue of their publication which, in this instance, ran to 159 pages, exclusive of the two back covers. The following sampling of scores from the study demonstrates consistent advertisement readership throughout the publication.

Page	Noted Score	Page	Noted Score
6	36	67	39
14	38	106*	40
24	35	118	30
30	38	121*	40
34*	58	139*	50
45*	47	143	32
47	35	151*	46
56*	58	155*	38
62	34		

*Insert

Generally speaking, advertising visibility does not seem to suffer because of the number of pages in a publication, and in many cases it actually does better.

A number of magazine studies by McGraw-Hill have supported this view, whether the measure of advertisement effectiveness was readership scores or actual sales resulting from the advertisement.

One note of caution must be intruded here, despite the results that have just been quoted. As a publication adds pages it becomes necessary for the advertiser to use every technique in copy and layout to make advertisements stand out. A poor advertisement will not stand up in the crush of competitive material.

Why Use Inserts? Use of inserts often will assure attention for advertising even in the thickest magazines. A glance back at the figures for advertisements Starched in *Purchasing* magazine reveals the best-read advertisements were inserts.

Despite the proved attention-getting power of inserts, too many inserts in a magazine become a distracting nuisance to readers. Inserts make the magazine "break" or open at the insert, stealing reader attention from other advertisements. Over-reliance on inserts to get attention may lure the advertiser into paying less attention to the advertising content. The intelligent buyer quickly distinguishes form and content, learning to ignore advertisements that do not quickly give important business information.

The advertiser must strike a balance. Inserts should be used occasionally for their attention-getting power. Ideally, the advertisement is inserted in a magazine issue with only a few other inserts. Equal attention should be paid to the advertising content.

Why Pay for Color?   Ever since color was first introduced into print advertising, color advertisements have attracted greater attention, developed higher readership, coupon returns, and (very often) direct sales. The increased cost for using color—typically 35 percent—requires that the use of color be justified.

As with consumer advertising, sometimes the advertiser has no choice. Products such as paints, dyes, rugs sold for office use, and numerous other products require color. Color may be ineffective for products sold in bulk. Each advertiser experiments to learn whether the additional cost for color justifies the additional expense.

Color in a business publication advertisement will have a better chance of attracting attention. Just how much more attention is indicated by the fact that in more than 2,500 advertisements tested by McGraw-Hill, the four-color pages had average noted scores 77 percent higher than black-and-white pages, and that spreads (two-page advertisements) averaged 63 percent higher. In both cases the increase in readership was greater than the increase in cost.

Is Timing Critically Important?   Most advertising budgets are approved around the first of the year. Some managements insist on seeing the report of the operations for the year ending December 31 before committing themselves to a budget of expenditures.

Before the advertising program is definitely set, therefore, it is often March 1, or later. Under such circumstances there is little or no advertising during January, February, and March. The time lag between approving an advertising budget and developing the yearly advertising program creates difficulties for the advertising department, especially in handling schedules with business magazine publishers.

Publishers operate on calendar-year contracts with rates and frequency discounts based on every-month insertions. Unable to advertise every month, the advertiser may not qualify for frequency discounts.

The advertiser in fact faces several penalties. Contact with buyers is lost for several months, the cost of space purchased increases, and readership may be lost during periods of intense buying activity.

The loss of readership is particularly painful to business advertisers. Unlike consumer advertising, business advertising draws consistent readership throughout the year, even when allowance is made for variations in monthly and seasonal response to advertising.

What can you as an advertiser do to maintain year-round advertising? You would attempt to get your annual advertising budget approved no later than November 1. This would permit your advertising for the coming year to start in

January without loss of continuity. This means work on next year's budget starts early in the fall.

Do You Use Photographs or Artwork?   Realistic photographs, in general, seem to draw higher readership than art. A photograph of a bulldozer or a power lift in action will usually draw more attention than an art rendition of the same units.

Yet it is dangerous to generalize in this matter. Many of the highest ranked advertisements in any given issue of a publication will have used artwork. Engineers, for example, will give rapt attention to cutaway diagrams, charts, graphs, and blueprints. Sometimes, in certain types of advertisements, photographs can actually be distracting elements.

But whether to use photographs or art is not very much a matter of choice these days, since business publication advertisers overwhelmingly choose photographs over art. An examination of a typical industrial publication, *Steel* magazine, that was made while this text was being written, showed the following choices between photographs and art:

- 57 advertisements that used photographs only
- 14 advertisements that used art only (half of these were small advertisements)
- 9 advertisements that combined photography and artwork

How Big Will Your Advertisement Be?   Readership of business advertising is strongly influenced by the size of the space used. Consistently, the larger space advertisements will draw better readership than those in smaller spaces. There are two important things to remember about this point, however:

(1) Usually, the added readership gained because of the bigger size of the advertisements will not be in proportion to the increased size of the space as is also true in consumer advertisements. A full-page advertisement, for example, will not consistently obtain twice the readership of a half-page—in fact, many more times than not, it will fail to do so. Likewise, a spread of two pages or more will not draw readership proportionally greater than that obtained by a single page.

(2) There will be many occasions when smaller advertisements, because of their subject matter, timing, or creative excellence, will outperform larger advertisements.

Despite the success of small-space advertisements, the business publication advertiser may choose full-page or larger advertisements. Bigger headlines and illustrations attract more attention. Details lost in smaller advertisements can be easily seen. Copy can thoroughly relate complex information. The company name is larger and more easily remembered. All these elements add to getting attention and telling the advertising story more completely and with greater memorability.

Institutional advertisement for a trade magazine.

Occasionally it is desirable to remind customers of a company's quality and dependability story, as this advertisement does. In the long run, confidence in the company helps sell its products.

COLORITE DELIVERS... P.D.Q.

Super Flexible Reinforced

50 Feet 5/8" Inside Diameter

Product. Colorite manufactures America's most complete line of garden hose.

Dependability. While many other manufacturers can't keep up with orders, Colorite can...and does! Colorite's two huge manufacturing/warehousing facilities — one in Ridgefield, New Jersey, one in Sparks, Nevada — produce garden hose 24 hours a day, 7 days a week, year round. Whenever you need garden hose, Colorite has it . . . and Colorite can deliver . . . fast!

Quality. Every Colorite Hose meets strict quality standards. In addition to ongoing factory testing, a continuous testing program is conducted for Colorite by Nationwide Consumer Testing Institute, a leading independent laboratory that performs monthly tests on Colorite Garden Hose obtained at random from retail outlets. When it comes to quality, Colorite delivers!

Our customers are our best recommendation.

Circle 171 on Inquiry Card

Small Advertising Budgets

As a percent of sales, advertising budgets for business and industrial advertisers are usually modest. As previously mentioned, advertising often plays a supporting role for the salesperson. The following figures, selected at random, are typical percent-of-sales advertising figures for more than 800 firms included in an analysis done by McGraw-Hill publications:

Industry	Gross Sales in Millions	Percentage Spent for Industrial Advertising
Textiles	50-100	0.09
Plywood	100-plus	0.3
Printing papers	50-100	0.45
Process chemicals	10-25	0.41
Industrial plastics	10-25	0.71
Synthetic rubber	100-plus	0.7
Ceramic coatings	5-10	0.7
Buffing and polishing compounds	½-1	0.45

These figures are median figures (based on a midpoint) and not averages. In some cases there are startling differences in how much industrial companies spend for advertising. In the "general industrial machinery" classification, for example, one company spent 25.3 percent of gross sales for industrial advertising, while another company spent only 0.1 percent.

The study did not seek answers for the large differences in advertising expenditures. A single example, however, may argue that even very large advertising investments as a percentage of sales costs are reasonable, if advertising does the entire selling job. For some small industrial advertisers this is the case. No salespeople are employed. Advertisements carry the entire selling burden.

The Relation of the Advertising Budget to Sales Costs

Sales cost analyses of industrial companies often reveal something we do not expect: The larger the advertising investment the lower the total selling costs. Why? Advertising makes salespeople more efficient.

Advertising locates and identifies prospective buyers. The sales call preceded by advertising is more likely to result in a sale than a "cold call" on a buyer who has no knowledge of a company or its products. The cost of advertising, in short, is an investment in making salespeople more productive.

The industrial advertising investment typically is a small portion of industrial marketing or selling costs. The following percentages include a portion of the total marketing expense represented by advertising and sales promotion expenses. The 2.2 percent figure includes all advertising production and media expenses. It does not include advertising department salaries and administrative expenses.

Based on the average marketing costs of 227 companies selling to business and industry, table 13-4, based on a McGraw-Hill study, shows the breakdown of total marketing costs.

TABLE 13-4
Total Marketing Costs

Category	Percentage of Costs
Salesmen's salaries, commissions, travel, and entertainment	7.0
Salaries and operating expenses of advertising and sales departments	4.4
Advertising and sales promotion expenses	2.2
Warehouse and delivery	1.5

Responsibility for Developing the Advertising Budget

Most industrial advertising managers are not members of top management, and advertising budget decisions are expressed as recommendations to top management.

Along with the advertising manager, the sales or marketing manager often is deeply involved in developing the advertising budget. Since advertising is developed to help achieve sales or marketing objectives, there is close cooperation between sales or marketing managers and advertising managers.

Once the general outline of the advertising budget is worked out with others in the company, the advertising budget is worked out with others in the company, the advertising manager consults with the account executive of the company's advertising agency. Because media costs are a major budgetary expense, allocation of money to various media is done in considerable detail.

The advertising manager again reviews the final proposed budget with the sales or marketing manager before submitting it for top management review.

Management and Advertising

Years ago the top management of companies that used business advertising, shared a "faith" in the effectiveness of advertising with the top management of companies that advertise in consumer media. Over the years this "faith" has been subjected to increasingly sharp questioning. This is reasonable. Every other business investment is expected to make a measurable return to company profits. Advertising investments could not remain an exception.

Management today increasingly demands precise results from advertising expenditures. One advertising manager expressed top management's viewpoint as follows:

> The problem is that management is result-oriented. The advertising manager who wants recognition should . . . recognize that . . . management, as a result of years of hearing that advertising is not just an expenditure but an investment that brings a return, now wants to know exactly what the return consists of.

The advertising manager who is unable to develop evidence of advertising effectiveness faces an increasingly hard-nosed top management.

Executive-Management advertisement.

Upper management is the particular target of this corporate advertisement.

IBM
DATA PROCESSING DIVISION

The corporate manager's need to know, when facing "what if" questions concerning a company's future, nearly always exceeds the information readily available.

But today management can call on a strong right arm, the computer, to assist in the process of planning and decision making.

No longer mainly an administrative tool, for many companies the computer has become part of the fiber of business itself.

Its steady migration into the operational aspects of business has produced, as an unprecedented bonus, an important new resource for the organizations it serves.

A resource of information—for evaluating, for projecting, for planning.

That is why more and more management people, from the board room and executive suite on down, are turning to the computer. To help keep the future in focus.

The future is a moving target. Computers can improve your aim.

CHARACTERISTICS OF BUSINESS ADVERTISEMENTS

Business publication advertising often is described in several broad classifications reflecting the production, distribution, or professional orientation of readers. The advertisements designed for each reading group tend to exhibit these different characteristics, points or emphasis:

Industrial Advertisements

Long-Range Investment. Industrial advertisements for very expensive but long-lasting machinery such as lathes and stamping machines discusses the performance of machinery over a productive life of ten, twenty, or more years. The initial cost of such equipment is high. Even more important may be energy costs associated with the equipment, frequency, and cost of planned overhauls, frequency of breakdowns, and speed with which the machine operates.

Technical and Engineering Facts. Often those with the greatest influence in buying machinery ignore cost and focus on the technical characteristics of the machinery. Because engineers and technicians may be the bulk of industrial magazine readers, often technical specifications are dealt with in detail and cost information is mentioned only casually or even ignored.

Management-Oriented. Industrial magazines are written for decision makers, including top management, plant managers, and engineers. The advertisements reflect the interests of these and other readers with management responsibility. Advertisements may relate the investment in production-line machinery to worker safety, lower production and maintenance costs, or to more rapidly moving production lines.

Long Copy. More so than in consumer magazine advertising, industrial advertisements often are filled with long, detailed copy. Some advertisers question the use of long copy, noting that only a small portion of the magazine audience reads most or all of the typical advertisement. The copy-length question has been studied in numerous surveys and through coupon response, mail-order inquiries, and actual sales. Many advertising managers believe copy length has little to do with readership. Advertising managers inclined to use long copy, however, argue that readers eagerly seek job-related information.

Schematic Drawings, Blueprints, Graphs, and Charts. Many readership studies show that leading advertisements attract readers with detailed and seemingly dry drawings, blueprints, and graphs. Consumer magazine readers tend to ignore such illustrative devices. Additionally, industrial advertisements may not use models to introduce the human factor or establish empathy. In some advertisements the use of a model would distract from rather than enhance the advertisement. Unless the use of a model is natural and meaningful, the model is often omitted.

Case Histories and Testimonials. The case history that shows how equipment and materials were used profitably is attractive to the industrial advertising reader. Even if the application is not exactly suited to the reader's problem, with some minor adjustment it might be. Since many industrial products are altered to a buyer's specifications, the industrial publication reader thinks in terms of modifying machinery and other equipment while reading advertisements.

Dominant Illustrations. More readership is obtained for advertisements that use illustrations that dominate the space and attract the attention of the industrial readers. A big illustration of what is being sold is not only attention-getting but also permits inspection of the product details and function so important to critical industrial readers. A dominant illustration may be used in an advertisement and still allow room for ample copy. As a rule, it is best to avoid all-text advertisements in industrial publications. Occasionally, an announcement of an important new process or product may be given impact through the use of an all-text advertisement, set in a typeface that is suitably "important looking," but the dominant-illustration approach gets higher readership in most circumstances.

Professional Advertisements

In many ways industrial and professional advertisements are similar. A number of professional advertisement characteristics, however, are distinctive and deserve mention.

"Professional Language." Far more often than not, the language in professional advertisements is highly technical. Frequently, the copy is not understandable to us as lay readers. Doctors and dentists, however, think and talk a specialized language during their working lives. Curiously, the longer the word used, the more precise the meaning, which accounts for the use of very long words in much professional copy. You can find samples of such language on even the most simple consumer product packages.

Advertisements that do not use the technical language appropriate to each profession frequently are ignored. Thus, you find medical publications, for example, filled with such language as the following:

Hyperbaric therapy gives promise of becoming an increasingly important adjunct to the management of a wide range of hypoxic conditions.

Its iodine content (400 mg/ml) provides a high degree of X-ray contrast, particularly useful in those instances where greater opacification of the renal collecting system is required.

Scientific Proof. Medical practitioners are responsible for our health. Advertised claims for any product affecting the well-being of patients must be backed by accurate proof. In fact, the law now requires that advertisements for drugs relate in great detail the number and types of studies done using the drug. Side effects must also be indicated.

Copy for advertisements in medical and dental publications (and in legal and architectural magazines, for that matter) is written by trained specialists who have other trained specialists check the accuracy of the advertisements. The advertised message must be unquestionably accurate to satisfy the most critical audiences in the business publication field.

No Puffery or Pressure. The professional reader is alienated by the general product claim and by high-pressure advertising. Professional advertisements are restrained, scientific, factual, and highly technical. The reader will not tolerate exaggeration.

Information. Most professionals attend seminars and other professional meetings and read journals and the business press to keep abreast of the latest developments in their respective fields. The life-long goal of professionals is improved service to clients. The reader with the true professional commitment is an avid seeker of new information. Any advertisements that show how a client may be better served will be avidly read and evoke a response.

Before Redi-Set went up in the hospital that was being built, it went up in the one that was being torn down.

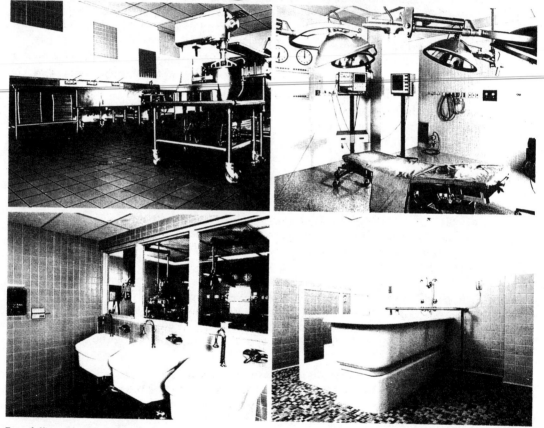

For a full year, hospital administrators in a large metropolitan area hospital watched how Redi-Set™ performed under normal hospital conditions, in a room in the old building, tiled just for that purpose.

One year later, Redi-Set ceramic tile was up in the new $30 million hospital. On the walls in the operating room suite and kitchen. And on the walls in the corridor bath areas.

Redi-Set is a natural for areas like these because its non-porous, water-repellent silicone rubber grout is easy to keep bacteria-free. So mold and mildew don't have a chance to grow either. And because it resists most stains, it stays bright and clean with routine hospital-accepted cleaning procedures.

There are economic advantages to Redi-Set, too. It comes in flexible, pregrouted tile sheets that go up quickly over just about any existing solid surface (old or new). So installation costs are held to a minimum. And it won't crack or powder out even with slight building movement.

Discover for yourself what many hospital administrators already know about Redi-Set. Mail the coupon for a free descriptive brochure on Redi-Set. It's ceramic tile plus.

Plate No. 691

Trade Advertisements

Advertisements in business publications serving the "trade" or distribution functions of business contrast strikingly with industrial and professional advertisements. Readers are urged to "act now" by advertisements written with unabashed enthusiasm. Trade or distribution advertising is quite unlike industrial and professional advertising and exhibits the following characteristics.

Profit Is Key Motive. Trade advertisers are not shy or given to euphemism. Profit is the motive most frequently tapped. Even if the word *profit* is not used, it is implied when the reader is asured the advertised product has high markups and sells quickly.

Trade advertising is addressed to the wholesalers and retailers who move merchandise toward final consumers. Low cost and high return is the almost constant theme of such advertising.

Promotional Support. No one is lonelier or more unhappy than the retailer without advertising to support the product with national advertising and cooperative advertising allowances. Information about a manufacturer's advertising and other promotional support is an inducement to stock the product. The small retailer with a limited advertising budget may then coordinate retail advertising with the national advertising and promotion.

Product Details. The retailer often is less interested in the product itself than in the profitability and advertising support given the product by the national manufacturer. If the product is strikingly new, the retailer may examine the product in detail to determine how the product "fits" existing store merchandise and whether the product lends itself to prominent in-store display.

Enthusiasm. In trade or distribution magazines the "lid is off." Copywriters can be as enthusiastic as they want. The dealer or retailer, after all, must believe enthusiastically in the product and its salability or the product will not be stocked. Retailers often comment that they buy from one salesperson rather than another because "That salesperson's so enthusiastic you just have to believe the product is good."

Trade magazine advertisers, therefore, fill their advertisements with such phrases as:

> Imagine anything so good being so profitable!
> For amazing performance in increasing store volume . . .
> Nationally advertised consumer offer of the biggest selling 89 cent brush
> Sales sparkers! For the 8 fastest selling manicure implements, call your Toiletry Merchandiser today!
> Over 50 percent profit with these two quality, eye-catching Christmas or year 'round assortments.
> Just set 'em up in their colorful, prepacked self-selling display shippers and see Christmas candles sell as never before!

Business Advertising Merchandising

"Merchandising" here has essentially the same meaning that it has in consumer advertising—making advertising do double work. It is an important

Radio commercial directed at businessmen.

Two entertainment personalities have been used for what has become a well-known campaign for dictating equipment. This campaign entertains while it sells and is done so well that even those in the general public who are not in the market for the product look forward to the commercials. Still, when radio is used to reach businessmen the advertiser must be aware that there will be substantial waste circulation.

MARSTELLER INC.   *Broadcast*

RADIO COPY

Client: LANIER   January 29
Program: "Workout"
Facilities: Stiller & Meara
Date:
Time: :60

ANNCR: Here's Stiller & Meara for Lanier Dictating Equipment.

STILLER: Up-down--1-2--up-down

MEARA: 1-2-1-2. Boss, a ~~secretary~~ shouldn't be in a men's
           exercise class at the Y. It's embarrassing. I want
           to get out of here.

STILLER: I need you here to take dictation. Take this medicine
           ball.

MEARA: Uhhhh!

STILLER: Sorry, now take a letter. Dear Fred...UGHHH.

MEARA: Let me read that back. Dear Fred. UGHHH. This is
           ridiculous.

STILLER: I just pressed 80 pounds.

MEARA: You just pressed your luck too far. No more exercise
           class for me. You need a Pocket Secretary.

STILLER: Great idea. Maybe I can get Olga Korbett to defect --
           does she take shorthand?

MEARA: Not a ~~secretary~~-secretary. I mean Lanier's new pocket
           dictating machine -- the Pocket Secretary. It uses tiny
           cassettes and weighs just 12-1/2 ounces. All muscle.

STILLER: I can take it where I can't take you. I could dictate
           in the sauna.

MEARA: Sure, and there's another advantage -- it doesn't need
           a sweatsuit. Can I put the medicine ball down now?

STILLER: Why don't you get off the rings first.

ANNCR: Get more done with Lanier's Pocket Secretary.
           In the Yellow Pages under Dictating Machines.

responsiblity of the advertising manager to "merchandise" the advertising program to the company management, the company employees, the sales organization, and distributors. Unless such action is taken, these various groups may have no idea of the extent or value of the advertising.

If an organization is small, the easiest, least expensive way to keep associates acquainted with the program is through the use of proofs, preprints, or reprints. "Preprints," properly identified to show when and where each advertisement is to run, may be posted on factory and office bulletin boards. They should be put up before publication date.

If the company has an employee house publication, stories about the advertising should be carried regularly. Employee readers should know the purpose as well as the results of the program—that it is a tool to increase and to stabilize the company's business, thereby helping to make jobs better and more secure.

FARM ADVERTISING IS CONSUMER AND BUSINESS ADVERTISING

Farm advertising is both consumer and business advertising because farming is a way of living and of work, and many products are purchased for family as well as working use.

The farm pickup truck may haul produce and serve as the family car. Larger trucks may haul livestock to market and the family pleasure boat to a nearby lake. Fertilizers and pesticides used for field crops may be used for flower gardens around the house.

Many other products are purchased for work only, including tractors, plow, combines, spreaders, conveyors to lift grain for storage, and fans to dry wet grain.

While business publication advertising typically focuses narrowly on the working life of readers, farm publications, and advertising usually address farmers in their dual roles as buyers of consumer products and of working farm machinery, chemicals, and other products.

Today's farmer is sophisticated. Although the farmer still must plow a straight furrow, it is equally if not more important these days for the farmer to balance books by established accounting methods. The farmer fertilizes fields after calculating the increased yield expected from the fertilizer investment in light of current and anticipated crop prices. The way machinery is depreciated for tax purposes may be more important than the purchase price of machinery.

The Changing Farmer

Farmers today are changing rapidly. Farms are growing in size and decreasing in number, with the remaining farms becoming more mechanized and efficient. Improved machinery, sophisticated chemicals, and new hybrid seeds are in part responsible for this efficiency. The farmer as a businessman (for farming now is often called agribusiness) allocates dollar resources in the constant search to raise crops and livestock more cheaply.

Because farmers often work alone, more so than other workers, they must seek out new information. County agents offer them short courses, as do agricultural colleges. Farm publications provide additional information.

Farmers have learned to calculate investment returns as carefully as professional cost accountants. Unlike the accountant, who is often an employee, the farmer bears the full and personal burden of poor decisions.

For years farmers were isolated by rutted roads that often became soggy and impassable during winter thaw and spring rain. Farmers were the last group of Americans to enjoy household electricity and to harness electrical power to run machinery. Today, highways and improved secondary roads give farmers quick, easy access to other farmers and to major markets. The natural production cycle of many northern farms permits farmers to follow the sun for long vacations in Florida, the Bahamas, or Arizona. Often warmer climes are reached in the plane used for farm work and family pleasure. Thus, we have organizations such as the Flying Farmers of America.

Radio commercial addressed to farmers.

Farm radio is an important medium because it reaches the farmer not only in his home but also where he works—the barn, on the tractor, and other places around the farm. He relies upon radio for news of agricultural developments, for latest quotations on farm products, and for meetings of interest to farmers. If commercials deliver useful messages he will listen to them with more interest than does the general radio listener.

FROM   ADVERTISING ▫ MARKETING

42 east genesee street, skaneateles, new york 13152 ▫ phone (315) 685-5778

commercial no. 6833-10   client BEACON MILLING

length 25 seconds (plus 5 sec tag)   product/service Silage Pre-Serv for corn silage

```
You're waiting to cut corn silage and the weatherman

says "Drying conditions poor."  That's one time you

should have Beacon Silage Pre-Serv* on hand.  With

Pre-Serv, you can cut corn silage with as much as 60 or

65 percent moisture.  Pre-Serv prevents heat build-up and

greatly reduces spoilage and shrinkage.  To get the most

out of your corn silage crop, try Beacon Silage Pre-Serv

this year.



*Pronounced "preserve"


5 second tag
```

Television commercial selling a business product.

Although television is by no means the basic medium for selling to the businessman, this humorous commercial will reach a wide range of businessmen because so many businesses now use photocopying machines. Furthermore, it is entertaining enough to prevent non-businessmen viewers from resenting the advertising of a product they have no interest in buying.

Needham, Harper & Steers Advertising, Inc.
909 Third Avenue, New York, N.Y. 10022
Telephone 212-758-7600
Cable: Neehars 422392 Telex: 12-6249

XEROX CORPORATION   NB-2196

"SAVER" :60   (AS PRODUCED)

VIDEO:	AUDIO:
INT. BUSY OFFICE DAY. A SWEET ELDERLY GENTLEMAN SITS ON COUCH IN WAITING AREA AS YOUNGER MAN CARRYING ATTACHE CASE ENTERS.	
AS THE YOUNGER MAN REACHES FOR A MAGAZINE, THE OLDER MAN SPEAKS TO HIM PROUDLY.	OLDER MAN: You know my son is the president of this company.
THE YOUNGER MAN LEAFS THROUGH HIS MAGAZINE, PATIENTLY ACKNOWLEDGING THE PROUD FATHER.	OLDER MAN: I taught him how to save. When he was six years old I gave him twenty cents...he brought back a quarter.
THE YOUNG MAN IS TRYING TO BEAR UP WITH IT ALL.	Smart. Very smart kid.
THE OLDER MAN POINTS OVER HIS SHOULDER AND THE CAMERA REVEALS A GIRL APPROACHING THE 4500 IN THE B.G.	OLDER MAN: He just got that Xerox 4500 copier. It copies on both sides...
CUT TO: GIRL PUSHING BUTTON.	of the same sheet of paper automatically!
ANOTHER ANGLE: TO FEATURE THE DOCUMENT ASSIST DEVICE IN ACTION.	It even takes out the old original and makes room for the new one.
CAMERA: FEATURES SORTING BIN.	(CONFIDENTIAL TONE) ...and then sorts what it copies.
THE YOUNGER MAN IS NOW TRYING VERY HARD TO BE CORDIAL BUT DOESN'T KNOW EXACTLY HOW TO REACT. SO HE LISTENS.	OLDER MAN: That Xerox 4500 saves paper, filing space, mailing costs...time...AND money!
THE GIRL HAS COMPLETED HER WORK AT THE 4500 AND APPROACHES THE YOUNG MAN.	I tell you...my son he really knows how to save.
AS THE YOUNG MAN LEAVES, ANOTHER MAN CARRYING AN ATTACHE CASE SITS DOWN ON THE COUCH NEXT TO THE FATHER.	OLDER MAN: You ought to see him play ball.
THE FATHER LEANS OVER AND SPEAKS TO HIM AS HE REACHES FOR A MAGAZINE.	OLDER MAN: (PROUDLY) You know my son is the president of this company?
SUPER: XEROX.	

Reaching Farmers Through Media

The days when the *Farmers' Almanac* and the Sears Roebuck catalog were the chief reading fare and advertising medium for the farm market are long gone. As farmers have become financially prosperous, the differences between the farm and city family have diminished. Farm families view the same national TV shows as city families. Both read many of the same consumer magazines.

Farm Publications. General farm publications, such as *Successful Farming, Progressive Farmer,* and *Farm Journal,* with circulations in the millions, serve the farmer nationally in both the farm field and the consumer field. There are other national publications in the farm field, but these are among the leaders in circulation.

A number of regional farm publications serve the agricultural interests of farmers in large geographic areas of the country. Examples of such publications are *Capper's Weekly* and *Wallaces Farmer.* The latter, for example, is a powerful influence in the Midwest, especially among the corn and hog raisers. Considered an authority by the farmers in the states it covers, the magazine is rated as a powerful advertising medium by farm advertisers.

The state farm publication classification includes the most farm magazines, as between national and sectional publications. Whether we are talking about the *Alabama Farmer* or the *Wyoming Stockman-Farmer,* the state publication narrows its focus to those problems of agriculture peculiar to a relatively small geographic area. Farmers, understandably, tend to be interested in the experiences of farmers who are close by, who suffer or enjoy the same soil and climatic conditions. A corn grower in Iowa, for example, may feel that corn growers in New Hampshire "speak a different language," as it were, from him. Thus an Iowa state farm publication is going to be of much greater interest to him. In each state having state farm publications, the same kind of narrowed-down interest is shown.

Although there are some very fine state farm publications, many are rather poorly executed on crude paper stock. Circulation is small for many of these magazines. Despite these handicaps, the magazines may have a reading audience so devoted that they are still a good place for agricultural advertising.

A number of farm publications are specialized in title and content in accordance with the specific agricultural specialty of their readers, whether that specialty be wheat growing, hog raising, cattle breeding, or dairying. These publications can be state, regional, or national. Examples are the *Soybean Digest, Hoard's Dairyman,* and *Shorthorn World.*

Radio. Despite the emergence of television as the most powerful broadcast medium, radio remains a potent force in farm advertising.

Radio has built listening loyalties over the years. Many stations offer early morning farm programming, complete with weather, farm news, and grain and livestock market reports. As a companion, radio accompanies the farmer through the day, in the house, the barn, and truck or automobile. Today's sophisticated tractors with enclosed cockpits resembling aircraft cockpits, include radio receivers as well as CB radio.

Farm directors on radio stations become neighbors over time. Often these radio announcers and personalities were themselves raised on farms. They know the farmers' concerns, speak the language of farm life and work. Often farm directors remain with stations for years. They become trusted information sources and ideal salespeople for farm products.

Television.   Stations are still experimenting with farm television. One of the problems of course, is that by programming directly to the relatively small farm audience, the station may lose the bigger audience that has no interest in agricultural matters. Country music shows and personalities often bridge the gap between the two types of audiences, but the problem still remains as to what type of commercials to use. A commercial for hog feed, for example, is going to cause great numbers of the nonfarmer listeners to lose interest, leave the room or start dial-twirling.

Despite these handicaps, farm television, in areas where there are sizable numbers of farmers within the station's signals, has had some fine successes, especially for demonstration shows and commercials. Also, the station's farm director (who may do double work when the television and radio station are under the same ownership) can build a good audience.

Television, nevertheless, does not do a better daytime job than can radio in the farm field when it delivers the news, market reports, and other fare that does not demand visual presentation. When nighttime comes, television takes over. Then the farmer relaxes and assumes the role of a consumer. What interests city TV viewers interests the farmer.

Newspapers.   Understandably, small-town dailies and rural weeklies provide the best place for agricultural advertising, among newspapers in general. These publications, however, while quite suitable for local firms, such as farm-equipment distributors and feed-supply firms, present problems for national advertisers. They are likely to:

(1)   Offer poor reproduction. Illustrations may come out badly, and, in general, the appearance of advertisements may be poor.

(2)   Fail to follow schedules. National advertisers have often commented bitterly on the nonchalant attitude of many small-circulation newspapers toward inserting advertising matter on scheduled dates.

(3)   Charge high rates. While the actual agate line rate for such newspapers may not be high, in terms of the milline rate the rate may be very high indeed. Since national advertisers measure the cost of advertising in milline rates, they wince at the high millines for the rural newspapers. If the advertiser is a tractor manufacturer or the manufacturer of some other product sold only to farmers, the advertiser accepts the high cost as necessary to reach farmers. An advertiser of a consumer product, however, may refuse to use small-town and rural newspapers because of the excessive milline and will look for less expensive media.

One of the advantages of the rural or small-town newspaper is the intensive readership they enjoy. Also, since there is usually only a small amount of advertising in these papers, and few pages, an advertiser is assured of greater visibility than in many-page newspapers crowded with advertisements.

Outdoor Advertising.   Hybrid seed corn, agricultural implements, and animal feeds are among the many products advertised on outdoor posters. Outdoor advertising has the advantage in the agricultural field of reaching farmers in the territory in which their farms are located. Thus, outdoor advertising campaigns can be adjusted to geographical variations, unlike the advertising in national farm magazines. Usually placed on the roads most heavily traveled by farmers, outdoors advertising serves as a constant reminder.

Talking To Farmers

Despite the fact that differences in farm and city life are breaking down in many ways, the farmer still has a distinctive outlook on life. The farmer often has a different set of personal and working interests, a different language, living environment, and way of doing things. Even today, contracts may be based on a farmer's *word* and handshake rather than an extensive written document signed before witnesses. Farm advertisers must understand this distinctive audience. Advertisers must talk to farmers in ways farmers find acceptable.

Provide Proof.   Traditionally, the farmer is a skeptic about product claims. Isolated and flimflammed in the past, the farmer views unsupported product claims with suspicion. Advertised claims are weighed against information provided by county extension agents and the extension information services provided by agricultural and veterinary colleges throughout the country.

Talk Farm Language. A farmer will snicker at and then dismiss an advertisement that does not show an understanding of farming. Writers of farm advertising therefore, often have had farm backgrounds, know the language and what the farmer is interested in and will believe.

Testimonials. Advertised testimonials from farmers in the same or a nearby county are very persuasive with farmers. The farther away the testimonial-giver is, the less persuasive the advertisement. The late, cold, wet spring of Minnesota is not experienced by the southern Alabama corn grower. Thus, testimonial given by a Minnesota farmer is irrelevant to the Alabama farmer. The weather, soil, and numerous other factors are too different.

Some testimonials will achieve widespread readership and belief. A tractor testimonial may be acceptable to farmers nationally. The key to the testimonial is the extent to which farmers can apply the facts and figures from the testimonial to their individual situations. Farmers can do this more realistically if the testimonial giver is nearby, perhaps even known personally to the farmer.

Try editorial techniques. An advertisement that looks like a news story, or like a picture-caption story from the news part of a magazine, will often carry more conviction for a farmer than the conventional advertisements. If, for example, an advertisement in *Wallaces Farmer* looks much like, or exactly like, the surrounding editorial content, it may attain readership that would not be achieved if it looked like an out-and-out advertisement. This suggestion applies especially to those farm publications that are considered strong authorities by their readers.

Farm magazine advertisement.

Advertisements such as this one in farm magazines are important to farmers looking for help, and news of developments in the agricultural field. The language in such advertisements should be that of the farmer.

Don't buy your neighbor's Feeding Program.

Get a Total Feeding System Planned for <u>Your</u> herd alone.

Profitable feeding is "no-nonsense" feeding—providing every cow in your herd with the nutrients she needs for profitable milk production. Not overfeeding. Not underfeeding. Not buying nutrients you've already grown yourself.

No-nonsense feeding begins with our free analysis of your roughage. We need to know such things as your herd's production record...Its potential...The stage of lactation for most of your cows...Is the herd grouped?

Our lab analysis of your roughage will show what nutrients you already have. Then we'll recommend whatever feeds and supplements are needed to insure proper nutrition and optimal income over feed costs for <u>your</u> herd.

Don't just buy feed on the basis of guesswork and the lowest cost per ton. Take advantage of our free, knowledgable planning service. The result will be a **total feeding system** that will enable you to get the most **profit** out of every dollar you spend for feed—and probably cost less overall. That is

If you don't know your Beacon Advisor or Area Dairy Specialist, call us collect at (315) 253-7331 for his name and telephone number.

Beacon Milling Company, Inc.
Headquarters at Cayuga, New York

Recognize the farmer-wife-children combination. On any given farm, different members of the family may assume different obligations. The farmer takes care of the heavy tasks; the wife may handle bookkeeping chores and care of the chickens (and perhaps some gardening for table vegetables) in addition to her normal household duties; the son may take care of the young livestock and may spell his father on the tractor; the daughter helps her mother in any of the extra duties. A farm writer will acknowledge this splitting-up of responsibilities. A farm family is much more of a partnership arrangement than is found in most city families.

FARMERS ARE IN THE POLITICAL MAINSTREAM

In recent years, farmers have become more aggressive politically. While the number of farmers is decreasing, the farm bloc still carries political clout. The farm vote is respected in Washington and when farmers strike or protest vigorously, political figures from the agricultural states come to attention.

Farmers, feeling victimized by low prices for their output and high prices for what they must buy, are increasingly strident in their demands. Such currents and changes in farmers' attitudes must be studied by advertisers who serve the farm field.

QUESTIONS

1. Distinguish between a horizontal and a vertical business publication.
2. Why are business advertising budgets smaller than consumer advertising budgets?
3. How does the business publication reader differ from the consumer magazine reader?
4. How do advertisements in business publications differ from those in consumer magazines?
5. There has been some shift in advertising from business publications to weekly news magazines. Why has this come about?
6. Advertisers often use business publications to achieve what are called "support objectives." What are some typical support objectives?
7. What is meant by the term "buying influence?"
8. Why do business publications develop more detailed audience information than consumer magazines?
9. Why are business publication advertisers more likely to stress advertising repetition than consumer magazine advertisers?
10. In what ways does professional advertising differ from trade or distribution advertising?
11. To advertise hybrid seeds to farmers, would you be inclined to use radio or television? Why?
12. How should advertisers talk to farmers?
13. What are the advantages and disadvantages of inserts in business publications?

14

RADIO ADVERTISING

RADIO ADVERTISING

Hum, whistle, or sing the first tune that comes to mind. The odds are you heard it on the radio. You remembered it. The tune may even be from a radio commercial.

You have also answered two questions advertisers often ask of radio: Does anyone listen? If so, do listeners remember what they hear?

RADIO IS EVERYWHERE

Regardless of what you have heard or read elsewhere, radio is alive and well and reaching tens upon tens of millions of people each day. In fact, you may be listening to radio while reading this page. Some people even read or study only after turning on two radios to different stations. They claim they study better when "company" is around.

This illustrates another point about radio: Radio is a constant companion you can turn on but tune in and out at your convenience, most of the time without thinking about what you are doing. Is this important? You may not think so. Yet, if you drive, the probability is overwhelming that you have a radio in your car. You have several radios at home. You also are likely to own a battery-operated radio to take with you to the beach or on picnics or camping.

You may wake up with a clock radio, decide what to wear after hearing the weather forecast. Without thinking, you tune in a radio traffic reporter when driving to work or class. You take radio for granted, unaware that it is a working information tool you use to get your day underway.

TELEVISION TOPPLED RADIO

If asked to name important advertising media, radio might be one of the last you mentioned. Many say radio is unimportant or ineffective or just background noise. Some even refer to radio as wallpaper for the ears, noticed at first and then fading into the background. Others say television replaced radio as the premier advertising medium. In a very real sense, television did just that. At one time, radio was king, day or night. Today television attracts millions of viewers with daytime dramas, or soaps, and tens of millions of viewers with evening programming from 7 P.M. to 11 P.M.

Television forced radio to change in numerous ways. National radio networks no longer provide entertainment programs for large evening audiences as they did in the years when Sunday evening meant families sitting around radio receivers to listen to Jack Benny. Youngsters today have never thrilled to the radio adventures of Jack Armstrong, The All-American Boy. The musical spelling of J-E-L-L-O, the frequently repeated LS/MFT for Lucky Strikes, and Johnny calling for Philip Morris are today recalled only occasionally by mature Americans, or in programs featuring old-time radio.

WHERE RADIO IS TODAY

Despite television's dominance, radio is more widely used by more Americans than ever before. No longer the premier medium that it was in the 1930's and 1940's, radio has adapted its programming and sharpened its appeal to sharply defined target audiences during different times of the day.

During a given week, radio reaches around 96 percent of Americans 12 and older, with about 83 percent tuning in sometime during the typical day.

Radio is attractive to advertisers because radio reaches so many people so frequently and inexpensively. Soft drink and other beverage advertisers are heavy radio users. Radio reaches life insurance owners, credit card users, people who buy recording tape, use shampoo frequently, and buy frozen baked goods. Radio also reaches most two-car families (both radio-equipped, of course) providing a selected audience for automotive products.

National Radio Networks

Radio audiences today are served by national and numerous regional networks. The radio networks primarily gather and distribute news to affiliated local stations. Several networks offer a lineup of additional services, such as covering sports events, interviews, special features, and news commentaries.

Most of the news for local stations is produced by ABC, NBC, CBS, and the Mutual Broadcasting System. Among the major radio networks, ABC has four separate radio networks, reflecting radio's sharply defined programming. ABC's Entertainment Network presents news, celebrity interviews, and features with broad appeal. ABC's FM Network is popular with stations programming for college and college-age audiences. The Contemporary Network is picked up by stations programming contemporary and rock music appealing to an audience 18 to 34. The Information Network is picked up by stations using a middle-of-the-road format appealing to listeners 25 to 49.

Special Markets And Radio

Certain groups continue to be reached by radio as well, or better, than by other media—among these are the farmers, the foreign language groups, the minorities, the late-at-night listeners, the teen-agers.

Farm Market. Although farms are decreasing in number the dollars spent by agriculture continue to mount. Billions are earmarked for operating expenses for such products as feed, seed, and farm machinery. Other billions are spent yearly for products consumed or used in daily living in the farm homes—food, clothing, insurance, transportation.

Comforting figures are available to advertisers anxious to know whether radio can reach the farm market. A 98 percent penetration of the farm population is achieved through the thousands of radio stations that carry farm programming. Although these radio stations are reaching a national market, they are run on the philosophy that while agriculture is national, farming is local. Station programming and operation in farm belts is always localized in conformance with the local or regional peculiarities in a station's listening area.

Not only does farm radio reach the farm families, but it commands their attention, too. Average listening time to farm radio is estimated at somewhat more than three hours daily. The compartmenting of radio listening, previously mentioned, is even more pronounced in the farm audience than in the city or suburban audience. Strong agreement exists that farm listening breaks down like this:

- 5-7 A.M. Listening is done before farmer leaves for barn chores—although much listening is done in the barn, too. Program content is strong on weather and opening markets.
- 11:30-1 P.M. Farmer is eating dinner, frequently in kitchen. News programs dominate.
- 5-7:30 P.M. This is the period of relaxation. Program content most often made up of weather and closing markets.

Although farm listening habits are well fixed for the foregoing periods, farm families listen at all other hours, too. Farmers, isolated as they are in so many areas, have developed strong loyalties to stations, programs, and personalities.

One of the oddities of farm radio advertising is the position of the radio station's farm director. No other member of a station's staff holds quite the same standing with the radio audience. To the farmers in his area, the station farm director is the station. Because he is almost always strong in agricultural background and training, he is a respected figure whose opinions are valued. When he delivers a commercial, it is not viewed so much as a "sales pitch" by the listener as sincere advice from one farmer to another. Glibness is not a weapon of the farm director delivering a commerical, but sincerity certainly is.

Part of the power of the radio farm director is derived from the work he does on the outside of the station. The energetic farm director calls on dealers, attends local sales meetings, is present at important farm meetings, state fairs, and other places where farm folk gather. During these activities he identifies himself with the product he advertises, develops a wide acquaintance with local farming personalities and, through all this, envelops the products he promotes with a local flavor.

Farmers, unlike most radio listeners, use radio listening as a working tool to become better farmers, and to obtain information that is useful daily—markets, weather, and news.

Farm radio at work.

A radio station farm service director interviews an Iowa farmer. The competent farm service director is a respected figure in the agricultural community he serves.

Although most advertisers see the farmer chiefly as the independent manager of a business, they also view him respectfully as an important purchaser of consumer goods. This point is shown in the findings concerning cake-mix usage among farm wives. Where a city housewife buys but one pound of mix, a farm housewife will buy five to ten pounds.

Advertisers have learned that the Spanish-language market cannot be treated as a single market. A single broadcast commercial will not be equally persuasive in Los Angeles, Miami, and New York City, because the Spanish spoken in each major market area derives from Mexico, Cuba, and Puerto Rico, respectively. While sharing a common language, idioms and pronunciations differ. The Cuban-American does not respond positively to a broadcast commercial delivered by a Mexican-American announcer. Three different voices and slightly different advertising appeals may be required for Spanish-language radio commercials used in different sections of the country.

Minority Market. Despite agitation in recent years for breaking down minority-white barriers, there is a definite feeling of "separateness" in the fact that many stations and many programs are slanted toward minority groups in different areas.

Hundreds of radio stations in states from coast to coast offer minority programming. Many of these stations devote their entire schedule to the minority market.

Because the minority market has a number of sensitivities it has been a tricky market to approach. Print advertisers, especially, have experienced difficulty. In illustrating advertisements, for instance, the print advertiser must be careful not only in his recognition of minority-white relationships but also in recognizing the strong class distinctions within minority groups themselves.

Much of this difficulty is eliminated in radio because of the absence of potentially offensive illustrations and because of its mass, instead of class, selling. Radio stations, however, that sell to the minority market must be especially careful in the choice of announcers and in program selection. In some areas it may be a real advantage to employ minority announcers to deliver commercials.

Future status of minority radio can only be conjectured in this period of boiling social change. If segregation disappears and white and minority families are intermingled in neighborhoods throughout the country, there will be no truly separate minority bloc to advertise to. If this is true, the need for separate minority programming will largely disappear. Social change moves slowly, however; minority radio thus will not disappear overnight.

Meanwhile, more than 200 stations regularly schedule black programming. Serving the black market are the Mutual Black Network and the National Black Network.

Regional Networks

Regional networks are found throughout the United States wherever there is sufficient common interest served by several scattered radio stations. The Tobacco Radio Network, with stations in six southeastern states, provides tobacco market prices and other information useful to tobacco farmers. The Amigo Network provides program material for Spanish-language stations from Texas to California.

Some networks are quickly patched together to carry the broadcast of a professional or collegiate athletic event and then quickly return to regularly scheduled programming, once the game is over.

Radio Stations

The success and vitality of radio today is evident in a variety of facts. There are more than 8,000 licensed radio stations in the United States, and the Federal Communications Commission, the federal agency which grants radio licenses, constantly receives applications to start additional new stations. More than 4,000 of the licensed stations are commercial AM's. About 3,000 are commercial FM's, with the remainder being noncommercial FM's of the type often associated with universities and other nonprofit organizations.

Radio Audiences

Radio's prime time is now drive time from 5 A.M. to 10 A.M. in the morning and 3 P.M. to 7 P.M. in the evening. The total radio audience is larger than the television audience from 6 A.M. until about 6 P.M., when television abruptly absorbs the attention of a larger total audience.

Some American Statistics

If Americans do not say radio is important, their actions suggest otherwise, as a look at these statistics testifies:

(1) According to the most recent figures available, almost 43 million radio sets are sold yearly.
(2) There are over 413 million working-order radio sets in the U.S., or about two per person.
(3) About 65 percent of radios sold yearly are AM/FM receivers.
(4) Close to 99 percent of all U.S. homes have at least one working radio. The average home has 5.6 radio receivers, and 45 percent of all homes have clock radios.
(5) About 92 percent of all new cars leaving American automobile factories are radio equipped. Surveys indicate car radios are used more than 62 percent of the time we drive.
(6) Over 17 million battery-powered radio receivers are sold each year, with 75 percent of teenagers, 53 percent of adult women and 55 percent of adult men currently owning battery-powered radios for personal use.

Radio's Continuing Growth

In recent years the FCC has granted a growing number of FM radio licenses. FM today is estimated to reach 45 percent of the total radio audience.

FM stations emit a higher-quality signal that carries over short distances than those on the AM band. Because their signals are limited to line-of-sight (straight-line) transmission, FM stations tend to be more innovative programmers, constantly testing new ideas in search of new audiences based on musical or other interests in their small coverage areas. FM is particularly attractive for classical music programming because the sound fidelity is superior to that on AM and FM stations have had exclusive FCC approval to broadcast in stereo—a two-signal system that adds another dimension to sound. FM will be more attractive to advertisers in the future because Congress is pressuring now to require FM reception in automobile radios, thereby increasing the potential FM Drive Time audience.

At the same time, the FCC may soon approve AM stereo broadcasting. AM stereo will be attractive for automobile installation because it is less subject to interference from radio wave obstacles, including tall buildings, and because the AM stereo signal reaches further than regular AM radio signals.

As the FCC grants more radio station licenses, there will be greater competition among radio stations for audiences, hence even more innovative programming. Simultaneously, the expansion of stero transmission, and reception promises added listening pleasure for audiences and opportunities for advertisers.

PROGRAMMING TO ATTRACT AUDIENCES

When television lured the large evening audiences from radio in the late 1940's and early 1950's, radio networks and stations were forced to seek new ways to attract audiences. Radio executives focused on those times of the day (called day parts in broadcasting) that would or could not appeal to audiences. Radio entered a period of intense experimentation with a variety of news, entertainment, and music formats designed to attract and hold listenerers. Music and news became the basic program ingredients, supplemented with sports, commentary, interviews, and public issue discussions.

Radio is programmed according to a format. A radio format is a way of presenting a combination of sound carrying information and entertainment, including music, news, voices, the emphasis or de-emphasis of announcer personality, the distinctive sounds serving as the station signature, and the tempo with which the entire programming is presented.

There are numerous ways of classifying radio formats, with many subtle and obvious variations within the formats to match musical and other interest preferences of audiences by region, urban vs. suburban, and even life styles.

Major Radio Formats

The Top 40 format is one of the oldest current radio formats and is popular with audiences up through the mid-40s. Stations programming in this format play current record hits, emphasize local personalities and attract sizable commuting audiences. The Top 20 format limits musical selections to the very current hits only and appeals to a younger audience 12 to 34.

Middle-of-the Road (MOR) radio formats tend to attract listeners 35 and over. MOR programming places heavy reliance on news and sports. Personalities are important, especially the morning announcer. Adult Contemporary programming is similar to MOR but tends to appeal to somewhat younger audiences from 25 to 49.

Album-Oriented-Rock (AOR) formats appeal to young men and women from 18 to 24. Disc jockey chatter is limited and the announcer personality is not emphasized. Current popular album artists are featured. Life style advertising appeals are popular in this format.

Soft Rock is a relatively new format that appeals to people who have outgrown the sounds of the Top 40 format.

Beautiful Music programming, often called background or doctor's office music, offers soft, easy-listening sounds. Beautiful Music stations offer less news and other information than other radio formats, even when audiences might desire news and travel advice during morning drive. Advertisers sometimes have reservations about the Beautiful Music format. The worry is whether commercials blend in so well with the background music that they are unheard by the listening audience.

News-and-Talk station programming works best in major markets and tend to appeal to mature audiences. Audiences tend to listen for reasonably long periods of time to talk shows. Stations programming only news tend to have rapid audience turnover as people quickly tune the news in and out.

Ethnic and Foreign Language Formats

Ethnic and Foreign Language formats guide radio programming in major cities and in smaller cities scattered throughout the U.S. The term *ethnic* is now used to describe all minority audiences and markets, some of which number in the millions and are distributed throughout the country, while others are isolated pockets, perhaps of recent immigrants. Because radio reaches to serve these markets, the number and location of stations reveals the dispersion or concentration and size of ethnic markets.

More than 200 stations regularly schedule black programming. The Spanish-language market is served by several networks. There are numerous ethnic and foreign language markets throughout the U.S., as revealed in the following sampling. In major markets, single stations often program in a variety of languages. WHBI in New York City programs in Spanish, Italian, Polish, Hungarian, Portuguese, Irish, Ukranian, Bulgarian, Arabic, Yugoslavian, Greek, Albanian, and Rumanian. WZAK in Cleveland, Ohio, broadcasts in several languages, including Bohemian, Croatian and Serbian. In the same market WZZP also programs in many languages, including Swiss, Lithuanian, and Estonian.

Many stations program primarily in English with special times and programs for ethnic audiences. WLPR (FM) in Mobile, Alabama, programs in Greek. KICY in Nome, Alaska, programs in Russian and Eskimo. KDJI in Holbrook, Arizona, programs in Navajo and Spanish. KQXE in Phoenix, Arizona, programs in Polish. KRDU in Dinuba, California, programs in Spanish, Japanese, and Armenian. WGBC in Spring Valley, New York, programs in Italian, Hebrew, and Haitian. KBOI in Boise, Idaho, programs in Basque.

The student of American society might watch television and surmise from the large evening audiences that everyone speaks, acts and thinks alike and enjoys the same entertainment. Were that student to listen to radio rather than watch television, an entirely different conclusion would be reasonable, because radio programming reflects greater diversity and innovation, and programming often targets on ethnic markets, many of which are addressed in a language other than American.

SOUNDS SELECT AUDIENCES

The person cooking and handing out breakfast sausage samples in the supermarket can appeal to all of our senses: we can see, feel, smell, and taste the sausage. We can hear other sausages frying in the nearby pan. We see and hear television. We see and feel print media. Direct mail advertising often offers fabric samples to feel or perfume samples to smell. Radio, however, is unidimensional. This is radio's strength and weakness.

Music Selects Audiences

Radio must attract our attention and engage our minds only with sound. For most of us radio means music.

It is not unusual when driving into a large city for the first time to hear several stations that sound alike. The stations probably are programming by one of the more popular radio formats, such as Top 40, the strongest overall radio format for attracting and holding audiences. Also you hear many other types of music. Some stations play only jazz, rock, hard rock, or Country and Western. You may also tune in disco, disco rock, or Dixieland. Softer musical sounds may come from stations programming Classical, Soul or Soul Disco, or Contemporary Oldies.

In major urban markets the musical programming seems infinitely varied. The musical spectrum of taste is well covered in Chicago with more than 50 radio stations and New York City with more than 70. The music programmed may be a variation of a basic musical format. Sometimes a single adjective, "Contemporary" for example, indicates how a basic sound is modified. Stations may program Contemporary Album-Oriented-Rock (AOR), Contemporary Black, Contemporary Country and Western, and so on. There are many Progressive variations, including Progressive Rock and Progressive Country. Still other stations may program Country Pop, Country Fresh, Country Gospel, Country Rock, Country Sunshine. There is Hard Rock, Light Rock, and Soft Rock.

Each musical format presents a different combination of muscial themes and programming designed to appeal to subtle differences in audience musical tastes.

Radio Voices Select Audiences

Radio voices are carefully chosen to fit station formats and programs. Voices may be described as friendly, insulting, hip, or sophisticated. Some announcers speak with machine-gun rapidity, while others speak slowly in low, resonant, and sympathetic tones. Long pauses may simulate a conversation with audience members. Some voices are neutral for announcing time and temperature. Other voices, such as the feminine personality voice for Culligan Water Softener Products, are unmistakable.

Not long ago in New York City there was a campaign called, "Your neighbor is a rat." Radio spots urged listeners to keep garbage cans sealed and take other steps to control the rat population. Just the announcer's voice alone suggested the grime and filth, the threat of having rats around. Listeners felt the degradation involved in the rat problem, even without paying attention to the words.

Radio Personalities Select and Build Audiences

Radio voices often reflect the personalities behind the voices. Arthur Godfrey started in radio and later became one of television's most enduring and influential personalities. At his peak, Godfrey talked commercial messages without a script. His rapport with large audiences made Godfrey the most sought after voice and personality to associate with products. His informal delivery made every commercial a testimonial.

Many radio station formats today emphasize local personalities at different times of the day for different subject matter. A local sports or weather announcer or traffic reporter may become a local personality, asked to head fundraising drives and crown high-school prom queens.

The larger the audience a personality attracts, the more valuable the personality to the local station. Sometimes personalities that are popular in one market do not appeal to many listeners if they move to other markets. The sports announcer in Minneapolis may not attract listeners in Philadelphia. The popular early morning personality in San Francisco may fizzle in Seattle.

Some stations do not seek or use radio personalities or distinctive radio voices. Classical stations tend to use announcers with neutral voices. Often, if the announcer is doing a commercial message on a classical station, it is obvious the commercial is being read.

Listeners Choose Sounds

When you slowly turn your radio tuning dial, you eavesdrop on the incredible diversity of sounds designed to appeal to different audiences. The selection of music, news, drama, features, sports, interviews, and the personalities projected by voices—all are sounds providing information, entertainment, and companionship. The distinctive way in which sounds are blended develops markets based on sound. Some people are content to listen to a single station and never tune in anything else. Others move the tuning control constantly.

If you want to relax, turn to a Beautiful Music Station for lush, down-tempo music that is low key and features strings and full orchestration. The radio commercials will not bother you, because they are produced to fit the station format and the specific program environment. Not incidentally, this is often called doctor's office music. It is soothing. Gospel or religious programming piped into a doctor's waiting room filled with anxious patients could be disturbing to both doctors and patients.

After a week of work or perhaps a full program of classes and study, you might choose Hard Rock and Disco music that expresses your relief that the week is finished. Or when tired and driving home late at night, you might select a talk format station and disagree violently with the on-air discussion for the sole purpose of staying awake while driving.

Whatever your mood or desire, radio offers a choice.

HOW ADVERTISERS THINK OF RADIO

Radio is like a constantly turning kaleidoscope. The medium is always changing. Despite this dynamism, advertisers are able to make some key assumptions about radio.

The National Advertiser

Low Cost. Compared with other media, radio is a low-cost advertising medium. An advertiser may buy small time units on individual stations for only a few dollars or spend thousands of dollars on radio networks. Whether buying individual station or network time, radio costs per thousands are low.

Flexibility. Because even long-established consumer products do not sell equally in all markets, the advertiser can easily tailor advertising media investments in radio to match current sales or to put added advertising weight against regional, urban, or other markets. The advertiser may lighten investment in one market and "heavy-up" in another. The advertiser also can quickly tie into special sales opportunities.

Timing.   Television network requires long-term commitment of advertising dollars. Some magazines have lead times longer than two months. An established advertiser can get radio commercials on the air within the hour to tie in with a weather crisis, sports event, or space shot.

Broad Reach.   Radio can reach the majority of consumers or prospects for most products—and do so quickly. Although the radio audience often is small on a station-by-station basis, radio accumulates audiences quickly, especially if numerous commercials are aired on several stations. Radio's reach varies by day-part and target audience segment, but radio research enables advertisers to calculate the number of commercials and commercial cost required to reach both broad and sharply defined target audiences.

Editorial and Programming Values.   The program environment in which radio commercials are placed adds to or detracts from the commercials' effectiveness. Radio offers a wide variety of program environments attractive to advertisers. Shock absorbers can be advertised before or after an air traffic report. Supermarkets can advertise following consumer service news. Ski slope condition reports often are followed by advertisements for ski equipment.

Frequency.   On a single station during a single day-part, it is possible to repeat a commercial several times to break through the clutter of competing messages. Used this way, radio commercials may serve as reminders or reinforce sales points or compel initial brand awareness. Frequent use of commercials simultaneously builds reach or the number of listeners contacted at least once.

Selecting Audiences.   National advertisers study audience information from syndicated research services such as TGI, Simmons, and others who perform research that profiles the audiences of particular stations or that are attracted by specific program formats. Advertising messages can be produced for heavy, moderate, or light product users for middle-or high-income families or for young consumers or by shopping habits. When buying radio time in a major market, such as Los Angeles with more than 70 AM and FM commercial stations, the advertiser requires considerable audience information in order to choose the right stations.

Effectiveness.   Radio is seldom the primary medium for the advertiser introducing a new consumer product where the advertiser requires package identification by consumers or offers couponed incentives to make initial use of the product. Radio can, however, effectively work in conjunction with other media for new product introductions. Numerous advertisers have used radio to gain consumer awareness of a product benefit and increased brand shares through the use of music, repetition, and humor in radio commercials designed to serve as consumer reminders.

Localizing National Advertising. Each commercial delivered on a local station by a local announcer is associated with a local institution and a local personality. To some national advertisers the local association is so desirable that only radio scripts are supplied to local radio stations with instructions that the "morning" announcer, for example, read the script casually during morning drive time. Where special effects or a musical signature (jingle) are necessary for commercial effect, the advertiser may supply recorded commercials.

The Only Way to Reach Some Markets. Some media buyers are convinced that radio is the only way to reach teenagers who spend more time with radio than television and who may pay little attention when television is on because the program is not of their choice. Radio also reaches an estimated 86 percent of working women during the average weekday, and 90 percent of professional and managerial men.

The Regional Advertiser

For both the national and the regional advertiser, radio offers geographic and time flexibility. Radio is also a desirable support medium when newspapers are the primary advertising medium in regional and local markets. Radio inexpensively fills gaps in the newspaper's reach of audiences. Radio can provide week-long continuity for newspaper advertisements run only once a week during a new product introductory period. Radio commercials can help consumers recall the newspaper advertisement seen several days prior.

The Local Advertiser

Greater effort by the sales staffs of radio stations is largely responsible for the year-by-year increase of local radio advertising volume. "Local" here refers to use of radio advertising by local industries—department stores, dairies, banks, dry-cleaning establishments, local breweries, hotels, and others. It will be noticed that these are industries that draw business from a wide area. Very small retailers drawing business from a small area usually shun radio despite its attractive time rates; they are paying for too much waste coverage.

Many local industries still use radio advertising only for "specials"—those unusual events that call for all-out effort. Such advertisers rarely give radio advertising men a chance to demonstrate what might happen if radio were used on a day-to-day basis over a long period.

Other businesses use radio simply as a supplement to newspaper advertising, especially those advertisers who stress goods with strong visual appeal. Those who use radio in a supplementary capacity on the local level are in the majority, since few advertisers can be found in each town who consider radio advertising their principal medium.

Local advertisers who dare to break away from the newspaper tradition often find strong appeals in radio advertising. Some of these are:

(1) The strong local personality who builds a large and loyal audience becomes a local celebrity whose recommendations carry word-of-mouth authority with local listeners.

Local radio commercial.

Where once radio was used almost entirely for institutional messages by department stores, it is now used frequently to sell items. It is still, however, a supplementary medium for most department stores because so many products require the visualization offered in newspaper advertisements.

```
MR-152  GOLD TOE SOCKS    :30 RADIO    WRITER: Bob


                    GET ON YOUR TOES AND DOWN TO MAY

                    COMPANY FOR THE ANNUAL SALE ON GOLD

                    TOE SOCKS...BECAUSE RIGHT NOW, YOU

                    CAN SAVE TWENTY PERCENT ON EVERY

                    STYLE AND COLOR IN STOCK...GOLD TOE

                    SOCKS ARE WELL-KNOWN FOR QUALITY AND

                    COMFORT...AND THEY'RE A MAY COMPANY

                    EXCLUSIVE...SO TREAT YOUR FINICKY FEET

                    TO GOLD TOE CREW SOCKS, DRESS ANKLETS,

                    MID-CALF AND OVER-THE-CALF STYLES --

                    ALL AT TWENTY PERCENT SAVINGS...DO

                    SOMETHING NEAT FOR YOUR FEET AND SAVE

                    MONEY AT THE SAME TIME...NOW AT MAY

                    COMPANY'S ANNUAL SALE ON GOLD TOE

                    SOCKS.
```

---

(2) The daily continuity that newspapers offer may be too expensive.

(3) The penetration into the suburbs. Coverage through a well-listened-to radio station may be much more dense in the suburbs than that afforded by even a well-read metropolitan newspaper. Such coverage, as previously discussed, has reawakened the appeal of radio for many regional and national advertisers.

(4) The creation of memorability for a slogan until it becomes a part of the local idiom. Every town and city has strong local users of radio who have pushed their slogans and basic selling messages for so long, and so constantly, that virtually no citizen of the area is unable to remember them.

(5) The fact that at the moment of impact—when the commercial is being delivered—the small advertiser's message has the stage to itself and sounds just as important as the message of the biggest advertiser.

(6) Because radio is basically a theatre of the mind, inviting listeners to become active participants in completing the sound-only message, advertisers may select radio to let listeners complete and tailor commercial messages to their own interests. Several women may shop the same department store, one in the bargain basement, one in ready-to-wear and one in the fur department. Each of these three women regard the same store in different ways. Sensitively written and produced radio commercials allow each woman to create a meaningful image of the store for herself.

RADIO ADVERTISING RATES

As with newspapers, radio stations long have offered lower rates to local advertisers—as much as 70 percent lower than would be charged national advertisers. There has been and remains considerable confusion about radio rates. When radio audiences shrank during television's rapid growth, published radio time rates for advertisers were largely ignored. Advertisers bargained hard and bought commerical time for substantially less than the published time rates.

What radio stations charge advertisers for commercial time reflects the commercial durations, typically 10 seconds, 30 seconds, or 60 seconds, with 30-second commercials the most often used. The frequency of advertising typically earns a discount from the charge for just one commercial, often called the "one-time" rate. If the advertiser buys a program, other rates apply.

Day-part influences the price of commercial time, typically reflecting audience size. As a rule of thumb, day-parts are AM Drive, Daytime, PM Drive, Evening, Overnight, Weekend Drive, and Sunday AM.

Various arrangements influence the price of time. Commercial time may be bought Run-of-Station (ROS), meaning the station manager places commercials to develop a cumulative audience size and demographic mix or profile. Radio frequently is bought on a Fixed Position basis, meaning the commercial must be aired at certain times. Radio time also is sold in Package Plans and Til Forbid, the latter meaning the commercials run according to some prior agreement until the advertiser orders the radio station to cease advertising.

Today, SRDS publishes radio station time charges and buying options. The advertiser may buy on the basis of SRDS-published rates or contact the radio station directly to request information or perhaps bargain for reduced prices.

CHOOSING AM OR FM

Anyone interested in radio advertising learns quickly that he can cover a wider geographical area if he uses an AM (amplitude modulation) station than if he uses an FM station (frequency modulation). AM radio waves follow the earth's curvature and thus may be heard as far as the strength of the station's signal (any sound that may be picked up from the station's transmitter) permits. In contrast, FM waves do not follow the earth's curvature. Thus, when they reach the horizon, they go off into space and cannot be picked up by radio receivers. This means, of course, that their range is the distance from the transmitter to the horizon.

As indicated early in the chapter AM stations greatly outnumber FM stations. Radio advertising's big money is spent in AM stations despite the relatively static-free reception of FM broadcasting, and despite FM's slectivity which defines sharply a station's coverage. This latter point is significant because FM stations on the same wave band will not interfere with each other if judiciously spaced. Perhaps because of the original difficulty of attracting advertisers, many FM stations have built a tradition or programming with relatively few commercial interruptions. Some FM station prohibit musical commercials. Because of outstanding sound production with stereo, FM often delivers small but high-income audiences, attractive to advertisers of many products.

AM Channels

"Channels" are the groups of operating frequencies or wavelengths assigned to radio and television stations. There are 106 channels for broadcasting. Through the regulatory power of the Federal Communications Commission stations are licensed. Under their licensing agreements they are assigned certain power, hours of broadcast, and locations. These regulations are levied with a very important objective—to enable the stations to provide clear, uninterfered-with reception in their broadcast areas.

Stations fall into three classes of channels—clear, regional, and local.

Clear: One on which the dominant station offers service over wide areas without interference in its primary service area. Much of its secondary service area is also free of interference.

Regional: Here several stations operate with powers not in excess of 5,000 watts. The primary service area may be limited, because of interference, to a given field intensity contour.

Local: One on which several stations operate with powers not in excess of 250 watts. Again, the primary service area of a station operating on such a channel is limited.

References to primary service area in the foregoing allude to that area surrounding a station in which it is heard strongly, and steadily. Secondary service area is applied to that area beyond the primary area in which reception is not consistent. It may be good at some times, not good others.

One of the exasperating aspects of radio advertising is the irregularity of a station's coverage pattern. For the advertiser it would be convenient for planning if a radio station's coverage reached out evenly in all directions. Unfortunately, however, coverage patterns are often highly irregular due to such factors as soil conductivity, or topographical variances in the area. A human factor enters into the situation, too, since many stations use directional antenna that send signals farther in one direction than another.

To compound the difficulties for the advertising planner there are sharp differences in a station's coverage contour for daytime and nighttime. Even the most unsophisticated listener has observed that stations that come in clearly in the daytime often fade at night, or are interfered with by other stations. Any consistent radio listener has also found that on any given night stations located at astonishing distances will suddenly boom in loud and clear.

RADIO REPRESENTATIVES SUPPLY STATION INFORMATION

The local advertiser can learn about radio by simply calling one or more local radio stations. The national advertiser, however, usually gets information about radio from firms of "radio station representatives." The number varies, but there are about 200 such firms, known familiarly in the broadcast business as national reps or radio reps. These firms represent individual and noncompeting radio stations in markets scattered throughout the U.S. A single representative may call on a major advertiser on behalf of 100 or more individual stations, no one of which could afford to support salespeople in the major markets where national advertisers are headquartered.

Calling upon both advertisers and advertising agencies, radio representatives sell station time by supplying information about rates, station power, merchandising assistance, scheduling, programming, and audiences. If an advertiser wants information about a single radio station, a call to a nearby radio representative usually will suffice.

Whether or not advertisers deals with a radio representative, they usually consider the following points when thinking of buying time on a radio station.

Coverage and Reach

"Coverage" describes the geographical area in which a station can be heard. On request, stations will supply field intensity maps whose irregular contours indicate the primary and secondary coverage areas. (See figure 14-1.) Because coverage simply indicates the capacity of the station to be heard by an audience, the advertiser then asks for more specific information about listeners, or the station's "reach." The numbers and types of listeners "reached" is primarily a function of station program format and individual program appeal.

Rate Schedules

Here is where the advertiser may become lost in a morass of discounts and special arrangements. Rates will be discussed in detail later in the chapter. At this point it is enough to say that a station's rate schedule must be studied minutely in order to determine what advantages may be derived through buying certain time periods, programs, or long-term contracts. Even after all this, the advertiser may find that the time or times wanted may not be available.

Merchandising Services

There is a decided unevenness in the amount and quality of merchandising service offered by different radio stations. This side of radio selection is hard to determine from a distance. Ideally, the advertiser should check the point with other advertisers who have used the station, or should make a spot check upon retailers in the station's home city to see how they rate the merchandising.

Station Personnel

Much information about station personnel is furnished by the station promotion department. From a distance, this material is often difficult to judge because every station lauds its own shows and talent.

In addition to studying the audience ratings developed by different performers, the advertiser should have some sort of personal check made by someone who actually listens to the station. If the performer or personality is attractive to audiences, the advertiser also wants to know about the performer's ability to deliver believable commercials. Disc jockeys, news commentators, and sports announcers, along with performers associated with certain day-parts, develop audiences. The advertiser attempts to choose that one "voice" or "personality" that best delivers the commercial message.

Network Affiliation

In the 1930s and 1940s a radio station's network affiliation was often more important than the station itself. Today, however, radio is increasingly a local or regional medium, and the advertiser is less concerned with a station's network affiliation.

Radio networks do continue to provide the bulk of radio news, and continue to develop attractive features, provide programming advice for the network lineup of stations. Networks provide audience information for national advertisers and a sales arm for affiliated stations.

DESCRIBING RADIO AUDIENCES

Information about radio audience size and characteristics is obtained from samples in several ways, including day-after personal interviews, telephone interviews, and listener-completed diaries, usually covering a period of a week. The listener diary used by the American Research Bureau (often called Arbitron) develops one of the most widely used sources of current radio audience information.

The Terms Used

There are several terms which are basic to program ratings research. They include (1) sets in use, (2) program rating, (3) share of audience, (4) cost per thousand, (5) cumulative or unduplicated audience, (6) frequency, and (7) audience turnover.

Each figure in a program rating report is an estimate, with each figure subject to a sampling error that can be computed mathematically. For example, a 2.3 program rating in a small sample might possibly range between a 2.1 rating and a 2.5 rating. For this reason any slight differences in ratings are seldom

FIGURE 14-1.
Day and night coverage contours.
Radio coverage map shows prospective advertisers where their message will be heard.

WKZOland is that richly diversified area lying mid-way between Detroit and Chicago. It is only natural that WKZOland's industrial output should reach to the far corners of the globe. Paper, pharmaceuticals, taxi cabs, fishing equipment, automobile parts and bodies, shoes, refrigerators, baby food and breakfast food are just a few of the items produced in WKZOland.

WKZOland is also a rich farming community. 46.97% of all farms in lower Michigan are within the WKZO primary area. Here, also, is diversification. Fruit, berries, grains, livestock and poultry are among the farm products that are sold on the Nation's markets everyday.

WKZOland means vacation land. Hundreds of lakes, attracting thousands of vacationers, are all within range of the WKZO transmitter. Both winter and summer vacationers and sportsmen find plenty to do in WKZOland.

All these factors contribute toward the steady employment and sound buying income of the 1,770,000 people who make WKZOland their home. Kalamazoo, ranks first among all Michigan cities in stability, cultural background and "goodness of life."

Primary

Secondary

See other side

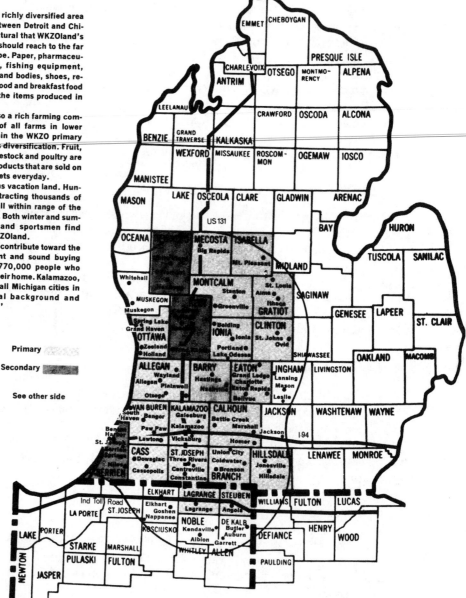

Humorous radio campaign.

Broadcast media have been useful to this advertiser because the use of humor and the human voice can deliver the message effectively and inoffensively. Notice the reference to the yellow pages and the descriptive material that identifies the company trucks for the radio listeners.

:30 "I hate Bugs"
     (WITHOUT BUG ON TRUCK)

Client   TERMINIX INTERNATIONAL
Medium   Radio
Date
Job Number

I hate bugs. I hate ants, roaches, ticks, fleas. I hate termites, mice, beetles - beetles, I hate them so bad I even busted up my kids' records of the Beetles. Me, I'm the best in the pest control business. 27-years top man wit minix. Top man, because I hate every kind of c   , crawly pest you can name. Yeah. If you hate s, call Terminix. We're in the yellow pages an   orange trucks.

:30 "I hate Bugs"
     (WITH BUG ON TRUCK)

Client   TERMINIX INTERNATIONAL
Medium   Radio
Date
Job Number

I hate bugs. I hate ants, roaches, ticks, fleas. I hate termites, beetles, mice. I hate every kind of creepy, crawly pest you can name and I'm the best in the pest control business. 27-years, top man with Terminix. Top man, and what do I get? A big plastic bug on top of my truck. It's embarrassing. If you hate pests, call Terminix. We're in the yellow pages and the orange trucks with the big bug on top.

John Malmo Advertising
Commerce Title Building Memphis, Tennessee 38103 (901) 523-2000

statistically significant, and those who use research information, as well as those who present research information, must interpret the findings with this fact in mind.

In the definitions that follow, reference is made to station ratings. In general, however, all the terms, with slight modifications in definition, are equally applicable to network radio program ratings.

Sets in Use. As the term suggests, "sets in use" is an estimate of the percentage of radio sets turned on in the sample area. It is reported as a percentage figure for half-hour or quarter-hour segments, and usually it represents an average for a certain time period. The terms "sets in use" and "homes using radios" are often used interchangeably.

Program Rating. The estimates most eagerly sought through radio rating reports, particularly by station sales people, are program ratings. Generally shown as a percentage figure, the program rating is an estimate of the percentage of radio homes (or of individuals, depending upon the research base) who heard a specific radio program or listened to a particular station at a specified time. The terms "station rating" and "program rating" are synonymous in local radio advertising research. In some rating reports the projected number of homes or listeners is shown rather than a percentage.

In most rating reports, Monday-Friday ratings are based on a five-day average and the total survey period may run for four or more weeks. Likewise, Saturday ratings or Sunday ratings are usually an average of several Saturdays or Sundays.

Share of Audience. "Share of audience" is a ratio between a program audience (or a station audience) and the number of sets in use. Thus the term "share" is used to evaluate both station and program ratings, particularly as they compare competing stations or competing programs on the air at the same time. For example, if the reported share of audience for a 7 A.M. to 7:30 A.M. morning show on WCBS is estimated at 11.6, this means that an estimated 11.6 of all the sets in use at that time of morning were tuned to WCBS.

Cost per Thousand. Cost per thousand (CPM) is a ratio between the cost of the radio time purchased and the size of the radio audience it reaches. The CPM is an attempt to evaluate efficiency. The formula for determining this cost is

$$\frac{\text{Cost per broadcast}}{\text{Audience per broadcast} \div 1,000}$$

It is helpful for station owners and advertisers to know how many different listeners or different families a station or an advertiser reaches over a one-week or over a four-week period. Such an estimate is commonly called a *reach*. Technically it is called a cumulative or unduplicated audience. These terms contrast with the term "gross audience," which defines the total number of listeners or home impressions (even though some of the impressions reach some of the same people or homes more than once) obtained over a given period of time.

In general, the more a radio advertising schedule is spread over the seven days of the week, daytime and nighttime, and the greater the number of announcements used, the larger the reach. Contrariwise, the more a schedule is concentrated in a single program, such as participation in the Monday-Friday noon news, the lower the reach.

One special study reported that one advertiser reached about 32 percent of all the homes in the area with his four-week radio advertising campaign. The campaign was scheduled on three different stations in the market. Fifteen messages a week were used on each station. The same research also showed that each family heard the campaign an estimated 8.8 times in a typical four-week period and about 3.5 times in a typical week.

Frequency "Frequency," as a radio advertising term, means the average number of times a typical listener or radio family is exposed to a given commercial or program, usually over a one-week or a four-week period. There is a direct relationship between gross audience, net audience, and frequency, as is shown by the following formula:

$$\text{Frequency} = \frac{\text{Gross audience}}{\text{Unduplicated audience}}$$

For example, if a Monday-Friday morning network newscast achieves an estimated gross weekly audience of 27,000,000 listeners and reaches an estimated 16,200,000 different listeners, the average frequency is estimated at 1.66 (rounded to 1.7 in practice). This means that the average person listening to this program is exposed to about 1.7 commercials per week. The terms "frequency" and "average episodes" are synonymous.

Audience Turnover Audience turnover is a ratio between the average number of persons that listen to a given radio program and the total number of different listeners that hear the program over a given period of time, usually one week. It is expressed by the formula

$$\text{Turnover} = \frac{\text{Unduplicated audience in one week}}{\text{Average-per-broadcast audience}}$$

If the Monday-Friday morning network news program (preceding example) research estimates that the average daily broadcast reaches about 5,4000,000 listeners, and if the unduplicated audience was researched at 16,200,000 different listening homes in an average week, then the listening home audience turnover is estimated at 3.0, or 16,200,000 ÷ 5,400,000. This means that the average-per-broadcast audience "turns over" three times in the course of a week. This is the equivalent of an entirely new audience on each of the first three days—on Monday, Tuesday and Wednesday—but with only some of the same listeners (and no new listeners) in the audience on Thursday and Friday.

Repeat Performance.

The ad above appeared in this magazine 10 years ago. The headline was a quote from one of the many letters WKZO received from grateful Western Michigan residents after the paralyzing snow storm of 1967.

On January 27, 1977, the tenth anniversary of the storm, the Western Michigan area was beset by another devastating snowfall. And once again Fetzer Broadcasting responded to the emergency. In fact, during a 17-day period, WKZO Radio carried over 17,000 announcements of school closings, meeting cancellations, road conditions and weather bulletins.

Today, just as in the past, responding quickly to the needs of our listeners is all part of the Fetzer tradition of total community involvement.

The Fetzer Stations

WKZO	**WKZO-TV**	**KOLN-TV**	**KGIN-TV**	**WJEF**
Kalamazoo	Kalamazoo	Lincoln	Grand Island	Grand Rapids

WWTV	**WWUP-TV**	**WJFM**	**WWTV-FM**
Cadillac	Sault Ste. Marie	Grand Rapids	Cadillac

RESEARCHING RADIO

The majority of radio research deals with audience size and demographics. Numerous other types of research also are conducted, often to assess what audiences think about a particular station or about the on-air personalities associated with the station. Advertisers can test the effectiveness of several different advertising appeals on several different stations. The effectiveness of radio in developing audience awareness or interest in a product can be tested, as can the extent to which radio makes an advertised claim believable. Sales may be the test when people are asked to send a money order to an address for a record or kitchen utensil.

Individual radio stations may survey listeners to learn whether the station is regarded as public spirited, important when the station's license comes before the FCC for periodic review and renewal.

BUYING RADIO—BY THE RATE CARD

Over the years, radio stations have for the most part sold their time by A-B-C units, each letter representing a different time segment during the day, with Class A time being the most expensive because the audience was largest. Many stations no longer use the traditional A-B-C classification. In some cases, time costs now are governed simply by the number of times station facilities are used. Some stations continue to use a combination of time classification and frequency of use to determine rates. Class C time, however, has virtually disappeared, replaced by some stations with AA as the most expensive time—typically morning or afternoon drive time.

For the advertiser of automotive products drive time remains the most desirable day-part. Mid-morning is desirable to advertisers of household cleaning products. Many advertisers are, however, abandoning the old concept of buying in specific time periods. Instead, they favor saturation campaigns. Under such arrangements they use a certain number of announcements each week. These are broadcast at station-determined times. Such technique is especially useful in new product promotion, or to shore up sales quotas for established products that have been doing poorly in regional markets. Sometimes, radio saturation may be used in a "blitz" campaign over a weekend.

RADIO COMMERCIALS—TO PRERECORD OR NOT

No one will ever be able to settle definitively whether live or prerecorded commercials are better. Considered quickly, it would seem as if everything would be in favor of prerecorded commercials. They are perfectly executed. They can be delivered with exactly the right kind of voice, plus the right music and/or sound effects. In addition, they can be put on whenever desired, at times when a station's top talent would not be available.

Yet, as previously indicated in this chapter, almost any station has one or two powerful personalities who command loyal and attentive audiences. These personalities can outpull any transcription. On the other hand, anyone who has heard commercials "murdered" by an unskilled station announcer may be forever unwilling to entrust commercial delivery to unknown announcers. For a big campaign it is almost impossible to make certain that the station's top announcer, in each case, will do the commercials. The present use of taped cassettes/cartridges has, however, made possible greater use of the top announcers at any time of the day or night.

Public service advertising.

Every commercial radio station is committed to devoting a percentage of its time to public service announcements. Here is a typical such announcement.

THE ADVERTISING COUNCIL, INC.

Help Fight Pollution

30-SECOND RADIO SPOT #2 - "Imagine"

ANNOUNCER

Imagine this land as it once was...

Imagine an Indian brave...riding through the wilderness.

Now imagine that scene superimposed over your community today...

Don't leave out the litter...the pollution...the noise.

Thinking about litter and pollution won't make them go away -- but getting involved can.

For the name of the KEEP AMERICA BEAUTIFUL community volunteer nearest you, write: KEEP AMERICA BEAUTIFUL, 99 Park Avenue, New York, New York 10016.

People start pollution. People can stop it.

A public service message of this station and The Advertising Council.

# # #

THE PROGRAM ENVIRONMENT FOR COMMERCIALS

Music and news remain the meat and potatoes of radio programming. Even more precisely, the Top 40 format stations continue to attract more than 30 percent of the radio audience.

Because radio is so quickly turned on and off, tuned in and out, charged with being background or "white noise" or "wallpaper for the ears" that you first notice and then ignore, advertisers are unsure just who is or is not listening. When radio was the primary evening entertainment medium, the overwhelming majority of the audience listened to each half-hour segment. The advertiser was reasonably certain of the audience size and characteristics. Today, many listen to radio in bits crowded between one activity and another. Today's radio audience is on the run, a moving target which advertisers attempt to reach through a shotgun strategy of numerous spots broadcast at many different times during the day.

SPOT RADIO

"Spot" as a term can cause confusion because the term has several meanings. One meaning is geographical. An advertiser may "spot" advertising in just one or several urban or regional target markets. Or, the advertiser may just buy individual time slots or packages of numerous time slots not associated with any particular program. Still another meaning is a time dimension. The advertiser may refer to spot announcements of a minute, 30 seconds, 20 seconds or 10 seconds as "spots." The advertiser may also refer to a "spot campaign," meaning an intensive use of commercials for a limited time period.

The young person starting out in advertising frequently can understand the particular way in which the word "spot" is used from the context in which it is used.

Common Questions When Buying Spot Radio

Buying radio time is a puzzling exercise in logic, figure juggling and hope. To pin down precisely what the radio time buyer is getting in return for the money spent, the time buyer asks many questions, such as the following:

(1) How big is your audience at different times of the day? What else can you tell me about this audience—age, income, occupation, ethnic composition, etc.
(2) What is your station "sound" or program format? Will this "sound" provide an attractive environment for my commercials?
(3) What coverage data can you furnish?
(4) Does your station furnish rating service information? Any other studies of audience reaction to your station?
(5) Do you have announcers who can effectively deliver my commercial?
(6) What merchandising help can you furnish?
(7) What can we buy for X dollars?
(8) Has our competition used your station? If so, how?

QUESTIONS

1. How did radio change as a result of the rapid growth and popularity of television?

2. How would you describe radio audiences today compared with the audiences for network television?

3. Is the audience for all U.S. radio stations ever greater than the audience for all U.S. television stations?

4. What arguments would you develop in support of the idea that radio today is more vital and vigorous than ever?

5. How would you describe a radio format?

6. What changes will make radio an even more attractive medium for advertisers in the future? Why?

7. What is meant when radio is described as unidimensional?

8. For what reasons do you tune into a radio station? (Think of as many as you can.)

9. How would you, as a national advertiser, reach large audiences through radio?

10. Why is radio seldom used as the primary advertising medium to introduce a new packaged consumer product?

11. When radio is called a "theatre of the mind," what does this mean to an advertiser?

12. What influences the rates advertisers pay for radio time?

13. How do "sets in use" differ from "program rating"?

14. For what reasons might an advertiser use only pre-recorded commercials?

15. During morning drive time, a 30-second commercial on a radio station costs the advertiser $60. If this commercial reaches 30,000 listeners, what is the cost per thousand for the commercial? Now assume the commercial is from a tire manufacturers who wants only commuters and not people listening at home. If there are 15,000 driving listeners, what is the cost per thousand for the commercial?

16. Assume an advertisement is aired 10 times during a given week, during which time it reaches a gross audience of 500,000. If the commercial reaches an estimated 250,000 different listeners during this time period, what is the frequency of the commercial?

17. If a daily mid-morning talk show reaches an estimated 400,000 listeners daily, and approximately 1,200,000 different listeners in an average week, what is the audience turnover rate?

Answer to:

question 15:

$$\frac{\$60}{30,000 \text{ divided by } 1,000} = \$2.00 \text{ (answer)}$$

$$\frac{\$60}{15,000 \text{ divided by } 1,000} = \$4.00 \text{ (answer)}$$

question 16:

$$\frac{500,000}{250,000} = 2.0 \text{ average frequency}$$

question 17

$$\frac{1,200,000}{400,000} = 3.0 \text{ audience turnover rate}$$

REFERENCES

1. Radio Facts (555 Madison Avenue, New York: Radio Advertising Bureau).
2. Often these accumulated audiences are referred to as *cumes* with advertisers more interested in cumes than big audiences for single programs.

15

TELEVISION – CONTROVERSIAL AND EXPENSIVE

TELEVISION – CONTROVERSIAL AND EXPENSIVE

The easiest way to get into an argument is to say you watch a lot of television and enjoy every minute of it, including the commercials. Your intelligence, if not your sanity, will be questioned by those around you.

Television is easily the most controversial medium. Television is called a babysitter, tranquilizer, electronic pacifier, entertainer, educator, purveyor of reality, and false reality. Television is loved, hated, revered, and despised. Perhaps opinions about television are strong because the medium is difficult to ignore. More than 98 percent of U.S. households have at least one receiver. More than 77 percent of U.S. households have color television.

A recent Superbowl game was seen by an estimated 85 million Americans. The cost per commercial minute exceeded $300,000. Is television advertising expensive? Yes! No other medium, however, develops such huge audiences. No other medium generates so much excitement. No other medium is so much like face-to-face communication with sight, sound, action, and color.

TELEVISION'S RAPID GROWTH

Today it is hard to believe that in the late 1940s television was regarded as an expensive toy with only a few hours of weekly scheduled programming viewed by a small family circle—small because early television screens often were five or seven inches, measured diagonally. In 1950 about nine percent of U.S. households had television. A mere four years later 56 percent of U.S. households had television. In 1958, household television ownership jumped to 84 percent. Currently, household television ownership—what advertisers call penetration—has stabilized at 98 percent. About 4 percent of households have two or more television sets.[1]

Television Viewing Times

Television viewing increases throughout the day, peaking between 8 and 10 P.M. and dropping sharply at 11 P.M. Viewing variations are minor in the morning year round. Viewing later in the day varies more sharply by season. (See figure 15-1.)

FIGURE 15-1
Percent of TV Households Using Television

For the average television household daily television usage is 6 hours and 19 minutes per day. In January, television usage is about 7 hours a day. In July, viewing drops to about 5½ hours a day. There are no dramatic differences in television viewing by household income, although households with incomes under $10,000 tend to view less than the average for all households.[2]

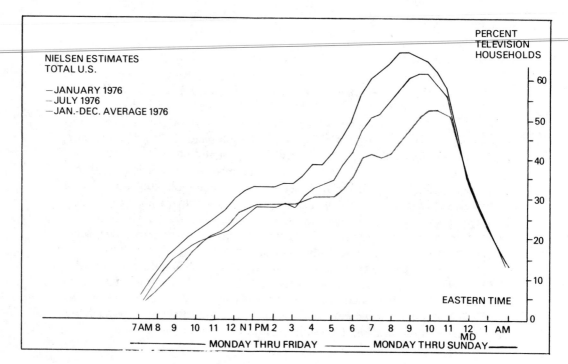

TELEVISION ADVERTISING CRITICIZED

Television by itself is controversial. Advertising by itself is controversial. Join television with advertising and the potential for discussion—often heated—is unlimited. As do most citizens, advertisers hold many of the same general opinions about television. Advertisers however, tend to have additional specific opinions based on detailed audience information and studies relating to advertising effectiveness and commercial costs.

Most advertisers agree that television advertising is as close as one can get to personal selling with a mass medium. Most advertisers also agree that personal selling is far more effective than advertising. It is also vastly more expen-

FIGURE 15-2
Stations Receivable (% Share of TV Households)

There are now approximately 740 commercial and 260 noncommercial television stations. Four or more stations can be received by 96 percent of all television households. Seven or more stations can be received by 66 percent of television households.[3] The continuing growth of cable television suggests that viewers will enjoy an even greater number of program options from which to choose.

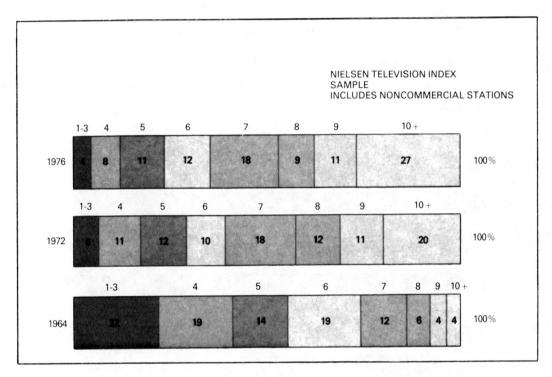

NIELSEN TELEVISION INDEX
SAMPLE
INCLUDES NONCOMMERCIAL STATIONS

	1-3	4	5	6	7	8	9	10 +	
1976	4	8	11	12	18	9	11	27	100%

	1-3	4	5	6	7	8	9	10 +	
1972	6	11	12	10	18	12	11	20	100%

	1-3	4	5	6	7	8	9	10 +	
1964	22	19	14	19	12	6	4	4	100%

sive, with a single sales call by a professional salesperson costing close to $80. A single prime-time 30-second commercial now costs about $80,000, or the equivalent of 1,000 sales calls.

Major Objections to Television Advertising

Advertisers, critics and many viewers share several common objections to television advertising. All of us, at one time or another, have discussed at least the following frequently mentioned objections.

Too Many Advertisements.   Many viewers object to the sheer number of commercials on television, what the industry calls commercial "clutter." Advertisers, themselves, are unhappy with the number of commercials run before, during and after programs. According to the National Association of Broadcasters Code, nonprogram time, which includes billboards, is limited to 10 minutes per hour for prime time. (Prime time is any consecutive three hours be-

FIGURE 15-3
Weekly Activity for Man, Women, Teens, and Children

The bar chart (Figure 15-3) indicates that women tend to view more television than men. Men and women over 55 tend to be the heaviest viewers. Teens and young men tend to be light viewers. Preschoolers are heavy daytime and early evening viewers.[4]

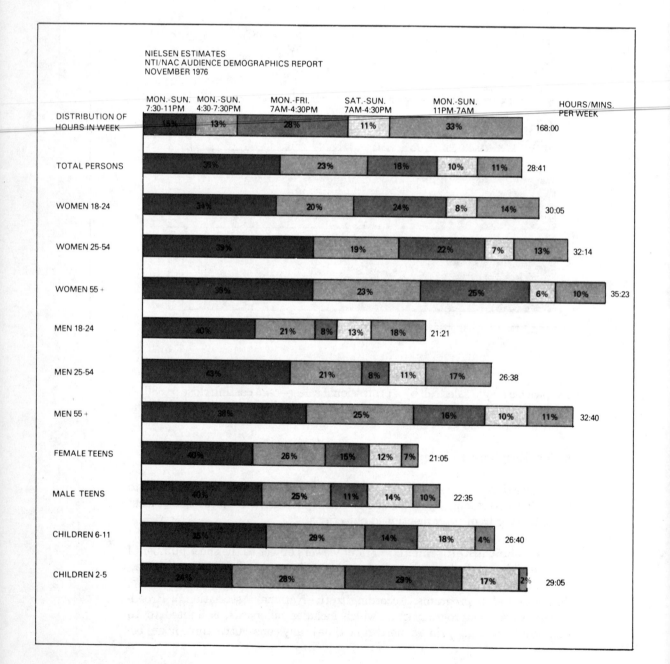

NIELSEN ESTIMATES
NTI/NAC AUDIENCE DEMOGRAPHICS REPORT
NOVEMBER 1976

	MON.-SUN. 7:30-11PM	MON.-SUN. 4:30-7:30PM	MON.-FRI. 7AM-4:30PM	SAT.-SUN. 7AM-4:30PM	MON.-SUN. 11PM-7AM	HOURS/MINS. PER WEEK
DISTRIBUTION OF HOURS IN WEEK	15%	13%	28%	11%	33%	168:00
TOTAL PERSONS	39%	23%	18%	10%	11%	28:41
WOMEN 18-24	34%	20%	24%	8%	14%	30:05
WOMEN 25-54	39%	19%	22%	7%	13%	32:14
WOMEN 55 +	36%	23%	25%	6%	10%	35:23
MEN 18-24	40%	21%	8%	13%	18%	21:21
MEN 25-54	43%	21%	8%	11%	17%	26:38
MEN 55 +	38%	25%	16%	10%	11%	32:40
FEMALE TEENS	40%	26%	15%	12%	7%	21:05
MALE TEENS	40%	25%	11%	14%	10%	22:35
CHILDREN 6-11	35%	29%	14%	18%	4%	26:40
CHILDREN 2-5	24%	28%	29%	17%	2%	29:05

tween 6 P.M. and midnight.) Up to 16 minutes of nonprogram time is permissible during other hours. Because of public pressure, the television industry has pulled back on nonprogram time during childrens' television on Saturday morning from 16 to 9½ minutes.

Advertising for Objectionable Products or Services. At one time or another we have all objected to television commercials for this product or that service. In fact, when you think about it, it is curious that television advertising, which enters millions of homes, has not raised more viewer objections than it has. While we have all grumbled in the past, the networks, local stations, advertising agencies, and advertisers have been sensitive to possible viewer objections, very much aware that commercials intrude into millions of American living rooms and are viewed in a family setting.

Increasingly, however, many viewers are objecting to commercials for new products and services. Viewers regard such commercials as an invasion of privacy. A commercial urging sex education in primary schools, for example, is viewed by many parents as a threat to family values and parental control. Many viewers object to commercials for products associated with emerging and controversial new values and lifestyles.

The advertiser's problem is that rapid, and in many ways, revolutionary, social change has engulfed America since the late 1970s. The traditional conventions dictating behavior have lost authority. In ever-growing numbers Americans are consciously opting for new lifestyles and represent a substantial market reachable by television.

Objectionable Commercial Techniques. We also object to the incessant hectoring that blares forth from many commercials. Broadcast industry codes preclude some practices, such as unusually loud sound tracks. Numerous other blatant and attention-getting techniques are unacceptable to network and local station standards of practice. Even so, many commercials are acceptable for broadcast, despite what might be tasteless repetition both in what we hear and simultaneously see printed on the screen.

What do we do? We frequently exercise our inalienable right to misperceive or ignore what we dislike, disagree with, or find distasteful. How well can we do this? If you viewed television recently, try jotting down as many commercials as you can recall. There won't be many.

NATIONAL TELEVISION ADVERTISING: DECISIONS AND DOLLARS

Why do national and regional advertisers spend many thousands of dollars for 30 seconds of commercial time? The basic reason is that the advertiser wants to reach large numbers of consumers quickly. The advertiser does not make television-buying decisions lightly because of the huge costs involved.

What the advertiser does is to relate television time costs to the audience size. The 30-second commercial time costing $80,000 is exposed to an audience of millions. The cost-per-thousand viewers may be between $4 and $5, which is typical of prime time television commercial costs. The cost of contacting each viewer is a few pennies.

For low-cost, widely distributed products bought frequently by millions of consumers, television may be the ideal medium. That is because the vast majority of those viewers who see the commercial are reasonable prospects to buy the product. For limited appeal products, such as luxury automobiles, very expensive jewelry or vacation steamship cruises, network television would not be a logical medium because it costs too much to reach the relatively small number of prospects for these products or services.

While reaching a mass audience at a low cost-per-thousand or per-prospect may be a national advertiser's basic reason for using television, national advertisers have many other reasons for choosing the medium, many of which are not related to cost. Following are some of the reasons as expressed by leading advertising people:

Advertising agency vice-president of marketing services:
"I distinguish between dynamic and static media. A dynamic medium is one in which the recipient has to make an effort to escape exposure to the commercial message. A static medium is one in which he has to make an effort to obtain exposure to the message. TV and radio, of course, are dynamic media. The newspaper is a static medium."

Advertising agency chairman of the board:
"The television advertising experience is a total experience, whereas advertising in newspapers and magazines usually occupies only a portion of the opened pages, and outdoor advertising is only a part of the scene."

Drug company advertising director:
"I don't look at TV the way a media man does, in terms of cost-per-thousand. What I'm interested in is cost-per-sales. That's why we think so much of TV. It's better for us than any other medium in terms of cost-per-sales. TV costs more than radio, for instance, but TV has an impact, a remembrance, that doesn't seem to come through in any other medium."

Insurance company vice-president:
"We must ask several things of our advertising. One is broad coverage, geographically. Another is a family audience. And, because our company renders a vital service to the public, we want our advertising to render a service. We have been able to accomplish these things through the use of television."

Utility company vice-president of merchandising:
"Television with its impact through sight, sound and intimate relationship with the family livng-room pattern is an increasingly important tool of marketing management. Its penetration into practically every segment of the total market gives a unique advantage to the advertiser who sells the general public."

Pen company marketing vice-president:
"TV is an invaluable medium in introducing new products, and particularly products with demonstration features."

Camera company sales and advertising vice-president:
"Television is perfect for us. We can reach the family together and demonstrate the ease of operation of our cameras."

Other advertisers say television advertising attracts attention by presenting the unexpected, often with human warmth and humor. Some believe the medium lends prestige and drama to products with low inherent interest. All agree that the combination of sight, sound, motion, and color make television the most effective medium for product demonstration.

Television Cost Comes First

The high cost of television advertising reverses the usual order in which many advertisers make media decisions. Traditionally, advertisers assess media options after setting a budget and developing a marketing plan and an advertising plan. Only then are individual media considered, whether outdoor, consumer magazines, newspapers, local radio, or any other medium.

If the advertiser wants to use television advertising, however, anticipated television costs are gathered even before the budget is developed. Suppose, for example, the cost of reaching target consumers three or five times a week through television is far more than the advertiser can afford. The advertising planner wants this information quickly. Today the already high and rapidly increasing cost of television advertising forces many advertisers to use less expensive media. Knowing in advance that television is too expensive, the advertiser can develop alternative message and media strategies that bypass television and the often staggering costs associated with the medium.

Sometimes television is not a desirable medium. Long advertising copy, for example, demands print rather than broadcast media, so there is really no television decision to be made when long and detailed advertising copy is required. Sometimes the advertiser feels pressured to use television, even when convinced that other media—singly or in combination—can reach target consumers with desired levels of frequency at lower costs. Often television time buying is done with an eye to enlisting dealer or retailer support and enthusiasm. Because of television's glamor and impact, dealers and retailers may be more impressed by television advertising than by advertising through other media that dealers and retailers may take for granted. The advertising director of a national advertiser makes this point: "When we run a newspaper campaign, or even a color magazine campaign, we'll hardly get a whisper from the dealers but if we run a television show, all the dealers are talking about it the next time the salespeople make their rounds. There's a lot of 'talk' value to advertising."

If the decision is to use television, then the advertiser must decide on the time of day (or night), audience size, and characteristics on a cost-per-thousand basis.

Television's Buying Options

The advertiser examines several television buying options to see if television reasonably fits a proposed budget. The advertiser may buy sponsorship of programs, invest in cosponsorship or alternate sponsorships, buy program segments, or spots.

Program Sponsorship. Sponsorship of a weekly prime time network television show is a realistic option only for advertisers with national product distribution. Even for large national advertisers, sponsorship of a network show is the major advertising expenditure in their budgets. Sponsorship offers the advertiser a number of benefits and advantages:

(1) Commercials can be shaped to fit the program.
(2) Listeners develop program loyalty and identify the product with the program and the sponsor. Also, there is less frantic tuning in and out of commercials than is the case with spot commercials placed at the end of programs.
(3) Program sponsorship impresses dealers, giving the company and the products prestige not only with the public but also with the dealer organization.
(4) Use of programs enables advertisers to analyze audiences more closely.

Program sponsorship does have drawbacks:

(1) Sometimes viewers just do not associate advertised products with sponsored programs.
(2) Sometimes audiences change, and large numbers of new viewers are not prospects for the advertised product.
(3) The advertiser's plans go awry if the network drops the sponsored program because the number of viewers is small or declining.
(4) Buying sponsorship of a successful show enables the advertiser to learn about the audience in advance, but sponsoring a new show involves the advertiser in some very real business risks. The audience size and composition attracted by the program is a guess.

Cosponsorship and Alternate Sponsorship. The advertiser may reduce the cost and risks of program sponsorship by buying cosponsorship of a program. Two advertisers share the commercial time and costs each week on a mutually agreed basis. Alternate week sponsorship is similar to cosponsorship. but each advertiser's commercials are shown in the program only during alternate weeks. Even large advertisers may choose to share program costs for one or more programs in order to reach more different viewers. Mystery fans can be reached on one show, and those who prefer humor, music, or news on other shows.

Alternate sponsorship does pose problems, of course. Network discount allowances, for example, are less favorable for the every-other-week sponsor than the weekly sponsor. Also, product identification or association with the sponsored program may be weak. Sponsors buying time on the same show on alternate weeks must agree on other, often ticklish, problems involving program format changes, settlement of credits for program interruptions, changes in the network lineup of stations used, and many other points.

Segments. Another option for the national advertiser is to buy segments of network shows, sometimes referred to as the "magazine concept" of time buying. Participations are one form of segment time buying. An advertiser, for instance, may take a six-minute segment of a show, the six minutes consisting of five minutes of show time and one minute of commercial time. The advertiser may segment in another way, buying only certain stations in the network, stations in the eastern daylight savings time zone, for example.

Spots.   A final option for advertisers is to buy spot television. Spot television may be bought in a "scatter plan" of announcements. The scatter package may be designed exclusively by the network or in conjunction with the advertiser. The advertiser's commercials are in one or perhaps several different time periods, perhaps early evening or fringe and prime time. Typically, the advertiser focuses on reaching large numbers of different viewers, foregoing identification with any television programs.

The advertiser may bypass scatter packages and buy precisely what is wanted. Buying spot television in this way means the advertiser is in control. The advertiser selects the markets—as many or as few as are wanted—and decides when to advertise by season, day of week, and time of day. The advertiser decides which commercial messages go to which markets and chooses the number of spots (often called advertising weight) to be used.

The advertiser, in short, tailors the advertising media schedule to fit marketing objectives. Using spot television, the advertiser can buy and run commercials quickly to meet specific market-by-market problems.

Primary or Secondary Medium?

In planning an advertising campaign, a given advertising medium may be selected as the primary advertising vehicle or it may be assigned a secondary or complementary role. Media themselves are not primary or secondary. Advertisers make such distinctions on the basis of their own objectives. An advertiser who wants to reach an audience of engineers with long, technical copy will invariably choose engineering magazines as a primary medium. An advertiser who wants to demonstrate the quickness and ease of making a new dessert product, at the same time making sure the consumers recognize the package on supermarket shelves, may choose television as the primary medium.

Because of the effectiveness of television as an advertising medium, it is usually selected a a primary medium, budget permitting. So effective is television in quickly reaching millions of consumers that even when a particular advertising budget will not permit a primary effort in television, the budget often permits the use of television in flights (short promotional periods) or on a seasonal basis to support whatever other medium was chosen as the primary medium. The small-budget advertiser, however, invariably chooses radio, newspapers, or magazines as the primary medium. Spending too little for television advertising is worse than spending nothing because the television investment is thus wasted. Television requires a certain level of use—some call this a threshold—before anything happens. Thresholds vary by product interest, the benefit and persuasiveness of the commercial. Major advertisers learn these thresholds in test markets. They know they have to invest a certain amount before they can get feedback from large numbers of consumers who know about the product and can correctly identify or associate the benefit before the product moves from the store shelves.

Television and Buying Judgments

Are television shows with the highest ratings the best buys? Sometimes a television show may be desirable to the advertiser, even though the show has an average rating. Perhaps such a show has a very loyal audience, or one which attempts to view the program each week. This gives the advertiser frequency with a stable audience. Or perhaps the show emphasizes basic, homespun values of family life. The association would be attractive to the advertiser of family games or food products which emphasize old-fashioned natural flavor and goodness.

When considering sponsorship of a program with an attractive and dynamic star, the advertiser is balancing a number of factors. The advertiser may want a show with a high rating. Such a rating means a huge audience and a certain prestige and visibility in the industry. Such a star may make so overwhelming an impression on audiences that sponsor and product identification are low. In prior research, 60 percent or more of the audience for top-rated shows have failed to identify sponsors. Also, the advertiser questions the durability of the star's appeal to viewers. Some stars are very durable, while others lose audience appeal during their first season.

PLANNING FOR TELEVISION ADVERTISING

The following four steps are considered in precampaign strategy planning:

(1) establishing television advertising objectives,
(2) setting the advertising budget, and selecting media,
(3) making precampaign recommendations and decisions,
(4) going on the air, and
(5) campaign coordination and follow through.

Establishing Television Advertising Objectives

In national television advertising, objectives are chosen to help achieve long- and short-range marketing goals expressed in the marketing plan. Television advertising is usually asigned one primary objective. One or perhaps two secondary objectives are also chosen for each campaign, usually to help achieve the primary objective. For new products, typical objectives are

(1) to develop awareness of the product and benefits from its use,
(2) to develop product identification so consumers will recognize the product on supermarket shelves, and
(3) to develop consumer belief.

Continental Dinners might have to convince consumers that a tasty meat dish in a foil pouch can sit on kitchen shelves for two years without spoiling. For well-known national products, the primary objective may be to remind people to use the product already on their kitchen shelves. V-8 vegetable juice television advertising has this primary objective.

In retail advertising, television objectives may be expressed as long- and short-term. Retailers are local institutions with reputations. One store may be known for having the latest fashions, another for the range of selection, another for delivery and repair service. Retailers may attempt to maintain such reputations with consumers over periods of time. Short-term retail objectives for television advertising are frequently expressed in terms of immediate sales.

Setting the Advertising Budget and Selecting Media

When allocating dollars to media, sufficient money should be invested in the primary avertising medium in order to do an effective advertising job. Three or four daytime network television spots weekly may be sufficient for reminder advertising for an established household product. For a product that sells evenly throughout the year, the advertising budget should contain sufficient funds to buy this level of continuous advertising.

Cold remedies, mosquito repellents, toys, and ski equipment all have strong seasonal sales patterns. Advertising for such products should be scheduled to precede and accompany peak selling periods.

If the advertiser with year-round sales cannot afford year-round advertising, the advertiser should consider using four- to six-week "flights" with each flight schedules several times throughout the year. Or, the advertiser may concentrate advertising only during the best sales months for the product. This type of concentrated use of media is often called "pulsing."

Experience has shown that an advertiser with a limited advertising budget can make effective use of the advertising budget by using television advertising dollars during preselected promotion periods. When used in this way, television advertising reaches a substantial audience with high frequency. In general, it is better to allocate television advertising in this manner rather than to run "thin" year-round schedule.

GRPs: a Planning Tool.   Numerous advertisers approach advertising with a coldly mathematical bent. When planning, such advertisers will ask, "How many Gross Rating Points (GRPs) will our advertising deliver?" GRPs are a quick way of expressing the cost of reaching a defined audience with a given frequency. For instance, assume that the cost of a rating point in a market is $30. Also assume that 15 television announcements are planned, each with an 11 rating (reach). The number of announcements multiplied by the rating totals 165 Gross Rating Points. At $30 per rating point, the planned cost of the media buy is $4,950.

GRPs are a useful tool in the early stages of marketing and advertising planning. The advertiser, using widely available industry figures, quickly learns whether reaching 50 percent of women 18 and older an average of 6 times with network television reasonably fits within a proposed budget.

If television time can fit within an advertising budget, the advertiser carefully studies GRPs on a market by market basis, probably focusing on demographic classifications within markets. Women 18 to 34 are household buying agents for young families and highly desirable target consumers for many advertisers. Gross Rating Points can express the cost of reaching such women with a desired frequency.

GRPs are a planning guide only. The price the advertiser actually pays to reach target consumers in broadcast or print media may be lower. Advertisers often can negotiate reduced time or space charges. Also, GRPs are based on one unit of space or time, and media generally offer generous frequency or volume discounts.

Making Precampaign Recommendations and Decisions

Only if an advertiser has sufficient dollars to do an adequate job in a primary medium should the advertiser consider a secondary advertising medium. In general, network television is a primary advertising medium for the national advertiser with national distribution for a widely used and frequently purchased product. Spot television may be the primary medium for the regional advertiser who wishes to reach selected markets. When television is used as a secondary advertising medium (radio, newspapers or magazines in the primary role, for example), network or spot television may be used in flights.

Going On the Air. In practice, the first precampaign phase of planning blends into the second phase of campaign development—getting the television commercial on the air. This campaign usually includes at least four phases: time buying, selecting what to promote for the retail campaign, creating the television commercial, and producing the television commercial.

Individual broadcast commercials can be tested in specially equipped theaters to which a sample of consumers are invited to view new television programs and commercials. Consumer reactions to the commercials tell advertisers whether the commercials accomplish the pre-established objectives.

In many instances, the campaign is then pretested in two or three test cities or sales territories. This is particularly true for new products and often the case when a major change in media or creative strategy is involved for an established national product. Depending on the success of the test, the campaign is adopted and goes national.

Coordinating the Campaign and Following Through

The print advertisements and broadcast commercials we see as consumers didn't just happen. The thinking and preparation may have been done over one or two years. Before major consumer advertising breaks, the advertising manager coordinates the preparation and placement of advertisements designed for distributors, wholesalers, and retailer. Sales promotion and other materials, including in-store displays, are distributed, typically by the sales force already trained to urge the stocking and prominent display of the new product.

The advertiser and agency monitor the consumer campaign as it "goes public." If print advertisements include coupons, the rate at which consumers redeem coupons is monitored. Warranty card return from consumers of small and large appliances provide additional information. What advertisers call "tracking" studies reveal by survey the speed with which consumers become aware of the advertised product or service. Surveys also reveal how much information consumers learned from the advertisements, whether they think the information important, and whether they believed in the advertisements. Nielsen surveys reveal the rate at which new products flow through stores. Feedback from the sales force reveals the smoothness of product flow through the distribution channel as well as problems with stores being out-of-stock. Surveys of consumers who bought and used the product reveal consumer satisfaction.

TELEVISION PROGRAMMING

Despite criticism of program content, television continues to attract the attention of millions of viewers, and many programs have enriched the lives of people.

The Bell Telephone Hour for years presented the best music from classical to popular. Great dramas were presented on Kraft Theater, Armstrong Circle Theater, Playhouse 90, and Studio One. Original dramas, such as *Requiem for a Heavyweight, The Miracle Worker* and *No Time For Sergeants*, were produced for television first and then went to the legitimate theaters on Broadway. The Hallmark Hall of Fame has presented outstanding programs year after year.

Most television programs are designed to have a broad appeal. The Western as a dramatic format has proved to be incredibly flexible. It can present humor or tragedy, or a combination of both in an infinite variety of ways. It can show superficial shoot-the-bad-guy action, or a person's struggle between ethical beliefs and dealing with reality, such as when a religious man has to pick up a gun. Sometimes, vengeance—with Biblical "eye for an eye" connotations—is the main theme in a story. The Western appeals to the viewing public because it can exploit every human emotion, bluntly or subtly.

At one time there were 39 Western series on television. Variety programs, musicals, action dramas, and situation comedies have also proved popular over the years. More recently, serialized novels produced for prime time showing in installments have attracted large audiences, with *Roots* developing one of the largest audiences in modern television.

While television program formats remain constant, the program content changes radically. Daytime dramas or soaps, for example, deal with family and interpersonal problems unmentionable five years ago. Situation comedies which formerly dealt with minor human foibles, now often present humor in the bittersweet context of family argument or social conflict. Action dramas, which portray the work of law enforcement agencies and private investigators, update successful plots with new personalities dealing with social tensions and problems.

Television has an incredible appetite for talent and new program ideas, many of which are presented within the traditional program formats or situation comedies, action dramas, and westerns. Critics prefer radical experimenting with entirely new program formats. Television, however, is the most expensive mass medium. Television must develop large audiences to cover high talent and production costs.

New programs, called slots, are constantly being tested with samples of typical television viewers invited to theaters to see and give their reactions to the pilots. In-theater testing is not infallible but often predicts how the American audiences will react to new programs. The proof of in-theater tests is the audience size or rating when the new program is introduced, traditionally in September but increasingly at any time during the fall and early winter.

Children's Television

Children are a special audience. Extra precautions are required to prevent deception in advertising intended for the very young. To some, this means that there should be no advertising aimed at children eight and under.

An FTC study group in 1978 argued that children are incapable of understanding the selling intent of advertisements. Children, it was said, lack the information, experience, and therefore the ability to distinguish advertisements from programs or to reasonably assess the safety of a product.

Self-regulatory guidelines developed by the Children's Advertising Review Unit of the Council of Better Business Bureaus likewise assume that children are a special audience. Rather than do away with the advertising directed to children 11 and under, the *Guidelines* provide specific directions to ensure that children-directed advertising is accurate, truthful, and fair.

The *Guidelines* detail desirable and undesirable practices under topic headings such as "Social Values." Good manners and obedience to parents are, for example, listed as desirable. The *Guidelines* also deal with comparative claims, pressure on parents to purchase advertised products, safety and the use of premiums, which, the Guidelines warn, should not be emphasized more than the advertised product.

The *Guidelines* specific suggestions as to "Presentation" in commercials made for children are as follows:

Presentation

Children have vivid imaginations. Use of imagination enables a child to project himself beyond his immediate capacities and reach for his future potential. Advertisers should, therefore, always respect a child's imagination. The use of imaginative situations, appropriate to the audience concerned, is an acceptable and normal communications practice. Implicit in the foregoing is the concept that fantasy, including animation, is an appropriate form of communication to any audience, including the very young. However, the use of special situations and fantasy in advertising should not suggest unattainable expectations of performance. To achieve this, presentations should not exploit the child's difficulty in distinguishing between the real and the fanciful. Therefore:

(1) Copy, sound, and visual presentations—as well as the advertisement in its totality—should not mislead (a) on performance characteristics such as speed, method of operation, size, color, durability, nutritional benefits, noise, etc., (b) on perceived benefits such as the acquisition of

strength, popularity, growth, proficiency, intelligence, and the like; or (c) on the expectation of price range or cost of the product.

(2) The advertisement should clearly establish what is included in the original purchase of a product. When items are to be purchased separately, the fact should be disclosed in a way that is clear to the child audience primarily addressed. Advertising for all products sold unassembled should indicate that assembly is required. If any other product is essential in order to use the advertised product—such as batteries—this should be disclosed.

(3) In general, information which requires disclosure for legal or other reasons should be in language understandable by the child audience to which the advertisement is addressed. In television advertising, audio as well as video disclosure is encouraged. In all media, disclaimers, when used, should be clearly worded, legible, and prominent.

(4) A clearly depicted presentation of the complete advertised product should be shown in the advertisement. Where appropriate to help identify the product, the package may also be depicted, provided it does not mislead as to product characteristics, content, or the price range to be expected.

(5) Advertising demonstrations should show the use of a product or premium in a way that can be duplicated by the child for whom the product is intended.

(6) An effort should be made to establish the size of a product clearly and adequately. This is of particular importance when size claims are being used, such as "giant sized," "monster size," etc.

(7) Representation of food products should be made so as to encourage sound usage of the product with a view toward healthy development of the child and the development of good nutritional practices. Advertisements representing mealtime in the house should clearly and adequately depict the role of the product within the framework of a balanced diet. Overconsumption of food products and beverages should be avoided, nor should it be implied that any one food provides all the nutrients contained in a well-designed daily food plan.

(8) To ensure truthful and accurate representations of playthings in television advertisements, they should be shown in mormal play environments and situations, except when the number of products to be featured exceeds what should be reasonably owned by the child or children shown in the play situation.

(9) Should a whole line of toys, or more toys than might reasonably be owned by the average child be featured in a television advertisement, limbo settings (which are defined as nonrepresentational settings with a plain background) or in-store settings are suggested. These settings might provide a better context for fair demonstration of such products to children. When representing large lines of products (in print or television) special care should be taken to ensure that the child will understand the separate purchase requirement.

(10) When toys or any other product can be purchased either individually or as a collection of related items, price representation, if any, should

clearly indicate to the child that the cost of collection is greater than the cost of the individual item.[5]

THE MONEY INVOLVED

No advertiser, no matter how fascinated with television's selling effectiveness, can ignore the high cost of commercial time. Trade publications frequently publish stories about already high and still rising costs. One advertiser who continues to use television advertising, despite the rising cost of commercial time, said: "While TV is good for us, we find that even with our very large volume of advertising in television, we cannot afford to keep any sort of status quo. We are spending 23 percent more money for 39 percent fewer commercials. This is not an encouraging trend."

While the total cost of television commercials has grown rapidly, on a cost-per-thousand basis, television remains a reasonable buy for many advertisers. For example, a 30-second commercial costing $45,000 during evening prime time on a network show with a rating of 20 costs $3.28 per thousand audience members. Daytime television, of course, is less expensive because talent and production costs (and audiences) are smaller. A 30-second spot might cost $7,000 for a program with a rating of 7. In this case the cost-per-thousand is about $1.46.

This, then, is the anomaly. Television is and is not expensive. It is expensive when you look at the cost of commercial time. It isn't if you're dealing with large audiences. However, many small and medium-sized advertisers and some large ones regard time costs as a barrier. Today, we're seeing a smaller number of large advertisers spending more money for less commercial time.

Determining Rates

Overall, television commercial rates are determined as radio rates are determined—by time of day or night used, by the length of time used and by the number of times used. This pattern is clearly shown in the rates for television stations listed in the television section of *Standard Rate & Data Service*.

Many other charges, not listed in the foregoing, may ultimately increase the sponsors cost. Some of these charges include use of special equipment, use of studios for rehearsals, and film editing costs. Although all stations set up rate schedules in the same general way, there are enough differences in each situation that the advertiser must consult *Standard Rate & Data Service* carefully or must talk to a station representative.

TELEVISION'S TECHNICAL SIDE

For a long time (as time is measured in television's history) an intra-industry battle has been fought between those who favor telecasting on very high frequency channels (VHF) and those who favor ultrahigh frequency channels (UHF). VHF channels (2-13) are up to this point used by far more stations than use UHF channels. UHF stations utilize channels 14-83.

All the first television stations were VHF. When UHF stations did begin, their operators found almost no sets in the telecast areas that were geared to tune in their channels. To convert a set so that it could receive UHF telecast costs more money than great numbers of the public were willing to pay. Without strong audiences for UHF stations, advertisers were unwilling to back them with advertising schedules. This unwillingness was enhanced by the fact that UHF stations offered considerable less coverage area than VHF stations. Networks, as well as advertisers, did not support UHF. Now that set manufacturers are required by law to make television sets that offer VHF and UHF capacity, a change in the VHF-UHF situation has been made possible.

LOCAL TELEVISION

Local television is used principally in the daytime or late night—and will probably continue to be so used.

Local television is characterized by use of spot announcement advertising or low-cost programs. The latter are dominated by live shows, local talent, or syndicated films. Television stations build local personalities for childrens' shows, morning talk shows; news personnel may do in-depth programs on local problems or issues. Sports reporters may host bowling or other sports programs.

Local television personalities may do on-camera commercials for local advertisers or stay off camera and do what are called "voice-overs," while the television video shows products in use.

Use of television by local advertisers is usually determined by what the advertiser can afford. Almost any local advertiser would like to use television advertising. Few, however, can afford to use television in the manner of a large clothing concern. This chain of 220 stores in 130 markets made year-long use of television on 85 stations in 75 markets. Nothing was spent on network television in this period.

Department stores advertise on local television because they draw customers from an entire market covered by local television stations. Small retailers serving neighborhoods obviously find television wastefully expensive.

Other retailers bypass television for other media because they sell products or services unsuitable for daytime audiences composed mostly of women. During evening or late night television, when audiences are large and heterogeneous, the higher commercial time costs effectively bar some retail advertisers.

TYPES OF COMMERCIALS

Great numbers of advertisers favor videotaped or filmed commercials—either live action or animated—for obvious reasons.

(1) They are more flexible. A filmed commercial can be telecast any time of the day or night.
(2) They permit greater variations and effects than can be obtained through live delivery. Music, sound effects, utilization of well-known

talents—all these are possible in any film commercial and, as indicated in the preceding point, these are available whenever and wherever the advertiser wants them.

(3) They require less supervision by the advertiser. Once a film commercial has been done to the satisfaction of the client, it can be sent to hundreds of stations with perfect assurance of suitable delivery of the message (except for an occasional mechanical breakdown) no matter how small the station. In live commercials there is always the chance that station announcers or station facilities will not be capable of first-rate delivery of the commercials.

Local advertisers, watching budgets closely, will often use slides that are usually explained by the voice of a station announcer. While slides can be effective, they are more often lacking in life and character, and even as good photographic reproductions.[6]

Television advertisers still have not found the perfect type of commercial. For some, it is the *demonstration* commercial. If the product lends itself to demonstration, there is no better commercial for holding and convincing (and selling) an audience.

Others prefer the *straight-sell* commercial delivered by one or more persons who usually are shown with the advertised product during at least part of the time that the commercial is spoken. This straightforward approach is heavily used and is highly acceptable, even if it does not have the high appeal of some of the other commercial types.

Still others favor *animated* commercials, often with a cartoon flavor. About 25 percent of filmed commercials are animated, despite the fact that animation may cost 75 percent (or more) higher than live action film commercials.

Lately, the *integrated* commercial is liked by many advertisers, especially those who employ "big-name" stars. Integration can be made either in film or live. Either way, the commercial is worked smoothly into the story line and delivered by the actors, often so entertaining that tune-out is thus prevented. Products are given an identity and personality that is a reflection of the identity and personality of the star who delivers the commercial. Critics of integrated commercials have, however, declared that sometimes the personality of the star may be so overwhelming that the audience listens to the star, not really to the commercial's message.

TELEVISION'S ADVERTISING PROBLEMS

Sometimes it is assumed that if an advertiser makes a commercial and then buys commercial time to air the commercial the commercial is assured of success. Nothing is further from the truth. Some commercials are more effective than others. All commercials, however, must compete for a slice of the viewer's attention, and all face some problems in common.

Viewer Tune-out

Estimates vary, but the average television viewer is bombarded with hundreds of commercials each week. The viewer (and that includes each of us) develops a psychological blindness and deafness to television commercials called "selective inattention." The inattention may be conscious or unconscious. We may recognize the commercial and decide to ignore it, or without thinking we may not see or hear the commercial.

If you have watched any television within the past 24 hours, try to remember the commercials aired in and around the programs. You'll remember very few. In fact, not many people remember commercials. Telephone surveys of television viewers the day following a telecast yield what are called commercial "day after" recall scores. Sometimes several thousand phone calls must be made to find 50 television viewers who remember the advertiser's television commercial.

The tendency of the television viewer to tune out unconsciously the commercial has caused advertisers to seek ways to improve commercials, to make viewers want to see and hear the commercial messages. Some advertisers have attempted to hold the listeners' attention through humor, others through cuteness, some through demonstration, and others through being noisy. Watch a dozen or so television commercials. Note the technique or combination of techniques advertisers use to get and hold your attention during the critical first five seconds.

Is there an underlying formula that would enable an advertiser to devise an effective commercial? No. Pretesting commercials with theatre audiences tells advertisers whether the tested television advertisement is likely to be successful, but offers no guarantee. Also, television advertisements are conceived and produced to meet different advertising objectives. Some advertisements introduce new products, others inform consumers about new uses for existing products, whie still others emphasize package identification. Some advertisements are designed to correct consumer misconceptions and others to achieve consumer belief that a product will perform as claimed.

Viewer Confusion

Television advertisement effectiveness also is influenced by the immediate program or commercial environment. No advertiser wants a commercial aired immediately before or after a commercial for a competitive product. Advertisers refer to this as the adjacency problem. Networks attempt to provide at least 15-minute separation between such heavily advertised products as headache remedies or shampoos. Networks can not guarantee this separation because many television commercials are bought on a regional or local spot basis.

Running several television advertisements, one closely after the other, for competitive products leads to viewer confusion. Claimed benefits from the use of one product are misidentified by viewers as benefits from a competitive product. You can investigate this for yourself. Analgesic and headache remedy advertisers are heavy users of television. Simply write or type a list of the names of these heavily advertised products down one side of a page. On the other side of the page, in random order, write the benefit or theme or slogan for each advertised product. Then ask some friends to draw a line from each product brand to the appropriate benefit, theme or slogan.

Compounding Viewer Confusion

A television viewer, it is sometimes said, considers each program a separate entity. The viewer breaks connections psychologically between each show; thus adjacencies (if this theory is to be accepted) on separate shows have little or no effect on the viewer. Many advertisers do not accept this theory.

Regardless of research findings of the foregoing type, most advertising people buying network time look with disfavor upon the custom that has grown of "triple-spotting," or putting three spot commercials into a station break period. Possibly these will be two back-to-back commercials plus an ID (identification commercial 10-seconds long). Other combinations are possible, of course. Actually, however, what with openings and closings, billboards, and triple spots there can be six or seven advertising messages in a four- or five-minute period. Advertisers fear that advertising remembrance is seriously affected when viewers are subjected to so many commercials in such brief time periods. In protest, some of the big advertisers are refusing to buy time on stations that engage in heavy triple-spotting. Numerous stations, in reply, refuse flatly to eliminate the practice unless advertisers are willing to accept a substantial rate increase that would be justified in terms of the revenue the stations assert they would lose were triple-spotting stopped. These stations argue that the spots must go somewhere and that the advertisers themselves have created the situation in their hunger for television spot time. Newspapers, the station personnel point out, can add pages when they need more room for advertising, but time cannot be added to a television station's telecasting day.

Overcommercialization

Television networks and stations accused of using too much time for television commercials invariably defend the time sold as being within allowable limits according to the NAB Television Code. The allowable commercial time varies by daytime and nighttime as well as by program length. Despite this defense, many viewers and advertisers believe too much time is set aside for commercials.

One reason for viewer discontent is the belief that commercials run more than the allotted 60 or 30 seconds. Viewers are oftentimes right. Traditionally, brief self-identifying opening and closing billboards (such as "Brought to you by the makers of Crest Toothpaste") are usually not considered part of commercial time. If, however, the advertiser writes a longer billboard ("Brought to you by the makers of Crest Toothpast, the dentifrice with the seal of approval of the American Dental Association"), the total billboard is then considered part of commercial time. This is accommodated by shortening one or more of the commercials within the body of the television program to 50 seconds rather than 60 seconds, for example. In general, most advertisers use short, self-identifying billboards and full-length television commercials within programs.

Because the FCC frowns on overcommercialization, and because the FCC takes this factor into serious consideration at license renewal time (television licenses must be renewed every three years), all television stations watch the total amount of commercial time in the daily and weekly schedule. In general,

Commercials for this product are fast-paced, lively and emphasize the fun and good times enjoyed by people who use the product. It is important to companies making a product of this type
to (1) Create a favorable atmosphere. (2) To provide strong identification of the product through
registration of the brand name. Both aims are accomplished in this commercial.

BBDO
Batten, Barton, Durstine & Osborn, Inc.
PEPSI COLA
PARENTS DAY :60
PEPA 7096
9/13
AS FILMED SCRIPT

VIDEO	AUDIO
CHILDREN GREETING PARENTS AT CAMP ON PARENTS DAY	(MUSIC UNDER)
MOTHER AND BOY EMBRACING	A smile can wake the sun up
DAT AND DAUGHTER EMBRACING	to what your world can be
GIRL CLIMBING ROPE LADDER	and with every brand new
GIRL AT TOP OF ROPE SMILING.	moment, you're alive.
KIDS GIVING MOM A BABY SKUNK	You're feelin' free. Make this day a celebration come and taste
COUNSELORS DRINKING BOTTLE OF PEPSI	the Pepsi way
CAMPERS PLAYING WITH A LARGE BALL	life is what it should be when you have
OTHER CAMPERS WITH PEPSI IN HAND CHEERING	a Pepsi day.
KIDS AT THE STARTING LINE OF A RACE	
CHILDREN JUMPING OVER ROPE OBSTACLE COURSE	C'mon, c'mon, c'mon and taste the Pepsi way.
CAMPERS AT FINISH LINE WITH LARGE BALL	C'mon, c'mon, c'mon and have a Pepsi day.
CLOSE UP OF GIRL SMILING AND PEOPLE GRABBING PEPSI	wrap a thirsty smile around it
COUNSELOR DRINKING PEPSI	Raise a Pepsi up and down it c'mon,
CAMPERS CONGRATULATING EACH OTHER	c'mon and have a Pepsi day.
CAMPERS AND PARENTS IN CANOE RACE	C'mon, c'mon and make
MOM CHEERING &GROUP CHEERING	this day a celebration
CLOSE UP OF DAD PADDLING	C'mon, c'mon
CANOE RACE COMING UP TO FINISH LINE	and join the Pepsi
MOTHER CHEERING	generation.
GIRL CANOEING AND SMILING	C'mon, c'mon
GIRL COMING INTO FINISH LINE	C'mon, c'mon
GIRL CHEERING AT FINISH LINE	Have a Pepsi day!
SUPER: HAVE A PEPSI DAY.	

Photoboard for 60 second commercial shown in FIGURE 00.

Photoboards, sent out for promotional and merchandising purposes—often to dealers and salesmen—are held to one page. Thus, a comparison of the scenes in the photoboard with the scenes shown in the script, reveals that there are far fewer scenes in the photoboard even though the word count in the audio portion is the same in both.

BBDO

Batten, Barton, Durstine & Osborn, Inc.

Client: PEPSI COLA		Time: 60 SECONDS
Product: PEPSI COLA	Title: "PARENTS DAY"	Comml No. PEPA 7096

A smile can wake the sun up to what your world can be and with every brand new moment, you're alive.

You're feelin' free. Make this day a celebration come and taste

the Pepsi way

life is what it should be when you have a Pepsi day.

C'mon, c'mon, c'mon and taste the Pepsi way.

C'mon, c'mon, c'mon and have a Pepsi day.

wrap a thirsty smile around it

Raise a Pepsi up and down it c'mon,

c'mon and have a Pepsi day. C'mon, c'mon and make this day a celebration

C'mon, c'mon and join the Pepsi generation.

C'mon, c'mon
C'mon, c'mon

Have a Pepsi day!

the ratio of entertainment matter to commercial matter is a variable factor. A good station usually avoids exceeding more than 14 commercial minutes during a typical daytime and late-evening hour, and seven commercial minutes during a prime nighttime hour. Despite the criticism of overcommercialization in television, most print publications carry a far higher ratio of advertising to commercial matter than does television. Print publications carrying 50 percent or more of advertising matter are well above the 15-20 percent normal commercial time in the Television Code. The prevailing opinion that television is excessively commercial is partially a reflection of the effectiveness of the advertising medium, whose messages reach both the passive and active viewer and are hard to ignore or avoid.

Commercial Length and Clutter

At one time, the 60-second commercial was the standard in television advertising. Then, gradually, the 30-second commercial was introduced until today the number of 30-second commercials is far greater than the number of 60-second commercials.

Several reasons account for the switch:

(1) Research showed that the shorter commercial was often just as effective, or even more effective, than the longer commercial.

(2) Since No. 1 was true, advertisers, cost conscious always, decided that it was sensible to use the less costly time unit if the same results could be obtained.

(3) Stations, always seeking more revenue, eagerly accepted and promoted the shorter units.

Naturally, when commercial length was halved, it was possible to sandwich more commercials between programs and between the various breaks within the programs. Furthermore, many advertisers use ID's enthusiastically (10-second commercials) which intruded even more commercials in any given hour. Then add to these commercials the station "promos"—telling about forthcoming programs—and station identifications and the listener is suddenly facing what has come to be known as "commercial clutter."

It is a subject that arouses the passions of advertisers who complain that greedy stations are running so many commercials that viewers cannot remember what they have heard or seen. Commercial recall is depressingly low in almost every research study dealing with television advertising effectiveness. Every meeting of advertising agencies and of advertisers results in proposed solutions, but nothing has been done to curtail clutter. Station owners assert that cutting down the number of commercials without raising rates to make up the loss would be ruinous.

Only limitations imposed by the FCC would offer any solution to the problem, but it is doubtful that the government will lower the current allowable commercial time.

As for the effectiveness of the 30-second commercial versus the 60-second commercial, it depends somewhat on what is being attempted. A demonstration commercial of an off-the-road vehicle, for example, can be interesting enough to hold a viewer for the full 60-seconds. Furthermore, it may be necessary to use every second of this time to develop the demonstration properly.

On the contrary, many products that do not require demonstration and that have no solid product points to register can get on and off the screen quickly and yet put the message over better in 30 seconds than in 60 seconds. Soft drinks, chewing gum, and many food products can be advertised successfully in 30 seconds or even 10 seconds. Therein lies the difficulty of ever curing commercial clutter. In fact, there has been some talk in the industry that at some future date the standard commercial unit will be 15 seconds. Should this occur, today's commercial clutter may seem as nothing to future viewers and advertisers.

DESCRIBING TELEVISION AUDIENCES

When reading newspapers or magazines, we often come across stories describing television programs. The growing or declining popularity of the programs is expressed as a rating, a shorthand way of expressing audience size. A rule of thumb for prime-time television is that when a program rating declines to about 18 the program is in trouble.

Figuring the Program Rating

More specifically, a rating is an estimate of the percentage of households in a survey area that report viewing a specific television program. The rating is an estimate because it is based on a sample survey.

There are two types of ratings:

(1) total audience ratings based on all television households viewing a program five minutes or longer, and
(2) average audience ratings based on the number of households tuned during an average minute of the program.

The formula used to determine the average audience rating follows: The estimated number of television households tuned to a specific program during the average minute is divided by the total number of television households in the research area. To illustrate: assume the research area is the entire U.S. Also assume an estimated 20,340,000 TV households are tuned to a specific program during the average minute, and there are an estimated 71,000,000 TV households in the U.S. Then

$$\frac{20,340,000}{71,000,000} = 28.6 \text{ Average Audience Rating}$$

Figuring Share-of-Audience

Advertisers are also interested in another way of describing television audiences known as share-of-audiences. The share-of-audience is defined as the proportion of all television households using television at any given time and viewing a specific television show. The share-of-audience rating is based on the average audience rating. Share figures are used by advertisers to compare programs telecast at different times of the day or night or during different seasons of the year. The share-of-audience figure more precisely expresses the attraction of a program based only on those households where the set is on, often expressed as sets-in-use or households using TV l(HUT).

$$\text{Share of audience} = \frac{14{,}200{,}000 \text{ Households viewing a specific program.}}{26{,}000{,}000 \text{ Households using television}}$$
$$= 54.6\%$$

Calculating the Cost of Television Advertising

The cost per thousand (CPM) is a ratio expressing the cost of a television buy in relation to the audience size. The cost per thousand calculation results in a dollars-and-cents description of the cost (and efficiency or lack of efficiency) of buying a television program or an individual television advertisement.

Cost per thousand may be computed using whatever denominator the advertiser desires. The basis may be the cost per thousand households or the cost per thousand viewers. An advertiser interested in reaching women may refine a CPM figure even further by computing a cost per thousand women viewers. An advertiser interested in reaching only the male audience may do exactly the same, using men viewers only in the computation. In general, however, most television research is based on the household unit.

Cost per thousand is usually computed on a commercial-minute basis. The formula is the cost of the program (per commercial minute) divided by the audience in thousands of television households, for the viewing area.

$$\text{CMP TV households} = \frac{\$80{,}000 \text{ Cost per typical nighttime network television commercial minute}}{18{,}000{,}000 \text{ Television households tuned to the program}}$$
$$= \$4.44$$

TELEVISION TRENDS

Rapid progress in television and television-related technologies has changed the way television material is produced, the way in which television reaches us and the uses we make of television.

Producing Television Programs and Advertisements

Videotape enables the television producer to record both sound and pictures on magnetic tape. Unlike film, which requires processing before viewing, videotape can be played back instantly. Imperfections in any commercial or show being recorded for broadcast can be edited instantly.

The use of videotape speeds production, thereby lowering production costs. A videotaped commercial can be done in one day instead of the weeks required

Department store television commercial (in storyboard form).

For those local advertisers who can afford television advertising, it is a very effective medium. In this instance, the product is well demonstrated and careful instructions are given about the selling points to be stressed. In short, careful planning is provided to make certain the commercial is effective.

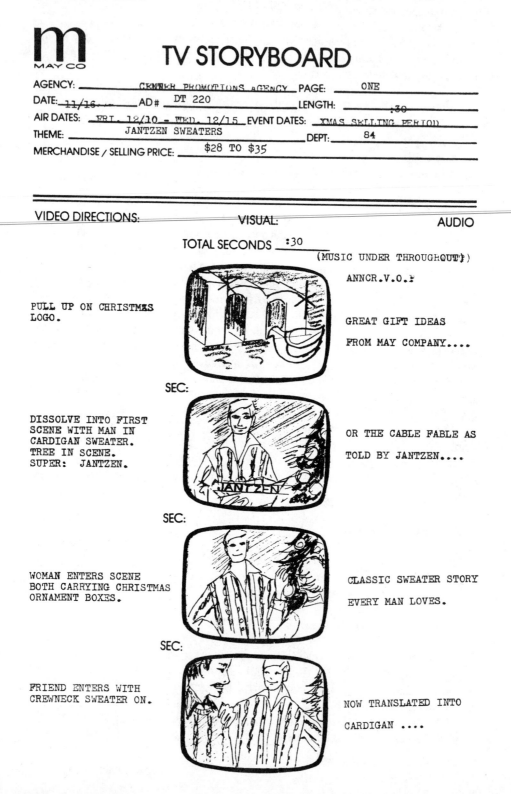

m
MAY CO

TV STORYBOARD

AGENCY: _____ CENTER PROMOTIONS AGENCY ___ PAGE: _____ ONE _____

DATE: _11/16_ ___ AD # ___ DT 220 _____ LENGTH: _____ :30 _____

AIR DATES: _FRI. 12/10 - WED. 12/15_ EVENT DATES: _XMAS SELLING PERIOD_

THEME: _____ JANTZEN SWEATERS _____ DEPT: _____ 84 _____

MERCHANDISE / SELLING PRICE: _____ $28 TO $35 _____

VIDEO DIRECTIONS: VISUAL: AUDIO

TOTAL SECONDS __:30__

(MUSIC UNDER THROUGHOUT)

ANNCR.V.O.:

PULL UP ON CHRISTMAS
LOGO.

GREAT GIFT IDEAS

FROM MAY COMPANY....

SEC:

DISSOLVE INTO FIRST
SCENE WITH MAN IN
CARDIGAN SWEATER.
TREE IN SCENE.
SUPER: JANTZEN.

OR THE CABLE FABLE AS

TOLD BY JANTZEN....

SEC:

WOMAN ENTERS SCENE
BOTH CARRYING CHRISTMAS
ORNAMENT BOXES.

CLASSIC SWEATER STORY

EVERY MAN LOVES.

SEC:

FRIEND ENTERS WITH
CREWNECK SWEATER ON.

NOW TRANSLATED INTO

CARDIGAN ....

VIDEO DIRECTIONS:	VISUAL	AUDIO

(ANNCR V.O.: Continued)

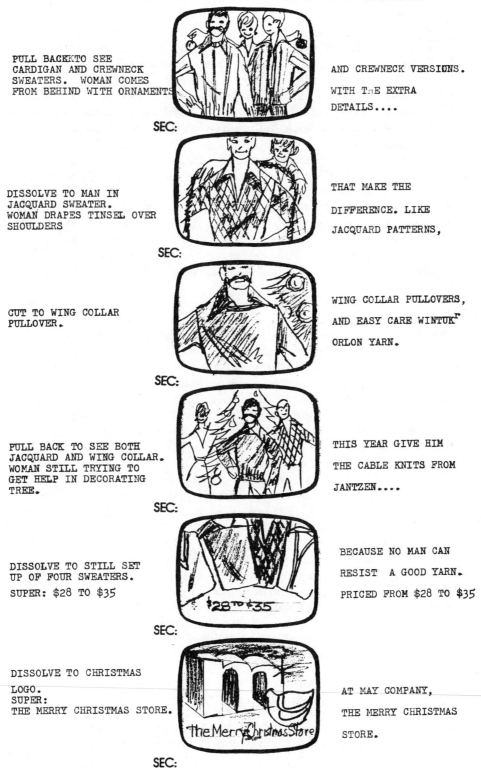

PULL BACK TO SEE
CARDIGAN AND CREWNECK
SWEATERS. WOMAN COMES
FROM BEHIND WITH ORNAMENTS.

AND CREWNECK VERSIONS.

WITH THE EXTRA

DETAILS....

SEC:

DISSOLVE TO MAN IN
JACQUARD SWEATER.
WOMAN DRAPES TINSEL OVER
SHOULDERS

THAT MAKE THE

DIFFERENCE. LIKE

JACQUARD PATTERNS,

SEC:

CUT TO WING COLLAR
PULLOVER.

WING COLLAR PULLOVERS,

AND EASY CARE WINTUK

ORLON YARN.

SEC:

PULL BACK TO SEE BOTH
JACQUARD AND WING COLLAR.
WOMAN STILL TRYING TO
GET HELP IN DECORATING
TREE.

THIS YEAR GIVE HIM

THE CABLE KNITS FROM

JANTZEN....

SEC:

DISSOLVE TO STILL SET
UP OF FOUR SWEATERS.
SUPER: $28 TO $35

BECAUSE NO MAN CAN

RESIST A GOOD YARN.

PRICED FROM $28 TO $35

SEC:

DISSOLVE TO CHRISTMAS
LOGO.
SUPER:
THE MERRY CHRISTMAS STORE.

AT MAY COMPANY,

THE MERRY CHRISTMAS

STORE.

SEC:

(MUSIC UP AND OUT.)

when film is used. Yet the tape quality is as good as live television. Taped material can be integrated quickly by stations and networks into any of their programs whether those programs are film, live, or tape.

Stations with tape equipment are now able to produce commercials by utilizing their studio and camera equipment. Increasingly, commercials put on film in the past are being put on tape. At least 100 repeats can be made from any one recording. Tapes, furthermore, are erasable and reusable.

One former limitation has been resolved with the use of optical effects. Such effects, which are possible in limitless variety in film commercials produced in studios, are now fully available to the advertiser using videotapes.

The extent of videotape's adoption by television is seen in estimates that up to 90 percent of daytime network television program trnsmissions and up to 70 percent of prime time night programming use videotape in some way.

Videotape, as indicated, offers competition both to live telecasting and to film. As an example of the latter is the beauty lotion advertiser who had found that repeated showings of a film commercial caused dirt to gather on the film and hence seemed to be on the skin of a girl model used in the commercials. A change to videotape gave a live quality to the commercials that conveyed the delicacy and softness of the model's skin as well as imparting the fresh cleanliness of the skin.

Another instance is in the use of videotape for ice cream commercials that had formerly been produced live. When the latter had been used the ice cream dishes had been prepared just before the news came on the air. Dripping and melting, the ice cream lacked appetite appeal. When videotape was used, the commercial was recorded at the station's convenience. The ice cream was prepared just when the camera crew was ready to record. To be sure of results, the tape could, of course, be played back immediately.

As for film competition, videotape commercials are almost always less expensive than those on film and often less expensive than live commercials. The latter would be true in cases where the same live commercial is repeated a number of times, each occasion requiring the use of studio and talent. In contrast, studio and talent are needed only once for videotape.

The majority of the nation's television stations now offer color videotape facilities. Combined with all of videotape's attributes, the addition of color has given television commercials and programs a new dimension.

Although most of film's special effects can be achieved on videotape such as wipes, dissolves, live action on miniature sets, and split-screen comparisons, film still has the edge in animation even though animation is possible in videotape. However, existing film of animated sequences can be combined with new live sequences on videotape.

Altogether, from the production standpoint, videotape has been the most significant develoment in television since the introduction of the medium itself unless, of course, we consider the advent of color on the same level of importance.

Community Antenna Television (CATV)

Early television viewers found that in some communities television reception was so poor because of the interference of mountains, or the distance from

Dramatic 30-second television commercial.

There would be fewer complaints about television advertising if more commercials used the format of this one. The video is utilized fully, almost no words are used, and the ending comes to a humorous climax. Thus, there is a combination of entertainment and good sales power.

"ICE MAN"
30 seconds
Bic Pen Corporation

SFX: (Grunting, Wind, Chipping)

CONTINUE

CONTINUE

CONTINUE

CONTINUE

CONTINUE

CONTINUE

CONTINUE (Music Under)

CONTINUE (Music Under)

CONTINUE (Music Under)

MONSTER (VO): Dear Bic.

You're probably not going to believe this, but...

the stations that their sets were useless. In fact, a number of communities could not receive television programs at all unless some special technique were devised. That "special technique" was Community Antenna Television, or CATV.

The heart of the system is a very high antenna, which very often is placed on the highest point in a section and usually near a town or city. This antenna catches the television signal and through special amplifiers retransmits to send it along to a nearby community. It may be "sent" through a microwave cable or through a coaxial cable that is itself connected to the homes and to power or utility poles. The latter procedure is much more common.

Once the homeowner has the set connected to a CATV system the homeowner pays a monthly fee plus a small installation fee. For this expenditure the homeowner receives from 10 to 12 outside channels (and even up to as many as 24 channels) and, in some cases may receive one or more FM music bands. CATV was originally welcomed by set owners, the networks, the advertisers, and even by the watchdog of the broadcast industry, the FCC. Set owners in poor television reception areas now enjoyed crystal-clear reception of many stations and completely without interference. All this was possible without unsightly and expensive outside home antennas.

Advertisers and networks viewed CATV set owners as a bonus audience. Where once there was no audience, there were now many more homes to receive the advertisers' commercial messages. The FCC, in turn, viewed CATV systems as a harmless public service.

Suddenly, however, without anyone seemingly aware of how quickly the change was being effected, CATV developed into a huge enterprise far beyond the public service industry originally viewed with such benevolence by the broadcasters, the networks, and the FCC. Only the set owners were still content with CATV and because CATV provides perfect reception for color telecasting, they were more satisfied than ever.

What had happened was simple enough. Enterprising business people saw that there was a huge market for CATV systems outside the trouble areas of television reception. Even in areas now serviced adequately by two, three, or more stations, television set owners were ready to welcome (and pay for) a CATV system that would offer them many more channels. Accordingly, new systems sprang up all over the country. There are now about 4,000 cable systems serving more than 8,000,000 subscribing households, or about 13 percent of all U.S. households.

Television networks, advertisers, and the FCC are now in a quandary. The continued growth in the number of cable systems could well mean the breakdown of the existing broadcast system.

A set owner who can twirl dials to bring in twelve or more distant stations can no longer be assumed to watch loyally the local television stations, even though CATV operators are required to include local stations among the channels they offer. Local stations may soon find it impossible to deliver a predictable and reasonably large number of viewers to advertisers. This, in turn, will decrease the size of audiences developed by networks. In short, for a modest monthly fee, cable subscribers can exercise greater program choice, while networks, local television stations, and advertisers grapple with the problem of smaller, more fragmented viewer audiences.

Another problem, not big now but likely to become so in the future, is the originating of programs by the CATV systems. These would be direct rivalry to network programs. Because of all these threats and developments, the FCC and other governmental bodies have been taking a second look at CATV and undoubtedly, restrictive legislation will be imposed on this husky youngster. Whatever happens, however, CATV is a strong and disturbing force in the television world.

Some have called it a form of pay TV and, in the sense that set owners do pay monthly charges, they may be said to be "paying" for their television entertainment. CATV is not, however, pay TV if considered in the context of the usual definition of pay TV. In this definition, pay TV is considered a programming service in which the subscriber pays for each program he selects. In contrast, the CATV subscriber selects the programs offered through the system and has an unlimited viewing time of any and all programs chosen. In contrast, for a monthly fee the CATV subscriber selects the programs offered through the system and has an unlimited viewing time of any and all programs. Some cable systems offer subscribers several options, one of the most popular being an additional fee to view a specified number of first-run movies each month. The subscriber does not, however, pay for each movie viewed. This "Home Box Office," as it is called, has grown rapidly

An interesting aspect of CATV has been the haste with which existing television stations have "joined the enemy" by buying CATV franchises in order to protect themselves againt this competition. A number of big corporations have entered the CATV acquisition race, too, including General Electric, and the Time-Life interests. If the CATV franchises continue to grow as they have in the recent past, the entire character of the U.S. broadcasting industry will change—and rapidly.

Syndicated "Mini-Networks"

In addition to CATV, viewer choice is further widened by the development of syndicated "mini-networks," which develop programs to entice viewers from the three major networks. Sometimes these networks are based on sports broadcasts with strong regional appeal; sometimes independent (nonnetwork-affiliated) stations band together to buy and air programs with strong viewer appeal.

NEW TECHNOLOGY, NEW USES

Not only do many viewers have greater choice of television channels than ever before, new and often striking technological innovations change the way we think of and use television.

For example, one characteristic of television has been control by the sender. If the viewer wanted to see a particular program, the viewer had to be free, to watch television when the program was broadcast. Home video recorders and videodiscs now give viewers control. Connected to the television receiver, recorders enable viewers to record a program while they are absent from the home or simultaneously to watch one program while recording another for later

Celebrity presenter television commercial.

One of the more effective ways to capture attention for a commercial is to have it presented by someone known widely by the general public. This particular campaign has been very successful for the company and has been merchandised heavily to capitalize on the name of the star. This commercial is intended to go beyond car rentals to other areas such as truck leasing, car leasing and used car sales.

"Hertz is The Superstar

O.J. SIMPSON: Speed, dependability, experience — when you've got it all —

and can stay in shape

to do it better than anyone else —

that's what makes for a Superstar — Hertz.

But not just in rent-a-car. Hertz know-how comes across in whatever they do.

Did you know Hertz sells cars? All year long, as new models come in,

Hertz sells last year's cars to families like yours at over a hundred locations.

And truck leasing:

Some of the nation's largest corporations rely on Hertz to handle their transportation,

so they can concentrate on what they do best.

And nobody takes care of them like Hertz,

with a unique nationwide maintenance system —

in everything they do!" *O. J. Simpson*

and 24-hour S.O.S. emergency road service.

And car leasing, too.

For a family or a

fleet of a thousand, open end or closed, Hertz can write the lease you need.

Truck leasing,

car leasing,

used car sales

or rent-a-car —

if it moves on wheels

and rolls on a road

it pays to go with

The Superstar — Hertz.

viewing. The viewer has the option of storing the program for viewing more than once. This has given rise to numerous copyright problems. To the viewer, however, an educational program may be rerun several times for study, giving the viewer the type of control over broadcast material that formerly was associated with newspapers, magazines, and books.

Video games add a new dimension to television. Rather than passively viewing the television screen, youngsters use the screen to play electronic games, solve puzzles, or perhaps do homework. Home-sized computers are now available that enable viewers to create and program their own games for projection on home television screens. New levels of involvement associated with these activities may carry over to regular viewing.

The most exciting television development is the first two-way cable system in Columbus, Ohio. Qube (pronounced cube) makes it possible for viewers, at the touch of a button, to "talk back." Qube programming is designed to invite participation. Viewers are asked to choose programs and give reactions during and after programs. Viewers may second-guess coaches on the selection of an upcoming play in a football game. Play selections chosen are projected on the screen, much like a vote, before the play is run.

A Qube subscriber can bid at televised auctions, vote during political debates, evaluate local newspaper features, vote during talent programs, order a table and a meal in advance at a restaurant, and give reactions to advertisements and comparison shop supermarkets.

When added together, these new technological developments suggest that while future audiences may be smaller because of greater channel choice, the way in which viewers regard television will change. Television is becoming an electronic news, entertainment, and nerve center in a growing number of homes. Some cable systems wire homes for emergency services, such as alerting fire and police departments. In many supermarkets the electronic calculating equipment already in use can be patched into CATV. Viewers will soon be able to order food from home, pay for it with a credit number, drive by, and have the food placed in the car—all without setting foot in the supermarket.

TELEVISION'S INFLUENCE

What is the influence of television? People are sure television's influence permeates almost every facet of American life because the medium is everywhere. Television is blamed for many things, but research designed to assess the influence of the medium often yields conflicting results. Curiously, although opinions are strong, nobody knows for sure just what is the influence of television.

Some who study television conclude that the medium presents traditional values and is therefore conservative. Others argue that television accelerates change and is revolutionary, presenting new ways of living and thinking, new values, and aspirations.

While some believe television is mindless, others believe television is provocative and stimulates thought. Television is charged with presenting overly simple resolutions to serious problems. Some believe television programming gears us mentally to think in 30-minute segments, with the young population segments convinced the world sychronizes time on the hour with commercial station breaks.

It is generally conceded that political candidates are selected and sometimes elected on their ability to campaign on television. Even products, it is claimed, are designed more to be attractive when presented on television than to be effective when used in the home.

Religious services are broadcast for shut-ins. Televised educational programs enable working people to pursue college coursework. Programs designed for very young children expose them to concepts that must be mastered for success in school. Groups protesting one issue or another await the arrival of television cameras before starting to demonstrate.

While many people think of television only as entertainment, television is the eye through which we learn about the world. Television presents the tragedies and triumphs of the human experience. Television news presents violent death, revolution, and the plight of people driven by flood and famine. The medium also presents the daring of skiers in Olympic giant slalom races. Millions of people throughout the world breathlessly watched the first walk on the moon.

THE RECURRING TELEVISION CRITICISM

Any discussion of television's influence usually narrows to the question of causality. Various public interest groups, persuaded that television changes the way we view ourselves, others around us and our environment, believe television causes both obvious and subtle changes in audience perceptions and behaviors.

Does It Stimulate Violence?

Several public interest groups, some critics, and many viewers believe there is a causal connection between television violence and social violence. Should, for example, a police program be viewed simply as action-packed entertainment? Does such a program instruct viewers to obey laws? After all, the criminal is invariably caught and punished. Or does such a program instruct some viewers in how to commit crimes?

The real or imagined connection between televised and social violence is a widely discussed concern. In 1977 a lawyer in a Florida murder case argued that hundreds of hours of watching violent television programs had caused a young male defendant to kill an elderly person. While the jury decided otherwise, many people are convinced that there is a causal connection between televised and social violence. Critics argue that in program after program conflict is simplistically resolved with fists or guns. The critics believe that television should provide a deeper understanding of the nature of conflict, developing nonviolent resolution to problems or issues.

Does It Hinder Education?

Another major current concern is the influence of television on the very young. Numerous studies indicate that preschool television exposure for children exceeds the number of hours of formal education through grade school. Some teachers are convinced that television changes the way children perceive and learn. The lack of motivation to read and reading problems are blamed on television, as are a host of negative attitudes toward learning.

Does It Stereotype People?

Numerous critics accuse television programs and advertisements of maintaining objectionable stereotypes. The stereotypes typically involve establishing a personality, situation, or setting through widely recognized and expected cues. Putting an Irish-American in a bar, having an Italo-American singing, or showing a black American working only at unskilled jobs are examples of traditional stereotypes. Some long-established product symbols, such as Aunt Jemima, now are regarded by some as demeaning. Hispanic-Americans are sensitive to commercial characters that make fun of Spanish-language pronunciation of English words.

Various minority and ethnic groups have argued strenuously against stereotypes they believe unflattering. Advertisers and television program producers are sensitive to the objections, trying to develop alternative ways of quickly establishing a personality or situation in a 30-minute drama, doing so instantly in a 30-second commercial.

Recently groups of elderly object to what they consider unfair portrayals. Women are especially sensitive today to being shown always in the kitchen. More than ever before, advertisers today are working in an environment wherein many American women are actively changing their self-definitions and their values.

Some women continue to work at home and care for their young children. Other women are both mothers and members of the work force, adding their paycheck to the family income. Still other women have strong career motivations, with marriage and family formation of secondary importance to their career goals. The traditional, the working, and the career-oriented women have different values.

In print media, particularly magazines, advertisers can design and place advertisements that fit the primary attitudes and values of audience members. A magazine for career women will carry career-related articles and advertisements. On television, however, the advertiser attempts to address all three groups of women without alienating any individuals or groups. This is increasingly difficult to do today.

REVIEW QUESTIONS

1. For what kinds of products are television commercials best suited?

2. For what reasons would a national advertiser choose television?

3. Discuss some of the major criticism of television programming and of television in general.

4. Why is spending too little on television advertising worse than not spending at all?

5. Why and how would you use Gross Rating Points as a planning tool?

6. Why are television audiences more fragmented today than, say, ten years ago?

7. Why are young children regarded as a special audience?

9. What does a share-of-audience figure mean to an advertiser?

10. Discuss the statement: television is and is not expensive.

11. Compare and contrast the role of women in commercials with that of today's changing woman.

12. What different options does an advertiser have when buying television time?

13. Discuss the recent developments in television and television-related technology that influence the way we use and think of television?

14. Why is it more economical to use video tape rather than film when making a television advertisement?

15. Approximately 16,000,000 TV households have their televisions tuned to a particular variety show during the average minute of a half-hour time period. Using an estimated figure of 71,000,000 TV households in the U.S., determine the average audience rating.

$$\text{Answer to question 15:}\quad \frac{16,000,000}{71,000,000} = 22.5 \text{ rating}$$

REFERENCES

1. A. C. Nielsen Company, *Nielsen Television 1977*, p. 5.
2. Ibid., p. 7.
3. Ibid., p. 5.
4. Ibid., p. 10.
5. Children's Advertising Review Unit, National Advertising Division, Council of Better Business Bureaus, Inc., *Children's Advertising Guidelines*, revised (September 1977).
6. Videotape commercials have been especially valuable to local advertisers who can afford television. They are flexible, eliminate the worry about delivery "Fluffs" and can be used at odd times like film commercials. They are especially well-suited to retail's fast pace.

16

GETTING ORDERS BY MAIL

GETTING ORDERS BY MAIL

At the moment you read this sentence it's a certainty that somewhere someone is asking for something by mail order. It might be a lonely rancher's wife in Wyoming who is many miles from a shopping area. Or it might be a man in Yonkers who views shopping through mail order as a substitute for the horrors of city traffic and parking. Or it could be a woman living in Winnetka, a Chicago suburb, who can't resist the attractive offerings of Carroll Reed's store in North Conway, New Hampshire. Somehow, while this suburbanite might very well obtain the same merchandise in Marshall Field's, she yields to the excitement of buying through Carroll Reed's colorful catalog.

Mail order, or direct-response promotion, as it is often called, is booming because of these and many other types. Buying through mail order, however, is not new. The present mail-order boom is simply a form of second wind for an old method of purchasing.

MAIL-ORDER ADVERTISING

Mail-order advertising is part of American folklore and tradition like corn on the cob, baseball, and county fairs. Catalogs from Sears, Roebuck and Montgomery Ward were an important part of rural America. In the days when America was not a nation on wheels, buying through mail order was not only a form of shopping adventure; it was also a *necessity* for millions of Americans.

Today, while not so large a percentage of Americans are actually dependent upon mail-order buying to supply their needs, mail-order selling continues to be a vital force in American economic life. Billions of dollars in goods are sold through mail order, and mail-order advertising runs into hundreds of millions of dollars.

There is still a feeling of adventure about mail order. A mail-order advertiser feels a tingle of mixed hope and apprehension when making a mail-order offer in the media. How many will respond to the offer? Will enough do so to cover the investment in product and advertising? Will the new technique pull better than the technique used in the last advertisement?

Meanwhile, the prospects see the mail-order advertisement and find themselves responding to the enthusiastic words of the advertiser."Shall I," they ask, "send money through the mail for this item? Suppose it's no good; suppose it doesn't do everything the ad says? Wonder if I'll really get my money back if I'm not satisfied?"

Mail-order buying is an act of faith on the part of the customer; it is a well-developed art on the part of the mail-order advertiser.

What's the Difference Between Direct Mail and Mail Order?

For years confusion has surrounded the terms "mail-order" and "direct mail." The terms are used interchangeably, and yet they do not have the same meaning. Direct mail is an advertising medium, just as radio, television, magazines, and newspapers are advertising media. These are vehicles for carrying the messages of advertisers.

Mail order is not an advertising medium. It is *not* a vehicle to carry advertising messages. It is, instead, a specialized form of advertising conveyed to prospects and buyers by almost all forms of media—catalogs, broadcast media, newspapers, magazines, telephone, and, of course, direct mail. Direct mail, in fact, is one of the most important media to the mail-order advertiser.

Mail-order advertising has two chief function: (1) to persuade readers or listeners to order a product or service, and (2) to persuade readers or listeners to inquire about a product or service.

Almost always the advertiser expects that the orders will spur action through the mail—hence the "mail" in mail order.

Mail Order Is Big Business

Were it not for mail-order advertising, thousands of businesses would not exist because they would have had no way to start in the first place. A small business in Vermont that has no way to make significant money on the sale of maple syrup in the local area can expand business a hundredfold if successful in making sales through mail-order advertising in national magazines. Likewise, a firm such as L. L. Bean, located in Freeport, Maine, a mere hamlet, can establish a world-wide reputation and business through mail-order. Had the company depended upon local customers it would undoubtedly be a small country store today.

Mail-order advertising was the foundation of the success of many giant businesses. While today Sears, Roebuck and Montgomery Ward do most of their business through their retail stores, it was their reputation established in their mail-order activity that made possible today's retail store empires. Furthermore, each of these firms still carries on a substantial mail-order business; a glance at the thickness of their yearly catalogs provides testimony.

Many magazines depend upon mail-order advertising for a sizable portion of their revenues. A look at the back pages of *Better Homes & Gardens* magazine provides an example. In short, ordering by mail is an important element in American business—a convenience for the consumer and a money-maker for the mail-order business.

Why Mail-Order Advertisers Feel Superior

Mail-order advertisers are inclined to look condescendingly upon other types of advertisers. They feel that they work from a standpoint of knowledge, in contrast to other advertisers who, they feel, are so often playing an expensive guessing game. These viewpoints have much validity as the following mail-order characteristics demonstrate.

Reasons for buying by mail.

In this discussion by one of the nation's leading mail order enterprises, we find an eloquent exposition on: (1) The delights of shopping by mail. (2) The requisites for success for companies that are engaged in the mail order business.

(1) Mail-order advertising is demanding because it depends upon direct results, not upon mere readership or recognition of the advertising.

(2) Mail-order advertising is the best tested and most thoroughly tested of all forms of advertising. Each mailing is a test in the sense that it is measured against past mailings and against future mailings.

(3) Mail-order selling demands absolute integrity upon the part of the advertiser. There is no place in mail-order advertising for the half-truth or hazy facts. When someone sends money through the mail for an item, he is entitled to complete honesty and accurate representations on the part of the mail-order seller.

PLANNING: AN IMPORTANT INGREDIENT OF MAIL-ORDER SURVIVAL

One mail-order authority has estimated that only 30 percent of those entering the field manage to survive the first year. Supporting this contention was a published report showing that of 87 mail-order firms only 10 were still advertising at the end of a 5-year period.

While the history of mail order shows some enormous successes, there are many quiet failures no one hears about. What keeps people going in a business in which there are more failures than successes? The answer is that the rewards *can* be so great that the failures are forgotten. When would-be mail-order people read about an advertiser receiving a half-million dollars in orders from one $1,500 mail-order advertisement, it is easy to play down the possibility of failure.

Some people, for example, when testing a new product become carried away by optimism and order heavily. A sensible procedure in new product testing is to buy as little merchandise ahead as possible. Basements all over America are filled with merchandise and packing materials that overenthusiastic mail-order beginners were unable to dispose of.

Although enthusiasm is a needed ingredient in the make-up of the mail-order people they should not go into the business without first doing some careful planning. This planning should consist of realistic dollars-and-cents calculations, of constant review, and scientific testing. Many of the mail-order failures have been the "wishful thinkers," the types that let enthusiasm rush them into a field for which they are ill prepared. Before starting a mail-order business, it should be decided what to sell and how to do it. Equally important is an estimate of costs, expenses, overhead, and margin of profit.

There are two reasons why an accurate analysis must be made in advance.

(1) Despite the excitement of the field, it is not easy to sell through mail-order because the prospect is being sold something that he never sees until it is delivered through the mail. Unless a profit margin permits the use of salespeople to follow up inquiries, the advertising must perform the entire selling job by itself without any supplementary personal sales help, unlike national advertising that depends strongly upon salespeople in retail stores to complete the selling job.

(2) Without careful advance analysis a mail-order enterprise can be a costly financial mistake since mail order is not an inexpensive way to sell.

Unless the mail-order enterprisers' arithmetic is accurate, they may find that the labor and money put into mail order is merely helping to finance the media, the production people, and the postal system.

What goes into planning? Some of the elements to be included would be:

Idea development	Development of research and testing procedures
Analysis of the worth of the ideas	
Product evaluation	Pricing decisions
Decisions as to markets to be developed	Development of budget and profit projections
Positioning of products in those markets	Media to be used

SELECTING THE ITEMS TO SELL

Selection of what to sell is the starting point of any mail-order business. All the knowledge of "how" to sell is meaningless if "what" is being sold is without consumer appeal.

So important is the offer—product or service—that mail-order people agree that a good offer can overcome the handicap of a poor presentation and copy. On the contrary, an advertisement complete with eloquent copy and outstanding illustration cannot sell an offer without appeal. The word *appeal* implies such elements as good value for the price, superiority, or point of difference over competitive products or services, and exclusiveness.

Although, of course, the number and kinds of items sold through mail order are limitless, for convenience here they are placed in three groupings: general merchandise, specialty merchandise, and service.

General merchandise. A glance at mail-order catalogs will show what is embraced by this grouping—clothing, furniture, foods, seeds, plants, wire fencing, radio sets, commonly used pharmaceuticals, and other articles generally considered necessities. Since retail stores sell items of this general nature it means that successful selling by mail of the items require that they be exceptional in style or quality in relation to the selling price. Another characteristic of such items is that they or their equivalents are unavailable at retail stores in sufficiently large numbers of areas throughout the country.

Specialty merchandise. These are products that serve a useful purpose but are not necessarily necessities. Their purpose may be the accomplishing of some function that people consider desirable or of correcting or ending some condition that people regard as undesirable.

In the specialty class are items that people might call "interesting" such as lobsters from Maine, fish from Gloucester, books on self-improvement or on making and repairing furniture, pecans from Georgia, pears or apples from Oregon, massaging or exercising devices designed to improve health, patented gadgets to regulate the closing of doors or to prevent them from slamming, attachments to control from a chair the sound of a radio or television program or to switch programs or commercials on a television set, a poultry tonic to increase egg yield, or specialized fishing or hunting equipment.

Because of a very strong appeal and obvious advantages, specialty merchandise is successfully and widely sold by mail. Since these articles are frequently copyrighted or patented, they need not be so competitively priced and sold as general merchandise.

"Specialty" mail order item.

An item such as this falls in the "interesting" class—a product that can be useful but cannot be described as absolutely necessary. From the striking headline through the enthusiastic copy it is sold with almost irresistible appeal.

6 pages from your daily newspaper can cook a steak to perfection in less than 6 minutes.

Completely portable and you'll never spend another penny on fuel.

About 15 years ago, on our first trip to Africa, we saw natives in the northern frontier district of Kenya broiling meat

You can use the Shikari Grill in your fireplace for delicious outdoor flavor anytime.

on strange looking pots with holes in the bottom. Using rolled up balls of grass for fuel, they were cooking up a storm.

Needless to say, we were intrigued. We did a little looking, and found that a British engineer stationed in Johannesburg had also observed this unusual device and perfected it by using a rolled steel barrel and newspaper. We know it's hard to believe, but this thing really works. We like to call it the Zulu's answer to microwave ovens . . . only a less expensive version. In fact, if you consider the money you'll save on charcoal and lighter fluid in just one season, Norm Thompson's Shikari Grill will literally pay for itself.

Fast and efficient . . . the Shikari Grill cooks just about anything.

We guarantee it . . . a succulent steak, medium broiled to tasty perfection over live flames in just 6 minutes. There's no charcoal or lighter fluid to mess with, no waiting for coals to glow. Just crumple newspaper into a ball, light a match, and instantly you're cooking.

Steaks, hamburgers, hot dogs, chops, spareribs, fish and chicken . . . you can even boil water. Meat cooks in its own juices over scientifically air-controlled flames. (The Shikari Grill works on the

Compact carry case measures only 12" x 12" x 8".

principle of controlled combustion. Natural fat dripping over charred paper keeps the fire going.) You get better tasting food and it's actually more healthful because you use fat for fuel instead of eating it.

Compact and completely portable.

Norm Thompson's Shikari Grill comes in a compact, heavy cardboard box that serves as a carrying case. It measures only 12" x 12" x 8" so it's really easy to take anywhere! It's great for just about anything from a summer picnic at the beach to a winter barbeque at a ski resort.

Safe and easy to use in your fireplace.

This is one outdoor grill you'll want to use year 'round. Use it in your fireplace for delicious outdoor flavor any time. And since combustion is complete, there's little or no mess to clean up. There's no need for forks or spatulas because the entire grid turns over rather than turning each piece of meat. The unique, "stay cool" handles simply don't get hot, so you won't even need hot pads. Order your Shikari Grill today. You'll get everything you need . . . 3 section barrel, nickel plated grid, and instructions.

No. 9005 . . . . **$15.00**

Service. A variety of services fall into this grouping; examples are correspondence courses, tax problem guidance, weekly newsletters out of Washington, bulletins prepared for business executives, periodic tree inspection by experts performing this service for property owners, or clearance of drains and pipes by firms specializing in removing obstructions in these locations.

Chief stress in selling a service is placed upon the need for the service and the competence of those performing the service. The physical value of whatever actual merchandise may be required as in the case of tax-bulletin forms may be practically nothing compared with the permissible tax savings that the service offers the business executive who has subscribed for the service.

IDENTIFYING ATTRIBUTES FOR SUCCESSFUL MAIL-ORDER ITEMS

Some mail-order items have great appeal at one period and none at all a short time later. Other items are consistent business pullers. Still others will always have limited appeal. In general, the following attributes are considered important for the successful mail-order item:

(1) *Has appeal for a great many people.* In this sports-minded nation of ours, mail-order items aimed at those who are interested in sports participation are often successful but usually when they are suited to a big enough group. Lures for bass fishermen might pull a profitable return but equipment for marlin fishermen is interesting to too limited a group.

(2) *Satisfies a definite need.* Although many mail-order advertisers have recognized the appeal of a novelty item and have profited from its short-run popularity, the mail-order man who takes a long-range view of the business will concentrate on items that satisfy a basic need. Such items will sell indefinitely and are the "bread and butter" products of the mail-order business.

(3) *Offers suitable profit.* The profit on mail-order items must be sufficiently high to cover such points as cost of item itself; wrapping materials and labor; postage; transportation; losses by damage, replacement or refusals; bank fees for depositing an abnormal number of checks; all costs from time of manufacture or purchase of item until the item is delivered to the purchaser.

As a rule of thumb, it has been estimated that if the total cost per unit does not exceed one-third the proposed selling price, the chances are all right that a reasonable profit will be yielded, but if the cost exceeds one-half, difficulties may be met.

(4) *Has repeat-sale possibilities.* This is not a "must," but many mail-order advertisers have depended upon repeat sales to insure their continued success. The Maine lobster firm previously referred to might survive if all its customers were one-time buyers, but it does much better financially when it can turn a first-time customer into a many-time customer. Mail-order booksellers have built fortunes on the repeat buyer.

(5) *Has the appeal of newness of the excitement of the moment.* Although, as said earlier, stability in mail order is achieved through the item that

fills a long-range need, there are many opportunist in the mail-order business who are ever on the alert for the fad that will be gone in a hurry but which will sell mightily and at high profit during its short life.

(6) *Is easy to handle.* If a product cannot be shipped, or cannot be shipped except at prohibitive cost, it will be impractical to merchandise it, no matter how appealing it is. A check with the post office will help determine this aspect. Then, too, there may be difficulties connected with packaging, wrapping, assembling, and the actual making of the product.

(7) *Is available.* The mail-order man's source of supply must be steady. Should the product be one that is bought from a manufacturer, assurance must be obtained that the merchandise will always be available for the filling of orders. The mail-order firm's customers will not be interested in excuses for nondelivery. They will blame the mail-order firm, not the manufacturer, for the former's failure to furnish the ordered item. The smart mail-order person obtains a Dun and Bradstreet credit rating on all suppliers. Nothing is more upsetting than to have an advertising schedule in a number of magazines only to find that a supplier has gone out of business and, at the same time, to have hundreds of unfillable orders coming each day in the mail.

Emphasis on product with current excitement.

Caught up in a sports craze that has engaged the enthusiasm of men and women the nation is receptive to products such as this. Men and women alike find pleasure in court games and are receptive to products that will be useful in such games. Long copy will be read for such products and, in fact, is necessary for the sale.

Nylon and leather team up for racketball, tennis, handball & more!

New this year for men and women . . . a lightweight shoe designed expressly for court sports.

Court sports like tennis, handball, and racketball are currently experiencing rapid growth in America as never before. In response to the increasing demand for footwear designed specifically for these sports, the people at Patricks have come up with a truly remarkable shoe. We call them Courts, because they're engineered inside and out for one purpose only . . . outstanding performance on a court surface. Whether you play tennis, handball, racketball, squash or badminton, we guarantee they'll add to your game. Already widely accepted in Europe (and currently worn by the European Badminton and Squash Champion), Courts are extremely lightweight yet durable. You'll experience real comfort, support, and sure traction with the sensation of weight almost non-existent!

Designed for lightness and durability.

The uppers on our new Courts are specially constructed for extreme lightness and maximum durability. Heavy-duty nylon is the primary material used. It's naturally lightweight, yet tough enough to take the continuous stress and strain it'll be subjected to during active play. This nylon is also specially woven to breathe, so your feet stay dry and comfortable. Special stitching along the side and over the in-

step provides strong support without adding the extra weight of reinforcing leather stripes.

Elsewhere on the uppers, you'll discover glove-soft, sueded leather. It's placed where necessary for added strength and reinforcement. You'll find this leather all the way around the shoe between the sole and nylon upper, on the heel and lace stays, and covering most of the toe and instep.

A sole that performs.

Underfoot, you'll experience a unique foundation of natural rubber that's proven to be long wearing and extremely durable. Its very special tread design provides sure traction without "sticking" (the cause of a lot of unnecessary stress and strain and twisted ankles).

The same natural rubber extends well up around the edges of the shoe for added protection from scuffs and wear.

Other special features.

■ An arch support you can feel working helps provide proper support and keeps your foot from sliding side to side.

■ A special heel cup cradles your foot

while holding it well back into the shoe.

■ An extra-thick textile insole is designed to prevent blisters and abrasion.

■ A sueded leather tongue is foam padded for extra comfort and features a slit for laces to keep it securely in place.

■ Backed by our "You be the Judge" guarantee (p. 2), so you risk nothing by trying a

pair yourself during your next game.

Color: White, with grey leather trim and blue and green accent stripes. Men's sizes: 6-12, 13. Women's sizes: 5-10. Available in one width to fit A-E. EE order ½ size larger for proper fit. Size 13, add $2.50.

No. 2750 (Men's) **$28.50**
No. 2759 (Women's) **$28.50**

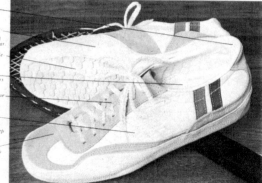

A special heel cup cradles your foot while holding it well back into the shoe

The natural rubber sole extends well up around the edges of the shoe for added protection from scuffs & wear.

The "competition" tread design provides sure traction without sticking

An extra thick textile insole helps to prevent blisters and abrasion

Foam padded leather tongue features slit for laces to keep it securely in place.

Uppers are constructed of heavy-duty nylon . . . lightweight, yet extremely durable. It also breathes to keep feet dry and comfortable.

Glove-soft, sueded leather has been added for strength and reinforcement of areas subjected to constant wear during court play.

Don't Guess — Test

Testing to a big mail-order house is multi-faceted. It can include such major elements as:

Time of the year to make the offer.

Type of media to use.

Type of product to offer.

Best geographical areas in which to make the offer.

Worth of prospect lists.

There are, of course, many other elements to be tested. For instance, offers made through direct mail can be affected by the size and color of envelopes used, as well as the messages printed on the envelopes. Types of stamps and postage can make a pronounced difference, too. Where the creative approach is involved, headlines and illustrations should be checked against each other. There have been many cases where the right headline has doubled (or better) the response to an offer.

The legitimate elements for testing are numerous. Although the big mail-order entrepreneur is constantly testing such elements for their effect upon response, the small mail-order business person is too busy with day-to-day tasks to have time for elaborate test procedures. Such a person learns through trial and error which of the major elements affect returns. Many of the mistakes uncovered through trial and error could be avoided, however, if the person were to follow well-known principles that have been discovered by the experts.

One such expert, who like many in the direct mail and mail-order fields has been generous in sharing hard-earned knowledge, is Robert Stone. His excellent book *Successful Direct Marketing Methods,* published by Crain Communications, can be an enormous help. Stone, who writes a column on mail order for the magazine *Advertising Age,* can help the mail-order user in deciding such matters as use of letterheads, mailing lists, envelopes, addressing, postage, color, follow-ups, timing, and creative approach.

A Vital Question: What Price To Charge?

As many mail-order operators have discovered painfully, it is generally risky to try to make a $2.00 sale—or, as often used, $1.95 to $1.98—pay its own way, without too great risk of loss or too utter dependence upon a follow-up sale.

Most mail-order people, after thorough testing, aim to sell at a price that is not so high as to cut down their volume of business and yet not so low as to involve a loss on the initial sale. Some are willing, in order to get business in sufficient volume, to seek initial orders on a break-even basis, or even at a slight loss. These compromises are made only if their own experience has proved that the necessary profits will come *after* the initial order.

Now, to talk about a figure that is contemplated with real pleasure by mail-order operators—the highest safe selling price that they can ask for an article of specialty merchandise.

Naturally, they must restrain both the desire for big profit and the usual enthusiastic impulses by recognizing that there are limits to the highest price that can be sought. In recent years, however, there has been a significant change in the prices that can be asked by the mail-order operator. At one time, the rule was that the person pulling for orders through publication space seldom tried to sell any item priced at more than $4.95. It was reasoned that the use of space in expensive publications made it too costly for the advertiser to give the full sales message that would make it possible to ask for more money than that.

Two factors have changed the old ideas—inflation and the almost universal use of credit cards. An advertisement for the Sunfloat Company provides an example. This advertisement, run in the *New Yorker,* pulled very profitably for an item selling at $95. Thus, we find high-priced items being sold in expensive mass media. At one time, such items would have been sold through direct mail. Letters, booklets, or brochures, it was felt, permitted the advertiser to use a sales talk ample enough to sell products of a higher cost.

Direct mail, furthermore, permits the use of specialized lists reaching people who are already known to be interested in—or who are purchasers of—products that represent the same broad category as the product being sold by the mail-order man. When general publications are used, this kind of pinpoint selectivity is not possible.

Why Seek Inquiries Instead of Orders?

If it were possible, of course, no mail-order creators would settle for inquiries if they could always draw a profitable number of orders instead. There are, however, certain conditions that make it necessary to seek inquiries—as when the product or service is too expensive to be sold wholly by advertisements pulling for orders. In such cases the advertisements instead seek to stir up requests for further information necessary to do the sales job. Again, advertisements may aim at obtaining requests for catalogs or booklets. These may describe a wide variety of general merchandise or a line of specialized merchandise such as health foods, books, holiday gifts, plants, or seeds.

Inquiry Advertisements Versus Order Advertisements

Both types of advertisements must sell hard. Both have common characteristics. Yet there are some differences caused by the fact that the order-seeking advertisement pays for itself many times over. Inquiry-producing advertising, in contrast, represents nothing but cost, unless the follow-up ultimately results in substantial sales.

Most conspicuous result of this delayed-profit aspect of inquiry-producing advertisements is that often they are likely to be smaller than order-seeking advertisements. This, of course, is not *always* true since many of the advertisements seeking inquiries are large-space types.

Naturally, mail-order advertisers are usually more likely to use large space units for obtaining direct sales. In such advertisements they use a full sales story which, in many instances, makes it necessary that they have ample space. Inquiry-seeking advertisements, on the contrary, are not usually expected to develop the entire sales story. That task will be left to the follow-up material, whether catalogs, folders, or booklets.

When advertisers *do* use larger space units for inquiry-producing advertisements, they may do so because they are looking for a larger than usual number of inquiries and/or because they want the people who inquire to be more fully sold in advance. Thus, the follow-up will not have to do so much of the sales job.

GETTING GOOD RESULTS FROM SMALL-SPACE INQUIRY ADVERTISEMENTS

Throughout all advertising, the smaller unit almost always requires an extra ingenuity to make it resultful. This is true whether talking about the 10-second "ID" in television, the tiny "reader" type advertisement in newspapers, or, in the mail-order advertiser's world, the small-space inquiry advertisement.

Some of the elements that are executed with especial care in these advertisements are the layout, the headlines, the coupons. Actually, all mail-order advertisement creators consider these elements with exceeding care no matter what types of advertisements they are preparing, but when small-space is used, the problems are intensified. Here, for example, they must guard against being "lost" on pages where there are larger advertisements. Also, the small-space unit must be super-efficient in putting across the message.

Some of the ways the mail-order operator makes advertisements more attention-getting or more efficient:

(a) Uses much "reverse" in which white is printed on black instead of the conventional black on white.

(b) Selects type faces that are clearly read and that are likely to be different from the usual typefaces.

(c) Uses a headline that is (1) just as big in physical size as is possible within the size limitations of the advertisement, and (2) just as challenging in what it says as is possible so that it will attract attention, create interest, and force readership of the message.

(d) Uses an attention-getting border that calls out to the reader from the pages of the publication. This procedure cannot always be followed if a publication has regulations relating to conspicuous borders.

(e) Pays especial attention to the coupon, not only in its construction but to what it says, and to the ways that the coupon can be "merchandised" in the advertisement itself.

INCREASING THE NUMBER OF INQUIRIES IN GENERAL

After mail-order people have made sure that the proposition they are making in advertisements have great appeal to consumers, they can then proceed to think of other actions to take to insure the highest possible number of inquiries. Some of these follow:

(1) *Put the inquiry-offer up at the top of the advertisement.* If what is being offered is a free booklet on knitting, a fishing guide, a scenic map, or some other free and useful item, the consumers' interest can be whet-

ted by letting them know about the offer immediately. In putting the offer at the "top," the mail order advertiser can well mention it:

- In the main headline
- In the subhead
- In the opening body-copy immediately under the main head, or the subhead, if there is one

This process is demonstrated by the following material that tells the reader immediately the reward in reading the advertisement. There is no need to "dig" to determine that there is a "payoff" in the advertisement:

Main head: Yours free—a guide to Canadian vacation spots.

Subhead: Tells you where to go whether you're a fisherman or city sightseer.

Opening body copy: Let your free 75-page "Guide To Summer Canada" be your travel agent for an exciting, out-ot-the-ordinary vacation.

(2) *Tell reader immediately both in body copy, coupon, and headline (if possible) that there is absolutely no obligation of any kind.* This is exemplified in the line from a coupon that reads;

Please send without obligation your free 10-page brochure about how to save money on taxes.

(3) *Include a copy line somewhere, whether in the body copy, or in the coupon, that assures the reader that no salesman will call.* A sure way to discourage many people from filling out a coupon is to fail to make it clear that there will be no personal follow-up by salesmen. Too often high-pressure salesmen follow every coupon lead. Some people have had so much trouble with such sales follow-ups that they never fill out coupons. This is unfortunate for the mail-order operator who has no sales force and who is doing all selling through advertisements. For such an advertiser the line "No salesmen will call" is strongly necessary to step up the number of inquiries.

(4) *Do everything possible with the coupon to make it a strong selling aid.* Inside and outside the coupon should be appealing and usable. Yet, many mail-order advertisers who are masters of their craft in every other respect, fall down in coupon construction and "merchandising." Some of the basic requirements in using a coupon:

(a) Make it action-inviting through the use of exciting, action-impelling words that urge the reader to do something: *Mail immediately. Don't wait. Act now. Send for today.*

(b) Include key in name and address. This is suggested for mail-order advertisers who use a number of publications and find it important to know from which publications the inquiries are coming.

(c) Repeat the terms of the offer clearly. Although the offer will be made in body copy it will be necessary to repeat it once more in the coupon to make certain that the respondent knows just what he is sending for. This is illustrated in the following:

> Please mail your illustrated book that tells in clear, readable explanations how I can do home repairs that will save the cost of the book over and over again.

(d) Make it easy to clip. This usually means that the coupon should be placed in the lower right-hand side of the page since, in this position, the coupon is easy to clip and its removal from the page does not mutilate the publication seriously. Although it is traditional for most coupons to be placed in this position, a mail-order advertiser can experiment to see what works best. Some coupons, for example, might better be placed in the left-hand corner in the case of left-hand pages, especially in magazines that have a strongly curving fold. Some coupon users have put coupons in the very middle of a page, a location highly recommended by a number of experienced advertisers who feel that in this spot the coupon will certainly stand out.

(e) Ask for the reader's zip code in order to facilitate replies.

(f) Put in a line above the coupon that stresses the offer or that uses the action-words suggested in point (a). Some examples:

> **Make money in your spare time.**
> **Mail coupon now.**
> **No salesman will call.**
> **Send coupon for 10-day trail.**
> **Learn to crochet.**
> **Head south to Sea Island–**
> **Two fabulous weeks for $559,**
> **everything included.**
> **Nobody can match this**
> **motor-coach tour of**
> **Western Europe.**
> **Here's all we have to**
> **know to open your account.**
> **Start a new career today!**

(g) Make the coupon stand out physically. This can be done in a number of ways. A heavy dotted line can make the coupon obvious. An arrow pointing to the coupon can draw the eye to it, as well as a pair of scissors that seem to be cutting it. Sometimes a tint block can be used for the coupon portion. Sometimes liberal use of white space in the coupon when the rest of the advertisement is heavy with print can draw attention to this portion of the advertisement.

(h) Have the opening copy in the coupon stress what the readers are going to get instead of what they must do to get it. The "doing is unpleasant; the "getting" is fun. Dangle the carrot before asking for action. Some examples:

> Sure. Tell me how I can make a big improvement in my tennis just by following your Game Plan.

> Fill out this coupon if you like the adventure of travel but don't have the money for plush tours.

> Yes. I'd like to learn how to grow flowers and vegetables that will make me the envy of my neighbors.

(i) Plan the coupon physically so that the respondent will have enough room to write. This means that the lines should not be too close together and most important it means that spaces should be adequate to contain the information that is required. On this latter point, too many mail-order advertisers provide absurdly small spaces for the city name in particular. If a coupon is designed, as so many are, like the example following, the coupon is worthless. The advertiser is forcing the respondent to write the information separately which means that it will thus reduce the number of inquiries:

> Name _____
> Address _____
> City _____ State _____ Zip Code _____

If the respondent lives in Philadelphia, San Francisco, or Minneapolis there is no space to write the city name yet time after time coupons allow no more space than is shown in the foregoing. It is one of the most baffling and foolish mistakes in the business world.

(5) *Feature the offer of the free booklet, or whatever it is, in an illustration if for some reason it cannot be stressed in the headline and subhead.* The greater amount of wordage and illustration space that can be given to the offer the greater emphasis will be placed upon the desirability of the prospects accepting it.

(6) *Give the free booklet a title that clearly and quickly tells the prospects that it contains interesting and valuable information for them.* If the booklet title is tied up with the use of the advertiser's product and makes the prospects feel that they will actually profit from having it, much of the advertisement's sales power is in that title. Inquiry totals are increased by titles such as the following:

> *Control Weight Without Dieting*
> *How to Invest Profitably*
> *26 Ways to Cook Meat Better*

Advertisement that dramatizes importance of mailing lists.

In this persuasive advertisement, strong reasons are given for the use of good, result-getting mailing lists. It is axiomatic that if a mailing list is no good, the mail order advertiser is almost certainly doomed to failure.

HOW TO GET RICH RENTING MY LISTS!

"The Mail Order Pros Have Kept This Secret To Themselves Long Enough"

This is a typical "opportunity" ad. It's an opportunity for you, a business for me.

I run ads like these all over the country offering a variety of money-making and self-improvement information. I also send out a load of direct mail month in and month out.

My promotions pull thousands of cash customers every year. That's where *your* opportunity comes in. You can get rich (or at least "comfortable") selling these super-buyers.

A dozen extremely knowledgeable, extra smart mail order pros are making a pot-full of money with my names.

Now it's time to share their secret and spread the wealth without revealing their prestigious identities.

The pros can hardly wait for me to release my lists of current buyers. Because my lists pull their respective heads off.

They work so darn well that these insiders use them a *second* or *third* time for the *same* offer. The pros know what they're doing.

If an offer pulls 10%, there's still *90% unsold*. And a *repeated* offer can still bring home the bacon — if the list has money pulling power.

I know that my lists have this kind of draw because they pull money for me. All the time. Again and again.

Other promotions may deal in "inquiries" or "send more information." Not mine.

My ads, my direct mail, all ask for the same thing: *Money up front before delivery.*

That makes a whale of a difference, as the pros know. My customers are the cream of the market, the elite. *Cash-in-advance customers.*

They're also something else. Most are not just "one timers." They are steady buyers for virtually any new offering I present. *Repeat* cash-on-the-barrelhead buyers. The kind beloved by mail order folk everywhere.

With customers like these, you make money on the front-end *and* the back-end. Multiplying profits every step of the way.

They're not stingy, either. They spend wads of greenbacks. Some of my programs go as high as $395 (again, payment in advance.) Of course, not all of my offers go that much. My prices vary to accommodate the market. By and large, they range over $20.

So how can *you* get rich renting my lists? That's easy. Just *do* it. *Rent* them!

If you have a solid opportunity deal, my Master List of 207,000 buyers is ready, willing, and waiting with cash in hand to hear from you.

And if you really want the hottest list in the business, my 72,000 Success-Power Motivation names will have your envelope-openers working extra hours.

Let's pause here for a word of advice. Don't spring for an *entire* rental unless you want to get rich *fast.* Better try a 5,000 test to make sure you're on target.

Unless you're trying to peddle cigarette lighters to non-smokers. I'll be quite surprised if you don't come back for a "continuation."

I've just up-dated my lists with my latest 1976 buyers. And I've printed up a List Fact Pack describing each of my six lists in depth.

GEORGE FELDMAN
When he speaks, the pros listen. His 30 years of successful mail order experience comes FREE with your list rental.

MY LISTS PUT MONEY IN YOUR BANK!

SUCCESS-POWER MOTIVATION— 72,000
Success-oriented buyers who want to multiply their personal fortunes quickly.

FINDERHOOD — 105,000
Trial and current members of the world-wide finders' club.

WHEELER-DEALER ASSOCIATION —36,000
Seekers of foxy-smart angles and little-known opportunities.

BUSINESSWISE — 11,000
Buyers of the manual, "How to Get Rich Reading Classified Ads."

GEORGE FELDMAN MASTER OPPORTUNITY BUYERS — 207,000
Merged/purged consolidation of spenders who purchased two or more times. Truly, "The Mailer's Money Maker."

All $40/M except Success-Power ($50/M). 5,000 minimum. Ask your favorite broker or write directly.

To get it, just drop me a line along with a buck to help cover the cost of printing, postage, and handling. (I told you that my ads *always* ask for money!)

I'll speed a Pack back to you by first-class mail, with this guarantee: If you rent any of my lists, I'll send you *two* bucks. That's 100% profit on your investment *plus* the chance to hit the big time. Just like the pros.

Here's my address. George Feldman, Liberty List Co., Dept. DH, 15 West 38th St., New York, N.Y. 10018.

If you want to talk, please phone me at (212) 279-3660.

© 1977 George Feldman

(7) *Tie an authority's name to the booklet being offered.* A booklet associated with a leading figure in sport, art, gardening, or some other skill or activity will draw more inquiries than one written by an unknown. Sometimes the famous person may merely write the foreword to the booklet; even so, merely having the name in conjunction with the booklet will give it extra appeal to prospects.

DECREASING THE NUMBER OF INQUIRIES

Very troublesome to the mail-order advertiser are the curiosity seekers, or professional coupon-clippers who cannot resist sending for coupon offers even if not truly interested. Some persons, with much time on their hands, become coupon-clippers; part of this group is the youngster who early in life becomes a collector of odds and ends.

When advertisers see that they are getting too many inquiries from people who cannot be candidates for their goods or services they will usually analyze the situation to learn how to cut down inquiries from nonprospects without cutting down inquiries from genuine prospects.

When sales literature is expensive and percentage-of-sales-to-inquiries is low, and the sales force is complaining about the poor quality of leads furnished through advertising, it is time for the advertiser to aim for fewer, but better, inquiries. Here are some ways to do it:

(1) *Make a small charge for the booklet or ask the reader to send a small amount to cover postage and handling charges.*

Before charging for booklets, the mail-order operator should test the effect or, instead of getting better-type inquirers, the operator may end up with no inquirers. Inquiries may not drop only slightly when the charge is applied; they may drop as much as 50 percent to 80 percent. The increase in sales closings from the remainder may not go up enough to offset the decreased volume of inquiries. It may be reasoned that mail-order enterprisers cannot work at all on the inquiries they do not get. Meanwhile, many good prospects reject the advertisements because they feel that they should not be required to pay for that which is offered free by the majority of advertisers.

(2) *Ask for information in the coupon that will have a weeding-out effect.* Inquirers, for example, may be asked to give more information than their names and addresses. They may be asked for occupation and age. In business mailings the inquirer may be asked to furnish a business card or a company letterhead, or may be asked for a title.

(3) *Eliminate the coupon.* This will have a strong effect on the number of inquiries because the inquirer must thus work harder to provide the information. Coupon-clippers will overlook offers made in couponless advertisements since their interest is flagged entirely by coupons.

(4) *Take special aim at youthful inquirers by inserting certain qualifying riders in the coupon.* An example is furnished by one mail-order advertiser who put at the bottom of the coupon next to a little box for checking—"If 18 years of age or under, check here for booklet A." Inquiries thus obtained may be handled in a different, less expensive manner.

(5) *Cut down on the hard sell for the free booklet being offered.* Instead of giving it a provocative title simply refer to it as a "Catalog" or entitle it "Better Golf" instead of "Here's How you Can Cut Your Score by 20 Strokes in One Summer."

(6) *Put certain "drawback" points in the copy.* Indicate that the product is not being offered on a price basis; that it is not possible to install it quickly; that its maintenance will require a certain amount of effort and time on the part of the purchaser. Obviously, as in the case of putting a charge on the booklet, this inclusion of "drawback" copy must be handled carefully or the mailer may kill prospects entirely.

(7) Make headline and copy selective in order to narrow the range of replies expected. If offering a home study course, for example, use a selective headline such as:

Learn The Electronics Field at Home in After-work Hours

Only those persons with a real interest in the field of electronics would bother to reply to the advertisement. Replies, thus, would be fewer but each inquiry would represent a real prospect for the home study course. A less selective headline such as:

**Here's How to Make a Good Living
in an Important and Growing Field**

would broaden the base of replies but the increased number would include many who had less interest in the field and thus could not be considered such good prospects.

Enthusiasm: No. 1 Quality in Mail-order Copy

Mail-order copy is bursting with enthusiasm. To cause readers to part with money for items they have not seen and advertised by companies which, in many cases, are completely unknown to them, requires copy that sounds as if the writer believed enthusiastically in what is being written.

There are certain words, for instance, that sound perfectly acceptable when used in mail-order copy that might be thought of as "too much" or "too high-pressure" when used in soberer copy for national magazines, or in television where announcers cannot use them without sounding like circus barkers.

Generally conceded to be mail-order advertising's most attention-getting and sales-getting words are these five: *Free • Amazing • New • Now • How.* Every one of these words, of course, can be used in other types of advertising, but in mail order they seem to carry a particular magic.

> Free—while supply lasts
> Amazing CB development
> New. An electronic breakthrough
> Now—freedom from cleaning drudgery
> How to find peace of mind

It would be easy enough to use all five of these response-evoking words in one fervid passage such as: Now! Free! An amazing new booklet that tells you how to restore furniture easily!

A mail-order writer's grab-bag is, of course, full of other "hot" words and phrases. A few of these:

Do it now.	*Bargain.*
Better.	*Bonus.*
Clip this coupon.	*Discover.*
Enjoy.	*At last.*
Extra.	*Learn.*
Surprise.	*Only.*
Proof.	*Tested.*
Try.	

Naturally there are many other words with great mail-order appeal but these are the ones that any reader will see time after time when he is reading mail-order advertising whether in letters or publications.

The question arises: "Can't these be overused?" It *may* be possible, but to this point the words have stood up well. Each one of the magic five, with the possible exception of "amazing," tells a story and does so quickly. Each one mirrors the enthusiasm of the writer.

Other Qualities Found In Mail-order Copy

1. *It can be (and usually is) long.* Mail-order copy, as previously mentioned, must do the entire selling job. This means that the use of a clever headline and a few clever sentences is not enough. Mail-order advertisements, consequently, are consistently longer than other types of advertisements.

Consider a mail-order advertisement for a Hudson Bay blanket. Here we must supply details: Weight. Length. Colors. Width. Materials. Cost. Savings represented in the cost. Superiority of this blanket. Illustration. Durability. How soon delivered. How to order. Manufacturer.

These details, and others, are interwoven into a copy message that is glowing with the promises of satisfaction that the buyer is going to experience because of possession of the item. There will be a promise of beauty; of snug, wintertime warmth; of long, economical use.

A mail-order writer must *prove* that the offer is worth the money the reader is being asked to send and proving requires a thorough sales message. Even business executives, supposedly too harried and hurried to read long copy will do so if it is interesting to them. One prominent mail-order organization, to illustrate, has found that some of its most successful mail-order promotions to business people have run to six pages.

(2) *It requires strong, inflammatory headlines.* "Inflammatory" may seem a peculiar word to attach to a piece of advertising writing, but the dictionary defines inflammatory as "tending to produce heat or excitement," and that is actually what the mail-order copywriter should aim for with the headline. Along with excitement is interest and the solu-

tion to a problem, the satisfying of a long-felt want, and the picturing of something that is of great, easily-understood use to the reader. Thus, a few mail-order headlines read like this:

Decorating ideas galore!
"We're enjoying winter for the first time . . ."

Red Glory living fence...
The only rose hedge created for this purpose alone...yours
for only pennies...and guaranteed

Giant dahlias
from seeds in 10 weeks

We're looking
for people who
like to draw

If you can thread a needle...
YOU CAN LEARN TO PAINT ROSES

This year fill your life with music
Take 4 RCA Victor records for only 98 cents

There are many mail-order advertisements, of course, that do not have headlines with the promise and excitement of the foregoing examples. Sometimes headlines in small-space advertisements are mere statements or labels because of the limited space. Thus, we find headlines such as:

For tall or big men only!
Save 50%
Eagle decals
500 zip code labels—50 cents

(3) *It should pack power into the first paragraph.* Even if copywriters have written the "inflammatory" headline previously mentioned, they have still wasted their time if the readers attracted read the first paragraph and give vent to a disappointed "Oh!" They should make them express a satisfied "Ahhh!"

When readers go through the first paragraph they should find that it has been worthwhile to read the headline and should feel, furthermore, it will be even more worthwhile to continue reading in order to get *all* the exciting details of the proposition that is unfolding. They will want to know the other advantages.

(4) *It should maintain interest with strong selling subheads.* All of us can remember that some schoolbooks were more interesting than others. It is pretty certain that our vote would not go to those books that went

page after page without breaking up the type mass with subheads. On the other hand, all of us follow news stories, sometimes very long stories, without trouble because they *do* have subheads to guide our reading and to break up long passages.

PROVIDING PROOF TO GET THE ORDER

Many times in a person-to-person sales interview a prospect will ask, "Are you sure this will do everything the ad says?"

An alert salesperson will reply: "It certainly will, and here's why." The customer's question provided a chance for the salesperson to prove why the advertising claims were correct.

In mail-order advertising the advertising not only makes the advertising claims but it also carries its own proof of those statements. Once more we see how the advertising situation differs when the whole sales process must be done through advertising, not through advertising *and* selling.

Facts are the sales stuff of mail order. Consumers are more interested in the performance of an item than in how it was made, or in broad statements about its excellence. In the following list of points, therefore, number 2, 3, 4 are especially important. In detailing performance and tests, tell specifically *how* they were conducted, *where* the action took place, exactly *what* occurred, and *who* tried the product or tested it.

Facts and proof should be presented in the consumer's language and point of view, not from that of the manufacturer. What is intensely interesting to the manufacturer may be boring to the consumer. A consumer's interest in the manufacturer's facts is limited to what those facts mean in the use of the product by the consumer. In short, "What will the product do for me?" is more important than "How is it made?" Specifications, therefore, should always be expressed in what they mean to the consumer.

Here are some ways to back up claims with proof and, incidentally, to clinch the order:

(1) *Use facts or figures supplied by acknowledged experts.* Educators, doctors, scientists, engineers, and many other people respected for their expertness and for their neutral attitude toward the product or service can provide great assurance to the prospect.

(2) *Provide a demonstration in pictures and words, or just in words,* that shows why and how the product mades possible the claims advanced for it. Such a demonstration should have been conducted under fair conditions and with scientific exactitude.

(3) *Show how the product performed under exceptional conditions.* Assume that the product is a flashlight, and the demonstration showed how it held up although used under water for an extraordinarily long period. This is sometimes known in advertising as the "swim-a-mile" technique, since the assumption made by the prospect is that the product that can keep going under difficult circumstances of long use, or use in cold, heat, wet, or other unfavorable circumstances will do well under ordinary conditions.

(4) *Include evidence of official recognition.* Perhaps the item won first prize in an important state fair, in laboratory tests, or in public tryouts. Naturally, the power of including such recognition is in the fact that the item won out over *competing* items.

(5) *Describe quality specifications.* Sometimes this may be all-important. Here would be included details of workmanship, materials, ingredients, and design. In selling clothes, watches, or any products where these elements are important, the specifications must be given carefully. In a camera sales, for example, the camera buff will want to know who makes the lens. A sports enthusiast buying golf balls will read with interest the details of the ball's construction, and will judge then whether claims for extra distance have any validity.

(6) *Furnish testimonials or praise from users.* Mail-order advertising makes much use of statements from typical users who have used the product under typical circumstances and have found it satisfactory. In some ways, comments from satisfied users make the most convincing proof of all—that is if the comments are believable and provided by believable people.

(7) *Give the background of the product maker.* A famous mail-order house is the L. L. Bean Company, Freeport, Maine. Mr. Bean, the founder, had a reputation as an outdoorsman. His long experience in fishing and hunting was mentioned frequently in the advertising copy of the Bean catalog. Readers of the catalog were assured because they felt that if Mr. Bean, for example, said advertised boots would stand up under the toughest conditions, they *would* stand up. A company's experience, reputation, financial standing, progressiveness, and standing in research and production all provide proof of advertising statements along with the reputation of top management, as in the case of Mr. Bean.

(8) *Stress of sales success.* Frequently, advertisers whose products are not selling so well are inclined to exaggerate how well sales are going. Thus this sort of "proof" is not especially effective unless supported by true facts and figures that prove that purchasers have been satisfied and that demand is either steady and heavy, or constantly growing. If, for example, the statement can truthfully be made that the item being offered became the best-selling product of its type within three weeks in a major marketing area, the prospective customer should feel that the product has merit.

(9) *Offer to give money back if not satisfied.* This approach has always been effective and will continue to be effective. It is not actually "proof" in the real meaning of the word, but it is proof in the sense that the advertiser "proves" strong confidence in the performance or quality of the product.

ASKING FOR THE ORDER

Many salespeople make good presentations but falter at the point when the order should be closed. Somehow, they become numb at the most important moment of their sales pitch. A mail-order advertiser can't afford such "numbness."

Since mail-order advertisements *must* stir action if they are to be successful, there is much more copy devoted to action-inducement and the use of strong action-arousing words is much more pronounced. In larger-size mail-order advertisements, whole paragraphs near the end feature action-talk—the same kind of talk a real-life salesperson might use in closing the order.

Intense, fast-paced, and even high-pressure, this copy often summarizes in different, more highly charged words some of the strongest selling points found earlier in the body copy of the advertisement.

Of course, action-talk is not solely at the end of the advertisement. It can be found anywhere—in the beginning, in the middle, or in the conclusion.

GETTING ACTION: SOME TECHNIQUES

Some of the techniques of the action-getting mail-order order "closer" are listed here:

Indicate time and/or supply is limited. Many people simply cannot resist the limited-offer approach. Suddenly, when they read that the item will not be offered at the current price beyond a certain date, or that it will not be offered after the current supply runs out, it seems very important to them to have it. Thus, we find great power in such action-talk as:

> You have nothing to lose.
> A whole world of benefits,
> goods, and services to gain . . .
> and precious freedom from
> financial care. So, please,
> while the introductory First
> Edition offer lasts, rush in the
> No-Risk Coupon today.

Point out that the price will go up. Everyone loves a bargain, it is often said, and many mail-order advertisers have made fortunes by never forgetting this principle. Examples of this form of action-talk follow:

> This gives you a chance to buy
> at low grower prices. But remember—
> in just two weeks prices go up and you
> will probably never see such a bargain
> again. Order NOW. Beat the price rise.

Point out that the price has gone down. Sometimes the mail-order firm picks up a genuine bargain that makes for a good mail-order situation. Then it can offer a low price but without any pressure copy saying that there will be a rise in price. Copy states simply that this is a one-time offer at this price. When the supply runs out, that is the end of the deal. This kind of situation is less common than the "price-rise" situation. An example:

> Because we were able to buy
> in large quantities (at a manu-
> facturer's close-out sale) we are
> able to offer these hand-crafted
> chairs to you at a price lower than
> you have ever seen before. And
> you'll never see . . .

Show how offer is special. Copy should tell quickly just what is so special about the offer being made. This is a form of "proof" previously mentioned but, handled with sense and enthusiasm, it is also a form of action-talk. It should be tied up closely to the money offer being made. Example:

> Only $2 at Bookstores or with Coupon
>
> Nowhere else in book form today can you find so complete, so timely and so *readable* an account of how America's faiths—major and minor—are meeting the challenges hurled at them by today's seething, fast-changing world. To get your copy now, visit your local book store or send $2 with the coupon direct to publisher.

Give a money-back assurance. When the mail-order company says:

> 10-day money-back guarantee . . .
> You must be satisfied or your money is refunded

it is often knocking over the last barrier to acceptance of the offer. That is the reason that this assurance is sometimes put at the beginning of the advertisement as well as at the end. It should always be at the end of the copy and, if there is a coupon, in immediate conjunction with the latter.

Hit hard with action-talk words. Throughout the copy, action-invoking, live, vigorous words should be sprinkled liberally. An example is afforded by one advertisement that used the following words and phrases:

> Turn the page to . . .
> Learn how . . .
> Please rush me . . .
> Rush in the coupon today . . .
> But there's more—much more!!!!
> Mail coupon today . . .
> Now quickly turn to page . . .
> Learn how . . .
> Write in immediately . . .

Include a coupon and stress its use. One mail-order authority has indicated a return expectancy four times as great when a coupon is used. To help achieve reader-reaction, a coupon is of great help. To make the coupon work to full efficiency, however, it should be played up in the body copy and in the material near it, and the coupon itself should be exciting and full of action-talk. Examples:

> Mail quick-action coupon now!
> Got a stamp? Mail this coupon now for the newest, most exciting vacation sampler you've ever seen! Don't delay. Fill out this coupon now, and this summer you'll be the envy of all your neighbors.

Offer rewards for acting quickly. The longer prospects delay in responding to a mail-order offer the more likely it is that they will not act at all. An extra inducement that causes them to make up their minds more quickly pays dividends in increased response. Example:

FREE

of extra cost—Preseason orders

before April 1st

get bonus of 3 Holland Peacock Orchid (Acidanthera) Bulbs

Offer a slight discount for multiple purchases. The offer of a discount for buying more than one of the units (say they are selling for $2 each and are being offered 3 for $5) will increase in most cases the number of units sold. The idea is worth testing even when the mail-order man's instincts might indicate that no one would buy more than one item.

Offer interesting incentives. A huge array of possible incentives are open to the mail-order operator who wants to stir action. Some of these include: free trial of the product, giving of samples, sweepstakes and contests, a discount for paying within 30 days, or making "charter" members out of those accepting offer. The foregoing are only a few of the almost limitless number of incentives that can be used by the imaginative and enterprising mail-order people.

Keying Advertisements to Check Origin of Orders and Inquiries

If a mail-order company uses a number of magazines, it has a strong interest in how well each magazine draws inquiries and/or orders. Should it, however, run the same advertisement in these magazines and subsequently draw hundreds or even thousands of coupons, it will be unable to judge which magazines are responsible for the business unless it has keyed the coupons in some way. Keying can be done in a number of ways as shown in the following examples:

Use a department number in the address. If, for example, "Dept. 29" appears in the address, the "2" indicates the name of the publication as it appears in the master list of publications used. This list is kept by the advertiser. The "9" shows the issue month of September.

If weekly magazines or daily newspapers are used, a different initial may be added (Dept. 29a) to designate the specific issue used during that month. Sometimes "Studio," "Block," or "Desk" may be used instead of "Dept."

Arrange to use variations of the advertiser's street number or box number. In small towns it is often possible to arrange with the post office to vary street numbers or post-office box numbers as key addresses. For one magazine the street address might be 188 Franklin Street, and for another magazine 199 Franklin Street.

Change room number of building for each advertisement. The first advertisement may be 800 White Building, the next 801 White Building, and on and on.

Vary the initials of the person to whom coupon may be addressed. One address may read: G. R. Robinson, President. The next might read G. R. Robinson. By transposing all the letters of the alphabet, the advertiser obtains a sufficient number of keys. It is sometimes suggested that the mail-order advertiser avoid the letters *I, J, O,* or *U,* since in the poor handwriting of many respondents these letters may look like something else. Another suggestion in the use of initials: Where a big number of keys is required, the use of three initials may be desirable.

Add a letter designation to the offer being made. By asking respondents to ask for Booklet A, or Booklet B, or Catalog F a great many magazines can be differentiated through the initials.

MEDIA SELECTION FOR MAIL-ORDER ADVERTISING

Selection here refers to magazines, the principal mail-order medium. Newspapers will be considered later, as will the broadcast media. Testing is the byword of the mail-order man who is choosing media. Even an operator of long experience moves slowly in selections, testing one or two publications at the outset. Then checks the results. Then tests a few more publications. Observes these. Then goes back to the good ones.

As a result of this analysis, the weak magazines are pruned and, a list of publications built up with a record of success in selling the specific product or service advertised.

Selecting media is one of advertising's hardest jobs. A roomful of experts will disagree vigorously with each other in media choices. But in making *preliminary* judgments about the magazines to put through the testing procedures described in the preceding section, the following steps are generally taken.

(1) Determine whether men or women are the most likely buyers of the product or service. Assuming that it is decided that women make up the best market, then proceed like this:

(2) Study magazines that reach the women's market. Circulation figures and editorial policy will reveal this. In the "study" of each magazine check it closely, not only in current issues but in back issues going back a year or more.

(3) Analyze the mail-order "track-record." Determine how much mail-order advertising they carry. List the mail-order advertisers. Note especially how many of these advertisers repeat their advertising regularly. It is especially important to find out whether the repeat-advertisers are selling products similar to those of the advertiser making the analysis. At the same time it should be noted whether those products are in the same general price range and whether the advertisements are designed to obtain orders. If it is discovered that these latter points are true, then the analysis being made will be that much more applicable to the prospective advertiser's situation.

(4) Spend no money on advertising until the preceding checkup and analysis has been made. A comforting assurance is found in the fact that established and successful mail-order advertisers have been running advertisements in certain magazines week after week or month after month. That they have done so is prima facie evidence that sales figures have proved that these publications have pulled well for them.

(5) Make the first selections among the smaller magazines. One or two publications with smaller circulation and lower rates should be selected before the advertiser tries the big publications. Even the small ones should not be used, however, unless they meet completely the requirements discussed in the preceding four points.

Take a hard-boiled look at circulation and rates. A mail-order person of experience knows that the higher the rate rises above a specified cost per-page-per-1,000-circulation (figured on the black-and-white rate) the less likely it will be that the publication will pay out satisfactorily. This can be true even though the appeal of the advertised product is powerful. This specified cost changes constantly and must be examined for fluctuation.

Timing of Mail-Order Promotion

First, it must be established that the timing of mail-order advertising is very often not in tune with the timing of other types of advertising. December, for example, a great month for the retail advertiser, is usually a poor month for the mail-order advertiser. The national advertiser of a nonmail-order product will also differ sharply from the mail-order advertiser in the choice of good months in which to advertise.

Mail-order people have found that the same advertising copy in the same position of the same publication can vary from 40 percent to 70 percent in actual results depending upon the months the advertisements are run. It is firmly established that some months are better for resultful mail-order advertising than others. There are some logical reasons for this:

(1) Many publications have higher circulations in some months than others.
(2) Reading is more thorough in some months than in others. In summer, for example, the lure of the out-of-doors is stronger than the lure, of reading. Many advertisers deny that "summer slump" is so formidable as has always been thought but still advertising must work extra hard to pull comparable results in warm-weather months, especially in areas that have hard winters and where so much of the outdoor living must be crammed into June, July, and August.
(3) Characteristically, all persons have a certain amount of inertia when it comes to acting upon the appeals of advertisements. This inertia varies sharply and often in direct ratio with busy holiday activities.

In trying to select the best month for mail-order advertising, the operator must go back to that old formula-testing. What works best for one advertiser may not work best for another who is selling a different product in different magazines, and in different ways.

A mail-order company whose stress is on gifts, for instance, may find that December—a poor mail-order month for many advertisers—is its peak month, or November may be "it," since the advertising will be run in advance of the big December rush.

In making a general assessment of what months are good, the mail-order company can analyze the mail-order linage month by month in the publications it intends to use. If it finds, for instance, that January is very bad but November is enormous, it certainly is being furnished with a clue as to what other advertisers are finding to be the best months.

A mail-order company that does not close the order in its advertisement may find a different monthly pattern than the compay that has no outside sales force but does all its selling within the advertisements.

Value of Position in Publication Advertising

That mail-order advertisers fail to go along with the "proof" offered by the media that shows position value is greatly exaggerated is found in the statement of one authority who has said: "I'd bet money any day that my poorest ad put on the first right-hand page will pull better than my best ad put in the worst position. Outside of what we have to offer, the most important factor in mail-order success is the position of mail-order advertisements."

Once more, however, each company must find out for itself which position works best for its products, offers, and magazine selections. As in the case of "when" to run mail-order advertisements there is endless disagreement about "where" to place them.

Although there are differing opinions among mail-order advertisers, often caused by the kinds of items being offered, there is rather general agreement that best results are obtained from advertisements placed far forward in publications. After that, positions far in the back such as the page facing the third cover are desirable. Right-hand pages are favored somewhat over left-hand.

It is *unanimously* agreed among mail-order advertisers that position *is* important and will influence returns. Thus, the mail-order advertiser disagrees with many media people who tend to discount position importance and with some nonmail-order advertisers who may not fight for specific pages.

Using Bigger Space for Testing

If the company is testing an entirely new offer, it is better to overspace than to underspace. It can well use more space than it actually needs. Later, when it knows better how the offer may go, it can cut down space. Behind the initial overspacing is the following logic:

(1) A larger test advertisement may help the advertiser obtain a better position in the magazine, an important consideration as the preceding material on position has stressed.

(2) A copy story can be developed better in the larger advertisement. It may help uncover a broader market than was originally thought possible. Although mail space copy can be very productive, no copywirter will work with a small space by choice.

(3) Should the test turn out well, it will have been learned early that the product advertised in large space will produce bigger sales volume—that properly presented it will do well.

(4) Should the test in large space do badly, the advertiser will not, at least, be tortured by the thought that the failure was due to the use of small space, which in turn caused the sales angles to be covered inadequately.

(5) Should results be neither good nor bad in relation to advertising cost, then experiments in smaller space advertisements can be conducted. Perhaps the proper profit margin can be obtained through lower-cost smaller units.

When Should an Advertisement Be Repeated?

In mail-order advertising, repeating of a good advertisement can be profitable but usually only if a long enough time elapses between insertions of the advertisement. Figures seem to show that when the same full-page advertisement is repeated in the same publication, and with all factors as similar as they can be, the results of the first repeat, if run within a period of from 30 to 90 days, will fall off 25 to 30 percent, or even more. A second repeat will also fall off another 25 percent or more as compared with the first repeat if run within a short period after it.

It is likely that the first repeat will do as well as the original insertion only if there is a rest of from 6 months to a full year between the original insertion and the first repeat of the same full-page advertisement in the same publication.

Successful mail-order advertisers using full-page advertisements rotate these advertisements in publications they use regularly. Since mail-order advertisements are so very selective in their appeals, full-page advertisements generally skim off the cream of the prospects interested in these appeals. Thus, it becomes unwise to repeat the same full-page advertisement too quickly in the same publication. Time must be allowed for another crop of prospects to grow.

Fall-off in prospects is not so severe in the case of small-space advertisements. The reason, obviously, is that smaller advertisements usually will not obtain the selective attention and readership of so many of the magazine's readers each time they appear.

Getting Mail Orders in Local Markets

Suburban growth and the trend toward retail decentralization have made mail-order advertising an increasingly important way to reach shoppers.

Mail-order newspaper advertising brings the merchandise to the shopper by capitalizing on newspaper circulation to reach out into fringe areas for customers. Establishment of a suburban or branch store can bring about an increase in mail-order customers. Studies show that branch store sales are not primarily a diversion from a store's downtown customers but come from consumers in the branch area itself, a great many of whom formerly purchased from small neighborhood stores. With the decline of the neighborhood store easy-walking-distance shopping has almost vanished.

It has been found that the mail-order sales check is higher than the store average and sometimes is twice as high. Return ratios average about the same. Careful accounting analysis has shown department store mail-order business to be profitable in relation to the cost of obtaining such business.

Easy care... wash & wear!

Norm Thompson's Ranch Pants...

Tougher than blue jeans and a heckuva lot better looking.

... unconditionally guaranteed for 6 months.

Made by Niver Western Wear, Ranch Pants are virtually immune to snagging by brush and thorns.

If your Ranch Pants rip, tear, wear through, or pull apart at the seams within six months of the date of purchase, we'll send you a new pair free or refund your money in full... no ifs, ands, or buts. Either way you risk nothing by trying them out yourself.

Rugged comfort that's more than good looking.

Ranch Pants are styled with a bold western flavor and made to withstand just about any kind of tough use you can give 'em. You'll enjoy the lightweight comfort of 50% cotton combined with the rugged durability of 50% Dacron® polyester. We think they're better than blue jeans for camping, hiking, riding... almost any outdoor adventure you have in mind. And what's more, they're completely machine washable and dryable.

Ranch Pants for men.

You'll appreciate the lightweight comfort for outdoor activities, and you can bet they're substantial enough for year 'round wear. They feature two flapped back pockets that fasten securely for carrying valuables. The roomy front pockets are a full 10" deep... ready to hold more than you'd expect. Seven heavy-duty belt loops can easily handle belts up to 2" in width.

Women's Ranch Pants.

Built for rugged use, women's Ranch Pants are cut and tailored especially for women ... not just adapted from men's pants. They're designed with a waistband

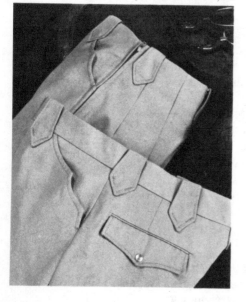

snap and locking side zippers to insure a proper fit around the hips. There are no back pockets on women's Ranch Pants ... just a plain, slimming design that can flatter a woman's figure.

Colors: Slate blue, or tan. **Men's** even waist sizes 28-50. **Women's** waist sizes: 22-30, 32, 34. Shipped unhemmed for easy adjustment to exact length.

No. 4382 (Men's) $23.00
No. 4389 (Women's) $23.00

In developing such business, department stores have followed certain ground rules:

(1) to work hard in the devising of a special mail-order coupon.
(2) to put major stress on the use of Sunday newspapers.
(3) to call attention to the store's eagerness for mail-order business.
(4) to not offer loss leaders as mail-order items.
(5) to offer merchandise that is easy to handle in that it is prepacked and marked.
(6) to avoid low-priced items unless they lend themselves to multiple-unit selling—sheets, curtains, and the like.

DIRECT MAIL

Direct mail to most people simply means letters. This is understandable because letters continue to be the dominant form of direct mail solicitation, whether personal or processed letters. Despite the dominance of letters the direct mail user has many other forms of direct mail to call upon. Although direct mail advertising totals hundreds of millions of dollars and could well be the single biggest advertising medium, no one knows for sure just how much is spent in this universally-used medium. The figures may be uncertain, but it *is* certain that direct mail is vitally important to thousands of small businesses as well as to giant corporations. For any type of direct mail user the starting point is the *mailing list,* or those individuals or firms who will receive the direct-mail solicitations.

Who Should Be on a Direct-Mail List?

There are many ways of building a mailing list but in general there are two groups of people that mail-order companies prefer to circularize:

(1) People who have bought something by mail before. Some people simply don't like to do business through mail-order; it is important to know and to do business with those people who are *willing* to order in this way.

(2) People who have previously bought by mail something similar in general purpose or appeal to what is now being offered them.

A mail-order company tries to hit the right people with its offer in order to avoid waste. To do this it makes up its own list or it may rent lists from list brokers who have ready-made lists or will compile lists to specifications.

Some of the possibilities for list-building by the circularizer include:

(1) questionnaires to present customers asking for names of prospects,
(2) names obtained through coupons.
(3) directories—these can be in business, professions, and other areas.
(4) list exchanging with other companies that promote related products.
(5) public records.
(6) club and association rosters.

There are many other possibilities, of course, but the foregoing give some idea of how an energetic mail-order advertiser can build lists.

Lists can be built up internally from its sales, credit and shipping records, general correspondence, the sales force, recommendations, and those who register at trade shows (see "Trade Show" section in chapter 19).

A list made up of individual names, not surprisingly, will usually pull better than a list not composed of individual names and should normally be more successful than a list composed of titles. The latter would, of course, apply to business mailings.

Check the list. Almost as soon as the direct-mail list has been assembled, certain tedious but important tasks must be performed. A system should be set up to: (1) Keep the list up to date by weeding out old names and adding new ones. (2) Keep a close check on the current buying patterns of those on the list; that is, to determine how recently they have purchased. (3) Evolve a demographic profile of those on the list in order to know what they might buy and the best way to approach them.

Because people change jobs and addresses so frequently, list checking is a never-ending task. Unless it is done, direct mail can be enormously wasteful. In a short time it is easily possible that a list can become 90 percent useless.

Doing Business with List Brokers. Seldom are lists sold. The price, however, includes addressing the material of the mail-order advertiser. The broker arranges with companies that have developed mailing lists and with those who wish to use the lists. His profit is on the commission paid by the list owner. Lists of this type may run from $10 to $50, and more, depending upon the size and selectivity of the list.

Since the costs for lists of names merely bestows the right to circularize the list once, without considering other costs such as printing and postage, it is clear that the mail-order advertiser must do much preliminary planning and figuring before plunging into the mailing.

How Many Orders or Inquiries Will Be Pulled?

One direct-mail expert when asked "What is a good percentage of response to a mailing?" Replied: "One that makes a profit."

This is a safe answer because response to direct mail is so uncertain. Still, it is reasonable to want *some* idea of what response might be. For instance, anyone going to the expense and trouble to set up a sweepstakes promotion might hope to get 20 percent, or more from a direct-mail solicitation but less if the sweepstakes is run in a publication. Of course, much of the response from the direct-mail sweepstakes might be made up of people who reply: "No. I don't want the product, but please let me know if I have won a prize."

An advertiser pulling for orders on a "cold list" of people who have not inquired about the product will do well if he pulls 3 percent or 4 percent; that is, 30 or 40 orders to the thousand.

Mailings pulling for inquiries may pull 15 percent, 20 percent, or even more, depending of course on the quality of the creative work, and the appeal of the product to those receiving the mailing.

Despite a high wastage of mailed material which mailers are prepared for, a certain percentage will read it thoroughly. For these important people a good selling presentation must be made.

As already explained, there may be many ways to increase response. For example, many direct mailers have strong faith in the power of first-class postage to increase response and have figures to show that the use of actual adhesive stamps, instead of postage meters, will help even further.

Other direct mailers attach less importance to first-class postage but generally concede that its use will bring quicker results than if third-class postage is used. When using first-class postage results can often be increased still further by calling attention on the envelope to the fact that first-class postage has been used.

Seasons and Days to Mail

As in mail-order publication advertising, endless differences of opinion exist on this point. If a product's appeal is seasonal, for instance, circularizing will be influenced strongly by this factor.

If the product has a year-round appeal, some mailers have found July 5 to July 15 good for early testing. Most mailers avoid mass mailing in summer months, with as much as 25 percent higher returns noted for the generally accepted months of September, October, and until about November 15.

After a gap for Thanksgiving and Christmas, many circularizers begin mailings again right after Christmas and continue until about the middle of February. Results, unless the product is seasonal, get progressively poorer until early in July; then they improve gradually.

Seasonal gift mail usually goes out as early as August or September for Christmas mailings. Paul Grant, a mailing authority, has named direct-mail mail-order months in order of effectiveness as October, November, January, February, September, April, March, May, December, August, July, June. This pattern fits in with the generalization that the summer months are the poorest, and the fall months the best, although often January and February are at the top.

A direct mailer should study the calendar for yearly events that might affect mailings. Income tax time is an example. Many taxpayers, distressed by their tax situation, are notably reluctant to spend any money at this particular period. On the other hand, those with sizable refunds coming may be in a buying mood.

Days. If mailings are going third-class the mailing company has little control over exactly when the mail will arrive at its destination. If it *does* know when it will arrive, it will most generally select Tuesday, Wednesday, and Thursday as the best arrival days for results. Mondays find a pileup of mail both in the home and office. Fridays in the home are shopping days and the start of weekend activities; in business, Fridays are cleanup days when the big rush is on to get the desk cleared before 5 P.M. It is not a good time for mail-order mailings.

Yet despite this logic a check of 100 mailers would undoubtedly find each day of the week named by one or more persons as the best day for mail to arrive. This is one more instance when the mailers' testing must discover which days are best for their mailings.

DIRECT-MAIL TECHNIQUES AND FORMATS USED FOR MAIL ORDER

Whole books have been written on the subjects covered in this subhead. Thus, we are touching only lightly here upon the topics. For the mailer the selection of the right form is important but nowhere near so important as its execution assuming, in the first place, that the offer is good and the timing suitable.

Selecting the Format

Personal Letters. Mass mailers simply can't afford to send out individually addressed, secretary-typed direct-mail solicitations. If, however, the list is very selective and the offer yields enough profit, the personal letter becomes direct mail's most powerful instrument. Such letters, sent with first-class postage, have a high percentage of careful readership, sales, and profit.

If the item sold is expensive enough, it might be profitable for the mailer to personalize the letter any way possible. One way, of course, is to simply fill in the name, address, and personal salutations. Some mail-order people will not use such personalizing unless selling items such as jewelry, power boats, or appliances. To determine the value of the fill-in the mailer should test the same letter with or without the fill-in.

Processed Letters. Even if the letter is quite apparently a form letter, results are better when letters are included no matter what form the mailing takes. A good letter and a good circular together will usually do better than the circular without the letter.

Unless written interestingly about an interesting offer the mailer should try to keep the letter to one page. If, however, the offer is good, the product appealing, and the writing excellent, letters can go two or three pages and will be read carefully.

Cards. Cards, in general, are used for obtaining inquiries, or for pulling orders for items of low cost that do not require a long copy story to sell them. Card mailings, too, are relatively low cost, thus make possible a profitability even though the margin may be small on the item being sold.

Not too many single cards are used because: (1) The room for copy is limited. (2) There is no reply card.

Double and triple cards, in contrast, offer room for copy and provide a way for the receiver to respond without finding and addressing an envelope.

Display Letterheads. Another device, the display letterhead, can be a factor in seizing the readers' attention at the critical moment when they have opened the mail and are ready to read it, or throw it away. Display letterheads take an infinite number of forms—pictures of the product, pictures of what the reader will get for buying the product, or certificates that show how much can be saved by using the product.

The point, of course, is to make the display letterhead interesting enough to stop the reader momentarily. On the negative side, the display letterhead looks very "addy" and robs the letter of any truly personal one-on-one flavor. Likewise, unless exceedingly well done, it can look cheap instead of inviting. If done well, however, it can be a stopper.

Envelope "Flashes". Using messages, or "flashes" on envelopes is a technique increasingly of interest to mailers who see how consistently such messages cause mail recipients to look inside. A strong promise on the envelope's outside, or a "teaser" phrase builds up enough curiosity to make it difficult for prospects to resist.

"Your window to the world of facts and ideas!"

The foregoing words appeared on a recent mailing for a "thought type" magazine. Another mailing for a product of interest to the parents of small children "flashed" this message on the envelope:

"Here's money-saving news for parents of small children"

Such captions on the outside of the envelope flag the attention of the receivers and may pique interest enough to cause them to open mail they might ordinarily throw away without opening. These "flashes" are especially valuable in the case of third-class mailings to a cold list. Usually they are printed on the left-hand section of the envelope's face, often in color. They contain a strong promise of benefit. An example:

> Corn growers!
> Increase yield 25% to 50% with Korn-Gro hybrids—learn how!

Flashes are almost always used in mailings to a specialized list, characteristics of which are known to the mailer. The flash aims at the known interest of the receiver. Another form of flash is the phrase "Here's the information you requested," used in order to let the receiver know that the catalog or other literature is not being sent unasked.

Follow Direct Mail For Results

A careful test conducted by the U.S. Department of Commerce showed that a one-day delay in answering inquiries resulted in 1 percent less business; two days, 2 percent; three days, 5 percent; five days, 7 percent.

Usually the first letter will be sent immediately by first-class mail. While mail-order people are agreed on the immediate mailing of the first follow-up letter, there is some difference of opinion about the sending of the second follow-up. Although most such follow-ups are sent a week after the first, some successful mailings have been sent as soon as a day or two after the first follow-up. After the second follow-up, two-week intervals are often allowed. Normally, all follow-ups after the first will go by third-class mail; this delays the arrival by several days.

In determining the proper follow-up intervals the usual advice must be given—the mail-order company must test to discover what system is best for it.

How Many Follow-ups?   Results produced by each mailing on its own will determine the number of mailings in a follow-up series. Only two or three mailings will suffice for some series while other, usually for expensive products or services, will require five or more mailings. Each mailing should be keyed and tested individually to enable the mailer to know what is best.

Such tests should be made simultaneously, not singly one after the other, because selling conditions change over a period of time. Separating the inquiries by publication or list is done because one individual publication or list may produce a higher sales percentage than another. If the mailer knows that each mail-

Processed letter.

Whether this should be called direct mail or mail order can be debated. There is no arguing, however, that this kind of letter used by most department stores obtains results. It follows the wise principle of inviting business from present customers, people already favorably inclined toward the advertiser.

4005 CRENSHAW BLVD., LOS ANGELES, CALIFORNIA 90008 (213) 293-4311

Dear Preferred Customer:

You are cordially invited to attend a special preview showing of our ONE MILLION DOLLAR FUR SALE on Wednesday, March 23 from 10:00 A.M. to 9:30 P.M. You won't want to miss it!

This is a special day set aside for you to shop and save from $151 to $300 . . . AND MORE . . . on a spectacular collection of luxury furs.

All furs will resume their regular prices after this event, which ends at 6:00 P.M. on Sunday, March 27.

You'll find enormous savings on hundreds of exquisite furs . . . among them mink, nutria, broadtail . . . all of superb quality to ensure enduring beauty. Traditional and contemporary styles . . . even some designer styles . . . impeccably crafted by master furriers. Rising world fur prices will make these savings impossible to offer later. Hurry in before the sale opens to the public Thursday, March 24.

Call the Fur Salon at Ext. 280 for your appointment, or stop by at your convenience.

We look forward to serving you.

Sincerely,

Robert Walker
General Manager
May Company-Crenshaw

P.S. You may charge your fur purchase now and not be billed until September.

ing is more than paying its own way, it does not matter how many mailings there are in a series. In determining whether follow-ups are paying their way it is important to assemble a full record of the cost of each item of expense in the follow-up series. These figures will make possible an estimate of what it is costing to follow up each inquiry, a figure that may run from 20 cents up to an amount two or three times higher.

A corollary question concerns the frequency limit for soliciting a customer list, not just the frequency for follow-ups to inquiries. The answer for many mailers is that if the former customers are still alive, they remain prospects for further solicitation unless, of course, you are selling a youth-oriented product and the customer has aged to the point where he or she is no longer a prospect. Some customers may not order for five years despite a steady stream of solicitations. Suddenly they order again. The profits from the resulting sales can pay for all those mailings many times over.

Expected Percent-of-Sales from Inquiry Follow-ups. A complete follow-up series sent to inquiries will normally produce a total percentage of sales that ranges from 7 to 12 percent. Except for home workshop machinery or other items where the product may quickly be turned to money-making advantage, it is unusual for the percentage of sales to be higher than the figures named.

Characteristically, follow-up series to women yield a smaller percentage of sales than those sent to men. On the contrary, inquiries followed by a personal salesman may yield a sales percentage as high as 25 to 50 percent. This figure will depend upon the appeal of the product offered, its cost, terms of payment, and the salesman's selling ability.

ADDITIONAL MEDIA FOR MAIL ORDER

Newspapers

Not many mail-order advertisers are enthusiastic about ROP newspaper advertising as a medium. Little mail-order advertising will be found in the general news sections of newpapers because:

(1) Only large-size, and thus *expensive* advertisements, can stand out on a big newspaper page. Although small advertisements can be successful in newspapers, the odds are with the big-space advertisements, especially when each small (comparatively speaking) mail-order advertisement must pay out in actual orders it brings in.

(2) A newspaper is read quickly and has a short life in the home. Most newspaper readers give their papers a total reading time of about 15 to 18 minutes daily, and the bulk of this time is given to the news and editorial content. Mail-order advertisements with their long, detailed copy simply do not fit into the reading patterns of the newspaper reader. Possibly even more important—a daily newspaper does not linger around the house. Magazines, in contrast, may be around for a month, or months. Unlike the newspapers, they are around long enough for the readers to mull over mail-order offers and to look at the advertisements several times before a buying decision is made.

A mail-order advertiser's best opportunity in newspapers is not in the run of the paper (ROP) sections of the newspapers but in special mail-order sections or departments. Shopping sections are most often found in Sunday supplements or magazines usually printed by rotogravure, or in letterpress sections printed by the newspapers.

Such special sections have the news flavor that comes automatically with newspapers and have, also, the shopping atmosphere that is inherent in newspapers. Some pages such as the garden or book page bring satisfactory mail-order results. These may appear during the week, but most mail-order advertising in newspapers appears on Sunday since certain sections of Sunday newspapers have a retention time that is more like that of weekly or monthly consumer magazines. Typical of such sections is the *New York Times Magazine* or that newspaper's book review section.

Thousands of mail-order advertisers do use shopping sections of regular magazines or newspaper-distributed magazines. Many of them use such sec-

Bean's Maine Hunting Shoe

Mr. Bean first developed this boot in 1912. He was tired of coming home with wet and sore feet from wearing the heavy leather woodsman boots then in common use. Rubber boots were clammy feeling and too clumsy for all day walking. He decided to combine lightweight leather tops with all rubber bottoms, incorporating the best features of both types of footwear and doing away with the disadvantages. He called his new boot the Maine Hunting Shoe.

Bean's Original Split Backstay Construction

The practical advantages of this design were readily apparent to hunters and woodsmen. For bare ground walking it was light in weight, snug fitting, had a cushioned innersole and a chain tread outersole for better traction. For wet going and walking on snow, the waterproof bottoms were ideal. Mr. Bean invented the split backstay to eliminate chafing and by keeping all parts as light and flexible as possible he had a boot that could be used all day in perfect comfort. The Maine Hunting Shoe was an immediate success.

Over the years continuous improvements have been made. The best full grain leathers from improved tanning processes are adopted. New developments in r u b b e r compounding provide l o n g e r wearing bottoms. But the basic design of Mr. Bean's boot has yet to be improved for all weather and all purpose outdoors comfort.

Today the Maine Hunting Shoe is the most widely used sporting boot in the world.

Bean's Chain Tread Outersole.

Uppers are of supple, long wearing full grain cowhide, organically treated in tanning process to resist water for life. Will not stiffen with wetting and drying. Tan or Brown finish. Bottoms are made on a swing last of tough, ozone resistant rubber compounded especially for us to provide longer wear. Cushioned innersole. Outersole of durable crepe is permanently vulcanized to the vamp and features Bean's famous chain tread.

**Mr. Leon L. Bean (1872 - 1967)
holding his Maine Hunting Shoe.**

tions just as much to obtain names at small cost for their mailing lists as for the profit to be made on merchandise sold.

One difficulty in using daily newspapers for mail-order offers is the general character of the newspaper audience. Specialized magazines preselect audiences. Newspapers, in contrast, cut across the entire local population. Only by asking for a special position, and paying a higher price as a consequence, can the mail-order advertiser partially overcome this difficulty. Thus we may most often find mail-order advertisements in the sports area, financial pages, and other specialized pages or sections.

Preprints, Syndicated Supplements, and Comic Groups. Much of the between $30 and $40 million spent in newspaper mail-order advertising in recent years has been assigned to preprints, syndicated supplements such as *Parade* and *Family Weekly,* and to groups of comic sections distributed to about 500 newspapers. One noteworthy type of mail-order/advertiser using the comic sections with great vigor, and success, is the photo-finishing firm. Such a firm will typically include a long copy message, enthusiastically presented and, possibly more important, an envelope in which the respondents can send in for processing the film they have shot.

All three of these possibilities—preprints, syndicated supplements, and comic groups—are expensive but resultful. For advantages, they offer color, room for a long copy message, large audiences, plus the exciting, invigorating news atmosphere of newspapers. Sometimes, to be candid, the news atmosphere can be a negative, because advertising readership tends to fall when truly cosmic news events fill the columns of newspapers. This does not occur often enough, however, to be an overriding concern of the newspaper mail-order advertiser.

Radio

While radio as a mail-order medium does not compare in importance with magazines or circularizing, it has had some notable successes. Like newspapers, however, its audience is so broad that it lacks the selectivity desired by mail-order advertisers. Only by tying in with specialized programs can the advertiser achieve any kind of audience focus.

Lack of a coupon is another serious limitation faced by mail-order radio advertisers. The transitory character of the radio message is another. Still another is the difficulty experienced by most people in following directions that are given quickly and that are heard, not seen. Complete absence of visual presentation handicaps many advertisers, especially mail-order advertisers, if the product they are selling demands to be seen.

Despite all these admittedly serious limitations of radio, it has these points in its favor:

(1) A human, enthusiastic voice can often arouse more excitement for an offer than cold print.
(2) Timeliness is important in mail-order selling and radio *is* timely. Radio commercials can be prepared quickly and delivered quickly to take advantage of a special situation. Magazine advertisements, on the contrary, are prepared weeks or months ahead of publication.
(3) Loyalty to certain radio announcers is an accepted fact in the advertising field; a good mail-order offer delivered by an announcer who has developed a large, faithful audience can bring great results.

Not all products are suitable for mail-order radio, of course. Costly items and/or items that require long and complicated explanations simply do not fit the radio medium.

What *are* some of the mail-order services or products that are sold successfully by radio? Musical albums or records are prominent. Books, flowering plants, and investment services may be included.

Mail order radio commercial.

Smithsonian Magazine
Radio: 60
Christmas Gift Subscription

ANNCR (LIVE):

A gift is an expression of your regard for someone--a symbol of your warmth
of feeling for a friend, an associate, a relative. This holiday season
there's an especially thoughtful gift you can give--a gift that will appeal
to virtually everyone on your list. It's a year's subscription to Smithsonian
Magazine. Every month Smithsonian will arrive to inform, entertain, inspire--
and remind the recipient of you. In vivid prose and exciting, colorful
illustrations, Smithsonian opens up a world of ideas and information as it
covers fascinating aspects of the sciences and arts, technology and nature.
Yet, a year's gift subscription costs only 12 dollars. And makes the
recipient an Associate Member of the Smithsonian Institution. A handsome card
announcing your gift will be sent. To assure arrival in time for Christmas,
please order no later than December 10th. Write Smithsonian Gift, WOR, New York,
10018   . Or call right now, 265-6500   . Send no money. You'll
be billed later.

Television

When television was young and rates were not so high, the medium was used to some extent by mail-order advertisers. Rates have now reached the point
where only "sure-thing" items will be advertised on the medium. One of these,
as an example, was the offer of six "giant cushion Mums" on the morning *Today*
show. Listeners were told that they were to pay nothing until they saw the
flowers actually growing. Then they would pay $6.95. Instructions were simply
to write:

Mums
"Today"
Box 676
New York, New York 10019

Date of the offer was April 27.

The foregoing illustrates several principles for the mail-order man using television.

(1) The item was timely.
(2) Cost was not prohibitive.
(3) Directions were simple.
(4) A trusted figure made the offer (the commercial was delivered by the master of ceremonies on the show).
(5) The product has wide appeal.
(6) The don't-pay-until-you-see-them-grow appeal created a feeling of trust.

All the limitations named for radio as a mail-order medium (except the lack of visualization) apply to television with the added negative of very high cost-per-thousand-actual-prospects for selective items because of the very broad reach of television.

If the address for a mail-order item is a local station rather than a far-distant station, or a network designation, it will often pull better simply becuase viewers have more confidence that the local station will be more likely to back up the offer than the distant organization that will not feel the same sense of responsibility to local viewers.

CATALOGS

Mention catalogs[3] and one instantly thinks of Sears, Roebuck and Montgomery Ward. This is natural since these are the giants of the mail-order business. A Sears, Roebuck catalog, for example, will run about 2,000 or more pages and will be distributed to millions of persons, and the number of copies shoots up every year.

"Sears" and "Ward's" are the giants of the mail-order catalog field, but there are many lesser firms that use the catalog to build profitable businesses through the mail. In addition, many other firms send out catalogs as one more device to bring in orders.

Sometimes these catalogs may be "homemade" affairs that may be produced cheaply. The store may boost its sales substantially through non-fancy but effective catalogs. Illustrations can be cut from folders or mat proof books supplied by manufacturers. These can be pasted on sheets of white paper with descriptive copy being typed in. Normally such a catalog is best used on a seasonal basis since the usual retail store proprietor does not have time to turn them out frequently. Spring sales, fall sales, and possibly special Christmas promotions will be the best times for catalogs of this type.

Although the emphasis in this text is not on big, expensive catalogs, it is worthwhile to discuss some aspects of catalog selling.

Considerations in Creating Catalog Advertising

(1)   Fascinating, provocative headlines are not quite so necessary as in magazine advertisements that must compete with advertisements for other products. A "label" headline that merely identifies the product or tells in telegraphic style its chief use will be sufficient in many catalogs. Here are some examples from a very successful catalog:[4]

Catalog advertisement that demonstrates all the important creative elements

A strong headline; long, enthusiastic copy, illustrations with captions and many selling subheads provide persuastive reasons for buying the product.

Stay cool and dry this summer.

Natural sheepskin for year 'round comfort and driving pleasure.

The car seat cover developed over 1000 years before the invention of the automobile!

We've gone back more than nine centuries into history to find the solution to the discomfort of modern car seats . . . a solution you might find hard to believe.

Hundreds of years ago, Mongol warriors put sheepskin over their saddles for comfort. (It didn't improve their dispositions, but at least they were comfortable.) In the not-too-distant past, sheepskin car seats were custom-made for high performance sport cars (Ferrari, Mercedes, Porsche) driven in long distance rallies by European drivers. Only the select few who knew and needed the unordinary comfort of these seat covers owned them.

Once a costly luxury . . . now a great value!

Today, natural fleece is a unique yet practical answer to the icy cold or blistering heat of leather or vinyl auto upholstery. The staff of Norm Thompson, working closely with consulting experts, has been able to produce a fine sheepskin cover that will fit any make or model of car . . . give you luxurious, long-lasting comfort . . . all at a very reasonable price.

Here's what you can expect.

▪ **New driving comfort . . . all year 'round:** The natural insulating properties of sheepskin will help keep you cool and dry while driving on a hot summer's day. You can even leave your car parked in direct sunlight without having your seat turn

Easy to install in just 5 minutes . . . sheepskin seat covers fit any car . . . bucket or bench seat.

into a frying pan. The soft, natural fleece simply doesn't get hot.

Next winter you'll discover just the opposite. These seat covers will insulate against the cold, even in extremely low temperatures. All you feel is soft, comfortable warmth.

▪ **Beautiful and unique:** The soft fur adds a touch of distinction to even the finest auto interiors.

Truly a unique gift . . . ideal for chairs at home or at the office.

Office chairs, planes, boats , . . makes just about any seat more comfortable.

We've had the opportunity to talk with a number of people who are presently using these seat covers for just about anything from private planes to their vinyl desk chairs at the office. They all seem to agree on one point . . . "these sheepskin seat covers invariably make sitting on any surface a little more comfortable."

Natural fleece keeps you warm when it's cold, cool and dry when it's hot.

▪ **Easy-care:** Dry clean or machine wash in cold water and air dry. (Do not bleach)

▪ **Less chance of shocks:** Natural fleece reduces static build-up to a minimum.

▪ **Durable:** They should last the lifetime of your car.

▪ **Interchangeable:** You can transfer them from your old car to a new one.

▪ **Minimizes clothing wrinkles.** Your clothing has less chance of wrinkling because these seat covers cut down on the problems caused by perspiration.

▪ **Fits any car.** Cadillac or Volkswagen . . . bench or bucket seat. We'll send you complete instructions for easy installation on any car in 5 minutes.

Made from a single hide.

Many sheepskin seatcovers on the market today are pieced together from scraps left over after the production of sheepskin coats. Ours is made from one complete hide. With no seams to come apart, you get a seatcover that's longer lasting and better looking.

A highly unordinary gift.

A good share of our sheepskin seat covers are sold to people who already have one or two of their own. They give them to friends and relatives, because as a gift they're not only unique, they're always appreciated.

Color: Natural shades ranging from white to rich beige. When you order two or more, we'll see that you get a matched set. Materials and instructions for easy installation are included at no extra cost.

No. 9106 (bench seat) **$38.50**
No. 9107 (bucket seat) **$38.50**

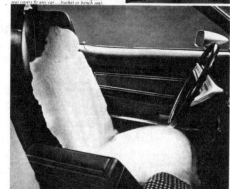

> **Dual Plant Shelves**
> **Snap-cut Telescoping Tree Pruner**
> **Imported Dutch and Edam Gouda Cheeses**
> **Magic Fingers Frencher-sheller**

(2) Description must be very precise. Mail-order copywriting for catalogs is considered superb training for entrance into advertising agency copywriting because descriptions and sales messages are so precise. Catalogs are expensive; a Sears Roebuck catalog, for example.

Much smaller catalogs may be even more expensive. Writing for this expensive form of mail-order advertising must be precise and resultful to make the catalogs pay off in orders.

(3) Copy may be long. Like other mail-order copy, that used in catalogs is doing the whole job of selling. Copy is not long for length's sake but because of the need to give all the facts needed to help the reader reach a buying decision. One of the famous catalogs—that of the L.L. Bean Company—uses fact-filled copy of only moderate length. Likewise, the small catalog put out by the well-known Sunset House uses concise copy of moderate length. Still other catalogs use very long copy for certain items. The rule, then, is that copy can be just as long as necessary to present the most efficient selling message.

(4) Price is stressed. Most readers of catalog copy are looking for bargains. Unless the reader uses a catalog only because he is so remote from civilization that he cannot shop in stores, he usually buys from catalogs simply to buy cheaper than he can in his local stores. It is very important for the writer to stress "good buy" in the copy. Otherwise, not, the reader will wait to buy the item on his next shopping trip.

(5) Need for timeliness not so great. Some catalog sellers put out seasonal catalogs, as in fall and spring. A number of items, of course, are especially suitable for those seasons. As a rule, however, timeliness is not so important in catalog selling as it is in magazine or broadcast media selling. Most catalog items are suitable for year-round sales, and the copy reflects this.

(6) Instructions for ordering must be clear. All that fine selling copy is nullified if the reader is puzzled by ordering directions. Anyone interested in catalog selling would profit from examining carefully the detailed ordering instructions included in Sears, Roebuck, Montgomery Ward, and Norm Thompson catalogs.

"800" NUMBERS FOR MAIL-ORDER RESPONSE

"Call us free on our 800 number" is a phrase heard increasingly these days as mail-order concerns invite prospects to order by toll-free numbers, or sometimes they call simply to obtain more information.

Because millions of people dislike writing of any type and are afraid to fill out forms, the use of 800 numbers has much customer appeal. Although many companies use the 800 number service merely as a means for helping customers locate local outlets for a company's products, the use by direct-response companies has been increasing because it is quick, dramatic, and eliminates much paper work.

Clear ordering instructions for catalog offers.

A catalog advertiser is dealing with masses of people with greatly varying ability to understand instructions. Thus, it is vital to be clear, as well as thorough, in those instructions. Notice how every question and contingency is anticipated on this page.

Help us give you a proper fit!

Chest or bust: Run a tape well up under arms, across shoulder blades, and over the fullest part of the chest. Hold the tape firm but not tight. Be sure it's straight across your back. Stand naturally. Give measurement in inches.

Sleeves: Measure in inches from middle of back of neck, across the shoulder and around point of elbow to wrist.

Waist: Measure in inches the waistband of same style slacks or skirt that fit properly. Or measure your waist in inches over a shirt or blouse. Measure at the position you normally wear your trousers or skirts.

Hips: Run a tape around the fullest part of hips which is usually 7"-9" below the waist. Give measurement in inches.

Neck: On a shirt of the same style that fits well lay the collar flat. Measure in inches from the center button to far end of button hole. Or run a tape around your neck at the level you'd usually wear your shirt collar. Please send measurement in inches.

Shirts: Send us your neck size, sleeve length, height, and chest or bust size.

Pants: Send waist (women also send hip) measurement. All Norm Thompson pants are styled with a medium rise and shipped unhemmed for easy adjustment to your exact length.

Belts: Send us waist measurement.

Jackets or coats: Send us your chest or bust measurement, sleeve length, and your height.

Hats: Measure in inches around the largest part of your head or where you plan to wear the hat.

Shoes or boots: Send us your regular shoe size and width (AAA to EEE, not narrow, medium, or wide). Please do not send a tracing of your foot.

Norm Thompson Gift Certificates.

Norm Thompson gift certificates are welcome on birthdays, anniversaries and special holidays. They make wonderful wedding gifts, especially for those young couples who get "two of everything for the house" when what they really need is clothing. A gift certificate is ideal for those who are just plain hard to shop for ... when you don't know the size or color ... and for those with decided tastes who would prefer to shop for themselves.

You can make Norm Thompson gift certificates for any amount from $10 right on up. If you want the gift certificate delivered on a special date, just let us know and we'll see that it gets there on time.

With each gift certificate we send a free Norm Thompson "Escape from the ordinary®" catalog.

Please include the name, address, and zip code of the recipient if you want us to send your gift directly to them.

GIFT CERTIFICATE

Norm Thompson P.O. Box 3999
Portland, Oregon 97208 Dept. SC.77

Order by phone TOLL FREE anytime 1-800-547-6712.
(Excluding Oregon, Hawaii, and Alaska)

☐ Mr.
☐ Mrs.
☐ Miss   1st initial   Last name

Address_____ Apt., Suite, or Room #____

City_____ State_____ Zip_____

Telephone # and area code (_____)_____
Where you can be reached

BANKAMERICARD

master charge THE INTERBANK CARD

☐ My personal check or money order is enclosed. (U.S. funds only)

Charge to my ☐ BankAmericard ☐ Master Charge___

Card number_____ 4 digit interbank No. for Master Charge___

X_____
Signature   Good thru date

☐ Send to: (if other than myself)

Name_____
Address_____
City_____
State_____ Zip_____

☐ I have moved since my last order. My former address was
Address_____
City_____
State_____ Zip_____

We want you to have the best possible fit. It'll really help if you can supply us with the following information.

Men: Height____" Waist____" Neck____" Sleeve____" Chest____"
Women: Height____" Waist____" Hips____" Sleeve____" Bust____"

Qty	Catalog #	Name of item	Size	Width	Color	Unit Price	Total Price

We want to give you the fastest and best possible service, so unless you specify shipment by parcel post your order will be shipped via United Parcel Service.

Air delivery:
For air delivery add charge listed in table at right.

Purchase	Add
1.00 to $26	$1.50
$26 to $54	$2.00
$54 to $75	$2.50
over $75	$3.00

Shipping, handling and insured delivery charges: +$1.50
Ship via air: Add +$
Total enclosed:

Thank you for your order

Prices effective until superseded by subsequent publication.

QUESTIONS

1. Which—direct mail or mail order—is an advertising medium? Why do you say this?

2. For what reasons do mail-order advertisers sometimes feel superior to other advertisers?

3. What are some of the elements that go into mail-order planning?

4. What are the attributes of a successful mail-order item?

5. Name some of the legitimate elements that enter into mail order testing?

6. What two factors have changed the old ideas about the maximum price that can be asked for a mail-order offer?

7. What are some ways to make small-space inquiry advertisements successful?

8. How do you increase the number of inquiries obtained by your advertisement?

9. What special points would you consider in constructing a coupon?

10. Why try to cut the number of inquiries, and how do you do this?

11. What are the five most attention-getting words in mail-order headlines?

12. List ways to back up copy claims with proof.

13. List several ways to get mail-order prospects to act.

14. Why are advertisements "keyed"? Name several ways to key an advertisement.

15. Name several steps to be taken in determining proper media selection for mail-order magazine advertisements?

16. What are some of the good and bad months for the magazine mail-order advertiser?

17. Name good positions in a magazine for the mail order advertiser.

18. Why is it desirable to use big space magazine advertisements for testing?

19. Discuss the desirability or undersirability of repeating magazine mail-order advertisements.

20. What are some of the mail-order guidelines established by department stores for developing mail-order business?

21. What two groups are especially desirable to include on a mail-order direct mail list?

22. Describe the activities of a list broker.

23. What are good seasons and days as viewed by those directing direct mail solicitations?

24. Under what conditions should a direct mailer use personal letters?

25. Distinguish between display letterheads and "flashes."

26. Discuss the topic of direct mail follow-up.

27. What advice would you give someone who was thinking of using newspapers for mail-order solicitations?

28. Name some positives and negatives for mail-order advertising in radio and television.

29. Offer five or six suggestions for creating catalog advertising.

REFERENCES

1. The adventure aspect is illustrated graphically by the experience of one firm which, in two different magazine advertisements, drew an order for 12 jars of English marmalade from the Queen of England and an order for a $1,985 jewelry item from the wife of the President of the United States.
2. Robert Stone, *Successful Direct Mail Advertising and Selling* (Chicago: Crain Communications, 1975).
3. The extent of catalog selling is dramatized by the present use of about 10,000 different catalogs. Many of these promote Christmas items, including such unusual suggestions as a $130,000 full-length lynx coat offered by Neiman-Marcus, Dallas, to a $1.12 million Discojet II that appeared in a catalog issued by Sakowitz in Houston.

   Such promotions yield big returns to thousands of catalog users who pull in an estimated $50 to $60 billion yearly. Even such an august enterprise as the New York Metropolitan Museum of Art gets about 75 percent of its sales from four catalogs a year that go out to a million households.

   Much of the boom in catalog selling is attributed to: (1) The great number of working women who have little time for the traditional store shopping, and (2) a sizble group of the elderly who have time for shopping but find it easier to stay in their homes and shop by catalog, and (3) high cost of gasoline for automobiles.
4. Some catalogs, however, use very exciting, colorful headlines. Each advertiser-company must learn what is suitable for its customers and prospects.

17

OUTDOOR AND TRANSIT ADVERTISING

OUTDOOR AND TRANSIT ADVERTISING

Anyone who has driven down country roads is constantly urged to chew tobacco, the exhortations appear in big letters on the sides of red barns. Such messages are an inevitable feature of rural America. Then, along the better-traveled highways, posters tell us that we're approaching gas stations or AAA-recommended motels. In the city, whether we look at street level, or up on the top of buildings, more posters tell us where to bank, buy milk, or to see the latest automobiles. And then, of course, there are those electrical displays of Times Square, a sort of unnatural wonder of the world that are part of the sightseers trip to New York City.

OUTDOOR ADVERTISING'S CONTROVERSIAL POSITION

Most Americans accept outdoor advertising as an element of the country landscapes or city life. Sizable numbers, however, resent the medium, especially for what they consider to be its desecration of the countryside. Consider, for example, the editorial comment of the *Times Record* of Brunswick, Maine.

Maine minus billboards

Despite claims by some that the bill to do away with billboards costs too much and could put some people out of work, the measure is a good one...

As one legislator remarked people don't come to Maine to learn, on the side of the road, about products that can be purchased in New Jersey. The traveler is not here to read about sun tan lotions, cigarettes and restaurants and has better things to do than look at the clutter of commercial messages lining the highways like so many over-sized cereal boxes.

Advertisements can be seen in any newspaper or magazine. They can be heard on radio stations. The same can't be said of the scenery in Maine, or elsewhere for that matter.

The bill will reportedly cost an estimated $950,000 over the next six years. $200,000 of this the next two. That does not seem a particularly high price to pay in light of the very obvious visual benefits the measure has to offer.

To the advertising man, outdoor's conspicuousness is its great virtue. To the environmentalist, nature lover and garden club member, the virtue becomes an intolerable affront; indeed, another form of pollution. Thus, the medium is assailed, reviled, and legislated against in all sections of the country. Laws and ordinances are levied against it on the village, town, city, county, state, and federal levels.

Oddly enough, it has simultaneously been praised for helping motorists stay awake, and attacked for causing accidents through its alleged distraction of drivers. Despite the "pollution" charge, in many city locations the responsible companies putting up outdoor posters have actually beautified rundown locations by cleaning out the trash, cutting down weeds, planting grass and bushes and then displaying attractive, colorful, well-maintained posters. Dreary corner lots have thus been given sparkle and interest.

The Real Enemy

Too often, the opponents of outdoor advertising don't know their real enemy—the small, unorganized outdoor firms which put up signs without regard for their spoiling of scenic views and then fail to maintain them properly. Such signs, furthermore, may be of all shapes and sizes and may not be well done to begin with. These unorganized elements of outdoor advertising are referred to contemptuously as "snipers" by the reputable outdoor advertising men.

In contrast to these companies that bring discredit upon the industry are the persons who constitute the *organized* outdoor industry. These people run firms that are public-relations conscious. Their outdoor signs are standardized in size and are placed where they will cause the least offense. They maintain the signs and surrounding area scrupulously. Furthermore, they belong to industry associations that insist that members have constant regard for the rights and sensitivities of the public. Unfortunately, opponents of outdoor advertising too seldom distinguish between unorganized and organized outdoor firms. As a consequence, the entire industry has suffered in recent years.

Despite its troubles with outdoor-advertising haters and with laws and rapidly disappearing spaces to put outdoor signs, the industry still enjoys a "sold-out" condition in most sections of the country. There is a lively interest on the part of national, regional, and local advertisers in the medium. There are some solid reasons for the continued vigor of outdoor advertising as the following material testifies.

Reaches People On The Move. An interesting difference between outdoor advertising and other media is that the prospects are carried to the outdoor advertising message, whereas in other media the message is brought to them. This characteristic is especially important in the case of out-of-town motorists

Inside and outside transit display units.

After a number of years of lack of uniformity, the transit industry has standardized the advertising cards used inside and outside on transit vehicles. Most such cards are shown here.

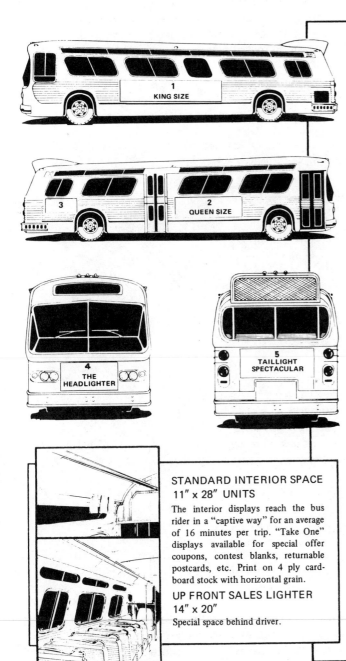

1 KING SIZE

30″ x 144″ Street Side of Bus

The largest poster on the bus—a moving billboard at eye level—carrying its sales message daily to people downtown, in plants or offices, in suburbs or shopping centers.

2 QUEEN SIZE

30″ x 88″ Curb Side of Bus

The Queen is located on the curb side of the bus between the entrance and exit doors. The Queen reaches people on the move whether walking, riding or boarding a bus. Sometimes used in conjunction with Kings to cover both sides of the street.

3 TRAVELING DISPLAY

21″ x 44″ Curb Side of Bus

The Traveling Display is our baby billboard used when high frequency and high reach is the priority but budget is tight. Can be used in conjunction with Fronts and Rears for outstanding results.

4 THE HEADLIGHTER

21″ x 40″ Front of Bus

The front display is called the Headlighter. Visible in any kind of weather, the Headlighter reaches pedestrians, bus riders and drivers or passengers of other vehicles.

5 TAILLIGHT SPECTACULAR

21″ x 70″ Rear of Bus

The rear spectacular offers high visibility and readability. Especially high impact and readership from auto drivers and passengers who follow immediately behind the bus. Highest exposure at traffic lights and intersections.

STANDARD INTERIOR SPACE
11″ x 28″ UNITS

The interior displays reach the bus rider in a "captive way" for an average of 16 minutes per trip. "Take One" displays available for special offer coupons, contest blanks, returnable postcards, etc. Print on 4 ply cardboard stock with horizontal grain.

UP FRONT SALES LIGHTER
14″ x 20″

Special space behind driver.

or other travelers who are in town temporarily. Such people can be a source of profit to local businesses, especially hotels and other businesses offering services, if the travelers can be made aware of the services offered. The advertiser's outdoor sign can give strangers that awareness.

The big sign, furthermore, creates confidence, a feeling that the advertiser is well established. Also, since transients will not have heard anything about the company on the radio, nor heard about it in television, newspapers, or direct mail, outdoor advertising may be its only means of bringing these transients as customers. Without outdoor advertising, motels, hotels, service stations, and local restaurants would lose an important source of new business.

Prize winning outdoor poster.

Effective combination of art and copy won an award in the annual competition sponsored by the Institute of Outdoor Advertising.

Shows Products In Color. To local advertisers especially, the advantage of color in outdoor advertising is important, since they may find newspaper color too expensive, or the newspaper may not offer color advertising. For the national advertiser or the regional advertiser who needs color in order to sell the product most effectively, outdoor advertising offers an opportunity to use color on the local level.

Color in outdoor advertising is, moreover, rich, true color that creates a smash impact when combined with the big size of an outdoor sign. Advertisers who sell packaged goods stress package identification almost above everything else in much of their advertising. Their packages, in color, on a huge outdoor sign help identify the packages for shoppers in retail stores and frequently do so at that critical moment just before the shoppers enter supermarkets, drugstores, hardware stores, or other types of retail establishments.

Offers Flexibility In Placement Of Advertising. Advertisers are often unable, because of costs, to advertise wherever they would like to be. In outdoor advertising, as in other media, therefore, they advertise in the places and at the times that will help them reach the maximum audience at the lowest cost.

Two points are noteworthy here: (1) The sliding scales reward advertisers who use the medium over an extended period. (2) Costs for the medium are low considering the number of people who are exposed to transit messages and who have a long time to read the advertising messages.

Rate Sheet

Poster	Production	Number of Units	Unit cost per month for:			
			1 Month	3 Months	6 Months	12 Months
KING SIZE 30″ x 144″ Street Side	For frequent copy changes print on 80 lb. paper. Copy which will remain in position for longer periods can be printed on pressure sensitive vinyl or directly on Duron board or Styrene.	80 or more 60 to 79 40 to 59 20 to 39 1 to 19	$44.00 46.00 48.00 52.00 54.00	$42.00 44.00 46.00 50.00 52.00	$40.00 42.00 44.00 48.00 50.00	$36.00 38.00 40.00 42.00 44.00
QUEEN SIZE 30″ x 88″ Curb Side		80 or more 60 to 79 40 to 59 20 to 39 1 to 19	32.00 34.00 36.00 38.00 40.00	30.00 32.00 34.00 36.00 38.00	28.00 30.00 32.00 34.00 36.00	26.00 28.00 30.00 32.00 34.00
TRAVELING DISPLAY 21″ x 44″ Curb Side	For frequent copy changes suggest printing on cardboard. Displays that will remain in position for more than 2 months, printing on styrene is highly recommended for all 3 of these positions.	80 or more 60 to 79 40 to 59 20 to 39 1 to 19	14.00 15.00 16.00 17.00 18.00	13.00 14.00 15.00 16.00 17.00	12.00 13.00 14.00 15.00 16.00	10.00 11.00 12.00 13.00 14.00
TAILLIGHT SPECTACULAR 21″ x 70″ Rear of bus		80 or more 60 to 79 40 to 59 20 to 39 1 to 19	34.00 36.00 38.00 40.00 42.00	32.00 34.00 36.00 38.00 40.00	30.00 32.00 34.00 36.00 38.00	28.00 30.00 32.00 34.00 36.00
THE HEADLIGHTER 21″ x 40″ Front of Bus		80 or more 60 to 79 40 to 59 20 to 39 1 to 19	20.00 21.00 22.00 23.00 24.00	18.00 19.00 20.00 21.00 22.00	16.00 17.00 18.00 19.00 20.00	12.00 13.00 14.00 15.00 16.00
BUS-O-RAMA 4 backlight panels 22″ x 122″ Rooftop	Print on translucent sprint materials.	*Bus-O-Rama available on 12 month contract only*				$ 60.00 each per month. $100.00 each for doubles. . both on same side.
INTERIOR SIGNS Backlighted 11″ x 28″ Both sides of bus	For best results print on a translucent styrene. Opaque cardboard accepted but not recommended.		4.00 each	3.80 each	3.60 each	3.20 each
UP-FRONT SALES LIGHTER 14″ x 20″ Inside back of driver			7.50 each	7.10 each	6.75 each	6.00 each
SPECIAL BUYS Basic Bus Total Interior			40.00 per mo.			
Total Bus All Exterior and Interior			140.00 per mo.			

COMMISSION: 15% to Agencies. No Cash Discount

Outdoor advertising gives advertisers unusual flexibility. Whether they are national, regional, or local, they can arrange to have posters in the precise locations needed; locations of high traffic of the very people they are trying to reach; locations situated in specific neighborhoods; locations near shopping centers.

If national or regional advertisers want to promote a product section by section, they can do so within a state, or they can move state by state with their outdoor campaigns. If they are selling a product to farmers such as seed, animal feed, or pesticide, outdoor advertising can be placed on the rural roads traveled by farmers.

Lets The Advertiser Repeat The Message.   Each day in the year the outdoor sign is delivering its message. If the sign is illuminated, the message is delivered 24 hours a day, 365 days a year. Furthermore, many prospects see the same message several times each day, until the point it makes is hammered home. This multiple impression is especially true of the working population because most motorists and transit riders tend to travel the same routes on their daily trips to and from their place of business. The outdoor industry, of course, knows these heavily traveled routes and places its signs in such areas for maximum exposure.

Clever twist.
In a subtle way the advertiser is saying that his car has surprising speed. Copyright: Volkswagen of America.

They said it couldn't be done.

Why Outdoor Advertising Is Seldom the Major Medium

Although outdoor advertising has been very effective for large and small advertisers of numerous products and services, it must be recognized that it is a supplementary medium in almost all cases. Because of a number of factors it is rarely the major medium for big-budget advertisers.

Foremost among these factors is the short copy message that lack of reading time imposes. Because outdoor signs are given flash reading, copy length must be limited to the number of words and ideas that can be taken in at a glance. Some products demand long, explanatory copy, especially new products. For such products, outdoor advertising can be used only to reinforce advertising that appears in other media.

Because most outdoor advertising is directed at people who are on the move in automobiles or public conveyances, it must necessarily be read under distracting conditions. The reader, often a motorist, usually divides attention between the advertiser's sign, traffic signals, the commercial on the car radio, and the pedestrians crossing in front of the car. Thus there is no time to savor the copy and to think about the advertiser's message.

Finally, there is the resentment against outdoor advertising. Although, as was explained, the responsible, organized members of the outdoor industry should not be blamed for the faults of the irresponsible elements many people resent *all* outdoor advertising—a resentment that may have some effect on the attitude toward products advertised on outdoor signs.

TYPES OF OUTDOOR ADVERTISING

Although people traveling around the countryside or in a city see a profusion of outdoor signs, when they eliminate the mass of small, cheap signs they will find that the signs put up by the reputable outdoor companies will generally fall into three types: posters, painted displays, and electrical or spectacular displays.

24-sheet posters

"Poster" is the newer way of saying "billboard," although many people still use the latter term. The most widely used form of outdoor advertising is the 24-sheet poster.* When most advertisers speak of outdoor advertising they are usually thinking of a 24-sheet poster because it is the most standardized form of outdoor advertising. Hundreds of thousands of these posters are displayed in the cities and the countryside of the United States. Dimensions of a 24-sheet poster are:

Printing surface:	8 ft. 8 in. high
	19 ft. 6 in. long
Outside dimensions:	12 ft. high
	25 ft. long
Number of sheets:	10 (usually)

Notice that only 10 sheets are used in making up "24-sheet" poster. The old-time posters did use 24 sheets, but with the new processes only 10 are needed. The "sheets" referred to are sheets of paper, most often printed by lithography or the silkscreen process, that are pasted on wood or steel panels.

Other Large Size Posters

Variations of the 24-sheet poster have been introduced until now the advertiser has an additional choice of 27-sheet posters, 30-sheet posters, and bleed posters. Of these, 30-sheet posters are very popular, with bleed posters coming up fast in advertiser favor.

A 30-sheet poster gives the advertiser about 25 percent more printed area than the 24-sheet poster, and the bleed poster gives 40 percent more. Posting charges are the same for the three types despite the greater printing area for 30-sheet and bleed posters. The differences in the various dimensions are shown in the following table:

**Three-dimensional painted bulletin that
creates a life-like display.**

**Table 17-1
Copy Space of Three Types of Posters**

	24-SHEET	30-SHEET	BLEED
COPY AREA (LENGTH)	19' 6"	21' 7"	21' 7" Live Area *
COPY AREA (HEIGHT)	8' 8"	9' 7"	9' 7" Live Area *
TOP AND BOTTOM BLANKING	10½" Top and Bottom (21" Total)	5" Top and Bottom (10" Total)	5" Top and Bottom (10" Total)
END BLANKING	19" (38" Total)	6½" (13" Total)	6½" Left and Right (13" Total)
FRAME WIDTH	11"	11"	11"

*"Live" area refers to usable copy space and is the same in the 30-sheet poster as the bleed poster. Bleed is the result of adding colored blanking paper to the basic 21'-7" by 9'-7" area.

Smaller Posters

At one time, a popular supplement to the larger poster sizes was the 3-sheet poster. Known as the "neighborhood" poster it was used as a point-of-purchase poster because it was put up near shopping centers or even mounted on the side of a retailer's building. It was much used by advertisers of grocery products. Other heavy users were banks, drug stores, laundries, grocery stores, bakers, and soft-drink bottlers. In recent years, however, the 3-sheet poster (with outside dimensions of 8' 7" high and 4'10" wide) has virtually disappeared. It has been replaced by the 8-sheet poster that serves essentially the same advertisers and same purposes. The 8-sheet poster has outside dimensions of 6' × 12' and a printing area of 5' × 11'. It was, at one time, called a 6-sheet poster. Very often the outdoor company that sells and puts up the larger poster sizes does not handle the smaller posters, leaving that business to small-poster specialists.

**Three-dimensional painted bulletin with clock,
located in a high-traffic area.**

Painted Displays

Painted displays are broken into two major classes: *painted bulletins,* in which the advertising message is painted directly on the galvanized-iron face of the poster panel, and *painted walls,* where the advertising message is painted directly on the wall surface.

Painted displays are meant for long usage. Once the advertising message is painted on a panel or wall, it usually stays on view longer than a month, the customary time for the use of 24-sheet posters. Painted displays are normally sold on a one-, two-, or even three-year basis rather than on a monthly basis as is done with 24-sheet posters.

Painted bulletins are frequently larger than 24-sheet posters, with sizes ranging up to 18 ft. high by 62 ft. 10 in. long. Size is usually determined by the location of the bulletin, the character of the advertising, the location available, and the amount the advertiser is willing to spend.

Some idea of the variety of painted bulletins may be gained by naming a few of the more common ones such as the Deluxe urban bulletin, standard highway bulletin, standard streamliner bulletin, junior highway bulletin, railroad bulletin, roof bulletins, store bulletins, and wall bulletins. Structurally, wall bulletins are the same as roof bulletins, except that they have no supporting framework. Wall bulletins are fastened to the faces of buildings and conform to standard dimensions as nearly as possible.

As for *painted walls,* the standardization in size is even less than in the case of painted bulletins. A painted wall is often more of a "permanent" installation than the painted bulletin. Unfortunately, many painted walls continue to deliver their sales messages years after the advertiser has gone out of business, and for this reason they are sometimes looked upon with disfavor by the public.

Selectivity and flexibility are attributes of painted displays. For general coverage the advertiser uses the bigger posters. To aim a message at a particular location the advertiser may select the painted display.

Painted bulletins and painted walls have the advantages of long life and custom-built character. Although much of the sales vitality and advertising appeal is lost when the public sees the advertiser's message in the same location year after year, there is a balancing factor of solidity. The advertiser creates an image of dependability. A retail store using such a long-lived sign becomes a part of the local scene, an institution.

Because the painted sign is individually created it is distinctive, unlike the mass-produced 24-sheet posters put out for national advertisers. The custom-built display can be made any size and shape to fit the copy message or the physical location.

Costs Of Painted Displays

In determining the costs of painted displays, several factors must be considered:

(1) Circulation (amount of traffic by the sign)
(2) Visibility
(3) Size
(4) Animation (light, neon, moving parts, and so forth)
(5) Amount of rental contract investment
(6) Labor costs (varies widely from area to area)

Retailers who want to use outdoor advertising will often settle upon a painted display because they feel they cannot afford a showing of 24-sheet posters. Consequently, at a substantial rental price, they put up one painted display. Because the basis of successful outdoor advertising is to command the traffic circulation of a retail area, this one sign is likely to fall far short of providing suitable market coverage.

If retailers can afford one sign, perhaps they can afford more signs. They may be wasting money to use just one sign in a weak effort at advertising, whereas three or four signs may cover their area effectively and be more economical in the long run. If retailers cannot afford several displays, it is possible they cannot afford one display (to take the opposite tack from the opening statement in this paragraph).

Rotating painted bulletin.

Appropriately enough, there are many colors shown on the paint-stirrer stick. This board, measuring 14 ● × 48 ● (a standard size) is purchased individually or in groups. The hand-painted face of the bulletin is moved to a new site every 30 or 60 days. Thus, the advertiser can vary his coverage in a market without having to buy many boards to do so.

Cooperative Outdoor Advertising

As is the case with other media, cooperative advertising is offered to retail advertisers who wish to use outdoor advertising on a share-the-cost basis. Under this arrangement the advertising message will be centered around the product made by the advertiser, and the dealer's name will appear on the poster as the local outlet for the product. Manufacturer and dealer will share the rental costs, with the manufacturer normally paying for the cost of the creative work and the lithographed sheets on which the advertising message appears. Usually the dealer's name will be imprinted or lithographed on the poster sheet. Or it may be put on overlay sheets, but sometimes these do not stay on the poster for the duration of the posting period. Therefore, the practice of using overlays is not recommended.

Rotating Painted Bulletins

A typical example of a rotating painted bulletin system is that provided by Foster and Kleiser, large outdoor organization. Under what the company calls its "Customized Coverage" plan, bulletin displays are rotated (physically removed) each month to boulevards and areas where the circulation is predominantly the type desired by the advertiser. Under this arrangement an advertiser can cover all of a market or just the segments containing the greatest sales potential.

A rotating bulletin generally 14' × 48' in size, consists of panels that can be removed from the molding and transported to another location, along with any "embellishments" used in connection with the display. (Embellishments consist of extras such as cutouts, neon letters, complicated animation, and plastic and metal constructions.) Depending upon how long a company's contract runs, it can expose its bulletin on some or all of a group of locations for periods of from one to four months at each location. In large markets, such as Foster and Kleiser's Los Angeles-Long Beach metropolitan area, a company can pick the locations best suited to its needs. Another possibility is to buy two or more bulletins which are moved around the circuit at the same time but on different patterns.

Although rotating bulletins do not offer the continuity advantage of a painted bulletin in a permanent location, they offer a considerable cost advantage to the advertiser. Permanent locations are relatively expensive. Actually, painted bulletins, whether permanent or rotating, are more expensive than 24-sheet posters, but rotating bulletins offer economies to those who can use this form of outdoor advertising.

Electrical Outdoor Advertising

If visibility is an outstanding characteristic of outdoor advertising in the daytime, this characteristic can be doubled, tripled, or even quadrupled at night. Neon signs, of course, have no standardization. They come in all shapes and sizes, and despite their high cost—as compared to electrical signs—they are used by small businesses as well as large. This is because they show up so brilliantly in good or in bad weather. To test this, look down from any hill rising above city streets where neon signs are used.

Although the neon sign is more common and used by more advertisers, the most talked about form of outdoor advertising is the electrical spectacular, which has achieved its greatest use and fame in the downtown areas of big cities, especially in the Times Square district of New York City.

Spectaculars have everything to make them live up to their name—huge size, movement, brilliance. They make pictures, they tell the time, they tell the news, they blow smoke; and in still other ways they amaze, inform, and entertain the spectators. Because spectaculars are invariably erected in high-traffic areas, they justify their high costs in the great number of people who will see their advertising messages, and also because of the "talk" value. A spectacular in Times Square, for example, may receive as many as 50 million exposures (number of people who pass the area) in a single month.

Tri-vision outdoor.

A portion of the surface rotates every few seconds to create the "growth" effect desired. The effect is humorous and attention-getting.

Only the fact that so many exposures are possible enables the advertiser to defend the high cost of electrical spectaculars. Construction of such signs may range from several thousand to several hundred thousand dollars. One New York spectacular, for instance, cost $400,000 to build. Added to construction costs are rental costs which, for high-traffic locations, can amount to many thousands of dollars yearly.

Because of the cost of constructing, renting, and maintaining spectaculars, they are primarily used by big-budget national advertisers. This cost can be justified for national advertisers because the big signs in Times Square, on

624

Michigan Boulevard in Chicago, or on Market Street in San Francisco have a nationwide impact and are eventually seen by millions of visitors to the cities who go back to their homes impressed by what they have seen, and who talk about the advertiser. It has been estimated by national advertisers that a spectacular on Broadway in New York City has 25 percent local value and 75 percent national value.

Because of high construction and rental costs, contracts for spectaculars are long-term. Usually, contracts are for three to five years, and they often extend to 10 years. Although advertisers of impulse items such as soft drinks, cigarettes, and beer are heavy users of spectaculars, the list of users of this form of advertising includes many others who do not sell impulse products. Automobile manufacturers, for instance, are prominent users of spectaculars. One thing is certain, however: spectaculars are not for the corner-store retailer. Their use is dominated by "blue chip" advertisers.

Electrcial spectacular.
Special effects, such as used in this spectacular, are in the tradition of the Douglas Leigh Organization famous for its realistic creations. They include cigarettes that "smoke" with live steam, soap bubble displays with steam, waterfalls using live water. Such signs have livened the New York City scene for years.

"PLANT" AND "PLANT OWNERS"

Each advertising medium develops individual terms peculiar to the medium. In outdoor advertising two such terms are plant and plant owner. Here the word *plant* refers to a business or to its buildings. In outdoor advertising, plants are the structures erected, maintained, and leased to advertisers—the structures that carry the messages known as outdoor advertising. The plant owner or operator is the company or individual running the outdoor business that owns the plant. In the United States there are about one thousand plant owners. Some are quite small, handling the outdoor activity in country towns. Others are huge enterprises with thousands of signs that may be found in a number of states. Small or large, however, the outdoor advertising company's work is just about the same. It includes:

Single-post construction.

Lack of ground space is answered by this single-post construction which puts a rotating painted bulletin 66 feet in the air and in clear view of motorists on nearby Santa Monica Freeway. Courtesy of Foster and Kleiser, A Metromedia Company.

(1) Locating and renting, from the owners, suitable locations. (Because of dense construction in cities and multiplying legal restrictions in the country, this first task has become one of the most difficult.)

(2) Putting up the outdoor structures, such as 24-sheet panels or painted bulletins.

(3) Contracting with advertisers for rentals of the posters, bulletins, or walls.

(4) Affixing the sheets on the 24-sheet or 30-sheet panels or painting the painted displays.

(5) Maintaining the outdoor structures, whether posters, painted displays, or spectaculars. Maintenance includes policing the areas, replacing defaced or torn sheets, and keeping the lighting in perfect condition. The trimming of obstructing trees and vegetation is also included in the price for which the outdoor advertising unit is rented to the advertiser.

Plant owners—and it must be remembered that these are the official and reputable representatives of the outdoor advertising industry—obtain most of their revenue from the rental of the standardized forms of outdoor advertising. Plant owners also obtain considerable revenue from all kinds of sign work, including neon signs, painted signs for storefronts, and all the other types of outdoor advertising that may be seen in or around a city. These nonstandardized forms of outdoor advertising are prepared in the same shop in which the bigger units are prepared.

Searching for properties on which to erect outdoor advertising has become almost a nightmarish occupation for plant owners, who in most areas have more advertisers who want to rent posters than they have posters available. Outdoor advertising continues to have a great appeal for advertisers, even as locations disappear in the face of zoning laws and the vanishing of empty city lots.

Getting Business

A plant owner's business will be local, regional, and national. Most local business will come in without solicitation or will be obtained through the efforts of the plant owner's salespeople. The bulk of the standardized business, however, will be from regional and national advertisers, and most of this business will be placed through advertising agencies.

If the outdoor advertising is for a local advertiser, the plant owner may supply the copy and artwork for the client. Regional and national advertisers usually have their creative work performed by their advertising agencies. In addition, the agencies, the outdoor representatives, and the advertisers will have previously worked out details of the budget, the kind of market coverage needed, and the duration of the outdoor campaign.

Showings

When talking about a poster "showing," the outdoor person refers to the number of 24-sheet posters being used to carry an advertiser's message during a contracted-for poster period.

Swept-wing panel.

Another double display of 24-sheet posters offers visibility at the top and additional display space at the bottom of the pole. Courtesy of Foster and Kleiser, a Metromedia company.

Intensity of market coverage is indicated by the numbers given the showings. A 100-showing, for example, is applied when the number of posters used is large enough to provide an even and thorough coverage of a market. Sometimes it is called a No. 100-showing and sometimes a 100-intensity coverage. Occasionally it may be termed "full" coverage. A company not wishing to spend so heavily in outdoor advertising may content itself with a 50-showing, or half the posters needed to cover the market thoroughly.

Market size, number of traffic arteries, and population density will determine the number of posters needed for different coverage patterns. In rural areas one or two posters may provide 100-coverage. In a market such as the Chicago area 300 posters will be needed for 100-coverage. For a crash campaign an advertiser may use as much as 150-coverage in order to saturate a market. Many advertisers, on the contrary, use a 50-coverage in numerous markets because they would rather cover more markets with 50-intensity showings than cover fewer markets with 100-intensity showings.

Counting Traffic

Quantity of circulation is determined by counting traffic passing a poster. Counting can be done by tabulators who record each passerby, or it can be done by mechanical counters. Traffic counts are made at certain intervals during the day and, to save a total count, the actual traffic results are worked out through an accurate mathematical formula.

No. 100-showing.

Some idea of the saturation achieved by a No. 100 showing is gained by studying the distribution of the 24-sheet posters represented by the dots. All important roads and streets have the advertiser's posters.

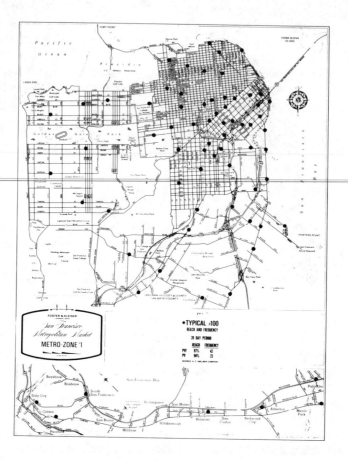

After making the count and adjusting certain factors, the outdoor companies can calculate the net advertising circulation, sometimes called NAC. In talking costs, an outdoor advertising man usually will not discuss actual costs immediately. Rather, he will mention costs in terms of cost-per-thousand net advertising circulation. Although total cost may be high, a poster showing may have such a good net advertising circulation that cost per advertising impression may be very low.

Quantity of circulation is not hard to discover, but to ascertain the quality of that circulation is a much more difficult task. Each person passing a poster cannot be stopped and asked if he or she is a potential customer for the advertised product. Although license plates may give strong clues, they leave some points unanswered. Again this question is of more concern to a retail advertiser than it is to a national advertiser.

Classes Of Traffic

An outdoor sign is evaluated in terms of the traffic that passes the sign. However, it is not enough to lump all vehicles in one designation of traffic, since there are several important differences. A passenger car, for example, will be valued more as traffic than will a truck.

Traffic is classed in the three following ways:

- Class A: Passenger automobiles dominate. A small mixture of truck, street car, or bus traffic might be found.
- Class B: A general mixture of passenger automobiles, trucks, and street cars, or buses, as compared to passenger automobiles, may actually dominate, the traffic, or they may constitute a considerably higher percentage than in Class A or Class B traffic.

Not only the kind of traffic but the kind of location or neighborhood must be considered when making an accurate evaluation of the worth of outdoor showings. In order to achieve such accuracy, posting areas are classified as residential, retail, and manufacturing.

Questions About Location Important To A Retailer

There are several important questions about location which should be answered before a decision is made to use outdoor advertising:

Should the outdoor poster be next to the store doing the advertising?

With 24-sheet posters the answer is not so simple. In a sense the storefront and the store sign constitute an outdoor advertisement. A 24-sheet poster doesn't add much to the store's present visibility. Placed down the street, on an approach to the store, the poster can cause people to think about the store's offerings before they reach the store. Then, when they are near enough, the store itself acts like an outdoor poster. Thus, the store's personality and its offerings have been registered twice. If, however, the storefront and its sign do not stand out from neighboring stores, the retailer could well use an adjacent poster.

Outdoor posters also have a psychological effect. For example, a major oil company found that within the company and among the company's dealers there was much debate over where to place 24-sheet posters that were used in large numbers by the company. The company had reached these conclusions:

- Our stations are distinctive because of their outside color and their architectural design.
- Prominent name signs give strong identification. Auto traffic, bus traffic, and pedestrian traffic can tell immediately what kind of gasoline is being sold.
- Sensible marketing strategy is not to put the 24-sheet poster next to the station, but down the street or road from the station. Then a prospect sighting the station itself will have had a double-reminder about the product.

What made sense to the company officials was not convincing to most of the company's station operators. They could not see the poster down the road, but they could see the poster next to the station. For this reason, and despite arguments from company advertising people, many of the company's posters were erected immediately adjacent to the stations. Somehow it was reassuring to station operators to have a big poster looming over their station even if logic said that the poster might do more good down the road.

Should a poster be located to be visible to traffic coming in or going out of the business district?

Many retailers prefer incoming signs. To most national advertisers, outgoing or incoming traffic is of equal value. Their desire is for heavy traffic no matter which way it is going. If traffic is outgoing, they have no worry, since the traveler can buy the product in the next town.

Retailers, in contrast, want the product bought locally and in their stores. Unless they have branches in the next town, they should think carefully before advertising to people who are leaving the business district. If they rightfully think of outdoor posters as point-of-purchase advertising, then the maximum benefit from an outdoor poster is gained when prospects are on the way to the stores, not when they are going away from them.

Should a poster be two or three blocks from one's place of business, or just outside town?

Size of the town will, obviously, affect the answer to this question. Assuming that the town is not a large one, there are several possible answers. If the poster is placed outside of town, it is likely to have fewer distracting influences around it, and to have a longer reading time. On the negative side, however, a poster's impression can be erased by other impressions that the viewer encounters before reaching the store.

Thus, if a sign is placed a few blocks from a store, it may account for the last advertising impression made before the store comes into view. If, on the other hand, the driver must go through heavy traffic, stoplight, pedestrian traffic, and business districts, then the retailer's poster may get little attention even if pedestrian and auto traffic are heavy. A retailer considering the use of outdoor advertising should drive by possible locations and imagine how a typical motorist would view it in order to evaluate the worth of a particular location.

Is it better to have the poster at a stop sign, or is it better to place signs in open stretches?

Outdoor advertising at a traffic light will in theory get longer reading, but many motorists waiting for the light to change watch the traffic and the signal, not the poster. The motorist driving on an open stretch sees the poster far ahead, and when the advertising message is close enough, the driver can read it and think about it, free from the distractions that bother people at traffic lights. Under open highway driving conditions, the reading of poster messages is almost inescapable.

Ethnic Outdoor Advertising

Sometimes, especially in certain big cities, the placement of outdoor posters will be determined by the presence of large numbers of non-English speaking residents. Coverage of ethnic markets can be important to advertisers. Once

again, the flexibility of outdoor advertising is demonstrated. Ethnic groups can be covered block by block with posters that have special graphics and are written in the language predominant in the neighborhoods where the outdoor advertising is placed. Putting up posters with copy written in English would largely be a waste in such areas.

Backing New-product Promotions

In backing a new-product promotion, a question arises. Must a poster campaign precede distribution of the product, or should posters appear only after distribution of the product is obtained? When the advertiser is not well known in a particular territory, it will be to the manufacturer's advantage to have the posters up at the same time that the advance salespeople make their calls. Dealers will be assured by the sight of the advertising backing the product. Since the advertiser will almost certainly be advertising in other media, the local outdoor campaign provides powerful backing for the other media, such as magazines and television.

If a product is known and has already obtained good distribution, the question of posters preceding the salespeople is not so important. Nevertheless it is usually desirable to tie in the outdoor advertising as closely as possible with other forms of advertising that may be breaking just then in behalf of the product.

Poster charges, unlike the charges in magazines that are tied closely to circulation, will not be higher or lower in exact accordance with the population density of areas. A high-traffic city area will, however, command more money for its posters than a lightly traveled rural area.

Repeating 24-sheet Posters

Readership, it has been demonstrated, actually increases when the good magazine or newspaper advertisement is run the second time. And, frequently, a continuing increase in readership will be noted when the advertisement is run more than two times.

Yet the almost unvarying procedure in outdoor advertising is to change the 24-sheet poster in a showing each 30-day period despite outdoor advertising research conducted by Daniel Starch and Staff that shows strong outdoor posters obtain improved observation scores with repetition. In a study of twenty-three food posters, for example, the average observation score was 20 percent higher on the repeat showing than on the first showing. This was true despite an interruption of a month or more between showings.

The reason for the increased observations on the repeat showing, according to Dr. Starch, is the fact that people do not immediately become aware of the existence of the poster. Over the course of time, however, many additional people begin to notice the poster. Some people notice the poster on the first day, some notice it for the first time on the second day, and so on.

Thus the level of perception of an advertisement is influenced by the number of repeat exposures that occur. It is logical to suppose, therefore, that by repeating an outdoor poster we can produce a rising level of perception. This is because a high percentage of the population becomes aware of the poster during the second 30-day posting period.

Rating System For Showings Of Outdoor Posters

The national advertiser who uses many outdoor posters should consider every factor that relates to the effectiveness of his posters. One of those factors, for example, is the way each poster is rated in terms of its physical circumstances. Over the years a rating scale has been developed that is useful for evaluating the total effectiveness of the posters making up an advertiser's showing. This scale is often used when the advertiser or a representative of his advertising agency "rides" a showing. ("Riding" a showing consists of inspecting each poster in the showing. The inspection is done by someone representing the advertiser and a representative of the plant owner.)

There is no complete uniformity in rating scales. Moreover, rating scales have an unofficial status in the industry because they vary from area to area, and because they vary according to the individual who is using them. However, they are used throughout the outdoor advertising business and no matter how they vary, they are usually concerned with certain physical factors such as:

- Length of approach
- Angle of poster panel to traffic
- Proximity of poster panel to others
- Distance of poster panel from the road (not the same as length of approach)
  - Character of obstructions (poles, girders, foliage, other signs)

A booklet of the Traffic Audit Bureau, *Standard Procedure for the Circulation Evaluation of Outdoor Advertising,* contains an official rating method. The method recommended by the booklet is much more precise.

CREATING OUTDOOR ADVERTISING

Overshadowing every other consideration in the creating of successful outdoor advertising is the fact that exposure time to the advertising message is so short. A motorist traveling at 35 miles per hour has only about five seconds to read the advertising message if the poster has a 250-ft approach, even less time if the poster shares the location with other outdoor advertising. Even the very short identification announcements on television give a longer exposure of the advertising message. A creative person approaching the task of making a good poster advertisement must never forget that the posters will be read hurriedly and often under the most difficult of conditions.

Keep Posters Simple

Simplicity in poster creation takes a number of forms. Simple ideas are easily grasped at a glance. When reading is so brief, and very often distracted, a subtle idea will not be understood, nor appreciated. Short, simple words and very few words should be used. It is difficult to say just how many words should be used in a poster. Some very successful posters have used just one word. Other good posters have used more than 10 words. Normally, however, the range will be 4 to 7 words. A good rule to follow is to use but one idea to a poster. Local advertisers, anxious to "get their money's worth" from a poster or a painted bulletin, will sometimes try to put over more than one idea, and the result is confusion.

Simplicity.

This painted bulletin creates appetite appeal through attractive visual treatment. No words are needed except those on the container. Courtesy Foster and Kleiser, a Metromedia Company.

Simple artwork is as important as simple words and ideas. There is no place in posters for complicated "arty" artwork. Lines should be clean-cut. Line drawings and clear simple photographs will stand out on a poster.

Use Ideas That Register Quickly

In outdoor advertising there are usually just two types of creative approach: posters with ordinary ideas, and posters with such striking ideas that the poster is read with appreciation, remembered, and talked about. The poster with the ordinary idea can still be effective for the advertiser simply because repetition of the main point will eventually register with viewers.

The posters that bring striking results, however, are the ones that carry ideas that cause instant reactions among the viewers—reactions of laughter, desire, appetite, thirst, excitement, and even fear. Because ideas must register quickly, emotional art and copy approaches serve well in outdoor advertising. Viewers respond instantly to emotional appeals and more slowly to logical ap-

Human interest appeal.

This poster's message uses only 7 words to draw strongly on the heart strings in order to loosen the purse strings.

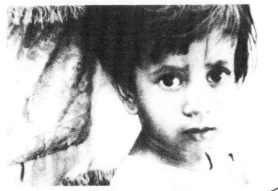

HUNGER IS ALL SHE HAS EVER KNOWN

Christian Children's Fund, Inc. Richmond, Virginia

peals. Babies, dogs, beautiful scenic views, pretty girls, appetizing foods, and shiny dream automobiles reach out powerfully from outdoor posters to evoke strong emotional response from those who pass.

The most powerful posters of all are those that combine a strong emotional appeal with a copy or an art twist that makes the total effect irresistible. These are the famous posters that are long remembered, and at the time they appear they are recognized instantly as having that magically different quality. It is this "difference" that every creator of outdoor advertising should strive for. Sometimes the "twist" is achieved without emotion.

Poster with a copy twist.

This award-winning poster uses simplicity and cleverness to deliver its strong message.

Shoplifters get free signed prints.

Make Suggestions

Some of the most powerful outdoor posters suggest that the viewer do something, such as, for example:

> Save shoe leather . . . Use the Yellow Pages
> Remember Holly Sugar
> Don't be a dishwasher . . . BUY ONE
> Trapped by bills? Get a Timeplan Loan!
> Put 'em up with cane . . . C and H sugar
> Have more fun going . . . go PHILLIPS 66
> Pick a Pack buy Bud
> Need protection? See your Prudential agent
> Keep freedom in your future
> BUY U.S. SAVINGS BONDS

One of the principles of good salesmanship is to ask for the order or at least to suggest either forcefully or gently that the prospect follow some course of action. Each of the foregoing examples has the vitality that is created through suggestion, from the ask-for-the-order Timeplan Loan suggestion to the mild reminders about Holly Sugar and Goodyear tires.

Use of suggestion.

This painted bulletin combines a suggestion with a play on words. Courtesy of Foster and Kleiser, a Metromedia Company.

Stress Visibilty

Humorous approach.

Clever humor is an ingredient of many successful outdoor posters such as this award-winning example. (Courtesy of General Telephone & Electronics Corporation).

Designs that are complicated, lettering that is hard to read, and colors that make the poster difficult to see from a distance should be avoided. Presumably, every advertiser is aware of these points. Yet, anyone seeing the parade of posters along the highway, soon realizes that the principles of poster creativity are constantly violated. Many times these difficulties are caused by artists who, in their anxiety to express themselves artistically, forget that the first purpose of an artist creating an outdoor advertisement is to make certain that it can be read easily, quickly, and from a distance. Abstruse designs, script and other forms of "fancy" type (and too much type), and background colors kill visibility of the copy message.

One of the surest ways to reduce the readability of the poster message is to make a bad choice of colors for the lettering and the background. Many experiments have been conducted to determine the relative legibility of various color combinations. In the main the experts agree which combinations are good and which are bad. The following list, which gives the relative legibility from the most legible to the least, of color combinations, can serve as a guide in the designing of an outdoor poster:

Relative Legibility of Color Combinations

1. Black on yellow
2. Green on white
3. Red on white
4. Blue on white
5. White on blue
6. Black on white
7. Yellow on black
8. White on red
9. White on green
10. White on black
11. Red on yellow
12. Red on green
13. Green on red

Another factor in visibility is the size of the lettering used for headlines, copy, and other matrial such as logotypes and figures. Following is a table (supplied through the courtesy of the Foster & Kleiser Company) that shows the legibility of lettering in different sizes:

Height of Letter	Will Read At
2 feet	840 feet
1 foot	420 feet
6 inches	210 feet
3 inches	105 feet
1 inch	35 feet

Should Posters Adapt To Other Media?

When approaching the task of creating a poster campaign, it is well to consider whether the campaign will be stronger if it is a direct adaptation of a campaign running in other media, or whether it should pay no attention to other campaigns and should blaze its own creative trail. There is no "right" answer to this question, since either course may be followed. Generally speaking, advertising is strongest when all media advertising is following the same campaign idea. If the outdoor campaign can do so without losing strength in its own right, good. If, however, the campaign approach does not adapt well to the peculiar limitations of poster advertising, then the creative person should be allowed to create the strongest campaign possible for the outdoor medium and connect as well as feasible to the campaign in other media, but should not be held rigidly to the campaign format employed in other media.

Realistic painted bulletin.

It is impossible to ignore this startling display. Courtesy Foster and Kleiser, a Metromedia Company.

Ready-Made Posters

Although most of the 24-sheet posters are made especially for the national advertisers displaying them, some posters are ready made. These stock posters are very useful to local advertisers, who can buy them in any quantity. This fact is important to an advertiser who wants the quality reproduction obtained through lithography, but who does not use enough outdoor posters to justify having specially lithographed poster sheets developed. Lithographers who produce stock poster sheets make them in large quanitites, thus spreading the high cost over many units. Since it is only the poster design that is reproduced, the local advertiser can have the correct name and address printed at the appropriate spot on the poster sheets.

In addition to being inexpensive, the stock poster is often created by very fine artists and is reproduced by first-rate lithographers. A local advertiser, therefore, can be proud to have the company name appear on such posters, since they are usually better than any posters produced locally.

Despite the fact that stock posters may lack the individuality of outdoor advertising made especially for the particular advertiser, they are often offered in a wide enough choice to enable the advertiser to find a design and copy message that suits company needs perfectly. This is especially true in the case of banks, dairies, bakeries, florists, furniture dealers, and others whose offerings are much like those of their competitors. Furthermore, only the advertiser and the supplier of stock outdoor advertising know that the outdoor posters are stock posters. As far as the general public is concerned, the stock outdoor display is simply an attractive example of outdoor advertising—often an unusually attractive example. Any local advertiser interested in 24-sheet posters in small quantities should investigate stock posters; that is, if desirous of first-class outdoor advertising at low rates.

RESEARCH FINDINGS FOR OUTDOOR ADVERTISING

For years the most-used data offered by the outdoor industry to advertisers who wanted to know the effectiveness of outdoor advertising in reaching their customers were the figures developed by the Traffic Audit Bureau and given to advertisers as "daily effective circulation." Such reports could not be connected with households, as could figures for magazines, newspapers, and other media.

Because outdoor advertising reaches people on the move, it was very difficult to pin down just where the outdoor audience was coming from, and until that information was obtained the advertiser could only guess at the composition of the huge number of prospects passing his outdoor signs.

The automobile accounts for about 90 percent of outdoor traffic. But simple traffic counting was not enough to trace automobile movement past the outdoor showings back to the households. Thus, license numbers came to be recognized as holding the key to where the drivers were coming from, permitting the evaluation of repeat trips past outdoor signs.

The importance of the license-checking method is proved by the fact that more than 90 percent of retail purchases are made outside the home, and that, in most cases, the automobile provides the means for the retail customers to travel between home and the stores.

"Teaser" outdoor poster.

A "teaser" poster usually has an intriguing line of copy and/or illustration but it is obvious that more is to come. The "teaser" is posted for about 10 days and then the message is completed. See the completed message in FIGURE 00.

Completed message for "teaser" outdoor campaign.

Here is the whole message and advertiser identification that followed the poster shown in FIGURE 00.

W. R. Simmons & Associates Study

An outdoor advertiser needs certain facts about the medium to determine the value of its use for his product or service. In addition to the usual demographic information, he wants to know how fast he can reach his market with outdoor advertising. There has been some suspicion that reaching the bulk of the market with an outdoor showing will take a long time.

According to research conducted by W.R. Simmons & Associates, and reported in the booklet "This Is Outdoor Advertising" (issued by the Institute of Outdoor Advertising), a No. 100 showing reaches more than 80 percent of the adults in a market during the first week of exposure. Such speed is especially important to an advertiser introducing a new product, or promoting a special offer, or a new label.

By the end of the normal 30-day posting period, the same message will have been exposed to 89.2 percent of the adults, the Simmons study revealed.

Frequency of exposure is considered in the same study. Here, it discloses, adults in the market will have been exposed to the No. 100 showing 31 times during the month.

As for the demographics of the market so reached, the Simmons study showed that the No. 100 showing reached 92.5 of the 18-34 age group 30.4 times a month and the 35-49 group attained even higher levels. This latter group had a 94.2 percent reach and a 36.1 frequency.

Likewise, reach and frequency rise as incomes rise. For example, reach was 95 percent and frequency 34.4 times per month in households with more than $10,000 per year.

Lastly, the Simmons study indicated a strong correlation between high reach and frequency and better education. This was demonstrated by a 96 percent reach for those who attended or were graduated from college. This is in contrast to the 76.9 percent reach for those who were not graduated from high school. Better educated people were higher in frequency ratings, too, with a 36.1 times per month figure for this group.

Further figures about the outdoor advertising market have been supplied in a 1975 study of TGI (Target Group Index). Among the highlights of the study:

- People who see the most outdoor advertising are almost 3 times as likely to earn $25,000 a year as the average person.
- The more a person sees outdoor advertising the more likely this person is to be a top-income adult, while the reverse is true for prime-time television and radio.

In 1978, another study by TGI offered proof of the accuracy of some of the earlier studies of TGI and Simmons. This latest study used a modest No. 50 national showing. Despite this below-normal showing, the figures indicated that such a showing will reach 80 percent of the population. Men will be reached an average of 15 times and women 13 times.

The same study showed that 87 percent of the 18 to 34-year-olds will be reached 15 times and 84.5 percent of the college graduates 15 times.

A significant change in the composition of the outdoor audience is the greatly increased number of working women who can be reached by the medium.

3-dimensional painted bulletin that makes strong positive suggestion.

Gross Rating Points

In order to enable advertisers to compare outdoor advertising more logically with other media, the industry has adopted a gross rating point system similar to that used in television advertising.

To demonstrate how this is applied to the outdoor advertiser, here is an example provided by the Outdoor Advertising Association of America.

Suppose, in a market of 1,000,000 population, a combination of poster panels provides 750,000 total impression opportunities each day. Such a showing would be delivering 75 gross rating points daily. Thus, in a standard 30-day contract, the showing would be earning 2,250 gross rating points monthly.

Application of the GRP system can give the advertiser a method for obtaining desired impression-weights on a comparable market-to-market basis.

In terms of cost efficiency, as expressed in cost per gross rating points, and cost per thousand, outdoor advertising asserts that it offers lower costs than any other medium. To support this assertion, the Institute of Outdoor Advertising says in its 1975 booklet "The First Medium" that outdoor advertising delivers its audiences in most places at less than 35 cents per thousand, compared to costs of $1 to $3 per thousand for network television.

Outdoor poster with humorous play on words.

TRANSIT ADVERTISING: INTRODUCTION

For years, people in transit advertising, when selling their medium, pointed with pride at the use of transit advertising by the William Wrigley Company. "Wrigley," they would say, "has a card in every transit vehicle in the United States. *There's* proof of the medium's worth."

Sad times came, however. Wrigley's commitment to inside cards in transit vehicles ended about the same time that many other transit advertisers disappeared. Today (at the time this revision is being written) to the elation of the transit industry, the Wrigley Company has once again plunged into transit advertising. Its initial commitment is $500,000, enough to enable the company to place four 11″ × 14″ cards per bus in 56 selected markets. This move followed research the company conducted.

Wrigley's confidence in the medium comes at a good time because the growth of superhighways and shopping centers, along with other developments, has decreased the use of public transportation, with an accompanying decrease in the use of transit advertising. Yet those engaged in the medium speak optimistically of the future. When they view the choked highways they visualize the revival of downtown shopping and improved public transit systems. Many urban planners believe that only public transportation can provide the solution to traffic problems. If public transportation makes the comeback so confidently predicted, transit advertising will also be revived because the medium has certain advantages that make it appealing to both national and local advertisers.

Improved research methods have contributed to increased interest in the transit advertising medium. Some of the most advanced research techniques have made it possible for advertisers to determine the readership for transit advertisements.

In discussing the medium, many writers have put transit advertising under a general heading of outdoor advertising. This was a peculiar handling in the period when transit advertising was almost wholly confined to inside transit cards. Transit advertising then had almost nothing in common with outdoor advertising except that it appeared on cards roughly the proportion of outdoor posters.

Today, however, there is more sense in the connection between outdoor advertising and transit advertising because of the intense use of advertising on the *outside* of transit vehicles. Still, there are many differences between outdoor advertising and transit advertising. The latter, found on buses, trains, street cars, subway cars, and other public conveyances is a most effective medium in its own right. It has earned the right to an independent status. About 65,000 moving public-transportation vehicles carry advertising messages either on the inside or the outside. More transit advertising appears in stations and platforms for railroads, subways, and elevated trains.

Outdoor message with positive suggestion.
A clever illustration and strong copy make this public service advertising notable.

Make America smarter.

Give to the college of your choice.

Characteristics of Transit Advertising

Transit advertising is the only national advertising medium whose capital expenses are not supported in a major way by the advertiser. Costs for the medium are low because the capital costs of the advertising space used are paid for by the fares collected. There is no investment needed to operate the basic business associated with the medium. In contrast, the outdoor advertising business has a huge capital investment in equipment.

Despite the impressive number of transit vehicles and the amount of yearly paid fares—about $2 billion and the approximately 7 billion riders—the total annual advertising billings of the industry (around $40 million) are tiny as compared with the billions invested in such media as newspapers and television. To most advertisers, transit advertising is not a truly major medium, either in total dollars spent or in the importance given to it when marketing and advertising plans are being formulated. The great majority of advertisers view it as a useful supplementary medium that can efficiently back up the advertising in other media.

Repetitve Value.   Men and women are creatures of habit. When they use the transit system they take the same routes day after day, and, as much as possible, they even take the same vehicle at the same time. Shoppers also travel the same routes many times, and because the inside cards in transit vehicles are usually shown for at least a month, riders are repeatedly exposed to the advertisers' messages.

This repetition was confirmed in a study of ridership of transit in urban Canada (1975) where it was found that the average member of the general population used transit 11 days a month. In a typical month the average person is exposed to transit advertising at least 11 hours during weekdays alone. On the average weekday this person makes more than two separate transit trips.

The importance of these findings does not rest in the fact that people ride but that the more frequently they ride the more often they are exposed to transit cards. This exposure soars of course in the case of the millions who ride back and forth daily to work.

Escape from Boredom.   People engaged in transit advertising seldom mention a point which could possibly be one of the strongest selling points for the medium. That is, with the exception of outdoor advertising, it cannot be said of any other medium that prospects seek out an advertiser's message eagerly in order to overcome the boredom caused by their surroundings. A daily transit ride is no pleasure jaunt for most adult passengers; it is something that must be endured. Transit advertising offers relief to the rider who is looking about for something to break the tedium of the journey. The atmosphere surrounding the reading of the transit message under these circumstances is certainly far more favorable to the advertiser than is a television commercial that interrupts a program the viewer is enjoying. A transit advertiser, in contrast, has an audience that likes to have the opportunity to read the message.

Long Exposure to Advertising Message. Many studies have measured the average length of transit rides. These have been conducted in various cities throughout the United States. The average ride reported is 22 minutes in duration. This figure is generally accepted, although some studies have reported a somewhat longer average ride.

The length of ride, therefore, presents a unique advantage for transit advertising. It has already been established that the transit riders making the same trip day after day read transit cards to escape boredom, and it is significant to the advertiser that transit riding prospects are given ample time to read and to reread messages. This long exposure time to an advertising message is unmatched by any other medium. Reading is almost forced on the captive transit audience. Riders moreover, not being able to escape the cards within vision, will often read them a number of times during one ride.

Although transit riders usually will not sit in the same seat day after day, transit companies rotate positions of cards from vehicle to vehicle. Such rotation helps assure all advertisers an equal opportunity to have their advertising messages read. Position of transit cards does not, however, have the importance imputed to position by advertisers in newspapers and magazines.

Low Cost. To get some idea of the low cost of transit advertising, an advertiser could simply tally how much it would cost to be on every radio station for a month, or every television station, or in every magazine, or every newspaper. No other medium can be bought in its entirety at such a low total cost a month, or at a lower exposure cost per 1,000 viewers.

Consistently the audience for inside cards can be reached for less than 20 cents per thousand viewers and for outside cards about 35 to 40 cents a thousand.

King-size outside transit unit.

Outside cards such as this are popular with advertisers and have been used with especial enthusiasm by banks and other media.

Shoppers' Medium.   Although it is difficult to praise transit advertising as a medium that is useful for reaching the supermarket shopper—because transit riding and carrying heavy bags loaded with groceries do not mix—many studies have shown that transit advertising reaches vast numbers of people who are on their way to shop downtown.

By providing continuity of impression for advertising messages right up to the point of sale, transit advertising becomes especially powerful for downtown stores and for nationally advertised products sold in those stores.

Humorous inside transit card.

Transit riders welcome entertainment as they ride. This card provides a light moment while putting across its main copy theme.

Use of Color.   Rich, full color is a characteristic of transit advertising. Where eye appeal and appetite appeal are important, transit cards offer opportunity for unexcelled color reproduction. Color opportunities offered in transit cards appeal especially to local advertisers, who often cannot afford the use of color in any other mass media, or who will not find color available even if they can afford and want to use it.

FACTORS THAT LIMIT USE OF TRANSIT ADVERTISING

Because transit advertising rarely requires a major promotional investment, most advertisers do not concern themselves with exhaustive analysis of the pros and cons of the medium. If the transit-riding market needs to be covered, or that part of the market that sees the *outside* cards, the medium is there to be used. Little thought is given to its limitations. Still, these should be considered.

Some Important Groups Missed

Although transit research has produced many impressive figures about the broad range of occupations, income levels, and educational groups represented in the transit riding audience, the fact remains that the transit advertising misses some important segments of the population. Included in these are rural dwellers; many of the important business, professional, and government leaders; and many suburban dwellers who use automobiles to get to work, and to do their shopping in suburban shopping centers.

In defense of transit advertising, its 7 billions of annual riders do include many of the "important" groups of people. And although it is true that rural dwellers do not use buses, this point is less important now than before because most of the people who live in the United States are concentrated in metropolitan areas.

Does Not Get Quick, Traceable Sales

Transit advertising is generally thought of as a long-range form of advertising, especially useful for reminder purposes. Wrigley Gum illustrates this use for the medium.

Most advertisers do not use transit cards for quick sales results. Yet, used vigorously and correctly, the medium offers opportunities for quick response. This was illustrated during a heavy campaign for Frito-Lay potato chips and corn chips, products bought on impulse. This company reasoned that since 85 percent of all supermarkets are located on bus routes, transit advertising could suggest purchase of their products right up to the time the housewives entered stores. The transit advertising was used to reinforce the company's daily radio and television advertising.

Lack of any noticeable effect on sales has discouraged many advertisers from continuing with the medium. This is especially true because advertisers often view transit advertising merely as a supplement to their major advertising efforts in other media. Because it is considered a supplementary medium, it is usually the first medium to be dropped, especially when nothing seemed to have happened as a result of using the medium. This harsh treatment is often unfair because the medium should usually be bought for long-range effect, not for direct-action results.

KINDS OF TRANSIT ADVERTISING

New Development

One of the most striking changes in transit advertising in recent years has been the intense interest in the use of outside displays. Once, when transit advertising was mentioned, it was understood that the discussion would be about inside cards. Today, because of the changed status of the outside displays the outside units have been standardized in size, and sales interest is often greater for outside displays.

Inside Cards. Just as the 24-sheet poster has become the standard size in outdoor advertising, so has the 11 × 28-in. card become the standard inside card for the transit advertising field.

The sizes most found commonly are 11 in. × 14 in., 11 in. × 28 in., 11 in. × 42 in., 11 in. × 56 in., and 11 in. × 84 in.

Subject to what is offered in the individual transit systems, other inside cards are available. Front-of-the-bus positions, for instance, often called "bulkhead" positions, are sold under special arrangement. Cards occupying these front positions are sold at a higher rate than the side cards and are not so standardized in size as the 11-in.-high cards.

An 11 x 28 in. INSIDE transit card.

This card uses poster technique.

Outside Displays. Outside displays, now a big money-maker, were a hodgepodge of sizes until recent years. Then the Transit Advertising Association recommended that outside displays—or posters as they are frequently called—be standardized not only in size, but also in name. Where once all outside units were called "traveling displays," they are now individualized by different names and sizes.

The industry still changes these names and sizes from time to time. Furthermore, not all the different types are offered by all systems. The following, however, represent the outside displays most often offered by transit systems:

King-size 30" × 144" (These displays are especially effective when they incorporate a play on words, or use humor to put over a point)

Queen-size 30" × 88"

Traveling displays 21" × 44"

Taillight spectaculars 21" × 70"

Headlighters (Headlight spectacular) 21" × 40"

A new development is the Metroform spectacular. This is printed on adhesive sheet plastic. It can be varied in shape and size. Usually, it takes up big space on the side of the bus; in fact, it can go all the way from the front to the back of a vehicle.

Merchandising Buses

An advertiser deciding to make dramatic use of transit advertising may use a merchandising bus. This is a public transit bus chartered by an advertiser and filled with promotional materials, displays, and product samples. Fitted with inside and outside posters, the merchandising bus carries its promotion of the advertiser's product directly to distributors and retailers.

King-size outside transit poster.

This 30″ x 144″ transit sign flags passersby and motorists. It is, in a sense, a moving outdoor poster. Such signs are very popular with advertisers because of the wide exposure they give their messages.

Station Posters

Station posters are found principally in and around big cities on station platforms for railroads, subways, and elevated railways. Although size may vary from city to city, posters are available in the following sizes in the New York City Market:

One-sheet: 46 in. high × 30 in. wide
Two-sheet: 46 in. high × 60 in. wide
Three-sheet: 84 in. high × 42 in. wide
Six-sheet: 66 in. high × 12 ft. wide

Some idea of the observation potential for station posters may be gained from the claimed monthly circulation figures for this media. In several metropolitan areas these posters are on suburban railroad platforms, and in rail, ferry, and bus terminals. The following circulation figures were supplied by Transportation Displays, Inc., a company that sells, puts up, and services station and terminal posters.

TABLE 17-2
Monthly Circulation Figures

Area	No. of Terminals	No. of Stations	Monthly Circulation
New York area	18	263	55,486,000
Philadelphia area	5	90	5,000,000
San Francisco area		46	12,000,000
Chicago area	5	100	12,526,000

Take-One Cards

A useful device is the take-one card, which is often really not a card but a sheet of paper that is part of a pad affixed to a transit card, or in other cases an actual card hung on a "vendor" hood near the transit card. Sometimes the "card" is contained in a pocket located on the transit card. Riders can tear off the cards, fill them in, and either mail them or bring them to the advertiser. "Take-ones" are used for the same purpose as a coupon and are often designed in the same way, but because they are bigger they can hold a greater sales message and can explain in detail just what the offer is about.

An astounding number of "take-ones" may be used up in a single week on a transit system but, unfortunately, all is not profit for the advertiser. Hundreds and even thousands may be torn off by curiosity seekers or by vandals. Take-ones are the special target of children. Still, despite the wastage that is almost inevitable, take-ones have a good record. As a promotional device for developing sales leads or for getting information into the public's hands, they can be quite valuable.

To obtain best results with take-one cards, there are two important rules to follow:

(1) Have an offer that is good enough to make it worth the reader's time to tear off and fill in the card.

(2) Promote the take-one in the copy and illustrations on the transit card. Call attention to the take-one and urge people to fill it in.

Take-one card.

There is plenty of time during the average transit ride for the rider to fill out the required information on this card. When the rider leaves the transit vehicle, the card can be dropped into the nearest mailbox—a tidy, easy operation.

FIRST CLASS
PERMIT NO. 1143
NEW YORK, N.Y.

BUSINESS REPLY MAIL
No postage stamp necessary if mailed in the United States.

Postage will be paid by

The Bowery Savings Bank
Life Insurance Department
110 East 42nd Street
New York, N.Y. 10017

Gentlemen: I would like your expert opinion about life insurance. Please send me more information.

Name_____
(please print)

Address_____

City_____State_____Zip_____Phone_____

Age_____ ☐ Married ☐ Single Number of children_____

I am interested in:

☐ Term Insurance ☐ Straight Life ☐ Endowment ☐ Family Plan
☐ I'm not sure which policy is best for me . . . please give me some ideas.

THE BOWERY
The Largest Savings Bank in America

M

SIZE AND CHARACTER OF TRANSIT AUDIENCE

Generally speaking, transit riders belong to what would be called the wage-earning working class of average education. Except for train-riding suburbanites around some of the very large cities, the transit vehicles are not heavily used by those of superior education and job status.

Still, as a group, transit riders (40 percent of whom own their own homes) make up an important buying segment of our population. Although their buying tendencies may not run toward art objects and other items of luxurious living, they provide a big market for goods and services needed in everyday living.

TABLE 17-3
Monthly Rides (12-month Average in Twelve U.S. Cities*)

City	Metro Area Population of Cities	Number of Vehicles	Rides Monthly
Atlanta	1,848,200	753	6,393,468
Baltimore	2,163,400	1,000	10,097,722
Boston	2,876,900	1,700	46,001,021
Chicago	6,960,300	4,000	51,744,924
Cleveland	1,966,000	1,000	8,314,071
Los Angeles	6,907,300	2,400	20,345,000
Miami	1,481,200	513	5,183,118
Minneapolis-St. Paul	2,024,200	1,000	6,831,162
Philadelphia	4,787,300	2,300	30,891,588
St. Louis	2,354,900	973	5,167,257
San Diego	1,564,400	300	2,979,051
San Francisco	3,163,200	900	13,921,095

*Based on 1977 SRDS figures

An idea of the impressive chances for the exposure of transit advertising messages is conveyed when one contemplates the New York City transit riders. Just on the subway system alone the monthly rides average between 140 million to 150 million, plus.

What About Recall?

A study in Canada by Daniel Starch (1975) revealed that among the heavy users of transit in Toronto, the recall for individual inside cards ranged from 32 percent to 93 percent with the majority of the scores running between 60 percent and 90 percent.

In almost every case, recall was in the higher levels when a full service run of cards was used. Few half-service runs achieved high recall figures.

Another study in Toronto (1976), also by Daniel Starch, of King-Size outside posters, showed a recall range for individual posters of 15 percent to 70 percent for men, and 13 percent to 73 percent for women. Most of the recall scores, however, were well above the minimum figures.

24-sheet poster.

Outdoor posters have been used for marriage proposals, for reconciliation attempts by husbands, for job-hunting and, in this case, by a person desperate for basketball tickets. Outdoor advertising is strongest when it plays upon emotion—humor, tragedy, suspense.

Income Levels Of Riders

Despite the rather firmly held opinion that transit riders are largely in the average-wage class, Brand Rating Research study in 1971 revealed that subway advertising in New York reached 43 percent of all adults in $10,000-and-up households in the 17-county New York-New Jersey area. The same study showed that the subway advertising also reached 52 percent of all adults in $25,000-and-up households.

Another study made in 1977 by Pulse, Inc. for Transportation Displays, Inc. (TDI) re-emphasized the point that much of the transit audience enjoys a high income level. This study, made of people who buy wine, found that the use of in-car displays and station posters reached the up-scale audience that dominates the wine market. Of this audience, 42 percent had incomes of $25,000 and over, and more than 47 percent had college degrees.

BUYING TRANSIT SPACE

Almost every city in the United States with a population of 15,000 or more has a transit system that permits advertising inside or outside its vehicles, and most of these systems are under contract to an advertising company that handles the sales of transit space. Occasionally, the transit system will handle

Long-copy inside transit card.

With 92 words and some numbers this transit card does not employ the brevity of an outdoor poster. The length of the copy will not daunt the transit rider who has ample time to read and think about messages posted near where he sits or stands.

advertising arrangements directly. However, this practice is unusual and normally found only in bigger metropolitan areas.

Each transit advertising company handles the sales and servicing of local accounts and the card arrangement in the vehicles. Sometimes the company will also handle the selling of national accounts, especially in the larger cities. Some companies engaged in the national sales field supply sales representation for individual companies, in the large advertising centers throughout the country.

Much of the national and regional advertising is placed with the local transit advertising companies by advertising agencies. Some local business is also placed this way, provided the advertiser employs an advertising agency. As compensation for its various services, the recognized advertising agency is given a discount from the list price of the service.

When an advertising agency is involved in the purchase of transit advertising it will almost always provide copy and artwork for its client. Likewise, it will handle production details, such as the selection of proper typography and getting transit cards reproduced by a suitable method. It will then have the cards delivered to the transit system for mounting in the spaces selected.

If the advertising is placed directly with the transit advertising company by the advertiser, the transit advertising company will help the advertiser by planning and placing the advertising. People not knowing the name of the transit advertising company in any city can obtain the information by asking the transit company.

Schedules

Advertising space in transit vehicles is sold in "runs." A full run is a card in every vehicle. If a card is placed in every other vehicle, it is a half-run. A quarter run placed a card in every fourth vehicle. These three "runs" are the most common. Some transit systems, however, use only full runs and half runs, and some offer only full runs.

Normally, transit advertising is sold by the month, with rates quoted on the basis of 12 months of continuous use. Higher rates go into effect should the contract be for fewer than 12 months. Short-term rate differentials are illustrated by the accompanying figures for a transit system in New York state:

Discounts Applicable to All Space

Months	Schedule In One Year	Discount
3	×	5%
6	×	10%
12	×	20%

Inside transit card with copy twist and take-one slips.

Transit riders with time on their hands can decipher the headline message and then decide whether to fill out one of the take-one slips in order to obtain more information about the service offered. This card offers another example of how differently the creative person can treat the transit card than the fashioning of an outdoor poster.

Three factors are behind the variations in transit advertising costs: (1) length of the run, (2) kind of run—whether full, half or quarter, and (3) size of the space used.

Rates go up, of course, in big cities that offer more vehicles as in the New York subway system with its 7,000 cars. Full service in 11" × 28" cards costs an advertiser $24,977 per month on a month to month basis. If the advertiser takes a yearly contract, the figure lowers to $18,733 per month. Contrast this with a yearly contract on the 45-bus Orlando-Disney World system where a full service run of 11" × 28" cards costs $72 a month. These figures are based on 1977 rates in SRDS.

Any advertiser wishing to discover rate information can ask the transit companies for rates applying to the towns in which advertising is to appear. Or can look up the rates and other date in the transit advertising section of the Standard Rate & Data Service (SRDS) rate schedule, which is published monthly and which carries rate information for all important transit systems in the United States.

Rates for outside space and for station posters are also offered by Standard Rate & Data Service's transit advertising section. A transit advertiser should realize, however, that complete as the listings in Standard Rate & Data Service seem to be, there are many individual arrangements that can be worked out by the transit advertising company. Spaces and schedules can be tailored to fit advertisers' needs. Outside bus posters, for example, can be changed in some special situations just as often as the advertiser wishes—daily if necessary.

Station poster.

Station posters such as this attract the attention of hundreds of thousands of transit riders in subway station, and railroad platforms. Humorous treatment of art and/or copy is desirable to catch the gaze of hurrying riders.

Outdoor poster with a clever art twist.
An interesting illustration can convey the outdoor message quickly and make even an ordinary piece of accompanying copy seem clever.

Producing Transit Cards

Advertisers supply the cards to be used, and either the advertiser or the advertising agency will place the printing order. An advertiser with no agency may ask the transit advertising company to handle this detail.

For national campaigns, fine-grade letterpress printing or lithography is used. Because their printing runs are shorter, regional and local advertisers may use silkscreen printing, which produces very acceptable cards at less expense. Nearly all transit cards use color, which means that the concern doing the printing should be carefully chosen. Much valuable information about production requirements may be found in the opening pages of the transit section of SRDS. Directions are given regarding proper paper stock, sizes, and printing.

The cost of producing cards varies according to the number printed, the colors used, the printing process employed, and the size of the cards.

When ordering a run of cards to be printed, the advertiser should ask the printer to make a slight overrun of cards for replacement purposes should cards be defaced in the transit vehicles.

A national transit advertiser will usually change cards monthly. A local advertiser, more cost-conscious, will very often change cards only every six months in order to cut down production expense.

Use Of Cards For Display

A local advertiser who wishes to obtain even fuller use of transit advertising cards should have a number of extra cards included in the usual printing overrun. These extra cards can then be used for window displays or for interior displays. Such displays can be especially useful to banks, one of the largest users of transit advertising. Most of the bigger banks have many branch offices, and transit cards can be very useful as display material in the branches as well as in the main office. Such double usage of the cards provides fine coordination of transit advertising with point-of-sale advertising. If a similar campaign theme is being used in newspapers, the coordination is even more complete.

CREATIVE IDEAS FOR TRANSIT CARDS

"Baby billboards" is a phrase sometimes used to describe transit cards. Persons using this phrase have given a somewhat erroneous idea of the creative approach applied in creating transit advertising. Transit cards are not "baby billboards." True, they have some points of similarity. They have essentially the same horizontal proportions. Both make extensive use of color. Some of the same creative ideas may be applied. Here and there an advertiser may use what might be called a "poster" technique in all his cards.

But despite the foregoing points of similarity, there is one factor that makes it unrealistic to apply literally the "billboard" concept to transit cards. That factor is the environment in which transit cards are read. Included in this environment are much longer reading time and different physical circumstances, which require that transit cards use different techniques in printing and artwork.

High-readership transit cards will, in general, have certain elements in common. Some will have several of these elements, some will have all the elements, and some will have only one or two. These elements include:

- Human interest
- Medium-length copy
- Simple layouts
- Strong color
- Illustration of product or package
- Interesting headlines
- Dominant illustration

As suggested, some of these same techniques are shared with outdoor advertising. The person creating transit advertising must, however, provide a number of elements as described.

Allow For Transit Reading Conditions

Before designing a transit card the creator should take many rides on buses, subways, or streetcars to study the physical circumstances under which riders read cards. It will be found that most cards are read by seated passengers, and that they will be read from an angle as the riders look upward. Standing passengers, likewise, view the cards from an angle an seldom from a full-front view.

Rate sheet for outdoor showings.

An advertiser wanting to know how much it will cost him for different types of coverage in a market will consult a rate sheet such as this. It shows the proportion of illuminated and un-illuminated posters, costs and the gross rating points earned by different showings.

SIZE	UNILL. PANELS	ILLUM. PANELS	TOTAL PANELS	COST PER MONTH	DAILY GRP
150	156	714	870	$164,640	
100	104	476	580	109,760	100
95	99	452	551	104,260	
90	94	428	522	98,760	
85	88	405	493	93,320	
80	83	381	464	87,820	
75	78	357	435	82,320	75
70	73	333	406	76,820	
65	68	309	377	71,320	
60	62	286	348	65,880	
55	57	262	319	60,380	
50	52	238	290	54,880	50
45	47	214	261	49,380	
40	42	190	232	43,880	
35	36	167	203	38,440	
30	31	143	174	32,940	
25	26	119	145	27,440	25
20	21	95	116	21,940	
15	16	71	87	16,440	
10	10	48	58	11,000	

SOUTHERN CALIFORNIA METRO-PLEX

Population: 10,683,400

Los Angeles -Long Beach; Anaheim - Santa Ana -Garden Grove; Riverside - San Bernardino -Ontario; San Diego, SMSA's.

When applicable a 20% continuity discount will be allowed.

Rates and Allotments quoted above are for general coverage showings only. Coverages other than general in composition are available on an individual quotation basis.

Our observer will note, too, that the cards in the sideracks are curved to fit the shape of the vehicle. In some vehicles this curve is strongly evident. Lastly, most reading is done at a distance, except for the occasional standing rider whose nose may be almost pressed against the card directly in front.

Now what effect do these factors have on transit card creation? First, because it must be assumed that all reading is done from a distance, headlines and copy must be in type that is of a legible design and is big enough for easy visibility. For lowercase type, 24- or 30-point size is usually recommended. Such a type size will be helpful to the person with poor vision, and about 50 percent of Americans are in this category. Eye tests show that the average person can read 3/8-in. type at 20 ft. but, despite this figure, it is best to test the visibility of the print on a number of persons before accepting it. Another rule of thumb is that a card obtains most of its readership from the three seats on either side of it. One simple test often made by creative people to check readership of type on a card is to drop the card on the floor and to view it from a standing position.

Second, because the cards are sometimes curved in the side racks at the top side of the transit vehicles, it becomes harder to read printed material at the top of the cards than at the bottom. Headlines, product names, or the advertiser's name will, in this situation, be better placed at the bottom or the middle of the cards than at the top.

Because of the unusual reading conditions, typography should be especially simple, with a minimum use of script type, capital letters, and italics. Too many different kinds of typefaces in one card are undesirable, too.

Entertain — Use Humor

If the product or the service is suitable, the transit advertising message can use humor or entertainment. Human interest cards, showing people in situations that arouse an instantly sympathetic response, have much appeal to a rider who, bored by the daily ride, is willing to escape by reading the advertising within sight. Humor is especially good in lifting the rider from the humdrum situation.

Time after time, the best-read cards are those cards that cause a chuckle, or which arouse sympathy or interest for the person's plight in the illustration.

Long copy inside transit card.

In this card we find a demonstration of the fact that transit cards are not "baby billboards." Because of long riding time, the transit card can use much more copy than a 24-sheet outdoor poster, or a painted bulletin. Riders often welcome long copy as an escape from the boredom of the ride.

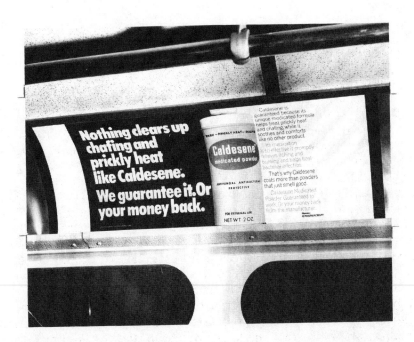

Keep Copy Short—Usually

Some of the outstanding transit cards have carried long copy messages, many running to more than 100 words and others carrying charts and tables in addition to lengthy copy. Copy for transit cards should, nevertheless, be brief unless there is a strong reason for being long. Here "brief" does not mean the five, six, or seven words usually carried on outdoor posters. Roughly, transit advertisers should limit their copy to about 25 words. If the advertiser's copy story cannot be limited so severely, it is possible to use much more copy than the 25 words, because the audience has more reading time than is available in outdoor advertising. Instead of the flash reading given outdoor advertising, transit advertising has one of advertising's longest reading exposure times, 25 to 30 minutes.

Readers have time to weigh every word, to read charts, and to study figures, and they will do so if the messages is interesting enough and the advertiser does not use so many words that type must be reduced to an unreadable size in order to crowd it in the space. Still, despite the possibilities for long copy, it is best to give the sales message cleverly, clearly, and briefly.

Make One Sales Point

Because copy is generally brief and because the card's working space is limited, it is important to make only one sales point to a card. To attempt more will only lead to confusion. To hold to one point in a transit card is simply following the principle recommended for any kind of mass media advertising; the only difference here is that because of space limitations the point is even more valid.

Taillight spectacular.

Placed on the outside of the bus this is, in a sense, a traveling outdoor poster that displays its message to motorists and pedestrians in all parts of the city.

Use Few Elements

Some transit cards are a hodgepodge. Others have a simplicity that causes their copy messages to flash out at the reader clearly and forcefully. The former may use a jumble of headlines and subheads, along with illustrations, company names, product names, slogans, and copy blocks. The latter may use only a package and a person in a happy or unusually interesting situation. This card may or may not use words. If the artist has done the job well, the picture may tell the entire story.

Two important prinicples should be observed in maintaining simplicity: (1) if in doubt, cut down the number of elements, and (2) while holding down the number of elements, make one element clearly dominant. By so doing the creator of the card is giving the reader something to focus upon.

Feature Packages

No better opportunity for package registration is available than that afforded by a long transit ride. Also, since almost all transit cards are in full color, the package can be shown just as it will look on the supermarket shelves. If a package product is being sold, the picture of the package may be the element about which the card's message is built.

Make A Suggestion

Remember that the rider may be taking the same ride from a half-hour to an hour or more every working day of the year. Time after time this person may be exposed to the advertiser's card for these long, unbroken periods. Even allowing for the fact that much of the time may be spent reading newspapers, sooner or later the rider is going to see the cards nearby. If each time a card suggests: "When you need a loan, see First National," "Drink Coca-Cola," "Change those old tires now"—the suggestion is going to be impressed strongly in the rider's consciousness with the result that it will be acted upon almost automatically the first time that the advertiser's product or service is needed.

Have A Twist, Angle, Or Gimmick

In this respect a transit card is like an outdoor poster. If it has the unusual turn of phrase, or an illustration with a striking unusualness, it has a chance to be a great card. It may be talked about, remembered, liked, and acted upon. Few cards have this difference. The card without the difference may do a very workmanlike job for the advertiser and may be a good business-builder. Yet anyone creating transit advertising should always try for the card with a twist, because it is that kind of card that stands out on the side racks and makes the rider respond.

Local Advertisers Can Use Stock Transit Cards

Local advertisers who wish to achieve the professional touch for their cards, but who do not want to spend the money necessary to accomplish this, can find stock cards that have been designed for a wide range of businesses.

These cards are obtainable at low cost because they are printed in great numbers. Copy and artwork, while not individualized to a specific advertiser, are well done. A space is provided for the dealer's name and address. When this information is printed on the card it is ready for use. The whole arrangement, of course, is similar to the stock outdoor posters described earlier in this text.

QUESTIONS

1. Opponents of outdoor advertising are misdirecting their attacks. Who should be the target of their anger?

2. For what reasons is outdoor advertising seldom the major medium for big-budget advertisers?

3. What are the three types of large posters?

4. Name and describe the two major types of painted displays.

5. What is an advantage of the rotating bulletin to the advertiser?

6. As an advertiser, what would you expect a plant owner to do for you?

7. Why are emotional appeals effective in outdoor advertising?

8. Is transit advertising usually considered a major or supplementary advertising medium? Explain.

9. What advantage does transit advertising offer that is unmatched by any other medium? Discuss.

10. In what sense is transit advertising a shoppers' medium?

11. What are two factors that limit the use of transit advertising?

12. Name common sizes for inside transit cards. What is the "standard" size of inside transit cards?

13. What is a "take-one" card? What are its pros and cons?

14. Describe the functions performed by transit advertising companies?

15. On what bases are rates determined that are charged buyers of transit advertising?

16. What kind of printing process is generally used for transit advertising cards?

17. What creative techniques does transit advertising share with outdoor advertising? In what respect does a person writing transit advertising depart from outdoor creative techniques?

18. Who uses stock transit advertising cards and why?

Section V
PROMOTIONAL AIDS OF ADVERTISING AND MARKETING

ADVERTISING'S SPECIAL MEDIA

ADVERTISING'S SPECIAL MEDIA

In a suburban home a 16-year-old boy flips open the telephone book to the yellow pages before heading for the nearby shopping center. He needs some work done on his Garrard turntable. Quickly, he finds a display advertisement that tells him that Simon's Stereo Shop sells and services the Garrard.

In the same home, the boy's mother makes a notation about a bridge date on a calendar page. Without thinking, and for about the fiftieth time, she sees the name Citizens National Bank. The bank gave her several such calendars on January 4.

Downtown, the boy's father opens a matchbook in order to light a cigarette before a conference. Idly, he notes a message on the inside flap that lists Italian food as a specialty of the Villa Venice restaurant.

That night the boy's older sister, soon to be married, watches the big screen at the drive-in theater. Showing now, after the feature film, is a theater-screen advertisement for Gibson refrigerators. This interests her because she'll be furnishing a new home in the near future.

A Mixture Of Advertising, Promotion, Marketing

Ask our family members to define advertising and all of them would undoubtedly refer to television, magazines and other mass media. Yet, all of them on this day, and many other days, have been helped by these less spectacular forms of advertising. And they *are* advertising, and they work. In fact, three that were mentioned—yellow pages, calendars, and matchbooks—work 24-hours-a-day.

Thousands of national and local advertisers will never use television or national consumer magazines. To them "advertising" means these special media, and nothing else. To others, the special media are properly put under a heading of "promotion." To satisfy both groups, think of the special media as part of the advertising-promotion-marketing mix. Many thousands of persons in the

United States make a profitable and interesting living as experts in the special media.

This chapter is especially concerned with:

- Telephone book advertising (Yellow Pages)
- Specialty advertising.
- Matchbook advertising.
- Theater screen advertising.
- Industrial directories and guides.

Lest anyone consider that these activities are in the minor leagues of advertising and promotion, it may be said that literally billions of dollars are spent in these areas of advertising and marketing. Likewise, in terms of the number of users, totals are impressive. Thousands of businesses, for instance, that use no mass-media advertising media make constant use of matchbooks, calendars, circulars, trade conventions, and other items in the foregoing list.

When an advertiser uses promotion vigorously, the media and aids mentioned here are not usually used as the major promotional effort but simply as supplementary backing to reinforce the advertising program. An advertiser may be willing to spend substantial sums in this backing but normally these sums will be a minor element in the total promotional budget.

Most often, then, the special media described in this chapter are considered *after* the money has been allotted for the major media. Few big advertisers, for example, will consider matchbook expenditures *first* in their planning, nor will they budget for specialties such as calendars and memo pads before they allot money for newspapers or magazines.

Then there are the advertisers who view almost all these special media as a deplorable frittering away of advertising funds. Such an advertiser may say: "Why water down the advertising budget with these frills? It makes more sense to concentrate advertising expenditures in the major media. These others are just extras that swallow your funds and cause you to wonder at the end of the year why you haven't gotten more for your money."

In some instances, such objections are valid. In other cases, they do not apply since the "extras" may be badly needed in order to make the major advertising media work to their full efficiency. Certainly this can be true in the case of telephone book advertising.

Yellow Pages Advertising

More familiarly, telephone book advertising is known as "Yellow Pages" advertising. Also, it may be called "telephone classified" or, more formally, telephone directory advertising. More than 150 million directories are distributed each year.

Whatever it is called, however, the advertising on the yellow pages of phone books is a powerful result-getter. It is such an obviously efficient and necessary form of promotion for local and national advertisers alike that it is baffling to consider that the medium needs to be sold, and sold hard. It would seem that it was the one form of advertising that should be bought automatically without any sales pressure needed.

Yellow pages display advertisement.

Much useful information is packed into this nonetheless very readable yellow pages advertisement. With its good copy and use of illustrations, it can serve as a model for advertising of its type.

Possibly the best way to determine what an enormous selling force is constituted by telephone directory advertising is to ponder some of the statistics of the industry gained from almost 20,000 personal interviews. Some of the facts especially interesting to advertisers:

- 93.2 percent of the time people who use the yellow pages take action by phone, visiting, or writing.
- 58 percent of yellow pages usages were for personal reasons.
- 42 percent of yellow pages usages were for work or for business.
- In 52 percent of the cases, people could have used the white pages but used the yellow pages because it was easier to do so.

It may be added that these figures were pertinent at the time of the book's 2nd edition. The Yellow Pages experts consulted for the 3rd edition reported that further surveys simply confirmed the original figures. Differences were so slight that the original survey is still valid except for minor variations in individual markets.

There is literally no product or service that is not offered in big city telephone directories where as many as 4,000 different headings may be listed.

In Chicago, long noted for the impressive thickness of its yellow pages book, subscribers are even given a choice of *two* "Red Books," as the business directory is called. These now smaller directories are:

(1) The "B" directory going to all Chicago subscribers, residence and business. It contains product and service classifications used by homes and businesses.
(2) The "C" commercial-industrial directory going to all business subscribers. It lists product and service classifications of manufacturers, wholesalers, distributors, fabricators and business services.

Yellow Pages Locate Outlets of National Advertisers

One of the vital tasks of every national advertiser is to make certain that people who read advertisements know where to buy the advertised goods or services in their local communities. For such an advertiser an advertisement in the Yellow Pages says: "You have a nationwide office when you let 'OPERATOR 800' handle your telephone calls and messages." In addition to being a useful method of increasing a company's direct response business, the use of free 800 numbers to locate local dealers has been increasing. Along with the supplying of the name and address to the inquirer, the service may also include forwarding such leads to the business concerned.

National advertisers use much space in print advertisements to list their dealers in different cities. This technique has been especially useful in the case of manufacturers who market a somewhat exclusive line that is not widely distributed in each city. Macintosh raincoats provide an example.

Although such dealer listings are powerful, localizing push has also been supplied by the "Consult your yellow pages, or, "Let your fingers do the walking" phrase which has come to be so familiar to millions of Americans faced with the problem of just where to get an advertised product, now that their desire for it has been aroused. Other advertisers may use the phrase: "Dealers are listed in most classified phone directories." Regardless of the phrase used, consulting telephone directories to find advertised products and dealers has become a way of life for most adult Americans.

How National Advertisers Use Yellow Pages Advertising

Thousands of companies use yellow pages advertising as part of their national advertising campaign, chiefly for the reason already discussed—to direct potential customers to local dealers.

Where once the details concerned with many telephone directories for national advertising were enormous, they have been simplified so that advertisers and advertising agencies are no longer so daunted by the job.

Although there are still some out-of-the-ordinary difficulties connected with the buying and placing of telephone directory advertising, the problem as a whole has been made markedly easier through the establishment of NYPS, or the National Yellow Pages Service. This service makes it possible for advertisers to buy display space or listings in as many as 5,000 different local classified telephone directories without arranging the purchasing with each of the numerous publishing companies involved. All the buying and placing procedure is handled through one local telephone company representative or selling agent who serves as the advertiser's account man.

If an advertising agency is involved it will find that regardless of the complexity of the program or the number and location of the directories, it is necessary to sign only one contract. Furthermore, the agency receives only one monthly bill. Likewise, the agency gets its usual commission on such business.

Take the situation of a typical advertising agency in the pre-NYPS days. Wanting to list its client's exclusive distributors in 350 local directories in 50 states, the agency was forced to negotiate with each telephone company, or even each directory. Mechanical and copy specifications, closing dates, and other details varied greatly. Hundreds of contracts would need to be signed. Likewise, hundreds of bills came from everywhere each month. Resulting paperwork was a huge and never-ceasing task.

Because of the change, agencies now are more willing to engage in telephone directory advertising even though this activity still involves some detailed work and a new vocabulary. Furthermore, the advertising agency is aware that if clients will plunge heavily into telephone directory advertising the results from national advertising may improve and the agency's position with clients will be firmer.

SPECIALTY ADVERTISING: A SUPPLEMENTARY MEDIUM BUT A BIG ONE

Each year thousands of business firms engage gladly or reluctantly in advertising's greatest giveaway. Millions of customers, prospects, or just plain people who are neither customers nor prospects, benefit from this large-handed generosity. What they will get from the business-firm donors is a fantastic variety of items ranging from the very useful to assorted gimcracks of minimum utility. Useful or useless, these items are referred to here as *specialty* advertising items although very often they are lumped under a heading of *novelty* advertising, or novelties.

Facts And Figures Of Specialty Advertising

Although most consumers cannot explain what is meant by the term specialty advertising the specialty advertising industry would obtain their respectful attention if consumers knew, for example, that about $2 billion are spent yearly on advertising-specialties, or that just one company has distributed $5 million in advertising specialties and gifts in one year. In calendars alone, that account for about one-third of the specialties, it is estimated that enough are produced each year to supply one to each person in the United States. Like telephone directory advertising, specialty advertising is often not used by advertising practitioners, especially advertising agency people who tend to concentrate their attention upon the so-called major media.

With 10,000 to 15,000 specialty items available to carry advertising messages, such advertising can be *target* advertising over which the user exerts direct control of circulation, distribution and cost, unlike mass medium advertising. It is often combined with another medium, direct mail, because many specialties are sent through the mail.

As a means for business people to advertise to other business people specialty advertising's impact was impressive as shown in a survey by Creative Research Associates, Chicago, that was discussed in a 1977 release of Specialty Advertising Association International. The survey reported that:

60% of the business people reported used specialty advertising.
98% had at least one specialty item available.
50% had nine or more specialty items in their offices or on their person.
70% recall was recorded for the advertiser's message on specialties received during the previous year.

Investigations indicate that most advertising specialties distributed are used. One company distributing 65 million advertising specialties in one year, for example, reported that an estimated 75 percent to 85 percent were used.

Although advertising agency people, and the big national advertisers may not view specialty advertising very seriously, their nonchalant attitude toward the medium is more than made up for by the hundreds of thousands of small and middle-sized advertisers who faithfully and enthusiastically use specialties each year. Banks, insurance companies, service organizations, and retail stores are just a few of the myriad of businesses that find specialties a valuable link with their customers and prospects.

Defining Specialty Advertising

Although it would be easy to define this medium by simply naming some of the objects that constitute specialties, it is necessary to be somewhat precise in the definition in order not to confuse specialties with premiums, a confusion that rather frequently occurs.

A specialty is an item, most often a *useful* item, that carries with varying emphasis and efficiency the name (and possibly) a selling message of an advertiser. As reminder advertising it is usually given free to customers and prospects, although the specialty is sometimes sold.

The principal difference between a specialty and a premium is that the specialty is imprinted; the premium is not. There is nothing on the premium to associate it with the advertiser. It is just the same as any other item bought from a retailer. In contrast, the specialty tells the recipient from what company it was derived.

Thus, the premium is a reward that carries no advertising message; the specialty's only reason for existence is to carry such a message from the donor to the recipient. An advertising specialty can be called a form of advertising medium; the premium is actually not an advertising medium but an inducement that causes people to read advertising and to take buying action. Unlike the premium, the advertising specialty user does not require recipients to buy any products in order to obtain the specialty.

Reasons For Using Specialty Advertising

Most obviously, specialty advertising is used as a reminder. It is hoped, of course, that goodwill will be created through this gift that says without words: "We appreciate your business." Such a gift also says wordlessly to prospective customers: "We'd appreciate *having* your business."

Another strong reason for the use of specialty advertising is to reach markets that may be difficult to reach with conventional media, or that might be better appealed to with specialties. Such is the children's market that is very responsive to certain types of gifts such as knives, rulers, notebooks, coloring books, and pencils. If a specialty is popular with the younger set, the specialty-giver can rely on word-of-mouth to help reach great numbers of young people swiftly, which means, of course, that the advertising message is being delivered where the advertiser wants it to be delivered.

Sometimes the market may be so very small and specialized that it would be too expensive to reach with mass media. Perhaps the target may be a group of company presidents, or possibly medical specialists. Direct mail and/or specialties might offer the most sensible ways to approach them, and, possibly, the only ways. A technique often used is to send out the specialty to such a group and then to follow up with direct mail. Sometimes, as previously mentioned, the specialty and direct mail go out at the same time.

Specialties have been useful for "softening" prospects that salespeople often find difficult to approach. An example: housewives. Another: retailers. If the call by the salesperson is preceded by the specialty frequently the reception is likely to be more cordial. This has been especially true in the case of door-to-door salespeople who so often are viewed with suspicion. The specialty not only helps in the first calls of these salespeople but also makes the second calls more agreeable to the housewives, or to the men of the house.

Lastly, the specialty may, because of its use, provide a valuable reminder of the specific products or service sold by the giver. Calendars for freight shippers or fishermen are in this category. Then there are paint stirring sticks, aprons, or caps given by paint advertisers, or by paint or hardware stores. Slotted cards, furnished by stationery stores, to help typists erase neatly are tied directly with the products sold by the specialty giver.

Sometimes, specialties reflect the fads of the moment such as imprinted T-shirts, currently popular. Other specialties have a seasonal slant; plastic wind-shield scrapers are an example. Ash trays and ballpoint pens, on the contrary, are in the "old reliable" class of specialty, always useful and acceptable.

Occasionally, a specialty serves an important, more subtle function than simply offering a good-will gesture. An example is afforded by Boise Cascade, a large lumber company. In their case, they used a specialty to counteract the widespread feeling that lumber companies that cut down trees are automatically insensitive to environmental concerns. The specialty they used was a Gro-Stik that resembled an ice cream stick. It was actually a planter that contained three pine seeds in a water-soluble base of fertilizer.

Once the stick was pushed into the ground, the seeds sprouted. A press release about the item resulted in 93,222 sticks being distributed in five month. Twice after that, the company reordered. With each stick bearing the name Boise Cascade and the company's slogan "Trees are America's renewable resource," the campaign brought a favorable image of the company to schools, youth groups, ecology groups, and others concerned with the environment.

What Makes A Good Specialty?

(1) *Real usefulness.* Puzzles and whistles fall within the novelty advertising category but their usefulness, in contrast to that of memo pads, letter openers, pencils, and many other specialty items, is limited. The useful specialty will be appreciated and retained longer.

(2) *Long-lasting.* The longer a specialty items lasts, the longer it will be reminding customers of the advertiser. Paper hats, matchbooks and memo pads are likely to be gone long before such items as ash trays, key tags, and calendars. On the other hand, to be fair to matchbooks, the cost is so little that one can afford to give them for a long time and still spend no more than is spent on some of the longer-lasting but more expensive specialty items.

(3) *Carries a real message.* The advertiser cannot put a very useful message or reminder on a pencil, a corkscrew, a mirror, an ice pick, a flyswatter, or a thermometer. If one *cannot* put a good message on the item, this item immediately becomes proportionately more expensive than the specialty that allows an adequate message to do its selling job for a long time.

(4) *Constant use and constant sight.* The item that is in constant *use* and constant *sight* is to be preferred. Card cases, buttons, license holders, souvenirs, and yardsticks might be appreciated but it is unlikely they will be seen often enough, or used often enough, to make them as vauable as other specialties to the advertiser.

(5) *Low-cost.* Specialty givers run the risk, if they give specialties to some customers and not to others, that they may offend those who were not recognized. If cost is the factor that causes the advertiser to omit some customers from giving, it might be wiser to give an item of lower cost and thus take care of *all* customers. The list of those who are scheduled to be given specialties tends to grow each year. Unless the advertiser keeps the cost of the specialty down the use of this advertising may be swallowing too much of the promotional budget.

(6) *Personalized.* If possible, the item should be personalized so that the recipient's name appears on it. Since this type of personalizing is likely to be quite expensive, this procedure is not mandatory but suggested, if possible.

(7) *Possible to mail.* Mailing charges for a heavy, bulky item can make a specialty too costly to use. Even a moderately heavy or bulky item might not be feasible if the list of recipients is very large and widely scattered.

Most specialty items cannot meet the seven qualifications just listed. The calendar does. It is, therefore, the most popular specialty, providing a good advertising vehicle for local and national advertisers.

Once You Give, Do You Dare To Stop?

One giver of specialties voiced the feelings of many who dispense specialties when he said: "I hate to think how long we've been sending out these things (calendars), but darned if I know whether one single person has done business with us because we hand him or her a specialty each year. You should hear the gripes though if we cut people off the list. I don't have the nerve to stop, but believe me I've thought many times about doing so."

Once committed to sending specialties to a regular list, it takes a brave business person to stop. Yet many would like to do so. Still, with all the doubts, advertisers continue their use, good times or bad. Annual figures, in fact, show a steadily increasing use. Giving and getting specialties are national habits.

SMALL, BUT BIG—MATCHBOOK ADVERTISING

Millions of pockets, purses, drawers, auto glove compartments, tables, desks, bars, hotel room, ashtrays, and counter tops hold the ubiquitous matchbook with its advertising message. No matter where you are, the question "Got a match?" produces an instant response because the 18 billion matchbooks distributed each year to 75 percent of the adult population find their way into all public and private places. And where the matchbook goes, there goes the advertiser's message.

No advertiser is too big, mighty, or dignified to use matchbook advertising. Such users are banks, investment houses, airlines, top corporations of all types, politicians, restaurants, and broadcast media. These organizations and individuals use two types of matchbooks: *reproduction* and *resale.*

Reproduction matchbooks. These are distributed by the advertiser. Hotels, restaurants, banks, and other local advertisers are the most frequent users of this type of matchbook.

Resale matchbooks. Unlike the reproduction matchbooks, advertisers do not buy the resale matchbooks, but instead pay for advertising space on a specified number of the books. Oddly enough, they never have them in their physical possession. After contracting for the space with the matchbook manufacturer, the latter then sells the books to a jobber, who in turn sells them to retailers who give them away to customers. National advertisers using resale matchbooks for promotion are estimated to spend around $3 million yearly for this form of advertising. Hundreds of national advertisers use matchbooks on a big scale.

When the other users of resale matchbooks are added, it is found that the total number of matchbooks on which they advertise (along with the national advertisers) amounts to many billions yearly.

Altogether annual distribution of resale matchbooks results in a total advertising expenditure of between $30 and $40 million by the more than 300,000 advetiser employing them.

A considerable money volume is represented, also, by the special reproduction matches that are made to order for individual business enterprises, including huge advertisers or down the scale to nightclubs and taverns.

In contrast to resale matchbooks that invariably contain 20 lights, the special reproduction matchbooks may have from 10 to 240 matches. Around 55 to 60 millions of dollars are spent on special reproduction matchbooks yearly. An estimated $40 million to $45 million of this sum is represented by advertising.

Determination as to whether an advertiser will use resale matchbooks or reproduction matches rests on how much control is needed over the distribution and placement of the books. Some of the big resale matchbook users such as cigarette companies or food companies look for wide distribution and saturation; the controlled circulation of reproduction matchbooks is not very important to them. Other advertisers, on the contrary, want close control since they send the matchbooks to a planned list of customers or prospects.

Appeals Of Matchbook Advertising

Matchbooks furnish these attributes to advertisers:

(1) They can flood a market with advertising reminders to everyone in that market.
(2) They can also provide those reminders *selectively* reaching only those prospects and customers the advertiser thinks are important in the promotion of his product.
(3) They provide an adequate space for a selling message. The number of words in the selling message is at least equal to the number found in many other advertising media.
(4) Because of low cost, advertisers can afford to put out enough matchbooks to provide almost endless repetition of their selling messages.
(5) Advertisers who are vigorous users of coupon offers find matchbooks a good location for coupons. An estimated third of matchbooks dispensed at cigarette and cigar counters contain coupon offers.
(6) They constitue a form of premium, an inexpensive gift that will be given to a retailer by a manufacturer for the placing of an order.

Is Matchbook Advertising Read?

There have been those in the advertising business who have had little belief that persons who carry matchbooks ever bother to read the advertising messages contained in the books. This judgment is made very often with the reasoning: "I never read the messages in matchbooks; I'd guess others don't either."

Yet every survey, in and out of the matchbook industry, seems to show that a sizable percentage of matchbook carriers—almost always smokers—*do* read advertising messages in their matchbooks. Quite a number do not, of course. Others read only infrequently. Others cannot remember the messages they have read or the names of the advertisers on the matchbooks they are carrying.

Despite the exceptions, enough men and women read matchbook advertising to make this form of promotion profitable to advertisers. Somewhat between 40 and 45 percent of the people who carry matchbooks are usually able to recall the advertising, according to studies. This figure compares favorably with the remembrance of advertising carried in other media.

While matchbooks cannot be considered a major medium and may actually be a waste of advertising funds for some advertisers, they are suitable as a low-cost supplementary medium for a good number of advertisers.

THEATER-SCREEN ADVERTISING: THE INESCAPABLE MEDIUM

In many motion picture theaters across the land, theater screen advertising is part of the scene, like popcorn and small boys running up and down the aisles. Yet, there are many residents of big cities who have never seen a theater screen advertisement. It is not generally a medium used in downtown theaters in big cities.

At some time or another however, theatergoers in most small-town theaters will be exposed between showings of the entertainment feature to a film that contains advertising for a national advertiser, and/or that sells the merits of a local business. This is theater-screen advertising.

Although such advertising is seen most often in small-town theaters, it will also be seen in outlying theaters in big cities, very occasionally in downtown theaters in big cities, and frequently in drive-in theaters.

Who Sees Theater-screen Advertising?

(1) *Number of theaters showing theater-screen advertising.* A majority of the thousands of theaters, including drive-ins, will regularly or occasionally show such films. The number of such theaters varies from week to week and from season to season, however, since many drive-ins close in the winter, some regular theaters close in the summer, and some theaters go on a reduced schedule at certain times of the year. Yet despite this uncertain pattern, opportunities for those who want to use theater-screen advertising are afforded from coast to coast.

(2) *Average number of people seeing motion pictures in a given week.* Although any theater owner can give advertisers a definite count of his audience for any given week—and this is one of the advantages for the advertiser since most media cannot give such precise figures—the figures on the national scale are not offered with such precision. Estimates for the number of persons seeing motion pictures nation-wide average over the year about 40 million weekly and about double that number in the summer months.

A Variety Of Advertisers Use Theater-screen Advertising

Although an almost endless number of local advertisers including banks and retailers of all types use this medium, there is an especially heavy use by the automobile companies which use theater films as part of national advertising or on a cooperative basis. Then, too, jewelry stores and jewelry store suppliers make strong use of the medium. Almost any type of advertiser, with exception of the "snob" type of advertisers such as the Rolls-Royce Company, the exclusive fashion shops, or ultra jewelry shops, can and does use theater-screen advertising.

What Does Theater-screen Advertising Offer The Advertiser?

(1) *Provides impact advertising.* There is probably no advertising that has more elements for creating impact than theater-screen advertising. A huge screen, brilliant color, motion that permits demonstration, and music and voices in sound provide more vigor possibly than any other form of advertising; it is bigger-than-life television, as it were.

(2) *Gives a captive audience.* Except for the children running up the aisle for popcorn, or the people who leave the theater between showings of the feature film, the audience rooted to the theater seats are compelled, willing or unwilling, to watch and hear the advertiser's message. Sometimes they show their resentment at being "captives" by talking during the showings of the commercial messages but in the main they see and hear what is being said. No other advertising medium quite duplicates theater-screen advertising in its captive audience aspects, even transit advertising.

(3) *Has a local flavor.* Advertising delivered in a neighborhood or small-town theater has a local intimacy. This aspect is especially true in the case of manufacturer-dealer advertising or films made especially for local advertisers. Many such films show local businesspeople whose faces are well-known to numerous persons in the theater.

Production And Showing Of Theater-screen Advertising

Production of this kind of advertising is usually handled by a firm that specializes in this work, not only in the production of the films themselves but in the booking of the films and in making all necessary arrangements with the theaters that show such films. Such a firm shoots the films, and makes all necessary contacts with motion picture theaters, manufacturers, and dealers. Different types of theater-screen advertising campaigns are as follows.

(1) *Manufacturer-dealer films.* This type of campaign is released in behalf of manufacturers who retail their products or services through dealers or distributors. The part of the film in each case that has to do with the manufacturer's product or service is 27 seconds long. In addition, another 13 seconds of film is spliced on to make a total length of 40 seconds. This second part is called a "personalized dealer signature trailer" and features the dealer. It may show the place of business and it may superimpose the address of the store over the picture of the place of business. Likewise, the audio message may give the name of the dealer and the address.

(2) *"Library" films.* The theater-film producer each year produces "open-end" films for a great many local businesses such as banks, drug stores, dairies, dry cleaners, florists, jewelry stores, and many other lines of business. These films concern these types of businesses but can be applied to any such type of business since they do not feature particular brands. Then, just as in the case of the manufacturer-dealer films, personalization is added through the addition of the signature-trailer.

(3) *National theater-screen ad films.* Some national advertisers have the film company produce one-minute, made-to-order films which are turned over to the film company for booking, shipping, storage, and theater-screening arrangements. Sometimes, of course, and this is true of the manufacturer-dealer films, the national advertiser may have films produced by an outside producer. In such cases, the company simply turns the films over to a theater-screen organization to handle all the other arrangements.

Advertisement with coupon.

Money-saving coupons flourish during competitive periods. They offer bargain to shoppers and increased sales to advertisers. In times of the present high prices, shoppers have become assiduous coupon clippers. In this instance, the coupon offer is handled well. Its generous size and attention-getting display are sure to obtain reader-attention.

Introducing Ken-L Ration Burger with Liver and Bacon Flavor Chunks.

INDUSTRIAL DIRECTORIES AND GUIDES

An unglamorous form of advertising, often not even mentioned in books on advertising, appears in books called "Directories." These books, chiefly used in the industrial field, give the names of manufacturers, location (or the names and locations of businesses offering services). Usually an adequate description of the product or service accompanies the other information.

Directories make a pronounced point of warning that they do not have "readers" in the usual sense. No one reads a directory as a magazine or book would be read. This person "refers" to it for information, usually in order to find someone who sells goods or services which the person is interested in buying. Many directories are "bibles" for certain industries and are referred to constantly; advertisers serving these industries simply cannot afford *not* to be in the appropriate directories.

Three Types Of Directories

In classifying directories, there are three types most numerous and most important—the general industrial directory, the vertical directory, and the functional directory.

General Industrial Directory.   This directory is referred to by all types of industries. In this category are the very largest directories that cover the nation and may contain hundreds or even thousands of pages of listings. Some of the more prominent directories of this type are:

- *Thomas Register of American Manufacturers*
- *Conover-Mast Purchasing Directory*
- *MacRae's Blue Book*

Vertical Directory.   Unlike the general character of the preceding directory, the vertical directory embraces specific industries. Big industries will almost always have a directory serving them. Advertisers with a very wide line of products may advertise in such directories only those products that would be of interest to the specialized industries referring to them. Advertisers with a very wide line of products may advertise in such directories only those products that would be of interest to the specialized industries referring to them. Some vertical directories are:

- *Post's Paper Mill Directory*
- *Composite Catalog of Oil Field Equipment and Services*
- *Electronics Engineers Master (EEM)*

Functional Directory.   This directory crosses industry lines but covers one function commonly found in the different industries. In the editorial material and the supporting advertising the person referring to such a directory will find products and sources that will help improve the performing of a technical or professional function. The directories are quite technical and speak the specialized language of persons working in the industries they service. Some idea of the specialized nature of functional directories is found in the titles of a few of them:

- *Hitchcock's Assembly Directory and Machine & Tool Buyers' Directory*
- *Data Processing Yearbook*
- *Telephone Engineer & Management's Directory and Who's Who of the Telephone Industry*

Taking *Thomas Register* as an example, we find one set of their directories simply furnishes listings. Another set provides specification sheets of numerous companies. In this set of catalogs, some advertisers mix in advertising copy with the technical information, thus selling as well as presenting. The catalogs are not, however, intended to offer advertising as their primary function.

QUESTIONS

1. Of what use is an 800 telephone number to a national advertiser?

2. What function is served by the National Yellow Pages Service (NYPS)?

3. Tell how a premium differs from a specialty.

4. Why is the calendar the ideal specialty?

5. What possible negative can be mentioned about the use of specialty advertising?

6. Name and explain the two types of matchbooks.

7. What percentage of recall is there for matchbook advertising?

8. What are three reasons for using theater screen advertising?

9. Define the different types of films available to theater screen advertisers.

10. What would you expect to find in an industrial directory such as the *Thomas Register* other than paid advertising?

19

TRADE SHOWS AND PREMIUMS

TRADE SHOWS AND PREMIUMS

Around the United States each year, a lot of business people can be heard making such remarks as the following:

"I'll meet you at the show."
"Look up our booth at the show."
"We're taking extra space at the show this year."
"It's pretty expensive, but I guess we'll be at the show again this year."

With about 5,000 trade shows going on each year, and billions of dollars spent in participation in such shows, these remarks could be made by persons representing many industries, but let's assume in this case they are from people planning to attend the big annual show of the hardware industry. Hundreds of firms will rent exhibit space to show new hardware items. Hardware retailers and wholesalers, wanting to look over the new lines, will come to the show from all parts of the United States. This annual show, like many others, is so important that exhibiting firms reserve exhibit space a year or more ahead.

THE IMPORTANCE OF TRADE SHOWS

In thousands of other industries, too, the trade show has an importance seldom realized by the general public that does not attend such affairs and knows little or nothing about them. To impart some idea of the meaning of a trade show to one industry, the following is presented as what could well be a typical conversation. Talking are two executives of a company that makes 16-mm motion picture equipment.

"What about the NEA meeting this year?"
"The National Education Association meeting?" "That's one we *have* to take part in. When you think of our sales to school systems with audio-visual programs we just can't afford public-relationswise *not* to be at the NEA. And think how it would look if all our competitors were there—and they darned

well *will* be—and we weren't? This gives us a chance to meet not only every important administrator in the school field, but also our dealers in that area—they'll all be there too! Most of the time the booth is jammed with them. And maybe you didn't know, or haven't got in on this side of things, but we always have a sizable dealer meeting in conjunction with our NEA convention participation.''

From this brief conversation we learn four reasons for participating in trade shows:

(1) for public and industry relations,
(2) for future sales to important persons in the industry,
(3) for dealer morale and participation, and
(4) for providing a time, place and reason for a dealer meeting.

Typical scene at trade show.

Some of the excitement of trade show is conveyed by this photograph of the crowds around the exhibits at the national Microfilm Association Convention in Dallas, Texas. It has been estimated that about $1.5 billion is spent on such exhibits but this figure does not include staffing costs and related travel and hotel expenses.

What Is A Trade Exhibit?

Many industries and professions conduct national or regional meetings (and the medical profession even breaks it down to county meetings) to exchange information, viewpoints, and to elect officers for their national associations. These activities are usually conducted on a yearly basis.

In the case of many of these meetings, a trade, industrial, or professional exhibit is run in conjunction with the former. Thus in the case of the National Education Association meeting, mentioned in the conversation between our two hypothetical executives, an entire convention hall might be engaged for the period of the meeting, usually about a week. Sometimes the meeting will engage the entire convention facilities of a large hotel or convention center. Big meetings, such as that of the National Education Association, will break the affair into two parts. (1) The meetings of the organization itself attended by teachers and administrators who will carry on their professional business. (2) The exhibit hall in which there may be hundreds of booths rented by corporations which make products or provide services connected with the field represented. In the booths will be exhibits of their products explained by company personnel who man the booths during the period of the meeting.

At the National Education Association meeting, for example, one will find the manufacturers of seats, textbooks, visual-aid equipment, and all sorts of school supplies and services. The show brings buyers and sellers together.

Long before the meeting, the companies have rented their booth space. If the school business is important to a company it will rent a number of booths, spending thousands of dollars on rental alone. Then, when the company adds up the cost of sending equipment to the booth and paying expenses of all the personnel manning the booth for the week, plus entertainment of important prospects, a very sizable sum will have been spent for the trade exhibit participation.

Such companies will attend meetings year after year and not only the big national meetings but the regional, state and county meetings. When a company has a wide range of products, it may exhibit in several hundred shows a year. The average number of participations a year by companies that consider shows important is seven.

What Goes On At Trade Exhibits?

At any given show, convention, or trade exhibit there will be a varying picture of activity. Some small booths, with one person in attendance, will have an atmosphere of failure. Nothing in the booth looks interesting; about all the advertiser seems to be achieving is identification through the sign giving the company or product name. In contrast, other booths are jammed with visitors. Personnel manning the booth may be demonstrating, talking to sales contacts, giving out literature and, in short, working up to capacity.

Here are some of the activities and purposes that will be typical of such exhibits:

Selling. Most exhibitors do not participate in shows in order to sell directly within the booths. Many, however, *do* take orders directly during the show and may do a very brisk selling business although they do not actually deliver the goods since merchandise is not brought to the meeting to cover sales.

Laying groundwork for future sales that will be placed through company dealers.   Perhaps the visitor to the booth came as a result of seeing company advertising. Once in the booth, the visitor may be given literature and samples and may see demonstrations of the product. Displays may be presented through continuous slide showings, or continuous motion picture showings. Sometimes there are working models of the unit, or three-dimensional slide viewers. Every technique, in short, may be used to interest the prospect who visits the booth. If thoroughly sold, this person will usually give a name and address to the booth attendant. This information will be sent to the dealer who operates in the prospect's territory. This dealer will call upon the prospect and, it is hoped, obtain an order from this presold contact.

New product introductions are especially important. Such introductions can be speeded up by months when products are shown at trade shows. People attending can see many new products quickly. There is no quicker way to achieve new product introductions. Knowing this, manufacturers plan their manufacturing schedules to bring out new products at the time of important trade shows.

Public relations and publicity.   Many persons who have a question about the company or its products, or possibly have long-time complaints, will never under ordinary circumstances talk directly to the company or its dealers because it is too much bother or is inconvenient. Such a person passing a company booth at a trade show will utilize this chance to voice the questions or complaints that have been stored up. Many situations can be smoothed out through the personal contact with company representatives attending the booth.

A public relations function is also served merely by the presence of the company in the exhibit hall. A certain amount of goodwill is achieved through this visible evidence of the company's support of the industry that has sponsored the convention. Without the support of the trade exhibitors, many national meetings could not be held, or at least not on the scale made possible through revenues provided by exhibitors.

News about new products or improvements in old products is speeded up through the publicity generated at trade shows by reporters and editors who attend such affairs. All of the trade press connected with various industries consider trade shows a must and are eager to report interesting developments in an industry. An exhibitor is wise to make the job of the press easier by preparing a publicity packet for use of press representatives. This will contain news releases, product information in booklets, leaflets, and specification sheets and data about the company.

Advertising product, and market research.   Response to the advertising is afforded by the comments and reactions of the many visitors to the advertiser's booth. Even more valuable is the market-research function served by the exhibit. An analysis of the complaints and praise for the company's products may have such value that this analysis alone might make the exhibit expenditure worth while. Visitors to the booth constitute a huge market-research panel of people who have an interest in the company's prospects. It would be impossible to assemble such a panel through conventional market-research procedures. The visitors not only provide a means for product research but also furnish the exhibitor with an idea of how the company's marketing and selling methods are viewed by prospects and customers for company products.

An exhibit is, in a sense, a research laboratory that enables prospective buyers to try out a number of products, make comparisons with competitive products. Product features and technical information can be supplied by company personnel, while the comparisons are going on. Scientists, professional people, engineers and business executives are thus served. Examples: a dentist can check with company designers of a new high-speed drill. An exhibitor's expert in sound systems demonstrates a new speaker assembly for dealers in stereo equipment. Camera shop proprietors learn the fine points of exotic new photographic equipment.

While all this is going on, the exhibitors are noting buying interests or product interests. These can be ascertained by the size of audiences attracted and by the reactions of the audiences.

An opportunity for a sales meeting. If the exhibiting company has a large sales force, participation in an important convention provides a suitable reason for conducting a regional or national sales meetings. Company salespeople often help staff booths, and in any case, use the meeting as a reason for consulting with company management personnel who usually attend important trade shows or conventions. Because salespeople are attending anyway, it is often convenient to hold a sales meeting in conjunction with the trade show.

A chance to improve dealer relations. Exhibiting companies usually notify dealers in the area of the convention site so that the dealers may attend the meeting and meet the "top brass" of the companies. When dealers come to the booth, they are entertained and given a chance to discuss matters that pertain to their distribution of the company products. If they have complaints or suggestions they will never find a better time to discuss them because normally top company executives will not visit them nor will dealers ordinarily travel to company headquarters for such discussions.

A chance to study competitors' products and methods. There is much visiting of competitors' booths by exhibitors. Sometimes this visiting is done openly and other times it is done without knowledge on the part of the firm being visited. Much can be learned by hearing the sales talk of representatives of rival companies. Under the convention setup, it is impossible to prevent this "snooping" on the part of competitors.

PREMIUMS

Certain marketing aids, tightly allied to advertising, cannot actually be called advertising, nor can they be called advertising media. Yet they may utilize the power of advertising and advertising uses *their* power. Likewise, advertising and selling campaigns may actually be built around them.

Such marketing, selling, and advertising aids are premiums. So, too, are contests, trade shows, packaging, and coupons. Almost all advertising people concerned with the marketing of a consumer product will be closely involved with one or more of these aids. Even the industrial marketer will be knowledgeable about one or two of these, usually trade shows and/or packaging.

Like specialties, premiums are big business, yet despite the great use of premiums the general public has no awareness just *how* extensively they are

Magazine advertisement with a premium offer.

In this advertisement we have the classic formula for a successful premium advertisement. A real value is offered. The premiums are seasonal. The premium offers are displayed prominently. There is a strong urge for quick action.

used and is barely conscious of the industry. The average consumer asked to define "premium" would probably say something like: "Are they those things they give away—like you see on the back of cereal boxes?"

Our consumer would not be quite right since premiums, unlike specialties, are not really gifts. Actually, the word "incentive" comes closer to describing "premium." Most often a premium is some item of merchandise. It may be given at a reduced price, or sometimes free, in order to encourage buying of a product or service.

Purpose of the premium is to attract consumers who would not normally buy a product, or service, or to encourage more frequent buying by those already buying the product. Insurance companies that promise a "handsome billfold" as a reward for supplying information and permitting a salesperson to call, illustrate the first purpose. The second purpose is clearly evident in the constant use of cereal packages as display areas for premium offers—or in the use of premium offers by other companies that assiduously employ premiums as a means of encouraging continued use of the brand. It can be seen from the foregoing description that a premium is usually offered in combination with an advertiser's product, or in addition to it. Very often premium discussion is connected with discussion of advertising media. While premiums, unlike advertising specialties, are not a form of advertising media, they exist in close conjunction with media that carry descriptions of premium offers.

How Important Are Premiums In Modern Marketing?

In addition to the $2 to $3 billion spent on the premiums themselves each year, more billions are spent for the goods or services that premiums encouraged consumers to buy. Beyond that, many millions are spent in media advertising that carries details of the premium offers. Since the big advertisers are the biggest premium users, media expenditures for this form of advertising are staggering. In a single year, for example, around 1,400 pages of premium advertising were found in just 24 of the leading magazines. Add to this figure, premium advertising in other magazines, in newspapers, direct mail, and the broadcast media, and some idea may be gained of the premium's impact on marketing.

When the Premium Show is held in New York City as many as 30,000 buyers crowd the aisles to see what is available. There is an insatiable hunger for customer-pleasing premiums among the aggressive marketers.

Cereals, coffee, tea, and other food products, especially those products of constant use, find premiums a valuable incentive for the purchase of their products. An example is furnished by a premium offer made by the advertisers of Flamingo frozen juices. To obtain a $4.98 can opener, users of the product were required to send in twenty-five cents and thirty Flamingo juice can tops. In two months, around 500,000 can tops were sent to the company.

This promotion was somewhat out of the ordinary because of the number of can tops required. This number was selected by the company because the purchase of that many cans of the product by consumers would help write off the entire cost of the promotion.

Although many premiums require the consumer to pay part of the cost of the premium, there are numerous "free" offers that generate great response. For instance, like the Flamingo offer, just described, there was the Diet Rite Cola promotion that required 12 can liners from the product to be sent in order for the consumer to receive free L'Eggs pantyhose. If only 50,000 took part in this promotion, it is obvious that considerable sales volume was achieved. Another "free" deal was offered by Nescafe that required the sending of two proofs of purchase of Nescafe to get the Guiness Book of Records, a $2.99 value. Still another such deal by General Mills offered free a $7.50 recipe file to persons who agreed to examine a set of Betty Crocker recipes.

Another classic story of the successful use of a premium promotion by a food advertiser is furnished by a Nescafe premium offer that pulled so powerfully that the company was forced to withdraw the offer until it could build up a big enough supply of the premiums to match the demand.

In less than a year, the offer attracted a million one-dollar bills, which were sent, along with a paper inner-seal from a jar of the product, in order to obtain a six-cup instant coffee maker customarily selling for $2.85 in retail stores.

Cereal box premium offer.

One of the best mediums for premium offers is the cereal box. Distributed by the millions and retained for a long time, they provide an ideal situation for premium merchandisers.

Why Are Premiums Used?

There are many lists of 50 to 100 reasons for using premiums. Following are a few of the major reasons for their use; many additional but less important reasons could be given. Most fundamental reason, of course, is the desire to increase sales, although sometimes premiums are offered in order to obtain other less direct objectives.

Cause product to be used more frequently. This objective is of supreme importance in the case of low-cost, mass-distributed products offering such a small profit-return that frequent use is necessary for the survival of the manufacturer.

Spur sale of product in a new form. Getting people to change buying habits along with a product change is one of marketing's difficult tasks. When Lifebuoy soap, for example, incorporated a new ingredient it would well expect that some buyer resistance would be encountered. A premium offer of a comb and brush set was made in order to encourage trial of the new-type of Lifebuoy.

Cut down substitution. One of the long-time users of premium offers was the Brown & Williamson company that included coupons in each pack of its Raleigh cigarettes. This coupon redeemable for premiums, when offered in specified numbers, helped to keep cigarette smokers loyal to the Raleigh brand and away from competing brands.

Introduce new products. This obviously is one of the more important reasons for the use of premium offers. Each year thousands of new products enter the market; many fail. Obtaining identity and use for a new product is one of marketing's most difficult tasks. A good premium may achieve this use and identity where ordinary advertising and marketing efforts might not succeed. A supremely important objective in advertising is to establish a "point of difference" between the advertiser's product and others—especially in new products. Premiums may be the only real point of difference for many new products and are purposely used to establish a difference.

Introduce new or old products in new territories. Even an established product that has been sold on a regional basis will find that it has all the usual difficulties of a new product when it aims at establishing a marketing foothold in a new marketing region. Premiums, deals, contests may be used to force successful entry into the new territories. A dog-food manufacturer in the northwest region of the country, decided to expand region by region. Premium offers in print and broadcast media advertising helped achieve consumer acceptance, and as this acceptance grew so did the acceptance of the supermarket chains that had to be sold in order to attain a profitable sales volume and wide distribution.

Persuade consumers to buy a family of products. A company such as Heinz has a number of products to offer but almost always finds that some product (or products) will be more popular than others in the line. Premiums help the advertiser to get the consumers to buy more widely in the line.

Provide extra appeal in special sales events. Many promotionally minded companies go from special event to special event throughout the year. Premiums can provide extra excitement for such events and can provide the "point of difference" for the event just as they help to differentiate between products.

Hasten selling of slow-moving items. Sometimes the product is the kind that always tends to be slow-selling. Sometimes its sales may reflect a seasonal lag, selling better at some times of the year than at others. Whatever the reason for the slow sales, premiums can sometimes provide a "hypodermic" that will speed up selling in the slow periods. A premium user who has a number of products may have a plan for regular use of premiums to accelerate sales.

Meet competitive prices. Some companies feel that it is bad for their reputation and standing to cut prices. Sometimes they cannot cut prices because they adhere to minimum pricing. In either case, the offering of a premium of real value constitutes a form of price-cutting that will not injure the company's reputation as a stable organization. A premium may be especially valuable in price competition occasioned by the low prices offered by discount stores.

Provide copy appeal. Especially in cases where a product is greatly like other products in the field, the premium gives the copywriter something to say in the advertising. In fact, successful premium promotions, like successful contest promotions, often require that the product description be minimized and the premium sell be maximized.

Promote large-size units. Since larger units mean larger profits to manufacturers (also, if consumers buy a larger unit it will be a longer time before they can buy a competing product) many inducements are offered to induce shoppers to take the larger size off the supermarket shelves. Premium offers are very often used for this purpose.

Help a small advertiser compete with big advertisers. A small company finds it necessary to use every stratagem to break into new markets when competing with much bigger companies whose products are well established. A good premium offer is one of the many marketing strategies to use.

Excite sales force. Every sales manager is aware that salespeople tend to "run down." A sales job has many difficult moments and one of the more difficult ones is that moment when prospects say: "What are you giving me—the same old story? Don't you have anything *new*?" An exciting premium offer *is* something new that can generate consumer and dealer enthusiasm and thus can wake up a dispirited sales force.

Kinds Of Premiums

Premiums must be broken into two principal classes—those for consumers and those for nonconsumers. Here we are concerned chiefly with consumer premiums. These are premiums used to encourage greater buying by members of the general public of those products (and sometimes services) that they use in their daily existence. Nonconsumer premiums would include premiums used to promote greater morale and efficiency among employees such as cutting down on waste, being more punctual, or attending regularly. These are the "incentive" premiums. Nonconsumer premiums have been used also as rewards to salespeople for meeting or exceeding sales quotas.

Although there might be some argument about terminology, it is generally agreed that there are four principal kinds of consumer premiums: (1) self-liquidating premiums, (2) package-band premiums, (3) coupon plan premiums, and (4) factory-pack premiums (called "in-pack" or "on-pack").

Self-liquidating premiums. About 50 percent of premium users it is estimated favor the self-liquidating type. This favoritism is understandable when one considers the significance of the name. In short, this type of premium is paid for by the money sent in by the consumers. The money sent in pays for:

- The item itself
- Taxes—if any
- Handling and mailing charges
- Packaging

Only the advertising promotion given to the offer is not cared for by the money sent in.

For this kind of premium, the consumer is asked to buy the advertiser's product and then to send in a label or boxtop and a specified amount of money. For this the person will receive the premium item, which will usually represent a very fine bargain since the consumer would not be able to buy the same item in the market place for the amount of money sent in with the boxtop.

This bargain is made possible because the company offering the premium buys the premium item in huge numbers and thus cuts down greatly the cost of the individual items. It is easy to understand how these savings can be made since big companies offering premiums may buy the premium items in lots going into the hundreds of thousands, or even millions.

A self-liquidating premium promotion that failed to attract consumers could be a financial disaster for the company, since it would have on its hands all the units that the consumers failed to send for. It is necessary, therefore, that the advertiser make certain in every premium promotion that:

(1) The premium itself not only represents an obvious bargain but also that it is the kind of item consumers find appealing.
(2) The advertising for the offer is not only skillfully and excitingly executed but that promotion is heavy enough to make impact on the market.
(3) The money they are asking for the premium is likely to be acceptable to the great mass of consumers. On this last point, it is difficult to name an "ideal" premium price. Such a price may vary with the economic times. Where once a quarter was considered to be the "right" price, the dollar then came into favor and considerably more has been asked in recent premium offers—at figures ranging from $10 and far more.

Two examples of the higher-value premium offer were the "Ginny Jogger" warm-up outfits offered by Philip Morris for $22.00 and two pack bottoms from cigarette packages, and the Chuck Wagon carving sets offered by Marlboro at $24.00. Each of these promotions tied in with the product campaigns; the first with the "You've come a long way baby" theme, and the second with the western feeling of Marlboro advertisements.

Another example that defied the "it's-best-to-keep-the-premium-price-low" philosophy was the Kool cigarette sailboat premium promotion. With the promotion requiring respondents to send in nearly $100 for the premium—a small sailboat—it would seem reasonable to expect very low returns. Instead, 20,000 consumers sent in the money and received their boats. Encouraged by this, the company then offered an even more expensive premium, a $699 catamaran.

Price, it may be concluded, depends upon the times and the nature of the offer. Normally, however, it takes considerable boldness to go beyond a $10 premium deal.

Despite all the good points for self-liquidating premiums, marketers have learned that this type of premium is not so good as in-pack and on-pack premium deals for getting consumers to try a product. Fewer than 10 percent of households respond to such premium offers. Still, with its relatively low cost and the fact that the presence of a premium in an advertisement can often double the readership, the self-liquidating premium continues to thrive.

Package-band premiums. Here again is a premium that in a sense pays for itself. Money sent for the premium items pays for the premium cost as well as the packaging and mailing. Actually, in terms of cost, the package-band premium has an added advantage—the fact that the advertising for such a premium is executed on the paper band wrapped around the package at the factory. It is often said, therefore, that a package-band premium is its own advertising medium, a strong point when considered in the light of the heavy media advertising expenditures for self-liquidating premiums.

In this day of self-service in the nation's supermarkets and grocery stores, the package-band premium offers strong selling at the most important point of all—the point of purchase. Usually, any item offering a package-band premium will be placed carefully on the shelves in order that the offer will be clearly visible and easily read. Not only is such a mass display appealing to the bargain-hungry shopper but also to merchants who favor any promotions that create store traffic and hence sales.

Unlike the coupon premium (to be described) the package-band premium is usually a "one-shot" promotion that does not develop customer buying habits. It is a temporary buying stimulus. It is, on the other hand, a low-cost, easy form of premium promotion that physically requires as its major requirement only the affixing of the package band—containing the advertising and details of the offer—to the package.

Coupon plan premiums. Chief objectives of the self-liquidating and package-band premium promotions are to obtain new users for products, or to cause former users to try the product again. In contrast, coupon plan premiums aim chiefly at holding present users and causing them to use the product again and again.

As a consistent part of a long-range plan, advertisers using a coupon plan premium put coupons in every package of the product, or may print the coupon on the package. This technique has been used frequently in the soap field and , as mentioned earlier, by Raleigh cigarettes. Usually it will take a good number of such coupons to entitle the consumer to the premium offer and the number will vary according to the worth of the premium. In coupon plans there will normally be a variety of premiums offered. These will be listed in a catalog and the number of coupons required for each will be given.

Sometimes the consumer can elect to provide a specified amount of cash and a smaller number of coupons, or can provide a larger number of coupons and eliminate the cash requirement.

No coupon plan will work successfully unless the product has enough merit to warrant continued purchasing. No matter how much a consumer likes to obtain premiums he or she will not, for example, continue to buy Raleigh cigarettes unless the product pleases. On the other hand, the kinds of products that use coupon plan premiums are usually the kinds from which users switch frequently. Thus the use of coupon plan premiums develop brand loyalty, or at least, brand habit, an enormously important factor in today's competitive market. As becomes apparent, coupon plan premiums and trading stamps have much in common.

Factory-pack premiums. In the other types of premium plans, the consumer is required to do some work in order to obtain the premium. This person may be required to mail in a request and to send money. Anyone in the merchandising field knows that when consumers are required to go to some effort, no matter how inconsequential, it will cut down on the number of persons who respond to an offer.

As its chief advantage the factory-pack premium eliminates any effort by the consumer, since the premium is either in the package or affixed to it. The consumer taking the package from the shelf now has the premium—no sending away of money and forms, and no waiting. Factory-pack premiums, therefore, have high shopper appeal.

Merchants quite aware of this appeal and aware of the traffic-building qualities of factory-pack premium deals will often build giant displays of packages featuring such premiums. Like bees drawn to pollen and nectar, shoppers will be lured to such displays since each package is shouting its message by either displaying visibly on the outside of the package the premium itself, or by an advertising band or illustration of the premium on the package.

Many items may be used as factory-pack premium incentives such as dishcloths, dishes, kitchen utensils, and other home items. Naturally, factory-pack premiums, while accepted eagerly by shoppers since they obtain the premium at no extra cost—or very little extra cost—add considerably to the advertiser's cost since there is no self-liquidating aspect.

Details about the premium offer are shown on the package itself which means more cost to the advertiser because special packaging must be executed. In order to amortize such costs, therefore, the advertiser usually permits the factory-pack premium deal to run for a lengthy period.

COUPONS AND COUPONING

In the descriptions of the various types of premium plans, the magic word "coupon" appeared. The discussion, however, was limited to the in-store package use of coupons. Another world of couponing exists outside of the in-pack type. These are the coupons distributed by direct mail, or promoted in advertisements (the type that are clipped to be sent to the advertiser or taken to the store for redemption).

Reasons for the intense interest in couponing are the same as for the use of premiums: (1) to induce people to try a product, (2) to keep people using the product, and (3) to add interest to a company's advertising.

Most consumers get their coupons through mass media. A 1975 study by A.C. Nielsen, the market research organization, showed that: 74 percent of coupons were delivered by newspapers; 14 percent by magazines; 8 percent through packages; and 4 percent by direct mail.

The same Nielsen study revealed that 65 percent of all American homes used coupons to save money on grocery products. A massive 34 billion coupons were distributed in that year. A profile of the biggest users of coupons: large families with good incomes and weekly grocery bills exceeding $50. Also, the biggest coupon user tends to be more mature—30 and above.

Couponing is often mentioned in the same breath with premiums and with sampling. The connection with sampling has a certain rough logic because the coupon is, in a sense, a less expensive form of sampling. Even with the cents-off feature, coupons are less expensive than samples.

Sampling can be very effective, especially for a product the attributes of which cannot readily be described in an advertisement (like the aroma of a soap or the taste of a toothpaste). Still, advertisers, choosing between coupons and sampling generally favor the former, not only because of the cost savings but also because coupons seem to get more people to become regular users of the promoted products.

QUESTIONS

1. Describe the various opportunities for public relations and publicity that are possible through trade shows.

2. Discuss the use of trade shows as a tool of research for a company's advertising, product, and marketing.

3. What is meant by saying that participation in a trade show creates an opportunity for a sales meeting?

4. Even when a premium is described in advertising as "free," why is it not really a gift?

5. Supply evidence for the statement that premiums are important in modern marketing.

6. Give five important reasons for the use of premiums.

7. Describe the four principal types of consumer premiums.

8. Why is the self-liquidating premium the favorite of premium users?

9. What medium is tops for delivering coupons to consumers?

10. Compare the relative cost and efficiency of couponing and sampling.

PACKAGES, SWEEPSTAKES, AND CONTESTS

PACKAGES, SWEEPSTAKES, AND CONTESTS

Imagine yourself in an old-fashioned grocery store. Pointing at a row of bins you say: "I'll take two pounds of sugar, a pound of salt, a pound of dried beans, and three pounds of rolled oats."

Having given your order, you wait while the clerk dips into the bins with a scoop and pours the various items into brown paper bags. After each has been weighed and string tied around it, you pay the clerk and carry your bags home.

That was the shopper's world before the modern package. No sturdy containers. No standardized weights and amounts. No unremitting standards of cleanliness. No breakdown of the ingredients. No helpful recipes and suggestions for use.

Without the package of today, the supermarket could not exist because there could be no self-service. The package has made possible the giant stores and food chains. But the package is not just for food products. Its development has revolutionized the retailing of all types of products. Furthermore, the modern package itself is a form of advertising and it has become just about the most important single element in the print and broadcast advertising for thousands of products, especially those in the food and personal products categories.

Such is the standardization of the package that wherever you go in the world, you expect to see familiar names—Campbell's, Heinz, Kellogg, Ivory Soap. You shop as confidently in some exotic land as you do in your home town when you see those packages that indicate quality, uniformity and cleanliness. All this is far different from the dusty bins of the earlier part of this century. No more clerks reaching with hands of questionable cleanliness into the murky depths of the pickle barrels, and no brushing off flies from food products as part of the service to customers.

698

PACKAGING

One marketing expert talking to a group of persons concerned with packaging declared that in the marketing stalemate that exists today for 75 percent of all consumer goods, that the package may be the only way to differentiate the product meaningfully in the eyes of the consumer.

Although packaging has always been an important part of overall marketing, there is no doubt that it has become increasingly important since the advent of self-service retailing, especially in the supermarket and drugstore fields. Later the coming of television heightened the attention given by marketing people to packaging.

Several media stress that they call attention to an advertiser's product just before the shopper enters the supermarket. This assertion has been made by transit, newspaper, outdoor, radio, and television. All of them, however, yield to the advertising on the package which offers truly the last chance for an advertiser to influence shoppers' decisions.

It is significant that there is a strong correlation between package recognition scores and good product sales. Memorable packages share certain characteristics such as the good illustrations of Charmin and Taster's Choice, distinctive colors as in the green Palmolive liquid dishwasher container, and a strong tie-in with advertising, Charmin's "squeezably soft" is an example. Lastly, a big, clear logotype can help, also.

Sweepstakes advertisement with timely appeal.
With food prices at an all-time high when this advertisement appeared, the prize structure was certain to appeal to a vast number of readers.

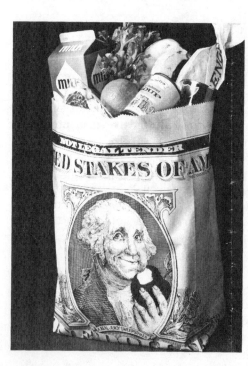

Functions of Packaging

From the standpoint of the packager, there are a number of reasons for packaging. Some of these have to do with promotion of the product, and some have to do with the physical aspects.

(1) *To protect the product.* Although this purpose has been obscured by the great stress on the promotional values of packaging, it is still the fundamental reason for a package's existence—to guard and hold the product until the consumer can get it home. Some packages in former days did a poor job of filling this fundamental purpose, but most modern packages not only protect the product well but also offer many ingenious innovations undreamed of a few years ago in the era of simpler package design.

(2) *To identify the product and/or advertiser.* In most cases this identification is of the product. Sometimes, however, especially in "family" packaging of a line wherein all packages (Campbell's Soups, for example) look alike, the company name may be featured. In modern supermarket merchandising, this package function is the most important to the advertiser because of the quick buying decisions made by the shopper pushing a shopping cart down the supermarket aisles.

Despite all the attention paid to the importance of quick product or advertiser identification, there are many examples of look-alike packages. Coffee, and instant coffee, packages look alike. Remove the labels and shoppers can't identify the products. This was demonstrated in a test with Wishbone salad dressing and a Kraft dressing. Shapes of salad dressing bottles are confusingly similar.

In contrast to the look-alike packages is the example of the Libby company that completely redesigned its big product line. Most prominent change was the use of the name Libby repeated three times in this manner on packages:

Libby

Libby

Libby

This technique provided superb name registration especially since the new, clean design provided ample white space around the name. Furthermore, when Libby cans were stacked, the repeating of name was even more evident.

(3) *To advertise and sell the product.* In many cases shoppers are still making up their minds after they have entered the store. What is said on the package may cause them to put one item into the shopping cart rather than another. Since clerks in the average supermarket are seldom able to talk knowledgeably about the thousands of items on their shelves, the package must be a silent salesman.

(4) *To help the consumer in using the product.* This function reaches its true importance once the product has arrived home. Wherever the point of use—kitchen, bathroom, laundry room, or in the garden—this function will sooner or later come into play.

(5) *To advertise and sell other products in the line.* Should users find that

they like the product contained in the package they have carried home, they will be open to suggestions that they use other products in the line. A listing of such products on the package is a strong selling agent and a help to the shoppers the next time they make up a shopping list. It is difficult to understand why *all* manufacturers of a multiitem line do not *always* use some portion of the package space to sell their other items.

(6) *To help in general promotions.* Millions of packages can be used for promoting and carrying the premiums offered in the premium deals. Similarly, millions of other packages can promote the company's latest contest or call attention to the stars advertising products on television. The latter is especially valuable in packages containing products used by children.

Easy-to-read package.

With food shelves jammed with packages fighting for attention, the advertiser should make his package easy to read in order that it will stand out. This package will have high visibility and readability wherever it may be used—on the supermarket shelf, in an advertisement, or in a television commercial.

Overall Importance of Packaging

This discussion will concern the importance of packaging:

(1) in the company's advertising plans,
(2) at the point of sale, where packaging must serve the wants of the consumer and the needs of the retailer.

In advertising. In every medium the package plays a central role. Any shopping day issue of a daily newspaper will, for example, feature hundreds of packages. In television, watch the announcers as they carefully turn the packages in order that the name and design may be seen. Even in radio, announcers will ask listeners to "Look for the package with the familiar red and gold stripe." In magazines, where reproduction, especially of color, is so good, the package is prominently used.

Just how important packages are in women's service magazines is revealed by an examination of three issues of *Family Circle* magazine, made at the time this book was being written. The record looked like this:

First issue:
93 packaged goods advertisers.

Of these advertisers 92 featured their packages. Many showed a number of their packages. The exception was Dial Soap that showed the product being used.

Second issue:
101 packaged goods advertisers.

Of these 99 showed packages, many more than one. Exceptions Dial Soap and Oscar Mayer.

Third issue:
85 packaged goods advertisers.

Of these 84 showed packages, many more than one. Exception: Oscar Mayer.

Marketing success stories often center around the package. One such story concerns Marlboro cigarettes which in 1954 had sales of only 0.3 billion cigarettes, tiny for the tobacco industry. In that year the company introduced its "flip-top" box and backed it with heavy advertising, including the now-famous Marlboro song featuring the new box. By 1956 sales had soared to 14.3 billion, almost directly attributable to the package improvement and the advertising backing.

Advertisers have been known not to include the package on the assumption that the package identifies the advertiser so quickly that the reader turns away from the advertisement. It is hoped that the packageless advertisement will hold the reader long enough for the reading of the copy. Unless the advertisement is a winner, however, chances are good that the reader won't read the copy anyway and, without the package illustration, the advertiser's identity may not be known. Thus, the advertisement rates zero. With the package included, the reader may at the least have been conscious of the product and/or advertiser.

Another point is that the package or bottle can be a natural part of the scene shown in an advertisement such as a bottle of barbecue sauce placed near some hamburgers about to be cooked on an outside grill, or beer on a food-laden picnic table, or potato chips with other items being eaten for a lunchtime snack. Often, in fact, the package can be the central character as in the case of advertisements that, through the use of stop motion, have the packages marching from the house, garage, or some other spot to the place where they are going to be used.

Packaging helps in the positioning of products. An example of this is shown in the marketing of several products of the Carnation company, all of them concerned in some way with persons who are dieting. "Slender," one of the products, is a substitute for a meal or snack and comes in a white package. "Instant Breakfast" is described as a low-calorie snack with a milk base. It has a chocolate package. Then, in a red package with a sun streak, is "Special Morning," that is said to be a bigger instant breakfast. Each, through its distinctive packaging, helps position itself in the market.

Many companies use their packages to help in their positioning efforts such as Campbell Soup that positions some of its soups for men and puts "Manhandlers" on the label to do so. Another is Lipton that positions its "Cup-A-Soup" for the person in a hurry and used a package showing a full color photo of soup being made in a glass cup.

Packaging furnishes much of the inspiration for creative people. New package designs provide overall themes for advertising. Marlboro cigarettes provide an example, along with the change in the Morton Salt package that enabled users to sprinkle salt as well as to pour it, or the company that devised the boil-in-the-bag frozen beans package, or the beer company that introduced the pop-top beer can or the throwaway bottles. Aerosol cans have provided copy for millions of dollars in advertising. An interesting change in the shape and appearance of a package can inspire copywriters, as witness advertisements for Janitor In Drum, and the Heinz bottle that gives an impression of an old-fashioned pickle barrel.

Currently, nostalgia is a big word in advertising and package design. Rural settings, grandmothers, and farms are grist for the copywriter's work. All of this is reflected in packages which also show the back-to-nature trend in such products as Earth Born Shampoo and Clairol's Herbal Essence. Some packages have merely retained their old-fashioned look with only minor updating needed. Examples: Arm & Hammer baking soda and 20 Mule Team Borax. A company such as Pepperidge Farm is fortunate in being able to associate its oldtime look with many products in addition to its distinctive packaging of its bread.

So important is the relationship between the creative side and packaging that a number of companies have changed their packages each time they change their creative themes. Among these are Revlon, Pillsbury Mills, Kellogg cereals, General Mills, National Biscuit, Eagle pencil, and Avon toiletries.

A company that changes its package and introduces its unique shape may establish a long-time theme for advertising because a unique shape makes possible the registration of the package as a trademark, or the obtaining of a patent good for 17 years. The shape gives a long-time advantage over conventionally-shaped competitive packages a dozen of which may look exactly alike.

On the other hand, relating a creative theme closely to the packaging may backfire if the theme proves unsatisfactory and is dropped before the packages conveying the theme can be replaced.

Most big advertisers of packaged goods have packaging committees that approach package design solemnly, since they know full well that the package that does not please the consumer or does not advertise well can cost the company millions in the marketplace. Joining the committee in its deliberations are packaging experts who work for the company's advertising agency. In addition, the company will undoubtedly call upon packaging consultants and designers for counsel and for help in designs. Likewise, the company will probably conduct careful and costly field research at the point of sale to test new colors, designs, and other elements before investing millions in package changes, or in packages for new products.

Any questions about the importance of packaging in the eyes of the modern marketer will be dispelled instantly if one can attend a meeting wherein a suggestion is made to change or modernize a package that seems to have been doing a successful job. Some advertisers would change their marital status before they would change one element in a reasonably successful package. In fact, some package changes have been delayed years after they should have been made, so fearful are certain advertisers about the possible harmful effects of package changes.

A big advertiser, for instance, whose product has a major share of the market may lose more customers than are gained when a package change is made. The firm with a small share of the market, in contrast, has much to gain in trying the package change. Furthermore, what happens depends on the nature of the change. Usually, nothing dire will occur if the changes are: minor legal points, the switching of a premium offer that was temporary anyway, a slight adjustment in the directions for the product use, or the use of a cheaper packaging material.

Customer sales may be seriously affected, however, if important changes are made in the packaging, changes that would include: a new name, a new package shape, a new dominant color, a new main illustration, and a new logotype.

At point of sale. Figures about shoppers, especially supermarket shoppers, are thrown around madly these days. The modern shopper has been analyzed, probed, studied, worried over, thought about, and dissected by every maker of goods sold on retail shelves.

Out of the thousands of studies made about shopping habits have come millions of figures that boiled down have much importance to the package planner. It is estimated for instance, that the average shopper buys about 2,000 packages in a year. Of these, according to the Grocery Manufacturers Association, 70 percent will be taken as a result of impulse. Sometimes the figure has gone up to 75 percent and sometimes down to about 40 percent. Whatever figure is chosen, the fact remains that impulse buying is a vital factor in shopping, whether in the supermarket or in the drugstore. The importance of good, attractive packaging in causing buying action on the part of the impulse buyer is obvious.

In one study of the Brand Names Foundation made several years ago (and the figures should be pertinent today), the woman shopper averages around 150 buying decisions in a shopping period lasting about 17.9 minutes. In this period the shopper will pass some 300 items per minute during a trip through the average supermarket. About 7 seconds is allotted to each buying decision in this shopping journey.

Again, if the figures are to be believed, the implications for the advertiser of a packaged item are obvious. An instant impression must be made on the quick-buying shopper. Anyone who has watched the shopper in the passage down supermarket aisles will note how many times such a person picks out a package, gives it a quick look, discards it, picks up another package, discards it, and continues until finally an item is put into the cart. Sometimes, however, the shopper's hand darts to the shelf. With no hesitation the package is seized and put into the cart—in considerably less than the quoted 7 seconds.

An important element in all this is shelf position. When, for instance, products have been moved from floor level to waist level, sales have risen more than 60 percent and to almost 80 percent when moved floor level to eye level.[1] Big names—Lever, Colgate, Procter & Gamble, Kellogg—are given good shelf position because their products are known sellers. Lesser-known products often get poor shelf position but an attractive package can frequently help the lesser-known firm get better position for its products. In any event, the more appealing package may enable the lesser-known products to compete better whether or not they are fortunate enough to enjoy good shelf position.

Some of the general and more unusual packaging likes and dislikes of consumers are that they

(1) like gold, silver, and metallic wrappings because they give a feeling of luxury,
(2) favor package colors that agree with package contents, such as steel blue for hardware, warm brown for coffee, and pink for cosmetics,
(3) are impressed by labels, seals, and crests on packages—such as gold seals suggesting "quality."

In general, color, a very important package element, seems to evoke responses from men and women that repeat the preferences found in other forms of advertising and promotion. Men react strongly to yellow, women to red. Getting the least response are greens and purples.

Package Elements That Please Shoppers

(1) *Multipacks.* Dog food, beer, and a good many other items are now sold in multiunit packages to conform to the once-a-week shopping habits of the consumer. The extra weight is of no consequence to the shopper who often has bundles carried to the car by store personnel or wheels them to the parking lot in a roomy shopping cart.
(2) *Easy-to-open cans, packages, and bottles.* Ease of opening alone will often sell one package rather than another. Despite many recent improvements in this direction, greater ease of opening is mentioned by many consumers when asked what improvements they would like in modern packaging.
(3) *Easy-to-read packages.* Around 70 percent of Americans wear eyeglasses part of the time and about 60 percent wear them all the time, according to the Better Vision Institute. Other people do not wear glasses who should, and others do not wear them in public because of vanity or forgetfulness. The moral is clear. Packages should

use legible and large type. If a shopper cannot read the name on the package, the contents, or the directions, a sale is lost. Hardly any type on a package should be less than 10-point, and much of it should be considerably larger. Furthermore, there should be short, snappy headlines and subheads that guide the reader, especially in the giving of directions, such as:

3 EASY STEPS

(1) Put 2 teaspoons in boiling water.

(2) Stir occasionally; reduce to low heat.

(3) In 5 minutes remove from heat and let cool.

Good illustrations can help put over points. Here again, if the pictures are supposed to be in sequence, number them.

(4) *Reusable containers.* Containers that can be used as glasses, as bowls, or for some other long-time purpose are great favorites with thrifty shoppers. They are especially attractive to the shopper if they can eventually be made into a set suitable for use by the family, or guests.

(5) *Larger packages.* As in the case of multipacks, the shopper is not daunted by large packages because there is almost no carrying of the groceries in this day of automobile shopping; a far cry from the days when persons shopped at corner groceries and walked two or three blocks with the order. Other factors contributing to the inclination toward bigger packages: higher income in U.S. families and bigger families.

(6) *Clear directions.* With all the corporate brains that are devoted to package construction it would seem that no shopper should ever be puzzled as to just how to use a product. Directions, it might be supposed, would be clear enough for a child to follow. Yet time after time a harried shopper is compelled to "read the mind" of the manufacturer in following directions.

Along with clarity in directions should be clarity about the amount in the package and/or the number of servings to be expected, a vital point for the person who cares for the needs of a family, or for guests.

Specific Package Elements That Please Retailers

(7) *Packages that stack well.* Odd shapes, and packages that have premiums attached to the outside, make even, easy shelf stacking difficult or impossible. In this day when every minute counts in store operation, a retailer simply will not bother with packages that cause him the slightest trouble in shelf stacking.

(8) *Packages that allow space.* The retailer needs space to stamp a price, a vital concern in self-service shopping.

(9) *Packages that have top or bottom package labeling to allow for side or flat stacking.* In short, a package should be flexible for the retailer's use. Often flexibility can be achieved by making the back exactly the same as the front so the package displays well no matter how it is placed. In any event, good use should be made of the back such as telling how to use the product, using it to advertise related products, making tie-in promotions of other products, displaying premium offers, and

furnishing guarantees.

(10) *Packages that are compact.* The package should not take up extra space—unlike pegboard-style packages that swallow valuable room.

(11) *Packages that group attractively.* Packages should look good in mass or jumbled displays as well as on the shelf.

(12) *Packages that are sturdy.* The package should stand up under supermarket wear and tear, including handling by store personnel as well as by shoppers.

(13) *Packages that have clear directions.* Directions should be clear in all respects so that the shopper will not need to take up the time of store people in order to be fully informed about contents, price, and use.

Special Demands of Television upon Packages

At one time package designers thought only of how their packages would look on the shelf. Next they became almost equally concerned with how it would look in print advertisements; eventually they were interested in its appearance in such other media as outdoor and transit advertising.

With the advent of the greatest visual medium of all, they had to readjust their planning all over again. Television has made demands upon the package designer undreamed of in the relatively simple prevideo days. Now, in designing for television, the packaging expert must:

(1) Give the product clear identity in large letters on four sides of the package, plus the top and bottom. Watch a television commercial in which the announcer or someone else picks up the package. The hand will probably obscure the name on one side of the package, and in the discussion, the person will probably turn the package. If the package has identity on all sides and sections, whatever the announcer does the name will *still* be visible.

(2) Make certain that the package identity can register in as little as 3½ to 4½ seconds, just about the time the television viewer will have to see the package in shown-in-use situations. It is vital to show the product name as the package is shown. This is especially true when the name sells the product on its own. An example is Make-A-Shake that identifies and positions the product instantly. No More Tangles, a hair-cream rinse, offers another example.

Recognize that television, especially color television, sometimes does strange things to color, washing out some colors and overemphasizing others. This adjustment for television color can cause trouble as the designer attempts to make colors suitable for shelf display also suitable for television.

(3) Be certain that the package demonstrates well. Will the package open easily, and *look* easy to open when seen on television?

Special Demands of Packaging for Children in a Television Age

From the very first moments of television, children became an enormously important factor in the sale of certain products among which, of course, cereals are prominent. Before they could read, children had learned to identify packages. Television advertisers wooed the youthful audience until pantry shelves were groaning with products that children had demanded of their mothers. In shopping trips, parents soon learned that small children could find their favorite packages faster than they could. What advertisers found appealing to children—especially television advertisers—included the following:

(1) *Pictures of other children.* Children identify themselves with other children who are their age and who are doing what they do. Packages must capitalize on this trait.

(2) *Easy-to-read message.* Big type, short words, and short copy. These ingredients are needed for these children who have learned to read. Even the nonreading child learns to identify a product name in big, clear, distinctive type. Be short and amusing because of child's short attention span.

(3) *Bright, cheerful colors.* Children in every area of their activity are attracted and activated by colors. Especially appealing to them are red, blue, yellow, magenta, orange, blue-green.

Although children prefer the primary colors they seem especially fond of green when they are quite young, probably because of its association with nature. Hot colors become favored, especially red, as they grow older.

(4) *Cartoons.* Up to about the time the child is 8, cartoons have pulling power.

(5) *Appeals to emotion.* Prizes, contests, excitement all draw children to packages. Most pronounced tendency of children that is utilized by packagers is the susceptibility toward hero-worship, especially the heroes of the moment such as spacemen, athletes, and current attractions on television. A point to remember in selecting subject matter is that girls will buy products contained in male-oriented packages but boys are negative to products housed in packages with a feminine slant.

Warning

Children's television, programs and commercials alike, have been the target of many groups. Exploitation has become a fighting word in the assault by critics. Packages, as a vital part of the advertising of children's products, are vulnerable when they offer premiums of dubious value, play upon hero-worship, and oversell products to impressionable youngsters. Those concerned with packaging in today's militant world should consider the social, economic and health issues implicit in the illustrations and written messages that are conveyed by packages.

Serious students of packaging should be sure to check item 2 in the "References" page 2 at the end of this chapter.

SWEEPSTAKES AND CONTESTS

A Las Vegas gambler, as accustomed as he is to fighting the odds, would blanch if in his daily wagering he faced the overwhelming odds so blithely accepted by those persons who fill out entry blanks for sweepstakes and contests. Yet, somewhere, this very minute, many people are at work filling out sweepstakes and contest requirements, and many other people are planning what they should do were they to win the ones they have entered. Winning a big consumer sweepstakes or contest is a form of the American dream—to be richly rewarded without having to devote a lifetime to winning the award.

Quite apart from the consumers entering sweepstakes and contests and dreaming about the prizes they might win are shrewd advertisers who use sweepstakes and contests as a part of overall marketing strategy. Their prize in the contest is a sharply increased demand for their products and, even more important from the long-range viewpoint, a number of people who, having tried their products for the first time because of the sweepstakes or contest, may become loyal to the brands.

Running a sweepstakes or contest is a huge guessing game. First, the advertiser must guess what prizes will be most likely to evoke consumer interest. Second is a guess about how many people will enter the sweepstakes or contest. If it is one that requires the sending in of product labels or box tops, it will have a strong effect on manufacturing and sales efforts must be supplied with sufficient amounts of the products. Third is a guess as to how many of the buyers of the product, once having tried the product, will continue to buy it.

When big national advertisers are playing this guessing game, the stakes are high. A successful sweepstakes or contest will draw millions of entries and will constitute a major factor in advertising and marketing plans. There are some advertisers, in fact, who base their entire marketing and advertising plans around sweepstakes and contests.

Why Use Sweepstakes or Contests?

Since contests disrupt regular advertising and marketing plans, and are likely to consume a great amount of money and time, no advertiser should decide lightly to use a contest as a part of his overall marketing strategy. One or more of the following reasons should be behind his decision to use this promotional device:

Can provide a quick stimulus to sales. This is the basic reason for the use of a sweepstakes or contest. When sales are lagging, a good sweepstakes or contest may be just what is needed to revive them. What a well-run contest can do to help sales is shown in the results of a giant contest run by Pepsi-Cola. Entry blanks for this contest were carton-stuffers, one for each six-pack carrier. More than 60 million of the stuffers had been turned in by the contest's end. According to contest experts, this was the greatest number of contest entries ever turned in for a contest.

Can furnish merchandising excitement for both dealers and salespeople. Every salesmanager is aware, especially if sales force is selling packaged goods in the drugstore, grocery, or supermarket field, that it is necessary at times to

Sweepstakes advertisement.

Excitement is the name of the game in a sweepstakes advertisement. In this one, as in most, the whole stress is on the promotion and the prizes, rather than on the product. An extra incentive is included with the offering of a coupon inducement. One of the most difficult aspects of sweepstakes promotions is the framing of the entry rules and qualifications.

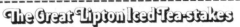

give salespersons something new to talk about and the dealers something new to hear and to think about.

Some of the leading manufacturers in the drug or grocery field plan so that each time their salespeople begin the complete swing around their sales territory again, they will have something new and interesting to tell their customers. This news may concern such developments as a premium offer, a change of prices, a new product line, a new package, or a sweepstakes or contests.

If the sweepstakes or contest is a good one that the company salespeople can merchandise well, the promotion can bring vitality and excitement into the sales presentation. An entire sales talk may be devoted to it.

Can give vitality and a theme to advertising. Just as the sweepstakes or contest is a hypodermic to sales, so it is to advertising. A copywriter, like a salesperson, is constantly looking for some way to make sales messages exciting and vital. It is the poor copywriter who cannot get a lift out of writing sweepstakes or contest copy. Such copy uses vigorous words, strong promises, and lyrical descriptions of the prizes and what it might mean to win them.

During the entire period of the sweepstakes or contest, the copywriter has a strong theme for advertising, something that may have been lacking in the regular campaign. What might have been a fairly dull and conventional campaign has developed into a slam-bang series of advertisements that infuse vigor whether presented in print or broadcast media.

Can open new markets. Assume that the manufacturer is making a grocery-store product for distribution in a several-state area along the Eastern seaboard. Assume further that having achieved distribution in that area, the company is now planning to open up new sales areas market by market. The company, however, is going to run into stern competition in these new markets from products that are well-established. The company's product, in contrast, is unknown even though it is as good, or better, than the already established products.

Faced with this set of circumstances, the manufacturer may decide that something drastic must be done to break into the new markets—such as running a sweepstakes or contest.

If the product looks good to the grocery store and supermarket people, and they know that the manufacturer is going to run an attractive sweepstakes or contest, and that this will be backed up with substantial advertising support (and this support must be spelled out in detail for the retailers) the company may be able to surmount that tough barrier—persuading the retailers to stock the product in sufficient quantity to cover those consumers who come looking for the product in order that they may send in labels or boxtops.

Can create interest for a product that itself is not interesting to consumers. To many people "salt is salt" or "sugar is sugar" or "bread is bread". Despite the efforts of advertisers of these products, consumers see little or no difference in the products. There are many other products that consumers think are the same as competing products despite the strong attempts of advertisers to make them think otherwise. Gasoline is such a product, for example.

Advertisers of such products may find that the only way to establish recognition for their brands is to run sweepstakes or contests. Normally, products are completely subordinated to details and rules. This is fine with the makers of nondistinctive products who run sweepstakes and contests.

Advertisement for company that judges sweepstakes, and contests.

Careful planning of a sweepstakes or contest is matched in importance only by the need for honest, impartial, and competent judging. The advertiser, in this instance, is one of the top firms offering help to companies engaging in sweepstakes and contest promotions.

WITH SWEEPSTAKES:
"Winning isn't the only thing; winning is keeping your job."

Old D. L. Blair Proverb

The biggest winner in a sweepstakes should be the brand manager—the guy who came up with the idea of having a sweepstakes in the first place. But if the sweepstakes is a bomb, it can blow up a promising career.

A successful sweepstakes can do many things. It can dramatically increase brand awareness. It can build up high levels of traffic. It can increase coupon redemption. It can create excitement. It can increase your share of market. A sweepstakes can do a whole bunch of good things. An unsuccessful sweepstakes, on the other hand, can cost your company a wad of dough and could cost you your job.

What's the best way to insure success?
With sweepstakes as in horse racing, it pays to go with a winner. And in sweepstakes the winner, hands down, is D. L. Blair.

That's why 35 of the top 50 package-goods marketers come to us. And 5 of the top 10 magazines. And that's also why, on a regular basis, 12 of the top 15 agencies work with D. L. Blair.

"Why?" you ask. It's simple. We do most of the work and all of the worrying. We create the sweepstakes or contest idea. We develop the theme. We work out the methodology. We get involved with all that legal stuff. We receive and judge all the entries. And we award all the prizes.

If you're thinking of a sweepstakes—a *successful* sweepstakes—think about giving D. L. Blair a call or dropping us a line. Before you can say "success," we'll sit down with you and spell out, in detail, what we can do for you, your product and your company. And, of course, all in the strictest confidence.

D.L.BLAIR

We're number one in more ways than one.

185 Great Neck Rd., Great Neck, N.Y. 11021 · (516) 487-9200 · 1548 Front St., Blair, Nebraska 68008 · (402) 426-4701

A good example of this attitude is provided in the advertiser for a regional sugar product who ran advertising in two periods of the year—in the winter and in the summer. During these two periods an intensive campaign revolved around a contest. Each contest lasted six weeks. Preceding the contest, however, were two months of advertising in trade magazines ready by grocers. This advertising gave contest details and urged dealers to stock heavily in anticipation of consumer demand. In addition, the company carried on intensive sales efforts among dealers, food brokers, and supermarket headquarters.

In between the two contests each year, the manufacturer did no advertising because it was not possible to compete with the big national advertisers, and in any event, nothing could be said about sugar that would especially interest consumers. Using the twice-a-year approach, however, the advertiser was able to obtain heavy sales in the states in which the product was distributed. Each time sales in the region began lagging the next contest brought them up to the desired level.

Can help counteract strong competition. A good, resultful sweepstakes or contest can take the momentum out of a competitor's sales drive. A new product promotion, for example, can lose much of its excitement if the chief competing product is running a big, glamorous sweepstakes or contest just when advertising is breaking for the new product. In certain fiercely competitive lines, each advertiser is engaged in an intense business chess game in which one move cancels another. A sweepstakes or contest run at the right time is a good weapon in this game.

Contests vs. Sweepstakes

Not too many years ago when the word "contest" was used it meant just what the word implied—that persons who entered were competing with each other on a basis of skill. This "skill" might involve the writing of a statement about the advertiser's product, or telling why the contestant favored a certain presidential candidate, or performing some other required task that demanded a display of judgment, writing ability, or some other attribute.

Of late, however, what is often loosely called a contest is actually a "sweepstakes" form of contest, the winning of which is determined by chance instead of skill. Normally, the winner will be chosen through a drawing and, in keeping with modern times, the drawing may be conducted electronically with a computer.

Those running a bona fide contest must be certain that they are not by law running a lottery. They may be doing so if they require a contestant to make a payment or outlay to enter the contest and then determine the winner by chance. In a legitimate contest the contestant is, as already indicated, required to demonstrate judgment or skill. In a sweepstakes the entrants usually are required to do no more than to write their names and addresses.

In discussing the matter of lottery, the Post Office Department has said:

> The scheme may be a lottery as long as some pay, even though others play free. One general exception to this rule would be a type of plan which is fully described in an advertisement, providing for entry with evidence of purchase, but also permitting entry by submission of nothing more than a plain

Contest advertisement.

Although the sweepstakes have become more popular with advertisers than contests, the latter still have their appeal for consumers. In this one, as is customary, the product sell is subordinated to the selling of the contest itself. An extra is the picturing of products of the advertiser instead of writing copy about them.

piece of paper or a coupon in the advertisement on which the contestant writes in his own handwriting, or plain block letters, the name of the product or some other specified term.

Here are the types of contests commonly used by advertisers in the past:

(1) *Statements*. Contestants are required to tell in a specified number of words why they like the advertiser's product. The statement, however, may ask the writers to express themselves on some topic of the day.

(2) *Jingles or limericks*. Usually the advertiser will help contestants by supplying the first two or three lines of a four-line jingle or limerick and then require that the last line or words be supplied by the person entering.

(3) *Word games*. These can take a number of forms such as unscrambling mixed up words, or deriving all the words possible from a word or sentence supplied by the advertisers.

(4) *Miscellaneous*. In this category are many types. Some of these include naming a new product, writing a letter on an assigned topic, furnishing a recipe, or working out puzzles (usually very simple).

A good general rule in making a contest popular is not to ask contestants to do too much work nor to think too much. The surge in the popularity of the sweepstakes confirms this rule. Moreover, all the other types are usually made so easy that the person of very average education can easily do whatever is needed.

In today's easier contests, the contestants may be asked to do nothing more difficult than to submit snapshots, answers to several easy questions, or favorite recipes. Currently, for example, the Lawry's $5,000 Burger Contest offers that amount to a contestant whose recipe for a hamburger (in which Lawry seasoning is used) is judged to be the winner.

Prizes That Lure Entries

Just as a number of advertising specialists are constantly studying the public's preferences in premiums in order that a premium offer may have the greatest possible drawing power, so are other specialists analyzing the public's interests in contest prizes. Unless the prizes offered by sweepstakes and contests are widely attractive, entries will be cut down and the event judged a failure.

Prizes, ranked in order of their appeal will vary, of course, but will usually be rated about in this order: cash, vacations, merchandise, automobiles, miscellaneous.

Lest anyone take an oversimplified view of sweepstakes and contest prizes by looking at the foregoing list, it must be recognized that most offer a combination of such prizes. It would be a rare sweepstakes or contest, for example, that would offer *only* cash prizes, or only vacations. Lists of prize popularity are usually based on the popularity of the *first* prize offered in each.

Taking a hard-boiled look at prizes, the advertiser finds that year after year the cash prize remains popular because everyone who enters sweepstakes and contests can use cash. In contrast, many people might find the vacation spot selected as the prize unacceptable either because of the location or because of the timing. In many cases, therefore, the advertiser will allow the winner to take cash equivalent of the vacation.

Likewise, merchandise, automobiles, speedboats and other such prizes may not be acceptable because the winner already has what he needs in these items.

Despite the universal appeal for cash prizes, advertisers have in recent years stressed the unusual and even the bizarre in prizes because these prizes have great talk value and make for exciting advertising.

Interesting Rewards in Sweepstakes and Contests

Imagination and, as said in the foregoing, an awareness of current interests of the public, dictate prize choices. The more interesting the prize, the easier it is for the copywriter to create an exciting and different advertisement. Think, for example, how much the copywriter has to say if, as in the Johnny Walker Black Label Scholarship Contest, the prize is the entire cost of a college education. Compared with this the copywriter who must write eloquently about the awarding of an automobile has the tougher task simply because automobiles have been offered so often and, furthermore, lack the human interest appeal of the scholarship.

Then there was the all-expenses-paid trip to Spain for two that rewarded the winner with a Chrysler Cordoba upon returning from the luxury vacation. Capitalizing upon the current tennis craze was a giveaway during National Tennis Week of a tennis holiday at a luxury tennis clinic. For the pet owners, there was the Win-Your-Dog's-Weight-In-Gold sweepstakes sponsored by Chuck Wagon.

For an especially exciting and long-range promotion, there was the Smirnoff "Lifetime of Summers" contest that offered a couple (you and the one you love most) $5,000 a year to spend on vacation every year for the rest of the winner's life. Contestants were required to match drink names with various Smirnoff ingredients. Although there was nothing mentally taxing in the requirements, they *did* make participants think about the company's products.

Entertainment-minded sweepstakes participants found appealing the promotion that offered a box seat weekly for one year at any event occurring in New York City. This was a local promotion that was advertised in the *New York Times Magazine.* For those yearning for faraway places, Bali Swimwear enticed sweepstakes participants with a trip for two to Bali, but for more home-minded persons there was the Bigelow Home Furnishings Shopping Spree Sweepstakes. First prize was $20,000 in furniture, accessories, and a Bigelow carpet. Ninety-nine second prizes in this promotion gave winners 20 square yards of Bigelow carpeting.

Sometimes the sponsoring company offers a choice of first prizes, a sensible way to broaden participants' interest. Brach's Pick-A-Mix Sweepstakes, as an example, offered the first three winners a combination of prizes worth $10,000, $5,000 and $2,500 respectively. Another sweepstakes offered a grand prize of a vacation for two in a choice of five locations, plus an American Motors Pacer automobile.

Another desirable procedure in sweepstakes and contests is to associate, if possible, the promotion with the company's product. Perhaps the entrant can be required to answer questions that require reading of a company advertisement or brochure. Even more desirable is the required use of the product as in the Burger contest that specified the use of Lawry's salt in the winning recipe. Another technique for product involvement in a promotion is to offer the company's product as one of the prizes. This technique is especially appropriate if the company makes a product of significant value and usable by large numbers of sweepstakes or contest participants.

Eventually, after all this thinking has been done about the prize structure and other facets of the promotion, a copywriter must work up an appealing campaign. When he does, he should depart from the usual copy platform in favor of putting the overwhelming emphasis on the promotion instead of the product. Furthermore, the stress should be on the grand prize. Such total emphasis on the promotion provides a strong reason why it is desirable, if feasible, to get the company product associated in some way with the sweepstakes or contest. In the days when contests were supreme and sweepstakes not yet used, the product association with the promotion was almost automatic. Most contests required participants to complete a statement in "25 words or less" why they liked Heinz Beans, Ivory Soap, or some other product. In short, they were forced to think about the product.

Negatives and Limitations of Sweepstakes and Contests

Many sweepstakes and contests have been costly failures. Others have bred ill will. Others have failed to accomplish any results beyond the duration of the sweepstakes or contest. Advertisers should think carefully before they offer a sweepstakes or contest. Some other promotional approach may be better for them.

Unless a product is unusually good, a sweepstakes or contest can provide only a temporary stimulus to sales. For example, one sweepstakes and contest expert, when asked how many new prospects are derived from a sweepstakes or contest, indicated that fewer than one-fourth of those entering would be usual. To demonstrate his point he explained that:

(1) 500,000 entries can usually be considered as the number of entries that mark a successful sweepstakes or contest.
(2) Out of these, 175,000 might actually be the number of entrants, since multiple entries are sent in by a great many persons. This, of course, cuts down on the total number of people taking part.
(3) Cutting the number down still further, it is estimated that about one-fourth of the 175,000 are persons who enter *any* sweepstakes or contest, and thus cannot be considered especially good prospects for the product. These are "professional" participants, not typical prospects.
(4) In the matter of multiple entries, it was found in one contest that the average contestant sent in 12 entries and that in sweepstakes and contests in general there have been a number of cases where as many as 200 entries will be sent in by some contestants.

Accordingly, although sweepstakes and contests can draw millions of entries, the number of actual participants may be significantly smaller. Furthermore, the total population is relatively untouched by such promotions as shown in figures that reveal that only slightly more than 20 percent of the public has ever entered a sweepstakes or contest. Of those that do, moreover, more than 75 percent accompany their entries with facsimiles, not proof of purchase such as labels or box tops.[3]

Dealers are often disgruntled by sweepstakes and contests. Picture the average grocer. For years he has had company salespeople bustling into his store to tell him about sweepstakes or contests their companies are running. Each one is described as a great boon to the grocer's sales. Each salesperson inevitably urges the dealer to stock the product in greater-than-usual amounts. If the grocer is an independent dealer, the salesperson will jam the store with displays that scream for shoppers' attention to the sweepstakes or contest.

After all this merchandising hysteria and the jamming of shelves and basement storeroom with the sweepstakes or contest product, the customer call for the product may be very light. Meanwhile, one or more additional sweepstakes or contests may break at the same time so that the dealer must decide whether to load up on these additional products, too. Also, he must decide whether the displays for the first sweepstakes or contest must come down in order to make room for the new one. Then there is the matter of the entry blanks that must be put near the checkout counter if they are to be useful.

If the dealer pays no attention to the sweepstakes and contests, he is certain to have customers asking for the product in order that they may obtain their required box tops or labels. Also, they will want their entry blanks. A dealer who fails to supply sweepstakes and contest products or entry materials loses not only the immediate sales, but also future business because of customer disappointment.

Because of all these various factors, dealers often "suffer" sweepstakes and contests rather than welcome them. They feel that for the various pressures and inconveniences they must endure that the increase in sales of the products are not especially worthwhile recompense. Furthermore, a dealer, unlike the advertiser, does not usually obtain new customers because of sweepstakes and contests.

Consumer ill will can be caused by a sweepstakes or contest. A good many people are suspicious about sweepstakes and contests. They believe that no one in their geographical areas ever wins. They feel the judging is superficial if, indeed, there *is* any judging. They think the names are arbitrarily selected rather than drawn by pure chance. If skill is involved, they fail to see how their entries failed to earn some sort of prize since, naturally, they feel they have done a superior job of filling out the statement, of making up a jingle.

Sweepstakes and contests can disrupt long-range campaign objectives. Advertising success is normally based upon carefully working out long-range objectives and then *sticking with the plan that has been decided upon.* Almost always a sweepstakes or contest represents a departure from a predetermined plan. Very often it is what advertising people call a "one-shotter," something that will not be repeated.

Overall Suggestions for Sweepstakes and Contest Planning

There is no way to assure 100 percent success in a sweepstakes or contest, but there are certain actions that may be taken to stay out of trouble legally to maintain good relations with consumers and to assure that the event is not just a flash-in-the-pan promotion but a solid contribution to the company's welfare.

Plan the sweepstakes or contest as part of the total marketing effort.

Possibly the first task here is to sell the dealers on the value of the sweepstakes or contest to *them* and not to the company. Previously, it will be recalled, it was pointed out that dealers often look sourly at sweepstakes and contests as a "nuisance." Some dealers will always dislike almost every sweepstakes or contest; but, if it is sold well enough to dealers in advance, most of them should be able to become at least mildly interested in the event, or at least not resentful of it.

Following this selling of the dealers, the company should work out the advertising carefully. Because there are so many sweepstakes and contests, everything should be done to do a better-than-usual job of advertising in the sweepstakes and contest advertising and this advertising should be timed exactly right.

Working hand in hand with the advertising department is the sales department. The sales department has as a "must" objective the complete sales coverage of the sales market in which sweepstakes and contest advertising will appear. This market may be regional or it may be national. Whichever it is, every outlet must be covered and a stock of the sweepstakes or contest product should be in the dealer's stores. Usually an "extra" stock is needed in order to take care of heavier-than-usual demand.

Along with stocks of the product itself, each store where store rules permit such promotion should be alive with displays that call attention to the sweepstakes or contest. Ample supplies of entry blanks must be placed for easy access by customers. Many supermarket chains do not permit manufacturers to place sweepstakes or contest displays in stores throughout the chain, at least not without clearing first through chain headquarters and very seldom even then.

Prices are sometimes reduced during the sweepstakes or contest period. Since pricing is such an important aspect of the total marketing process, the matter must certainly be considered by the sweepstakes or contest advertiser.

Check all legal rules. Some states prohibit sweepstakes and/or contests. Others permit them, but have established special regulations that apply. Making certain the event is legal in every respect is a job for lawyers with experience in these matters. Not only must they be aware of state and national regulations, but also they must check post office regulations carefully. No one who has any respect for the law ever enters upon a sweepstakes or contest lightly.

Pick prizes with utmost caution. As already indicated, prizes must be significant nowadays to be able to lure entries; and in addition, they should show imagination. Because winning prizes is the only reason for a consumer to enter a sweepstakes or contest, the advertiser should examine the prizes used in successful promotions and consider what prize or combination of prizes is most likely to draw the largest number of entries.

Limit sweepstakes and contest duration. Although there is some debate on the point, most sweepstakes and contest users seem to favor an event of eight weeks. On the assumption that it may take two or three weeks to get the sweepstakes or contest rolling full speed, a month is viewed as too short a time span, whereas any period after eight weeks seems to find a falling off in interest.

Follow-up after a sweepstakes or contest. If the entries are not too numerous, it is a fine public relations policy to send thank-you-for-entering letters to entrants who have not won anything. An expression of regret from the advertiser can soften the disappointment and even bitterness felt by many contestants who fail to win anything. Sometimes it is possible to publish a list of the winners, or to offer to send a list of winners. This helps to allay suspicions of those who begin to wonder if any prizes were *actually* awarded.

Consider use of a sweepstakes or contest planner. Many companies, feeling inadequate to handle all the technicalities connected with sweepstakes and contests, settle their problems by turning over the entire planning and management of sweepstakes and contests to firms that specialize in this activity. Best known of such firms are Reuben H. Donnelly, D. L. Blair Corporation, and Advertising Distributors of America. Other firms also known for their work in this field are R. L. Polk, Price Adams, Spotts Corporation, and Marden-Kane.

Some advertisers who use enough sweepstakes and contests may employ specialists on their staffs, just as a number of companies set up premium departments headed by persons who have established reputations in the premium field.

QUESTIONS

1. What, despite other reasons, is the fundamental reason for a package's existence?

2. Why is the statement made that without modern packaging today's supermarket could not function as it does?

3. How can a package contribute to the positioning of a product? Name some examples.

4. What is the danger in relating packaging closely to the creative theme of a product advertising campaign?

5. What kind of package changes should not seriously hurt customer sales of a product?

6. What are the effects of moving packages from floor level to waist level and from floor level to eye level on supermarket shelves?

7. What would you use in the design and copy of a package to make it appealing to children?

8. What is the basic reason for use of a sweepstakes or contest?

9. Why are makers of products such as sugar and salt sometimes inclined to use sweepstakes or contests for promotion?

10. What seems to be the trend in today's contests insofar as what the advertisers require the contestants to do?

11. Of the various prizes, which seem to have the greatest appeal for sponsors of sweepstakes and contests?

12. Should, or should not, a copywriter put major emphasis on the details of a sweepstakes or contest and thus neglect the usual product selling and/or copy platform?

13. Why are the big figures quoted for participants in sweepstakes or contests not so impressive as they seem?

14. About how long should a sweepstakes or contest last?

REFERENCES

1. Walter P. Margulies, "Plan Packages to Fit into Their Retailment Environment," February 2, 1970, p. 51.
2. It is recommended that the serious student of packaging refer to the many excellent articles on packaging that have appeared in the magazine *Advertising Age* under the authorship of Walter P. Margulies. The authors of this book are themselves indebted to him for many interesting points.
3. William A. Robinson, "*12 Basic Promotion Techniques,*" Advertising Age, January 10, 1977, P. 50.

Section VI
CREATING
ADVERTISING

FROM LAYOUT TO FINISHED ART: HOW AN ADVERTISEMENT IS FORMED

FROM LAYOUT TO FINISHED ART: HOW AN ADVERTISEMENT IS FORMED

Every advertising artist starts on an even basis with other artists—with a blank piece of paper. But true creativeness, imagination, and ingenuity enable one artist to make much better use of that blank space than another artist. In preparing an advertisement, the creative process begins with a *layout*, a drawing that indicates the placement of the various elements that make up the whole. These elements include such items as headlines, subheads, illustrations, company signature, price figures, and others. (While layout artists work with many forms of printed advertising such as booklets, catalogs, posters, direct-mail pieces, and others, this chapter is concerned chiefly with layouts as used in magazine and newspaper advertisements. Most of the principles of layout design, however, can be applied in the other forms of printed advertising.)

A layout artist may work anywhere that advertising is done but most discussions of layout artists seem to concern those who work in advertising agencies. The agency layout person may simply turn out rough layouts that illustrate the ideas of the copywriter for presentation to the client, or in some agencies the artist may take the layout through all the layout stages. Other layout artists are *free lancers*, who are hired for their skill by the advertising agency. Such artists may turn out more polished layouts, possibly in some specialty such as furniture, clothing, or machinery.

Depending upon who is doing the layout, it may serve one, or all, of the following purposes:

- It lets everyone concerned with the advertisement, particularly agency clients, see just how it will appear in print.
- It is a guide to those who do the physical work of preparing an advertisement: the artist, the copywriter, the platemaker, the printer, and the bindery worker.
- It provides a basis for estimating costs.
- It is a gauge of whether all the material that must go into an advertisement can fit into the space provided.

- It provides a clue to whether the idea that sounded so good during the "talk" stage can actually be utilized successfully in an advertisement.

Illustration using line art.

Such illustrations reproduce well in newspapers. The repetition of the figures in this instance creates an interesting effect. This advertisement, incidentally, ran in the United States edition of Christian Science Monitor.

LAYOUT STAGES

Layouts go from the very rough basic forms to elaborate work that sometimes falls in the expensive, fine-art category. Not all of the following stages are used for all advertisements, depending upon the artist and the nature of the assignment. Still, everyone deeply involved in layout preparation knows about these stages and has probably, at one time or another, been directly involved with them.

Thumbnail

Simplest of all the layout forms, the thumbnail is often a part of the initial "doodling" process in which the artist is, as it were, thinking out loud on paper. It is a very sketchy indication of the form of the advertisement and the placement of the major elements therein. As the name implies, thumbnails are small, possibly one or two square inches but there is no established size.

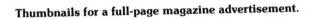

Thumbnails for a full-page magazine advertisement.

Anyone involved in advertising, whether artist, copywriter, or account executive, may have occasion to make thumbnails. This chapter will refer to this individual as the designer, no matter what the formal job title may be.

The designer will draw countless thumbnails in order to evolve one usable idea. In these simple drawings will appear the basic elements of the advertisement. Sometimes that "usable idea" will seem to be an accident. In a sense this may be true, but it is a controlled accident that the designer made happen.

Thumbnail sketch.

A competent artist may "doodle" on his pad for sometime making sketches such as this before he makes a full-size rough layout. Also, the thumbnail is often done by a copywriter who is trying to visualize the placement and proportion of elements. Even persons wholly inept in drawing can find it useful and possible to devise thumbnails in order to know what direction the layout should take.

Rough Layout

Evolving a good usable idea from all the thumbnails is a process similar to that of the person who writes scores of trial headlines. Suddenly, as if the artist has been smiled upon by some kind superior being, the "right" headline appears. When the "right" thumbnail idea appears on the artist's drawing pad, it is converted into a rough layout. Again, the drawing is a sort of visual shorthand; this time the artist constructs "complete sentences" instead of the fragments of the thumbnail.

The work is free and fast. Spontaneity is an essential ingredient and this comes from swift, though controlled, sketching.

The rough is done on any suitable paper. Usually it is in pencil, but it may be in any medium, especially when done in color. For a color advertisement, the designer begins using hues at this stage.

The rough is always the same size as the finished advertisement. Illustrations are shown in sketchy form, but their tonal values are shown quite accurately. Headlines are sketched in quickly and without detail. Copy blocks are shown to the extent that their tonal value is clearly apparent.

The rough may be reworked several times. In the larger size it is possible to show the relationship of details within the advertisement that are not included in the thumbnail. The final rough may accordingly be drastically different from the first rough or the thumbnails.

Rough dummy developed from thumbnails shown in Fig. 27-1.

Comprehensives

When all the problems have been solved in the rough, a more detailed plan is prepared. This is the comprehensive, or "comp."

The comp resembles, as closely as possible, the finished advertisement. The artwork will be shown in approximately its final form, whether black-and-white or color. There will still be refinements made by the artist in the final version, but these will be comparatively slight. The size of the copy block and the tonal value of the type will be exact. Headlines will be carefully traced or reproduced by other means, which we shall soon consider.

For tracing, the designer uses a type specimen book or cards that are especially printed for this purpose. The desired word or phrase is outlined on transparent tracing paper. Then the reverse of the tracing paper is covered by wide (chisel-point) pencil strokes which, in effect, convert it into "carbon paper." Laying the tracing paper on the comp and again tracing the letters transfers them to the dummy. Often a good letterer will do the work freehand with felt-tip pens.

The degree of polish will depend on the person who must approve the advertisement. For typical clients, business persons who have little or no experience in graphic arts (often unable to visualize beyond what has been done), the comp must be very detailed. This can be quite expensive.

Materials for Comprehensives. If art is already available, a photostat may be made in the right size and pasted into position. Headlines may actually be set in type, or they may be done in stick-on or transfer letters.

Material to show copy blocks is also available in stick-on form. These are lines of symbols that look like words at a glance but merely suggest mass and position. This material is called "Copy Block" by Zip-A-Tone, and similar names by other manufacturers. It is available in three different sizes to represent the most commonly used body types.

In some instances the designer will have a Polaroid picture made for the comp because it is difficult to duplicate the tone and texture of a photograph in a pencil drawing.

Recurring elements—signature, trademark, product, and so forth—are clipped from previous advertisements, and pasted in. Reverses are in the form of negative photostats. Color is shown in its exact hue and value.

Mechanicals

The final layout is the mechanical. This may be the finished copy for the platemaker or the detailed instructions for the printer and photographer.

The mechanical is usually the same size as the finished advertisement. (For platemaking it may be a little larger.) All the elements, in the form of "repro" (reproduction) proofs, finished hand arts, or stats or Veloxes (prints made on special photographic paper) of it are pasted in precise position. If the advertisement is to be in color, overlays are used for mechanical separations.

In some instances, notably for letterpress, the mechanical can be replaced by the comp.

Finished advertisement developed from rough shown in Fig. 27-2.

We have no way to make you richer. That's up to you.

We do have an unusual savings plan to help keep you from suddenly getting poorer. The plan does three things for you and your family.

▸ It pays you a weekly income if you get sick or hurt — without touching the money you save.

▸ It helps you save for the future any amount you choose.

▸ If you don't live, this plan will automatically complete itself and pay to your family the money you hoped to save.

We call this plan The Security Mutual Accumulator. It works for you no matter how much you earn, how much you can save or how much insurance you now own. It's a way to save for the future and make sure that you don't have to spend your savings if you get sick or hurt.

If there's a representative of Security Mutual Life listed in your phone book, call him. He will give you more details. Or write us for "The Accumulator" booklet. No representative will visit you unless you say so.

"FOR RICHER. . .
FOR POORER"

SECURITY MUTUAL
Life Insurance Company
BINGHAMTON, NEW YORK
"For the man who knows what 'always' means"

Each of these "blueprints" may have other names. Often an advertising department or agency will have its own set of terms. *Layout* may refer to the comp or mechanical. *Visual* is used for a rough or comp. Preliminary *sketch*, or just plain sketch, is a common name for the rough.

In the final two stages, the layouts have done their job of showing the client how his advertisement will appear, and of directing the graphic arts workers in the actual making of the printing forms or plates. Already in rough form the cost estimator can accurately determine the expenses involved.

The final two functions of a layout—fitting and blending the material—are even more important. The designer must, of course, arrange the necessary materials in the designated area. If copy blocks will not fit, copy must be revised or smaller type used. Pictures must be scaled to appropriate sizes. Elements must be arranged in logical order.

These tasks can all be done in a mechanical way, without imagination. An example is the typical advertisement for a cut-rate drugstore. The designer squeezes dozens—or scores or even hundreds—of items into the space. While the advertisement does its job with reasonable efficiency, it lacks that sparkle of creativity that makes an outstanding advertisement.

Mechanical pasteup.

Note instructions in margin and reuse of artwork from advertisement shown in Fig. 27-3.

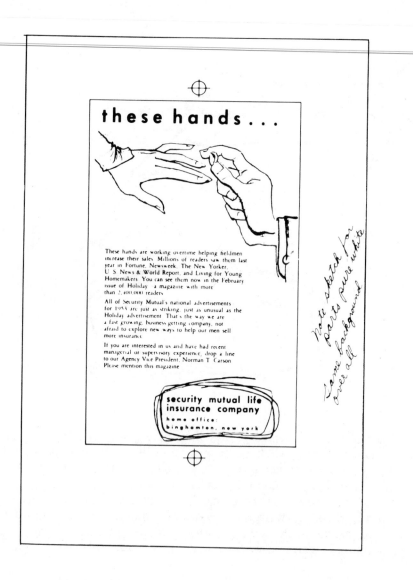

Visualizing The Appeal

Creativity is needed to visualize the appeal of an advertisement. This is the biggest challenge to the designer.

A good advertisement is more than a mere arrangement of typographic elements. It is a communication that reaches deeper into the subconscious of the reader than the individual elements can, singly or in total.

The creative process that makes an advertisement requires talent, skill, and knowledge. The result is a message that is instantly grasped—and that motivates the reader to action. Yet, not all advertisements succeed in getting their message across.

This chapter looks at the creative process primarily as it relates to preparing print-media advertisements. But the principles of the process, with only little modification, apply to all visual advertisements: outdoor posters, booklets, letterheads, three-dimensional packages, point-of-purchase displays, and television commercials.

COMPONENTS OF AN ADVERTISEMENT

All print advertising has some of these elements: headlines, copy, blocks, illustrations, signatures, trademarks or emblems, borders, and rules.

No one will deny that signatures, trademarks, and emblems are legitimate and necessary elements of an advertisement. Too often, however, the client will insist that too many of these constants be used in a single advertisement. By the time the designer has worked in an oversized signature, a slogan or two, several emblems, a picture of the factory, and "Our Founder," there may be little room for the sales message. And then the client decides to add a coupon!

Signatures

Signatures (signs) are trademarks. As such, they derive value from continuity and public acceptance. This does not mean, however, that a signature cannot be touched. If a "sig" or signature, is not functional, it should be changed. It is interesting to note how even the most familiar trademarks on the American scene have evolved over the years. Usually the change is slight; sometimes it is drastic.

A signature should be evaluated regularly. Even the good ones need refurbishing or redesigning at intervals. These are the criteria:

- *A signature must be legible.* The function of a signature is to identify an advertisement immediately and unmistakably. Of course, the reader who is familiar with a signature will recognize it, as a symbol, without actually reading it. Among any readership, however, there will always be a large percentage of new readers who must read the sig to comprehend it.
- *A signature must be distinctive.* The signature on an advertisement must be like the signature on a check—as different as possible from any other signature. Distinction is the quality that makes it recognizable over and beyond its legibility. An unusual silhouette, for instance, is an assurance of this distinction.

Rough layout for newspaper advertisement.

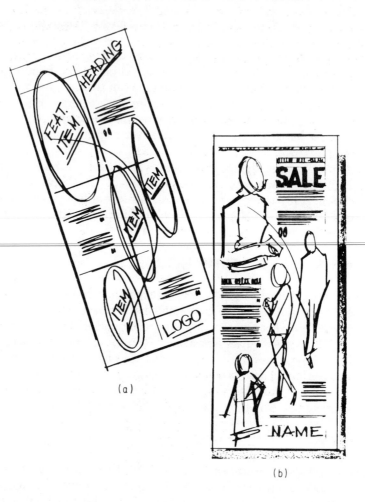

(a)

(b)

- *A signature must be usable in many sizes.* A signature can range in size from the small one used on a business card to one that occupies the whole side of a delivery truck or even a building.
- *A signature must be appropriate.* Without knowing anything about an advertiser, the reader ought to be able to tell much from the signature alone. Is this a manufacturer of heavy road-building equipment or a retailer of women's wear? Is this a high-quality, high-priced store, or is it one that stresses bargains? Is this an old, established firm whose stability is a major asset, or is it a new firm that caters to the fashions of the moment?
- *A signature should be handsome.* Appearance, of course, may be a matter of personal taste. The advertiser (and his readers) will have to live constantly with his sig. It is the one element that will appear in every advertisement, and it will be used constantly on business forms. Certainly it must be a design that is going to wear well.

- *A signature should be simple.* Simplicity is a fair guarantee of beauty; it is also an assurance of legibility and distinction. It is much harder to design a good, simple signature than ornate one. Decorations and frills tend to hide weaknesses in basic design. Such disguise offers only a short-lived advantage; poor design does not wear well, despite any attempts to disguise it.

Comprehensive dummy for newspaper advertising.

The designer must keep in mind all the elements that go along with the signature: the address, the phone number, and information such as store hours, credit plans, and parking. A pattern must be evolved for using these addenda without detracting from the sig itself.

Another consideration, associated especially with simplicity, is how well the signature (and this applies to the trademark designation discussed in the following material) will show up in the different media. A signature used in a newspaper advertisement or a magazine advertisement sits on the page, available for long inspection, or rereading. In television or outdoor advertising, in contrast, flash reading is all that will be possible. Thus, the simpler the better. This is true, likewise, of any such items appearing on a package because here, too, the hurrying shopper reads quickly and makes fast decisions as she goes down the aisles of the supermarket. The designer should make reading easy.

Varying sales approach using same layout.

Varied weights of rules and type make (A) a "hard-sell" layout; (B) a "middle-of-the road" advertisement; (C) a "soft-sell approach," almost "high fashion."

Placement of Signature.   Some advertisers contend that the sig should be at the very top of an advertisement to identify the advertiser immediately.

Others insist that the signature is just that—the signature that appears at the end of a written message of any kind. Like any other signature, they say, the sig should be at the bottom of the page.

Sometimes a Solomonic decision is to place the sig in both positions, top and bottom. In the case of a full-page newspaper advertisement, this is usually a wise decision. Newspaper pages are normally folded, so that only half of the advertisement is exposed. Using two sigs assures that at least one of them will be visible at all times.

Typical "schlock" or "borax" advertisement.

This is difficult to read because of distracting elements and lack of convenient pattern.

Trademarks

A trademark must, in general, meet the same standards as a signature. Often the trademark is an ideogram; it passes along its meaning without the use of words. Thus it need not be legible in the same sense that a sig must be legible. Yet it must be legible in the sense that the reader will recognize the "picture" of an idea as quickly and as definitely as the letters of the word. The famed trademark of International Harvester is an interesting example. Most people recognize the mark as a monogram of a lowercase *i* and a capital *H*. Other people see a stylized "picture" of a farmer riding a tractor. The monogram is adequate as identification; the "picture" expands the message by suggesting the kind of business or merchandise.

LAYOUT CREATIONS

The layout artist seeks an arrangement of typographic elements that makes it easy, convenient, and pleasant to read an entire printed message.

There is a running argument as to whether layout or copy is the more important component of a printed advertisement.

While it is primarily the copy that persuades the reader to buy merchandise or services the best copy in the world is useless unless, and until, it is read. The primary function of layout is to assure this readership.

Anyone who has studied Starch readership reports and other readership analyses, cannot fail to notice that readership of body copy is quite low in most advertisements. The big figures in the reports are obtained by the headlines and illustrations, usually in combination. These two layout elements normally account for figures that are so much higher than those earned by the body copy

International harvester trademark.

It can be read as a monogram of i and H or as a stylized picture of a farmer riding on a tractor.

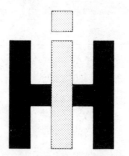

that the results tend to discourage talented and hard-working copywriters.

What is done in the layout can showcase the copy and help bring up the readership figures, or it can result in copy earning even lower readership scores than usual. No one denies the importance of the copy message but the reading public is captured first by the layout. Clients, too, tend to make their judgments largely on how they react to the headline and layout. Thus, the general appearance of the advertisement is the first consideration. After this impression has been made, the copy is read.

With so much riding on the creative excellence of the layout, the layout designer has a clear-cut responsibility for the success of an advertisement. In the following section you will read about the layout approaches that help the layout artist achieve *selling* advertisements. To accomplish this, the artist first of all makes certain that the layout is functional *and* organic.

A *functional* layout is one that does a specific job well and one in which each element does a job. Each element in a layout must be assayed. We must ask: "Does this element do a good job?" If the answer is in the negative, we throw out that element as quickly as possible.

Product alone.

It was important to feature the product in this 2/3-page magazine advertisement. Thus, no other layout elements were introduced. Notice the effective use of takeout lines to call attention to four product features.

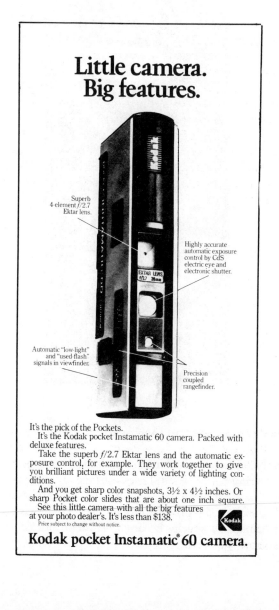

When we say a layout must be *organic,* we mean it must grow like a living organism. Veteran advertising people often say: "This advertisement laid itself out." What they mean is this: There was such a logical interrelation between all the elements of an advertisement that there was only one pattern in which they could be disposed.

Blacking out.

By blacking out the background the advertiser concentrates the reader's attention on the product. This technique, in alliance with an attention-getting headline and an interesting copy line, give this small advertisement good impact.

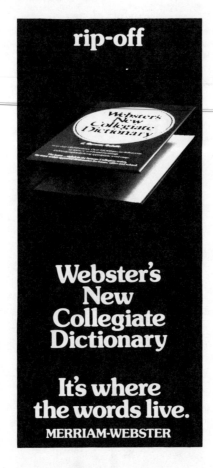

Establishing Basic Premises For The Layout Design

No matter just how the designer does it, the task is to establish basic premises by answering these or similar questions:

(1) Shall I illustrate the product alone?
(2) Shall I emphasize special features?
(3) Shall I show the product in use?

(4)   Shall I picture the benefits of use?
(5)   Shall I show new uses?
(6)   Shall I provide a setting for the product?
(7)   Shall I use magnification?
(8)   Shall I make comparisons?
(9)   Shall I feature symbols?
(10) Shall I feature the disadvantages of not using the product?

Show The Product Alone? The simplest illustration is of the product alone. This can be effective despite, or because of, its simplicity. Often it is the appearance of the product that produces the sale. In wearing apparel, china and silverware, furniture, and many other lines, the reader must see the product, or a picture of it, to decide whether to buy it.

Often the inherent beauty of the product, even if it is not in a changeable style, is a pleasant attention-compeller. Such is Steuben glass. For packaged

FIGURE 00.
Transit card layout—a challenge.

Designed to jar riders from their daily boredom, transit cards often have a creative twist. In this instance, a strong message is conveyed with minimum copy.

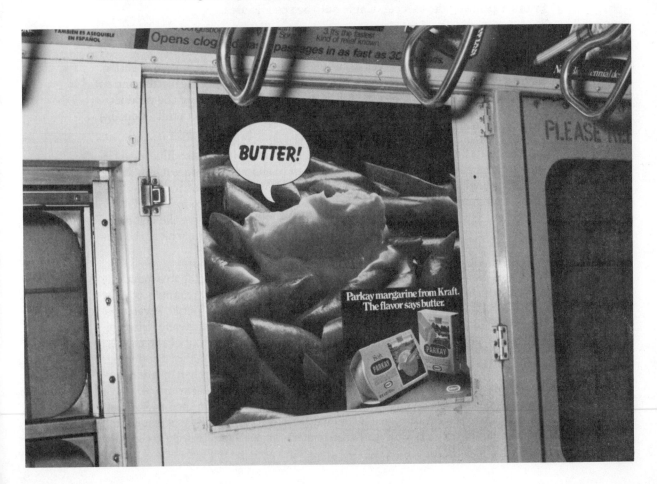

goods, the picture in the advertisement provides the reader with identification to seek out the product on crowded shelves or to recognize it when it comes within view.

If the product is small in size it is almost imperative to show it alone. Background or accessories, even though appropriate, would dwarf a diamond ring, wristwatch, or hearing aid. Small advertising space also requires that the product be shown alone. If the area is limited, there just is not enough room to show anything except the item itself.

Emphasize Special Features? Few items of merchandise on today's market are exclusive. Almost always the reader has several or many other automobiles, blouses, television sets, or pens to choose from. The decision to buy a particular brand or make is often based on some feature unique to that one line. Illustrations can persuasively call the reader's attention to such features.

The product, in small size, may be shown as if under a magnifying glass, with the unique feature greatly enlarged. Or the detail may be removed from the product and illustrated in a more illuminating way.

The rest of the product may be ghosted, or grayed down, with only the special feature in full tonal value. A tint block may be used under the feature alone, or the tint may be shown under all the product except the feature. Arrows or other pointing devices can single out the specific area.

Show The Product In Use? Showing the product in use is an excellent way of creating interest.

Readers can put themselves in the picture when they see a human in action. Psychologically, the viewer "trade places" with the human in the picture and so uses the product himself. In effect, it is a way of demonstrating the product.

At the least, showing a product in use suggests, or even details, benefits that accrue from the use of the product.

Picture The Benefits Of Use? Often it is more effective to illustrate the benefits that come from using a product than to show the product itself. In the case of intangibles, we cannot show the product; we must illustrate something else. Sometimes there is nothing new left to say about the product itself.

For such products the illustration becomes a little narrative the last scene of which tells the readers: "Then Mrs. Jones used Slim-Trim, and look at the nice thing that happened."

Show New Uses? A basic sales technique for any product is to expand the uses to which it can be put. Scott Towels are an excellent example of this. Originally they were used only for drying hands, mostly in public lavatories. Because there is a definite ceiling on the number of hands washed and dried daily in public lavatories, there was a ceiling on the sales potential of the towels.

The manufacturer sought new uses in order to increase sales. Soon paper towels were advertised, and used, for drying dishes in the kitchen, draining excess grease off fried foods, wiping windows, and polishing glassware. A whole new market, the private home, was opened. Users were encouraged to find new uses and share their discoveries through other advertisements. As a result a roll of towels lasted only a few days instead of a few weeks; again the market was expanded.

Provide A Setting For The Product? Many products are in themselves neither beautiful nor interesting. For such a product, interest and pleasure can be provided by the setting in which the product is shown. Many products, though not necessarily ugly, have no appeal by themselves. A rug, for instance, can be monotonous when shown all alone. The proper furniture brings out the beauty of the rug.

The setting must be appropriate. A very expensive Oriental rug should not be shown in a casual basement game room; neither should a medium-priced rug be shown in a setting so luxurious that the reader is led to believe, without even reading the copy, that she cannot afford it.

Use Magnification? Probably most items that the average American buys are of a size that demands reduction in advertising pictures. But there are some products so small that even were they shown life-size, detail would be lost. For these products, dramatic enlargement can add interest and significance.

When size is exaggerated, it is best to eliminate any extraneous detail of surroundings. When the setting is important, it can be shown in reduced size, with the product illustrated separately and in much larger proportions.

Make Comparisons? Before-and-after techniques have been used since the days of the medicine show. Often such advertising is crude, unconvincing, and of dubious taste. Handled with care and taste, it is an effective device because it persuades in a simple and believable way.

The technique may be actually that of before-and-after. One picture may show an automobile that is dull and dirty. The second shows the same car bright and gleaming, the result of using So-Glow polish.

A variation is to show a 10-year old car that has been kept sparkling by using So-Glow, while another car, same make and same age, is drab and dreary because its owner used Brand X polish instead of So-Glow.

Feature Symbols? Symbols have a deep appeal for most people. The cross of Christianity means more in itself than thousands of words of exposition. When we see Santa Claus, we need not be told that the Christmas season is at hand. When we see the skull-and-crossbones device on a poison bottle, we draw away instinctively.

Many things that are advertised are so intangible that we must either symbolize them or use many words of explanation that may well be ignored by the reader.

Insurance companies, because they must sell perhaps the most intangible of all services, have been leaders in using symbols. The Travelers' uses a ubiquitous red umbrella to symbolize the protection its policies give. All-State shows a home held in a protective pair of hands. Prudential has the Rock of Gibraltar for a salesperson, testifying to the stability and strength of the company.

Feature Disadvantages Of Not Using The Product? The lawn that's grown out of control; the house with peeling paint; the woman with a blotchy, sunburned skin; the unhappy child who stands alone, while others play nearby; the attractive girl (with bad breath) who never dates the same man twice—all

Layout designed for quick reading.

Outdoor layouts must be attention-getting because they are given glance reading by hurrying motorists. Simplicity in layout design, and brevity in the copy are mandatory, as in this outdoor poster.

these are stock characters in advertising. All, advertisers assure readers, have problems that use of the advertiser's product can solve.

Showing what happens if a product is *not* used can be dramatic and gives full scope to the advertising designer's imagination. It can also be a dangerous technique because it may be too negative. Also, if not handled well, it can be overly-exaggerated and, hence, unbelievable.

Other Considerations for the Designer at the Start

(1) *Photography vs. artwork.* Generally, photographs are used where absolute realism is needed, as in an industrial advertisement showing a man in a factory who is telling why he uses the advertiser's product.

Sometimes exact details must be shown of a machine or tool. If lifelike details will sell an item, photography can be an imperative. Automobiles and many other items sold through detailed pictures find photographs best for illustrations. Such photographs are usually cheaper, but not always. Also, they can be executed more quickly except possibly for elaborate color work.

If an impression is wanted, sometimes artwork can supply it better. Ultra-smartness and sophistication can sometimes be conveyed through the exaggerations of artwork. Lifelike qualities can be sacrificed by the artist in order to focus attention through exaggeration on the item sold, or the person featured. Artwork, likewise, can create exactly the characters needed for a copy situation—a dynamic business-executive type, or an idealized, silver-haired couple for a retirement-fund. Finding such persons for photographic illustrations is often difficult, but the competent artist can draw them endlessly from his imagination.

(2) *Use of children and/or animals.* It is said that no one can resist a picture of a child or a dog. When the youngster and the animal are joined in a photo, the photo is irresistible.

The appeal of the child's picture comes from the human need for progeny. Children make perfect models. They are not self-conscious, and they instinctively assume graceful and interesting poses. Even when shown in less than idyllic circumstances, the child is attractive. The reader is drawn as much by the dirty-faced little tyke as by the angelic one in spotless dress.

The appeal of animals, on the other hand, is not universal. There is, in fact, a considerable segment of people who actively dislike animals. Even people who love dogs may dislike cats, and vice versa.

There certainly is, however, a fascination with animals. Animals are much like children, in that they habitually assume pleasing poses. Animals are useful, too, as symbols. The elephant typifies strength; the cat, elegance; the dog, devotion. The tiger, unlike most of the felines which ordinarily have feminine connotations, has a strong masculine appeal. During one advertising season there were successful advertising campaigns for automobiles, gasoline, hairdressing, tires, and perfumes all based on the tiger.

The designer must remember to show a logical connection between the animal and the product or lose all the animal's potential appeal.

(3) *Use of humor.* Humor puts the reader in a pleasant and receptive mood but humor must, of course, have some connection with the sales message, and it must be in the best of taste. There are some products and services that just do not lend themselves to humorous advertising. Heaven help the funeral director who attempts even the slightest levity in advertising.

Once, however, an acceptable humorous format has been established it sets the stage for an inexhaustible supply of situations for an enduring campaign. Consider Benson & Hedges with the bent cigarettes, or Tareyton's characters with the black eyes because they'd rather fight than switch. And then the humor-in-advertising backers can point to the long-lasting New England life campaign that demonstrated to the skeptics that life insurance advertising *could* use humor. Young people have gone to school, married, had children and become middle-aged while the *Philadelphia Bulletin's* advertisement assured readers that nearly everyone in Philadelphia does, indeed, read the *Bulletin.* Still, despite these long-time successes, humor can backfire, and it is extremely difficult for the advertising designer to think of a humorous format that can hold up as a long-time campaign. It's easy to run dry of humorous situations.

Centered layout pattern

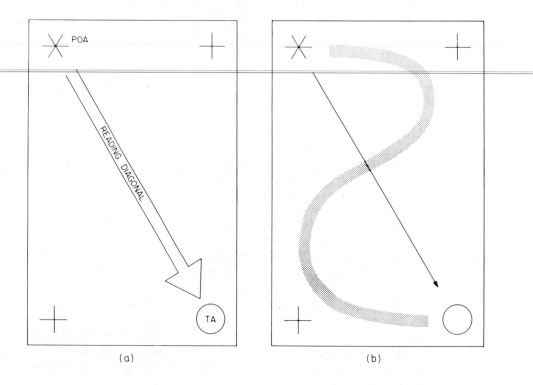

(a)   (b)

LAYOUT PATTERNS

The simplest pattern is the symmetrical, with its subdivisions of centered balance and formal balance (figure 21-1).

Every element in the advertisement is centered on the vertical at the middle of the area. Such a layout is simple to prepare. Centered advertisements are easy to set.

Formal symmetrical layouts balance some elements in mathematical precision and center the rest. If a mirror is placed on edge at the vertical or horizontal center of the advertisement, or diagonally either way, the exposed half of the advertisement and its mirror image will look just like a symmetrical advertisement. This pattern, too, is easy to lay out and to make up. All the necessary placement can be done with a ruler.

FIGURE 21-1
Centered layout pattern.

Symmetrical layouts, whether centered or formal, have both strengths and weaknesses. Symmetrical advertisements stand solid and dignified. They give the impression of strength, permanence, and authority. Because this is exactly the impression that many advertisers seek to convey, symmetrical patterns are ideal for their use. Churches, financial institutions, funeral directors, and law firms can use this layout effectively. A person in the market for stocks and bonds is looking for solidity and security. An advertisement that gives the impression of firm dependability will help the reader decide, often subconsciously, that this is the broker with whom to deal or that this is the company in which to invest money.

These very strengths of symmetry are also its weaknesses. The line between dignified and stodgy, conservative and reactionary, authoritative and aloof is a fine one. It does not take much to turn a favorable impression into a poor one. Like people, advertisements that demonstrate these admirable qualities are not very exciting. A dignified college dean will not attract as much attention as a colorful halfback.

A virtue of symmetrical advertisements is their simplicity. A sales message delivered in a straightforward manner has built-in effectiveness. Advertisements without illustrations lend themselves to centered layouts. Tall, narrow advertisements are often used to the greatest advantage in formal balance or centered, because the layout artist does not have much room for maneuvering elements.

Informal-balance Layouts

All layout patterns other than symmetrical are called informal-balance, dynamic, or asymmetrical.

When the layout artist begins to assemble one of these patterns, it is important to visualize an imaginary pivot at the optical center of the adver-

FIGURE 21-2
Formal layout patterns.

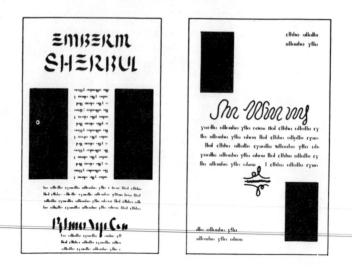

tisement—that is, at the horizontal center but six-tenths of the vertical distance from the bottom. Then the elements are placed as if they had physical weight and in such a way that the advertisement hangs almost but not quite straight up and down.

Imbalance lends a dynamic, exciting quality to a layout, a fact that can be demonstrated by analyzing a familiar and pleasing picture. Almost invariably, it will be noted that it doesn't "stand straight."

Classic Layouts

A classic layout gets its name from the fact that great artists of the past developed the characteristic patterns, and that they have been in use ever since. Age has not diminished their usefulness.

Classic layouts are usually in the basic shapes of letters of our alphabet. The most famous, and most useful, is the reverse S. The regular S is another favorite. Triangles can be as powerful in advertisements as they are in paintings; the renowned "Mona Lisa," for example, is triangular in composition. The triangle need not be equilateral, with all sides equal, or isosceles, with the two rising sides equal.

An L, facing either way, is an effective classical composition. Whistler's "Mother" is designed as a backward-facing L. The letters T, Y, and U are also classical bases. They may face in any direction.

The classic layout, in addition to being pleasing to the eye in its gracefulness, also *leads* the eye to the places in the layout that are important—sometimes the price; sometimes the signature, or the item being advertised.

FIGURE 21-3
Classical Layout Patterns. (a) reverse-S; (b) pyramid; (c) reverse-L.

(a)   (b)   (c)

READING PATTERNS

As you turned to this page, where did you look first? At the upper left corner, of course. You gave this no thought; you knew instinctively that this is where you start to read. If you had been taught to read and write in Arabic, you would have just as instinctively looked at the top right corner, for the Semitic languages read right to left.

The top left corner, for those using the Latin alphabet, is the primary optical area (POA). Each page and each subdivision of a page has its own POA. On first looking at a newspaper page the eye moves to the top left of the page. When we look at an individual advertisement the POA tends to be somewhat different as will be explained.

By continuation of habit and instinct, we always know what the goal of our reading is on any page or subdivision of a page. It is the lower right corner, the terminal area. Whether we read or write, we know that when we reach that lower right corner, we have completed the page or the advertisement. So it is to this goal that we always move. The basic path of the reading eye, then, is this southeasterly sweep, the reading diagonal.

Analyze any advertisement, newspaper page, or magazine spread that you find pleasant and inviting. About eight times out of ten, you'll find that the reading diagonal is well defined.

A reverse S lures and directs the eye by taking advantage of these ingrained reading patterns. Beginning at the POA, it ends in the terminal area. Thus, the lessons learned from the fine artist are utilized by the advertising layout man.

One observation should be made here. Very often readers when turning a page and seeing an advertisement, will find their eyes settling upon the optical center of the advertisement instead of the upper left-hand corner. The latter is a natural starting point for a printed page but in advertisements the situation is different because strong headlines in big type, or a big, interesting illustration, may be placed near, at the center of the page. Thus, the eye may settle on that point. In fact, advertising readers have formed the habit of looking at the optical center (slightly above and to the left of the exact center). This is a logical starting point for most advertisements. It is also called the *focal point* of an advertisement.

Once the eye has settled on that point, it may jump to other areas of the advertisement but the general tendency is to follow the reading diagonal, previously discussed. It would be a mistake, however, to assume that because we are used to starting the reading of printed pages in the upper left-hand corner that this is automatically the case with advertisements. Regardless, the reading diagonal principle is sound once the initial starting point has been established, and certainly there is no question that overwhelmingly most Readers of body copy will begin their reading in the upper left portion of the copy.

Layout Movement and Eye Flow

Just as the layout artist uses the classical layout patterns for almost forcing readers to look at an advertisement in a certain way, so he uses other arrangements of layout elements to direct eye flow. For instance, the gaze of one of the figures in an illustration may direct the reader's eye to an item, price, or copy block. This *gaze motion,* as it is sometimes called, can be accomplished, also, through the use of a pointing hand, lines, arrows, dots, or a moving object such as a boat, an airplane, or an automobile.

Usually, the movement is from top to bottom, or left to right to conform to normal reading patterns. Beginners in layout work are warned quickly not to have the reader's gaze directed *out* of the advertisement as might be the case if a person in the illustration is looking, or pointing, at something out of the advertisement. Axiom: Generally, face people and objects *into* an advertisement as often as practical.

More about eye flow. A layout designer usually avoids erecting "dams" across an advertisement, elements that cut off one part from another. Example: heavy lines separating the illustration from the copy.

In fact, to achieve eye flow, the designer is well advised to relate copy blocks close to high interest spots in the layout in order to obtain highest readership. Preferably, they should be directly below the major illustration because illustrations attract the eye and obtain the highest readership in most advertisements. Copy near illustrations, accordingly, benefits automatically.

LAYOUT PATTERNS

One Element

In a layout pattern, one element must definitely dominate. This element acts as the starting point for the conscious scrutiny of an advertisement by the reader. If there is no dominant element, then the reader must choose between two, or among several, elements as the starting point. This decision he is reluctant to make. Often the result is that he will leave that advertisement and go on to another where the choice has already been made for him.

To many people it will seem almost incredible that the reader should be so reluctant to choose between two equal elements. After all, this decision is slight compared to many others that the average person must make constantly. Still it is a fact that the reader must be led, by the figurative hand, into and through a layout. Some element must tell beyond any doubt, "This is where you start looking or reading!" Others must tell, "This is where you go now" and "Here is the next thing you're supposed to look at." Much of this leading is subtle, but it must be built into every layout with "lines of force" or artist techniques that pull a reader's eye in a desired direction.

One of the most pronounced faults found in the layout work of the advertising amateur is the failure to provide a dominant element. Typically, the amateur scatters many objects of approximately equal size about the layout so that there is no focal center and no logical place to begin reading or looking. Poor local advertising is often guilty of this fault, too, as a glance at almost any newspaper will reveal.

That such procedure is folly is demonstrated over and over again in readership studies which give better readership for dominant-element advertisements than for those that split the gaze. What about picture and caption advertisements that have no dominant element, yet frequently obtain good readership? Do such advertisements refute the dominant-element principle? No. Picture and caption advertisements are an exception because, if well-handled, they tell a story interestingly (or present a number of different points) and lead readers logically and clearly from the top to the bottom of the advertisement. If a picture and caption advertisement is *not* well done, the advertisement-designer would be better advised to stick with the dominant-element principle. Make no mistake about it. Having a dominant element in an advertisement should be one of the designer's most important objectives whether that design element is an illustration or an unusually strong headline.

Unity

The principle of unity may be illustrated by a handsome tree. The observer does not see the individual branches and leaves; he does not distinguish between the wood and the foliage. He sees the tree as a single whole. A designer, in the same way, links all the elements of an advertisement into a logical, integrated, organized whole.

Balance is one factor that gives unity to a layout. The disposition of white space is also important. White space should be used primarily on the outside of an advertisement. This does not mean that all elements must be crowded together. There must, for instance, be adequate space between a headline and the copy block or between art and copy, but large masses of white should not be allowed to accumulate within a layout. This trapped space, a hole in the doughnut, tends to break down the layout. The reader gets the impression that the elements of the advertisement are exploding from the void in the center.

White space is more effective in a large single unit than when broken up into smaller segments. It should be regarded as the beam of a searchlight, acting to focus attention on a printed element. An advertisement, or an element within the advertisement, will also gain attention from white space that points to it, or surrounds it.

Layout with dominant element.

Good layouts give the reader a single dominant element upon which to focus. This principle is demonstrated in this advertisement in which the container pulls the reader's eyes.

Marked-up copy sheet for a newspaper advertisement.

All these instructions are needed to get the copy set in print. You see here the copy sheet exactly as it was handled by the newspaper production people. Not fancy, but effective.

EDWARDS — Sun. Herald SOCIETY JUNE 29 — 2x140

1 Good news! Our expert in — 18' TM
HAND-CUTTING CRYSTAL — 24' Alternate Gothic
is here to serve you — 18' TM

2 This fine craftsman will be happy to help you with your selection of crystal glassware and discuss the various types of monogramming available. — 12' TM

3 Major fig 48' TB Condensed
$7.99 — 30' TB Condensed
DOZ. — 10' TEB — 69¢ EA. — 10' TEB
OF ONE STYLE — 10' TM — MIX OR MATCH — 10' TM

4

5 24-PC. SETS...$13.95 — 24' TB Condensed
(8 EACH of 3 STYLES SHOWN) — 10' TEB

6
A America's perennial favorite—12-oz. sham-bottom tumbler. Heavy, tip-resistant bottom.
6' lead — X
B 13-oz. stax beverage tumbler for extra sparkle, easy space-saving storage.
6' lead — X
C 11-oz. roly-poly tumbler for sophisticated entertaining.
— 12' TM (w TEB key letters)

7 Edwards Glassware, Street Level, Syracuse Mall — 10' TM Ital Delete "Syracuse Mall" if necessary to hold to 1 line

8 A   B   C   Mr. DUNCAN GORDON — 10' TM

8 9 10

11

DOZ. EA.

Rough layout and type mechanical for newspaper advertisement.

In FIGURE 00, you saw the marked-up copy sheet. In the normal procedure in newspaper advertising, the following steps occur: (1) The copy is written and a rough layout is executed (or the layout is done first and then the copywriter writes the copy). (2) The copy sheet is marked up to indicate the size and kind of type to be used. (3) A type mechanical is prepared in which all the type is set and pasted on the page. (4) The advertisement is printed.

Repetition as a Part of Unity. Repetition of a motif is an excellent contributor to unity. The motif may be verbal as in the repetition of the words *SAFE SAFE SAFE,* or the repetition may be of a visual shape.

Dividing an advertisement weakens unity. if an advertisement is divided into four areas, the reader may believe that he sees four separate advertisements. This danger may be avoided by keeping the areas in markedly different sizes. Another way to retain unity is to have boxes or elements overlap.

Rhythm. Just as undefinable, but just as discernible as unity is the rhythm of an advertisement. This is the utilization of lines of force to lead the eye through the entire advertisement in a series of smooth sweeps. As already learned, there is an instinctive movement of the eye through any area, and there is also a movement which can be guided by lines of force and typographic magnets.

Elements in Sequence

Elements placed in sequence will guide the eye in the proper direction. If a series of approximately equal elements are placed side by side, the eye will instinctively move from left to right, reading each in turn. If equal elements are placed vertically, eye movement will be from top to bottom. The picture-caption technique previously discussed demonstrates the placement of elements in sequence.

A comic strip offers another excellent demonstration of elements in sequence. The reader knows through long acclimatization that the panels are arranged in a series of horizontal rows, and he will read in that order.

Using numbers, especially large ones, to identify elements in an advertisement is a common and useful technique. The eye will go from 2 to 3 with little temptation to skip over to 6 or 8.

A series of short paragraphs, each begun with a paragraph starter, will usually be read in top-to-bottom sequence.

Contrast

Contrast may be defined as "change of pace." Designers use contrast in several ways. They may use it as an accent typeface. In an advertisement basically Roman they will use a word or two in sansserif. They will use contrast in shape. If an advertisement has many rectangular pictures, they will use a silhouette as contrast. They will use variations in tonal value; a paragraph of boldface or italic will break the monotony of masses of normal type.

Changing tonal or chromatic values creates pleasant contrast. In an advertisement with several high-key photographs, a picture with a black background will have added impact.

Contrast can come from changing an axis. If most elements in an advertisement are horizontal, a tall, thin element will add interest.

Contrast in content is achieved by "before-and-after" pictures in ads.

A picture can contrast with the headline. If the headline says, "The Happiest Moment in My Life," and the picture shows a man in a dentist's chair, the contrast will lure even the most blase reader.

White spaces creates impact.

Attention is focused on the illustration and the print elements because of the intelligent use of the white space surrounding them. This was one of ten advertisements run in major news weeklies, *Business Week* and *Nation's Business*. Each featured a different vocational area in which NCR had skill. Before and after studies were made to measure the campaign's effectiveness in building awareness among the company's major prospects.

NCR makes sure retailers aren't left holding the bag!

NCR retail terminal systems help department and discount stores operate more profitably. Other NCR systems produce similar results for many different industries. NCR knows from years of experience what you need in electronic business systems to earn more profits. Of course, a good business system is more than a computer. NCR provides you with data terminals, peripherals, and computers to help you run your business better. You get the help of NCR representatives who are trained in your industry and devote their efforts solely to your business. And over 7,000 field engineers provide service coverage for your NCR system. You're in good company with NCR, the complete systems company.

Proportion

The reader is most receptive, to a printed message when it "looks right" even though not being able to define what is "right" about it. The designer has almost as much difficulty reducing to a formula that quality in a layout which we call proportion—the quality that makes the layout "right."

Ancient Greeks did reduce the quality of "looking right" to a mathematical formula when they set up the famous golden rectangle, the approximate 3-to-5 ratio. Thus, an advertisement 6 inches wide will be 10 inches deep.

Obviously, the column and page widths of a publication will be a major determinant, but the designer still has a choice. One choice is to avoid a square. Also, the designer will probably try to get as close as possible to the 3-to-5 proportion but often will have to decide whether that rectangle should be horizontal or vertical. Many publications insist on vertical advertisement, but even without this restriction, the designer would usually choose the vertical anyway. Newspapers require, in fact, that in general, advertisements should be deeper than wide in order to fit the pyramid design of page makeup.

A major consideration in proportion is the size of display type used in an advertisement. The designer knows that type can become illegible from excessive size as well as in too-small sizes. Typical readers hold a newspaper or magazine some 15 in.—give or take 1 or 2 in.—from their eyes. If type is too large the eye sees only a small portion of the total picture and is irritated to a point where it refuses to make the effort of reading the whole word or phrase.

COLOR IN ADVERTISING

Terminology of Color

Red, blue, and yellow are the primary colors. Mixing two primaries produces a secondary color; red and yellow make orange; red and blue, violet; blue and yellow, green. A primary and a secondary make an intermediate color. The result of mixing any two colors is a new hue. Black, white, and gray are achromatic colors; they are not actually colors. Neither are the metallics, which include gold, silver, bronze, and so forth.

Adding white to a color produces a tint; adding black produces a shade.

Hue has another meaning, too. It is that quality which makes "color;" hue is the quality, for instance, that makes red what it is—red.

Tone or value is the quality which indicates a dark or light color. The deeper the tone—or the lower the value—the more closely a color resembles black. As the tone or value becomes higher, the color more closely approaches white.

Chroma designates the intensity of a color. A color we would call "bright" has high chroma. If the chroma is low, we would call the color "dull," "muddy" or "washed out."

Function of Color

The designer must consider color as a component of the layout; color must, in itself, be functional and organic, and it must contribute to those same two requisities for the layout as a whole.

Golden rectangle.

Golden rectangle is shaded portion of (a). Note how closely common 3x5 proportion for cards and phots adhere to this ideal. Arrow in (b) shows line of golden proportion.

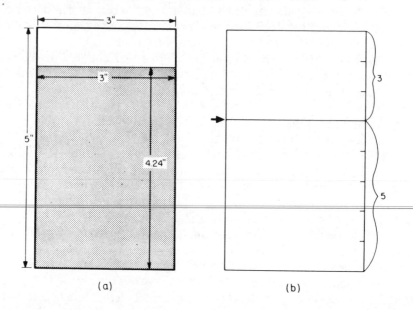

(a)   (b)

The functions of color are:

(1) To augment the written word. Few colors can be described verbally. The reader may recognize robin's-egg blue or fire-engine red from the words alone; but the terms "veldt green" and "bark" are meaningless. If, on the contrary, the reader sees a picture of a product printed in the exact color of the original, the message is swift, clear, and unmistakable.

(2) To attract attention. like all attention-compellers, color must be used logically and in good taste. Improper use of color backfires more quickly and more disastrously than does the misuse of black-and-white elements.

(3) To guide the eye through an entire layout. Spots of color are strong magnets that create lines of force to direct the eye's motion.

(4) To create a pleasant mood and increase the reader's receptivity to the message.

One blanket admonition covers all situations: *Color should be used sparingly.* As with all powerful elements, it is easy to overdo color. Too much color loses the values of contrast and emphasis. At worst, it can actually confuse the reader and irritate the reading eye.

Psychology of Color

The psychological impact of color is great, and it must be well understood by the designer. For every desirable psychological attraction to color there is an equal revulsion. A picture of a T-bone steak makes the mouth water when printed in red ink; in green ink it may cause acute nausea.

It was the designers who first classified colors as warm and cool. Those hues close to red—yellow, orange, and violet, as well as red itself—are warm colors; the others are cool. Speaking broadly, warm colors are exciting and cheerful, cool colors are calm and quiet.

The "temperature" of colors must be appropriate to the advertised merchandise. Air conditioners are best presented with cool colors; furnaces with warm ones. Cool colors are used for positive sales approaches and warm ones for negative appeal. This will vary, of course. Cool blue can have strong negative force in a blizzard scene that warns the reader to buy anti-freeze.

Cool colors generally make better tint blocks than warm ones. For cool colors tend to recede and thus do not compete with the type that is printed over them.

Children and adults who are low in education, culture, and the economic scale will prefer bright primary and secondary colors. Older and better-educated people will usually prefer cool and soft colors. Of course, there are many exceptions. Just as a gourmet will occasionally choose the unsubtle taste of a hot dog and mustard, so the sophisticate will on occasion sometimes get pleasure from raw, vibrating colors.

Women prefer pure colors in this order: red, blue, violet, green, orange, and yellow. Men's preferences are: blue, red, violet, green, orange, and yellow.

Women prefer violet in both tints and shades; they like tints of yellow much more than the pure color or shades thereof. Men prefer blue above all other tints or shades.

Red means power and boldness. Because of its great strength, it must be used sparingly. Overuse of red creates "schlock" or "borax" advertisements.

Blue is the favorite color of all people, without distinctions of age, economic level, and sex. It connotes hope and patience. Notice that these are "quiet" virtues, just as blue is a quiet color.

Yellow is a happy color with its suggestion of sunshine. It has low value, though, and consequently cannot be used to print any but the very largest type. It is most effective in large masses.

Orange is another happy color. It is used much as yellow is, except that, as it swings toward the red part of the spectrum, orange gains strength. Then it can carry medium-sized type, but the danger of overuse increases.

Brown is a color of many uses. Most people like it. It can carry type well; in its deeper shades it has almost as much strength as black but none of the irritation of red.

Green is as versatile as brown, probably because green foliage appeals to everyone. It is effective in large masses or as small, sharp accents. In most of its values and tones, it can carry type legibly.

Violet suggests richness and dignity, especially in its purple shades. In its tints—the lavenders—it is too feminine to have appeal for men, but women love it.

Use of Color Combinations

The most legible combination is black on yellow. So a yellow tint block can add reading ease as well as attract attention. Yellow on black is almost as legi-

All-type layout.

Occasionally an illustration will be eliminated in order to achieve dramatic effect. In this instance, an illustration might have detracted from the impact of the blunt message. The use of reverse printing was suitable here not only because of the short copy in big type but also because the blackness was appropriate for the grim message.

If you don't like thinking about safety, think where you might be without it.

**National
Safety
Council**

ble; so reverse can be printed in black on a yellow tint block. Black on red is almost illegible and must be avoided. If red is used as a tint block, it must be screened down to a pale pink. White on red has enough legibility to be used as the product of a reverse block printed in red. The type must be fairly large and without fine lines or serifs.

Red-and-green combinations must be approached warily. Some combinations of red and green clash so badly that the eye actually aches. yet the two colors are favorites for Christmas themes. For Yuletide use, it is best to keep green in masses and use the red sparingly.

Whenever a cool and a warm color are used in combination, one color should definitely be used in such mass that it gives the overall effect; the other is used sparsely for accent. If a layout looks basically blue, a little yellow will add pleasant interest. If blue and yellow are used in equal or near-equal amounts, the effect will be almost of green; the eye will begin to mix the two colors optically, as it does when reading process color. Unfortunately, the mixing will be incomplete and the effect will be unpleasant.

In any combination, the best effect is obtained when one color is pure (that is, unscreened) and the other is a tint or shade; or, especially when using intermediate colors, a shade can be combined with a tint.

There are pleasant combinations that use the noncolors as well. Black-and-red is probably the most widely used combination for advertising purposes. Much of this use is anything but good. The bad effect is due to overuse of color and poor balance between the two, rather than to the combination itself. A red-orange will be more effective with black than pure red.

Gray is particularly pleasing with yellow in combination with bright pink or blue.

Gold and silver will harmonize with all colors. Gold and purple produce the most elegant and the richest of all combinations.

Consider Use of One Color At Times

Although much attention is given to four-color process advertisements, it is often better (and less expensive) to use one color in an advertisement. This one color, especially on a newspaper page that has no competing color, will stand out. Furthermore, if it is used to feature an important element in the advertisement such as the package, a new shade of lipstick, or a special color of paint, the use of one color can focus the reader's attention on the element. Under the circumstances, four-color process might actually be distracting.

Using one color in the manner suggested is to use color *functionally* instead of merely for attention-getting or aesthetic decoration. Some products or services do not require color for sales power—for attention, yes, for selling, no. A book, a pencil, or an ordinary can opener are such products. On the contrary, many products are actually sold through color. Drapes, rugs, floor coverings, foods, clothes, cosmetics, roofing, and furniture are in this category. For such products, color serves a functional purpose. if hesitating about using color because of cost, ask yourself: "Does it serve a functional purpose in the sale of the product?" If the answer is, "No," it may be advisable to use a black-and-white advertisement, or to use one color simply for attention-getting purposes.

DESIGNING THE ADVERTISEMENT

Ability To Draw Is Useful

Designers must be able to indicate artwork to the extent that another person can visualize the finished job which some artist will eventually do. Thus, designers should think of themselves as visualizers rather than as artists. They must remember that simplicity is the secret of a good visualization. The beginner is tempted to include too many details; visualizers must steel themselves to eliminate details—to work only in masses.

Stick Figures. The designer will find many uses for the simple stick figures. These figures are not childish really; they are quite sophisticated in that they look beneath distracting details and discern basic shapes. The human body consists of a head; a torso (reduced to a straight line); arms (two lines for each to indicate the bend at the elbow); hands (simple square or circle); legs (also in two sections), and feet (done the same as hands).

Even in this simplest form, the stick figure indicates action or pose. Later the figure can be elaborated into a series of boxes or cylinders. Shading can be added to show bulk or source of light.

FIGURE 21-4
Stick figures.

Even copywriters with no art ability can learn to draw stick figures that will help demonstrate layout ideas.

The results will certainly not be drawings like those of Leonardo da Vinci or Rembrandt, but they will be entirely adequate for visualization.

If designers do not have the time or inclination to master stick figures as a basic tool, they can always find a suitable picture in the swipe file (an idea file, also called a "crib" file) and trace it, then make changes or additions to fit the needs of the moment.

Campaign Thinking Is Important

In practice the designer rarely works with a single, independent layout. In many instances the layout must be part of a long-time advertising program, the individual layouts of which must have a family resemblance in order to build and maintain the proper image of the advertiser.

Headline reinforcement.

Drawing of hands reinforces message of headline in this full-page magazine advertisement.

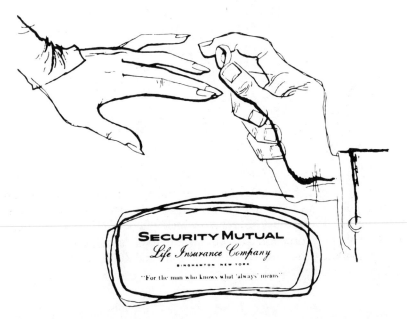

Other uses for drawings.
Same drawing, as used in Fig. 27-2, is effective on booklet cover.

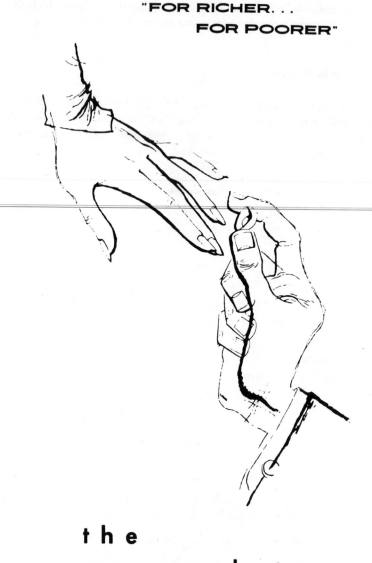

"FOR RICHER. . .
FOR POORER"

the
accumulator

The designer working on a layout always keeps in mind the question, "What will you do for an encore?" Knowing that tomorrow, or next week, or next month another layout must be created which will develop the same theme which will be an obvious companion to the current advertisement, yet will be different enough to attract the reader, and which will contribute to the cumulative effect of all previous advertising.

A campaign is built around a continuing theme that develops from a job of selling that must be done at the moment. In the case of perfume advertising, the sales department may have reached the conclusion that "we must sell perfume for everyday use instead of just for gala occasions." Once the theme, has been adopted, it is easy to develop pleasing variations.

Simple layout in small space.

A picture on the top, the headline following immediately and the copy just below the headline—this is a high readership formula even though such layouts become tiresome to art directors who like more challenge to their artistic ability.

No one wakes up thinking, "Today I'm going to abuse my child."

Abuse is not something we think about, it's something we do.

Last year in America, an estimated one million children suffered from abuse and neglect, and at least 2,000 of them died needless, painful deaths.

The fact is, child abuse is a major epidemic in this country.

The solution? Part of it lies in your hands. With enough volunteers, local child abuse prevention programs could be formed to aid parents and children in their own communities. With your help, eighty percent of all abusers could be helped. Please. Write for more information on child abuse and what you can do.

What will you do today that's more important?

A Public Service of This Magazine & The Advertising Council   **Ad** Council

We need your help. Write:

National Committee for Prevention of Child Abuse, Box 2866, Chicago, Illinois 60690

CHILD ABUSE CAMPAIGN
MAGAZINE AD NO. CA-2612-76   B-67
2¼"x10" [110 Screen]

Build a Family Resemblance. For campaign continuity, the designer must build a family resemblance in every advertisement devised for an account. This family resemblance is compounded from *consistent* use of a number of elements. Note the stress on "consistent". The campaign strategy is usually the result of long planning. During the planning sessions it is decided that certain layout and copy elements will be present in each campaign advertisement. A "copy platform" spells out what these elements are and then serves as a guide to everyone who works on the account such as the account executive, the copywriters, and the artists.

A client advertising manager will insist that agency personnel observe conscientiously the requirements of the copy platform. Each advertisement, therefore, time after time includes the elements decided upon. Quite apart from the copy requirements that embrace such points as marketing and legal musts, there are many layout elements that help make up the "campaign look" or family resemblance. Some of these are:

- A signature cut that provides a constant, if unobtrusive, similarity and carryover in advertisement after advertisement.
- The use of one family of type for all advertisements.
- Similar headlines in size of type and length (and the copy department will make certain that the thought of the headline is similar in each case).
- An illustration in each advertisement that is similar in size, subject matter, action, and the type of rendering; that is, drawing or photograph.
- Amount of copy used and arrangement of the copy blocks.
- Balance of the advertisements, either consistently formal or informal.
- A border that is distinctive and marks the advertisement as different. Very often users of smaller space will use such borders consistently to give them a competitive chance against advertisers using bigger space.
- A trademark character used in the same place and in the same size, time after time.
- A slogan, if any, set in the same size type and shown in the same location in the advertisement.
- Use of color, or black and white. If in color, colors should be similar.

All, or most of these elements, used constantly will develop an image that is reinforced by each advertisement. That image can indicate that the company stresses quality to the point of snobbishness, or quality in a middle price range, or a company stress on progressiveness that uses up-to-the-minute, modern techniques. Eventually, readers recognize this image and learn to recognize the advertiser and his message without even reading the signature cut. They can play back the sales message without even reading the copy block.

A side benefit of the campaign approach is the reusing of elements of the campaign advertisements such as the art and certain typographic sections. Not only is money saved through such reuse but also art time is saved because the artist doesn't need to strain to come up with a new approach each time. Instead, he or she works within the established framework.

Editorial Layouts For High Readership

Give the reader what is familiar. Readership is more assured if the layout conforms to established reading habits than if the layout designer has tried to lure the reader into the unfamiliar. Following are some known, and tested, editorial-type techniques that get good readership, as many studies have revealed.

News format layout.   Used to introduce new products, or significant improvements in established products, the news format uses banner headlines and an open, newsy appearance.

Narrative format.   A dominant illustration dramatizes the story in this format. A generous amount of copy is directly under the picture and a headline that promises an interesting narrative to follow. Balance is usually formal. The top of the advertisement is devoted to the picture; the bottom half by copy and perhaps a supporting illustration.

Cartoon format.   Usually this style is used for well-known products. The advertiser is aiming for high "Noted" scores while, at the same time, he offers a simple one-or two-thought sales message.

Believe-it-or-not format.   An artist using this format should be certain that the product has amazing features or benefits and that the story about the product is more important than showing the product itself, or many a number of sales points. The format will fail if a striking copy story and illustration aren't provided.

Picture-page format.   Editors of picture-page sections of newspapers and magazine draw good readership. Layouts for advertisements can apply these principles, especially if the product can be demonstrated or can be the subject of a how-to-use-it, or testimonial approach.

Sunday comics format.   Placed in the comic strip section, this layout format will work if, like the nearby strips, it offers a story well-told in pictures and copy. This story can be dramatic or comical but unless the designer is careful, the story can smother the sales message.

What Pulls Readers to Illustrations or to Headlines

Once more, we can refer to readership studies to learn what works consistently. This time we are concerned not, as in the foregoing, with the layout as a whole but some of the components.

First, in discussing illustrations, we assume that generally people like to see people in advertisements if those people are in familiar surroundings and they are doing something relevant to the reader's interests and knowledge. Products by themselves rarely are comparably interesting. Furthermore, a person using the product has more interest for the reader than a still life of the product, or the package by itself.

Space limitations, or a desire to dramatize the product or package, may cause many layout designers to desert the people-doing-things format. Often the designers are successful. Still, if you want to "ride a winner" stay with the people approach as much as possible. Many of those successful advertisements featuring the product alone could have been more successful had they used people.

Second, the chief aim in headlines (physically speaking) should be to make them easy to read. After picking a popular type face, avoid long headlines in reverse and make few changes in the style of type or lettering in the same headline. As much as possible, avoid the all-capitals headline and long, script-type headlines. Make headlines continuous, not started in one place in the layout and finished in another because, for example, the illustration has separated them.

QUESTIONS

1. What purposes are achieved by making a layout?

2. Name the criteria for good signatures?

3. Distinguish between functional and organic layouts.

4. List the strengths and weaknesses of formal layouts.

5. Name 3 "classic" layout patterns. Why are they used?

6. Define POA.

7. Where is the optical center of an advertisement?

8. What was said about "functional" color?

9. What are some means by which a layout artist builds a family resemblance into campaign advertisements?

22

PRINTING AND ENGRAVING FOR ADVERTISING

PRINTING AND ENGRAVING FOR ADVERTISING

A careless, indifferent or insensitive worker in an engraving plant can diminish the superb work of an advertising artist. Likewise, harm can be done by advertising people who do not understand the mechanical processes through which words and artwork finally reach the pages in magazines, newspapers, and other printed media. Without intelligent cooperation between the production worker and the advertising people, the appeal of artwork and the nuances of the copy message are not fully realized in the finished advertisement.

Quite apart from the aesthetics of advertising production, there is the more mundane consideration of cost. An agency account executive, for example, is expected to know enough about production to save unneeded expense for clients and to get them the best possible work at the lowest prices.

In daily work the account executive seldom meets the printers and engravers but transmits wishes through the production department. Sometimes this will be a sizable department headed by a production manager. Other times, it will be a one-person department. In very small advertising agencies an artist may take over the production chores, along with art duties. Thus, the artist will decide the type faces, sizes, and printing processes to be used. This person will also select the firms to do the work, sometimes on a bid basis.

An account executive should be knowledgeable enough to supervise such work whether he deals with a full-sized production department or a one-man, art-production department.

PRINTING PROCESSES

Changes in printing technology change so rapidly these days that it is difficult to keep up with them. Electronics, computers, and satellite communication have in the newspaper business, for example, forced editors to spend much of their time learning about mechanical production. Still, the basic printing processes fall into about five types that will be discussed briefly in the following pages. These are letterpress, lithography, gravure, stencil, and electrostatic.

Letterpress

Letterpress, also known as "relief" printing, is demonstrated in its simplest form by the rubber stamp. The raised characters on such a stamp capture ink and deposit it on paper.

In letterpress printing using machines, type and other printing elements are placed in a steel frame called a chase. Height of type elements is referred to as "type-high" and is 0.9186 inches. Paper thickness is so uniform that the printer can use a "kiss" impression, or the minimum contact needed to transfer ink from type to paper.

Several types of presses are used in letterpress printing. They are the: cylinder press, platen press, and rotary press.

Cylinder Press. In the simplest form of cylinder press— that used by printers to pull proofs—the inked form lies on a flat bed, the paper is laid on the form, and pressure is applied by a cylinder that rolls across the surface.

For printing commercial quantities, rather than one or a few proofs, the paper is wrapped around a stationary cylinder and the form, on the bed, is moved under the roller to create the impression.

FIGURE 22-1
Schematic of cylinder press.
On bed of press a, type b lies flat. Paper c is pressed down by impression cylinder d to transfer ink from type to paper.

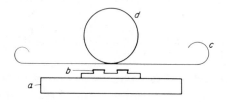

Cylinder presses are usually sheet-fed, with a single sheet at a time, either manually or automatically. The printed sheet is removed from the cylinder by mechanical fingers and deposited on the delivery table or taken directly to a folder.

Platen Presses. A simpler press is the platen. In this press the form is locked vertically and inked by rollers that move across a large flat plate on which ink is placed, at intervals, by hand. The paper is carried on the platen, a flat surface that is hinged at the bottom.

FIGURE 22-2
Schematic of platen press.
Into immovable frame of press a, type b is locked vertically. After inking by roller c, form and paper f are brought into contact as platen e moves on hinge mechanism d.

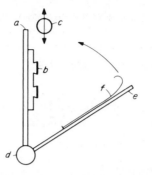

The *stereotype* process makes the necessary curved form needed in rotary press printing. A form is made up in the conventional chase on a flat surface. On the form is laid a *flong,* which is a piece of rather thick, soft cardboard of several sheets of paper pasted together. Intense pressure is applied, either by a roller or by a plate driven by hydraulic force. The flong is pressed onto and around all the relief elements in the form: type, rules, and borders, and engravings of illustrations. The flong becomes a perfect matrix, or mat, a mold of the original form.

Now the moist matrix is bent to the same curve as the cylinder on the rotary press and dried, or scorched. Then it is placed in a metal "box" curved to precisely the same arc. Molten type metal is poured into this box, and the result is a curved metal printing plate which, except for its curve, is an exact duplicate of the original form. This "half-around," named for its shape, is then placed on the printing cylinder.

Schematic of rotary press.
On cylinder A, type B is raised. It is inked by roller C and pressed against paper E by impression cylinder D. When paper, feeding from endless roll, reaches F, it is folded or cut into pages G.

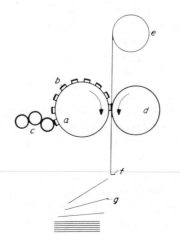

The stereotyping process is used by numerous big newspapers with their many pages and huge press runs. Often two or more casts are made from the same matrix so that, in a typical newspaper plant, several complete copies of an edition are printed at one time.

The capacity of rotary presses is great—40,000 copies per hour, and up. They are used not only for newspapers, but whenever a large number of copies must be printed.

Lithography

Offset lithography, also called photo-offset, is a thriving branch of the printing industry. Lithography utilizes the well-known fact that oil and water will not mix. In its original form (still employed in fine arts) lithography uses an image placed by hand, with a greasy crayon, pencil, or ink, on a smooth slab of stone. When water is sloshed over the surface, the stone is thoroughly wetted but the greasy image repels the water. Then ink is rolled across the surface. The wet stone repels the oily ink, but the greasy image receives a coating of ink. When paper is pressed onto the stone, the added ink—in the exact form of the original image—is transferred to the paper.

Photo-offset.   Lithography became photo-offset by adopting the two principles the new name suggests. Today the original stone has been replaced by metal plates, usually aluminum, on which the image is placed by photography instead of by hand. This is a major saving in time essential for modern commercial processes.

The plate is wrapped around a cylinder and dampened and inked by rollers. Then the image is "lithographed"—not onto paper, but onto a rubber blanket. From there it sets off (offsets) to the paper, just as an inky image written by hand is transferred to a blotter.

The introduction of the offset operation is the key to the success of the process. The blanket is resilient and adapts itself to coarse paper, so that fine detail can be printed on cheap material. Offset can print on almost any surface: metal (where it was first used), cloth, wood, or glass. By way of demonstration, offset printers sometimes use sandpaper as their "stock."

Offset uses a lightweight plate for its original image. It does not require metal type, with its attendant weight and problems. It is ideally capable of using cold type produced photographically, and the growth of phototypesetting has expanded the potential of offset.

Paste-ups.   A form for offset is assembled by pasting up images of type into an exact duplicate of the final job. Type may be cold type, that from a photocomposition machine, or it may be a carefully produced reproduction proof, a repro, from metal type. Line art is pasted directly into position. Halftone art is converted into a screened negative and later combined with the negative for line work. The assembled paste-up is photographed. The resulting negative is exposed to a metal plate on which the action of light creates the needed ink-attractive image.

Lithography and offset are planographic printing processes; the image is not raised, as for letterpress, but is on the same plane as the plate that bears it. The simplest offset press is the duplicator used in many offices.

Gravure

The basis of gravure printing goes back to the word intaglio (pronounced in-Thal-yo) which means "incised." Etchings like those done by many famous artists, are the simplest form of intaglio. The artist covers a sheet of copper with an acid-resistant ground. Into this he scratches the lines of his picture. The plate is immersed in acid, which etches the exposed metal under the scratched lines. By varying the time of exposure to the acid, the artist controls the depth of the incision.

After the ground has been washed away, the artist inks the plate, then wipes its surface, so that only the incisions remain filled. When paper is pressed onto the plate, the ink adheres to the paper and is removed from the incisions.

In the gravure method, sheet-fed gravure prints single sheets from a thin copper plate wrapped around a cylinder. *Rotogravure* uses the rotary press principle by printing from an incised cylinder onto a continuous roll of paper.

The printing image of a gravure plate consists of many tiny holes—almost 20,000 per square inch—all of the same area but of varying depths. Because gradations of gray, or of any other color, can be finely controlled, gravure is the almost-ideal method of reproducing photographs and other continuous-tone pictures.

For advertising, gravure's major asset is the ability to reproduce fine detail on cheap paper, such as newsprint. Sunday magazines, such as the *New York Times Magazine* and nationally printed supplements distributed with local newspapers, are excellent examples of the superb work, in black and white and in color, that rotogravure produces.

Forms for rotogravure are pasted up the same as those for offset. Preparatory costs for rotogravure are high. Thus, it requires a long press run to bring the cost per unit low enough to be competitive.

FIGURE 22-4
Schematic of rotogravure printing.

Metal cylinder a, with incised image, turns through ink fountain b. Ink c covers surface of plate but is removed by doctor blade d, leaving ink only in incisions e. At point f, ink is placed on paper g, feeding from endless roll, by pressure from impression cylinder h. At point i, paper is folded or cut into sheets j.

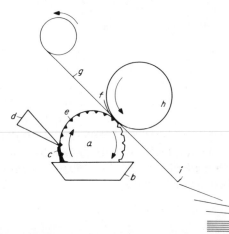

Stencil Process

Silk screen, also called process printing, is a stencil process and embodies the principles of the simple stencil used to put shipping addresses on crates and boxes.

Silk screen is most advantageous when the run is short but the area of the printed sheet is large. (Printing plates are sold by the square inch; if the total impressions are low, the cost per unit may be exorbitant.)

Silk screening is used for book covers, point-of-purchase displays, posters, car cards, and similar jobs, and it can produce low-cost 24-sheet outdoor posters. Its applications in advertising are obvious and multitudinous. Local advertising campaigns often utilize this process to develop the comparatively small amounts of materials used.

Electrostatic

Electrostatic, or xerography, are used interchangeably to refer to "dry" printing, or printing that does not use conventional liquid inks to make the impression. Used in a massive way for office duplicating purposes, the process has been making great progress and may become a major method of reproduction for color and black-and-white work.

Inserts, Preprints, and Tip-ins

Anyone concerned with newspaper and magazine advertising soon becomes involved with production techniques and costs connected with the use of inserts, preprints, and tip-ins. Each provides a potent way to add power, sales effectiveness, and attention for his advertising messages. The following discussion points out some of the advantages of these techniques and their involvement with printing methods.

Inserts. Sometimes advertisers will require better printing quality than the publication itself can provide. Or they may want advertisements printed on special paper or with special ink. In this case they can use preprints or inserts. They will have advertisements printed on the proper size sheets, which are then delivered to the publication for inclusion with its regular pages.

Rates for inserts vary, of course, but the net effect is usually the regular cost of the space if the advertisement were printed by the periodical, plus a premium for the extra work of handling the sheets in a separate binding process, plus the cost of the paper and printing for the inserts.

To offset the added cost there is the advantage of being able to use special paper or printing materials, or die cutting. Foil, fabric, and even wood veneers have been used for inserts. The advertiser can control the quality of the printing, and almost always orders extra inserts, which are used for direct mail or other advertising purposes. Often the cost of distributing materials as inserts is far lower than by any other method. The advertiser, in effect, gets the use of an extensive mailing list at a negligible cost. Many manufacturers have distributed catalogs and similar booklets as inserts.

Preprints. A variation of the insert is the preprint, whose use in newspapers grows constantly. The advertiser has advertisements printed on a roll of paper by rotogravure, which permits more brilliant colors and finer detail than the newspaper can produce on its rotary presses. The roll is then given to the newspaper. It prints the reverse side by its normal letterpress methods and may even imprint names and addresses of local dealers onto the rotoprinted sheet.

Preprints need not always be done by roto. A bread manufacturer captured wide attention when he had a roll of waxed bread wrappers fed through a newspaper press. Paper toweling and aluminum foil have also been used with marked effectiveness in this manner.

Tip-ins. Tipping-in is the process of pasting a single sheet of paper into a book or magazine. Tipping-in fastens a sheet onto another page. The process may be machine or manual. Tipping-in is used to bind a single-sheet insert into a magazine. It also has effective use as a means of showing samples of merchandise to periodical readers. Advertisers have tipped in swatches of fabrics, wallpaper, plastics, foil, and other materials to newspaper and magazine advertising.

Tipping-in is sometimes used to add a full-color illustration to a black-and-white advertising job.

PAPER

The four most common kinds of paper all have uses in advertising.

Newsprint is one of the cheapest of printing papers. It is composed of about 80 percent ground wood (for opacity and smoothness) and 20 percent chemical pulp (for strength). It soon grows yellow and brittle; it is never very white, and it will not accept fine halftones. With sizing to give it a smoother finish, newsprint becomes roto paper. In advertising, newsprint has its major use for short-lived material where quality is not essential.

Book papers are most often used in advertising. There are many kinds, with texture the main point of difference. Antique papers are soft, and are comparatively rough and bulky—sheets are thick in comparison to weight. Woven paper is smooth, with a surface that resembles that of fine fabric. Laid paper has an overall watermark that looks somewhat like the pattern of Venetian blinds.

Book papers are often coated with a thin layer of a mineral substance, usually clay, which produces a smooth surface. Coated papers may have a glossy or dull finish. That with extremely high luster is called enamel.

English finish (E.F.) combines a high content of mineral, which adds solidity and a smooth surface, with heavy calendering. It is a favorite for quality advertising printing.

Writing papers are sized with a glue solution to create a smooth surface and to prevent ink from penetrating and spreading in the fibers of the paper. Flat writing paper is made of wood pulp, sized and well calendered. Bond, used for letterheads and similar purposes, usually contains varying percentages of cotton or linen fibers. Ledger, too, often has a high rag content. It is a smooth, durable paper, highly receptive to writing by pen.

Cover stock is a heavy weight of paper, designed to take the added wear of the outside of books.

Paper is sold by weight. This is based on its substance, the weight of 1,000 sheets of paper in a basic size. Catalogs and price lists show paper by size and substance: 25 × 38-60M means that a thousand sheets in that size weigh 60 pounds.

RELATIVE COSTS OF PRINTING PROCESSES

Printing costs are a major item in today's advertising budgets. Before approving the use of one printing process over another, a hard-boiled analysis should be made and questions asked. Some of the many questions should be:

- How much quality do we really need? Should we pay "extra" for this quality?
- Could a less expensive process serve just as well?
- How long a run will we need?
- How fast should the job be done?

To answer these questions certain factors are certain to be considered such as composition, paper used, pictures.

Composition

For jobs that require a galley or less of type, linecaster composition is usually the fastest and least costly, and this points to letterpress. In quantities greater than a galley, phototypesetting becomes more competitive, and no flat rule can be established on which kind of composition is the more economical.

For offset and gravure, photocomposition has advantages. Depending on the form, of course, cold type can be produced on film and go directly to the platemaker. For letterpress, cold type is less advantageous because a relief plate must be made.

If type is already set—it may have been used totally or in part in a previous job—letterpress is often indicated. If it is expected that type will be used in the future with no change, or with only small changes, letterpress again has an edge.

Paper Used

The kind of paper specified for a job has a bearing on the printing process. If the paper is smooth, letterpress or offset can reproduce both type and pictures with crispness. If the paper is rough, offset is probably the only economical way to maintain fine detail.

Gravure can use rough, poor-quality paper with results as good as those obtained from offset. But the preparatory costs for gravure are high, and so it is usually not considered unless the run is around 100,000 and the total printing area is at least as large as that of a newspaper page.

Pictures

Speaking broadly, for comparatively short runs of jobs that have a large area of pictures in relation to the type, offset will be considered first. But if photoengravings are already available, the balance may tip to letterpress.

If new art will be used, its technique will tend to indicate the method of reproduction. Line art is sharpest in letterpress. On the other hand, "soft" art media—washes, pastels, pencil drawings, and so forth—are ideal for reproduction by offset or gravure.

If the area of a job is large and the run is short, and especially if color is to be used, silk screen is an obvious choice.

SUMMARY OF FACTORS CONSIDERED IN SELECTING PRINTING PROCESS

Generalizations are dangerous. Still, there are some overall guides to help the person faced with decision relating to the production of his advertising. Here are the guides:

Letterpress should be considered first when:

(1) deadlines are tight;
(2) standing forms can be used with few, if any changes, especially when the form is an intricate one;
(3) the run is comparatively short, 100 to 10,000;
(4) crispness of type and line work is essential;
(5) envelopes are to be run in jobs of up to 10,000.

Offset is considered first when:

(1) there are many pictures in relation to type and the run is under 10,000;
(2) halftones must be run on rough paper;
(3) reprinting is to be done and good camera copy is available;
(4) soft art techniques are called for.

Gravure has advantages when:

(1) fine detail and color are to be used on cheap paper;
(2) the job is primarily pictorial;
(3) the press run is a long one, above 50,000.

PHOTOENGRAVING

Advertising uses pictures to show the product in use, to suggest benefits therefrom, to capture attention and create interest, and to direct the eye through a layout. The advertiser must be familiar with the methods of placing pictures on the printed page.

Photoengravings are relief printing plates. But their principle is used, with only minor variations, in all the other printing processes. Examination of the methods of photoengraving, even simplified to the bare essentials, enables us to understand all methods of printing pictures.

Linecuts

The simplest photoengraving is a linecut—also called a line etching or a zinc etching. These are relief plates, not the intaglio "etching" of the fine artist.

As its name implies, a linecut reproduces original art that consists of black lines, dots, or masses. Pen-and-ink drawings are typical of artwork so reproduced.

Line engravings have many uses in advertising. They are particularly useful when printing is on poor-quality paper, such as low-grade newsprint. They can retain finer detail than might other engravings.

The original art is placed before a camera, which "takes a picture" of it. The result is a film negative. Here the tonal values are reversed (hence the name *negative*). The original black lines of the drawing appear as transparent areas on the negative; the original white background is opaque black on the film.

Reverse Plates

A variation of the line etching is the reverse plate, which gives the effect of white letters printed on a black background. The original art is again a line drawing.

Line cuts.

(a) Fine detail in pen-and-ink technique. *(b)* Cartoon style. *(c)* Pen drawing in technique resembling wood engraving. *(d)* Hand lettering.

(a)

for an
inside
report
on the
outside
world

(b)

(c)

Fiesta of Values

10.11 SEP   Form 17

(d)

Reverses are often used for small ads or for emphasis in advertisements that stress price. Since they make effective attention-compellers, they are a much-used device for signatures in advertising.

Reverse printing and dramatic use of black.

Reverse printing can be attention-getting and effective when the advertiser, as in this instance, holds down the amount of copy uses the black background to dramatize the product.

Halftones

The reproduction of photographs or other continuous-tone material, such as paintings, depends on an optical illusion.

A photograph consists of the black of pure silver, the white of the paper, and intermediate tones of gray produced by light reflecting from the paper through varying thicknesses of silver.

Schematic of line-engraving process.

(a) Original art, black on white. *(b)* Negative of original art. *(c)* Negative flopped to create mirror image. *(e)* Flopped negative exposed to sensitized plate *(d)*. *(f)* Photographic image printed on metal plate will become an acid resist before plate is etched by acid.

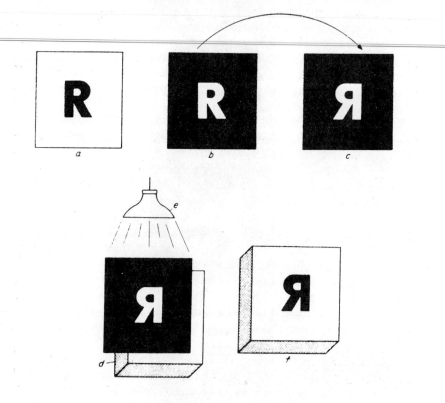

To create grays in printing from black ink requires magic. This magic is achieved by printing dots of various sizes in black ink. Test the theory. With a ball-point pen, draw a square of about 2 inches. Along the left edge put in a great many dots, as close to each other as possible without actually touching each other. Then do a strip where the dots are only half as many in a given area, and a third strip where the dots are widely dispersed. Leave the right margin of the square untouched. Now look at the result. It will seem that the square graduates from dark gray at the left to white at the right.

The foregoing illusion of gray is used in what might be termed a transitional engraving form, linking line art with continuous tone.

By using dots in the manner just described, or by using fine lines, either roughly parallel or in crosshatching of tiny squares, the artist could give the effect of various values of gray though he used only black ink.

Where large areas of gray were required, the hand technique had obvious disadvantages.

BEN DAY PROCESS

When in 1881 Benjamin Day invented a mechanical method of applying shading, his process, now called benday, found instant and manifold uses.

In the original process (rarely used today because largely supplanted by mechanical tint patterns like Zip-a-Tone applied in film form to the artwork) a regular pattern of dots or lines was printed onto the entire surface of a line etching before it was placed in the acid bath. The unwanted areas were washed away and the remaining pattern converted to an acid resist. Thus, a mechnical shading screen was added to the original line work. The pattern was printed from a relief plate of celluloid.

Today there are a great many shading or tinting patterns available in sheet or film form, and the artist chooses his pattern(s) from a catalog. More than one pattern can be used in the same area, offering opportunities for many effects. However, these films or sheets cannot produce true halftones—which are continuous gradations of tone images produced only from the original copy itself.

If the benday is applied to the negative instead of to the plate, the result is a pattern of white on a black background. This is especially useful for converting an overpowering mass of black into a more pleasant gray. The background of reverse cuts is often made lighter in this way; in fact, many newspapers will not accept a pure black reverse but insist that it be screened down to gray, usually of 80 to 85 percent value and sometimes even lighter. Large type is often screened down in the same way.

The same effect as that of benday, which we call a shading screen, is also possible with shading sheets. Of these, "Zip-a-Tone" is such a popular trade name that it has become almost generic.

Shading sheets are thin, clear, self-adhesive plastic on which is printed a dot or line pattern, identical with those of the benday process. They are affixed directly to the artwork and are available in either black or white.

The advantage of tint films or shading sheets as opposed to the original benday shop operation is threefold. First, the artist does all the work himself; he need not trust to the skill of the engraver. When the area in which the shading is to be applied is indicated by the lines of the original drawing, it is no problem to apply the "benday" pattern precisely. But when there are no ink lines to guide him, the engraver must be a freehand artist as he traces, on the plate, an area the artist has painted onto his drawing.

Perhaps the greatest advantage of shading sheets is that artists can see immediately what the effect of the shading will be. If it is not what they want they can strip off the sheet and start all over again with a different pattern.

Halftones made with contact screens.

The range of contrast and sharpness can be varied considerably. The halftones here were printed from velox negatives.

ROUND DOT (100)

SQUARE DOT (100)

ELLIPTICAL DOT (100)

MEZZOTINT (75)

STRAIGHT LINE (62)

SUNBURST (100)

MEZZOTINT (150)

STEEL ETCH (50)

WAVY LINE (60)

CONCENTRIC CIRCLE (60)

STEEL ENGRAVING (50)

LINEN (50)

NEW HALFTONE MADE FROM OLD HALFTONE WITH CAPROCK RE-SCREENER FILTERS

Original 100 Line Halftone

100 Line Halftone Re-Screened
With 60 Line Screen

60 Line Halftone Not Re-Screene

Screening type.

(a) type printing in full 100 percent value. *(b)* Same types screened down to 60 percent gray.

Halftone Screens and Their Use

When engravers start to make a halftone, they place the glass halftone screen ("crossline screen") in front of the film negative as they take a picture of the original photograph. The screen breaks the continuous tone down into a series of dots. The black areas will be converted into large dots, so close together that they overlap at the corners. White areas on the original will show only very tiny dots. Gray will have dots of varying sizes, depending on the tonal value of the original.

Screens vary in fineness and are designated by the number of lines of dots per linear inch. Thus a 55-line screen, the one commonly used in newspapers, will have 55 lines of dots horizontally and vertically per inch, or a total of 3,025 dots per square inch.

The dots of such a screen are visible to the naked eye, but at about 140 lines per inch the dot pattern becomes invisible without a glass. Actually, we are rarely aware of the pattern even at 65 or 85 lines. Turning the screen so that "vertical" rows of dots run at a 45-degree angle makes the pattern less apparent, too.

Newspapers use 55- or 65-line screen if they use the stereotyping process; 85-line if they print directly from the plate. "Slick" magazines use 110-, 120-, or 133-line screens. Extremely smooth paper can accept 150 and up to 200; screens as high as 350 have been used with highly coated stock but only in exceptional cases.

Order Screen with Care

When advertisers order engravings for use in publications, they must specify the proper screen. That screen depends upon the quality of the paper used. If a fine screen is used on coarse paper, such as newsprint, the tiny dots may fall on a "valley" in the paper and thus not print. Sometimes the lint that flakes off newsprint will fill in between the dots, capture ink, and create a smudge on the paper. If, on the other hand, a coarse screen is used on smooth paper, fine detail will be lost and the dot pattern will be unpleasantly conspicuous.

Halftone dot pattern.

Outlined area of 85-line screen *(a)* has been blown up six times by linear measurement to show dot pattern *(b)*.

(a)

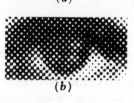

(b)

KINDS OF HALFTONES

A square halftone need not be square; it can also be rectangular, and it can have 90-degree corners. Round and oval halftones are so named for obvious reasons.

If the background has been removed from an engraving, so that the subject appears against plain white paper, it is a silhouette engraving. A vignette is a plate that prints with the effect of the tone of the picture blending almost imperceptibly into the white of the paper. Vignettes are difficult to produce by letterpress and so are most often seen in offset, where they create no production problem.

If a silhouette or vignette has one to three straight edges, it is modified. Sometimes a picture is silhouetted in one area and vignetted in another.

Mortising is cutting out a portion of a halftone plate so that type or another engraving can be placed in that area. The simplest mortise is the notch, a rectangle removed from one corner. An internal mortise is one in which the opening is completely surrounded by the halftone. Mortises are usually rectangular, but internal ones are occasionally irregular. Notches are comparatively easy and inexpensive to make; they can be sawed. Internal mortises, however, require considerable handwork, especially if they are irregular.

Halftone screens.

Four examples of the same subject show effect of varying screen fineness. *(a)* 55-line. *(b)* 65-line. *(c)* 85-line. *(d)* 100-line.

(a)

(b)

(c)

(d)

Combination Plates

Particularly in advertising use, line work is often combined with continuous tone (halftone). This is probably most frequent where a headline prints, in black or reverse, across a photograph.

If the type were printed right onto the original photograph and the whole thing reproduced as a halftone, the type would be neither black nor white. For, as has been seen, even the darkest area of a halftone has some tiny white areas where the dots do not completely meet. The "white" areas are not truly that, for they carry the tiny highlight dot. Thus, a combination plate is made by using two negatives, one in line, the other screened. The line work is then pure black or white, while the halftone has its normal pattern of dots.

Variations of Halftones.
(a) Silhouette. *(b)* Vignette. *(c)* Oval halftones. *(d)* Modified shilhouette.

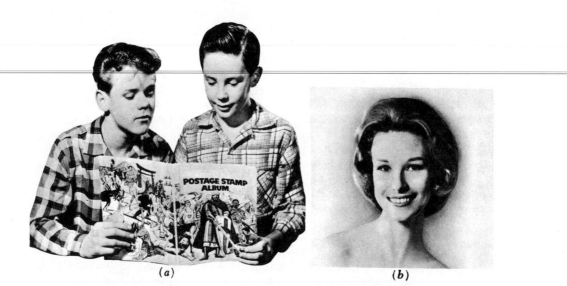

(a)   (b)

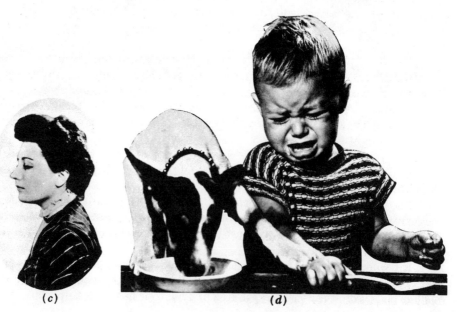

(c)   (d)

Highlight or Dropout Halftones

There are no areas of pure white in a halftone; even photographs of bonewhite areas will produce "pinpoint" dots. Yet often it is desirable to allow the paper to show a 100 percent white area. If silverware is shown in an advertisement, for instance, the silver will reproduce as a light gray. To create a sparkling highlight, it is necessary, or at least desirable, to eliminate the dots entirely in certain areas.

The resulting plate is called, appropriately enough, a highlight, dropout, or facsimile halftone.

Wash drawings, so popular in fashion advertising, must be reproduced by halftone. Yet the entire background must be silhouetted out and highlight areas within the drawing can have no halftone dots. To minimize the work required, a photographic process, Kromolite, has been developed.

COLOR

Although the first color advertisement in a newspaper was run as recently as 1937 (magazine color work had preceded it by about two decades), color is now accepted as a basic tool of the advertiser. Color is a most potent tool, and its use grows constantly as its dividends increase.

Process Color

Process color utilizes two to four halftone plates to reproduce the spectrum of nature. Original art is a full-color continuous tone.

A painter with only the three primary colors on his palette can, at least in theory, mix them to create all the hues apparent to the eye. Red and blue, for instance, make violet or purple, depending on the ratio of the pigments; blue and yellow make green, and so forth. The printer also utilizes this principle of mixing primaries.

The first step in color reproduction is to break down, by filtering, the original full-color art into its component primary colors. If an artist draws a picture in yellow crayon and then lays over the drawing a piece of plastic in the same value of yellow, the drawing will disappear. If the yellow plastic is placed over a green drawing, the artist will see it as blue, for the plastic has blocked all the yellow light rays.

If a yellow filter is placed before a color photograph, the same effect is achieved. if a blue filter is also placed before the photo, the result will be that only the red rays will be visible.

The two filters are combined into a single green one when a screened negative is made. The result is a halftone negative of only the red components of the original, whether the component is a pure red or an orange, a violet, or any of the other myriad of hues that contain portions of red.

An orange filter (the equivalent of a yellow and a red) allows only the blue rays to create a halftone negative. A violet filter (red and blue) separates out the yellow elements of the picture.

The three negatives just described are called *color separations*. They are used to make three individual halftone plates. Printed with the proper inks, the plates will again combine the primaries to produce all the colors of the original.

Checking the Quality. To determine the quality of color plates, the engraver pulls a proof of each plate, singly and in combination. First the yellow plate, then the red; then the engraver combines the two. Next he or she proofs the blue plate and combines it with the yellow-red proof. Thus the set of progressive proofs (progs) numbers five.

Corrections are made by staging and re-etching or burnishing, just as for black-and-white plates.

A new method allows proving before the plates are made. Each of the separation negatives is exposed to a sheet of special film which produces a photograph of the screen pattern in the proper color. When the three transparent prints are superimposed, the effect is approximately that which later will result from printing the three plates.

Errors detected at this stage can be corrected on the separation negatives, either by reshooting the negatives or by using a process called dot etching. (It must be stressed that dot etching is done on negatives, not on plates, and should not be confused with the etching of metal.) Dot etching reduces the area of dots by dissolving their edges with an acetone solvent.

Ability to work on the negative, preliminary to making the plate, saves time and money. For this reason the new method is fast gaining popularity.

Another function of the "progs" is to show the printer precisely the colors of ink to use. These must match the original filters. Usually the inks come in standard process colors. Instead of using the pure primary colors, the platemaker and printer use magenta, a slightly bluish red, instead of violet; cyan, a greenish blue, instead of green; and yellow instead of orange.

Getting Color Plates in Register. When color plates are printed, they must be in exact register. Colored comic strips often show the sorry results of printing out of register. A character often has two mouths because the red plate was out of position and printed the lips somewhere in the cheek.

To assure perfect register, the platemaker places a register mark on each plate. There are variations, but the most common mark is a circle with a cross on it. When this device, in each color, prints exactly over those of the other colors, the printer knows the job is in register. If a plate is improperly positioned, the platemaker can easily measure the degree of error and correct it.

The register mark is placed somewhere where it can be cut off the finished job. If there is no extra paper, the register mark is chiseled off the plate after positioning.

Black Plates. For perfect reproduction of full-color art, the printer adds a black plate. This is produced without filtering. Its function is to add black and grays to the picture and also to help toward sharper definition of shapes in the picture.

When a black plate is used, it adds two more proofs to the set of progs—that of the black plate alone and that of the other three in combination with it.

Four-color process printing (using yellow, red, blue, and black plates) gives perfect reproduction. It is commonly used in magazines and fine books. Three-color process (without the black plate) is more commonly used in newspapers.

Overlays.   The elements for one color are drawn on cardboard. This is the key plate that carries the greatest detail; usually this is the plate that will print in black, although it can be for any color. Over this board the artist affixes an overlay of clear acetate plastic and draws the elements for the second color, placing them in exactly the right position.

Additional overlays are used, one for each color. Register marks are drawn on the original and each overlay; they must, of course, superimpose precisely. The engraver then makes a plate from each piece of art.

Overlays, of plastic or tracing paper, are also used to give instructions to the printer or platemaker. Cropping or mortises on straight halftones are so shown. So is the mechanical separation if this is done from a single piece of art.

If a large area is to appear in one color, the artist often does not fill it in entirely in India ink but draws the outline and, on the overlay, tells the platemaker to finish it up on the negatives.

The artists does each overlay in black ink, no matter what color the resulting plate will be printed in. To see the final color effect, the artist may use transparent plastic sheets with duplicate standard printing inks. The sheets are placed over each other to obtain the right effect. Then the proper value of each color is obtained by benday or mechanical shading.

Best known of such color sheets are those of the Bourges (pronounced "Burgess") system. Its plastic sheets show ten standard printing ink colors in five values from 10 to 100 percent. There are also pencils and inks which are exact duplicates of standard printing inks.

Tint Blocks.   Tint blocks are printing plates that lay down a large, simple area of color. They carry no detail and no gradation in tone, although they may be in full value or screened down to a light tint.

The simplest tint block is a rectangle of color over which is surprinted type or pictures. Usually a block like this must be screened down to afford the necessary contrast between background and surprinting. Full-bodied colors like red and blue must always be screened down to keep the overprint legible. Yellows can usually be in full value. The screening of other hues depends, of course, on the depth of their full value.

Sometimes tint blocks are silhouetted as simples shapes—a Christmas tree or a jack-o'-lantern, for instance. A tint block may be an internal silhouette. In this case it will make a background for a silhouetted halftone, which will then print, not on the color, but on the paper itself, with the color surrounding it in lap or loose register.

A typical use of tint blocks in advertising is to set off a coupon. The tint block can also set off some elements in an ad from the others. This is the same function a box often performs, but there are none of the dangers that often beset the use of a box.

DUPLICATE PLATES

Many occasions arise where duplicate plates are needed. Advertising regularly requires duplicate plates, for black-and-white as well as process and flat color work.

Suppose an auto company wants to run an announcement of a new model in each of the daily and weekly newspapers of the country the same day or week. It could send out comprehensive layouts, with copy and photographs, and have each newspaper plant make up its own advertisement. But the advertiser would then lose the ability to check each proof and would be at the mercy of the type resources and craftsmanship of thousands of composing rooms with varying standards of performance.

To keep control, and to ensure uniformity, the advertiser will have a single form set up and will make duplicates, which are mailed to each publication.

Flat Casts or Stereotypes

The simplest duplicate plate is the stereotype. The process for producing the curved plates needed for rotary presses has been discussed. This process is used at least as frequently for making flat casts (or stereotypes) that, as the name indicates, are not in curved form.

In our example the advertiser would have flongs rolled to the number required. These are light and durable and can be sent by mail with minimum postage or damage. The newspaper flat-casts from the matrix and the resultant plate is locked up in the form. Then the entire page is again matted and cast, this time as a curved plate.

Other materials used in many places at the same time are similarly matted: comic strips, cartoons, syndicated feature material, pictures without a pressing time element, and so forth. Both type and engravings can be matted, of course.

Major users of stereo mats are companies that issue advertising mat services. One point should be made again at this point: A mat is *not* a printing plate. It is a mold from which a printing plate can be made. This caution is given since a mat is often referred to carelessly as a "plate."

Plastic Plates

The plastic plate is cast from a stereotype flong but uses a lightweight plastic instead of type metal. Results are good. The plate is so light that mailing costs are not high. Some national advertisers prefer to send out the plates rather than stereo mats because this eliminates one-step, flat casting, where poor craftsmanship can reduce the quality of the advertisement.

Electrotypes

The highest quality duplicate plate is the electrotype. It carries extremely fine detail; 140-line engravings can be reproduced faithfully by electrotypes, while stereotypes are limited to 65-line.

To make an electrotype, the platemaker prepares a mold of wax, lead, or plastic. By the same electrolytic process by which automobile bumpers are chromium-plated, the matrix is copper plated. This coating of copper is very thin, less than one-sixteenth of an inch. To give it needed strength, the copper is reinforced with a heavier layer of type metal. The entire electrotype is less than a quarter inch thick and must be mounted on a suitable base to bring it type high.

Electrotypes are constantly used in advertising. Even if a single advertisement is to run in only one magazine, the advertiser will send the publication an electro rather than the original form of engraving. Electros can be curved to fit rotary presses, and all but the smallest magazines print from electros rather than original type. Then, if the plate is damaged or worn during or before printing, it is comparatively easy to make a duplicate.

If nickel instead of copper is used for plating the mold, the result is a nickeltype. This is far more durable than electrotype and is used for elements, such as signatures and trademarks, that are used on many occasions.

While an electro weighs many times more than a stereo flong or plastic plate, it still does not involve exorbitant mailing costs. Duplicate plates are used for both black-and-white and color printing.

Of particular interest is the use of computers in typesetting. By the use of these electronic machines any typist can produce tape to actuate typesetting machines, hot or cold.

The use of plastic instead of metal in making printing plates holds many benefits, especially in the use of wraparound plates, as we have already seen. Xerography shows indications of rapid and important advances within the next few years. Offset continues to grow, but letterpress and gravure volume is increasing, too.

Offset Printing and Duplicate Plates

In the last few years there has been a great movement in the newspaper field toward the use of offset. Letterpress printing of newspapers has been vanishing, especially among the smaller and medium-circulation newspapers. These publications have found offset's economies appealing, as well as its superior reproduction of photographs and advertising material.

Naturally, the trend toward offset has created significant changes in the use of duplicate plates. Such plates are not needed by newspapers using the offset process. Neither do such newspapers require the use of mats. Mat service companies, for example, continue to provide mats for newspapers still using letterpress printing but need only supply glossy proofs to the newspapers using offset.

ODDS AND ENDS OF PRINTING

Even persons wholly engaged in printing and engraving admit that they will never learn all there is to know about their craft. Furthermore, new techniques and new equipment appear almost daily. The ordinary advertising person, to whom mechanical reproduction is only a portion of the daily work, may feel overwhelmed at times by this aspect of an advertising job. Still, there are terms and figures he must learn if this part of the job is to be done competently. A few of these are discussed here.

Type Specimen (Type Style) Books.

Even long-time printers cannot learn all the varieties of type. It is madness for the advertising person to attempt to do so. Instead, to help, there is the type specimen book supplied by newspapers and printing houses and used in advertising agency production departments. These are consulted in order to select type of the size and kind needed. There is no need to memorize type styles with such books handy.

Type Schools, Families and Faces

Of these three classifications, the broadest is the school of type, also called race or style. The schools are listed so differently by typographers that it is almost impossible to produce a list over which arguments will not start. Despite all the differences of opinion and terminology, the following list of five schools is offered as embracing just about all type.

Text (or blackletters)
Roman
Italic

Block (Gothic, sans serif, square serifs)
Script-cursive

Of these, Roman is the most important in terms of the number of type families it represents.

This is Text type
This is Roman type
This is Italic type
This is Block type
This is Script type

Here is Text type (Old English)
Here is Roman type (Century)
Here is Italic type (Century)
HERE IS BLOCK TYPE (HELIOS)
Here is Script type (Commercial Script)

Familes. A family of type consists of all the variations in width and weight within a basic type design. There is, for example, the Times Roman family.

This is 10-point Times Roman Bold Italic
Here is 10-Point Times Roman Bold Italic

Faces. Variations within a family are called faces. Most type faces used in advertising are cut in three weights—light, medium and bold. As used in another type family, here are the three weights:

Helios Light ...... 10 point
Helios Medium .. 10 point
Helios Bold ..... 10 point

Units Of Type Measurement

Following are terms that even a nonprinter may use or see everyday if the person is in the advertising business. This will be true if the person has merely a slight contact with printers or agency production personnel.

Point. Depth of type is measured in points. By "depth" is meant the thickness through the type body top-to-bottom. There are 72 points to the inch. Point sizes likely to be found in any one type family are: 6-8-10-12-14-18-24-30-36-42-48-60-72.

Other sizes may be found in a printer's shop from a tiny 4-point to 144-point. Off sizes of 9- and 11-point are found frequently because these are often used in books and magazines. Type is offered sometimes in half-points such as 9½-point.

Body type in an advertisement can be set in a range of sizes but usually doesn't go beyond 12- or 14-point type. Sizes of 18-points and more are called display type (sometimes 14-point type is considered display size) and will be used for headlines, subheads, and other copy outside of the copy blocks such as price figures, logotypes, and slogans. Much of the editorial material in a newspaper is set in 8- or 9-point type. Ten-point type (frequently 11-point) is often used for advertising body copy.

Pica. To measure the width of a type column, the pica is used. An inch is six picas. A printer will say that a line is 12-picas wide (two inches), or he might say it is 12 ems, or even 12 pica-ems. The latter description causes much confusion to advertising beginners because printers also use em to refer to the square of a body of type. Thus, a 12-point em is 12 points high and 12 points deep.

Leading. Spacing between lines is accomplished by placing strips of lead between the lines. This is called leading, pronounced led-ding. This size of the lead strips determines the spacing and is measured in points. Accordingly, a printer who says "10-point, 2-point leaded" means that the copy is set in 10-point type, leaded 2 points. To determine how much 10-point type, leaded 2 points, will go into a given space, the printer will calculate on the basis of 12-point type *set solid*. This term refers to type that is set without any leading between lines. Unless otherwise specified, a lead is assumed to be two points thick.

Readability of Type: Ways to Achieve It

Most of the suggestions you will read here are based on common sense (backed by many studies). Still, even a quick look at advertisements makes it distressingly clear that advertisers are approving thousands of advertisements that common sense should have warned them are not readable. Why lose readership (and sales) because of obvious faults so easily avoided? Here are some suggestions:

Lead sensibly between lines. Material set solid is disliked by most readers. Two-point leading encourages reading. Leading beyond 3 points, however, doesn't necessarily help readership and need be used only when copy is set in long lines. Excessive leading can actually hurt readability when lines are of ordinary length.

Limit number of type styles in one advertisement. This warning has been given before. Normally, limit type in an advertisement to one family and make type variations only within that family. Some advertisers use a rule of thumb to use no more than three faces in an advertisement. Too many faces and too many sizes of type can hurt the readability of the best-written advertisements.

Hold down use of boldface, italics, and capitals. Useful as these can be, their excessive use hurts readability because each is less familiar to the eye than conventional type. Even attention value is diminished when too much type screams for attention. Printing in all-capitals is especially bad for readability.

Break up long copy blocks. Type masses, unbroken by white space, daunt even the most eager of readers. Readability of long copy material can be increased through use of subheads, use of paragraphs, or layout techniques that separate the copy. The advertising person can profit from an examination of how editors handle the long-copy problem.

Use flush left-hand margins. In an effort to be artistic, advertisers frequently use irregular left-hand margins. From the readability standpoint, however, the advertiser only succeeds in making his copy more difficult to read. Faced with irregular margins, the reader's eyes must jump back and forth in order to fix upon the spot where the reading begins. Why cause this extra effort?

Avoid overly-delicate type in newspaper advertisements. Type with thin, delicate hairlines often breaks down in newspaper printing; legibility is thus reduced. Small type, too, may fill with ink. High speed presses and coarse paper stock can cause trouble. Big dailies are less likely to be troublemakers than the small papers. Much improvement has occurred, however, with the use of offset printing by so many newspapers. Thus, this warning is not as valid as it once was.

QUESTIONS

1. What kind of letterpress press is used by newspapers generally? Why?

2. Under what circumstances would silk screen printing be used? What kind of advertising media are especially big users of this method?

3. Why would an advertiser use an insert? What would be the charge for this?

4. For what reason would you use benday? What is Zip-a-Tone?

5. What is meant by "out of register" in speaking of color work?

6. What is a: (a) combination plate? (b) mat? (c) electrotype?

7. What effect has the trend toward offset printing by newspapers had on the use of mats? Why?

23

THE SELLING MESSAGE: ADVERTISING COPYWRITING—PART 1

THE SELLING MESSAGE: ADVERTISING COPYWRITING—PART 1

Universal language? There is none. But advertising copy comes close because it is, in a sense, the universal language of the marketplace.

A copywriter in Bombay uses it in much the same way as any counterpart in Tokyo, London, Buenos Aires, Berlin, Tehran, Johannesburg, Athens, and New York. There are differences, of course, caused by cultural variations and local customs. Still, people everywhere eat, drink, want comfort, have curiosity, seek learning, are profit-motivated, and want to be loved, attractive, and popular. A copywriter, thus, wherever located, caters to consumer habits, needs, and desires whether writing in Chinese, English, or Swedish.

Universally, too, when advertising is criticized it is copywriting that is the target because copywriting is so very visible and so very revealing of the purposes and aims of the advertiser.

"COPY" A DEFINITION

Words used in print or broadcast advertising are "copy." Often, however, the term is used collectively. If an advertising person asks for the copy, it may well include more than the words in the body text. Included, also, may be the artwork or, in television, the storyboard.

Such sterile definitions do not do justice to the word because a difference in the copy approach may result in a million dollar success, or a multimillion dollar flop. Good copy can become a part of the language and can be parroted by most of the population. Bad copy can rouse the ire of the Federal Trade Commission. Poor creative work is the single most important reason for a client to fire an advertising agency.

Before Writing—What Must Be Done

Writing an advertisement is often the easiest step. The prewriting thinking may well be the hardest part of turning out the finished advertisement. In this pre-writing thinking, the persons responsible for overall planning will decide:

(1) the people likely to buy the product or service;
(2) the media to be used;
(3) the basic appeals to which human beings react;
(4) the long-range advertising plan or campaign thinking; and
(5) the art and production factors as they relate to the copy.

PEOPLE

Income

Income levels automatically stratify great numbers of people. A copywriter for Black, Starr & Gorham is not writing for the person whose income is under $3,000 any more than the writer for Rolls-Royce, or Tiffany's. Although it is not always true, income has a powerful effect on what is bought. Likewise (and this again is not always true) there is a fairly strong correlation between income level and education level. It is generally assumed that high income and higher level education go together. Thus, knowledge of the income of the prospects for a product or service will cause the copywriter to write at what is assumed to be the proper language level for this income bracket.

Social Class

In the foregoing discussion of income level, it was indicated that at times the writer, misled by a high income level, may write above the audience. A blue-collar home may have the same income as the home of a teacher or accountant, but members of the two homes are in different social classes. Because they have different interests, different educational backgrounds, and different attitudes, the writer would make a great mistake in writing the same way to these groups. Advertisements to women of the working class, for example, should not use too sophisticated terms or stress motives of status seeking. It becomes obvious, therefore, that income level, while an important guide to the copywriter, cannot be the sole determinant of the writing style and the appeals used; social class must be considered, too.

Education and Job Position

A writer can consciously write for the easy comprehension of the different educational levels; this is done by observing well-established formulas. Sometimes a college graduate will work on the assembly line, or as a mailman, or as a laborer, but generally the kind of job a person has will provide a fairly accurate indication of income, social class, and education. If the copywriter knows that the majority of the audience are professional people, engineers, professors, factory workers, or farmers, a strong clue is provided as to how to write the copy.

Sex

Naturally, the sex of the audience is one of the most important factors. This factor, in a great many cases, is the very first considered. After it has once been decided that the audience will be mostly or entirely male or female, the others will then be considered.

Men and women look for different things in advertisements. In a study made by the research firm of Daniel Starch and Staff, for instance, it was discovered that in appliance advertising men are principally concerned about price and the available discounts, while women are most interested in advertisements placed by stores that offer guarantees of satisfaction.

Further, the report went on, men are most attracted by products offering comfort, pleasure, and convenience, such as air conditioners, radios, and television sets. Women are most attracted to appliances that save work, such as automatic washers and dryers.

Men, it was found, do not mind going carefully through advertisements showing many items and many brands. Women, however, prefer fewer items, much white space, and a minimum of reverse printing (white on black).

Location

Actually, where people live is not so important as where they buy, though the first often affects the second. A regional farm program, for example, is addressed to people who may do all their buying in smaller, rural communities. Their purchasing may be done largely in farm stores and in Sears Roebuck outlets. Suburbanites do most of their purchasing in outlying shopping centers, while city dwellers buy clothes and other big-ticket items in department stores in the central business district. While these differences have little effect on the writing of national advertisements, they can affect sharply the writing of regional and local copy.

MEDIA

Audience of Medium

Sometimes a medium is so specialized that it becomes the primary consideration in helping the copywriter determine the nature of the audience. The character of the medium makes it easy to determine just who the prospects are and how to write to them. As the medium becomes less specialized (as in radio and television) however, the copywriter finds it harder and harder to analyze the audience in terms of the medium.

A magazine such as *Reader's Digest* reaches so broad a group of readers that the copywriter preparing copy for an advertisement to appear in this magazine must write to a huge, faceless audience. To a lesser degree the copywriter has a problem with advertisements for *Time*, which also reaches a broad spectrum of readers. If, however, the advertisement is to appear in the business section of this magazine, it helps to know that this section has a big readership among corporation management men.

A copywriter who prepares advertising for *Better Homes & Gardens* begins to have a better idea of the audience when research shows: that the group has more than the usual interest in the home; that it has a somewhat better-than-average income; that it has many specialized home interests such as gardening, decorating, and do-it-yourself activities. Other home-service magazines, or "shelter books" as they are called, will provide the copywriter with these same clues as to the nature of the audience. These include *House & Garden, House Beautiful*, and others.

Then there are those magazines that single out unmistakably the interests and character of the readers. So clear-cut are these that the copywriter's job becomes relatively simple. The copy aims directly at these interests and appeals strongly to the reader. Some magazines in the consumer magazine field that pinpoint reader interests are *Country Club Golfer* and *American Rifleman*. Likewise, writers of business magazine copy can aim directly at their audience in such publications as *Cheese Reporter, Resort Manager*, and *Southern Building*.

BASIC APPEALS

All human beings act as they do because of certain stimuli. In advertising, these stimuli are usually referred to as copy appeals. Such stimuli are working on each one of us throughout our conscious hours. Some of them are more powerful than others, but each is powerful to a degree if it is used in the right place at the right time.

A beginning writer should think of these appeals before starting to write, and should decide which one will be most effective for the audience, medium, and product. The copy should then use this appeal just as powerfully as possible. Often an advertisement will feature one basic appeal while employing subordinate appeals to widen its attraction. An electric shaver advertisement, for example, might appeal to male egotism (satisfaction in the clean-shaven appearance), but at the same time might use, in a subordinate way, a sensory appeal.

What Are the Basic Appeals?

Basic appeals in the literal sense refer to primal appeals such as those connected with hunger, thirst, and the sex drive. The copywriter refines these appeals and greatly expands them. When writing, he generally does not think deliberately about what appeal to use, but a writer simply chooses the appropriate appeal automatically.

Yet, even an experienced copywriter may find it useful to look over the basic appeals occasionally for help in achieving a copy direction. The following list is given to show the different avenues available to the copywriter. Appeals represented here embrace most of the appeals that motivate people to buy.

(1) *Profit motive.* The desire for monetary gain is one of the strongest of appeals. The headline **Earn Big Money as a TV Repairman** illustrates the use of this appeal.

Naturally the profit appeal can take many forms other than the direct promise that one can earn more money. An advertisement that stresses car care in terms of a product that will make the car last longer and perform more economically is certainly stressing profit. Likewise, an insurance policy with various benefit features falls into the "profit motive" category. Two other products that can be sold through the profit appeal: (1) a new design of refrigerator that keeps foods better and cuts down wastage. (2) An electric clock thermostat that is advertised with a headline that promises: **You Can Cut 40% From Your Fuel Bill This Winter.**

In short, there are literally thousands of products and services that will in some way offer a profit. An enormous number of advertisements stress the profit-motive appeal, capitalizing on the very human desire to make more money, to keep from losing money, or to keep intact the money or investment that one has.

(2) *Health.* **Prevent Tooth Decay Now** is a headline that stresses the health appeal.

Although this appeal is naturally uppermost for medicines and drug products, it is not always the strongest appeal when used with products such as cereals, which are normally eaten for their good taste rather than for health-giving benefits.

(3) *Love and sex.* Love, in this instance, is romantic love, rather than family love.

This appeal is exemplified by the headline **Evenings That Memories Are Made Of.** The sex appeal, on the other hand, is illustrated by the headline **Tigress: Because Men Are Such Animals.** Cold creams, cologne, perfumes, and many other personal products use the sex appeal constantly with telling effect.

(4) *Fear.* **A Poor Diet Plan Can Wreck Your Health.**

This headline illustrates the appeal that plays upon physical fear. There are other fear appeals that are strong, too. There is the fear of social embarrassment, fear of failure (in a job or in school work), fear of growing old. Yet, though the fear appeal is strong, it must be used with discretion, or it may backfire by giving the advertisement such a negative tone that people will not read the copy because it seems too unpleasant.

(5) *Admiration.* Football players who smoke cigarettes, daring adventurers who drink whiskey highballs, and society leaders who use certain brands of cold cream are featured in advertisements because many people admire them and want to be like them.

Admiration appeal can also be called emulation appeal or hero-worship appeal. **There Must Be a Good Reason.** _____ _____ **Used Ever-Last Shoes in the NBA Playoffs.** Such an appeal will influence thousands of youngsters who imitate the professional basketball stars in equipment as well as playing style.

(6) *Physical comfort.* The desire to be warm, cool, or just in between is the appeal that sells millions of air conditioners, dehumidifiers, hot-water bottles, electric blankets, electric fans, heaters, and other assorted products that make people physically comfortable.

Our caveman ancestors huddling over their fires knew this appeal even though they could not articulate it. The desire for comfort is one of the most fundamental of all appeals and will always remain so. **Now, Light Protection So Comfortable You'll Wear It Any Time.**

This headline demonstrates the comfort appeal as applied to clothing.

(7) *Sensory appeals.* Here again are appeals that are as fundamental as life itself. These are the appeals to sight, taste, touch, smell, and hearing. The following headline appeals to two of the senses.

You'll Like the Feel of this Sweater As Well As Its Bright Beauty.

A sensory-appeal headline can, if the copywriter is ingenious, be written for almost any type of product. In this case, it is a sweater but it could well be a piece of farm machinery, an automobile, or a toaster oven.

Downy-soft wool comforts the skin while colors such as heather-blue please the eye. Run your hand over the soft fabric. Notice, as you do, how the sheen captures the light and intensifies the color. Here is a garment to delight the senses.

This advertisement in head and copy goes all out to stress the sensory appeals of touch and sight.

Still another example of the senses approach:

ARE THESE SALADS IDENTICAL TWINS?
YOUR EYES SAY: YES.
YOUR MOUTH WILL SAY: NO.
DON'T BE CASUAL
WHEN YOU READ THIS BOOK:
IT MAY CHANGE
YOUR WHOLE WAY OF THINKING.

While the appeal to mental stimulation is not one of the truly fundamental appeals, it is nevertheless a strong appeal to the relatively few people who enjoy using their minds. Schools and makers of mind-using games employ this appeal.

(8) *Desire for new experiences.* Seeking for adventure and the different, and breaking away from the humdrum, have been strong in man from the earliest times. They supply, of course, the strongest appeal in travel advertising. This headline from an advertisement for travel exemplifies the appeal:

MARCO: IT'S A FAMILY ADVENTURE
ON A SUMMER ISLAND

(9) *Fun and pleasure.* Most people do not live for work alone. The pursuit of fun and pleasure is growing all the time as people have more and more leisure and enough money to make the most of their extra time.

Fun is stressed strongly, for instance, in the sale of beverages, many foods, and other accompaniments of relaxed living. A headline for a Kodak film advertisment demonstrates one version of the fun appeal:

*GORDON GETS TO FLY A KITE. NATHAN GETS TO WEAR A
WIG, AND I GET TO MAKE THE FLAG.*
BOY, IT'S FUN STARTING A COUNTRY.
KODAK FILM FOR THE TIMES OF YOUR LIFE.

Much of today's advertising uses the appeal that says, in effect (if
not directly): "You've worked hard; you deserve fun and the good
things in life. Have them."

(10) *Family affection and togetherness.*

MAKE FRIENDS WITH YOUR WIFE AND KIDS AGAIN.
AT SEA PINES.

This headline is a headline for a resort area that is typical of many
advertisements that appeal to the love of parents for their children.

Other powerful appeals stress the affection of a man for his wife or
pride in the home, but children are sometimes stressed as in the
following:

"ALMOST 50% OF AMERICA'S CHILDREN DON'T GET
ENOUGH VITAMIN C."
"THAT'S WHY I'M GLAD MY CHILDREN LOVE
THE TASTE OF TANG."

(11) *Egotism and vanity.* Suntan oil, cosmetics, clothes, and a whole host of
other products are sold largely through this appeal, which has been
strong from the beginning of man.

Even appeals for cultural pursuits, such as schooling, books, and
music, are frequently rooted in appeals to egotism and vanity.
Sometimes advertisements are said to have a snob appeal—in different
ways and for different products:

"MY PARKING TICKET SAID CADILLAC
BUT MY CAR IS A FORD GRANADA"
GET RID OF THAT GRAY HAIR.
IN 10 DAYS LOOK 10 YEARS YOUNGER.

Even the armed services have used these appeals by saying, in effect (or actually): "If you think you're good enough, try the Marines."

(12) *Self-gratification.* Vacation trips, the possession of luxuries, eating at
fine restaurants, jewelry—all of these are the stuff of which advertisements using the self-gratification appeal are made.

New products with features are often likely to be advertised
through the self-gratification appeal—the desire to have the new even
though sometimes there are no truly significant differences between
the new product and the old product. New car sales are based largely
upon this appeal or sometimes upon the vanity appeal. An example of
the "new" appeal that falls into the self-gratification area is this
headline:

WHY SHOULDN'T YOU HAVE AN EXCLUSIVE?
IT'S YOUR MONEY.

(13) *Convenience.* While not a fundamental human appeal in the sense that it can be traced back to caveman days, convenience has nonetheless become a basic appeal in this era when thousands of products and services cater to the widespread desire to have things easier, quicker, closer, and with less trouble.

This appeal is illustrated by this headline:

DISPOSE OF TRASH NEATLY AND EASILY
WITH A TIDEE COMPACTOR

Another example is afforded by an advertisement that features a cake mix that can be prepared in two minutes. The headline for this product sounds almost apologetic:

ANYTHING THIS MOIST, THIS DELICIOUS
SHOULDN'T BE THIS EASY.

(14) *Altruism, patriotism, kindness.* Most people read advertising to satisfy certain selfish and personal desires.

Appeals to altruism, patriotism, and kindness are not likely to gain the interest that is automatically given to appeals that are aimed at selfish motives. Still, within almost all of us lies the wish to do something, at least occasionally, for some reason other than personal advantage. Were it not for this fact, there would be no advertising for churches, for charities, for hospital funds, for schools, or for government drives. In terms of total advertising, these appeals to unselfish motives are not important, but they are present and must be mentioned. Typical of such appeals is a headline for an advertisement that reads:

READ THIS AND CRY.
FOR THE LOVE OF A HUNGRY CHILD.

A somewhat similar approach, only for trees instead of people, was successful in raising a considerable sum for the "Save-the-Redwoods League."

CAMPAIGN THINKING

The Campaign Plan

Although there are many retail advertisers, and some national advertisers, who prepare their advertising on an advertisement-to-advertisement basis, without establishing any overall theme or campaign plan, most advertisers who have a substantial investment in advertising do think in terms of a long-range plan. In advertising terminology, this thinking is summed up in the term "campaign." The advertisements used in a campaign have certain characteristics in common. These characteristics may include the style of writing, the kind of typography, the size of the advertisements, the borders used, the illustrations, the logotype, the use of color, and the headline style. All of these may be used consistently, or only certain ones.

The Copy Platform

Big-budget national advertisers and regional advertisers will almost invariably think in campaign terms. Almost always the campaign approach will be outlined in a short summation, called a "copy platform," which is prepared by the advertising agency, the company, or both. This "platform," serves as a guide to copywriters, as well as to anyone else who works on the account. It tells what is not to be done in the campaign, as well as what is to be done. Some copy platforms are elaborate, but most are quite brief because they are more usable that way. Generally they consist of the following statements and listings:

(1) An overall statement that expresses the philosophy, theme, or rationale of the campaign.
(2) A statement of the specific objectives to be achieved by the campaign.
(3) A listing of the copy points, statements or claims that must be used in every advertisement.
(4) A listing of important points that can be used frequently in the campaign.
(5) A listing of points, statements, or claims that should not, for copy reasons or company reasons, be used.
(6) A listing of the points that must be made for legal reasons.
(7) A listing of the points that, because of legal reasons, should not be made.

Not every copy platform, of course, includes all these items. Some companies, for instance, do not have legal problems with their products. Other companies, on the contrary, are more conscious of legal aspects than of any other consideration when they devise a copy platform. Patent medicine, cigarettes, cosmetics, soaps, health foods, and farm animal feeds are some of the products for which the advertising may run into legal difficulties. Platforms for these products are certain to include legal points to be observed.

Looking For and Stressing the Point of Difference

Almost always, a product has a point of difference from other products that should be stressed by the copywriter. Usually, this difference will be emphasized in the headline and in the opening copy. In a television set, it might be freedom from repair, superior brightness, easier tuning, handsomer appearance, or some other point important to set owners.

In a power mower, it might be quieter operation, ability to cut grass even when it is wet, a sure start every time, or a unique safety feature.

Sometimes a new feature is introduced into a product for the sole purpose of giving advertising writers and salesmen something special on which to base their selling presentation. Without a point of difference to exploit, copywriters have a desperate writing job. Their first question, in fact, before they write the copy is: "What's different about the product or service?" They are likely to be gloomy if told there is no difference.

If the latter is true, then the copywriters have two recourses:

(1) To study the product, the service, or the advertising company intensively to see if some point of difference has been overlooked. If one is found, and it is sufficiently significant, that will probably become the key point in the advertisements.

(2) If it is impossible to find a significant point of difference, then the advertising itself may become the point of difference. This might mean, for example, that an unusual character will be used in the advertising.

In television and radio, unusual visual and/or sound effects or music may create the point of difference. An unusual art style or typography might help create the difference.

It is better, of course, that a genuine product (or service) differentiation be used than to simply try to establish that difference through the character of the advertising. Yet, many selling successes have been based upon the latter.

Unique Selling Proposition

U.S.P. flashed across the advertising sky some years ago when it was featured in the book *Reality in Advertising* by Rosser Reeves, a well-known advertising agency head.

Actually, the phrase was a dramatic way of saying 'point of difference' and was based upon the author's assertion that every product or service has an exploitable feature that is its alone, and that advertising for this product or service must be built around this unique selling proposition.

As Reeves said, the U.S.P. is often not apparent. It must be sought out through intensive study of the product, the service, or the advertiser himself. It is found most often through the hard work and imagination of the creative man working on the account. Once discovered it should be stressed hard in the advertising and, if it is truly an important U.S.P., it can be featured in the advertising over a long period since Reeves maintains, with justification, that good U.S.P.'s are often not used long enough because the advertiser tires of their use long before the public is generally aware of the point being made.

Suffering Points

Allied to the 'point of difference' and 'U.S.P.' is the suffering point approach to the writing of advertising. This approach is based on the assumption that users of products find in those products the answers to problems they have experienced. Before writing, the copywriters ask: "What are the suffering points answered by the use of the product?"

In a paint, for instance, the suffering points could be:

- Paint leaves brush marks.
- Paint takes too long to dry.
- Paint goes on hard.
- Paint requires two applications.
- Paint is too runny.
- Paint is too hard to clean from brush.

If copywriters find that the paint they are writing about answers one, or more of these suffering points, they have a basis for writing appealing advertising. It might be that the quality of a product that answers a suffering point might also be a U.S.P. but not necessarily.

Copywriters who stress the suffering point approach can be sure of one thing—they are talking consumer language, because consumers do not buy products just to buy products; they buy answers to problems.

ART AND PRODUCTION CONSIDERATIONS

The Writer's Concern with Art and Production

With great frequency it is found that when people pass judgment upon an advertisement and say, "'I don't like it," they are judging the advertisement according to their feeling about the illustration and the main headline—especially the general layout and illustration. These are the most obvious features to consider in an advertisement, whether the person doing the judging is a client of an advertising agency or a reader of a publication.

A writer, therefore, must be deeply concerned about art and production. ("Production" refers here to the selection of typography, printing process, and engraving procedures.) No matter how fine the copy, it will not succeed if the first impression of the advertisement is negative because of factors other than the copy.

Unless copywriters have strong artistic talent or are working in small organizations where they double as artists-copywriters, they will (and should) have little to do with the actual execution of layouts and artwork. Their time is better spent on copythinking and copywriting.

Writers, nevertheless, especially in an advertising agency, will need to make many decisions regarding layout and art direction because it is impossible to write copy without considering the illustrating technique that will be used with it. In the retail field this is not much of a problem for department-store copywriters, for example, since they most often write the copy in the spaces left by the artist. According to the usual procedure, the layout will be done first; then the copywriter goes to work. In the advertising agency, the copywriter works up the headline and illustration idea and then does one of two things:

(1) turns both over to the artist and asks him or her to do a layout;
(2) finishes the copy and then gives headline, copy, and illustration ideas to the artist. However, there can be many variations in the procedures followed.

The copywriter's illustration idea, as mentioned in the layout chapter, may simply be conveyed through a thumbnail sketch, which is a small, very rough sketch that does no more than indicate the placement and relative size of elements. Another procedure is to do an extremely rough layout in full size. For the many copywriters who have no artistic ability whatsoever, there is a third course—to tell, in written or oral instructions, what kind of illustrative and layout treatment the copywriter would like.

HEADLINES

Writing Headlines: the Starting Point

After doing the prewriting thinking, the copywriter is ready for the real starting point of the writing—the headline. A simple little headline that the reader skims over without giving it any real attention may have taken the writer some days to achieve. This hard worker may have written and rejected pages and pages of headlines. Perhaps the headline represents not only the copywriter's thinking, but also the thinking of many other persons drawn into the effort.

The headline sets the theme of an advertisement. Actually it *is* the theme in many instances. Until the headline is written, it is impossible for the artist to proceed intelligently; the illustration and the headline work together. A good headline and a good illustration, plus an identifying logotype, can carry the major portion of the creative burden of an advertisement even before copy is written.

Most copywriters find that once they have written a headline that satisfies them, writing the body copy may be relatively simple.

"Rules" for Writing Headlines

Quotes have been used around the word "rules" to indicate that there are no fixed rules in headline writing. Just as soon as some advertising expert says that something must always be done or not done, in headline writing, some clever copywriter breaks the rule successfully.

Put a Benefit in Your Headline. The benefit you put in your headline will usually be the chief benefit. It answers a "suffering point" of the reader. It indicates, in other words, that something that has been a source of trouble, inconvenience, or annoyance to the reader can be solved or alleviated through the use of the advertised product or service. Gillette's headline asks: "Why buy a blade that gives you fewer shaves?" This is clearly a benefit headline. The suffering point is the quick-wearout factor in razor blades. The benefit is a blade that gives more shaves.

People almost always read headlines and copy because they hope that the product advertised will answer some problem. Benefit headlines talk directly to people with problems. A straight benefit headline is seldom clever and it is not talked about, yet it is the most reliable in sales power. That is because it is written first in terms of people, not chiefly in terms of things or products.

Suppose Gillette had written: "Here's the sharpest blade of all—the new

Headline that gets attention through physical size and clever twist.

Big headlines look important. In this case, impressive physical size is combined with a twisting of a familiar phrase to engage reader attention. The accompanying copy gives a straightforward, information-packed message.

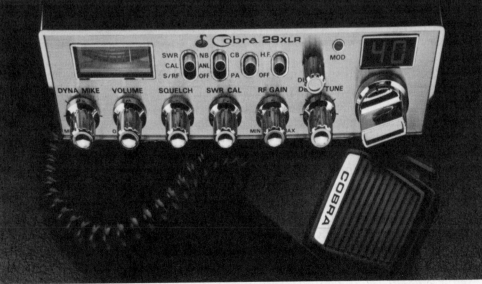

The 40-channel Cobra 29XLR. From the sleek brushed chrome face to the matte black housing, it's a beauty. But its beauty is more than skin deep. Because inside, this CB has the guts to pack a powerful punch.

The illuminated 3-in-1 meter tells you exactly how much power you're pushing out. And pulling in. It also measures the system's efficiency with an SWR check. In short, this Cobra's meter lets you keep an eye on your ears.

The Digital Channel Selector shows you the channel you're on in large LED numerals that can be read clearly in any light. There's also switchable noise blanking to reject short-pulse noise other systems can't block. The built-in power of DynaMike Plus. Automatic noise limiting and Delta Tuning for clearer reception.

And the added protection of Cobra's nationwide network of Authorized Service Centers with factory-trained technicians to help you with installation, service and advice.

The Cobra 29XLR. It has 40 channels. And it has what it takes to improve communications by punching through loud and clear on every one of them. That's the beauty of it.

Cobra

Punches through loud and clear.

Cobra Communications Products
DYNASCAN CORPORATION
6460 W. Cortland St., Chicago, Illinois 60635
Write for color brochure
EXPORTERS: Empire • Plainview, N.Y. • CANADA: Atlas Electronics • Toronto

PUNCH AND BEAUTY

Super Blue Blade." This is a product-oriented headline. The benefit to the reader is only implied. There is no direct promise.

Despite the obvious virtues of benefit headlines, readers will see many advertisements that seem to work hard to avoid a direct statement of benefit. Sometimes the writer feels that a special approach will attract more attention than the relatively colorless benefit headline. Other times this writer may feel that direct benefit headlines are too easy to write and have therefore been used so much by the competition that they lack freshness and appeal. If, for example, every tire advertisement headline were to promise safety and long wear, it would become difficult to differentiate one advertisement from another.

Make Your Headlines Short (or Long?). "Make your headlines short", for many years was one of the most-quoted maxims of headline writing. It was felt that the headline should not "give away" the copy story—that, instead, it should lead readers into the body copy by teasing as it were. A long headline, it was thought, would be sure to steal the thunder from the following copy. Also, and this is a reason that is still valid, when a headline is very long it must be printed in small type unless the advertiser is using a big space and is willing to take up most of that space with the headline.

Yet the long headline can be defended. Readership figures show that if the long headline is interesting and contains benefits, it will gain attention and readership. Because the average person has so much advertising to read and listen to these days, he or she has become a headline reader who will pause only over those advertisements striking enough in headline and illustration to seize attention and partly sell. Thus, today the headline carries more of the selling task than in the days when it was only an attention-getter. The function of many of today's long headlines is to presell the readers before they begin reading the copy.

In small-space advertisements the copywriters are often faced with a problem:

(1) They want to use a headline in a type size big enough to stand out in rivalry with the big type used in surrounding large-space advertisements.
(2) If they do use a big type in the headline, they must cut the number of words severely.
(3) If they cut the number of words, they cannot achieve the kind of selling message they would like in the headline.

There is an answer to this problem that should be used more often than it is. The writer can use an overline above the main head, and a strong subhead under the main head. Suppose, for example, the copywriter is writing copy for a new battery-powered lawn mower to be advertised in *Better Homes & Gardens*. First comes the writing of a main headline that gives the big news—that there *is* a battery-powered electric lawn mower. The mere announcement of such a development will seize the interest of homeowners. Because the writer is simply making an announcement in the main headline, it can be kept short and thus a large type size can be used to create impact, drama and importance.

In order to expand upon the announcement and make the readers of the magazine appreciate just what this new unit will mean to them, the copywriter accompanies the main headline with an overline and long subhead. The trio of headlines looks like this:

Overline: *An electric mower without cords*

Although the advantages of electric mowers have always been apparent, the umbilical effect of the electric cords made grass-cutting awkward and sometimes dangerous because of the possibility of the blades cutting the cords. Thus, the overline stresses what may be the biggest advantage over other electric mowers.

Main head: At last—Electro-Kut— the *battery-powered* lawn mower.

In this headline we offer news of a startling advance in lawn mowers. Electric mowers have been around for years but always their use was limited because they had to be plugged into an electric socket. The mower could operate only within the length of the cord. And the cord caught on bushes, trees, and other objects. Accordingly, the head features the main point—the use of a battery. This is the U.S.P. and point of difference.

Subhead: Just think—noiseless, odorless grass cutting and, unlike ordinary electrics, no cords to hamper you. Here's the ultimate lawn mower.

This subhead attacks all the competition. First, it spells out the advantages of Electro-Kut over gas-powered mowers and then repeats the big advantage over electric mowers, the elimination of cords. At this point, the reader should be eager to get full details such as size of the cut, weight, length of battery charge, and unit price.

Sometimes, of course, when there is much to be said, the copywriter might amplify the main head only with an overline, or only with a main subhead. If using only the overline, the writer is almost forced to write a long main headline. This is demonstrated in the following overline-main head combination for the electric lawn mower:

Overline: *Now, the ultimate in lawn mowers*

Main head: New! Electro-Kut, the *battery-powered* lawn mower—outdoes the ordinary electric mower because it has no cords. Outdoes gas-powered mowers because it's incomparably quieter, and odorless.

Use Verbs in Headlines.   There is a logical reason behind this rule even though it is constantly broken. Verbs are action words. They create movement, life, and vitality. In many advertisements they urge the reader to do something and get him to act.

Still there have been hundreds of resultful headlines that have not used verbs. Here are a few that are typical of the many that can be seen in any national magazine:

NEW LIFE FOR OLD CLOTHES

ORIENT HOLIDAYS WITH FRIENDLY FACES AND EXOTIC PLACES

THE CURE FOR BEEF BLAHS

A BEAUTIFUL INTRODUCTION—TO THE TRANQUIL, LINGERING BEAUTY OF MASUMI BY COTY

Even though these are effective headlines, and it is not difficult to write a good headline without using a verb, the copywriter should use verbs in headlines whenever possible.

Relate Headlines to Illustrations

Although advertisements are often seen in which the different elements seem to be going at cross-purposes, the best advertisements tie together the headline, the illustration, and the opening copy.

This is demonstrated by an advertisement for Chap Stick Lip Balm:

Main head: **PROTECTION MONEY.**

Subhead: Chap Stick Lip Balm will give you $1.00 to protect your lips from the sun.

Opening copy: Imagine! Buy two different flavors of Chap Stick Lip Balm and get $1.00 back with proofs of purchase plus a 10¢ off coupon toward your next purchase.

(Illustration)   Woman in sun hat holding up facsimile of a dollar bill in one hand and four flavors of Chap Stick in the other hand.

Such coordination of these three important elements gives unity and persuasiveness to an advertisement. Too often, however, writers will tie the illustration and headline together but digress in their opening copy.

Feature Product Name or Advertiser   At one time people who gave rules for headline writing declared that the name of the advertiser or the product should never appear in the headline, because the headline containing such a name was inclined not to be written from the reader's viewpoint but from that of the advertiser.

Thinking has shifted on this matter. Because of the cursory reading given so many advertisements, the advertiser may derive some advantage from flagging the reader with the company name or product name. Certain company or product names, furthermore, are so well known and so prestigious that their presence in the headline automatically ensures attention and interest for the headline. Companies such as General Motors, General Electric, and Westinghouse have so established themselves in the minds of the public that they would be remiss not to use their names at least occasionally in headlines.

With so many products being advertised and product and advertiser identification so low among consumers, the use of the product or company name in the headline, as well as in the logotype, can help increase identification. Examples of identifying headlines follow:

TAKE A QUICK LOOK AT BISQUICK® THIS SUMMER
ATMOS. THE ONLY CLOCK IN THE WORLD POWERED BY AIR.
ROLLS-ROYCE BRINGS BACK A GREAT NAME.
SILVER WRAITH II.

Get Attention by Physical Size   The technique of getting attention by physical size applies to big-space advertisements of a page or more. Big, bold headlines command attention and create importance for the headline message. On the other hand, if big headlines are used too often by too many advertisers, they will lose their effect. Likewise, for many classes of advertisers, they are unsuitable, since big, bold headlines clash with the reserved atmosphere sought for these products or advertisers. A delicate perfume, for example, or a store such as Tiffany's could not appropriately shout its message in big headlines.

Sometimes the same effect of emphasis can be achieved in headlines of smaller physical size by (a) using a clean, individual type and (b) surrounding the type with ample white space. This technique is shown here in the following headline for a quality product. Give a headline in small type enough breathing space and automatically it achieves the visibility of a headline set in larger type that does not have the benefit of white space around it.

The French have a way with timeless elegance. Lanvin.

On the other hand, sheer type size alone can command attention as in the case of the following headline for sizing, a product used in connection with ironing. For this kind of product and the copy approach used in the advertisement, a big headline of this type is quite suitable. A glance at magazines, especially those carrying numerous utilitarian products, reveals that many advertisers use headlines of similarly impressive size.

FOUND!
New life for tired-looking clothes

When to make a headline big physically depends, as has been shown, on the type of product or advertiser. A copywriter at the "doodling" stage of writing an advertisement will do well to make some very rough layouts in order to experiment with headlines and illustrations, keeping in mind the competitive situation. With respect to competition, there is no special problem if the advertiser has a full page. If, instead, the advertiser shares the page with others, as so often occurs in newspaper advertising, then it must be made certain that the advertisement is competitive in physical impact with other advertising.

A way to determine whether the advertisement *is* competing is to clip the rough layout to a typical newspaper page containing other advertisements. One can thus tell whether the headline and illustration are submerged by other items on the page. By experimenting with headline and illustration size, the writer can make certain that the advertisement will be competitive.

Avoid Boasting Headlines. Readership studies show consistently that what are called "brag and boast" headlines do poorly as compared to the more modest headlines that are reader-centered rather than advertiser-centered (as boastful headlines invariably are).

Sometimes it is difficult to draw the line between an honest pride in performance—a performance that will be of interest to prospects for a product or service—and outright boasting. Suppose, for instance, that a headline reads:

> *Ten years in blistering sun*
> *and salty air—but Durex Paint*
> *hasn't faded*

Can this be called boasting, or is it excusable pride? Advertisers call such a headline an honest statement of fact that will create buying interest among prospects. In this instance, prospects for paint are ever interested in paint that will stand up against the punishment meted out by the elements. Such "honest" statements, however, mean nothing if they are not backed by facts presented clearly in the body copy of the advertisement. Only specific evidence will make the statement impressive to discerning prospects.

Use Quotation Headlines Occasionally.   Readability experts have found that quoted material attracts readers and makes material achieve higher readability scores. A quotation headline attracts readership simply because it is in quotes. Sometimes the quote is from a real person shown in the advertisement, and it will be especially attention-getting, of course, if the person in the illustration is a well-known person. Sometimes, however, the supposed direct quote is straight from a copywriter's imagination. Advertisements using this technique may be called quasi-testimonials.

Direct quote example: *"My skin was always dry and itchy but 10 days of using your moisturizer has given me relief"*

(The illustration shows an actual person and gives her name.)

Quasi-testimonial quote: *"For Father's Day I want a new lamp for my den"*

(The illustration uses a model and no name is supplied.)

Use Subheads.   Anyone who has ever been a newspaper writer or editor knows the value of subheads in breaking up tiring masses of type, and in helping carry stories along excitingly and with a rush.

In advertising, however, the subhead within the body copy has not been used to the extent that it should be. Long, unbroken passages of body type are seen time after time. National and retail advertisers are especially remiss in not using subheads. In contrast, mail-order advertisers learned long ago that subheads help readership and sales. This is especially true if the copywriter writes selling subheads, not just dull labels, as is so often done in retail advertising.

CLASSIFYING HEADLINES

With headlines, as with anything else in advertising that is classified, the experienced writers rarely say as they set about creating an advertisement: "Now, where's that list of headline types? I'm going to write a novelty headline." Copywriters of long experience have probably written every kind of headline type, but they simply do not consciously classify headlines when they write any more than an auto mechanic consciously thinks of the classification of tools to be used to repair a car. Yet it is convenient to have names for the different types of headlines. Also, it is helpful for the beginner to know the relative merits of the headline types in order to decide which type will fit best in certain situations. Likewise, when stuck for a headline idea, the beginner can think over the different types of headlines and perhaps get some starting thoughts.

News Headline

Since advertising is essentially news—news about new products, news about changes in old products, news about companies—it is not surprising that an enormous number of advertisements either use a straight news headline or use benefit headlines that have a strong news flavor. Some straight news headlines are illustrated by the following:

ASK ANY DATSUN DEALER
"WHAT'S NEW?"

RIVAL'S NEW "REMOVABLE" CROCK-POT® SLOW COOKERS
HAVE STONEWARE BOWLS THAT LIFT OUT.

A standard way to tell quickly that you have something new is to begin the headline with "Introducing..." This is an old reliable that is used by many copywriters. There is nothing wrong with its use, but with so many advertisers using the approach, your advertisement may not stand out. In one woman's service magazine examined at the time of the writing of this book there were 15 advertisements with headlines beginning with the word "Introducing." Perhaps, if the copywriters had worked a bit harder they could have said "new" with more flair.

The news headline is an "old reliable." If there is something new about your product, the news headline "writes itself." Readers, especially businessmen, are always looking for new equipment or processes in their fields, as are professional people in theirs. Knowing this, the copywriters in the different fields use the news approach and the word "new" constantly in advertisements.

Direct-Benefit Headline

Young copywriters seem to go out of their way to avoid writing benefit headlines. In their efforts to be clever they avoid the straight headline because it is not "different," "cute," or "original." While originality is always welcome in writing headlines, it is best for the inexperienced to concentrate on benefit headlines.

Here are some examples of benefit headlines:

AFTER 45 YEARS
WE STILL GUARANTEE ANY ZIPPO LIGHTER *EVER MADE*...
TO WORK ALWAYS OR WE'LL FIX IT FREE.

IT COULD TAKE ONE WHOLE WEEK OF SUNNY
AFTERNOONS TO GIVE YOU AS MUCH TAN AS YOU CAN
GET IN JUST ONE SUNNY AFTERNOON WITH
OT SUNTAN LOTION

KLEER GLASSES FILTER OUT HARMFUL RAYS WITHOUT
CUTTING CLEAR VISION

If in doubt, use the direct-benefit headline. It always has something to say, and it will always be of interest—despite the feeling of the young copywriter that it is not interesting. When a couple are interested in a refrigerator, for example, cleverness in the headline is certainly no substitute for telling them that this model has a revolving shelf that makes items easy to reach, or that it has more cubic feet of freezer storage space than any other model in the market, or that it does not need to be defrosted.

Maker's—Pride Headline

Many headlines reflect the pride of the advertiser offering a product or service. In their most extreme form such headlines can be called open boasting. In their more subtle form they express quiet satisfaction. Often they convey, directly or indirectly, a benefit to the reader.

The chief criticism of headlines of this type is that so many of them fail to offer any benefit to the reader himself. Accordingly, they lack the direct appeal of the straight benefit headline and even of the news headline.

Very often such headlines tend to be stuffy and even arrogant in their assumption that the world is interested in what the advertiser feels is a singular accomplishment. A headline of this type follows:

JASON & WEBSTER PROUDLY ANNOUNCES
AN IMPORTANT NEW SERIES FOR LOVERS
OF CERAMIC ART

Suggestion Headline

The suggestion headline is a good headline for copywriters to use frequently for three reasons:

(1) It is an action headline that asks the reader to do or think about something.
(2) It generally suggests a use for the product, or a way of using the product (or service). Thus it is quite often an "idea" headline, contrasting, for instance, with the maker's-pride headline.
(3) Usually it is a benefit headline, since the suggestion of use or the suggestion of action indicates directly or indirectly a benefit that might come to the reader as a result of the use or action.

There is a vitality in the suggestion headline that starts an advertisement off fast and positively. By supplying an idea to the reader it immediately creates interest.

The following headline for a denture cleanser illustrates the point:

PROVE HOW WELL ANTI-ODOR POLIDENT® CLEANS.
SCRATCH AND SNIFF

Curiosity Headline

In the curiosity headline the copywriter may or may not give some information that will help the reader to make a buying decision. The chief purpose of this headline is to stop readers and impel them through curiosity to read into the copy so that they can give the headline complete meaning.

Sometimes the headline has relevancy to the illustration and the copy, as does this headline:

AN INTERESTING PROPOSITION
FROM TWO NICE LITTLE
OLD LADIES

The "interesting proposition" in this advertisement was that the reader would get 20¢ off Mrs. Paul's Light Batter Seafood if a purchase was made of Mrs. Filbert's Margarine.

Another curiosity headline with relevancy but less oddity is the following headline that followed an illustration of a doctor's bag and stethescope.

WHY DOCTORS
RECOMMEND TYLENOL® MORE THAN ALL
LEADING ASPIRIN BRANDS COMBINED

A reader needs to be of stern fiber to resist reading the body copy to learn why the product is so heavily endorsed.

Curiosity headlines can often be used to combat the indifference of readers to the many advertisements they see. Any time an advertisement can cause a considerable number of readers to stop long enough to read the copy it has achieved a small triumph. The curiosity headline plays upon the widespread desire of human beings to find out the answer to a statement that has piqued their curiosity. An important consideration, therefore, is to make the curiosity headline relevant to the illustration and the copy so that the readers do not feel that the writer has tricked them into reading an advertisement which has no message, or a message that is not related in any manner to the headline.

Question Headline

The question headline is the easiest of all headlines to write. Almost any writer finds it easy if all else fails, to put headlines in the form of a question. There is a certain school of advertising people that frowns upon the use of question headlines. But judging from the number of such headlines in every issue of various magazines, there is another school that is enthusiastic about their use.

Question headlines such as these fill the pages of business and consumer publications. The technique should be used whenever it does the job required; the writer should not let the prejudice of some advertising people bar the use of this useful headline style.

Consider, for example, the following question headlines:

CAN'T TAKE A BATH?
WILL THIS BE THE BIGGEST FREE SAMPLE
YOU'VE EVER RECEIVED?
WHY IS BANK AMERICARD CHANGING ITS NAME?
THIS MORNING THE PATTERSONS WOKE UP TO PERFECT COFFEE.
DID YOU?

To obtain answers to these questions, the reader must read the copy. In each case, the answer is given in the opening words which is as it should be. There should be no delay in answering a headline question. Many such headlines, in fact, answer the question in the latter part of the headline such as:

SHOULD YOU BUY A GOOD USED CAMERA?
ASK THE THREE MILLION USERS.

Objections to question headlines are sometimes raised by those who say they are often unspecific and that they lack benefit. Also, they are criticized because sometimes they invite a flippant answer by readers who will answer "No" when a "Yes" reaction is desired. Still, the question headline has its uses and will always be with us.

Label and Logotype Headlines

"Label" headlines usually consist of one or two words and depend largely on the power of the illustration to give them meaning. Sometimes an entire campaign will feature a label-illustration duet in each advertisement.

Thus, a product might carry a headline word **FAST** in one advertisement, **VERSATILE** in another, and **RELIABLE** in the third advertisement in the series. If the one-word headline is set in big, black type and is explained quickly in the opening copy, considerable power can be generated, especially in industrial magazines.

Other examples follow:

REJOICE!   (for a champagne advertisement)
280-ZZZAP   (for a Datsun 280-z)
SUPER BOWLS   (for sterling silver reproductions of Paul Revere bowls)

Logotype headlines, consisting largely or entirely of the name of the advertiser, should be used sparingly except under one of the following circumstances:

(1)   The company is so big or newsworthy, or both, that its name carried in a headline automatically ensures a certain amount of readership.
(2)   A new product is being introduced, the sale of which will be increased by having it connected with a well-known company name.
(3)   The advertiser is not known but is desperate to build recognition by splashing his name anywhere and everywhere.

FINAL NOTE ON HEADLINES

Once more, the importance of headline writing should be stressed. Think back to the discussion of basic appeals. To show the appeal in action, it was necessary to give examples of headlines that conveyed the appeals. Headlines express basic appeals conspicuously and succinctly. Headline *types* themselves are merely techniques—ways of achieving attention. The real importance of the headline is to flag readers with a basic appeal, or so engage interest that they will be led into the copy where they will find the appeal.

QUESTIONS

1. What are five decisions to be made by persons responsible for the overall planning of advertising before any copywriting is done?

2. Distinguish between a basic appeal and U.S.P.

3. What are some characteristics that advertisements in a campaign may have in common?

4. Explain "suffering point."

5. What is the current thinking about the use of long headlines?

6. Why is the "suggestion" headline considered desirable?

24

THE SELLING MESSAGE: ADVERTISING COPY-WRITING—PART 2

THE SELLING MESSAGE: ADVERTISING COPYWRITING—PART 2

If we were to use a military analogy here, we could say that the analysis of the proper copy appeals in the preceding chapter constituted the strategy planning of the general staff, and the headlines the softening-up process that could be likened to attacks by aircraft and swift-moving tanks.

Now, we're ready for the "convincer," the ground troops, or, in advertising, the body copy where we bring to belief the promise of the headline.

BODY COPY

Selling takes place in the body copy. Although good headlines, especially long ones, can carry a heavy portion of the selling burden, the final sale is made when the prospect reads the proof, the evidence, the additional facts in the body copy. Many persons assert they don't read body copy, especially if it is lengthy. If product interest is lacking, or if the body copy is badly written, it is true enough that many persons read only the headlines in advertisements and notice the illustrations. Such persons will not read body copy whether it is long or short.

Skillfully written copy that concerns products of high interest to readers *will* obtain strong readership no matter how long it is or where it appears in a publication. The principle holds true for the broadcast media, too. Thus, we must start out with the factor of product interest because an advertisement for a new washer-dryer, to illustrate, will obtain zero-readership from persons who have just bought such an appliance even if the copy is written in letters of fire.

After product interest, follow effective writing techniques and three fundamentals—believability, naturalness, and modesty—that are so *very* fundamental they will be discussed only briefly here.

Believability

Believability is really another way of saying "honesty." This honesty is not only found in the use of claims and statements that are wholly accurate and true legally and morally but also in the portrayal of people who are supposedly users of the product or service advertised. The latter would, of course, eliminate many advertisements that portray silly people making silly statements about products they've bought. Unfortunately, belief in advertising is low among great numbers of the public, especially among young people who tend to be skeptical of advertising claims just on general principle and because they distrust or don't understand business. Believability is the first requirement in advertising copy because without it, there is nothing else.

Naturalness

Copywriters should write "like people." If they pretend they are talking to friends about a product they may avoid "copywriterish" language full of "cozy-warms," "sparkle-clean," and other artificialities. They may also avoid the pompous, board-of-directors approach typified by 'We-here-at-Mammoth-Corporation-take-pride-in" copy. They should write like real persons, not like copywriters who are writing for other copywriters. They should avoid "ad-dy" language found only in the never-never land of advertising.

Our skeptical young people, described in the preceding section about believability, tend to think of two types of people. *Real* people such as themselves and people they know. Then, there are those *stilted, odd-talking* people in advertisements whose language and reactions are not theirs. Thus, we have a "we" and "they" situation—almost an adversary relationship.

Modesty

No one likes a braggart and this includes readers of advertisements. "Brag and boast" copy, as it has been called, consistently rates low in readership and conviction. Instead of superlatives the copywriter should supply benefits and enthusiastically related facts that supply prospects with solid reasons for buying. It is rarely necessary to use superlatives if the copy has convinced the reader that possession of a product will be of benefit. This conviction can be achieved by vigorous but modest language.

WRITING SUGGESTIONS

It is absurd to offer rigid writing rules. Certain writing suggestions offered here might be followed some of the time and others all of the time.

Tie Opening Copy to the Headline

If the headlines stresses one point and the opening copy another, the advertisement lacks unity. Actually, there is a third element that must be tied in with both of these—the illustration. Tie-in of the three elements is demonstrated in the following:

Headline	*Opening copy*	*Illustration*
Royal Doulton Stoneware. It isn't our traditional look. It is our traditional quality.	Don't be misled by its rather informal appearance. Royal Doulton Stoneware is made with all the expertise that goes into the making of our English fine bone china. But it is created for the way you entertain now. Whether it be informally, on a terrace, or elegantly in your dining room.	Attractive table setting in color of the stoneware.

Start out Fast and Interestingly

It seems difficult for many novice copywriters to start quickly. Advice: Do not be leisurely. Satisfy the impatient reader who asks: "What are they selling?" "What's the point?" "What are they getting at; why do they waste my time?" Usually, if the opening copy ties in immediately with the headline and illustration, the writer will automatically start out fast and interestingly, as the following example shows:

Headline	*Opening copy*	*Illustration*
Why our scotch rules in England.	The English have acquired quite a taste for Teacher's. In fact, they like it so much, Teacher's has become the king of scotches in England.	Several Englishmen drinking Teacher's scotch in an English pub.

Identify the Product Immediately

Tell immediately what you are selling if the product is not clearly mentioned in the headline. High in the copy use the brand name of the product and tell what the product actually is (except for products known to everyone such as "Ford" or "Coca-Cola"). After once using the brand name in connection with the product high in the copy, then use the brand name alone henceforth. The immediate-identification principle is shown in the following:

Headline	Opening copy
Flexknit. Not just easy to work with, but easy to live with.	"Flexknit" zippers are designed to work in any garment, from the most rugged to the most delicate. They're easy to live with because they will keep on working smoothly for the life of your garment. That's unconditionally guaranteed.*

In the foregoing example, the product is identified by brand name in the headline. Then, to make identification swift and certain, the opening words use the brand name in direct connection with the product. The reader thus knows that "Flexknit" is the name of a zipper. No guesswork here.

Avoid Making Opening Paragraph Overly Long

One almost certain way to discourage readership is to make an advertisement look like heavy reading by hammering the reader over the head with heavy-as-lead opening paragraphs. It has already been suggested that copy should begin "fast and interestingly." There is nothing fast about a long opening copy paragraph. At the beginning of an advertisement it is still uncertain that the reader, momentarily attracted by the headline, will go deeply into the copy. Help readership along by making the top of the advertisement look easy and inviting. Here is how experienced copywriters have handled this critical point of the advertisements they wrote:

Headline	Opening copy	Illustration
Don't let the energy crisis squeeze you into a small car.	Well, friends, you heard what the man said. Some sacrifices will have to be made. But getting into a Volkswagen won't be one of them.	Four tall members of a basketball team about to get into a Volkswagen Rabbit.

Most copywriters prefer to break up copy by paragraphs, but many of them do not paragraph enough. Relatively few, as was said in the section on what a copywriter should know about typography, use subheads as frequently as they should. Newspaper editors learned long ago that they could obtain more readership by interspersing news stories with subheads. Most copywriters should pay more attention to the lessons to be taught by newspaper and magazine editors.

Any examination of advertising reveals that advertisements do not have enough paragraphs, and that subheads are rarely used. In looking for examples of paragraphing and subheads to show here, it was necessary to go through many advertisements. Much of the difficulty traces back, not to the copywriter, but to artists or production people, or both, who are less concerned with readership and readability than with creating an advertisement that overall is pleasing aesthetically.

Use the Singular "You"

One of the first lessons a public speaker learns is that it will be more effective to address the talk to individuals instead of to masses of people. Experienced speakers look for friendly faces in the different parts of an auditorium and then talk to those individuals.

Copywriters should follow the same procedure, though very often they do not. And while the singular "you" is highly important in print copy, it becomes even more important in the broadcast media. A commercial that begins with the salutation "Ladies!" is not achieving the intimacy of the commercial that opens with "If you've been finding your skin chapping because of the raw November weather, here's a suggestion." The "you've" aims right at every woman who is listening. "Ladies!" lumps her with all the other women listeners or viewers and, in consequence, is that much less personal.

Following is a piece of copy that is as personal as a person-to-person conversation. Notice how the writer has put the copy on a completely individual plane.

> A shirt that doesnt' fit
> right makes us both look bad.
>
> When you buy a Van Heusen shirt, there's one thing you can't get. A bad fit. Because a shirt that clutches your middle or pulls across your chest is as damaging to our reputation as it is to your looks.
> So to protect both of us, we've instituted a Consumer Sizing Information Program. It gives you the one thing you really want to know about a shirt before you buy it. The truth.

Sell, Dont' Just Tell

Too often the beginning copywriter, given a number of facts, merely fires those facts at readers or listeners or viewers without any attempt to use selling words and phrases. Almost anyone who has adequate writing skill and ordinary intelligence can assemble facts and then present them in a reasonably orderly manner. This, however, is not good enough in writing advertising copy. There is an added ingredient that must flavor these facts, and that ingredient is sales power. A reporter gives facts; a copywriter not only gives the facts but also adds persuasion to those facts.

Back up Positive Claims Quickly

An ordinary assertion that is self-evident does not require formal proof. When, however, an important, non-evident statement is made the writer should anticipate the natural question of the reader by supplying proof. This proof can take many forms: quoted statements; testimonials; photographs (before-and-after photographs, for example); case histories. Here is an advertisement that supplies proof.

Headline	Statement Requiring Proof	Proof	Illustration
Norm Thomp-	A 10-oz reversible	When we first	Several pic-

son's Apollo... jacket that keeps you just possibly *warm when it's cold* the most usable *and cool when it's* jacket you can *hot.* own! heard claims about this unique jacket we simply couldn't believe our ears. After receiving a few samples, we tested it around the world in places ranging from a ski resort in Switzerland to tropical Tenerife in the Canary Islands. Everything that had been said about the Apollo jacket was true, and then some. tures of jacket show—it normally, reversed, and rolled up.

Avoid Being Needlessly Negative

Some campaigns are built on negative appeals. The famous "B.O." campaign of yesteryear, which warned of the perils of the body odor, was such a campaign. So was the "halitosis" campaign, which warned possessors of bad breath that they might well incur social ostracism. "Denture-breath" is a current fear exploited among the users of false teeth and plates.

These are but three of the enormously successful campaigns that have used a negative approach. They have been cited merely to point up that at times the negative approach is a very good one. Still, in day-to-day writing it is better, as a rule, to write positively rather than negatively.

Naturally, no advertisement is totally negative. It may begin with a negative illustration showing someone in pain and be accompanied by a headline that is also negative, but then the negative yields to the positive when the body copy explains how the advertiser's product or service can bring relief. So it is with sunburn remedy, hair preparations, sleep pills, headache tablets, and ulcer remedies. The question, then, is whether it is better to create a first impression that is negative, or positive. The answer must be that if you are in doubt, be positive right at the start. Is it better, for example, to use a headline that says:

> "Heartburn is a permanent
> part of my life."?

or to say:

> "Here's a way to make certain
> that heartburn won't be a
> permanent part of your life."?

Observe the Rules of Good Writing and Good Grammar

The writers of copy have come in for a certain amount of criticism from grammarians and others who want the rules of good English and good grammar followed strictly in all writing intended for reading by the general public. "Winstons taste good, like a cigarette should" jarred these people and caused them to renew their charges that advertising copywriters were debasing the English language. Actually, the language has been enriched by many of the phrases and words used by advertising writers. Also, most advertising copy meets the rules for good writing. Most copywriters are good writers and know their rules of grammar, or they would never have entered the field. Occasionally, however, writing and grammar rules are broken deliberately for effect, in the same manner that poets break rules to achieve their effects. But poets are said to be merely exercising "poetic license" when they depart from the rules of grammar.

Despite the occasional, deliberate lapses from the strict rules of grammar, the copywriter should, in day-to-day work, write copy so that it is right with everyone. Some of the rules to be followed with great strictness may be found in any book on writing or grammar; other rules are especially adapted to the writing of advertising copy.

Advertising copy is generally conversational and informal. Sometimes, advertising writers carry informality to excess, especially in their use of sentence fragments and their habit of starting sentences with "and," "but," and other unconventional words. Such informality is more acceptable in broadcast writing that *should* be totally conversational. In print advertisements, however, the writer should show some restraint in the relaxed writing style. Make it simple and make it easy to read, but don't make advertising copy sound like the conversation to two juveniles discussing the latest rock concert.

A-I-D-A Copy Formula

For years, the A-I-D-A formula has been the bible of the beginning copywriter. While the application of this formula to a piece of advertising copy does not insure the success of that copy, even those persons most critical of formula-writing admit that the A-I-D-A formula is sound and has merit.

Here it is:

> A .... Attention
> I .... Interest
> D .... Desire
> A .... Action

It is expected that the headline and illustration will capture attention. Interest will be aroused by these elements and by the opening copy. Desire is aroused when the copy makes clear the benefits that will be bestowed by the product. Action results from the action-provoking words and phrases that have already been discussed.

Not all advertisements will incorporate these four elements in an orderly, progressive way. Advertisements, for instance, that consist of only a few headline words and nothing else do not serve as models for the writer attempting to use the A-I-D-A formula literally, but even here it is possible to fit the elements into the advertisement.

Following is copy from an advertisement that incorporates the A-I-D-A elements, even though it is quite likely that the writer was not deliberately writing to the formula when preparing the advertisement.

Illustration: Main illustration shows book cover with title. Small illustrations show man doing various repair jobs around the home.

Attention

Headline: Amazing how-to-do-it manual for the home: 1,000 tips for home maintenance and repair.

Interest

Copy: You may be an old hand at fixing things, or you may be all-thumbs when you're faced with a home repair problem. Either way, you'll find this 1,500-page book so valuble you'll wonder how you ever got along without it. There simply isn't any home situation it doesn't cover—electrical connections, plumbing, carpentry, use of tools, painting, furniture repair—an endless list of household tasks. And every tip is illustrated. Hundreds of drawings and photographs make simple work of what used to be hard tasks.

Desire

Now—*you* can do those jobs yourself

Once you have this beautifully organized book, you'll be able to tackle jobs you used to pay big money to have done. And if emergencies arise, you can handle them right on the spot, and in a hurry. No waiting around for the plumber, the electrician, or furnace man to show up—if you can get one. Think of the peace of mind you'll have and the money you'll save.

Action

Act now!

Fill out the coupon below today. Get your copy of HOME REPAIR AND MAINTENANCE MANUAL before the next home "situation" comes up. You'll find that the low $9.95 cost of this book will be the best home investment you've ever made. The book will pay for itself over and over again. So don't delay sending for your copy.

TYPES OF BODY COPY

As the list of body copy types develops it will be noticed that while the list parallels to some extent the list of headline types, it also adds classifications of its own. The types described in the following examples embrace most advertisements, except for a rather large group that fall in no classifiable category.

Straight-Selling Copy

Despite all the stress on cleverness, ingenuity, and being different, the bread-and-butter advertisement of the advertising industry is the straight-selling (sometimes called "straight-line") advertisement. Such an advertisement uses logical, expository writing. With no embellishments, it carries the reader along through a straightforward, no-nonsense sales talk.

Where is the magic in straight-selling body copy that causes it to be used more than any other? There is no magic—just common sense. It should be remembered that most people read advertising copy for information, not for entertainment. Above all, the straight-selling advertisement is informative. Recognizing that most people read advertising in a hurry, the copywriter gives facts in a hurry in the straight-selling advertisement. Following is an example of a straight-selling advertisement that delivers its message without any attempt at entertainment or fanciful language, but which, in its relating of useful information, will be read with as much, or more, interest than the numerous advertisements that work very hard to be cute, different, or amusing.

> *Headline:*   Double or triple your picking speed
> *Copy:*   With a King-Way® Order Selection System, every order picker can do the work of two or more people. All goods are displayed in a straight line, so pickers don't have to go back and forth in aisle after aisle. Also, frontage per item is kept to the minimum, saving your pickers 3 out of 4 steps—easily doubling their output.
>
>   etc.

Straight-selling copy is especially useful and desirable when the advertiser has a product or service that offers competitive advantages or, regardless of competition, has interesting points in its favor. A straight forward relating of these points will make interesting reading. As people in the business might ask: "Why gimmick up your copy style when you have a good story to tell?"

Mood-building Copy

A great body of products and services are sold, not through a logical progression of facts, but through words that build a feeling or mood about them. How, for instance, would a copywriter sell perfume by telling in a cold, logical way (or even in an enthusiastic way) the chemical composition of the perfume, or by giving a point-by-point analysis of its superiority over other brands? The following copy for a perfume illustrates the point:

> Very pretty.
> Very feminine.
> Very, very exciting.

Another example shows a beautiful model wearing a diamond stick pin and the copy beneath the jewel reads:

You sure know how to stick pins
in that old feminine mystique.
A diamond is for now.

Some of the products for which mood-building body copy is especially suited include perfume, jewelry, certain types of feminine clothing, bath or complexion soaps, and most soft drinks. Details, as in the case of the advertisements cited, are not needed in the usual advertisements for these products. Likewise, certain services require mood-building, rather than factual copy.

Hotel and travel copy is mostly of the mood-building type.

Picture-caption Copy

Useful for many products and easier to write than some of the other body copy types, the picture-caption approach is quite popular with copywriters, as a look at magazines and newspapers will testify. High readership, furthermore, is earned by most picture-caption advertisements.

With this technique, pictures are usually of the same, or approximately the same size. The "captions" are small blocks of copy which usually appear under the pictures, but which may also appear alongside or above the pictures. For best readership it is wise to place the captions under the pictures, because it is this placement that is familiar to readers, and readers tend to follow accustomed patterns in their reading.

For a big-ticket item, such as an automobile or a refrigerator, or for some other item that must be seen in a big illustration to be fully appreciated, the picture-caption technique may not afford the best way of selling the product. For certain other items, such as shoes, which must be shown in detail so that styling and workmanship are made clear, the picture-caption technique might also be avoided.

Institutional or Image-building Copy

For years the institutional advertisement was described simply as an advertisement that sold the company instead of its product and this description still holds for most such advertisements. In recent years, however, institutional advertising has acquired other names which, in themselves, indicate expanded uses for this form of advertising. Now it is known also as "image" advertising, "corporate" advertising, or "public relations" advertising.

Because this kind of advertising has nothing specific to sell the reader—a coat, an automobile, a box of cereal—it lacks appeal to the selfish nature of readers and thus very often achieves poor readership. A copywriter, therefore, must work extra hard to make institutional copy interesting and easy to read, starting with a challenging headline and combining this headline with an unusual illustration and sparkling copy. Otherwise, the result is another dull institutional advertisement. This will be unfortunate since such advertising often

Institutional (corporate) advertisement with emphasis on an individual.

People like to read about people. Thus, institutional advertisements that focus on individuals working for a big company make the company seem more human and approachable.

I never heard a passenger say:"I like to fly Pan Am because of the mechanics." But I have heard a lot of pilots say it.

After 16 years on the job, helping maintain the largest fleet of 747s in the world, somebody's bound to pat you on the back.

When it's the pilots, it's a real compliment. For they fly those planes to every continent in the world.

Of course, we mechanics don't deserve all the praise. All our people do their job well.

So the next time you're going overseas, fly Pan Am. Even if it isn't just because of the mechanics.

America's airline to the world.

See your travel agent.

has an important message to deliver. Also, many companies, discourgaed by the task of identifying their multiproducts in the face of thousands of advertisements for other products, find institutional advertising important to their success. Such advertising, creating confidence in the company, persuades consumers to buy any product of the company because of this confidence. A copywriter creating such an "image" for a company has a challenging creative task.

Case History or Testimonial Copy

Why do copywriters use case-history or testimonial advertising?

(1) They may have an unusually skeptical audience.
(2) They may have collected some interesting case histories or testimonials.
(3) They may need to do something to dramatize and humanize the campaign.

Industrial advertisements using the case history approach.

Case histories, that talk lowered costs and savings, interest economy-minded industrial management men. Notice how specific the figures are in headline and copy.

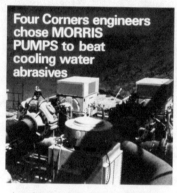

Four Corners engineers chose MORRIS PUMPS to beat cooling water abrasives

Arizona Public Service Company gets its cooling water from the San Juan River near Farmington, N.M. And what they get with it is sand and pea-sized gravel—7200 tons of it every 24 hours. That's too much abrasion for any ordinary pump.

And, that's why the engineers on the job chose Morris pumps—two sets of staged NC's, the horizontal units serving as boosters for the vertical models. Driven by 1250 HP motors, each set pumps over 20,000 GPM. Heads of nearly 450 feet are met at only 710 RPM.

Long life with minimum downtime.

These NC's run virtually unattended. That's why such wear-reducing features as low RPM operation, hardened chrome iron impellers, and chrome iron wear rings are so important. Peak performance is simple to maintain as wear occurs, because the NC's impeller clearance is quickly adjustable via external screws. When pumping abrasives is part of the job, you can't afford anything less than a Morris pump.

WRITE FOR FREE BULLETIN PACKAGE

MORRIS PUMPS, INC.
BALDWINSVILLE, NEW YORK 13027
You Can't Match a Morris Pump

But before they use a case history or testimonial, they must recognize certain facts:

(a) Good case histories are difficult (and sometimes expensive) to collect. Furthermore, it may take months or years to collect them.

(b) A copywriter expecting lucid, articulate, and useful statements to be given by people who are asked to offer testimonials will be disappointed. Usually the copywriter is going to have to write the statements for the testimonial givers, who will then be asked to verify that these statements express their experiences, or beliefs, or both, where the product is concerned.

(c) Case histories are rather limiting. A reader, in short, is likely to lose interest in the case history very quickly if the situation described is not familiar, or if the conditions are different. Suppose, for example, that a case history appearing in a construction magazine tells about the use of equipment in road building. Readers who are concerned with bridge footings or with building construction will give scant attention to the case history as soon as they find that it does not apply to their specialized interest, even though the equipment might be useful to them.

Announcement Copy

A copywriter must decide whether to go all-out for the announcement and skip the usual selling facts in the advertisement, or whether to begin with the announcement approach and then work in a straight-selling section at the middle and end of the advertisement. Another approach is to write a straight-selling advertisement which has an announcement flavor, but which is much more of a selling advertisement than an announcement.

In writing an announcement advertisement the copywriter should employ a genuine news style, after first making certain that what is being announced is new and important enough to announce. Above all, the announcement copy should convey an air of importance.

Oddity or Novelty Advertisement

Sometimes novelty and oddity advertisements are called "gimmick" advertisements. Whichever of the three terms is used it refers to the offbeat, unclassifiable approach that may rely on a "way-out" use of words or layout, or both. Generally the oddity or novelty advertisement will be conspicuous immediately because of its illustration, which will be so unusual that the effect would be spoiled by the use of too much copy; thus, the copy may consist of nothing more than a headline or at the most, of but a few words of body copy in addition to the headline.

An illustration of this approach is the advertisement for vodka. Total copy in the advertisement consisted of the words:

It takes your breath away.

Very often such a technique is used for products about which there is not much to write, or sometimes the oddity or novelty advertisement is planned solely to attract attention. Hard selling is not the object. Because this type of advertisement can take an almost unlimited variety of forms, it is impossible to offer a formula that can be applied to such advertising.

N·W·AYER & SON INC.

CLIENT U.S. ARMY
PRODUCT U.S. ARMY

TITLE "INFANTRY"
COMM'L NO. QQAI0175

0870

LENGTH: 60 SECONDS

1 (SFX & MUSIC UNDER)

2. ANNCR: In Infantry, you have to own more than a good pair of boots. MAN: Go!

3. ANNCR: You have to own the nerve to rappel from a helicopter,

4. and the stamina to survive in the wilderness.

5. You need the savvy to find water where it hasn't rained, food where you can't see any,

6. and your way home where the stars are your only road map.

7. You also need the skill to turn ropes into bridges,

8. ponchos into rafts,

9. and Personnel Carriers on a dime.

10. Infantry in today's Army isn't easy,

11. but then hardly anything worthwhile is.

12. CHORUS: Join the people who've joined the Army.

13. You could start building your tomorrows today.

14. Join the people who've joined the Army.

Join the people who've joined the Army.

800-523-5000

15. You could go a long, long way...ANNCR: For more information, call 800-523-5000.

Editorial-style Advertisement

Some editors of magazines and newspapers will not permit advertising that looks exactly like the editorial material. Most publications will permit a limited number of editorial-type advertisements but would bar the practice if too many advertisers used the technique. The usual editorial practice is to put the words

ADVERTISEMENT   ADVERTISEMENT   ADVERTISEMENT

at the top and or bottom of such advertisements.

Sometimes if the writer just puts the small abbreviation "Adv." at the bottom of an editorial-type advertisement the editor, if friendly to the advertiser, may let this suffice as a warning to readers that the advertisement is not part of the magazine's editorial content.

If the object is to obtain top readership for an editorial-type advertisement, the writer should see (1) that the story is written in authentic news-story or feature-story style; and (2) that the copy is, typographically speaking, just like editorial material in the publication.

A completely editorial-style advertisement, furthermore, will eliminate the usual logotype. Few advertisers have the courage to omit the logotype, but they will compromise by permitting the size and style of the logotype to be changed in order to make it unobtusive.

Sometimes the editorial-type advertisement can be in the form of a column not unlike the other columns usually found in magazines and newspapers. Heavy readership can be developed for such advertiser columns if the writer will remember that the first obligation is to be interesting and to be interesting news material should be supplied first and advertising material second. There is no point in using the news format if the news is much subordinated to the advertising. A writer might trick readers into reading a news-type advertisement one time even if it turned out to be mostly advertising, but would not trick them twice. Steady readers are developed by providing, time after time, interesting news items in the column.

Sometimes the news-type advertisement set up as a column will use a byline (the author's name at the top) of a person who does not exist. This fictitious byline gives a feeling of genuineness to the writing. So real does the name become to readers that successful columns of this type have brought heavy mail addressed to the byline name. The fictitious byline is useful because it can be used for many years; meanwhile, the writers of the column may have changed many times.

A last remark about editorial-type advertisements. Even if the writer does not wish to go "all out" by incorporating certain editorial techniques in the writing and in the mechanical format, the copy is in a sense, "picking the brains" of editors who, through years of experimenting have learned what produces high readership for their magazines or newspapers. It would be foolish for the advertising writer not to profit from their experiences.

Combination Advertisement

As might be expected, many advertisements combine two or more of the styles described in the foregoing pages. A natural combination, for example, is

Advertisement

IBM Reports

How one company's people and products are helping find the answers to some of the world's problems

Airline keeps down cost of keeping planes flying

It's an axiom of the airline business that you can't make money when your planes are on the ground. So tying up a plane periodically for two or three weeks to do a complete overhaul can be extremely costly.

To keep its planes flying, North

Computer-organized "mini-overhaul" will have this North Central Airlines jet flying again in hours instead of weeks.

Central Airlines, a regional carrier in the Midwest, has developed a system called SCEPTRE that helps management schedule maintenance so efficiently that the airline has been able to eliminate complete, time-consuming overhauls entirely. The system uses an IBM computer to keep a running file on everything that affects the

maintenance of the fleet, including the maintenance history of each plane, use of all components, parts inventory, warranty data and replacement forecasts.

Now North Central can bring in a plane once every 4 or 5 days for a "mini-overhaul," knowing exactly what service needs to be done and that the parts are on hand to do it. The mini-overhaul is performed in just a few hours after 1 A.M., when fewest flights are scheduled.

"With this system," says John Pennington, SCEPTRE project administrator, "we need one less jet to provide the same level of service. That saves us $7,000,000 right there."

With up-to-date information always available on the computer, North Central has eliminated redundant and unnecessary servicing.

Making rice paddies more productive. *As rice is the main diet of a growing percentage of the world's people, bigger and more frequent rice crops are urgently needed. In several countries, people are using IBM computers to help make rice fields more productive. In the Philippines, for example, a computer is being used to keep track of variables in soil chemistry, climate, pest resistance and plant genetics involved in the development of a strain of rice which has increased yields in some areas by as much as 100 per cent.*

Probing mysteries of kidney transplants

If a patient's body is to accept a kidney transplant, his or her tissue type should match that of the donor as closely as possible. A UCLA research team, headed by Dr. Paul Terasaki and Dr. M. R. Mickey, has developed a computer-based test for identifying the blood characteristics that define human tissue types. So far, 30 distinct tissue types have been identified, making it necessary to perform as many as 180 tests of white blood cells (as shown here) to assure a match between donor and recipient. The number of possible combinations is so great, reports Dr. Terasaki, that the task of analysis would be virtually impossible without the computer.

Hawaii taps geothermal potential

Engineers at the University of Hawaii are investigating the most efficient ways to use heat energy from the earth's interior to produce electricity.

Using an IBM computer, Dr. Ping

Cheng of the Hawaiian Geothermal Project has created a computer model of the island of Hawaii to learn where a geothermal reservoir is likely to be and to simulate the flow of underground water in a heated area. Based on these simulations and other geological information, an actual thermal well is now being drilled near Hilo.

Depending on the temperature of the geothermal resource, it may be used either to drive steam turbines directly or to heat a secondary fluid that will drive the generators. The computer model will help the engineers determine the best way to proceed.

If the experiment is successful, it may be able to produce 10 per cent of the island of Hawaii's electricity requirements, according to a university spokesman.

the announcement-type advertisement in an all-out editorial style.

Many times, too, the copywriter may decide to use an oddity- or novelty-type headline. The illustration and the opening copy will conform to this headline, but then, after attention has been obtained, the remainder of the copy will be the down-to-earth straight-selling kind. An example of this technique is the campaign showing Sherlock Holmes and Dr. Watson. The top of the advertisement had headlines in the form of several quotes:

"Fiendish, Holmes.
Ford and Chevy owners
disappearing without
a trace."

"Watson, I fear
they have been
car-napped
by the Diplomat."

"Diplomat.
That fiendishly seductive
new car by Dodge."

After this attention-getting array of headline quotes, the copy that follows is straight-selling. This combination makes sense, because it would be distracting to keep up the Sherlock Holmes-Dr. Watson novelty approach throughout the copy as well as the headlines. The purpose of the advertisement is to sell the automobile; this is better done with the combination.

Most copywriters do not set out deliberately to write a combination advertisement. But as they think of ways to be "different" and to obtain attention they find that the combination of the factual and the fanciful is a natural development. There is nothing in the rule book that decrees that an advertisement must stay consistently within one style throughout. Sometimes a blend will be preferable.

SLOGANS

Slogan writing is unimportant so far as the copywriter's daily life is concerned. Some copywriters may never be asked to work up a slogan. For others, slogan writing may come along once in a year or once in five years.

One reason for the infrequency of slogan-writing assignments is the longevity of good slogan. Once a slogan has been adopted by a company it has just about the same life span as the company trademark or the company logotype. How often, for example, would the copywriter be asked by General Electric to write a replacement slogan for "Progress Is Our Most Important Product"? How many times in a lifetime would Ivory Soap's "99 and 44/100% pure" be replaced, or Westinghouse's "You can be sure—if it's Westinghouse"?

Some companies do not use slogans. Either they feel that a slogan cannot be devised that is good enough for the company or product, or they are opposed to committing themselves to an element in their advertising that must be included every time.

Slogans may be born by chance, of course. Often a good slogan will pop right out of the copy that has been written. There was no intention of writing a slogan; the copy was good, and it produced the slogan as a sort of bonus. Many slogans have begun as headlines. The headline was written, and suddenly someone said: "Say, that headline of ours would make a good slogan." Then down to the bottom of the advertisement will go the headline.

Many slogans have become successful because they were used so often, not because they were especially clever or original. "It floats," famous slogan of Ivory Soap, certainly would win no awards in the sparkling-copy category, but by constant use the company succeeded in making it a part of American folkways. The same might be said of "99 and 44/100% pure," long considered to be one of the best-known slogans in the world.

Heavy use of a slogan is, in fact, almost more important than its cleverness. An ordinary phrase can become a part of everyone's language if it is repeated often enough, whereas a truly clever phrase will have no impact if the phrase is seen so seldom that it fails to register in the mind of the public.

Points to Observe

While no one can offer a sure-fire formula for slogan writing, any more than anyone can blueprint just how to write a beautiful piece of music, there are points that can be observed by the slogan writer.

(1) *Keep them short.* This is, of course, only a general suggestion. Many famous slogans have not been short, such as Hoover's "It beats, as it sweeps, as it cleans." Still, it is best to hold down the number of words, both for memorability and for ease in fitting the slogan into the advertising layouts. Five words usually are considered just about right for most slogans.

Examples of short slogans: from the past and present:

Chases dirt	Drink Coca-Cola	Oshkosh B'gosh
They satisfy	It's Toasted	Only at Sears

(2) *Give them rhythm or alliteration.* Most of the best-remembered slogans use both. Throughout history the use of rhymes has helped put over major ideas. Also, alliteration has been a useful technique for creating memorability.

Examples of rhyming slogans:

You can't beat Neat for feet

Solarcaine stops sunburn pain

Don't compromise—Midas-ize

Small advertisers can well use rhyming slogans to make themselves distinctive in their area. An example is the laundry in a small town that suggested to villagers that "When things look black, call Jack."

Examples of alliterative slogans:

Babies are our business

Speed Queen
Built better to last

When you can your best,
can with the best—Ball

(3) *Give them an easy, conversational feeling.* Slogans become a part of the language. They are the language of the people. They are often used in jokes or to illustrate a point. If they are in the vernacular, or even somewhat ungrammatical, such as "Winston tastes good, like a cigarette should," they may register better than if they had been phrased in faultless English. Most good slogans sound as if one person were talking to another:

Action television commercial in photoboards.

Printed photoboards such as this are used in a number of ways: In sales meetings with distributors. By distributors on sales calls. For brewery promotion and public relations. Notice how few words are used in the audio portion; the message is conveyed mostly by the video scenes.

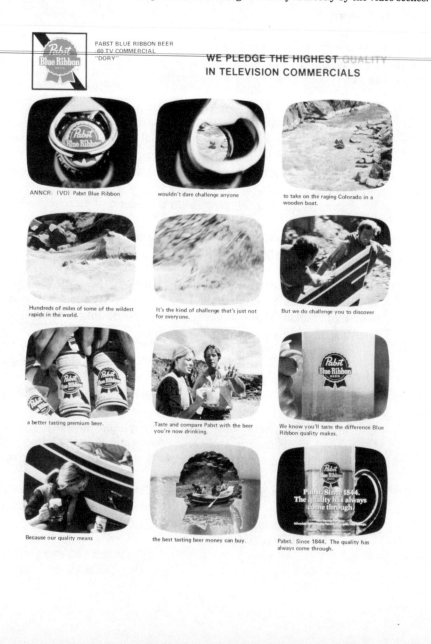

PABST BLUE RIBBON BEER
.60 TV COMMERCIAL
"DORY"

WE PLEDGE THE HIGHEST QUALITY
IN TELEVISION COMMERCIALS

ANNCR: (VO) Pabst Blue Ribbon

wouldn't dare challenge anyone

to take on the raging Colorado in a wooden boat.

Hundreds of miles of some of the wildest rapids in the world.

It's the kind of challenge that's just not for everyone.

But we do challenge you to discover

a better tasting premium beer.

Taste and compare Pabst with the beer you're now drinking.

We know you'll taste the difference Blue Ribbon quality makes.

Because our quality means

the best tasting beer money can buy.

Pabst. Since 1844. The quality has always come through.

Animated television commercial.

Animation calls for a peculiar set of skills in whimsy, art, and off-beat imagination. Skill in print copywriting may not necessarily equip a copywriter for preparing television commercials, especially for creating animated commercials.

N.W. AYER & SON, INC.
111 EAST WACKER DRIVE, CHICAGO, ILL. 60601

CLIENT: Illinois Bell Telephone
PRODUCT: Touch-Tone (R)
LENGTH: :30

TITLE: "Little Telephone Cars"
COMM'L NO.: AXIL3317

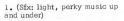

1. (Sfx: light, perky music up and under)

2. (Anncr VO) Here comes a very touching offer from Illinois Bell...

3. ...our special pushbutton package deal.

4. You get three Touch-Tone phones--...

5. ...any style, any color... at a bargain price.

6. Save up to $1.15...

7. ...every month...

8. ...on equipment charges.

9. And up to $15...

10. ...on initial one-time charges.

11. Why not...

12. ...touch up your home...

13. ...with Touch-Tone phones?

14. Just call Illinois Bell.

15. And ask about our touching offer. (Music up and out)

Eventually, why not now?

Ask the man who owns one

Make the bite test

Yes, I said 10 cents

These slogans, all famous and long-lasting, have that easy, friendly style which fits the product. While none of the four embodies all the principles for successful slogans, each has been perfect for its own particular use. None of them boasts. None of them is like any other. All have a "talk" feeling that makes them easy to say and to remember. Other slogans that talk:

Take AIM against cavities   A diamond is forever

Long distance is the next best thing to being there

SIMPLICITY. We make beautiful

use of your time

(4) *Suggest something.* Elsewhere it has been pointed out that it is desirable to ask readers or listeners to do something. This command or suggestion to take action has been urged for headline writing, and especially for the endings of advertisements. In slogans, too, the action feeling is desirable.

Another advantage of the action-suggesting slogan is that it can be worked into hundreds of advertisements as a sort of tag line. To do this, the writer should write the last few words to "build up" to the slogan. A copywriter for a school for example, might end the copy with the words:

... and at *this* school, it's not all outgo because you can work at a paying job in between classes. It's the school where you—

Earn while you learn

Consider almost any suggestion-type slogan. Note how easily it can be made into a punch line if the copywriter writes copy at the end to lead to the use of the slogan. This is making full use of the slogan.

(5) *Be competitive.* Many slogans highlight a difference that is enjoyed by a product or service. Sometimes the difference may not be 100 percent, yet the product has an advantage over its competitors to which the slogan can call attention. An example of this is the slogan "In Philadelphia, nearly everyone reads the *Bulletin.*" Another example of a newspaper slogan illustrating the same principle is "Covers Dixie like the dew."

One danger in the competitive slogan that must be faced is the fact that some day the advantage or unique quality stressed by the slogan may no longer exist, or it may be questioned on legal grounds. A great slogan was Old Gold's "Not a cough in a carload." This truly became a part of the American vernacular. Once, however, the government ruled that the claim would be impossible to substantiate for all smokers, the slogan disappeared from the advertising scene.

Occasionally a slogan is continued in use despite the fact that the product may be even better than the slogan implies. An example is Ivory Soap's "99 and 44/100% pure." "Pure," in this instance, refers to freedom from inert matter that does not contribute to the washing action of the soap. Today, in fact, Ivory Soap is quite capable of quoting a higher percentage of purity. But so ingrained is the slogan in the American consciousness that Procter & Gamble would not consider changing this household byword. Furthermore, most people would not be attracted to any greater degree if the purity percentage were raised to a higher figure.

Other (all famous) competitive slogans:

When it rains, it pours

It floats

Hasn't scratched yet

More people ride on Goodyear than any other kind

All the news that's fit to print

When you care enough to send the very best

Aren't you glad you use Dial Soap!
(don't you wish everybody did?)

Dutch Boy paints more years to the gallon

One of the important purposes of the competitive slogan is to prevent substitution by the consumer. By constant reiteration the consumer becomes aware that there is a difference between the "sloganized" product and other similar products. Sometimes the suggestion to avoid substitution is implied in the mere statement of a product's unique quality, as in "It floats." Frequently, however, the advertiser considers it necessary to be more direct. The "direct" type of "don't substitute" slogan is illustrated by "If it isn't an Eastman, it isn't a Kodak," or "Be sure with Pure."

(6) *Try to get in the name of the company, product, or service.*   Obviously there are many times when this cannot be done. The name may be too long or too difficult or pronounce. Or it may not fit in with the rest of the slogan message. Ideally, however, the name of the product, company, or service should be in the slogan, since the constant repetition of the name, allied with the outstanding selling point, makes a strong combination. Looking back over the examples already quoted in this slogan section, we find the names of the following products or advertisers mentioned in their slogans: Kodak, Goodyear, Dial, Ball, *The Bulletin,* Luckies, Simoniz, Coca-Cola, and Oshkosh. It is apparent from this list that many top advertisers have found it helpful to include the name in the slogan.

Other examples of "name" slogans are these:

6-12 PLUS. It could save your skin.

French's—we make your life delicious.

Ramada Inn. We're *building* a reputation, not resting on one.
Campbell's makes your cooking M'm! M'm! Good!

BROADCAST MEDIA

Writing for radio and television brings up a special set of problems. Still, the commercial writer is first of all, an *advertising* writer. Thus, the copy utilizes a knowledge of basic appeals, as in print writing. The copy must follow the same principles of selling that make printed advertisements successful.

Yet it does not follow that the competent writer of print advertisements will be equally competent in the broadcast field since the copy is now operating in different dimensions of sight and of sound. In both of the broadcast media, there is more of "show business" than is found in print advertising. There are characters who act, who sing, who perform. There may be bizarre sound effects, and certainly there will be much music that must be correlated with selling messages.

A television writer, in particular, often possesses a peculiar array of talents and background. Ideally, this person has had art background, dramatic experience, musical training, along with a sense for business. If asked to create animated commercials, such a writer will, in addition, often call upon a wild, way-out imagination that goes beyond any requirement for print writers. This includes an unerring sense of timing and the dramatic impact conveyed by a nod, a leer, a wink, or a slight movement. It also includes knowing how to hold dialogue to a minimum while wringing the maximum out of motion.

Since broadcast advertising is tolerated but very seldom sought out, the writer has an obligation to sugar coat selling with entertainment whether that entertainment is conveyed by humor, by slice-of-life drama, or by interesting demonstrations. In the effort to entertain, the broadcast writer too often becomes carried away and commercials may be downright silly and definitely irritating if viewed more than once. Thus, the broadcast writer runs a much greater chance of annoying or disgusting the audience than does the print writer.

While, of course, radio and television writers must observe the usual rules for good writing, there are, in addition, technical aspects that make broadcast writing a different writing form than print advertising. A few of these aspects are listed here. Boiled down, the chief point for radio is that writers must never forget that they are writing for the ear; the video writer for motion coupled with sound.

Radio

(1) Above all, write for an audience that is "hearing" your message, not seeing it.
  (a) Even more than in print copy, build copy around one central idea.
  (b) Make listeners "see through their ears."
  (c) Write "talk" language in contractions and often in sentence fragments.

Radio commercial with contemporary slant.

Because this advertiser does considerable business with truck stops across the country, they devised a commercial featuring truckers typically calling to each other on their "CB's" and utilizing a reference to the "Smokeys." The combination of rhyme, music and contemporary patter should hold listener's attention.

SSC&B Inc. Advertising

ONE DAG HAMMARSKJOLD PLAZA, NEW YORK, N.Y. 10017

BROADCAST

SSC&B JOB NO. 76-380
CLIENT S&H
PRODUCT Green Stamps
BROADCAST MEDIUM Radio
LENGTH OF COMM. :60
DATE TYPED 2/3

SHR 7376   "TRUCK STOP"   (WITH DONUT)   AS RECORDED
. . . .

(MUSIC UP AND UNDER)

MAN: Well I heard a breaker callin'
There's Green Stamps up ahead
So I kept it on the double nickel
"Break one nine", I said.

He said go ahead break I'm out here
Headin' for the Southern sun
Got gas in my tanks and stamps in the bank
It's another S&H run.

I said, "How about it good buddy?
Are the smokey's close behind" ?
He said nope the stamps I'm pickin up
Are the lick 'em, stick 'em on kind

(D O N U T   )

Yeah S&H Green Stamps
Make this truckin' fun
I can bring home a little extra
With S&H, on my run.
I keep my family happy
They sure like it fine
When I bring home S&H Green Stamps.
The lick 'em, stick 'em kind.

APPROVED: LEGAL _____ MEDICAL _____ CLIENT _____
           DATE _____   DATE _____   DATE _____

    (d) Use conversation bridges instead of paragraphs—such phrases as "And listen to this"..."Here's another point"..."Remember, too"..."But that isn't all."

(2) Assume listeners are giving half-attention.
    (a) Work especially hard to achieve attention-getting openings.
    (b) Repeat important ideas, words or phrases.
    (c) Picture the typical listener when writing the commercial.

(3) Disregard print rules about starting the selling immediately.
    (a) "Slide" into the selling message instead of stressing main sales point in the opening words.
    (b) Use a line or two to *set the stage*.

(4) Don't write too much but don't write too little.
    (a) Pace commercial to announcer, product and situation; in some cases, write as little as 100 words a minute or fewer but in most others write 150 to 170 and even up to 185 or more for very hard-sell commercials (but very seldom should you use this many words).
    (b) Study announcer's style and cater to that style.

(5) Use music and sound effects to gain interest and attention, and to lessen irritation.

(6) Make copy come to a climax.
    (a) Ask for the order or some other kind of action.

Television

To varying degrees the television writer applies all the rules just given for radio writing to commercials for television. In addition, there are some special considerations to be observed in writing for television. Some of the important ones follow.

(1) Demonstrate, if possible.
    (a) Use demonstrations (normally) within the experience range of the major portion of the audience.
    (b) Consider the demonstration as a form of "proof in motion."

(2) Use a production technique that will best convey the sales story—videotape, live action on film, animation on film, or live presentation.
    (a) If slides must be used because of budget restrictions, show enough slides to create action and use sound effects and music, if possible.

(3) Let the video (pictures) carry the burden of the selling.
    (a) Use few or no words for many commercials.
    (b) Think first in pictures, then in sound.
    (c) Stress *moving* pictures full of action and not "still lifes."
    (d) Make television commercials a blend of sight and sound.

(4) Use fewer words than for radio with a maximum of around 135 per minute for live action commercials, but usually much fewer.

(5) Plan the number of scenes carefully.
    (a) Figure 5 or 6 seconds to average scene and not less than 3 seconds normally. Many 30-second commercials use 9 to 10 scenes these days.

(b) Base footage devoted to scene on: importance of scene, whether a demonstration is being used, whether a character is being established. In both of the latter, use more footage. A good demonstration, for example, might take up almost all of the footage in a 60-second or 30-second commercial.

Examples of Broadcast Principles As Applied to Radio and Television Commercials

60-second Radio Commercial (summer screenhouse)

A straight commercial of this type may sometimes be announced by station announcers in which case the stations are sent a script by the advertiser's advertising agency. It is more likely, however, that a tape will be sent. The first procedure is less costly but subject to risk because station announcers vary so much in ability.

Summer's the time for outdoor living but bugs have other ideas. Don't let bugs keep *you* from enjoying those backyard barbecues this season—not when an Ezy-Use screenhouse will let you use your backyard fully without being bothered by insects. Just think. You can put up your Ezy-Use in just fifteen minutes anywhere you want it. It'll completely screen in an area big enough for several chairs, a picnic table, your barbecue equipment, and even a cot if you'd like to sleep outside on warm summer night. Imagine how this will increase your use of the backyard this summer. Even if it *rains* you're all set because Ezy-Use comes equipped with handsome, easily-installed panels to keep you snug against wind and rain. Plan on more backyard fun this summer. Now that warm weather's here, don't miss a single day enjoying outside living. Pick up an Ezy-Use screenhouse today at any department store. If you buy it in the morning, you can use it in the evening. Why wait?

(1) *Write a "hearing" message.*   In addition to using conversational language with contractions and bridges between ideas, this commercial concentrates on one idea—to get a screenhouse in order to increase enjoyment of outdoor living in the summer.

(2) *Assume half-attention.*   Repetition of the main idea and of the product name insures that even those listening carelessly will know the product and what it's for. Furthermore, the use of phrases such as "Just think" and "Imagine" ask for the listener's attention.

(3) *Disregard print rules.*   The writer has set the stage by talking about a familiar problem, the bug nuisance when one wants to enjoy the backyard in the summertime. Thus, the listener is "warmed up" to the introduction of the product as an answer to the annual problem. Unlike most print advertisements, the commercial does not plunge into a sales pitch immediately, nor does it mention the product name immediately.

(4) *Write enough but not too little.*   Most announcers can handle the approximately 170 words in this commercial quite comfortably. The pace is brisk but not overpowering. Most of the words are simple and short, another factor to consider in the timing.

(5) *Use music and sound effects.* Whenever possible, the writer of a straight commercial such as this one should employ music or sound effects to capture initial attention, to keep the message from being boring, and to enhance the total commercial.

(6) *Come to a climax.* There is a strong urge to action in this commercial. The whole bottom of the commercial is devoted to suggestions to the listener that he get the unit, that he buy the unit, and that he not delay.

60-second Radio Commercial (commercial bank)

Banks fight on the local level for the patronage of the general public. Once the effort was dignified, restrained, and centered mostly on acquiring more savings accounts. Today, banks offer many services and sell them vigorously. Loan business is especially lucrative. The following commercial is typical of bank commercials heard in cities and towns from coast to coast.

(SFX wind howling followed by 5 seconds of "I've Got My Love to Keep Me Warm") Music under announcer's voice.

That tune, in case you don't recognize it is the old standby, "I've Got My Love To Keep Me Warm." But with winter coming on you may need something more substantial to keep *you* warm—like a new furnace, or insulation, or a space heater. That's why you should be looking into a home improvement loan from People's National Bank. This low-cost loan that can be paid back over a long time will help make this a comfortable winter no matter how hard the wind blows, or how far down the temperature goes. Look over your home. Need storm windows, a fireplace, a bigger hot water heater? Get any or all of these items through a home improvement loan from People's National. Zero weather may be here before you know it. See People's National now for that loan, and then be comfortable no matter what the winter weather.

(1) *Write a "hearing" message.* Sentence fragments, contractions, and an easy personal style make this a hearing commercial and, as is appropriate when delivering a message to be heard, only one idea is delivered—to get a home improvement loan in order to prepare for the cold of winter.

(2) *Assume half-attention.* In addition to repeating the name of the advertiser and the main message (to get a loan) the copy has used other techniques to make the listener aware. It talks directly to the listener as in the line: Look over your home. Also, it asks some direct questions that are pertinent to the subject matter of the commercial.

(3) *Disregard print rules.* A warm-up of several lines precedes the "sell" although, of course, the warm-up is a part of the selling. There is a buildup, however, before the advertiser is mentioned and what the advertiser is offering. With no headline and illustration to set the stage, the radio writer seldom can start copy with the abruptness desirable in the opening copy of most print advertisements.

(4) *Write enough but not too little.* Because of the musical introduction and sound effects, the commercial runs just under 150 words, enough

to sell the service but not so many that the announcer cannot deliver a clear, sincere message. Furthermore, bank advertising should not be written for the push-push-push style of used-car commercials.

(5) *Use music and sound effects.* Because this is a straight commercial without any other embellishments, the music and sound effects in the beginning can make it livelier and can snare listener attention at that critical point, the beginning.

(6) *Come to a climax.* Several action words at the end afford a vitality to the ending and "ask for the order." Those words are "get," "see," and "now." In addition, the writer pictures for the listener the result of taking action.

60-second Radio Commercial (dictating equipment)

Much criticism is voiced about straight commercials of the type you have just read. Copywriters feel that straight commercials offer little creative challenge and, because such commercials bore *them*, they are convinced that they bore audiences, too. Despite such reservations, straight commercials *do* sell, are listened to, and continue to be the dominant form of radio commercials.

There is much room, however, for a high degree of creativity in radio commercial writing as the following humorous commercial demonstrates. Few writers, unfortunately, can write humorous commercials that sell as well as entertain. The following commercial, like so many of its kind, owes as much to the performers as to the writer for its success.

ANNCR:	Here's Stiller & Meara for Lanier Dictating Equipment.
MEARA:	Hi. I'm Donna Sue Billie Jean Garbonzo from Dial-a-secretary.
STILLER:	You're dressed like a mechanic.
MEARA:	I work nights in a body shop.
STILLER:	Great. I needed a secretary.
MEARA:	Today I'm all yours.
STILLER:	Listen, wash your hands. Put your tool kit in the corner. Sit here. Take a memo.
MEARA:	Take it where? I'm not a messenger.
STILLER:	You don't take dictation?
MEARA:	You don't use dictation equipment?
STILLER:	This is a small company.
MEARA:	Maybe it's small because you don't use Lanier dictating equipment. I know, I've been around.
STILLER:	I can see that.
MEARA:	You could take Lanier's pocket-sized portable with you on trips and work while you're away from work. Lanier's standard cassette units could help you and your secretary get more done while you're in the office.
STILLER:	With Lanier, I won't need you. But maybe you could take a look at my car.

MEARA: I already did. It looks like it was attcked by sharks. You need our weekend special. I'll do your points, plugs, shocks, and throw in a lube job—$800.

ANNCR: You can get more done with Lanier Business Products. Look for Lanier in the Yellow Pages under dictating machines.

STILLER: Get outa here! Hey! You got grease all over my lap!

(1) *Write a "hearing" message.* Despite the humor and the by-play between the two characters, no listener could fail to get the one idea that is stressed—that Lanier makes dictating equipment. Furthermore, the writing is wholly conversational and easy to comprehend through the ear.

(2) *Assume half-attention.* One advantage of a skillfully done humorous commercial is that attention is assured, especially in this commercial where there is a story line that makes the listener want to follow the plot, as it were. Thus, this type of commercial does not have the problem of holding attention as does the conventional straight commercial. On the other hand, a humorous commercial if not well done may turn off the listener at the beginning and never capture him again. Also, even a fairly good humorous commercial has a short life and can stand only about two or three airings. The skill of the performers determines whether such commercials have short lives or long lives.

(3) *Disregard print rules.* There is, of course, nothing about the format of this commercial that resembles print advertising. Thus, there is no relationship between the "rules" for this commercial and that of any print advertisement.

(4) *Write enough but not too little.* You find in this commercial a case where the number of words far exceeds the maximum of 170 suggested for most commercials. That is due to the rapid-fire delivery of the performers and the entertainment value of the material.

(5) *Use music and sound effects.* In a commercial such as this that is entertaining throughout, it is not necessary to employ devices to make it more appealing.

(6) *Come to a climax.* There are two climaxes. One, when the announcer suggests action. Two, when the entertainer hits an ending humorous note.

30-second Radio Commercial (trading stamps)

Music and sound effects are very important in this commercial which is of the type classed as a "production" commercial. Lively, light-hearted commercials like this are the favorite of the soft drink companies and other companies that sell products through reminder messages rather than with message that provide information and details.

MUSIC UP AND UNDER.

SFX: KIDS VOICES, LAUGHTER, SPLASHING.

BOY: Watch me dive, Dad!

SUNG: Hey, live a little!
SFX: LAUGHTER, APPLAUSE.
MAN: Beautiful!
WOMAN: Terrific!
SUNG: C'mon, live a little.
WOMAN: Up here at the lake, we live a little.
MAN: And before that, we save a little. Meaning S & H Green Stamps.
WOMAN: I always shop where they give'em. By vacation time . . . we've got books full.
MAN: This year, S & H got us the rubber raft.
MUSIC UP.
SUNG: Save a little . . . live a little.
              S & H Green Stamps . . . for life's extra pleasures.
TAG: Shop at (STORE NAME). We give S & H Green Stamps.

(1) *Write a "hearing" message.*   Music, sound effects and easy conversation make for easy listening plus the fact that the message is simple—save Green Stamps for the extras that such saving can bring.
(2) *Assume half-attention.*   Four repetitions of the product name in a 30-second commercial, plus the fast-moving character of the commercial, should insure listener attention. There is no place for the attention to bog down.
(3) *Disregard print rules.*   Once again, the commercial delays getting into direct product sell until the audience has been warmed up.
(4) *Write enough but not too little.*   Including the song verses and the dialogue this commercial has 86 words, about the usual for a sincerely paced 30-second commercial.
(5) *Use music and sound effects.*   As a production commercial, this is alive with music and sound effects. Both lend sparkle to the presentation.
(6) *Come to a climax.*   Both the ending song and the spoken tag make suggestions to supply plenty of action at the bottom of the commercial.

Television

In the following pages will be presented television commercials that will be analyzed in the same manner as the radio commercials just presented. There will, of course, be different criteria. These criteria are:

(1) Demonstration.
(2) Production technique.
(3) Video selling.
(4) Use of words.
(5) Planning of scenes.

60-second Television Commercial (U. S. Army) . . . see FIGURE 24-1.

All the armed services are engaged in a stern battle for recruits. In this commercial, shown in photoboard form, the Army uses something of the approach of the Marines in which the prospect is challenged to live up to the tough standards. It will be examined here to see how well it measures up in reference to the five criteria listed in the foregoing section.

FIGURE 24-1.
Photoboard for Army recruiting commercial.

Solving the energy problem will be expensive. For you as well as for us.

More costly fuel supplies, construction schedule delays, high interest rates, inflation and the increasing costs of protecting the environment all add up to higher utility rates.

At PG&E we're doing everything we can to provide you with reliable gas and electric service and to keep rates as low as possible. But rates are higher today and they'll continue to increase.

Here's a closer look at the reasons why:

Higher fuel costs.

Natural gas from Alaska and other distant points will be far more expensive.

The search for new gas supplies, including exploration in Canada and the Alaskan north slope, is expensive. Such gas will cost more and bringing it from greater distances will add to its price. Alternatives such as synthetic gas, gas made from coal, and importing liquefied natural gas could cost even more.

Besides natural gas, only low-sulfur oil is acceptable as fuel in steam-electric power plants under present air pollution control standards. And we have to pay high premium prices for low-sulfur oil.

(When the costs of oil and natural gas go up, so must electric rates, because most of our steam-electric power plants are fueled by gas or oil.)

Construction schedule delays.

Regulatory procedures, involving up to 30 or more public agencies, are taking longer and longer. And new laws and regulations have established more complicated procedures for plant siting and construction. All these slow down construction schedules, and inflation alone is adding substantially to costs during these periods of delay.

Last year we spent $48 million to help improve the environment, including undergrounding power lines.

Environmental costs.

It costs more to put power lines underground, to build and landscape esthetically pleasing plants, to minimize stack emissions and to cool the water discharged from power plants. During the period 1973-76, PG&E's environmental expenditures will exceed $300 million.

Higher interest rates.

1965	1973

Interest rates have almost doubled during the last ten years.

Utilities are "capital intensive" industries. That means money to build new facilities must be raised—in vast sums. Our construction program this year will exceed $600 million. And interest rates have risen from about 4½% in 1965 to about 7¾% today, which adds more millions to the cost of gas and electric service.

All these things, plus the inflationary pressures which affect every business, add up to higher costs for us and higher rates for our customers.

The era of plentiful energy at bargain rates is ending. Our job is to hold down costs wherever possible, without sacrificing the environment or the quality and reliability of your service. We're working hard to meet that challenge.

You can help—by not wasting gas and electricity. **PG and E**

(1) *Demonstration.* Most of this commercial consists of demonstration because it shows by example just what is expected of a man in the U.S. Army infantry. The technique is effective in recruiting because every person about to take on a career has the question: "What's it like?" Nothing answers the question better than an actual demonstration.

(2) *Production technique.* Live action, whether on film or videotape, is the best technique for a demonstration commercial. Real people doing the kind of work they'll do in the Army provide the information that is needed, better than animation, for example. The latter technique simply would not provide the realism and hard-boiled feeling required.

(3) *Video selling.* Exciting video scenes carry this commercial even though the words are necessary. Conceivably this commercial could have been quite effective if no words had been used except for the words shown on the screen in the last frame. This is a test of video effectiveness often suggested by television experts.

(4) *Use of words.* Although the video action is dominant here, 133 words are used, just about the maximum recommended for a live-action commercial. The words, however, are used well to give full meaning to each of the video scenes.

(5) *Planning of scenes.* A photoboard often does not picture all of the scenes in a commercial but the 15 shown here make it evident that the commercial will have good movement and action. Numerous scenes are required to give the recruit an idea of the many demands and opportunities of the Army.

30-second Television Commercial (instant soups)... see FIGURE 24-1 and FIGURE 24-2.

Presented here are the script and the following photoboard of a commercial featuring a celebrity whose background qualifies her to discuss the product intelligently and believably.

(1) *Demonstration.* A quick, graphic demonstration is the heart of this commercial which shows the presenter making a cupful of instant soup. This is a product that *must* be demonstrated because the ease and speed of preparation give the product a talking point against such soups as Campbell's that require more preparation time.

(2) *Production technique.* A live-action film in color offers the best way to present the preparation of a food product, especially when a celebrity is used to put on the demonstration. Appetite appeal is possible through live-action film; it would be greatly lessened by the use of animation. Videotape could, of course, also be used.

(3) *Video selling.* Through the first nine frames the video works hard and full use is made of the action that is television's strongest attribute. The last three frames, used for package and name identification, require no action and could be presented just as well by slides.

(4) *Use of words.* Words are important whenever a celebrity presenter is used because the audience wants to hear what the celebrity says. In this case, words are especially important because the celebrity is ac-

FIGURE 24-2.
Photoboard of commercial featuring woman celebrity.

CLIENT: THE NESTLE CO. INC.
PRODUCT: NESTLE'S SOUPTIME

TITLE: "KIM HUNTER"

LENGTH: 30 SECONDS

1. KIM HUNTER: When Nestle asked me to com-pare my

2. homemade soup with their instant Souptime with home-style stock,

3. I said, "You're kidding, how could an instant taste as good?"

4. Well, it was close.

5. Oh, I think mine is a little better,

6. (VO) but that Souptime came so close

7. and took just 10 seconds is astounding.

8. They say their secret is home-style stock.

9. (DV) Made a believer out of me.

10. ANNCR: (VO) Nestle Souptime

11. instant soups with home-style stock.

12. Look for our faces on the shelf.

N W Ayer ABH International

0873

1345 Avenue Of The Americas, New York, N.Y. 10019

CLIENT	NESTLE'	PROGRAM	
PRODUCT	SOUPTIME	FACILITIES	TV
TITLE	"KIM HUNTER"	DATE	
NUMBER	NESO 6309 As Produced	LENGTH	:30

	VIDEO		AUDIO
1.	OPEN ON KIM HUNTER BEHIND ISLAND TYPE STOVE IN KITCHEN SETTING. ON THE STOVE IS A KETTLE WITH BOILING WATER. THERE ARE ALSO VARIOUS MEATS AND VEGETABLES ON WORK SURFACES. SHE HAS PACKAGE OF SOUPTIME AND MUG IN FRONT OF HER. SUPER: KIM HUNTER, ACTRESS/COOKBOOK AUTHOR - "LOOSE IN THE KITCHEN."	1.	(PULL UP)
2.	AS SHE SPEAKS SHE MAKES THE APPROPRIATE GESTURES -- FIRST TO HER OWN SOUP . . .	2.	KIM: When Nestle' asked me to compare my homemade soup . . .
3.	THEN SHE HOLDS UP PACKAGE OF SOUPTIME.	3.	with their instant Souptime with home-style stock, I said:
4.	CUT IN TO CU OF KIM WITH PACKAGE UP BY HER FACE.	4.	"You're kidding. How could an instant taste as good?".
5.	CUT TO KIM WALKING TO OTHER SIDE OF COUNTER. SHE PICKS UP ENVELOPE AND TEARS IT.	5.	KIM VO: Well . . . it was close.
6.	CUT TO ECU OF KIM AS SHE POURS CONTENT AND WATER INTO MUG.	6.	Oh, I think mine's a little better,
7.	DISSOLVE TO ECU OF MUG AS SHE STIRS FINISHED SOUP.	7.	KIM: but that Souptime came so close and took just 10-seconds is astounding. They say their secret is home-style stock
8.	CUT BACK TO CU OF KIM'S FACE AS SHE RAISES MUG FOR TASTE.	8.	KIM: They made a believer out of me.
9.	MATCH DISSOLVE TO CU OF WOMAN IN SAME ATTITUDE ON SOUPTIME PKG.	9.	ANNCR VO: Nestle' Souptime instant soups with home-style stock.
10.	PULL BACK TO REVEAL ARRAY OF SOUPTIME PKGS.	10.	Look for our faces on the shelf.

F-440

tually endorsing, using, and presenting the product. The commercial would make much sense even without the words, but it is much stronger because of the audio. Furthermore, there is a disarming honesty in the underselling of the product with the celebrity maintaining that her own soup preparation is better than the advertised product.

(5) *Planning of scenes.* There is enough movement in the commercial to keep the viewers awake. It should be noted, however, that in some instances there is not an actual scene change, simply a change from a long shot to a close-up or a change of camera angle as in Frames 6 and 7. Good product identification is achieved with the package and product name easily identifiable in seven frames.

10-second Television Commercial (combination garden-tiller and lawn mower)

Ten-second television commercials,called ID's (short for station identifications, or identification spots) are very useful for saturating a market at a lower cost than 30s or 60s. Furthermore, with availabilities in television commercial time so limited in many markets, the advertiser has a better chance of placing ID's than longer commercials.

One caution to be observed by the writer: In a 10-second commercial there are only 8 seconds of sound track (the same caution is true for 60-second commercials that have only 58 seconds of sound track, and for 30s which have 28 seconds of sound). Following is a 10-second television script:

Video	*Audio*
1. Man using item as a garden-tiller. It is churning up earth.	Mower-Till. Plows hard-packed garden soil. Flip a switch and ...
2. Unit is now cutting grass on what is obviously a well-kept lawn.	... it's a superb lawn mower.
3. With unit still in action, a TCU (tight close-up) of name plate shows product name.	See Mower-Till at your garden supply store.

(1)   *Demonstration.*   Brief though it must be, the demonstration is all-important in the case of this product. With more time, it would be desirable to show the switching operation that converts the unit from a garden-tiller to a lawn mower, but the words "Flip a switch" and the demonstration of the unit serving both functions put the point across. Remember, that the ID would be part of a print campaign backed up by longer commercials. The ID, therefore, is a reinforcement for other advertising. It can't do the complete selling presentation.

(2)   *Production technique.*   Although this is a unit that *could* use animation to show its dual function, the demonstration is handled better with live action film, or videotape. The sight of the hard-packed dirt being broken up by the tiller would be deeply meaningful to gardeners who have used a hoe for this work, and then the lawn cutting that follows is more impressive if shown on an actual lawn.

(3)   *Video selling.*   Strong video scenes do the selling here. In only three scenes it is established what the unit does and what it is called. The commercial can just about tell the whole story without the use of audio.

(4)   *Use of words.*   With 22 words, we're tight. It would be inadvisable to use more than this in the 8 seconds. In the foregoing discussion of the video selling, it was said that the video scenes can "just about" tell the whole story. The qualification is included because the sentence "Flip a switch and it's a superb lawn mower" help explain how the unit converts from one function to the other. Because of the limited number of scenes in an ID, the help of the audio explanation is needed.

(5) *Planning of scenes.* Three scenes should be the maximum in an ID. Any more and the time allotted to each would be so brief as to be meaningless. Furthermore, since demonstration is important in the sale of this unit, enough time must be allowed to give scope to the demonstration. Even more than in the longer time units, the ID should cover just one point. In this instance that point is the fact that Mower-Till serves a dual function. Often an ID shares between-program time with a number of other commercials, most of them longer. Unless it makes its one point clearly and forcefully, it will be lost in the parade of competing commercials.

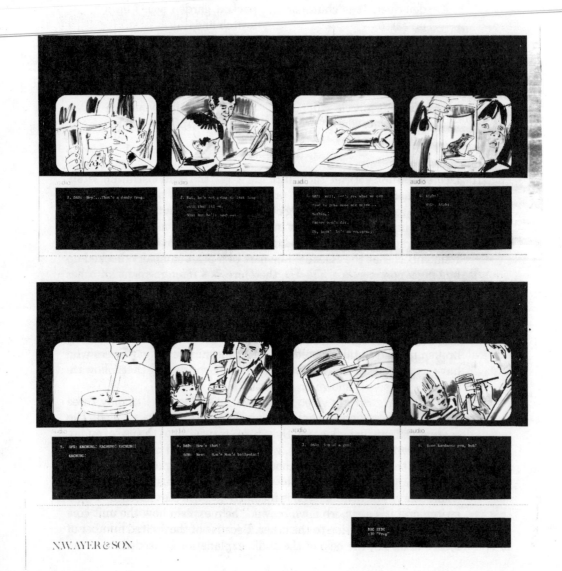

N.W. AYER & SON

N.W. AYER & SON

The Script or Storyboard — Only the Beginning

One point a television commercial writer soon learns: the preparation of a script or storyboard is the merest first starting step. First, must come approval by the client who looks at the commercial, not only for its creative appeal but also considers it as a sales vehicle. Does it fit in with the marketing and sales objectives? Dazzling creativity means nothing if the commercial doesn't sell the product and service and if it doesn't mesh with overall marketing strategy.

Second, comes the long production process. This is initiated by a preproduction meeting of the personnel of the client, advertising agency, and the television producer. Here the commercial is "costed." That is, the money requirements are considered. These embrace such considerations as the type of production technique, the elaborateness of sets and backgrounds, the number and quality of actors taking part, the charges of the director and assistants, musical scores, sound effects, and whether shooting will be in the studio or on location (more expensive). And there are many other considerations too lengthy to be listed here.

Every item is weighed in the preproduction meeting. By the end of the meeting, the script and/or storyboard, may be greatly changed, even though the basic idea remains intact. Even more changes may occur when the actual shooting takes place.

The copywriter—man or woman—often takes little part in all these deliberations. Oddly enough, even the copywriter may find it difficult to envision the final version of a commercial because of all the production techniques that can be incorporated and, even more important in many cases, because of the way the talent hired for the speaking and acting roles can bring distinction to ordinary ideas.

An unusual voice or acting ability can make what looked conventional on paper so gripping or interesting that a commercial can achieve national impact almost overnight. So it has been with scores of products such as Tareyton, Alka Seltzer, Volkswagen, Charmin, and Winston.

To repeat: the work of the television copywriter is only the beginning, but an important beginning.

QUESTIONS

1. What should be the copywriter's thinking about the use of negative approaches in copy?

2. In observing rules of grammar as one writes copy, what distinctions should be made between broadcast and print copy?

3. Of what use is the A-I-D-A formula to a copywriter?

4. What is the virtue and possible criticism of the straight-selling type of copy? For what type of products is it best suited?

5. What difficulties are found in the use of testimonial copy?

6. In giving advice to a radio writer, what is the most important suggestion you can offer?

7. What should a television commercial writer use as a rough guide for the number of scenes and words he uses in: (a) A 60-second commercial? (b) An ID commercial?

APPENDIX A

MAGAZINES SERVING THE ADVERTISING
AND MARKETING FIELD

Advertising Age, 740 N. Rush Street, Chicago, Ill. 60611

Advertising and Publishing News, 51 Upper Montclair Plaza, Montclair, N.J.
  07043

Advertising World, 1718 Sherman Ave., Evanston, Ill. 60201

Agri-Marketing, 5520 Touhy Ave., Skokie, Ill. 60077

Art Direction, 19 W. 44th St., New York, N.Y. 10036

Broadcasting, 1735 DeSales St., N.W., Washington, D.C. 20036

Communication Arts, 3437 Alma, P.O. Box 10300, Palo Alto, Calif. 94303

Editor & Publisher, 575 Lexington Ave., New York, N.Y. 10022

Incentive Marketing, 633 Third Ave., New York, N.Y. 10017

Industrial Marketing, 740 N. Rush St., Chicago, Ill. 60611

Journal of Advertising, School of Business, Brigham Young University, Orem,
  Utah

Journal of Advertising Research, 3 East 54th St., New York, N.Y. 10022

Journal of Marketing, 222 S. Riverside Plaza, Chicago, Ill. 60606

Journal of Marketing Research, 222 S. Riverside Plaza, Chicago, Ill. 60606

MAC/Western Advertising, 6565 Sunset Blvd., Los Angeles, Calif. 90028

Madison Avenue, 750 Third Ave., New York, N.Y. 10017

Marketing Communications, 475 Park Ave. S., New York, N.Y. 10016

Media Decisions, 342 Madison Ave., New York, N.Y. 10017

Potentials in Marketing, 731 Hennepin Ave., Minneapolis, Minn. 55403

Premium/Incentive Business, 1515 Broadway, New York, N.Y. 10036

Reporter of Direct Mail Advertising, 224 Seventh St., Garden City, N.Y. 11530

Sales & Marketing Management, 633 Third Ave., New York, N.Y. 10017

858

Signs of the Times, 407 Gilbert Ave., Cincinnati, Ohio 45202
Southern Advertising/Markets, 75 3d St., N.W., Atlanta, Ga. 30308
Southwest Advertising & Marketing, P.O. Box 2276, Dallas, Tex. 75221

Television/Radio Age, 1270 Avenue of the Americas, New York, N.Y. 10020

Variety, 154 W. 46th St., New York, N.Y. 10036

APPENDIX B

ASSOCIATIONS OF ADVERTISING AND MARKETING

ADVERTISERS

American Advertising Federation, 1225 Connecticut Ave., N.W., Washington, D.C. 20036

Association of Canadian Advertisers, Suite 620, 159 Bay St., Toronto, Ontario, Canada

Association of National Advertisers, 155 E. 44th St., New York, N.Y. 10017

Association of Railroad Advertising Managers, 3706 Palmerson Rd., Shaker Heights, Ohio 44122

Business/Professional Advertising Association, 205 E. 42d St., New York, N.Y.

Life Insurance Advertisers Association, 1040 Woodcock Rd., Orlando, Fla. 32803

National Agri-Marketing Association, Suite 516, 800 W. 47th St., Kansas City, Mo. 64112

Public Utilities Communicators Association, c/o Minnesota Gas Co., Minneapolis, Mn. 55402

ADVERTISING AGENCIES

Advertising Women of New York, 158 E. 57th St., New York, N.Y. 10022

Affiliated Advertising Agencies International, 13693 E. Cliff Ave., Aurora, Col. 80014

Institute of Canadian Advertising, 8 King St. E., Toronto, Ontario, Canada

League of Advertising Agencies, 205 West 89th St., New York, N.Y. 10024

Mutual Advertising Agency Network, 5001 West 80th St., Minneapolis, Minn. 55437

National Advertising Agency Network, 420 Lexington Ave., New York, N.Y. 10017

National Federation of Advertising Agencies, Inc., 1605 Main St., Sarasota, Fla. 33577

Western States Advertising Agencies Association, 5900 Wilshire Blvd., Los Angeles, Calif. 90036

MEDIA

Agricultural Publishers Association, 111 E. Wacker Dr., Chicago, Ill. 60601

American Business Press, Inc., 205 E. 42d St., New York, N.Y. 10017

American Newspaper Publishers Association, 11600 Sunrise Valley Dr., Reston, Va. 22070

Association of Newspaper Classified Advertising Managers, Inc., P.O. Box 223, Danville, Ill. 61832

Association of Publishers Representatives, 850 Third Ave., New York, N.Y. 10022

Audit Bureau of Circulations, 123 N. Wacker Dr., Chicago, Ill. 60606

Business Publications Audit of Circulation, Inc., 360 Park Avenue So., New York, N.Y. 10010

The Canadian Assoc. of Broadcasters, Blackburn Bldg., 85 Sparks St., Ottawa, Ontario, Canada

Canadian Business Press, 100 University Ave., Toronto 1, Ontario, Canada

Canadian Circulations Audit Board, Inc., 44 Eglinton W., Toronto, Ontario, Canada

Canadian Community Newspaper Assoc., 12 Shuter, Toronto, Ontario, Canada

Canadian Daily Newspaper Publishers Assoc., 321 Bloor St., Toronto 5, Ontario, Canada

Canadian Direct Mail Association, 130 Merton, Toronto, Canada

Direct Mail Marketing Association, 6 E. 43d St., New York, N.Y. 10017

Exhibit Designers and Producers Association, 521 Fifth Avenue, New York, N.Y. 10017

Exposition Management Association, P.O. Box 669, Westport, Conn. 06880

Farm Publications Reports, Inc., 111 E. Wacker Dr., Chicago, Ill. 60601

Inland Daily Press Association, 100 W. Monroe St., Chicago, Ill. 60603

Institute of Outdoor Advertising, 485 Lexington Ave., New York, N.Y. 10017

International Advertising Association, Inc. 475 Fifth Avenue, New York, N.Y. 10017

International Newspaper Advertising Executives, P.O. Box 147, Danville, Ill. 61832

International Newspaper Promotion Association, P.O. Box 17422, Dulles International Airport, Washington, D.C. 20041

International Radio and Television Society, 420 Lexington Ave., New York, N.Y. 10017

Magazine Advertising Bureau of Magazine Publishers Assoc., Inc., 575 Lexington Ave., New York, N.Y. 10022

Magazine Association of Canada (The), 1240 Bay St., Toronto, Ontario, Canada

Magazine Publishers Association, 575 Lexington Ave., New York, N.Y. 10022

Magazine Publishers Association of Canada, 100 University Ave., Toronto 1, Ontario, Canada

Mail Advertising Service Association, 7315 Wisconsin Ave., Washington, D.C. 20014

National Association of Advertising Publishers, 313 Price Pl., Madison, Wis. 53705

National Assoc. of Broadcasters, 1771 N. Street N.W., Washington, D.C. 20036

National Assoc. of Display Ind., 120 E. 23d St., New York, N.Y.

National Assoc. of Exhibit Managers, 1101 16th St. N.W., Washington, D.C. 20036

National Outdoor Advertising Bureau, 810 Seventh Ave., New York, N.Y. 10019

National Premium Sales Executives Inc., 240 Park Ave., Rutherford, N.J. 07070

Newspaper Advertising Bureau, 485 Lexington Ave., New York, N.Y. 10017

Outdoor Advertising Assoc. of America, Inc., 485 Lexington Ave., New York, N.Y. 10022

Periodical Press Assoc., 100 University Ave., Toronto 1, Ontario, Canada

Point-of-Purchase Advertising Institute (The), 60 E. 42d St., New York, N.Y. 10017

Premium Advertising Assoc. of America, Inc., 420 Lexington Ave., New York, N.Y. 10022

Promotion Marketing Association of America, 420 Lexington Ave., New York, N.Y. 10017

Publishers Information Bureau, Inc., 575 Lexington Ave., New York, N.Y. 10022

Radio Advertising Bureau, Inc. 555 Madison Ave., New York, N.Y. 10022

Second Class Mail Publications, Room 405, 1627 K Street N.W., Washington, D.C. 20006

Specialty Advertising Association International, One Crossroads of Commerce, Rolling Meadows, Ill. 60008

Station Representatives Assoc., Inc., 230 Park Ave., New York, N.Y. 10017

Television Bureau of Advertising, Inc., 1345 Avenue of the Americas, New York, N.Y. 10019

Traffic Audit Bureau, Inc., 708 Third Ave., New York, N.Y. 10017

Transit Advertising Assoc., Inc., 1725 K St., N.W., Washington, D.C. 20006

Tub of Canada, Inc., 65 Queen St., W., Toronto, Ontario, Canada

Western Society of Business Publications, c/o Grayce Ross, 4041 Marlton Ave., Los Angeles, Calif. 90008

PUBLIC RELATIONS

Bank Marketing Assoc., 309 W. Washington, Chicago, Ill. 60602

Public Relations Society of America, 845 Third Ave., New York, N.Y. 10022

ADVERTISING-MARKETING-MEDIA RESEARCH

Advertising Research Foundation, Three East 54th St., New York, N.Y. 10022
America Marketing Assoc., 222 S. Riverside Plaza, Chicago, Ill. 60606

Bureau of Broadcast Measurement, 120 Eglinton Ave. E., Toronto 12, Ontario, Canada

Canadian Advertising Research Foundation, Inc., 159 Bay St., Toronto 1, Ontario Canada

Marketing Communications Research Center, 575 Ewing St., Princeton, N.J. 08540

Marketing Media Research Associations, 598 Madison Ave., New York, N.Y. 10017

Media Research Directors Association, c/o McGraw-Hill Research, 1221 Avenue of the Americas, New York, N.Y. 10020

Radio and Television Research Council, c/o Broadcast Advertising Reports, Inc., 500 Fifth Ave., New York, N.Y. 10036

TRADE ASSOCIATIONS OF ADVERTISING AND MARKETING

Advertising Council, 825 Third Ave., New York, N.Y. 10022
American Advertising Federation, 1225 Conneticut Ave. N.W., Washington, D.C. 20036
Association Third Class Mail Users, 1725 K Street N.W., Washington, D.C. 20036

Brand Names Foundation, 477 Madison Ave., New York, N.Y. 10022

Canadian Advertising Advisory Board, 1240 Bay St., Toronto, Ontario, Canada
Council of Better Business Bureaus, Inc., 845 Third Ave., New York, N.Y. 10022

Institute of Canadian Advertising, 8 King St. E., Toronto, Ontario, Canada

National Cable Television Assoc., 918 16th N.W., Washington, D.C. 20006

Sales and Marketing Executives International, 330 Lexington Ave., New York, N.Y.
Specialty Advertising Assoc. International, 1 Crossroads of Commerce, Rolling Meadow, Ill.

APPENDIX C

SOURCES OF INFORMATION
(ANNUALS, DIRECTORIES, AND REPORTS)

Advertising Checking Bureau, Inc. (ACB) 353 Park Avenue South, New York, N.Y. 10010. Newspapers use this service to supply tear sheets to their advertisers as evidence that the advertising has been run and to give advertisers and their agencies an opportunity to check production quality.

Broadcast Advertisers Reports (BAR), 500 Fifth Ave., New York, N.Y. 10017. Provides network television schedules and expenditures. Monitored on tape off the air. Furnishes commercial differences in network programs in 75 key cities.

Broadcasting Yearbook, 1735 DeSales St., N.W., Washington, D.C. 20036. Gives facts and figures about broadcasting industry for the year just concluded. Included are list of stations, key personnel, and the organizations that serve the industry.

Leading National Advertisers, Inc. (PIB), 347 Madison Ave., New York, N.Y. 10017. Measures network television schedules and expenditures and reports weekly program logs for each network which indicate commercial placement by advertiser and brand. Obtains information through off-the-air monitoring of network broadcast.

Media Records Report (American Fulfillment Corporation), 370 Seventh Avenue, New York, N.Y. 10001. Provides record of space run and dollars spent by more than 40,000 advertisers in 650 trade, industrial, business, and professional publications.

Media Records, Inc., 370 Seventh Ave., New York, N.Y. 10001. Provides monthly and yearly reports on newspaper lineage figures. Figures are based upon advertising in leading newspapers and are broken into various classifications such as retail, general, automotive, financial, legal, classified, and total advertising. Newspapers on which reports are based account for about 85% of total U.S. newspaper circulation.

N. C. Rorabaugh Co., Inc., 347 Madison Ave., New York, N.Y. 10017. Gives information on local market television competition activity and expenditures. Stations report to company. Covers about 200 markets and provides information on number and length of commercials and how much is spent by various national advertisers. Concentration is on spot television.

N. W. & Sons Directory of Newspapers and Periodicals, 210 West Washington Square, Philadelphia, Pa. 19106. In addition to providing information about newspapers and periodicals, the directory furnishes information about the marketing areas in which the listed publications circulate.

National Trade Show Exhibitors Association, 4902 Tolleview, Rolling Meadows, Ill. Organized in 1966. Members of NTSEA exhibit in more than 1,000 trade shows to market products and services (excludes hotels, exhibit designers and builders, association sponsors, or any service firm deriving financial benefit or revenue from trade show exhibitors.)

Publishers Information Bureau (PIB), 575 Lexington Ave., New York, N.Y. 10022. Provides competitive information by totaling lineage figures for a number of leading national consumer magazines and Sunday supplements. Indicates expenditures by company, product classifications, and brand.

Sales & Marketing Management Survey of Buying Power, Sales & Marketing, Inc., 633 Third Ave., New York, N.Y. 10017. Gives current figures on population, effective buying income, retail sales by types of markets-city, county, metropolitan, state, and regional. Issued yearly in May.

Standard Directory of Advertisers, National Register Publishing Co., 5201 Old Orchard Road, Skokie, Ill. 60076. Lists advertisers, their executives, their advertising agencies (for each product they advertise), and the general class of media they use. Sometimes the advertising budget figures are also included.

Standard Directory of Advertising Agencies, National Register Publishing Co., Inc., 5201 Old Orchard Road, Skokie, Ill. 60076. Contains a listing of advertising agencies with addresses of main offices, branch offices, and foreign offices. Names key personnel, various media groups conferring recognition. Usually lists accounts of the individual agencies and their branches.

Standard Rate & Data Service, Inc., 5201 Old Orchard Road, Skokie, Ill. 60076. This "service" consists of monthly publications that provide rates and other data needed by time and space buyers in order to place an individual medium on a schedule. Individual monthly publications are furnished for newspapers, consumer publications (farm publications are included in this section), business publications, radio, television, weekly newspapers, and transit advertising.

Television Factbook, Television Digest, Inc., 1836 Jefferson Place N.W., Washington, D.C. 20036. Published annually. Contains general facts about the industry, including equipment, finances, networks and trends. Has a television catalog section.

Thomas Register, Thomas Publishing Company, One Penn Plaza, New York, N.Y. 10001. A purchasing reference used by industrial purchasers to locate sellers of industrial goods. Comes in a number of tightly packed volumes.

Index